COMPUTERS AND THE LAW

An Introduction to Basic Legal Principles and Their Application in Cyberspace

Computers and the Law provides readers with an introduction to the legal issues associated with computing – particularly in the massively networked context of the Internet. Assuming no previous knowledge of the law or any special knowledge of programming or computer science, this textbook offers undergraduates of all disciplines and professionals in the computing industry an understanding of basic legal principles and an awareness of the peculiarities associated with legal issues in cyberspace. This is not a law school casebook; instead, a variety of relevant cases are presented in redacted form with the full cases available at an ancillary website.

The pervasiveness of computing in modern society has generated numerous legal ambiguities. This book introduces readers to the fundamental workings of the law in the non-virtual world while suggesting the opportunity to create new types of laws with nontraditional goals to fit the demands of cyberspace.

The late Robert Dunne was an Attorney and Senior Lecturer at Yale University's Department of Computer Science, specializing in legal problems arising from the use of computers in contemporary society. He wrote on alternative paradigms for behavioral control in cyberspace, the impact of cyberspace on the legal profession, and Internet crime. Dunne was also Co-Director of Yale's Center for Internet Studies and a Fellow of Yale's Silliman College.

Computers and the Law

AN INTRODUCTION TO BASIC LEGAL PRINCIPLES AND THEIR APPLICATION IN CYBERSPACE

Robert Dunne
Yale University

Published under the auspices of  Rights International
The Center for International Human Rights Law, Inc.

 CAMBRIDGE
UNIVERSITY PRESS

CAMBRIDGE UNIVERSITY PRESS
Cambridge, New York, Melbourne, Madrid, Cape Town, Singapore, São Paulo, Delhi

Cambridge University Press
32 Avenue of the Americas, New York, NY 10013-2473, USA

www.cambridge.org
Information on this title: www.cambridge.org/9780521886505

First published 2009

Printed in the United States of America

A catalog record for this publication is available from the British Library.

Library of Congress Cataloging in Publication data

Dunne, Robert, 1949–2008.
Computers and the law : an introduction to basic legal principles and their application
in cyberspace / Robert Dunne.
    p.   cm.
Includes bibliographical references and index.
ISBN 978-0-521-88650-5 (hardback)
1. Computers – Law and legislation – United States.   I. Title.
KF390.5.C6D86   2009
343.7309′99–dc22   2009005672

ISBN   978-0-521-88650-5 hardback

Cambridge University Press has no responsibility for the persistence or
accuracy of URLs for external or third-party Internet Web sites referred to in
this publication and does not guarantee that any content on such Web sites is,
or will remain, accurate or appropriate. Information regarding prices, travel
timetables, and other factual information given in this work are correct at
the time of first printing, but Cambridge University Press does not guarantee
the accuracy of such information thereafter.

For my favorite person, my daughter, Julia

Contents

Preface

This book is intended to provide its readers with an awareness of legal issues associated with computing – particularly in the massively networked context of the Internet. It assumes no previous knowledge of the law or any special knowledge of programming or computer science. It is not a law school "casebook," although there are many cases presented here (in redacted form). The unredacted cases are available at a website (www.cambridge.org/9780521886505) associated with this volume, with the portions that were ultimately redacted highlighted to make them easy to find.

Of necessity, the book contains a considerable amount of very basic legal information on a variety of topics. It is impossible to consider the workings of the law in cyberspace without at least some knowledge of the fundamental workings of the law in physical space. Again, this information is unsuitably elementary for the professional lawyer or the law student. They have enough information tailored to their needs. My hope is to reach people who do not have much legal knowledge.

Because the book is aimed at a more general audience, the format of the presentation of the cases is unusual. Judicial opinions can be very difficult reading for the non-lawyer or non–law student. Therefore, in the text of the cases, I have included in bold print comments on what is happening, on the importance of a particular statement, or on the importance of the case to "cyberlaw" in general. Many of these comments might suggest interesting topics for essays or discussion.

The pervasiveness of computing in modern society has generated numerous legal questions. Computers and computing are different enough from the kinds of devices and activities with which the law has previously dealt that in many circumstances (not all, but many) it is difficult to know how existing law should or can be applied.

Most often, these circumstances arise when computers are used in a networked environment, so this is the focus here. Indeed, most legal problems arise in a "networked environment," that is, when people interact. A person stranded on an uninhabited island is unlikely to have many legal problems. Wash another person ashore, and it won't be long before they are both hoping a lawyer washes ashore too. However, although the focus in this book is on networked computing, readers should be aware that use of computers in other ways could also raise legal questions. For example, if an un-networked, "standalone" computer running an artificial intelligence–based expert diagnostic system in a hospital fails, and a patient dies, where does liability lie? With the programmer? The hardware manufacturer? The hospital?

The goal of this book is to provide an understanding of some basic legal principles and an awareness that cyberspace can add peculiar twists and turns that sometimes make the application of those legal principles very tricky. However, it is a mistake to think of applying law in cyberspace as a problem. Rather, I think, it is an opportunity to apply law in new ways, and even to create new types of laws with nontraditional goals.

Acknowledgments

I am grateful most of all to my friend, colleague, and former student, Virginie Marier, currently a student at the McGill University Faculty of Law in Montreal, for her advice in general and her extraordinary help in redacting the cases that appear in this volume. I have long been familiar with her excellence, thoroughness, attention to detail, and enthusiasm, but she amazed even me here.

I also thank my many colleagues in the Department of Computer Science at Yale for their support and valuable suggestions, especially Stanley Eisenstat, Avi Silbershatz, Robert Bjornson, and, of course, Martin Schultz, to whom I owe so much for bringing me to Yale in 1986 and who has been my friend and mentor ever since.

Finally, I am grateful to my family, especially my brother Richard and my aunt Lorraine, and to my friends Judy and Roger Smith and Beverly Thalberg, all of whom listened patiently when I complained about the effort needed to get through the project, encouraged me, and prodded me whenever I needed a push.

Robert Dunne
New Haven, CT
2008

There are many people who have worked hard to ensure the completion of this project. I would like to first and foremost thank Virginie Marier, who lived up to the above praise and went beyond all expectations that were placed on her. Without her there would be no book, and for that I am forever grateful.

Secondly, I would like to thank Heather Bergman of Cambridge University Press, who never gave up on the idea that this book could still be published. She was patient with me in making decisions and helped me every step along the way.

Lastly and most importantly, I am grateful to my friends and family, many of whom have already been named above, and also to my grandfather, Cy Lishnoff, for reminding me not long ago of the importance of seeing this through.

The words in this text belong to my father. It had always been his dream to be a published author and I could not be more proud of him for making that a reality.

Julia Dunne
Milford, CT
2009

1. The Common Law and Statutory Law

Introduction

"Common Law" is frequently characterized as "judge-made law." It is the law of precedent, created through a process of constant evolution as courts interpret and apply previous judicial decisions. While it is true that, as many people insist, judges do not make laws (lower case "l") but legislatures do, judges do shape society's legal fabric – its Law (upper case "L") – through this interpretive process.

"Statutory Law" is the law of "statutes" or what we commonly refer to simply as "laws," created by legislative bodies such as Congress, state legislative counterparts of Congress, or other such bodies. Unlike Common Law, Statutory Law is a product of attempts to take a broad view and, usually, to make major adjustments to the Law. Common Law is built in a more piece-by-piece fashion, one brick at a time, by practitioners who are not concerned with the big picture, but rather with the case at hand.

The U.S. Federal Court system is essentially a three-tiered system, resembling a pyramid. At the lowest level are the District Courts, scattered all over the country. There are currently ninety-four federal District Courts. Each state has at least one, as do the District of Columbia and Puerto Rico. Three Territories of the United States also have Federal District Courts – Puerto Rico, Guam, and the Northern Mariana Islands. The District Courts are usually the starting point for litigation or prosecution if federal courts have jurisdiction over a case (which will be discussed in Chapter 15).

The middle level of the U.S. judicial pyramid consists of the Circuit Courts of Appeals. There are eleven regional judicial Circuit Courts of Appeals, each encompassing several states (and in some cases a U.S. Territory), listed in Table 1, which hear appeals from the District Courts in those states and territories. There is also a Circuit Court of Appeals for the District of Columbia, as well as a Federal Circuit Court of Appeals, which hears appeals on specific issues such as those involving patent, trademark, and copyright matters. Cases brought before the Circuit Courts of Appeals are typically heard by a panel of three Circuit Court judges.

At the apex of the judicial pyramid sits the United States Supreme Court, comprised of nine Justices, which hears appeals it chooses to accept from the Circuit Courts of Appeals.

Most state judicial systems mirror the three-tiered federal model.

It is important to grasp the organizational structure of the court systems in order to understand how the Common Law's precedent-based model works. Judicial decisions by courts of equal stature in the hierarchy, or from different circuits, are not binding on

Table 1: The Regional Federal Judicial Circuits

First:	Maine, Massachusetts, New Hampshire, Puerto Rico, Rhode Island
Second:	Connecticut, New York, Vermont
Third:	Delaware, New Jersey, Pennsylvania, Virgin Islands
Fourth:	Maryland, North Carolina, South Carolina, Virginia, West Virginia
Fifth:	Louisiana, Mississippi, Texas
Sixth:	Michigan, Kentucky, Ohio, Tennessee
Seventh:	Illinois, Indiana, Wisconsin
Eighth:	Arizona, Iowa, Minnesota, Missouri, Nebraska, North Dakota, South Dakota
Ninth:	Alaska, Arizona, California, Guam, Hawaii, Idaho, Mariana Islands, Montana, Nevada, Oregon, Washington
Tenth:	Colorado, Kansas, New Mexico, Utah, Wyoming
Eleventh:	Alabama, Florida, Georgia

one another. In other words, if the Federal District Court for the Southern District of New York decides a case, and a case with very similar facts is later brought before the Federal District Court for the Eastern District of Pennsylvania, the Pennsylvania court is free to disagree with the outcome decided upon by the New York court. Even if the Second Circuit Court of Appeals has already affirmed the decision by the New York District Court, the Pennsylvania court may *still* decide otherwise because the Pennsylvania court is in the Third Circuit, not the Second.

However, if a district court is presented with a case in which the facts closely resemble those of a case previously decided by the Third Circuit Court of Appeals – in which the Pennsylvania court is located – the Pennsylvania District Court is *bound* by the appellate court's decision and must follow its lead and apply the same reasoning. Similarly, this notion of "binding precedent" applies to all courts in the judicial system – appellate as well as district courts – once the United States Supreme Court has ruled on a particular issue.

The attorneys for the parties in a common law case devote a great deal of time and effort to unearthing cases similar to the one before the court, which support their arguments and which might weaken the cases relied upon by the other party.

The idea of a generalized "theory" of common law dates from the second half of the eighteenth century, when recorded judicial opinions became broadly available. "Case-based" arguments and decisions could be possible only if previous decisions were available to both judges and attorneys. The hypothesis was that the same "scientific approach" could be applied to both physical and social phenomena: regularities could be found and patterns discovered, yielding predictability.

American common law differs from the common law of England, from which it is descended, in several ways. American legal professionals approached the creation of their legal system with the idea and belief that it should all somehow make sense. Thus, the American system is more rigid and tends to have more abstract, universal "rules."

Partially, this rigidity comes from the American practice of publishing *one* opinion, which is the official opinion, or "holding," of the court. (Although concurrences and dissents are commonly published along with the holding, their content is not binding on any other courts.) In England, every judge on the panel hearing a case writes a separate opinion, and all the opinions that agree with the majority result are considered authoritative; that is, they constitute the official opinion of the Court for the purposes of precedent. Change is therefore harder to achieve in American common law because once the Court settles an issue, attorneys have fewer judicial points of view to use and interpret in framing subsequent arguments.

In the early part of the twentieth century, there was a general belief that a sharp line could be drawn between the courts and the legislatures. Legislatures, it was felt, made the laws and could change the rules, while courts primarily carried out those legislative "commands." This turned out to be an erroneous view of the way things worked.

Courts *interpret* statutes and thus often make statutes just another tool to be used in building the common law. Statutes, in fact, are often attempts by legislatures to curb some direction the courts seem to be taking. We will see many instances of such attempts later in this book. Nonetheless, it is true that courts are more tied down in making their decisions when the cause of action arises from a statutory, as opposed to common law source. With fairly explicit instructions from a legislative body, it is harder for a court to find a way to reach a decision it might believe to be the most reasonable and just in the circumstances.

The following two cases (presented in redacted form, meaning that they have been edited down to their relevant parts, as have all the cases in this book) illustrate the different ways in which courts approach analysis of (1) a common law matter (*Peevyhouse v. Garland Coal and Mining Company*) and (2) a statutory issue (*In re Phillip B.* and its continuation, *Guardianship of Phillip B.*). Reading judicial decisions can be daunting for a novice unfamiliar with the style of writing. It is important to remember that the cases are about real people, and it is helpful to try to picture those people and get a feel for what they are doing and the situation in which they find themselves. One should always ask, "Why are these people in court? No one wants to go to court. It is expensive, time consuming, and stressful. What is the story that brought the parties before a judge and jury?" In an attempt to clarify the story underlying the litigation, and to make the cases easier to understand, comments on the text of the cases have been indented and are in bold face.

The Common Law and Statutory Law: Case 1

Willie PEEVYHOUSE and Lucille Peevyhouse, Plaintiffs in Error, v.
GARLAND COAL & MINING COMPANY, Defendant in Error

No. 39588

Supreme Court of Oklahoma

382 P.2d 109; 1962 Okla. LEXIS 554

December 11, 1962

OPINION: JACKSON, Justice:

I. Facts

Briefly stated, the facts are as follows: plaintiffs owned a farm containing coal deposits, [...]

> **Willie and Lucille own a farm. It is at least 120 acres (it is hard to tell for sure from what we have in the decision), most of which, Willie says, is "in good grass." So, it is pasture land.**

> **In 1951 Willie builds a home on the property.**

[. . .] and in November, 1954, leased the premises to defendant for a period of five years for coal mining purposes. A 'strip-mining' operation was contemplated in which the coal would be taken from pits on the surface of the ground, instead of from underground mine shafts.

In 1954 a guy from Garland comes knocking at the screen door. He wants to propose a deal. Garland wants to strip-mine some sixty acres of Willie and Lucille's land for coal. Garland offers to pay Willie and Lucille some amount (unknown) for a five-year license to strip-mine the land.

In addition to the usual covenants found in a coal mining lease, defendant specifically agreed to perform certain restorative and remedial work at the end of the lease period. It is unnecessary to set out the details of the work to be done, other than to say that it would involve the moving of many thousands of cubic yards of dirt, at a cost estimated by expert witnesses at about $29,000.00. However, plaintiffs sued for only $25,000.00.

Garland also offers Willie and Lucille some amount of royalties on the coal produced, and promises specifically in writing to restore the land when the work is done (which we know will cost some $29,000 to perform).

During the trial, it was stipulated that all covenants and agreements in the lease contract had been fully carried out by both parties, except the remedial work mentioned above; defendant conceded that this work had not been done.

Note that the parties are not arguing about whether the contract was breached, only about the amount of damages.

Plaintiffs introduced expert testimony as to the amount and nature of the work to be done, and its estimated cost. Over plaintiffs' objections, defendant thereafter introduced expert testimony as to the 'diminution in value' of plaintiffs' farm resulting from the failure of defendant to render performance as agreed in the contract – that is, the difference between the present value of the farm, and what its value would have been if defendant had done what it agreed to do.

Once the coal is removed, Garland refuses to do the restoration work, claiming the cost of restoring the land far outweighs the actual diminution in value of the land ($300). Garland feels that is all it should have to pay Willie and Lucille. What Garland is saying here is that the market value of the land in its restored state would only be $300 more than its market value in its unrestored state.

Willie & Lucille sue Garland. They want [almost as much as the] "cost of performance" ($25,000) as damages for breach of contract. Garland obviously wants damages to be only $300.

II. Procedural Story

The trial court (the lower, entry-level court in which the suit was initially brought) actually instructed the jury that it must return a verdict for the plaintiffs and should solely consider the amount of damages (i.e., breach of contract is admitted by the defendant, so only damages are at issue).

The jury awarded $5,000 to Willie and Lucille. Great discretion was given by the judge in instructions to the jury, telling them they were at liberty to consider the "diminution in value" of the land as well as the cost of "repair work" in determining damages.

Willie and Lucille were unsatisfied and so appealed. (They based their appeal on erroneous jury instructions, although this is not explicitly stated in the decision. You cannot just appeal because you are unhappy with the decision. There must be legal grounds for an appeal.)

Garland was also unsatisfied with the verdict and so cross-appealed (on the same grounds).

III. What Kind of Sources Does the Appeals Court Use?

On appeal, the issue is sharply drawn. Plaintiffs contend that the true measure of damages in this case is what it will cost plaintiffs to obtain performance of the work that was not done because of defendant's default. Defendant argues that the measure of damages is the cost of performance 'limited, however, to the total difference in the market value before and after the work was performed'.

It appears that this precise question has not heretofore been presented to this court. In *Ardizonne v. Archer*, 72 Okl. 70, 178 P. 263, this court held that the measure of damages for breach of a contract to drill an oil well was the reasonable cost of drilling the well, but here a slightly different factual situation exists. The drilling of an oil well will yield valuable geological information, even if no oil or gas is found, and of course if the well is a producer, the value of the premises increases. In the case before us, it is argued by defendant with some force that the performance of the remedial work defendant agreed to do will add at the most only a few hundred dollars to the value of plaintiffs' farm, and that the damages should be limited to that amount because that is all plaintiffs have lost.

So, the first thing the Court does is look at other cases with similar facts although it notes these *precise* facts have not arisen before.

Plaintiffs rely on *Groves v. John Wunder Co.*, 205 Minn. 163, 286 N.W. 235, 123 A.L.R. 502. In that case, the Minnesota court, in a substantially similar situation, adopted the 'cost of performance' rule as-opposed to the 'value' rule. The result was to authorize a jury to give plaintiff damages in the amount of $ 60,000, where the real estate concerned would have been worth only $ 12,160, even if the work contracted for had been done.

It may be observed that *Groves v. John Wunder Co.*, supra, is the only case which has come to our attention in which the cost of performance rule has been followed under circumstances where the cost of performance greatly exceeded the diminution in value resulting from the breach of contract. Incidentally, it appears that this case was decided by a plurality rather than a majority of the members of the court.

Defendant relies principally upon *Sandy Valley & E. R. Co. v. Hughes*, 175 Ky. 320, 194 S.W. 344; *Bigham v. Wabash-Pittsburg Terminal Ry. Co.*, 223 Pa. 106, 72 A. 318; and *Sweeney v. Lewis Const. Co.*, 66 Wash. 490, 119 P. 1108. These were all cases in which, under similar circumstances, the appellate courts followed the 'value' rule instead of the 'cost of performance' rule. Plaintiff points out that in the earliest of these cases (Bigham) the court cites as authority on the measure of damages an earlier Pennsylvania *tort* case, and that the other two cases follow the first, with no explanation as to why a measure of damages ordinarily followed in cases sounding in tort should be used in contract cases. Nevertheless, it is of some significance that three out of four appellate courts have followed the diminution in value rule under circumstances where, as here, the cost of performance greatly exceeds the diminution in value.

The Court looks at cases presented by both the plaintiffs and defendants in support of their positions. The Court "distinguishes" (i.e., points out why the precedent's facts differ from the facts in this case) *Groves v. John Wunder Co.,* **the plaintiffs' chief case in support of their position, but approves of the defendant's cases.**

Even in the case of contracts that are unquestionably building and construction contracts, the authorities are not in agreement as to the factors to be considered in determining whether the cost of performance rule or the value rule should be applied. The American Law Institute's Restatement of the Law, *Contracts,* Volume 1, Sections 346(1)(a)(i) and (ii) submits the proposition that the cost of performance is the proper measure of damages 'if this is possible and does not involve *unreasonable economic waste*'; and that the diminution in value caused by the breach is the proper measure 'if construction and completion in accordance with the contract would involve *unreasonable economic waste*' (emphasis supplied). In an explanatory comment immediately following the text, the Restatement makes it clear that the 'economic waste' referred to consists of the destruction of a substantially completed building or other structure. Of course, no such destruction is involved in the case now before us.

On the other hand, in McCormick, *Damages,* Section 168, it is said with regard to building and construction contracts that 'in cases where the defect is one that can be repaired or cured without *undue expense*' the cost of performance is the proper measure of damages, but where 'the defect in material or construction is one that cannot be remedied without *an expenditure for reconstruction disproportionate to the end to be attained*' (emphasis supplied) the value rule should be followed. The same idea was expressed in *Jacob & Youngs, Inc. v. Kent,* 230 N.Y. 239, 129 N.E. 889, 23 A.L.R. 1429, as follows:

> The owner is entitled to the money which will permit him to complete, unless the cost of completion is grossly and unfairly out of proportion to the good to be attained. When that is true, the measure is the difference in value.

It thus appears that the prime consideration in the Restatement was 'economic waste'; and that the prime consideration in McCormick, *Damages,* and in *Jacob & Youngs, Inc. v. Kent, supra,* was the relationship between the expense involved and the 'end to be attained' – in other words, the 'relative economic benefit'.

In view of the unrealistic fact situation in the instant case, and certain Oklahoma statutes to be hereinafter noted, we are of the opinion that the 'relative economic benefit' is a proper consideration here.

Then the Court looks at other cases, mentioned in the Restatement of Contracts (the American Law Institute's summary of the state of the law), finding a couple of cases 'on point' (i.e., having similar facts). It also takes a statute into consideration.

This is in accord with the recent case of *Mann v. Clowser,* 190 Va. 887, 59 S.E.2d 78, where, in applying the cost rule, the Virginia court specifically noted that 'the defects are remediable from a practical standpoint and the costs *are not grossly disproportionate to the results to be obtained*' (emphasis supplied).

23 O.S.1961 §§ 96 and 97 provide as follows:

> § 96. Notwithstanding the provisions of this chapter, no person can recover a greater amount in damages for the breach of an obligation, than he would have gained by the full performance thereof on both sides.

> § 97. Damages must, in all cases, be reasonable, and where an obligation of any kind appears to create a right to unconscionable and grossly oppressive damages, contrary to substantial justice no more than reasonable damages can be recovered.

Although it is true that the above sections of the statute are applied most often in tort cases, they are by their own terms, and the decisions of this court, also applicable in actions for damages for breach of contract. It would seem that they are peculiarly applicable here where, under the 'cost of performance' rule, plaintiffs might recover an amount about nine times the total value of their farm. Such would seem to be 'unconscionable and grossly oppressive damages, contrary to substantial justice' within the meaning of the statute. Also, it can hardly be denied that if plaintiffs here are permitted to recover under the 'cost of performance' rule, they will receive a greater benefit from the breach than could be gained from full performance, contrary to the provisions of Sec. 96.

[T]he obvious and well known rationale is that, insofar as they exceed the actual damages suffered, the stipulated damages amount to a penalty or forfeiture which the law does not favor.

The Court cites this statute, used mostly for tort cases (i.e., civil cases other than breach of contract), but says it is applicable to contracts too, and points out that the "cost of performance" measure would amount to a "penalty or forfeiture" against Garland since the amount would so grossly exceed the actual damages suffered.

Then comes the "holding," the official statement by the Court of what it has decided. Note how the Court "narrows" the holding by making it very specific to the facts in this case.

We therefore hold that where, in a coal mining lease, lessee agrees to perform certain remedial work on the premises concerned at the end of the lease period, and thereafter the contract is fully performed by both parties except that the remedial work is not done, the measure of damages in an action by lessor against lessee for damages for breach of contract is ordinarily the reasonable cost of performance of the work; however, where the contract provision breached was merely incidental to the main purpose in view, and where the economic benefit which would result to lessor by full performance of the work is grossly disproportionate to the cost of performance, the damages which lessor may recover are limited to the diminution in value resulting to the premises because of the non-performance.

We are of the opinion that the judgment of the trial court for plaintiffs should be, and it is hereby, modified and reduced to the sum of $ 300.00, and as so modified it is affirmed.

The Court modifies the trial court's judgment in accordance with Garland's request to $300.

Four members of the Oklahoma Supreme Court dissent.

WILLIAMS, C. J., BLACKBIRD, V. C. J., and IRWIN and BERRY, JJ., dissent.

DISSENT: IRWIN, Justice:

By the specific provisions in the coal mining lease under consideration, the defendant agreed as follows:

> 7b Lessee agrees to make fills in the pits dug on said premises on the property line in such manner that fences can be placed thereon and access had to opposite sides of the pits.
>
> 7c Lessee agrees to smooth off the top of the spoil banks on the above premises.
>
> 7d Lessee agrees to leave the creek crossing the above premises in such a condition that it will not interfere with the crossings to be made in pits as set out in 7b.
>
> 7f Lessee further agrees to leave no shale or dirt on the high wall of said pits.

Following the expiration of the lease, plaintiffs made demand upon defendant that it carry out the provisions of the contract and to perform those covenants contained therein.

Defendant admits that it failed to perform its obligations that it agreed and contracted to perform under the lease contract and there is nothing in the record which indicates that defendant could not perform its obligations. Therefore, in my opinion defendant's breach of the contract was wilful and not in good faith.

The dissent takes the older traditional view of contracts:

- **Garland admits it failed to perform its agreed-upon obligations.**
- **Nothing in the record indicates Garland could not perform those obligations.**
- **Therefore the breach was willful and not in good faith.**

The cost for performing the contract in question could have been reasonably approximated when the contract was negotiated and executed and there are no conditions now existing which could not have been reasonably anticipated by the parties. Therefore, defendant had knowledge, when it prevailed upon the plaintiffs to execute the lease, that the cost of performance might be disproportionate to the value or benefits received by plaintiff for the performance.

Defendant did not have the right to mine plaintiffs' coal or to use plaintiffs' property for its mining operations without the consent of plaintiffs. Defendant had knowledge of the benefits that it would receive under the contract and the approximate cost of performing the contract. With this knowledge, it must be presumed that defendant thought that it would be to its economic advantage to enter into the contract with plaintiffs and that it would reap benefits from the contract, or it would have not entered into the contract.

Garland knew, when it "prevailed upon" Willie and Lucille to sign the lease, that the cost of performance might be disproportionate to the value of benefits received by the Peevyhouses for performance.

It must be assumed that Garland thought it would be to its economic advantage to enter into the contract with Willie and Lucille and that it would reap benefits from the contract, despite the cost of restoring the land to its original state, or it would not have entered into the contract.

Therefore, if the value of the performance of a contract should be considered in determining the measure of damages for breach of a contract, the value of the benefits received under the contract by a party who breaches a contract should also be considered. However, in my judgment, to give consideration to either in the instant action, completely rescinds and holds for naught the solemnity of the contract before us and makes an entirely new contract for the parties.

If the value of performance of a contract should be considered in determining the measure of damages for breach, so too should the benefits received by the breaching party be considered. That is, if the strip mining produces no profit for the coal company, should it be excused from the contract and not have to pay the Peevyhouses at all?

But, the dissenting judge asserts, considering either of these things ignores the "solemnity of the contract."

I am mindful of Title 23 O.S.1961 § 96, which provides that no person can recover a greater amount in damages for the breach of an obligation than he could have gained by the full performance thereof on both sides, except in cases not applicable herein. However, in my judgment, the above statutory provision is not applicable here.

In my judgment, we should follow the case of *Groves v. John Wunder Company*, 205 Minn. 163, 286 N.W. 235, 123 A.L.R. 502, which defendant agrees 'that the fact situation is apparently similar to the one in the case at bar,' and where the Supreme Court of Minnesota held:

> The owner's or employer's damages for such a breach (i.e., breach hypothesized in 2d syllabus) are to be measured, not in respect to the value of the land to be improved, but by the reasonable cost of doing that which the contractor promised to do and which he left undone.

Therefore, in my opinion, the plaintiffs were entitled to specific performance of the contract and since defendant has failed to perform, the proper measure of damages should be the cost of performance. Any other measure of damage would be holding for naught the express provisions of the contract; would be taking from the plaintiffs the benefits of the contract and placing those benefits in defendant which has failed to perform its obligations; would be granting benefits to defendant without a resulting obligation; and would be completely rescinding the solemn obligation of the contract for the benefit of the defendant to the detriment of the plaintiffs by making an entirely new contract for the parties.

I therefore respectfully dissent to the opinion promulgated by a majority of my associates.

The dissenting judge thinks the Court should follow the holding in *Groves v. John Wunder Company*, the Peevyhouses' main case, and apply the "cost of performance" rule in assessing damages.

Willie and Lucille's lawyers tried to get a rehearing to recalculate the damages based on the diminution of value of the *whole farm*, not just of the sixty acres used by Garland. They were denied this opportunity because they did not object early on in the proceedings, when the Garland lawyers insisted that only testimony about the sixty acres was admissible in the trial.

~

What is going on here? Is this a "good" decision?
What is a good decision?

 – A "fair" one?
 – A "just" one?
 – One that provides a useful template for future behavior?

What is that template here?

The template provided by this case is that in situations where the cost of breaching a contract will be less than the cost of fulfilling the contract, the "proper" or perhaps "smart" choice is to breach the contract.

This is now called "efficient breach of contract" and is largely smiled upon today. Garland's lawyers were way ahead of their time.

The Common Law and Statutory Law: Case 2

In re PHILLIP B., A Person Coming Under the Juvenile Court Law.
RICHARD W. BOTHMAN, as Chief Probation Officer, etc., et al., Plaintiffs
and Appellants, v. WARREN B. et al., Defendants and Respondents

Civ. No. 44291

Court of Appeal of California, First Appellate District, Division Four

92 Cal. App. 3d 796; 156 Cal. Rptr. 48; 1979 Cal. App. LEXIS 1717

May 8, 1979

OPINION: CALDECOTT, Justice:

A petition was filed by the juvenile probation department in the juvenile court, alleging that Phillip B., a minor, came within the provision of Welfare and Institutions Code section 300, subdivision (b), because he was not provided with the "necessities of life."

The petition requested that Phillip be declared a dependent child of the court for the special purpose of ensuring that he receive cardiac surgery for a congenital heart defect. Phillip's parents had refused to consent to the surgery. The juvenile court dismissed the petition. The appeal is from the order.

Phillip is a 12-year-old boy suffering from Down's Syndrome. At birth, his parents decided he should live in a residential care facility. Phillip suffers from a congenital heart defect – a ventricular septal defect that results in elevated pulmonary blood pressure. Due to the defect, Phillip's heart must work three times harder than normal to supply blood to his body. When he overexerts, unoxygenated blood travels the wrong way through the septal hole reaching his circulation, rather than the lungs.

If the congenital heart defect is not corrected, damage to the lungs will increase to the point where his lungs will be unable to carry and oxygenate any blood. As a result, death follows. During the deterioration of the lungs, Phillip will suffer from a progressive loss of energy and vitality until he is forced to lead a bed-to-chair existence.

Phillip's heart condition has been known since 1973. At that time Dr. Gathman, a pediatric cardiologist, examined Phillip and recommended cardiac catheterization to further define the anatomy and dynamics of Phillip's condition. Phillip's parents refused.

In 1977, Dr. Gathman again recommended catheterization and this time Phillip's parents consented. The catheterization revealed the extensive nature of Phillip's septal defect, thus it was Dr. Gathman's recommendation that surgery be performed.

Dr. Gathman referred Phillip to a second pediatric cardiologist, Dr. William French of Stanford Medical Center. Dr. French estimates the surgical mortality rate to be 5 to 10 percent, and notes that Down's Syndrome children face a higher than average risk of postoperative complications. Dr. French found that Phillip's pulmonary vessels have already undergone some change from high pulmonary artery pressure. Without the operation, Phillip will begin to function less physically until he will be severely incapacitated. Dr. French agrees with Dr. Gathman that Phillip will enjoy a significant expansion of his life span if his defect is surgically corrected. Without the surgery, Phillip may live at the outside 20 more years. Dr. French's opinion on the advisability of surgery was not asked.

We are in court in June 1979 in the Court of Appeal of California.

Phillip is twelve years old.

The state's juvenile probation department has filed a petition under the Welfare and Institutions Code asking that Phillip be declared a "dependent child of the court" so that he can receive cardiac surgery, which his parents have refused to approve.

The petition alleges the circumstances fall under the Code because Phillip has not been provided with the "necessities of life."

So we see here a case brought by the *State* based upon powers conferred upon it by legislative fiat. In reaching its decision, the Court will look primarily to statutes and their interpretation.

I

It is fundamental that parental autonomy is constitutionally protected. The United States Supreme Court has articulated the concept of personal liberty found in the Fourteenth Amendment as a right of privacy which extends to certain aspects of a family relationship.

Inherent in the preference for parental autonomy is a commitment to diverse lifestyles, including the right of parents to raise their children as they think best. Legal judgments regarding the value of child rearing patterns should be kept to a minimum so long as the child is afforded the best available opportunity to fulfill his potential in society.

Parental autonomy, however, is not absolute. The state is the guardian of society's basic values. Under the doctrine of *parens patriae*, the state has a right, indeed, a duty, to protect children. (See e.g., *Prince* v. *Massachusetts, supra*, 321 U.S. 158 at p. 166 [88 L.Ed. 645 at pp. 652–53].) State officials may interfere in family matters to safeguard the child's health, educational development and emotional well-being.

The Court turns immediately to our foundational legal text, the United States Constitution, and says that parental autonomy is constitutionally protected.

***BUT* the Court also says that parental autonomy is not absolute. The state, under the *parens patriae* (parent of the country) doctrine, has a right and a duty to protect children.**

Several relevant factors must be taken into consideration before a state insists upon medical treatment rejected by the parents. The state should examine the seriousness of the harm the child is suffering or the substantial likelihood that he will suffer serious harm; the evaluation for the treatment by the medical profession; the risks involved in medically treating the child; and the expressed preferences of the child. Of course, the underlying consideration is the child's welfare and whether his best interests will be served by the medical treatment.

The Court lists relevant factors to be considered when contemplating overruling parents regarding medical treatment:

– **the seriousness of the harm the child is suffering;**
– **an evaluation for treatment by medical professionals;**
– **the risks involved in such treatment;**
– **the expressed preferences of the child; and**
– **whether the "best interests" of the child will be served.**

Section 300, subdivision (b), permits a court to adjudge a child under the age of 18 years a dependent of the court if the child is not provided with the "necessities of life."

The trial judge dismissed the petition on the ground that there was "no clear and convincing evidence to sustain this petition."

The lower court dismissed the petition on the ground that there was "no clear and convincing evidence to sustain the petition," that is, that there was no proof that Phillip had not been provided with the "necessities of life."

SIDEBAR: Burdens and standards of proof

"Clear & convincing" evidence is the civil trial analog of the criminal law standard of "beyond a reasonable doubt." It is thus a very high standard. More typically in civil trials the standard is "by a preponderance of the evidence," which means that one outcome is 'more likely' than the other. The difference in the standards of proof is illustrated by the two O.J. Simpson trials. He was found "not guilty" of murder because the prosecution failed to prove his criminal guilt "beyond a reasonable doubt," but he was "liable" for the tort (the civil wrong) of "wrongful death" because the jury felt his liability had been established "by a preponderance of the evidence," that is, it was more likely than not that he was responsible.

The rule is clear that the power of the appellate court begins and ends with a determination as to whether there is any substantial evidence, contradicted or uncontradicted, which will support the conclusion reached by the trier of fact. (See 6 Witkin, Cal. Procedure (2d ed. 1971) Appeal, § 245, p. 4236.) The "clear and convincing evidence" standard of proof applies only to the trial court, and is not the standard for appellate review. (See *Crail* v. *Blakely* (1973) 8 Cal.3d 744, 750 [106 Cal.Rptr. 187, 505 P.2d 1027].)

The Court points out that (*by statute*) in reviewing a lower court decision, it can look only at whether there is "any substantial evidence, contradicted or uncontradicted, which will support the conclusion reached by the trier of fact." If there is, the appellate court cannot reverse or remand. Its hands are tied.

Turning to the facts of this case, one expert witness testified that Phillip's case was more risky than the average. Another expert witness testified that one of the risks of surgery to correct a ventricular septal defect was damage to the nerve that controls the heartbeat as the nerve is in the same area as the defect. When this occurs a pacemaker would be required.

The trial judge, in announcing his decision, cited the inconclusiveness of the evidence to support the petition.

On reading the record we can see the trial court's attempt to balance the possible benefits to be gained from the operation against the risks involved. The court had before it a child suffering not only from a ventricular septal defect but also from Down's Syndrome, with its higher than average morbidity, and the presence of pulmonary vascular changes. In light of these facts, we cannot say as a matter of law that there was no substantial evidence to support the decision of the trial court.

The Court says that the presence of expert testimony on the record detailing the dangers of a surgical intervention for Phillip is sufficient evidence for the lower court to have reached its decision. (There is a 5–10% mortality rate.)

II

In denying the petition the trial court ruled that there was no clear and convincing evidence to sustain the petition. The state contends the proper standard of proof is by a preponderance of the evidence and not by the clear and convincing test. The state asserts that only when a permanent severance of the parent–child relationship is ordered by the court must the clear and convincing standard of proof be applied. Since the petition did not seek permanent severance but only authorization for corrective heart surgery, the state contends the lower standard of proof should have been applied.

In the case of *In re Robert P.* (1976) 61 Cal.App.3d 310, 318 [132 Cal.Rptr. 5], the court pointed out that a dependency hearing pursuant to section 600, need not result in a permanent severance of the parent–child relationship. Section 366 (formerly § 729) requires subsequent hearings at periods not exceeding one year until such time as the court's jurisdiction over such minor is terminated. *In re Robert P.* held that even though the severance need not be permanent the standard of proof was "clear and convincing" and not a "preponderance of the evidence." The "clear and convincing standard" was proper in this case.

The state here tries to argue that the "clear & convincing" standard is inappropriate and the standard should instead be "preponderance of the evidence" because, by statute, the former should apply only in cases where the separation of the minor from his or her parents is to be permanent.

The Court, however, interprets the statute differently based on an earlier decision, *In re Robert P.*

III

Amicus Curiae contends the judge erred in failing to notify Phillip of his right to counsel, thus Phillip was not properly represented.

A minor has a statutory right to counsel. (§ 318.5.) If a minor is already represented by counsel, it is not crucial that a judge inform a minor of his right to counsel. "[If] either the minor or his parents appear without counsel, the judge shall advise the *unrepresented* party of his rights under this section." (§ 318.5, subd. (d); italics added.)

In the present case, the facts show that a deputy district attorney was representing Phillip at the hearing. He was introduced to the judge as Phillip's attorney. The deputy district attorney proceeded to make an opening statement and continued to represent Phillip throughout the entire hearing.

"Amicus Curiae" ("Friend of the Court") is a party not directly involved in the case but who has an interest in it (often because of public policy issues) and who writes "briefs" in support of one side's position or the other.

Amicus Curiae apparently filed a brief contending the lower court erred by not *informing* Phillip of his right to counsel. However Phillip *had* counsel, and there was no separate requirement that he be informed of his right to have what he already had.

The order dismissing the petition is affirmed.

The Common Law and Statutory Law: Case 3

The Phillip B. saga continues.

Guardianship of PHILLIP B., a Minor. HERBERT H. et al., Petitioners and Respondents, v. WARREN B. et al., Objectors and Appellants

Civ. No. 53419

Court of Appeal of California, First Appellate District, Division One

139 Cal. App. 3d 407; 188 Cal. Rptr. 781; 1983 Cal. App. LEXIS 1339

January 25, 1983

OPINION: RACANELLI, Justice:

We are in the same court in January 1983, four years later. Phillip is now sixteen years old.

Few human experiences evoke the poignancy of a filial relationship and the pathos attendant upon its disruption in society's effort to afford every child a meaningful chance to live life to its fullest promise. This appeal, posing a sensitive confrontation between the fundamental right of parental custody and the well being of a retarded child, reflects the deeply ingrained concern that the needs of the child remain paramount in the judicial monitoring of custody. In reaching our decision to affirm, we neither suggest nor imply that appellants' subjectively motivated custodial objectives affront conventional norms of parental fitness; rather, we determine only that on the unusual factual record before us, the challenged order of guardianship must be upheld in order to avert potential harm to the minor ward likely to result from appellants' continuing custody and to subserve his best interests.

Phillip B. was born on October 16, 1966, with Down's Syndrome.

Appellants, deeply distraught over Phillip's disability, decided upon institutionalization, a course of action recommended by a state social worker and approved by appellants' pediatrician. A few days later, Phillip was transferred from the hospital to a licensed board and care facility for disabled youngsters. Although the facility was clean, it offered no structured educational or developmental programs and required that all the children (up to eight years of age) sleep in cribs.

The Bs (the appellants here, i.e., the parties appealing to the Court to have the first instance decision reversed) initially visited Phillip in his board and care facility frequently, but soon their visits became less frequent and the Bs became "detached" from him.

When Phillip was three years old a pediatrician informed appellants that Phillip had a congenital heart defect, a condition afflicting half of Down's Syndrome children. (Smith & Wilson, *supra*, p. 41.) Open heart surgery was suggested when Phillip attained age six. However, appellants took no action to investigate or remedy the suspected medical problem.

After the board and care facility had been sold during the summer of 1971, appellants discovered that the condition of the facility had seriously deteriorated under the new management; it had become dirty and cluttered with soiled clothing, and smelled strongly of urine. Phillip was very thin and listless and was being fed watery oatmeal from a bottle. At appellants' request, a state social worker arranged for Phillip's transfer in January 1972, to We Care, a licensed residential facility for developmentally disabled children located in San Jose, where he remained up to the time of the trial.

Unfortunately, at the time Phillip is transferred, "We Care" doesn't seem to care very much.

At that time, the facility – which cared for about 20 children more severely handicapped than Phillip – operated under very limited conditions: it had no programs of education or therapy; the children were not enrolled in outside programs; the facility lacked an outdoor play area; the building was in poor repair; and the kitchen had only a two-burner hot plate used to cook pureed food.

This is like something out of a Dickens novel.

In April 1972, We Care employed Jeanne Haight (later to become program director and assistant administrator of the facility) to organize a volunteer program. Mrs. Haight quickly noticed Phillip's debilitated condition. She found him unusually small and thin for his age (five); he was not toilet trained and wore diapers, still slept in a crib, walked like a toddler, and crawled down stairs only inches high. His speech was limited and mostly unintelligible; his teeth were in poor condition.

Mrs. Haight, who undertook a recruitment program for volunteers, soon recruited respondent Patsy H., who had helped to found a school for children with learning disabilities where Mrs. Haight had once been vice principal. Mrs. H. began working at We Care on a daily basis. Her husband, respondent Herbert H., and their children, soon joined in the volunteer activities.

Mrs. H., initially assigned to work with Phillip and another child, assisted Phillip in experimenting with basic sensory experiences, improving body coordination, and in overcoming his fear of steps. Mr. H. and one of the H. children helped fence the yard area, put in a lawn, a sandbox, and install some climbing equipment.

Mrs. Haight promptly initiated efforts to enroll Phillip in a preschool program for the fall of 1972, which required parental consent. She contacted Mr. B. who agreed to permit Phillip to participate provided learning aptitude could be demonstrated. Mrs. H. used vocabulary cards to teach Phillip 25 to 50 new words and to comprehend word association. Although Mr. B. failed to appear at the appointed time in order to observe what Phillip had learned, he eventually gave his parental consent enabling Phillip to attend Hope Preschool in October 1972.

Respondents continued working with Phillip coordinating their efforts with his classroom lessons. Among other things, they concentrated on development of feeding skills and toilet training and Mr. H. and the two eldest children gradually became more involved in the volunteer program.

Phillip subsequently attended a school for the trainable mentally retarded (TMR) where the children are taught basic survival words. They are capable of learning to feed and dress themselves appropriately, doing basic community activities such as shopping, and engaging in recreational activities. There is no attempt to teach them academics, and they are expected to live in sheltered settings as adults. In contrast, children capable of attending classes for the educable mentally retarded (EMR) are taught reading, writing, and simple computation, with the objective of developing independent living skills as adults.

Over the next several years, the Bs became more detached from Phillip while the Hs established a close and caring relationship with him.

Beginning in December 1972, Phillip became a frequent visitor at respondents' home; with appellants' consent, Phillip was permitted to spend weekends with respondents, a practice which continued regularly and often included weekday evenings. At the same time, respondents maintained frequent contact with Phillip at We Care as regular volunteer visitors. Meanwhile, appellants visited Phillip at the facility only a few times a year; however, no overnight home visits occurred until after the underlying litigation ensued.

Respondents played an active role in Phillip's behavioral development and educational training. They consistently supplemented basic skills training given Phillip at We Care.

Phillip was openly accepted as a member of the H. family whom he came to love and trust. He eventually had his own bedroom; he was included in sharing household chores. Mr. H. set up a workbench for Phillip and helped him make simple wooden toys; they attended special Boy Scout meetings together. And Phillip regularly participated in family outings. Phillip referred to the H. residence as "my house." When Phillip began to refer to the H.'s as "Mom" and "Dad," they initially discouraged the familiar reference, eventually succeeding in persuading Phillip to use the discriminate references "Mama Pat" and "Dada Bert" and "Mama B." and "Daddy B." Both Mrs. Haight and Phillip's teacher observed significant improvements in Phillip's development and behavior. Phillip had developed, in Mrs. Haight's opinion, "true love and strong [emotional] feelings" for respondents.

The Hs even asked the Bs to share a picture of themselves so they could show Phillip who his parents were but the Bs never provided one.

Meanwhile, appellants continued to remain physically and emotionally detached from Phillip. The natural parents intellectualized their decision to treat Phillip differently from their other children. Appellants testified that Phillip, whom they felt would always require institutionalization, should not be permitted to form close emotional attachments which – upon inevitable disruption – would traumatize the youngster.

In matters of Phillip's health care needs, appellants manifested a reluctant – if not neglectful – concern. When Dr. Gathman, a pediatric cardiologist, diagnosed a ventricular septal defect in Phillip's heart in early 1973 and recommended catheterization (a medically accepted presurgery procedure to measure pressure and to examine the interior of the heart), appellants refused their consent.

In the spring of 1977, Dr. Gathman again recommended heart catheterization in connection with the anticipated use of general anesthesia during Phillip's major dental surgery. Appellants consented to the preoperative procedure which revealed that the heart defect was surgically correctible with a maximum risk factor of 5 percent. At a conference attended by appellants and Mrs. Haight in June 1977, Dr. Gathman recommended corrective surgery in order to avoid a progressively deteriorating condition resulting in a "bed-to-chair existence" and the probability of death before the age of 30. Although Dr. Gathman – as requested by Mrs. B. – supplied the name of a parent of Down's Syndrome children with similar heart disease, no contact was ever made. Later that summer, appellants decided – without obtaining an independent medical consultation – against surgery. Appellants' stated reason was that Dr. Gathman had "painted" an inaccurate picture of the situation. They felt that surgery would be merely life-prolonging rather than life-saving, presenting the possibility that they would be unable to care for Phillip during his later years.

What's the difference between 'merely life-prolonging' and 'life-saving'? Is any medical treatment truly 'life saving'?

A few months later, in early 1978, appellants' decision was challenged in a juvenile dependency proceeding initiated by the district attorney on the ground that the withholding of surgery constituted neglect within the meaning of Welfare and Institutions Code section 300, subdivision (b); the juvenile court's dismissal of the action on the basis of inconclusive evidence was ultimately sustained on appeal (*In re Phillip B.* (1979) 92 Cal.App.3d 796 [156 Cal.Rptr. 48]; cert. den. *sub nom. Bothman v. Warren B.* (1980) 445 U.S. 949 [63 L.Ed.2d 784, 100 S.Ct. 1597].

In September, 1978, upon hearing from a staff member of We Care that Phillip had been regularly spending weekends at respondents' home, Mr. B. promptly forbade Phillip's removal from the facility (except for medical purposes and school attendance) and requested that respondents be denied personal visits with Phillip at We Care.

Although respondents continued to visit Phillip daily at the facility, the abrupt cessation of home visits produced regressive changes in Phillip's behavior: he began acting out violently when respondents prepared to leave, begging to be taken "home"; he resorted to profanity; he became sullen and withdrawn when respondents were gone; bed wetting regularly occurred, a recognized symptom of emotional disturbance in children. He began to blame himself for the apparent rejection by respondents; he began playing with matches and on one occasion he set his clothes afire; on another, he rode his tricycle to respondents' residence a few blocks away proclaiming on arrival that he was "home." He continuously pleaded to return home with respondents. Many of the behavioral changes continued to the time of trial.

Appellants unsuccessfully pressed to remove Phillip from We Care notwithstanding the excellent care he was receiving. However, in January 1981, the regional center monitoring public assistance for residential care and training of the handicapped, consented to Phillip's removal to a suitable alternate facility. Despite an extended search, none could be found which met Phillip's individualized needs. Meanwhile, Phillip continued living at We Care, periodically visiting at appellant's home.

The Bs visited Phillip rarely and never brought him to their home for an overnight visit *until this litigation began.*

But throughout, the strong emotional attachment between Phillip and respondents remained intact.

Evidence established that Phillip, with a recently tested I.Q. score of 57, is a highly functioning Down's Syndrome child capable of learning sufficient basic and employable skills to live independently or semi-independently in a noninstitutional setting.

Procedural Background

In August 1981 the Hs filed a petition for appointment as guardians of Phillip, who was fourteen years old at that time.

The trial court, after a twelve-day hearing, agreed with the Hs and issued an order appointing them as guardians and giving them the authority to have the heart catheterization done.

That same day the Bs filed notice of an appeal and asked for writ of supersedeas (staying the power of the lower court to enforce its order while the appeal is made).

The California Supreme Court issued a stay and retransferred the case to the appellate court, which is where we are now.

Appellants raise several claims of reversible error relating to the sufficiency of evidence to support the findings, the admissibility of certain evidence and procedural due process. For the reasons which we explain, we find no error as claimed and affirm the order or judgment appealed.

Note that the appellate judge says right off the bat that he finds no error. This is typical legal writing. Courts generally avoid writing mystery stories in which we do not discover what happens until the end.

We consider the claims asserted in a sequence promoting clarity and convenience of discussion.

I

Sufficiency of the Evidence

Appellants' dominant claim of insufficiency of substantial evidence to support the critical findings below triggers settled principles of review which may be briefly set forth:

When a finding of fact is attacked on the ground that there is not any substantial evidence to sustain it, the power of an appellate court *begins* and *ends* with the determination as to whether there is any substantial evidence contradicted or uncontradicted which will support the finding of fact.

Courts generally may appoint a guardian over the person or estate of a minor "if it appears necessary or convenient." (Prob. Code, § 1514, subd. (a).) But the right of parents to retain custody of a child is fundamental and may be disturbed "'only in extreme cases of persons acting in a fashion incompatible with parenthood.'" (*In re Angelia P.* (1981) 28 Cal.3d 908, 916 [171 Cal.Rptr. 637, 623 P.2d 198], quoting *In re Carmaleta B.* (1978) 21 Cal.3d 482, 489 [146 Cal.Rptr. 623, 579 P.2d 514].) Accordingly, the Legislature has imposed the stringent requirement that before a court may make an order awarding custody of a child to a nonparent without consent of the parents, "it shall make a finding that an award of custody to a parent would be detrimental to the child and the award to a nonparent is required to serve the best interests of the child." (Civ. Code, § 4600, subd. (c); see *In re B.G.* (1974) 11 Cal.3d 679, 695-699 [114 Cal.Rptr. 444, 523 P.2d 244].) That requirement is equally applicable to guardianship proceedings under Probate Code section 1514, subdivision (b). The legislative shift in emphasis from parental unfitness to detriment to the child did not, however, signal a retreat from the judicial practice granting custodial preference to nonparents "only in unusual and extreme cases." (*In re B.G., supra,* 11 Cal.3d 679, 698, see *Guardianship of Marino* (1973) 30 Cal.App.3d 952, 958 [106 Cal.Rptr. 655].)

The judge has to wrestle with the language of the statute, which specifies when a court may appoint a guardian over a minor. Note how he "interprets" the statute in such a way as to favor the "best interests of the child."

The trial court expressly found that an award of custody to appellants would be harmful to Phillip in light of the psychological or "de facto" parental relationship established between him and respondents. Such relationships have long been recognized in the fields of law and psychology. As Justice Tobriner has cogently observed, "The fact of biological parenthood may incline an adult to feel a strong concern for the welfare of his child, but it is not an essential condition; a person who assumes the role of parent, raising the child in his own home, may in time acquire an interest in the 'companionship, care, custody and management' of that child. The interest of the 'de facto parent' is a substantial one, recognized by the decision of this court in *Guardianship of Shannon* (1933) 218 Cal. 490 [23 P.2d 1020] and by courts of other jurisdictions and deserving of legal protection."

The Court weighs the Hs' "de facto" parental relationship with Phillip heavily.

Appellants vigorously challenge the evidence and finding that respondents have become Phillip's de facto or psychological parents since he did not reside with them full time, as underscored in previous California decisions which have recognized de facto parenthood. (See, e.g., *In re Lynna B.* (1979) 92 Cal.App.3d 682 [155 Cal.Rptr. 256]; *In re Volkland* (1977) 74 Cal.App.3d 674 [141 Cal.Rptr. 625]; *Chaffin v. Frye* (1975) 45 Cal.App.3d 39 [119 Cal.Rptr. 22]; *Guardianship of Marino, supra,* 30 Cal.App.3d 952.) They argue that the subjective concept of psychological parenthood, relying on such nebulous factors as "love and affection" is susceptible to abuse and requires the counter-vailing element of objectivity provided by a showing of the child's long-term residency in the home of the claimed psychological parent.

We disagree. [T]he record contains uncontradicted expert testimony that while psychological parenthood usually will require residency on a "24-hour basis," it is not an absolute requirement; further, that the frequency and quality of Phillip's weekend visits with respondents, together with the regular weekday visits at We Care, provided an adequate foundation to establish the crucial parent–child relationship.

Appellants also challenge the sufficiency of the evidence to support the finding that their retention of custody would have been detrimental to Phillip. In making the critical finding, the trial court correctly applied the "clear and convincing" standard of proof necessary to protect the fundamental rights of parents in all cases involving a nonparent's bid for custody.

The record contains abundant evidence that appellants' retention of custody would cause Phillip profound emotional harm. Notwithstanding Phillip's strong emotional ties with respondents, appellants abruptly foreclosed home visits and set out to end all contact between them.

The judge says the record provides lots of evidence showing that if the Bs retain custody Phillip will suffer profound emotional harm. Thus the trial court had sufficient basis for its decision.

There was uncontroverted expert testimony that Phillip would sustain further emotional trauma in the event of total separation from respondents: the testimony indicated that, as with all children, Phillip needs love and affection, and he would be profoundly hurt if he were deprived of the existing psychological parental relationship with respondents in favor of maintaining unity with his biological parents.

We strongly emphasize, as the trial court correctly concluded, that the fact of detriment *cannot* be proved solely by evidence that the biological parent has elected to institutionalize a handicapped child, or that nonparents are able and willing to offer the child the advantages of their home in lieu of institutional placement. Sound reasons may exist justifying institutionalization of a handicapped child. But the totality of the evidence under review permits of no rational conclusion other than that the detriment caused Phillip, and its possible recurrence, was due not to appellants' choice to institutionalize but their calculated decision to remain emotionally and physically detached – abdicating the conventional role of competent decisionmaker in times of demonstrated need – thus effectively depriving him of *any* of the substantial benefits of a true parental relationship. *It is the emotional abandonment of Phillip, not his institutionalization,* which inevitably has created the unusual circumstances which led to the award of limited custody to respondents. We do not question the sincerity of appellants' belief that their approach to Phillip's welfare was in their combined best interests. But the record is replete with substantial and credible evidence supporting the trial court's determination, tested by the standard of clear and convincing proof, that appellants' retention of custody has caused and will continue to cause serious detriment to Phillip and that his best interests will be served through the guardianship award of custody to respondents. In light of such compelling circumstances, no legal basis is shown to disturb that carefully considered determination.

The Court zings the Bs when it says, "it is the emotional abandonment of Phillip, not his institutionalization, which inevitably has created the unusual circumstances which led to the award of limited custody to the respondents." The Bs' loss of custody was their own fault.

II

Due Process

Appellants assert several claims of due process violations. Our examination of each discloses no merit.

In the final analysis, due process is a flexible concept which calls for such procedural protections as each case demands.

The Court dismisses the Bs' due process claim (essentially a Fifth Amendment constitutional requirement that we be treated fairly). The Bs' claim here largely involves alleged errors in the pleading process, but the Court sets aside the contention surprisingly glibly, opining that "due process is a flexible concept."

Appellants' remaining due process complaint is directed to the trial court's receipt of a confidential juvenile probation department report bearing upon respondents' suitability as guardians. (See Civ. Code, § 4602; Prob. Code, § 1513, subd. (b).) The report, a copy of which had been mailed to appellants, was received and reviewed by the court after its August 7 decision without hearing. However, the report was never admitted into evidence.

Due process considerations generally mandate the right to an evidentiary hearing to question the contents of the report or to permit counterevidence. (*Wheeler* v. *Wheeler* (1973) 34 Cal.App.3d 239, 242 [109 Cal.Rptr. 782].) But the failure to object to the report or request a hearing effectively waives such right. (*Long* v. *Long* (1967) 251 Cal.App.2d 732, 736–737 [59 Cal.Rptr. 790].) Here, although appellants were well aware of the report and its contents with ample opportunity to register objections or demand a hearing (as late as the Sept. 24 final guardianship order), appellants waived their right by choosing to remain silent. Thus, they cannot now be heard to complain of the lack of a hearing.

The Bs apparently also claim that the lower court erroneously excluded certain evidence that they wanted to present about the Hs' unfitness to be guardians. The Court here says the Bs did not handle this appropriately, that is, the Bs tried to do it too late in the litigation. There was no error.

Appellants' showing of diligence was minimal at best.

In view of our determination, we need not discuss the remaining arguments raised in the briefs.

The order or judgment from which the appeal is taken is affirmed. The purported appeal from the interim order of immediate delivery and findings and conclusions, and each, is dismissed.

And so Phillip got his operation.

∽

Follow-up:

– In 1984, when Phillip was still sixteen years old, the Hs tried to adopt him formally but got nowhere (presumably because they would have needed the Bs' consent).

– When Phillip turned eighteen he got the right to choose for himself, *by statute*. He chose to become the son of the Hs.
– Phillip made progress and eventually got a job at the Santa Clara Medical Center cafeteria, busing tables.
– He lived with the Hs, whose name is Heath.
– He learned to read, use a computer, became a 49ers fan, and participated in the Special Olympics.

Remember:

– Both the *Peevyhouse* and *Phillip B.* cases illustrate that the law at its most important level is about people, not simply money or corporations or abstractions. This is easy to forget, particularly when we are dealing, as we will be, with law in cyberspace, where abstraction is the rule.
– The Phillip B. story should remind us that, contrary to popular belief, sometimes the law works the way we all hope it will.

2. Contracts

Definition

The most common response to the question "What is a contract?" is "an agreement," but a contract is more than that. The generally accepted legal definition of a contract is that it is a promise, or set of promises, that the law sees as a duty, for the breach of which the law will provide a remedy in the form of an action for damages. Thus a contract is a *legally enforceable* agreement.

Some Contracts Terminology

Promisee – A person to whom a promise is made
Promisor – A person who makes a promise
Offeree – A person to whom an offer is made
Offeror – A person who makes an offer

Contract Formation: Elements of a Contract

In order to make an agreement legally enforceable, three elements must be present – offer, acceptance, and consideration.

Offer

What is an offer? An offer is simply a manifestation of an intention to form a contract. The legal test of whether something is an offer is whether a reasonable person in the position of the offeree believes that acceptance creates a contract.

SIDEBAR: The reasonable person

The "reasonable person" is heavily relied upon by the law. No one can say with any specificity who this person is or what this person thinks, but the "reasonable person" might best be thought of as describing the "average" person, or perhaps the "normal" person. We will spend much more time examining this concept in the portion of this book that covers negligence.

Advertisements, as a general rule, are not considered to be offers, but rather "invitations to deal." The reason for this is primarily one of policy. It would not be desirable, or even realistic, to expect merchants to provide the goods advertised to every person who responds to an ad. If advertisements were considered offers, then every person who responded to the ad would be an offeree who could bind the offeror (the merchant) to the contract. But in most cases merchants are dealing in tangible goods and may simply run out or not have the right size, etc. (Of course, this is often less problematic when the merchant is selling "intangible" digital goods that can be easily and quickly reproduced. However, the same rule regarding ads applies in cyberspace.) So if a person sees an ad for, say, leather boots on sale at Bloomingdale's for $200 and then goes to the store to buy the boots, the customer is the offeror and Bloomingdale's is the offeree, free to accept the customer's 'offer to buy' if boots are still available in the customer's size, or to reject the offer if they are not.

If specific enough, though, advertisements *can* be offers. In particular, ads that specify quantity available and indicate who can accept the offer can put a merchant in the position of offeror, who will be bound to supply the goods to offerees. We will discuss this further later in the chapter.

Termination of Offers

Offers may be terminated in four ways:

1. *Termination of an offer because of lapse of time.* If a person offers to sell you a Trek mountain bike for $250 but does not mention how long the offer will last, can you accept two years later? No. An offer that does not specify how long it will be kept open must be accepted within a "reasonable time." "Reasonable time" is a flexible concept, but generally it is interpreted as meaning "within about a month or less."

2. *Revocation of an offer.* Revocation can be by words (i.e., the offeror explicitly tells the offeree the offer has been revoked) or by conduct, as long as the offeree is *aware* of the conduct indicating revocation. For example, Jane offers her golf clubs to Susan for $450. Later that day, Jane has second thoughts while sitting at home in her study and says aloud, "I don't want to sell those clubs to Susan." Can Susan still accept? Yes. She doesn't know about Jane's change of heart.

   On the other hand, if Jane offers to sell her golf clubs to Susan and the next day Susan sees Emily playing golf with Jane's clubs and Emily tells her that Jane has sold them to her, Susan cannot accept Jane's offer because she is aware of conduct by Jane that revokes the offer – namely selling the clubs to Emily.

   Note that a revocation sent through the mail is not effective until it is received.

   Note also that an offer cannot be revoked *after* it has been accepted.

3. *Rejection of an offer by the offeree, either directly by words or indirectly.* Rejection terminates all rights by the offeree to accept the offer. An example of indirect rejection is a counteroffer. A counteroffer acts as a rejection of the original offer, *but bargaining* does *not* terminate an offer and the difference between a counteroffer and bargaining can be very subtle.

   For example, Jane offers to sell Susan a thirty-foot sailboat for $10,000. Susan responds that she will only give Jane $9,000. Can Susan later accept the offer at the original price of $10,000? No. Susan has probably made a counteroffer and has therefore rejected the original offer. *But,* if Susan's response to Jane is "Will you take $9,000?" Susan is probably bargaining and may still decide to accept the original offer.

   Note that, like a revocation, a rejection sent through the mail is not effective until it is received.

4. *Termination of an offer because of death of a party prior to acceptance.* Death or incapacity of either party terminates the offer. For example, on September 15th Jane sends Susan a written offer. Jane dies on September 16th. Susan, not knowing of Jane's death, accepts the offer on September 20th. Is Susan's acceptance effective? No. When the offeror dies the offer dies too, whether the offeree knows about the death or not.

Acceptance

"Who can accept an offer?" may sound like a silly question, but it is an important one. Not just anyone can accept. Generally speaking, only a person to whom the offer is made and who knows about the offer can accept. That may sound even sillier, but let's look at an example of a couple of situations in which this issue comes into play.

Example: Suppose my dog wanders away and I place an ad in the local newspaper offering a reward of $500 for the dog's safe return. Not knowing about the ad, you find the dog on the street, read its tag identifying it as mine, and return it to me. I just say, "Thanks." When you get home your spouse asks if you got the reward and tells you about it. You return to my house and ask for the $500. Am I obliged to give it to you? No. Only if you know about the offer (the reward) at the time you perform the act can you say that the act (returning the dog to me) was an acceptance.

Example: I offer to sell my golf clubs to Joe for $200. Henry hears about the offer. Can Henry accept and bind me to the deal? No. Henry was not someone to whom I made the offer.

Note: Unlike rejections and revocations, acceptances are good when they are mailed. (The time at which something was mailed is often difficult to establish, but *proof* is an issue entirely separate from the underlying legal principles. Of course, the time of mailing should be easier to establish in the context of e-mail.)

Consideration

The third element required to form a contract is "consideration." An offer plus an acceptance adds up to an "agreement," but not one that is legally enforceable, that is, a contract.

Consideration is very difficult to define, but essentially it is a requirement that the agreement include some "bargained-for exchange" between the parties. That is, each party gives something up in return for something from the other party.

Consideration can be many things, including performance (doing something the party is not legally obliged to do), forbearance (not doing something the party is legally entitled to do), and even a promise to perform or a promise to forbear.

Luckily, in most contractual settings the consideration is obvious, for example, the exchange of money for a product or the performance of a task.

Perhaps the best way to grasp the concept of consideration is to look at a situation in which it is not present, and therefore there is no contract. A promise of a gift is such a situation.

Example: You give up smoking and I am so happy for you that I tell you I will give you $400 when I get paid at the end of the month. Payday arrives and you demand your $400. Am I obliged to give it to you? No. There has been no bargained-for exchange. You did not give up smoking *because* I promised you $400. You just gave up smoking. You did nothing in return for my promise. The agreement lacks consideration.

On the other hand, I offer you $400 when I get paid at the end of the month *if you give up smoking until then.* Payday arrives and you demand your $400. Now I *am* legally obliged to pay you the $400. There has been a bargained-for exchange. You have given up something you are legally permitted to do (although in fewer and fewer places) in return for my promise to pay you $400. The consideration is the exchange of my promise to you and your performance of a task.

Contracts: Case 1

Batsakis v. Demotsis

No. 4668

Court of Civil Appeals of Texas, El Paso

226 S.W.2d 673; 1949 Tex. App. LEXIS 1910

November 16, 1949

OPINION: McGILL, Justice:

Plaintiff sued defendant to recover $2,000 with interest at the rate of 8% per annum from April 2, 1942, alleged to be due on the following instrument, being a translation from the original, which is written in the Greek language:

Peiraeus
April 2, 1942
Mr. George Batsakis, Konstantinou Diadohou #7, Peiraeus
Mr. Batsakis:

I state by my present (letter) that I received today from you the amount of two thousand dollars ($2,000.00) of United States of America money, which I borrowed from you for the support of my family during these difficult days and because it is impossible for me to transfer dollars of my own from America.

The above amount I accept with the expressed promise that I will return to you again in American dollars either at the end of the present war or even before in the event that you might be able to find a way to collect them (dollars) from my representative in America to whom I shall write and give him an order relative to this. You understand until the final execution (payment) to the above amount an eight per cent interest will be added and paid together with the principal.

I thank you and I remain yours with respects.
The recipient,
(Signed) Eugenia The. Demotsis.

A consideration problem.

George Batsakis (plaintiff) sues Eugenia Demotsis (defendant).

Batsakis alleges Demotsis owes him $2,000 plus interest due on a loan (contract) made to her by him when they were residents of Greece.

Demotsis says that the contract should not be enforceable because there was inadequate consideration (i.e., that the Greek money she got from Batsakis was

so little compared to what she had promised in return that it cannot support the contract). Demotsis proposes that she repay $25 plus interest.

Further, in connection with this plea of want and failure of consideration defendant alleges that she at no time received from plaintiff himself or from anyone for plaintiff any money or thing of value other than, as hereinbefore alleged, the original loan of 500,000 drachmae. That at the time of the loan by plaintiff to defendant of said 500,000 drachmae the value of 500,000 drachmae in the Kingdom of Greece in dollars of money of the United States of America, was $25.00, and also at said time the value of 500,000 drachmae of Greek money in the United States of America in dollars was $25.00 of money of the United States of America. The plea of want and failure of consideration is verified by defendant as follows.

The lower court (without a jury, so what is referred to as a "bench trial") awards Batsakis $750 plus interest ($1,163.83).

Batsakis appeals.

Defendant testified that she did receive 500,000 drachmas from plaintiff. Her testimony clearly shows that the understanding of the parties was that plaintiff would give her the 500,000 drachmas if she would sign the instrument. She testified:

Q. Who suggested the figure of $2,000.00?

A. That was how he asked me from the beginning. He said he will give me five hundred thousand drachmas provided I signed that I would pay him $2,000.00 American money.

The transaction amounted to a sale by plaintiff of the 500,000 drachmas in consideration of the execution of the instrument sued on, by defendant. It is not contended that the drachmas had no value. Indeed, the judgment indicates that the trial court placed a value of $750.00 on them or on the other consideration which plaintiff gave defendant for the instrument if he believed plaintiff's testimony. Therefore the plea of want of consideration was unavailing. A plea of want of consideration amounts to a contention that the instrument never became a valid obligation in the first place. *National Bank of Commerce v. Williams*, 125 Tex. 619, 84 S.W.2d 691.

Mere inadequacy of consideration will not void a contract. 10 Tex.Jur., Contracts, Sec. 89, p. 150; *Chastain v. Texas Christian Missionary Society*, Tex.Civ.App., 78 S.W.2d 728, loc. cit. 731(3), Wr.Ref.

During World War II in Greece, Demotsis borrowed 500,000 dr ($25) from Batsakis because she could not get at her funds in the United States.

Batsakis made her sign a letter that said she had actually received $2,000.

The Court here holds that the contract providing for Demotsis giving $2,000 in American money to Batsakis in return for the 500,000 drachmas amounted to a *sale* by Batsakis of the Greek money in *consideration of the execution of the loan instrument, not the promise of paying him back $2,000*. Demotsis's plea of lack of consideration was therefore not valid. (Identifying the consideration can obviously be important.)

Since the parties both *knew* that Demotsis was signing an instrument that stated incorrectly that Batsakis was giving her $2,000, it was not fraudulent (although this is not said explicitly by the Court). The drachmas had value. On that day that value to Demotsis was $2,000.

Nor was the plea of failure of consideration availing. Defendant got exactly what she contracted for according to her own testimony.

Duress does not work here as a defense because duress must be personal or physical (gun to the head), not economic.

Fraud does not work because it applies only if there is either fraud in factum (the person did not know he or she was signing a contract) or fraud in inducement (the person was deceived about material terms).

The court should have rendered judgment in favor of plaintiff against defendant for the principal sum of $2,000.00 evidenced by the instrument sued on, with interest as therein provided. The judgment is reformed so as to award appellant a recovery against appellee of $2,000.00 with interest thereon at the rate of 8% per annum from April 2, 1942. *As so reformed, the judgment is affirmed.*

The Statute of Frauds

Some contracts must be written and signed (at least by the party against whom enforcement of the contract is sought). Contracts in this category are said to fall within the Statute of Frauds.

A number of types of contracts fall within the Statute of Frauds, but two are clearly the most important in cyberlaw-related situations.

The first of these is *service contracts* not *capable* of being performed within a year from the time the contract is formed. The word "capable" is key. The focus is not on what *actually* happens, but what *might* happen.

Example: I verbally contract with the owner of six thousand acres of forest land to cut down all the trees on his property. Fine. That contract is not within the Statute of Frauds and does not have to be written because it is *capable* of being performed within a year. Somehow it could be done, not by me alone with my Boy Scout hatchet, but I could hire an army of lumberjacks and get the job done.

Suppose it actually takes me two years? It doesn't matter. The contract did not have to be written because it *might* have been done within a year.

Example: My employer gives me a lifetime contract. The contract does *not* have to be written for me to enforce it because it *might* be performed within a year. (I could die!) BUT, if my employer gives me a contract for three years of employment it *must* be written if I wish to enforce it because it *cannot* be performed within a year. (I can't work three years in one, although most employers wish we all could.)

Another type of contract that falls within the Statute of Frauds and that is relevant to many commercial transactions, including those involving software, is contracts for the sale of goods for a price of $500 or more. These must be written and signed by the party against whom enforcement of the contract is sought.

"Ambiguity"

A contract may not be "ambiguous." "Ambiguity" in the contract law sense does not mean simply "vague" or "unclear." "Ambiguity" is a term of art. A contract is void because of ambiguity if:

- the parties use a material (i.e., "important") term open to at least two reasonable interpretations,
- each party attaches a different meaning to the term, and
- *neither* party knows or has reason to know of the meaning attached to the term by the other party.

Contracts: Case 2

RAFFLES v. WICHELHAUS

In the Court of Exchequer, 1864

2 Hurl. & C. 906

An ambiguity case.

Legal historian and scholar Grant Gilmore wrote that this case was as "to the ordinary run of case law as the recently popular theater of the absurd is to the ordinary run of theater."

OPINION: *PER CURIAM*:

Declaration. For that it was agreed between the plaintiff and the defendants, to wit, at Liverpool, that the plaintiff should sell to the defendants and the defendants buy of the plaintiff, certain goods, to wit, 125 bales of Surat cotton, guaranteed middling fair merchant's hollorah, to arrive ex Peerless from Bombay; and that the cotton should be taken from the quay, and that the defendants would pay the plaintiff for the same at a certain rate, to wit, at the rate of 17 $\frac{1}{4}$ d. per pound, within a certain time then agreed upon after the arrival of the said goods in England. Averments: that the said goods did arrive by the said ship from Bombay in England, to wit, at Liverpool, and the plaintiff was then and there ready and willing and offered to deliver the said goods to the defendants, etc. Breach: that the defendants refused to accept the said goods or pay the plaintiff for them.

So, we have a contract for the sale of 125 bales of cotton to be shipped from Bombay, on a ship named the Peerless ("to arrive ex Peerless") and delivered to the dock in Liverpool.

The price specified is 17.25 pence per pound.

The plaintiff (Raffles, the seller) says the cotton arrived in Liverpool on the Peerless from Bombay, that he had offered to deliver the cotton, and that the defendant (Wichelhaus, the buyer) had breached by refusing to accept or pay for it.

Plea. That the said ship mentioned in the said agreement was meant and intended by the defendant to be the ship called the Peerless, which sailed from Bombay, to wit, in October; and that the plaintiff was not ready and willing, and did not offer to deliver to the defendants any bales of cotton which arrived by the last-mentioned ship, but instead thereof was only ready and willing, and offered to deliver to the defendants 125 bales of Surat cotton which arrived by another and different ship, which was also called the Peerless, and which sailed from Bombay, to wit, in December.

The defendant says the ship *he* intended when he made the contract was the Peerless that sailed from Bombay in *October* (and on which the seller had shipped no cotton), while the cotton the plaintiff was talking about was cotton that had been shipped on a Peerless from Bombay in *December.*

Demurrer, and joinder therein.

SIDEBAR: *The demur*

Plaintiff demurs.

The "demur" is a form of summary judgment motion. What is summary judgment? A motion for summary judgment says to the Court that the facts as they have been presented to the Court, even taken in the light most favorable to my opponent, must result in judgment for me as a matter of law.

One form of motion for summary judgment is the demur, also called a motion to strike for failure to state a cause of action upon which relief can be granted. It means just that: that even if everything my opponent says is considered true, his contentions do not form the necessary elements of a successful legal claim. In other words, he can't win.

SJ motions are very common, since there is nothing to lose. If they are denied, one just proceeds with the trial.

A similar motion can be made at the end of the presentation of the other party's case. This is called a directed verdict.

In fact, initial SJ motions are almost always made because they are strategic. If one does not make an SJ motion, one cannot invoke a similar motion at the end of a case, called a Judgment Non Obstante Veredicto (notwithstanding the verdict), which claims essentially that no reasonable jury could have concluded from the facts as presented that my opponent won, and therefore the Court should grant me judgment anyway.

In this case, the demur means that the plaintiff concedes that the defendant meant to contract for the goods carried on the October Peerless, not the December Peerless, thinking, no doubt, that since the contract did not specify a time of sailing, shipping the cotton on *any* ship named the Peerless from Bombay would satisfy the contract. This tactic turns out to be a mistake for the plaintiff.

Mistake or ambiguity can justify rescission only when it relates to some fundamental aspect of the contract's performance. The big question in this case will turn out to be whether the identity of the ship was a fundamental term of the contract. The Court seems to assume that if the contract said "Peerless," then the identity of the ship must be a fundamental term.

Milward (the plaintiff's attorney) argues in support of the plaintiff.

Pollock and Martin, two of the judges, speak for the Court.

Milward, in support of the demurrer. The contract was for the sale of a number of bales of cotton of a particular description, which the plaintiff was ready to deliver. It is immaterial by what ship the cotton was to arrive, so that it was a ship called the Peerless. The words "to arrive ex Peerless," only mean that if the vessel is lost on the voyage, the contract is to be at an end.

Pollock, C.B. It would be a question for the jury whether both parties meant the same ship called the Peerless.

Milward. That would be so if the contract was for the sale of a ship called the Peerless; but it is for the sale of cotton on board a ship of that name.

Pollock, C.B. The defendant only bought that cotton which was to arrive by a particular ship. It may as well be said, that if there is a contract for the purchase of certain goods in warehouse A, that is satisfied by the delivery of goods of the same description in warehouse B.

Milward. In that case there would be goods in both warehouses; here it does not appear that the plaintiff had any goods on board the other Peerless.

Martin, B. It is imposing on the defendant a contract different from that which he entered into.

Pollock, C.B. It is like a contract for the purchase of wine coming from a particular estate in France or Spain, where there are two estates of that name.

That is, the Court means that the two ships, though they bear the same name, are different.

Milward. The defendant has no right to contradict by parol evidence, a written contract good upon the face of it. He does not impute misrepresentation or fraud, but only says that he fancied the ship was a different one. Intention is of no avail, unless stated at the time of the contract.

SIDEBAR: *The parol evidence rule*

The "parol evidence rule" is fairly complex but essentially says that, except in certain special circumstances, the only evidence that can be used to interpret a contract is the language of the contract itself. "Parol evidence" is evidence other than the language of the contract.

Pollock, C.B. One vessel sailed in October and the other in December.
Milward. The time of sailing is no part of the contract.

Again, the requirements for contractual ambiguity are:

1. **The parties use a fundamental term open to at least two reasonable interpretations;**
2. **Each party attaches a different meaning to the term; and**
3. **Neither party knows or has reason to know the meaning attached by the other.**

Mellish (the defendant's attorney) speaks in support of the plea, stating why parol evidence is admissible here.

There is nothing on the face of the contract to show that any particular ship called the Peerless was meant; but the moment it appears that two ships called the Peerless were about to sail from Bombay there is a latent ambiguity, and parol evidence may be given for the purpose of showing that the defendant meant one Peerless and the plaintiff another. That being so, there was no consensus ad idem, and therefore no binding contract. He was then stopped by the Court.

PER CURIAM. *There must be judgment for the defendants.*

The Court finds in favor of the defendant as a matter of law because, in the opinion of the Court, this is a situation in which the requirements for legal ambiguity have been met.

It is interesting that no one asks: Shouldn't a cotton merchant, who probably engages in a lot of transactions that involve the shipping of goods, know of the existence of two ships named Peerless?

If the October ship arrived first, why did the buyer not protest the seller's failure to deliver? Perhaps the October Peerless *did* arrive first (without cotton) and, knowing that another Peerless would soon come, the buyer did not protest. But between that time and the arrival of the second ship the market price of cotton dropped drastically and by December the buyer no longer wanted to buy at the original price (and have to market the cotton in England at a loss). So the buyer tried, successfully in this case, to avoid the contract.

Contracts in Cyberspace

For quite a while, it was unclear whether and, if so, how contracts could be formed online. Now it is well settled that so-called electronic contracts can be formed in a variety of ways, including by e-mail, interactive websites, online conduct, or computer-to-computer interaction, commonly referred to as "electronic data interchange" or "EDI."

EDI is intended to streamline the process of doing business. It is most often employed between parties with a continuing business relationship who create a "master trading agreement" that will govern their EDI transactions.

In the physical world, the typical business-to-business ordering and purchasing process involves many steps and, consequently, a lot of overhead. Buyer creates a purchase order and sends it to Seller; Seller enters the data from the purchase order and sends an acknowledgment to Buyer; Buyer records the acknowledgment; Seller bills Buyer; Buyer sends Seller payment; and Seller ships the goods.

An EDI transaction deals with these steps automatically – and quickly – by letting Buyer's and Seller's computers handle the transaction. Again, usually EDI is used by parties with a continuing business relationship. For example, suppose Buyer routinely orders some number of widgets every month from Seller, the number of widgets varying depending on the state of Buyer's inventory. Rather than go through the relatively laborious and time-consuming purchase order process, Buyer's computer automatically assesses the number of widgets Buyer has on hand and then orders the appropriate amount needed from Seller each month. The computers record the order, acknowledgment, payment, and shipping of the widgets automatically.

EDI is used in numerous contexts, including processing insurance claims and funds transfers – known as "financial EDI." Legal issues arising from use of EDI include, of course, security, but also allocation of risk of loss from error. What happens when something goes wrong? Suppose Buyer's software develops a "bug" and one day orders 1,000 pints of ice cream from Seller, instead of the 100 it should have ordered? Buyer has no need for all that ice cream and it will spoil. Who bears the loss? How should the parties deal with such a situation? As with most things in contract law, the parties must make arrangements *in advance*. That is, the issue should be anticipated and addressed in the master trading agreement controlling the EDI. This is one of the great powers of contract law. The parties can foresee problems and agree on a reasonable resolution. Perhaps, in the ice cream scenario, this might be to agree that any such losses will be shared equally by the parties. Why would the parties want to go to court, and potentially sever what is presumably a mutually beneficial business relationship?

Online Offers

Recall that a valid offer is one that a reasonable person in the position of the offeree would believe will create a contract if accepted, and that advertisements are typically not considered offers, but rather invitations to deal.

In general, a website merely displaying product information is considered an advertisement but, as with physical world advertisements, an ad that is sufficiently specific can be an offer. The analysis is the same in cyberspace as in the physical world, as illustrated in the following two cases.

Contracts: Case 3

Morris Lefkowitz v. Great Minneapolis Surplus Store, Inc.

No. 37,220

Supreme Court of Minnesota

251 Minn. 188; 86 N.W.2d 689; 1957 Minn. LEXIS 684

December 20, 1957

OPINION: MURPHY, Justice:

This case grows out of the alleged refusal of the defendant to sell to the plaintiff a certain fur piece which it had offered for sale in a newspaper advertisement. It appears from the record that on April 6, 1956, the defendant published the following advertisement in a Minneapolis newspaper:

Saturday 9 a.m. sharp 3 Brand New Fur Coats Worth to $ 100.00
First Come First Served $1 Each

On April 13, the defendant again published an advertisement in the same newspaper as follows:

Saturday 9 a.m. 2 Brand New Pastel Mink 3-Skin Scarfs Selling for $ 89.50
Out they go Saturday. Each $ 1.00
1 Black Lapin Stole Beautiful, worth $ 139.50 $ 1.00
First Come First Served

The record supports the findings of the court that on each of the Saturdays following the publication of the above-described ads the plaintiff was the first to present himself at the appropriate counter in the defendant's store and on each occasion demanded the coat and the stole so advertised and indicated his readiness to pay the sale price of $ 1.

On both occasions, the defendant refused to sell the merchandise to the plaintiff, stating on the first occasion that by a "house rule" the offer was intended for women only and sales would not be made to men, and on the second visit that plaintiff knew defendant's house rules.

Lefkowitz sued the store for breach of contract. The lower court awarded him $138.50 in damages. The decision is on appeal here in the Supreme Court of Minnesota.

The trial court properly disallowed plaintiff's claim for the value of the fur coats since the value of these articles was speculative and uncertain. The only evidence of value was the advertisement itself to the effect that the coats were "Worth to $ 100.00," how much less being speculative especially in view of the price for which they were offered for sale. With reference to the offer of the defendant on April 13, 1956, to sell the "1 Black Lapin Stole *** worth $ 139.50 ***" the trial court held that the value of this article was established and granted judgment in favor of the plaintiff for that amount less the $ 1 quoted purchase price.

1. The defendant contends that a newspaper advertisement offering items of merchandise for sale at a named price is a "unilateral offer" which may be withdrawn without notice. He relies upon authorities which hold that, where an advertiser publishes in a newspaper that he has a certain quantity or quality of goods which he wants to dispose of at certain prices and on certain terms, such advertisements are not offers which become contracts as soon as any person to whose notice they may come signifies his acceptance by notifying the other that he will take a certain quantity of them.

What's wrong with this argument? It applies only when the persons to whom the offer is made are unspecified – and thus potentially unlimited. The argument fails when you specify a number of offerees such that you cannot be put in a position of having too few of the offered item.

Such advertisements have been construed as an invitation for an offer of sale on the terms stated, which offer, when received, may be accepted or rejected and which therefore does not become a contract of sale until accepted by the seller; and until a contract has been so made, the seller may modify or revoke such prices or terms.

It is true that such an offer may be withdrawn before acceptance. On the facts before us we are concerned with whether the advertisement constituted an offer, and, if so, whether the plaintiff's conduct constituted an acceptance.

There are numerous authorities which hold that a particular advertisement in a newspaper or circular letter relating to a sale of articles may be construed by the court as constituting an offer, acceptance of which would complete a contract.

The test of whether a binding obligation may originate in advertisements addressed to the general public is "whether the facts show that some performance was promised in positive terms in return for something requested." 1 Williston, Contracts (Rev. ed.) § 27.

The authorities above cited emphasize that, where the offer is clear, definite, and explicit, and leaves nothing open for negotiation, it constitutes an offer, acceptance of which will complete the contract.

Whether in any individual instance a newspaper advertisement is an offer rather than an invitation to make an offer depends on the legal intention of the parties and the surrounding circumstances.

So, when is an ad an offer?

"Where the offer is clear, definite, and explicit, and leaves nothing open for negotiation, it constitutes an offer, acceptance of which will complete the contract."

Here, the offer for the sale of the stole "was clear, definite, explicit, and left nothing open for negotiation."

The plaintiff having successfully managed to be the first one to appear at the seller's place of business to be served, as requested by the advertisement, and having offered the stated purchase price of the article, he was entitled to performance on the part of the defendant. We think the trial court was correct in holding that there was in the conduct of the parties a sufficient mutuality of obligation to constitute a contract of sale.

2. The defendant contends that the offer was modified by a "house rule" to the effect that only women were qualified to receive the bargains advertised. The advertisement contained no such restriction.

What about the "house rules"?

This objection may be disposed of briefly by stating that, while an advertiser has the right at any time before acceptance to modify his offer, he does not have the right, after acceptance, to impose new or arbitrary conditions not contained in the published offer.

Affirmed.

Contracts: Case 4

Mary Mesaros and Anthony C. Mesaros, Plaintiffs-Appellants, v. The United States of America, The United States Department of the Treasury, Bureau of the Mint, James Baker, Secretary of the Treasury and Donna Pope, Director of the United States Mint, Defendants-Appellees

No. 88-1012

UNITED STATES COURT OF APPEALS FOR THE FEDERAL CIRCUIT

845 F.2d 1576; 1988 U.S. App. LEXIS 6055

May 6, 1988, Decided

OPINION: SKELTON, Judge:

On May 23, 1986, plaintiffs Mary Mesaros and husband Anthony C. Mesaros filed a class action lawsuit for themselves and others similarly situated (thirty-three of whom were named) in the United States District Court for the Southern District of Georgia, Savannah Division, against the United States of America, the United States Department of the Treasury, the Bureau of the Mint, James Baker, Secretary of the Treasury, and Donna Pope, Director of the United States Mint (defendants) seeking damages for an alleged breach of contract by defendants in failing to deliver a quantity of Statue of Liberty commemorative coins they had ordered from defendants pursuant to an advertisement mailed to plaintiffs and published in newspapers and other news media by the United States Mint. In the alternative they sought mandamus relief for the delivery of the coins. Plaintiffs also filed a motion for certification of the class.

Plaintiffs are suing for damages or "mandamus". A mandamus is a command by a court to do what was not done, (i.e., mint the coins necessary to fill the orders).

The defendants filed a motion to dismiss plaintiffs' suit, or in the alternative for summary judgment.

As introduced above, a motion for "summary judgment" is a procedural device to dispose of a controversy quickly if the Court determines that no material facts are in dispute and that the moving party will win as a matter of law. Another way of thinking about such a motion is that the moving party is saying that even if the facts are taken in the light most favorable to the other party, the moving party must win as a matter of law. This will be the case, for example, if the non-moving party has not provided facts that will support the required elements of a particular legal claim.

On April 13, 1987, the court granted judgment for defendants on their motion in its entirety. No action was taken by the court on the class action motion because it was moot after the other action by the court. The plaintiffs filed an appeal (No. 87-8445) in the United States Court of Appeals for the Eleventh Circuit. On motion of defendants, the case was transferred to this court.

The facts in the case, as stated in an order of the district court dated April 13, 1987, (with a few omissions and additions), and as shown by the record are as follow.

In July 1985, Congress passed the Statue of Liberty-Ellis Island Commemorative Coin Act. Pub.L. No. 99-61, 99 Stat. 113 (July 9, 1985). The purpose of the Act was to provide funds, through the sale of a limited number of specially-minted commemorative coins, "to restore and renovate the Statue of Liberty and the facilities used for immigration at Ellis Island," and to establish an endowment to provide for the upkeep and maintenance of these national monuments. The Act, which by modern standards is a commendable example of brevity, instructed the Secretary of the Treasury: to mint a stated number of coins; to follow certain procedures with respect to the marketing of the coins; to disburse specified surcharges included in the price of each coin to the Statue of Liberty Foundation; and to take all actions necessary to ensure that the project would result in no net cost to the government.

Perhaps in this day and age it will surprise no one that such a laudable piece of legislation has spawned a civil action against the government. More accurately, the manner in which the coins were sold to the public, rather than the legislation itself, led to the initiation of this lawsuit by the plaintiffs. In all fairness to the plaintiffs, the court must take judicial notice that the marketing of the coins may not have been a perfectly administered process.

The Mesaroses (plaintiffs) allege breach of contract by the United States in failing to deliver a quantity of Statue of Liberty commemorative coins they had ordered in response to an ad mailed to them and published in newspapers and other mass media by the U.S. Mint.

SIDEBAR: Judicial notice

Judicial notice is an act by which a court will recognize the existence and truth of certain facts without requiring the production of evidence as, for example, when facts are commonly known.

The provision of the Act that is directly implicated in this action is § 105(c), which reads: "The Secretary [of the Treasury] shall accept prepaid orders for [commemorative] coins prior to the issuance of the coins. Sales under this subsection shall be at a reasonable discount to reflect the benefit of prepayment." A related provision, § 105(d), authorized bulk sales of commemorative coins at a discount. Pursuant to these provisions, in November and December 1985, the Mint mailed certain advertising materials to persons, including the plaintiffs, whose names were included on a list of previous customers/coin collectors. These materials described the various coins the issuance of which was authorized by the Act, and encouraged potential purchasers to forward early payment for commemorative coins.

Was there a specific number of coins? Congress instructed the Mint to make a "stated number of coins" to commemorate (and raise money for) the restoration of the Statue of Liberty, but this number did not appear in the ad.

(The Court now knows that Congress authorized no more than 25 million half-dollar coins, 10 million one-dollar coins, and 500 thousand five-dollar gold pieces.)

The materials represented, *inter alia*, that "if [the Mint] receives your reservation by December 31, 1985, you will enjoy a favorable *Pre-Issue Discount* saving you up to 16% on your coins." Payment could be made either by check, money order, or credit card. Apparently, the Mint had not previously dealt with credit card sales, and the processing of credit card orders, which in this case turned out to be an almost impossible ordeal, was contracted to the Mellon Bank in Pittsburgh, Pennsylvania.

The materials included an order form. Directly above the space provided on this form for the customer's signature was the following:

VERY IMPORTANT – PLEASE READ: YES, Please accept my order for the U.S. Liberty Coins I have indicated. I understand that all sales are final and not subject to refund. Verification of my order will be made by the Department of the Treasury, U.S. Mint. My coins may be delivered in multiple shipments. If my order is received by December 31, 1985, I will be entitled to purchase the coins at the Pre-Issue Discount price shown. I have read, understand and agree to the above.[1]

Demand for the coins far exceeded the Mint's expectations. According to the Mint's "knowledge and belief," the last order for gold coins that was filled was accepted "some time between December 31, 1985, and January 6, 1986."

Oddly, the Mint does not know exactly when it accepted its last order. (!)

This exhausted the supply of 500,000 gold coins the issuance of which was authorized by the Act.

---

1 On the opposite side of the form the following language appeared: "Please allow 6 to 8 weeks for delivery after issue date of January 1, 1986. The U.S. Mint reserves the right to limit quantities shipped, subject to availability."

   Here was a disclaimer. But note how this language might be argued to apply to shipping some buyers *some* coins, not *no* coins. Better contractual wording might be, "coins are limited in quantity and not all orders may be filled."

   Mint may discontinue accepting orders should bullion prices increase significantly. Credit card orders will be billed upon receipt by the U.S. Mint.

A great many would-be acquisitors of gold coins were disappointed by the news of the sell-out. These individuals, many of whom were coin dealers, developed a more serious case of disappointment when it became apparent that the gold coins had increased in value by approximately 200% within the first few months of 1986.

Many lawyers and judges will acknowledge that the legal profession does not distinguish itself by its members' brilliance in mathematics. Here, for example, it is unclear if the Court means that the coins doubled in value (i.e., that their new value is 200% of their original value) or that the coins in fact tripled in value (i.e., that they acquired 200% of their original value.)

Notwithstanding the foregoing facts, which understandably would be cause for tears on the part of those turned away, collectors and dealers alike, it is quite possible that no legal action against the Mint would have been contemplated had not certain matters concerning the treatment of credit card orders come to light. In this regard, the ordeal faced by plaintiffs Mary and Anthony Mesaros appears not to have been atypical.

What happened to the plaintiffs?

11/26/85: They ordered coins for a total of $1,675 by credit card.

12/30/85: They placed orders on behalf of other family members for eighteen more gold coins, paid by nine separate checks.

2/18/86: They got a letter from the Mint that said the Mint "had tried but was unable" to process the 11/26/85 credit card order. The letter said to contact their bank, leaving the impression that they had bad credit and that the bank had bounced the request to charge their card.

Anthony was so enraged that he wrote "BASTARDS" across the face of the original order.

4/7/86: The bank said it *did* authorize the coin charge on 12/27/85.

May 1986: Plaintiffs received the 18 coins that had been ordered on 12/30/85 and had been paid for by check.

During the early months of 1986, rumors and information began to filter through the ranks of coin collectors and dealers concerning rejections of credit card orders under circumstances similar to those faced by the Mesaroses. It was becoming apparent by March or April that persons who had paid by wires, money orders or checks, dated as late as the end of December, were receiving their coins from the Mint, while many persons who had submitted credit card orders (in November in certain cases) were not receiving their coins. These disappointed credit card customers were sent form letters by the Mint informing them either that the Mint had "tried but was unable" to process their orders (such as that received by the Mesaroses, *see supra*), or that their order could not be processed because the gold coins had sold out. According to plaintiffs, the rejection of their credit card order, and the rejection of other collectors' and dealers' credit card orders, is inexplicable on any reasonable basis, in that there existed no inaccuracies in the information provided to the Mint and no shortage of credit on the part of those submitting orders.

According to the Mint, over 756,000 orders for Statue of Liberty coins had been received as of May 30, 1986, 186,000 of which were credit card orders. According to plaintiffs, approximately 13,000 credit card orders were rejected. However, the record shows that many of the credit card orders were insufficient or incorrect for one reason or another. For instance, some were illegible or mutilated, others did not include the expiration date of the credit card, some were unsigned, and on others the standard check with the issuers (Visa and Mastercard) showed that the purchase would exceed the customer's credit limit. On still others there was no matching account number shown in the credit card companies' records. In many instances there was a discrepancy between the number of coins or sets ordered and the amounts specified by the customer. Some of the orders did not have the full credit numbers inscribed thereon.

The Mesaroses' order was slightly irregular, in that Mary ordered the coins and used her name and address, but the credit card she used was her husband's and the form was signed by him.

Credit card orders were processed slowly because they went first to the Mint, which then sent them to the Mellon Bank for verification, and then back to the Mint.

The record shows that the Mint and the Mellon Bank were simply swamped with a deluge of 756,000 orders, of which 186,000 were credit card orders. On May 23, 1986, plaintiffs filed suit in the district court, seeking either damages on a breach of contract theory or, in the alternative, mandamus relief in the form of a court order forcing defendants to accept plaintiffs' credit card order. Such mandamus relief would ultimately require, according to plaintiffs, the government to deliver the plaintiffs the gold coins that they ordered in November 1985.

Breach of Contract

The plaintiffs claim that the Mint breached an express contract with them and that they are entitled to recover money damages from defendants for this breach.

The plaintiffs contend that the materials sent to them by the Mint, including the order form, constituted an offer that upon acceptance by the plaintiffs created a binding contract between them and the government whereby the government was bound and obligated to deliver the coins ordered by them. The great weight of authority is against the plaintiffs. It is well established that materials such as those mailed to prospective customers by the Mint are no more than advertisements or invitations to deal. They are mere notices and solicitations for offers which create no power of acceptance in the recipient.

A basic rule of contracts holds that whether an offer has been made depends on the objective reasonableness of the alleged offeree's belief that the advertisement or solicitation was intended as an offer. Generally, it is considered unreasonable for a person to believe that advertisements and solicitations are offers that bind the advertiser. Otherwise, the advertiser could be bound by an excessive number of contracts requiring delivery of goods far in excess of amounts available. That is particularly true in the instant case where the gold coins were limited to 500,000 by the Act of Congress.

The Court looks at the test for whether an offer has been made: would a reasonable offeree believe acceptance would create a contract?

- **Here, the Court says no.**
- **The order form says: "YES, Please accept my order...", which was an offer**
  from the plaintiffs **to the Mint to buy the coins.**

This is in accord with the following statement from I Corbin, *Contracts*, 375-76 § 88 (1963):

> Where one party solicits and receives an order or other expression of agreement from another, clearly specifying that there is to be no contract until ratification or assent by some officer or representative of the solicitor, the solicitation is not itself an offer; it is a request for an offer.

The plaintiffs rely on *Lefkowitz v. Great Minneapolis Surplus Store*, 251 Minn. 188, 86 N.W.2d 689 (1957).

Plaintiffs' case is, you guessed it, *Lefkowitz*, but the Court distinguishes it:

Here the Mint had 35,500,000 coins for sale to the general public for which it received over 756,000 orders. The Mint advertisement did not state that the coins would be sold on a first-come, first-served basis, as in *Lefkowitz*, or on any other particular basis. Since the coins could be paid for with checks, money orders or credit cards, it would have been impossible for the Mint to have processed the sales on a first-come, first-served basis.

Why? Difficult, maybe; impossible, no.

The situation in *Lefkowitz* was so different that it is of no help to the plaintiffs.

We hold that the Mint advertisement materials were not an offer of sale of the coins that could be accepted by the plaintiffs to create a contract, and that no contract was made between the plaintiffs and the government with reference to the coins.

Mandamus

Then, in pursuit of mandamus, the plaintiffs argue that the *statute* ordering the Mint to prepare the coins amounted to an order (a statutory duty) to the Mint to fill orders for the coins on a first-come, first-served basis.

It is clear that the district court would not have jurisdiction of the mandamus claim apart from the breach of contract claim unless the Mint had a statutory duty that it owed to the plaintiffs. The plaintiffs are asking the court for an order requiring the government to enter into a contract with them and ordering the government to deliver to them the gold coins they had ordered.

The court is without authority to order the Mint to deliver the coins to the plaintiffs for several reasons. In the first place, all of the coins have been sold and no more are available. In the next place, such an order would require the Mint to produce more gold coins, which would violate both the Constitution and the Coin Act. Article 1, Section 8, Clause 5 of the United States Constitution vests the power to mint coins exclusively in the Congress. The Mint has no power to mint coins unless it has been authorized to do so by Congress. Furthermore, an order by the court requiring the government to mint more coins to fill plaintiffs' order would force the Mint to act beyond the authority granted to it by § 102(a)(1) of the Coin Act, which authorized the production of no more than 500,000 gold coins. It is well settled that an agency's power is no greater than that delegated to it by Congress. *Lyng v. Payne*, 476 U.S. 926, 934, 90 L. Ed. 2d 921, 106 S. Ct. 2333 (1986).

There is nothing in the Act that imposed a duty on the Mint to enter into contracts on a first-come, first-served basis, or in any other particular sequence or manner. The plaintiffs rely on language in the statute that states that "the Secretary shall accept prepaid orders for the coins prior to the issuance of the coins. . . . " We find nothing in this language nor in any other language in the statute that creates a duty on the Secretary or the Mint to handle coin orders in any particular way

The decision of the district court in his well-written order is affirmed.

Affirmed.

∼

Online Acceptances

An offer can be accepted "by any means reasonable in the circumstances." Electronically, this may mean by e-mail, by clicking on a "button," by downloading, or through other actions by the offeree.

Note that acceptance of an offer made via one medium may not be valid in some circumstances if the acceptance uses a different medium. For example, if an offer is made by fax and acceptance is made by e-mail, the acceptance may not be valid if the offeror is not in the habit of regularly checking e-mail. To be safe, it is best to accept an offer using the medium in which the offer was made.

Clicking on a button or downloading a file is a valid acceptance if the offer invites acceptance by that action. In the physical world, if an offeror says, "If you paint my house, I will give you $500," the offeror is inviting the offeree to accept by performance. Similar reasoning applies to acceptance by performance in cyberspace.

Note also that usually silence cannot be acceptance. So if an offeree fails to respond to an offer that says, "Here is some demo software, if we don't hear from you by Friday we will consider our offer accepted," the offeree is not bound to a contract. The offeree has done nothing to solicit or acknowledge the reception of the software. On the other hand, if the offeror says, "If you download this demo software, you agree that you will let us know by Friday if you wish to reject the offer," an offeree who downloads the software *might* be bound by failing to respond by Friday. It was the offeree's choice in this instance to put him or herself in the position of *agreeing* to respond to the offeror by Friday.

The Statute of Frauds in Cyberspace

The two most common types of contracts formed in cyberspace that must be written and signed – that fall under the Statute of Frauds – are service contracts not capable of being performed within a year of the date of contract, and contracts for the sale of goods for $500 or more. But are *any* electronic contracts "written"? Yes. In other contexts, courts have defined "written" to mean "reducible to a tangible form." There have been cases regarding contracts formed by telexes, telegrams, mailgrams, and even tape recordings.

The requirement that a contract that must be written must also be signed – at least by the party against whom enforcement is sought – also arises as an issue with electronically formed contracts. What is a signature? Legally, it is *any* sign made *with the present intention* of authenticating a document. So names on telegrams, faxes, mailgrams, even letterhead paper – are considered "signatures" if the party *intended* by use of its name or letterhead to authenticate the document. Thus, even a name typed at the end of an electronic document should suffice.

Shrink-Wrap and Webwrap Contracts or Licenses

Software license agreements (just another flavor of contract) that come in shrink-wrapped boxes containing software are referred to as "shrink-wrap contracts" or "shrink-wrap licenses." Similarly, software license agreements formed electronically, usually using the World Wide Web, have come to be called "webwrap contracts" or "webwrap licenses."

For a long time most courts found that the terms contained in a shrink-wrap license were not enforceable because the buyer did not have knowledge of those terms until *after* the contract was formed. The contract was thought to be created when the buyer handed over the purchase price to the seller, who then gave the software to the buyer. The pendulum has begun to swing to some extent toward enforceability of shrink-wrap licenses, although the question is not entirely settled. The *Arizona Retail Systems* case provides an example of the older view, while the *ProCD* and *Hill* cases illustrate the newer trend.

Contracts: Case 5

ARIZONA RETAIL SYSTEMS, INC., an Arizona corporation, Plaintiff, v. THE SOFTWARE LINK, INC., a Georgia corporation, Defendant.

No. CIV 91-1553 PHX RCB

UNITED STATES DISTRICT COURT FOR THE DISTRICT OF ARIZONA

831 F. Supp. 759; 1993 U.S. Dist. LEXIS 14535; 22 U.C.C. Rep. Serv. 2d (Callaghan) 70

July 27, 1993, Decided
July 29, 1993, Filed

OPINION: BROOMFIELD, Judge:

Plaintiff Arizona Retail Systems, Inc. (ARS) has brought claims against Defendant The Software Link, Inc. (TSL) arising out of certain purchases by ARS of software from TSL. ARS has moved for partial summary judgment on the issue of whether TSL effectively disclaimed implied warranties and alleged oral representations through provisions in a license agreement that accompanied each delivery of software. TSL responded to ARS's motion and filed a cross-motion for summary judgment, contending that, as a matter of law, the license agreement provides the exclusive remedy for plaintiff's claims.

> **ARS has moved for partial summary judgment (see *Raffles v. Wichelhaus* earlier for a definition of summary judgment) on the issue of whether TSL effectively disclaimed implied warranties and alleged oral representations through provisions in a license agreement that accompanied each delivery of software.**

Background

TSL designs and sells software. This lawsuit regards the sale of a software operating system designed and sold by TSL known as PC-MOS. PC-MOS is designed to allow multi-user systems to access software applications from a central host computer, thereby eliminating the need to purchase individual software for each user.

ARS is a value-added retailer that, among other things, configures, markets, and services multi-user computer systems. Sometime in 1989, ARS' system manager, Allen

Rude, contacted TSL to obtain information about PC-MOS. Approximately two years earlier, Rude had evaluated PC-MOS but, for a variety of performance-related reasons, decided not to purchase the system. Rude contacted TSL in 1989 because he had seen a magazine advertisement for an updated version of PC-MOS.

TSL telefaxed to Rude various advertisements and other promotional literature describing the new version of PC-MOS. The literature stated that the program was now operational and compatible as a multi-user operating system. Rude claims that he interpreted these representations to mean that the problems present in the earlier version had been corrected. The representations interested Rude because ARS had clients in need of an effective program to support multi-user networks.

After reading the information sent by TSL, Rude contacted TSL and discussed the updated PC-MOS with TSL employees. The contents of the discussion are debated. TSL alleges that PC-MOS was discussed only in general terms; ARS contends that the employees assured Rude that the software would be compatible with DOS operated programs and that the problems with the earlier version of PC-MOS had been corrected. In addition, ARS contends Rude informed TSL of the specific type of system ARS wanted to support with PC-MOS and that TSL representatives assured Rude that PC-MOS would work with that system.

Rude ultimately ordered a copy of PC-MOS. It is unclear whether Rude ordered an evaluative copy of the system, which came with a live copy of the system, or whether Rude ordered a live copy and an evaluative copy accompanied the live copy. In any case, the materials Rude received stated that ARS could return the materials after a specified time period if ARS was not satisfied. Rude admits that he did not decide to keep the live copy of PC-MOS until he tested the evaluation disk. The materials were wrapped in "shrink wrap" plastic, upon which was fixed a Limited Use License Agreement. The Limited Use License Agreement (license agreement) included, among other things, the following provisions relevant to this case.

1. A clause stating that the customer has not purchased the software itself, but merely has obtained a personal, nontransferable license to use the program;
2. a disclaimer of all warranties, except for a warranty covering physical defects in the program disks;
3. a clause purporting to limit the purchaser's remedies to repair and replacement of defective disks, and to exclude all liability for damages caused by using the program;
4. an integration clause providing that the license was the final and complete expression of the parties' agreement;
5. a provision prohibiting the assignment of the program or license without the express prior consent of TSL; and
6. a provision purporting to trigger the purchaser's acceptance of the license upon opening the package.

After evaluating the system for about two hours, Rude decided to keep the system. Rude admits that he read the license agreement but thought that it was unenforceable and incapable of overriding the specific representations made to him by TSL employees.

Rude had probably heard that shrink-wrap licenses were unenforceable.

ARS purchased many copies of PC-MOS from TSL over the next year. With respect to these purchases, ARS usually initiated the procedure by telephoning TSL to place an order. During the order calls, ARS and TSL agreed on the specific goods to be shipped by TSL, the quantity of the goods, and the price for the goods. TSL then would ship the goods together with invoices. It does not appear to be disputed that neither party made any reference to the warranty disclaimers or liability limitations during either the calls or on the invoices. The license agreement, however, appeared on the face of the packaging of each set of software sent by TSL to ARS.

> **ARS proceeded to install the software on a number of its clients' systems, but the clients began experiencing problems.**

> **TSL recommended purchasing additional software to upgrade PC-MOS.**

> **One client, a law firm, suffered frequent crashes and lock-ups of its system and lost hundreds of pages of documents.**

> **After several months ARS gave up trying to repair the damage done by PC-MOS and filed suit.**

> **The Court notes that TSL has also been sued in the 3rd Circuit, where the Court ruled (in *Step-Saver Data Systems v. Wyse Technology*, 939 F.2d 91 (3d Cir. 1991)) that the license agreement did not constitute a part of the contract between the parties. ARS says the facts here are the same. TSL says they are not.**

Legal Analysis

The parties appear to agree that Georgia law governs this dispute. Georgia has adopted all provisions of the Uniform Commercial Code that are relevant to this dispute. For sake of simplicity, the court when possible will refer to the relevant provisions in the U.C.C. rather than the corresponding provisions in the Georgia Code.

A. The Relevant Provisions of the U.C.C.

An understanding of two U.C.C. provisions is necessary to resolve the issues before the court.

1. Section 2-207

Section 2-207 provides:

Additional Terms in Acceptance or Confirmation
(1) A definite and seasonable expression of acceptance or a written confirmation which is sent within a reasonable time operates as an acceptance even though it states terms additional to or different from those offered or agreed upon, unless acceptance is expressly made conditional on assent to the additional or different terms.
(2) The additional terms are to be construed as proposals for addition to the contract. Between merchants such terms become part of the contract unless:
  (a) the offer expressly limits acceptance to the terms of the offer;
  (b) they materially alter it; or

(c) notification of objection to them has already been given or is given within a reasonable time after notice of them is received.

(3) Conduct by both parties which recognizes the existence of a contract is sufficient to establish a contract for sale although the writings of the parties do not otherwise establish a contract. In such case the terms of the particular contract consist of those terms on which the writings of the parties agree, together with any supplementary terms incorporated under any other provisions of the [Code].

Section 2-207 thus controls the situation in which the parties at some point in time come to a general agreement but have failed, in that oral or written agreement, to come to a mutual understanding on various terms requested by the parties. Under such circumstances, a contract is formed when the parties reach the general agreement and all other material terms not agreed upon are supplied by the Code's "gap fillers." *See* U.C.C. § 2-207(3).

2. Section 2-209

Section 2-207 addresses situations in which various terms proposed by the parties in the offer and acceptances processes were not agreed upon before the contract was formed under section 2-207(1). Section 2-209 picks up where section 2-207 leaves off – i.e., after the formation of the contract. Section 2-209 thus sets forth rules for modifications of existing sales contracts.

B. The Initial Purchase

The parties treat the issues in this case as if only one contract existed between the parties. It appears to the court that the parties actually engaged in a number of separate contracts, and that the first contract entered into by the parties involves facts and circumstances materially different than the subsequent contracts. The court, therefore, will evaluate the initial purchase of software separately from the subsequent purchases, which appear to all have been conducted under similar circumstances.

First transaction

- **ARS gets demo and live copy and the license agreement**
- **evaluates demo**
- **reads license agreement**
- **decides to keep live copy**
- **therefore ARS had notice of license terms before acceptance**

The Court holds that on these facts, the contract was not formed when TSL shipped the goods (i.e., not before ARS had notice of the terms of the license). Rather, the contract was formed after ARS opened the shrink wrap on the live version. ARS thus had notice that opening the shrink wrap would result in the formation of a contract (i.e., that opening the live version, with its license terms on the outside, was acceptance – which is what the envelope containing the live version said on the outside.)

The court holds that if ARS requested an evaluation diskette and then, by keeping the live disk, agreed to purchase the copy of PC-MOS that accompanied the evaluation diskette after evaluating PC-MOS, the license agreement applies to the initial transaction. Under such facts, the contract was not formed when TSL shipped the goods but rather only after ARS opened the shrink wrap on the live version of PC-MOS, which ARS had noticed would result in a contract being formed.

The court's decision in this respect is not inconsistent with *Step-Saver*. The *Step-Saver* court addressed the situation in which a contract had been formed by the conduct of the parties – i.e., through the ordering and shipping of the agreed-upon goods – but the goods arrived with the license agreement affixed. In such cases, the contract is formed before the purchaser becomes aware of the seller's insistence on certain terms.

With respect to the initial purchase in this case, TSL made the offer by including the live copy of PC-MOS with the evaluation diskette. The live copy appears to have been sealed in an envelope, the outside of which stated that by opening the envelope the user acknowledges "acceptance of this product, and [consents] to all the provisions [of] the Limited Use License Agreement."

C. The Subsequent Purchases

The Court says that the circumstances of these other purchases are more similar to the facts in *Step-Saver*.

ARS contacted TSL by phone and ordered the goods (offer). TSL accepted the orders (acceptance) before shipping the goods. Each package of the software contained the license agreement on the outside. The parties did not discuss the license agreements during the ordering process. That is, TSL did not say, "We accept your offer to buy these goods subject to your acceptance of the same license agreement you have previously seen."

TSL makes three arguments as to why the license agreement is part of the agreement between the parties. First, TSL argues that the license agreement constituted a proposed modification of the original contract pursuant to U.C.C. § 2-209, and that ARS accepted the modification by opening the shrink wrap package.

The Court disagrees. It counters that TSL's last input into these contracts occurred when it agreed to ship the goods or, at the latest, when it shipped the goods.

Second, TSL argues that the license agreement constituted a conditional acceptance of ARS's offer to purchase, and that ARS accepted TSL's conditional acceptance by opening the shrink wrap package.

The Court responds that the purposes of the section of the Uniform Commercial Code (UCC) on conditional acceptances would not be served by assuming that package disclaimers that arrive only after the parties have reached a general agreement are anything but proposals to modify the agreement.

Besides, the Court says that TSL is misreading the UCC, and that the conditional acceptance analysis is not to be used when acceptance was by performance and a later writing (the license agreement) seeks to add terms to the agreement. That is, TSL's "acceptance," its shipping of the goods, did not include additional terms – it hardly could since acceptance was by performance, not by writing – and therefore the conditional acceptance analysis is inappropriate.

The Court says, "By agreeing to ship the goods to ARS, or, at the latest, by shipping the goods, TSL entered into a contract with ARS. After entering into the contract, TSL was not free to treat the license agreement as a conditional acceptance, which is essentially a counter-offer. The license agreement thus is best seen as a proposal to modify the contract between the parties, which, as the Court has discussed, was not effective because ARS never specifically assented to the proposed terms."

Third, TSL argues that if the court applies U.C.C. § 2-207 to this dispute as did the *Step-Saver* court, the court should hold that the terms of the warranty of the license agreement became part of the contract between the parties because the terms were not material.

The Court says the *Step-Saver* court rejected this idea and so does this court.

The license agreements attached to each box, then, amount to a proposal to modify the contract, to which ARS never assented and by which ARS is not bound.

Thus, the court concludes that the terms of the license agreement are not applicable. In all material respects, the subsequent purchases in this case are equivalent to the purchases in *Step-Saver*. This court finds that regardless of whether the terms of the license agreement are treated as proposals for additional terms under U.C.C. § 2-207, or proposals for modification under U.C.C. § 2-209, the terms of the license agreement are not a part of the agreement between the parties. *See* U.C.C. §§ 2-207(2)(b); 2-209. Having not expressly agreed to the terms of the agreement, ARS was not bound by those terms.

Partial summary judgment in favor of ARS, therefore, is appropriate on the issue of whether the license agreement was part of the contracts between TSL and ARS subsequent to ARS's initial purchase of PC-MOS.

Contracts: Case 6

PROCD, INCORPORATED, Plaintiff-Appellant, v. MATTHEW ZEIDENBERG and SILKEN MOUNTAIN WEB SERVICES, INC., Defendants-Appellees.

No. 96-1139

UNITED STATES COURT OF APPEALS FOR THE SEVENTH CIRCUIT

86 F.3d 1447; 1996 U.S. App. LEXIS 14951; 39 U.S.P.Q.2D (BNA) 1161; Copy. L. Rep. (CCH) P27,529; 29 U.C.C. Rep. Serv. 2d (Callaghan) 1109

May 23, 1996, Argued
June 20, 1996, Decided

OPINION: EASTERBROOK, Judge:

Must buyers of computer software obey the terms of shrinkwrap licenses? The district court held not, for two reasons: first, they are not contracts because the licenses are inside the box rather than printed on the outside; second, federal law forbids enforcement even if the licenses are contracts. 908 F. Supp. 640 (W.D. Wis. 1996).

Plaintiff (ProCD) says that Zeidenberg has breached a contract (license) by using a copy of software bought for consumer use for commercial purposes.

Defendant (Zeidenberg) says there is no contract restricting commercial use since the license agreement terms were inside the box and thus had not been revealed at the time the contract was formed by his purchase.

The parties and numerous amici curiae have briefed many other issues, but these are the only two that matter – and we disagree with the district judge's conclusion on each. Shrinkwrap licenses are enforceable unless their terms are objectionable on grounds applicable to contracts in general (for example, if they violate a rule of positive law, or if they are unconscionable). Because no one argues that the terms of the license at issue here are troublesome, we remand with instructions to enter judgment for the plaintiff.

I

ProCD, the plaintiff, has compiled information from more than 3,000 telephone directories into a computer database. We may assume that this database cannot be copyrighted, although it is more complex, contains more information (nine-digit zip codes and census industrial codes), is organized differently, and therefore is more original than the single alphabetical directory at issue in *Feist Publications, Inc. v. Rural Telephone Service Co.,* 499 U.S. 340, 113 L. Ed. 2d 358, 111 S. Ct. 1282 (1991). ProCD sells a version of the database, called SelectPhone (trademark), on CD-ROM discs. (CD-ROM means "compact disc – read only memory." The "shrinkwrap license" gets its name from the fact that retail software packages are covered in plastic or cellophane "shrinkwrap," and some vendors, though not ProCD, have written licenses that become effective as soon as the customer tears the wrapping from the package. Vendors prefer "end user license," but we use the more common term.) A proprietary method of compressing the data serves as effective encryption too. Customers decrypt and use the data with the aid of an application program that ProCD has written. This program, which is copyrighted, searches the database in response to users' criteria (such as "find all people named Tatum in Tennessee, plus all firms with 'Door Systems' in the corporate name"). The resulting lists (or, as ProCD prefers, "listings") can be read and manipulated by other software, such as word processing programs.

The database in SelectPhone (trademark) cost more than $ 10 million to compile and is expensive to keep current. It is much more valuable to some users than to others. The combination of names, addresses, and zip codes enables manufacturers to compile lists of potential customers. Manufacturers and retailers pay high prices to specialized information intermediaries for such mailing lists; ProCD offers a potentially cheaper alternative. People with nothing to sell could use the database as a substitute for calling long distance information, or as a way to look up old friends who have moved to unknown towns, or just as an electronic substitute for the local phone book.

ProCD engages in "price discrimination." It sells its database (slightly modified) for $150 to consumers, with license terms stating that the purchaser will not use it for commercial purposes.

Commercial customers pay more.

Judge Easterbrook spends a fair amount of time talking about why it is important for companies to be able to do this. It results in market efficiencies, like lower prices for both consumers and commercial users, since if consumers don't get to

buy at a lower price, commercial buyers would have to bear the full cost of ProCD making a profit.

If ProCD had to recover all of its costs and make a profit by charging a single price – that is, if it could not charge more to commercial users than to the general public – it would have to raise the price substantially over $ 150. The ensuing reduction in sales would harm consumers who value the information at, say, $ 200.

To make price discrimination work, however, the seller must be able to control arbitrage. A producer of movies segments the market by time, releasing first to theaters, then to pay-per-view services, next to the videotape and laserdisc market, and finally to cable and commercial tv. Vendors of computer software have a harder task. Anyone can walk into a retail store and buy a box. Customers do not wear tags saying "commercial user" or "consumer user." Anyway, even a commercial-user-detector at the door would not work, because a consumer could buy the software and resell to a commercial user. That arbitrage would break down the price discrimination and drive up the minimum price at which ProCD would sell to anyone.

Instead of tinkering with the product and letting users sort themselves, ProCD turned to the institution of contract. Every box containing its consumer product declares that the software comes with restrictions stated in an enclosed license. This license, which is encoded on the CD-ROM disks as well as printed in the manual, and which appears on a user's screen every time the software runs, limits use of the application program and listings to noncommercial purposes.

Matthew Zeidenberg bought a consumer package of SelectPhone (trademark) in 1994 from a retail outlet in Madison, Wisconsin, but decided to ignore the license. He formed Silken Mountain Web Services, Inc., to resell the information in the SelectPhone (trademark) database. The corporation makes the database available on the Internet to anyone willing to pay its price – which, needless to say, is less than ProCD charges its commercial customers. Zeidenberg has purchased two additional SelectPhone (trademark) packages, each with an updated version of the database, and made the latest information available over the World Wide Web, for a price, through his corporation. ProCD filed this suit seeking an injunction against further dissemination that exceeds the rights specified in the licenses (identical in each of the three packages Zeidenberg purchased).

The trial court held that the license terms were ineffective because they did not appear on the outside of the boxes. This is the "traditional" approach to the question.

Judge Easterbrook reverses here.

II

Following the district court, we treat the licenses as ordinary contracts accompanying the sale of products, and therefore as governed by the common law of contracts and the Uniform Commercial Code. Whether there are legal differences between "contracts" and "licenses" (which may matter under the copyright doctrine of first sale) is a subject for another day.

The trial court held that the "offer" was made by ProCD when it put the software up for sale on a shelf in a store and that Zeidenberg's "acceptance" was paying the price and taking the goods from the store.

Judge Easterbrook disagrees.

In Wisconsin, as elsewhere, a contract includes only the terms on which the parties have agreed. One cannot agree to hidden terms, the judge concluded. So far, so good – but one of the terms to which Zeidenberg agreed by purchasing the software is that the transaction was subject to a license. Zeidenberg's position therefore must be that the printed terms on the outside of a box are the parties' contract – except for printed terms that refer to or incorporate other terms. But why would Wisconsin fetter the parties' choice in this way? Vendors can put the entire terms of a contract on the outside of a box only by using microscopic type, removing other information that buyers might find more useful (such as what the software does, and on which computers it works), or both. The "Read Me" file included with most software, describing system requirements and potential incompatibilities, may be equivalent to ten pages of type; warranties and license restrictions take still more space. Notice on the outside, terms on the inside, and a right to return the software for a refund if the terms are unacceptable (a right that the license expressly extends) may be a means of doing business valuable to buyers and sellers alike. Doubtless a state could forbid the use of standard contracts in the software business, but we do not think that Wisconsin has done so.

> **Judge Easterbrook makes analogies to other "common" transactions in which the exchange of money precedes communication of detailed terms:**
>
> - **Insurance. An agent tells the buyer the essentials (amount of coverage, years, etc.), sends the premium to the home office, which then sends the detailed policy and its terms. Justice Easterbrook says the trial court's decision would mean that those terms are not effective.**
> - **Airline tickets. A traveler orders a ticket and pays, gets the ticket, and on the back finds detailed terms that the traveler is free to reject by canceling the reservation. Using the ticket is acceptance of the terms.**
> - **Concert tickets. The back of the ticket lists things like a prohibition against taping.**
> - **Consumer goods. A consumer buys a radio and inside the box are warranty terms. The trial court decision would mean that only standard UCC implied warranties would apply, which no state holds.**
> - **Drugs. Ingredients are listed on the outside but inserts usually warn of possible negative drug interactions and so on.**
> - **The software industry itself. Customers order by phone or over the Net. Often the product does not even come in a box, but arrives electronically. A buyer over the Net buys a serial number that activates the product's features – including the terms of sale. The trial court's decision implies that such sales have no terms.**

On Zeidenberg's arguments, these unboxed sales are unfettered by terms – so the seller has made a broad warranty and must pay consequential damages for any shortfalls in performance, two "promises" that if taken seriously would drive prices through the ceiling or return transactions to the horse-and-buggy age.

To judge by the flux of law review articles discussing shrinkwrap licenses, uncertainty is much in need of reduction – although businesses seem to feel less uncertainty than do scholars, for only three cases (other than ours) touch on the subject, and none directly addresses it. See *Step-Saver Data Systems, Inc. v. Wyse Technology*, 939 F.2d 91

(3d Cir. 1991); *Vault Corp. v. Quaid Software Ltd.*, 847 F.2d 255, 268-70 (5th Cir. 1988); *Arizona Retail Systems, Inc. v. Software Link, Inc.*, 831 F. Supp. 759 (D. Ariz. 1993).

Now Judge Easterbrook distinguishes the three other cases on this topic.

As their titles suggest, these are not consumer transactions. *Step-Saver* is a battle-of-the-forms case, in which the parties exchange incompatible forms and a court must decide which prevails. Our case has only one form. *Vault* holds that Louisiana's special shrinkwrap-license statute is preempted by federal law, a question to which we return.

The preemption argument is essentially that federal laws on a particular topic trump state laws that are incompatible.

Here, the contention is that if shrink-wrap licenses are contracts, they might extend protection to materials that are legally in the public domain under the (federal) Copyright Act. (Note that this is not an argument that the ProCD materials are in the public domain, only that enforcing shrink-wrap licenses might in other circumstances produce results inconsistent with the Copyright Act.)

Judge Easterbrook says the Copyright Act protects the copyright's owner against the world, whereas contracts affect only their parties. Thus, the Copyright Act does not apply to private contracts between parties. That is, if someone enters into a contract by which he or she gives up his right to copy material that is actually in the public domain, that is not a concern of the Copyright Act.

And *Arizona Retail Systems* did not reach the question, because the court found that the buyer knew the terms of the license before purchasing the software.

What then does the current version of the UCC have to say? "A contract for sale of goods may be made in any manner sufficient to show agreement, including conduct by both parties which recognizes the existence of such a contract." A vendor, as master of the offer, may invite acceptance by conduct, and may propose limitations on the kind of conduct that constitutes acceptance. A buyer may accept by performing the acts the vendor proposes to treat as acceptance. And that is what happened. ProCD proposed a contract that a buyer would accept by *using* the software after having an opportunity to read the license at leisure. This Zeidenberg did. He had no choice, because the software splashed the license on the screen and would not let him proceed without indicating acceptance. So although the district judge was right to say that a contract can be, and often is, formed simply by paying the price and walking out of the store, the UCC permits contracts to be formed in other ways. ProCD proposed such a different way, and without protest Zeidenberg agreed. Ours is not a case in which a consumer opens a package to find an insert saying "you owe us an extra $ 10,000" and the seller files suit to collect. Any buyer finding such a demand can prevent formation of the contract by returning the package, as can any consumer who concludes that the terms of the license make the software worth less than the purchase price. Nothing in the UCC requires a seller to maximize the buyer's net gains.

Reversed and Remanded.

There was, therefore, a contract, and Zeidenberg breached its terms. Judge Easterbrook remands the case with instructions to find for the plaintiff. (Why doesn't he just do it himself? Because it is up to the lower court, not the appellate court, to determine damages.)

Contracts: Case 7

RICH HILL and ENZA HILL, on behalf of a class of persons similarly situated, Plaintiffs-Appellees, v. GATEWAY 2000, INC., and DAVID PRAIS, Defendants-Appellants.

No. 96-3294

UNITED STATES COURT OF APPEALS FOR THE SEVENTH CIRCUIT

105 F.3d 1147; 1997 U.S. App. LEXIS 176; 31 U.C.C. Rep. Serv. 2d (Callaghan) 303

December 10, 1996, ARGUED
January 6, 1997, DECIDED

OPINION: EASTERBROOK, Judge:

A customer picks up the phone, orders a computer, and gives a credit card number. Presently a box arrives, containing the computer and a list of terms, said to govern unless the customer returns the computer within 30 days. Are these terms effective as the parties' contract, or is the contract term-free because the order-taker did not read any terms over the phone and elicit the customer's assent?

One of the terms in the box containing a Gateway 2000 system was an arbitration clause. Rich and Enza Hill, the customers, kept the computer more than 30 days before complaining about its components and performance. They filed suit in federal court arguing, among other things, that the product's shortcomings make Gateway a racketeer (mail and wire fraud are said to be the predicate offenses), leading to treble damages under RICO for the Hills and a class of all other purchasers. Gateway asked the district court to enforce the arbitration clause; the judge refused, writing that "the present record is insufficient to support a finding of a valid arbitration agreement between the parties or that the plaintiffs were given adequate notice of the arbitration clause." Gateway took an immediate appeal, as is its right. 9 U.S.C. § 16(a)(1)(A).

The Hills say that the arbitration clause did not stand out: they concede noticing the statement of terms but deny reading it closely enough to discover the agreement to arbitrate, and they ask us to conclude that they therefore may go to court. Yet an agreement to arbitrate must be enforced "save upon such grounds as exist at law or in equity for the revocation of any contract." 9 U.S.C. § 2. A contract need not be read to be effective; people who accept take the risk that the unread terms may in retrospect prove unwelcome. Terms inside Gateway's box stand or fall together. If they constitute the parties' contract because the Hills had an opportunity to return the computer after reading them, then all must be enforced.

ProCD, Inc. v. Zeidenberg, 86 F.3d 1447 (7th Cir. 1996) holds that terms inside a box of software bind consumers who use the software after an opportunity to read the terms and to reject them by returning the product.

Judge Easterbrook thus cites himself.

Likewise, *Carnival Cruise Lines, Inc. v. Shute*, 499 U.S. 585, 113 L. Ed. 2d 622, 111 S. Ct. 1522 (1991), enforces a forum-selection clause that was included among three pages of terms attached to a cruise ship ticket. *ProCD* and *Carnival Cruise Lines* exemplify the many commercial transactions in which people pay for products with terms to follow; *ProCD* discusses others. Gateway shipped computers with the same sort of accept-or-return offer *ProCD* made to users of its software. *ProCD* relied on the Uniform Commercial

Code rather than any peculiarities of Wisconsin law; both Illinois and South Dakota, the two states whose law might govern relations between Gateway and the Hills, have adopted the UCC; neither side has pointed us to any atypical doctrines in those states that might be pertinent; *ProCD* therefore applies to this dispute.

Plaintiffs ask us to limit *ProCD* to software, but where's the sense in that? *ProCD* is about the law of contract, not the law of software. Practical considerations support allowing vendors to enclose the full legal terms with their products. Cashiers cannot be expected to read legal documents to customers before ringing up sales. If the staff at the other end of the phone for direct-sales operations such as Gateway's had to read the four-page statement of terms before taking the buyer's credit card number, the droning voice would anesthetize rather than enlighten many potential buyers. Others would hang up in a rage over the waste of their time. And oral recitation would not avoid customers' assertions (whether true or feigned) that the clerk did not read term X to them, or that they did not remember or understand it. Writing provides benefits for both sides of commercial transactions. Customers as a group are better off when vendors skip costly and ineffectual steps such as telephonic recitation, and use instead a simple approve-or-return device. Competent adults are bound by such documents, read or unread. For what little it is worth, we add that the box from Gateway was crammed with software. The computer came with an operating system, without which it was useful only as a boat anchor. See *Digital Equipment Corp. v. Uniq Digital Technologies, Inc.*, 73 F.3d 756, 761 (7th Cir. 1996). Gateway also included many application programs. So the Hills' effort to limit *ProCD* to software would not avail them factually, even if it were sound legally – which it is not.

For their second sally, the Hills contend that *ProCD* should be limited to executory contracts (to licenses in particular), and therefore does not apply because both parties' performance of this contract was complete when the box arrived at their home.

SIDEBAR: Executory contracts

Executory contracts are contracts that have not as yet been fully completed or performed.

This is legally and factually wrong: legally because the question at hand concerns the *formation* of the contract rather than its *performance*, and factually because both contracts were incompletely performed. *ProCD* did not depend on the fact that the seller characterized the transaction as a license rather than as a contract; we treated it as a contract for the sale of goods and reserved the question whether for other purposes a "license" characterization might be preferable. 86 F.3d at 1450. All debates about characterization to one side, the transaction in *ProCD* was no more executory than the one here: Zeidenberg paid for the software and walked out of the store with a box under his arm, so if arrival of the box with the product ends the time for revelation of contractual terms, then the time ended in *ProCD* before Zeidenberg opened the box. But of course ProCD had not completed performance with delivery of the box, and neither had Gateway. One element of the transaction was the warranty, which obliges sellers to fix defects in their products. The Hills have invoked Gateway's warranty and are not satisfied with its response, so they are not well positioned to say that Gateway's obligations were fulfilled when the motor carrier unloaded the box. What is more, both ProCD and Gateway promised to help customers to use their products. The document in Gateway's box includes promises of future performance that some consumers value highly; these promises bind Gateway just as the arbitration clause binds the Hills.

Next the Hills insist that *ProCD* is irrelevant because Zeidenberg was a "merchant" and they are not. Section 2-207(2) of the UCC, the infamous battle-of-the-forms section, states that "additional terms [following acceptance of an offer] are to be construed as proposals for addition to a contract. Between merchants such terms become part of the contract unless. . . . " Plaintiffs tell us that *ProCD* came out as it did only because Zeidenberg was a "merchant" and the terms inside ProCD's box were not excluded by the "unless" clause. This argument pays scant attention to the opinion in *ProCD*, which concluded that, when there is only one form, " § 2-207 is irrelevant." 86 F.3d at 1452. The question in *ProCD* was not whether terms were added to a contract after its formation, but how and when the contract was formed – in particular, whether a vendor may propose that a contract of sale be formed, not in the store (or over the phone) with the payment of money or a general "send me the product," but after the customer has had a chance to inspect both the item and the terms. *ProCD* answers "yes," for merchants and consumers alike.

At oral argument the Hills propounded still another distinction: the box containing ProCD's software displayed a notice that additional terms were within, while the box containing Gateway's computer did not. The difference is functional, not legal. Consumers browsing the aisles of a store can look at the box, and if they are unwilling to deal with the prospect of additional terms can leave the box alone, avoiding the transactions costs of returning the package after reviewing its contents. Gateway's box, by contrast, is just a shipping carton; it is not on display anywhere. Its function is to protect the product during transit, and the information on its sides is for the use of handlers ("Fragile!" "This Side Up!") rather than would-be purchasers.

The Court says the Hills "knew" before ordering the computer that the box would contain some important terms and they didn't try to discover them in advance.

How would they know? The ads stated that the computer comes with limited warranties and lifetime support. "Obviously" questions like how limited the warranties were, and how much support, would be answered by some written information coming with the computer.

Shoppers have three principal ways to discover these things. First, they can ask the vendor to send a copy before deciding whether to buy. The Magnuson-Moss Warranty Act requires firms to distribute their warranty terms on request, 15 U.S.C. § 2302(b)(1)(A); the Hills do not contend that Gateway would have refused to enclose the remaining terms too. Concealment would be bad for business, scaring some customers away and leading to excess returns from others. Second, shoppers can consult public sources (computer magazines, the Web sites of vendors) that may contain this information. Third, they may inspect the documents after the product's delivery. Like Zeidenberg, the Hills took the third option. By keeping the computer beyond 30 days, the Hills accepted Gateway's offer, including the arbitration clause.

The Hills' remaining arguments, including a contention that the arbitration clause is unenforceable as part of a scheme to defraud, do not require more than a citation to *Prima Paint Corp. v. Flood & Conklin Mfg. Co.*, 388 U.S. 395, 18 L. Ed. 2d 1270,

87 S. Ct. 1801 (1967). Whatever may be said pro and con about the cost and efficacy of arbitration (which the Hills disparage) is for Congress and the contracting parties to consider.

The terms contained in the box were part of the contract and must be enforced.

The decision of the district court is vacated, and this case is remanded with instructions to compel the Hills to submit their dispute to arbitration.

∾

"Webwrap" contracts formed using websites generally are enforceable *if* the website is designed in a way that calls the buyer's attention to the terms of the contract (for example, making the customer scroll through the contract terms) and the buyer takes some sort of affirmative step to indicate acceptance (such as clicking on a button or downloading).

Warranties and Disclaimers

There are two types of warranties: implied and express. There are two types of implied warranties: the warranty of merchantability and the warranty of fitness for a particular purpose. The former is automatically included in all sales of goods by merchants; the latter is included in certain circumstances.

The implied warranty of merchantability is a promise that the goods being sold are fit for their *ordinary* purpose. So a bicycle will roll, a database will enable the buyer to store and manipulate data, a spreadsheet program will behave like a spreadsheet.

The implied warranty of fitness for a particular purpose is present only if the seller knows what the buyer intends to do with the goods (more specifically, in other words, than simply to use the goods for their *ordinary* purpose), and the buyer relies on the seller's expertise in selecting the goods.

For example, if the buyer goes to a yacht brokerage and tells the broker he wants to buy a boat suitable for a trans-Atlantic sail and the broker sells the buyer a twenty-five foot plywood sloop that breaks up in the first large wave the buyer encounters, the buyer (or more likely the buyer's estate) will have a claim against the yacht brokerage for breach of the implied warranty of fitness for a particular purpose. The key to deciding whether the implied warranty of fitness for a particular purpose is present in a transaction is often to look for the "reliance" by the buyer.

Express warranties are simply that. They are explicit statements by the seller about what is guaranteed. ("We warrant this car's drive train and engine components to be free of defects or failure for 30,000 miles or three years from date of purchase.")

Implied warranties *can* be effectively disclaimed, if done in the proper way.

The implied warranty of merchantability is effectively disclaimed only if the disclaimer language actually uses the magic word "merchantability." The implied warranty of fitness for a particular purpose is effectively disclaimed by language such as that the product is sold "as is," or "with all faults," or, of course, by language actually referring to the warranty of fitness for a particular purpose.

So, a disclaimer like "We disclaim the implied warranties of merchantability and fitness for a particular purpose" effectively eliminates those warranties from the transaction and the buyer cannot rely on them.

Express warranties can *never* be effectively disclaimed. After all, why should we permit a seller to make a specific guarantee to the buyer at one point and then permit the seller to declare it wasn't really true a little later in the contract?

Why then do so many contracts contain a statement that the seller "disclaims all express warranties"? Probably because some buyer may actually believe it is legally effective and will not try to enforce the express warranty.

A disclaimer that says, then, "We disclaim all warranties implied and express" is legally completely ineffective. It does not use the word "merchantability," it does not name the implied warranty of fitness for a particular purpose or use language such as that the product is sold "as is," and express warranties can never be effectively disclaimed.

3. Torts Introduction

Definition

This chapter provides a broad background about torts as well as about the elements of a number of specific torts. Some torts may seem unlikely to apply in cyberspace – and they may not – but that is what was once thought regarding the tort of "trespass to chattels," which was ultimately used quite creatively as a tool of cyberlaw.

In their famous legal treatise on torts, Prosser and Keeton wrote, "Broadly speaking, a tort is a civil wrong, other than breach of contract, for which the court will provide a remedy in the form of an action for damages." So note that torts are *civil* wrongs, as opposed to criminal wrongs. No one goes to jail for committing a tort, although the same behavior that resulted in a civil tort suit may separately also be the basis for a criminal action. For example, if person A stabs and kills person B, person A may be convicted of the crime of murder and be punished accordingly. However, person A may separately be found liable to the estate of person B in a civil suit for the tort of wrongful death, and have to pay damages to the estate.

The fundamental issue of torts is whether and when losses should be shifted from the victim of an injury to the person who inflicted the injury or some other source of compensation – often an insurance company. The tort suits of which the public is most generally aware are probably personal injury suits based on negligence.

The traditional goal of tort law has been to restore the injured party, as nearly as possible, to the equivalent of his or her condition prior to the harm. In the case of physical injury, of course, it is often impossible to achieve this goal fully. If a person has lost a leg or an arm in an accident and it is determined that the fault rests with the other party, no amount of money will ever *actually* restore the injured party to his or her previous condition. Nonetheless, a damage amount intended to compensate the injured party must be calculated. This amount should include compensation for tangible losses, such as hospital expenses, as well as "intangible" losses, such as the victim's pain and suffering.

Tort suits differ from contract suits in that the latter generally involve lots of documents as evidence. Tort suits most often do not. A suit based on a personal injury suffered in an accident, for example, generally arises from something that happened suddenly and without warning. The parties typically do not know each other before the accident occurs. They have no reason to have documented their relationship in any way. This also explains why tortious disputes are more likely to go to trial than contract suits. Parties to tort suits have no existing relationship to preserve. On the other hand, the parties to a contract generally expect to see each other again after the dispute has been resolved. Instead of engaging in costly and bitter legal battles, they may enter into a settlement because it provides foreseeable benefits. If they are commercial trading partners, they have strong incentives to reach a settlement of a dispute that preserves the mutually advantageous relationship.

At trial, the plaintiff in a tort suit has the burden of proving the essential facts of his or her case "by a preponderance of the evidence." That is, is it more likely than not that the defendant is liable for damages? Note how, as explained in Chapter 1, this standard of proof differs from the "beyond a reasonable doubt" standard used in criminal trials.

The common law permits a plaintiff to sue only once for harm suffered. After a suit, the plaintiff will have no further legal recourse for damages even if the plaintiff suffers further unanticipated harm as a result of the original tort. There are statutes of limitations, differing in duration from state to state, that define the window of time in which the plaintiff must bring a suit. As a result, tort suits for personal injuries, for example, are often not filed until the statute of limitations has almost expired if there is any chance that further complications from the original injury might develop.

In the United States, attorneys who represent plaintiffs in personal injury suits typically are paid on a *contingent fee* basis. That is, the attorney gets a previously agreed upon percentage of the amount recovered by the plaintiff, but gets nothing if his client loses. In many other countries, the contingent fee system is considered at least unethical, and is sometimes specifically prohibited by law. The feeling outside the United States is that if the plaintiffs know they will have to pay their attorneys whether they win or not, only those plaintiffs with serious and legitimate claims will sue. But that puts the decision of whether or not to sue in the hands of those who are least able to assess a case's likelihood of success – the plaintiffs themselves. The contingent fee system makes the courts more accessible to people in general by saving clients the trouble of paying any money upfront. The system also leaves the decision of whether or not to sue in the hands of the experts – the attorneys. An attorney is unlikely to accept a case based on a contingent fee unless the attorney is reasonably sure the plaintiff's case will be a strong one.

Employers are sometimes held liable for the torts of their employees, if the tort occurred in the course of employment. Employer liability is an extension of the rule of *respondeat superior*, which for centuries made masters liable for the misconduct of their servants. At one time, the master was legally entitled to be indemnified by the servant for any money the master was required to pay for the servant's misconduct, although this aspect of the rule is no longer invoked.

The doctrine of *sovereign immunity*, founded on the ancient principle that "the King can do no wrong," precludes bringing suit against the government, in the person of its officers and agents, without its consent. The federal government waived its right to invoke sovereign immunity for its torts in the Federal Tort Claims Act of 1946. However, the Act does provide that only federal courts, applying the state law of the state in which the suit is brought, will have jurisdiction over cases against the federal government; that there will be no jury trials in such cases; and that no punitive damages will be assessed. (There will be further discussion of punitive damages a bit later.) The Act also specifically excludes certain federal government activities from coverage (i.e., the government retains immunity). These include matters involving the Treasury, injuries to military personnel, and discretionary functions or duties.

State governments have generally waived sovereign immunity along lines similar to the federal government's waiver. (Most of us have become so used to thinking of the United States as one entity that we have lost sight of the fact that every state is a separate sovereign entity. The law has not. State court opinions will often refer to "foreign" corporations, individual, or entities. They are referring to those outside the state, not just those outside the country.) Some states have retained sovereign immunity but have created state commissions to handle claims against the state. Some have waived immunity in specific types of cases.

Some Intentional Torts and Their Common Law Elements

Intentional Infliction of Emotional Distress: requires *outrageous* conduct by the defendant and harm to the plaintiff.

"Outrageous conduct" is conduct that transcends the bounds of decency. Alternatively, it can be mildly unpleasant conduct that becomes outrageous by its relentless or repetitive nature. The type of plaintiff may affect the interpretation of "outrageous conduct" in a given case. For example, behavior that might not rise to the level of "outrageous" if directed toward an adult might satisfy the requirement if directed toward a child. Similarly, the type of defendant involved may be important. Defendants such as common carriers or innkeepers have a stricter than average behavioral duty toward their passengers or guests.

The plaintiff must also prove that he or she has suffered real harm from the outrageous conduct. U.S. and other common law courts are very wary of claims like emotional distress, in which the alleged harm is intangible. If someone has been physically injured in some way, the harm is usually either obvious or can easily be substantiated by hospital reports or the like. In an emotional distress claim substantiating the harm is less simple, and courts often require proof in the form of reports from a therapist or psychiatrist describing the nature and extent of the harm to the plaintiff. Of course, the more outrageous the conduct, the less difficult it is for the plaintiff to convince a jury that there was emotional distress.

Intentional infliction of emotional distress (which we can distinguish from its "negligent" version, discussed later) will often be used as a "fallback" tort. Most cases alleging any kind of injury to the plaintiff will also include an allegation of emotional distress, whether intentional or negligent.

Trespass to Land: requires "invasion" by the defendant of the land of the plaintiff.

The "invasion" by the defendant must be physical, although not necessarily by the defendant's person. The defendant could, for example, invade the plaintiff's property by throwing some physical object onto it. In actions alleging "computer trespass," courts have held that the electronic impulses used to instruct and run a computer are sufficiently "physical," and that the computer itself is comparable enough to a form of "land" or property, to hold a computer hacker liable under this tort for wrongfully accessing another computer. Most states also now have passed statutes criminalizing "computer trespass."

Trespass to Chattels (personal property) and Conversion (theft): require trespass to another's personal property by the defendant that affects the value of the property to the plaintiff.

These are two distinct torts that are best thought of together. If the trespass to the property diminishes the value of the property to the owner, you have trespass to chattels. Once the level of trespass increases to a point at which the property is no longer of any value, you have conversion – the common law term for theft.

Trespass to chattels has been used successfully as a tool to prevent spammers from sending unsolicited e-mail advertising to users of services such as America Online. The theory is that the spam adds a great deal of load to the service provider's systems. This affects the performance of the systems and therefore lowers the value of the owner's property. We will study the leading case on spamming in Chapter 14.

Miscellaneous Torts to Economic and Dignity Interests

This type of tort is very common in cyberspace. Some examples include the following:

Defamation: Slander or libel of another. Defamation is very common and easy to do in cyberspace. It is the subject of Chapter 4.

Invasion of the Right of Privacy: This actually consists of four torts, including appropriation of the plaintiff's name or likeness for the defendant's commercial advantage, unreasonable intrusion into the plaintiff's privacy, placing a plaintiff in a "false light," and publication of private facts about the plaintiff. Each of these four torts is more fully described and explained in Chapter 9, "The Right of Privacy."

Intentional or Negligent Misrepresentation: This requires misrepresentation of a fact, not merely sharing of an opinion, unless it is an opinion based on superior skill in some area. The misrepresentation must be made intentionally or recklessly. The defendant must intend to induce reliance by the plaintiff, and the plaintiff must then rely on the misrepresentation. Finally, the plaintiff must show harm.

Negligence

Many tort suits are based upon an allegation that the harm the plaintiff suffered was a result of negligence by the defendant. The general standard of care used in determining whether or not a defendant was negligent is that of the "Reasonable Person."

Who is the Reasonable Person? He or she is a creature of the law. Certainly, the Reasonable Person is not infallible or perfect, but rather represents a standard reflecting the moral judgment of the community – what the community feels *ought* ordinarily to be done, as opposed to what ordinarily *is* done. This approach to determining liability of the defendant implies that *conduct* is the deciding factor and that conduct is to be measured against external "norms."

Justice Holmes, in *The Common Law*, wrote, "The law considers what would be blameworthy in the average man, the man of ordinary intelligence and prudence, and determines liability by that." However, he added, "There are exceptions . . . which illustrate the rule," citing as examples a blind man or a child, who are judged by a standard other than the general Reasonable Person rule.

Prosser and Keeton note, "As to his physical characteristics, the reasonable person may be said to be identical with the actor," and that "Conduct of the handicapped individual must be reasonable in the light of the person's knowledge of his infirmity."

So, the defendant's conduct is judged by what it is reasonable to expect that particular defendant to have done in the given circumstances. Professionals engaged in performing their professional tasks are, of course, held to a higher standard of care than an ordinary person would be if required by circumstance to perform the same tasks. For example, a doctor who happens upon a car wreck and administers aid to the victims will be expected to do so more expertly than, say, a computer programmer who happens upon a wreck and tries to help.

Children have traditionally been held to standards of care appropriate for their age, although many courts have modified this to allow for adult standards of care to be applied to children performing "adult" activities, such as driving motorboats.

Custom can play a role in determining the standard of care to be applied. Proof of a common practice helps in formulating the general expectation of society. However, it is for a jury to determine if the defendant's conduct satisfies that expectation. Courts have rejected the argument that a prevailing custom absolutely defines the standard of care. That being said, custom may play an important role in a jury's determination of the standard of care. For example, proof that a defendant's care fell below an industry standard may be a good argument for the plaintiff since it shows that experienced industry members – the defendant's peers, if you will – would agree with the plaintiff's claim that the defendant's behavior was subpar.

Statutes and regulations play less of a role than one might think in determining whether a defendant has been negligent. Courts have not been willing to use statutory violations as the basis for a decision in which the harm that occurred was not the harm that the statute was intended to prevent. Licensing standards have similarly not been used to define negligence. For example, in a motor vehicle accident involving a driver without a license, the criminal act of driving without a license does not automatically imply negligence. The two issues are separate. Similarly, compliance with licensing or mandated operational safety requirements does not automatically mean that a party has satisfactorily fulfilled his or her obligations as a reasonable person and is thus immune from liability for negligence. So, a restaurant that has satisfied numerous health department inspections might nonetheless be liable for negligence in a case involving food poisoning.

Proof of Negligence

There are five elements of a "cause of action" based on negligence by the defendant:

1. Duty
2. Breach of Duty
3. Cause in Fact
4. Proximate Cause
5. Damage

The burden is on the plaintiff to establish ALL FIVE elements. If the plaintiff fails to establish any one of them, the defendant is not liable, as a matter of law.

Duty

"Duty" is relational. The question is whether the defendant has any obligation to the plaintiff. The common law rule has long been that no one has a general duty to protect others. Courts, however, have been chipping away at this rule by establishing exceptions, commonly based on a "special relationship" of some sort, such as, for example, a spousal relationship. Spouses have a duty to one another, just as parents have a duty to protect their children. Duty can, of course, arise contractually. A lifeguard has a contractual duty to assist those in distress in the water. Legislatures have also established exceptions to the common law rule of no duty by passing so-called good Samaritan laws that require people to provide assistance to one another so long as there is no potential danger to the person who tries to help.

The issue is always, "Did the defendant have a duty to the plaintiff?" The issue is not whether the defendant acted reasonably. Whether a duty existed is a question of *law*, and therefore is decided by the court (i.e., the judge); *Breach of Duty* is a question of *fact*, and is therefore decided by the trier of fact – usually a jury.

Breach of Duty

Once the plaintiff has established that the defendant did indeed have a duty to the plaintiff, the question becomes whether the defendant met the standard of care that applies. The most convincing proof a plaintiff can use is "documentary" or "real" evidence. This includes things like tire marks, a broken bottle, and so on. It is evidence that is hard to dispute – although, of course, the meaning of the evidence may be a point of argument. "Direct" evidence – that is, testimony by witnesses and others – is more easily challenged. One can cross-examine a witness, or cast doubt on his or her credibility far more easily than one can attack "real" evidence.

"Circumstantial" evidence, while commonly believed to be worthless ("the entire case is circumstantial"), can actually be just as strong as direct evidence. It depends on the strength of the inference that can be drawn.

An example of strong circumstantial evidence is the doctrine of *Res Ipsa Loquitur*, which translates as "the thing speaks for itself." (Law students routinely wonder why the thing doesn't speak English.) Res Ipsa, as attorneys refer to it, is a way of proving breach of duty circumstantially in certain cases. There are two key elements of Res Ipsa: the accident or event must be of a kind that does not usually happen without negligence, and the negligence must be the defendant's. For example, picture a plaintiff who suffers emotional or psychological harm as the result of finding a human toe in a tin of chewing tobacco. This is clearly a type of event that does not usually happen without negligence, and if the defendant is the manufacturer of the chewing tobacco the plaintiff has a very strong Res Ipsa case.

Cause in Fact

Some people like to consider cause in fact and proximate cause as one analytical step. I think it is clearer to consider them separately. The question we ask is "Was the breach of duty by the defendant a cause of the alleged harm to the plaintiff?" Some hypothetical situations might help understand the issue.

Suppose the harm was death by smoke inhalation in bed during a smoky hotel fire. The decedent's estate brings a suit for the tort of wrongful death as plaintiff against the hotel. The plaintiff succeeds in establishing that the hotel's fire escapes were inadequate. Did the hotel have a duty to the plaintiff? Yes, as a customer and guest of the hotel, the plaintiff was owed reasonable care. Did the hotel breach that duty by not providing adequate fire escapes for its guests? Yes. Is the hotel liable for the wrongful death of the plaintiff? No. The inadequacy of the fire escapes was not a cause *in fact* of the plaintiff's death *in bed* by smoke inhalation.

Consider another example. The plaintiff (an estate of a decedent again) proves that the defendant rounded a dangerous curve in his car, ignoring a sign that instructed drivers to honk their horns when rounding the curve, and hit the deceased's car head on. The deceased was listening to her radio at such a volume that all outside sound was drowned out. Did the defendant have a duty? Yes. Drivers have a duty to drive as safely as possible in order to avoid injuring others. Did the defendant breach that duty by ignoring the sign? Yes. Is the defendant liable for the death of the plaintiff because he failed to honk his horn? No. The fact that the defendant failed to honk his horn was not a cause of the death because the decedent would not have heard the horn if it had been honked. There was no causal connection between the alleged act of negligence and the harm.

In other words, in a negligence case, the defendant's negligence is *not* a cause in fact of the harm if the harm would have occurred in spite of that negligence.

Note the indefinite article "a" in describing cause in fact. For any event, there are innumerable causes in fact. This idea could be taken to an unreasonable extreme – for example by arguing that the defendant's birth was a cause in fact of the harm! And, of course, it *is* **a** cause in fact. The question becomes then how far back in the chain of causation are we willing to go? At what point should liability not be based? That is the question of "proximate cause."

Proximate Cause

Generally, two views are applicable when analyzing the question of whether the cause in fact was close enough to the harm to be a suitable basis for imposing liability for negligence on the defendant. Both views were articulated in the well-known case of *Palsgraf v. The Long Island Railroad Company*, which was decided by the Court of Appeals of New York (New York's highest state court) in 1924.

On a Sunday morning, Helen Palsgraf and her two daughters were waiting on a Long Island Railroad platform in Brooklyn for a train to go to the beach at Rockaway, New York. The platform was crowded. A train pulled in (not the train that Mrs. Palsgraf wanted to take). As the train was leaving the station a man carrying a package jumped aboard, being pulled up by one railroad guard and pushed by another. He dropped his package, which fell between the platform and the train and onto the tracks below where it exploded. According to reports, it was a package of fireworks of particularly great strength. The force of the explosion knocked over a number of penny scales on the platform. (Penny scales are the large, metal scales, about five feet in height, that are still often found in amusement parks – and in the Yale University gymnasium!) A scale fell over on Mrs. Palsgraf, causing the harm for which she brought suit: a stammer that developed several days after the accident.

The decision, by a vote of 4–3, was in favor of the railroad. In the majority opinion written by the now famous Chief Judge Benjamin Cardozo, the Court applied what has come to be called the "Reasonable Foreseeability" test for proximate cause. Under this test, the defendant is responsible for any harm resulting from his or her negligence only if the defendant should reasonably have foreseen the harm. In the *Palsgraf* case, Judge

Cardozo stated that the LIRR was not liable for Mrs. Palsgraf's alleged injuries because it was unreasonable to think that the harm was one that the railroad should have foreseen.

Judge Andrews, writing on behalf of two other dissenting judges, articulated what is now referred to as the "Direct Consequences" test, which takes a broader view of liability for the defendant, who is said to be responsible for any harm proximately resulting from his or her negligence. Of course, this is just another way of saying that a proximate cause must be a proximate cause, leaving the matter in the hands of a jury based on the circumstances of every case. Where in the chain of events should the line of liability for causing the harm be drawn?

The Direct Consequences test is used in the majority of states today, but there are many that prefer Cardozo's Reasonable Foreseeability test.

Damage (Harm)

Whichever test for proximate cause has been used, if the plaintiff has succeeded in proving that the defendant had a duty and breached it in a manner that was a cause in fact and a proximate cause of the alleged harm, the plaintiff still has to establish that there actually *was* harm. Usually this is not difficult. Most causes of action for negligence arise from tangible harm like damage to property or personal injury. A broken leg and a hole in a house's wall caused by a car driving into it are easy to see. *Intangible* harm, such as emotional or psychological distress, is much harder to establish. Courts are very wary of intangible harm, and the plaintiff will have to provide convincing proof, such as testimony of therapists or psychiatrists, records of numerous visits to their offices, and so forth, in order to sway the judge.

Damages

If the plaintiff has succeeded in establishing all five elements of negligence, the jury may award damages to the plaintiff. Plaintiffs may recover *actual* damages for tangible aspects of the harm (the cost of hospital bills and visits to the doctor, for example) and also for intangible aspects of the harm, such as pain and suffering. The jury will try to award the plaintiff some amount for what the plaintiff has been through. Obviously, this is a highly subjective question, but juries generally have substantial leeway in determining an amount.

Probably the most hotly contentious form of damages that may be awarded to the plaintiff is *punitive* damages. Punitive damages are the target of many of the "tort reform" bills that have appeared over the years in legislatures, usually with a goal of capping the amount of damages that may be imposed.

The danger in capping punitive damages is that it reduces their potential effectiveness. Punitive damages are supposed to be *punitive*, that is, they are supposed to *hurt* the defendant enough that the defendant will be compelled to alter his or her behavior. The goal is to ensure that the same harm will not befall other potential plaintiffs. Obviously, if the defendant is some small, family-run business, a punitive damage level that will lead to a change in the defendant's behavior will not have to be very high. However, if the defendant is a large, multinational corporation, the amount of punitive damages awarded will have to be extremely high to have any effect on the defendant's future behavior.

This can lead to windfalls from punitive damages for plaintiffs who are bringing suit against large corporations. To many, it seems unfair that one plaintiff, suing a large company for harm based on a particular kind of behavior by the defendant, should be "rewarded" with a large damages award, whereas another plaintiff, suing a small company for the same kind of harm resulting from the same kind of behavior, gets a much smaller amount. And, of course, in a way it *is* "unfair." But if punitive damages are to achieve their goal of behavior modification, the amount awarded must be proportionate to the defendant's means. Unlike compensatory damages regularly awarded in tort suits, which focus on the needs of the plaintiff, punitive damages focus on the defendant's assets. The aim is to get the attention of the defendant to an extent that will encourage the defendant to change.

One idea might be to use punitive damages awarded in tort suits for the public good – for example for medical research or for funding public education – rather than give the amount to a plaintiff. But as far as I know this idea has never been seriously considered.

Defenses to Negligence

Defenses to negligence take two forms: "Simple Defenses" and "Affirmative Defenses." The simple defenses are, well, simple. The defendant argues either that the defendant had no duty, or, if so, that it was not breached, or, if so, that the breach was not a cause in fact of the harm, or if so, that the cause in fact was not a proximate cause of the harm, or, finally, that there was no harm done. The burden of proving the five elements, as noted above, falls on the plaintiff.

If the defendant invokes an affirmative defense, the burden of proof of the affirmative defense falls on the defendant. Two common affirmative defenses are *contributory negligence* (i.e., the plaintiff was also negligent) and *assumption of risk* (i.e., the plaintiff knew that the plaintiff might suffer harm).

Under the traditional common law, *any* contributory negligence on the part of the plaintiff meant the plaintiff simply could not recover anything for the harm suffered. Clearly, this is pretty harsh since there are few situations involving negligence in which the parties do not share responsibility at least to some extent. As a result three forms of *comparative negligence* have developed over the years and have largely replaced the common law rule of contributory negligence. States have individually adopted one of these variations. They are:

- *Pure Comparative Negligence* – The parties share fault on a strict percentage basis as decided by the jury, and the plaintiff's recovery is reduced by the amount of his or her contributory negligence. So, if a plaintiff would have recovered $100,000 but is found to have been 20% contributorily negligent, the plaintiff recovers only $80,000.
- *Modified Not As Great As (NAGA) Comparative Negligence* – The plaintiff recovers fully if the plaintiff's contributory negligence is *less* than the negligence of the defendant.
- *Modified Not Greater Than (NGT) Comparative Negligence* – The plaintiff recovers fully if the plaintiff's contributory negligence is *not greater than* the defendant's negligence.

The important distinction between the NAGA and the NGT versions of comparative negligence is what happens when a jury determines that both the plaintiff and defendant were equally negligent. This is a very common outcome. In a state using the NAGA version of comparative negligence, the plaintiff does not recover (i.e., the plaintiff's negligence *is* as great as the defendant's and that bars recovery). In a state using the NGT version of comparative negligence, the plaintiff recovers fully (i.e., the plaintiff's negligence, while equal to the negligence of the defendant, is *not* greater than the defendant's negligence).

Assumption of risk as a defense is premised on the idea that the plaintiff knew or should have known of the risks inherent in whatever activity led to the harm. Assumption of risk can be "express," that is, the plaintiff signs a waiver or release form stating that the plaintiff understands that risks are present. (This is quite common when, for example, engaging in activities like an organized rafting trip down a river or skydiving.) But often the assumption of risk is implied, meaning that the defendant argues that any reasonable person would have realized that the activity involved risk. For example, a reasonable person attending a baseball game assumes the risk that if sufficient attention is not paid to what is going on there is a risk of being hit by a very hard object (the ball) flying at high velocity. Similarly, as one court ruled, eating freshly made fish chowder involves the risk of finding a fish bone in the chowder so caution should be used in eating it. If the plaintiff is determined to have assumed the risk, the plaintiff does not recover for the harm.

Strict Liability

An alternative to negligence as a theory of recovery for a harm suffered is the doctrine of *strict liability*. In circumstances permitting recovery under strict liability, the plaintiff need only establish causation, not duty or breach of duty. Some specific sorts of activities by a defendant, such as liability for "unnatural hazards" created by the defendant (chemical leaks), or liability for activities that the law classifies as "abnormally dangerous" (activities involving explosives, for example or, interestingly crop dusting) fall under this category.

The most frequent use of strict liability as a theory of recovery is in cases involving liability for products. Usually, these are cases in which the plaintiff alleges that the product was defectively designed or manufactured, or that the defendant failed to provide adequate warning of potential hazards in using the product. *Res Ipsa Loquitur* (see earlier) is often a doctrine that comes into play in strict product liability cases. However, strict liability can also be established by applying the *consumer expectation test*, which says that a manufacturer is liable for harm caused by a product if the product fails to perform as safely as an ordinary consumer would expect. Another commonly applied test is the *risk/benefit test*, which asks whether the product created excessive preventable dangers. If the latter test is used, the defendant must prove that the product's benefits outweigh its risks; so it is therefore not "defective."

Defenses to allegations of strict product liability include proof by the defendant that the product was "state of the art" at the time it was designed or manufactured and that it was therefore impossible for the defendant to have known at that time about the alleged defect. Alternatively, the defendant might try to establish that the product did not, in fact, cause the harm. Finally, of course, in cases involving allegations of inadequate warning, the defendant can attempt to establish that, on the contrary, an adequate warning of the products dangers was properly provided.

4. Defamation

Introduction

Defamation can be either written (called "libel") or spoken (called "slander") but for the purposes of this discussion we will simply refer to both types as "defamation," since whatever form it takes, the same elements and analysis apply. Defamation is a very large problem in cyberspace both because it is so easy to distribute statements widely and quickly, thus inflicting great harm on a person who is defamed, and because of the ease with which anonymity can be achieved.

There are four elements required to establish defamation. The first of these sounds obvious: the statement must be "defamatory." To be defamatory, the statement must assert some defamatory fact. Mere "name calling" does not qualify. If a statement is not obviously defamatory then its defamatory nature must be established by interpreting the facts of the case. The plaintiff has the burden of establishing that in the context of the facts, the statement is defamatory by implication. Even a statement made in jest can be defamatory if it is not understood that way by the recipient of the statement.

"Opinion" is not always a protection against an allegation of defamation. Once again, it depends on how the statement is interpreted. However, a statement that is merely an opinion, and is interpreted as such, is not defamatory. A statement that implies an allegation of some undisclosed defamatory fact or facts that are the basis for the statement is not simply an opinion. So, for example a statement such as, "Dr. Smith is incompetent," might be merely an opinion. However, "I'm not going to get into the specifics, but let me tell you, Dr. Smith is incompetent," might be defamatory.

Quoting a statement made by a person is usually *not* defamation of that person. However, the quotation must be accurate and must be presented in context.

Photographs that place a person in an unflattering light can be defamation. (They may also lead to a claim of liability under one of the four privacy torts that will be discussed later in Chapter 9, in this case the tort of placing a person in a false light.) It is wise to be aware of this visual form of defamation because computer graphics technology makes misrepresenting a person so easy to do.

The second element of a claim of defamation is that the defamatory statement must be about *this* plaintiff. If the statement does not clearly refer to the plaintiff, the plaintiff must establish that he or she was intended as the object of the defamation. Once again, the focus is on how the statement is received, not on the intention of the speaker or writer. Courts look at what a reasonable person in the intended audience would conclude.

Any living person or corporation can bring suit for defamation; estates of deceased persons cannot. However, only individuals or entities (such as corporations) can sue for defamation, not groups. No individual in a group is defamed if the group is large enough that there is no likelihood that a reader or listener would understand the statement to refer to any particular member of the group. (Generally, if the group is larger than twenty-five members, there is no recovery for a defamation claim.) So, for example, an individual attorney will not be able to recover based on a claim of defamation when someone opines, "Lawyers are thieves," because there is no likelihood that any reasonable person would understand the statement to refer to any lawyer in particular.

The third required element of a defamation claim is that the statement must be "published." This does not mean "published" in the common sense of that word, but rather simply means the statement must be communicated to a third person by any means. The communication of the statement can happen intentionally or negligently. It doesn't matter.

So, at a fund-raising cocktail party Mr. Smith tells Senator Tomato that Smith knows Tomato takes bribes. Mr. Brown overhears this. Has the statement been "published" (i.e., communicated to a third party)? Yes. Negligently, in this case, but the required element of defamation has been met. However, suppose Mr. Brown speaks and understands only Norwegian. Has the statement been published? No. The recipient of the statement must understand the statement.

In our world of rapid-fire forwarding of e-mail, it is important to remember that the reprinting or forwarding of a defamatory statement subjects the reprinter or forwarder to liability for defamation too. However, liability may be avoided *if* reasonable steps are taken to ascertain the truth of the statement. It is wise, however, to be aware and cautious.

Finally, the fourth element of a defamation claim is that the defamatory statement must injure the plaintiff's reputation. This is presumed when the statement concerns some specific things that are considered defamation *per se*. These include statements regarding a person's business or profession, statements involving crimes of "moral turpitude," statements alleging a person to have a "loathsome disease," or, in some states, statements imputing unchastity to a woman!

Statements regarding so-called public figures (a definition of which will be explored in more detail in Chapter 9 but, for now, think "famous person") are defamatory only if the statements are published with the knowledge that they were false or at least with a reckless disregard as to whether or not they were false, not merely published negligently. The reasons for this are primarily support for the freedom of the press, plus an assumption that public figures are able to get media attention to counter stories they feel are defamatory. Private figures have, therefore, an easier time proving defamation.

Whether being "well known" on the Internet makes a person a public figure is a question that remains open.

Defenses to Defamation

Consent

Consent is a valid defense to many causes of action, including defamation. If, for example, a person consents to being included in, perhaps, a documentary film, that person is unlikely later to be able to allege that he or she has been defamed in the film, so long as the person has been portrayed and quoted accurately and in context in the film.

Truth

The most common defense to an allegation of defamation is that the allegedly defamatory statement is true. Under the common law, to use this defense the defendant is required to prove the truth of the statement made about the plaintiff. This continues to be the rule today in the United Kingdom. However, in the United States, the Supreme Court held in 1985, in the case of *Philadelphia Newspapers, Inc. v. Hepps*, that the plaintiff is required to prove the statement is false. The rule, though, is still unclear. In 1986, a New York State court, in the case of *Pollnow v. Poughkeepsie Newspapers, Inc.*, held that the burden to prove falsity falls on the plaintiff only *after* the defendant has asserted some facts tending to show the truth of the statement.

But, in general, it is said that the rule is that in the United States the plaintiff must prove falsity, whereas in the United Kingdom the defendant must prove truth. The distinction on where the burden of proof falls is an important one because it is often extremely difficult to prove the truth or falsity of a statement. The global nature of the Internet often broadens the impact of allegedly defamatory statements and usually, when possible, a plaintiff will try to bring a defamation suit in the United Kingdom, where the defendant will have the burden of establishing the truth of the statement that led to the suit.

Privilege

Statements made in certain settings, such as judicial proceedings or in legislative session, are privileged and cannot be the basis of a defamation claim.

Fair Comment

Comments made on matters of legitimate public interest cannot be the basis of a defamation claim, unless made maliciously. This defense arises frequently in allegations of defamation against newspapers, periodicals, broadcasters, and, perhaps one day, against "bloggers."

Parody

Parody is a defense in defamation suits (and many other types of allegations as will be shown later in this text). However, usually the parody must be so obvious that no one could reasonably believe it to be based on fact.

Let's look at some cases on the topic of defamation.

Defamation: Case 1

C. Ivan GORDON, D.O., Appellant, v. LANCASTER OSTEOPATHIC HOSPITAL ASSOCIATION, INC.; Professional Staff of Lancaster Osteopathic Hospital; Berel B. Arrow, D.O.; Norman M. Axelrod, D.O.; Joseph Gordon; G. Richard Hartz, D.O.; Seymour S. Kilstein, D.O.; Robert C. Scott, D.O.; and Lewis M. Yunginger, D.O., Deceased and his successor, Ethel M. Yunginger, Executrix, Appellees

Superior Court of Pennsylvania

340 Pa. Super. 253; 489 A.2d 1364; 1985 Pa. Super. LEXIS 5916

August 23, 1984, Argued
February 13, 1985, Filed

OPINION: OLSZEWSKI, Judge:

Appellant, C. Ivan Gordon, D.O., practiced as a pathologist at the Lancaster Osteopathic Hospital ("LOH") from March of 1976 until October of 1980. From July 1, 1978 until June 30, 1980, appellant was employed by LOH; the terms of employment were defined by a written contract, renewable annually for a one year term. On April 29, 1980 appellee Joseph Gordon, Executive Director of LOH, notified appellant of the hospital's intent not to renew the contract. On October 31, 1980, appellant delivered a letter of resignation to Dr. Gordon, effective as of that date.

This action arose as a consequence of a series of letters written by appellees Berel B. Arrow, D.O., Norman M. Axelrod, D.O., and G. Richard Hartz, D.O. to the Executive Director, the President of the Medical Staff and members of the Board of Directors of LOH in the early spring of 1980. These letters stated in pertinent part:

> [W]e are totally unhappy and would like to present a vote of no confidence in Dr. Ivan Gordon. We all feel that we lack trust in the reporting of Dr. Gordon. We feel that the Pathology Department should be stronger as the institution grows. At this point, we would not like to go into absolute detail, but just inform you of the above opinion.
>
> Letter of February 14, 1980.

> [T]he department concludes that because of the difficulty in communication and lack of confidence in Dr. Ivan Gordon's work, that we regretfully recommend to you that under no circumstances shall Dr. Ivan Gordon accede the chairmanship of the department of Pathology at the Lancaster Osteopathic Hospital, and we further feel that attempts at recruitment of a pathologist should be actively carried out by the institution.
>
> Letter of March 7, 1980.

> On March 10, 1980 a letter from Dr. Hartz to the Executive Board stated: "A resolution of no confidence in the above individual was passed by a unanimous vote." On October 10, 1980 a letter from Dr. Arrow to the Grievance and Ethics Committee stated: " . . . Dr. Gordon's attitude and performance over the past several years warrants our opinion. We still feel that a vote of 'no confidence' is indicated."

Appellant alleges that these letters and other communications to the Executive Board were written in retaliation for his attempts to improve the quality of medical care provided by LOH.In the fall of 1979, appellant, as part of his duties as Chairman of the Professional Development Committee, had gained approval of a plan to increase the number of specialists at LOH over a period of five years. Appellant charges that appellee-physicians resisted implementation of that plan based upon fears of increased competition among specialists at LOH. He further contends that appellee-physicians were fearful of and disturbed by his accurate and proper surgical tissue and autopsy reports which documented appellee-physicians' "improper medical procedures and the substandard care provided to their patients."

Appellant's complaint levels seventeen charges including counts in libel and slander, intentional interference with employment, intentional interference with future economic opportunities, wrongful termination, violation of common law and procedural due process, corporate negligence, intentional infliction of emotional distress, restraint of trade, civil conspiracy, and a claim for breach of contract. Following appellees' preliminary objections in the nature of demurrers, the court below dismissed all counts now before us. This appeal follows.

Gordon raises ten issues, but only a few are relevant to our defamation discussion.

First, appellant argues that the lower court erred in finding the publications not defamatory as a matter of law. We hold that the communications were not capable of a defamatory meaning.

... Under the circumstances of this case, we recognize that a communication is defamatory which "ascribes to another conduct, character or a condition that would adversely affect his fitness for the proper conduct of his proper business, trade or profession." *Thomas Merton Center v. Rockwell International Corp.*, 497 Pa. 460, 463, 442 A.2d 213, 216 (1981), *cert. denied* 457 U.S. 1134, 102 S.Ct. 2961, 73 L.Ed.2d 1351 (1982), *quoting* Restatement (Second) of Torts § 573 (1977). The comment to section 573 elaborates:

> The imputation must be of such a character as to disparage the other in his business, trade, profession or office or tend to harm him in it. ... When peculiar skill or ability is necessary, an imputation that attributes a lack of skill or ability tends to harm the other in his business or profession. Restatement (Second) of Torts § 573, comment (c) (1977).

If the court has any doubt that the communication is defamatory, then the issue must be given to the jury for them to determine whether the defamatory meaning was understood by the recipient. *Vitteck*, 256 Pa.Super. at 431, 389 A.2d at 1199. The court must be guided by consideration of the expertise and knowledge of those to whom the publication is circulated, and by consideration of the effect it is fairly calculated to produce. *Corabi v. Curtis Publishing Co.*, 441 Pa. 432, 273 A.2d 899 (1971). "The test is ... the impression it would naturally engender in the minds of the average persons ... among whom it is intended to circulate." *Id.*, 441 Pa. at 447, 273 A.2d at 907 (citation omitted). Here, those 'average persons' are appellant's fellow physicians and the professional community at LOH, particularly persons involved with personnel decisions. Even where a plausible innocent interpretation of the communication exists, if there is an alternative defamatory interpretation, the issue must proceed to the jury. *Zelik v. Daily News Publishing Co.*, 288 Pa.Super. 277, 431 A.2d 1046 (1981); *Brophy v. Philadelphia Newspapers, Inc.*, 281 Pa.Super. 588, 422 A.2d 625 (1980).

We agree with the lower court which held that the words complained of by appellant bear no reasonable interpretation which would render them defamatory. The phrases "a vote of no confidence", "lack of trust in the reporting ability of [appellant]", "lack of confidence in [appellant's] work", and "[appellant's] attitude and performance over the past several years ... [indicates] ... a vote of 'no confidence,'" if believed, do not impute a charge of incompetency or unfitness. ...

We agree with the court below that, even under the assumption that appellees were possessed of the motives and malice towards appellant as alleged, the letters state no more than in the most general terms that appellees, speaking for their departments, lacked confidence in appellant's professional ability and could not recommend that his contract be renewed. As stated by the lower court, appellees "cunningly or unwittingly stopped short of committing acts susceptible of defamatory meaning."

We believe that the only reasonable interpretation of these letters is that they are expressions of opinions. Opinion without more is not actionable libel. *Bogash v. Elkins*, 405 Pa. 437, 176 A.2d 677 (1962); *see also* Restatement (Second) of Torts § 566 (1977) (a statement in the form of an opinion is actionable only if it implies the allegation of undisclosed defamatory facts as the basis for the opinion) adopted in *Braig v. Field Communications*, 310 Pa.Super. 569, 456 A.2d 1366 (1983). While the record shows that appellees specifically refused to elaborate on the basis of their opinion in response to a request from the Executive Board, we cannot say, as a matter of law, that the letters imply undisclosed defamatory facts.

Further, our court has held that communications which may annoy or embarrass a person are not sufficient as a matter of law to create an action in defamation. . . . We must conclude, after review of the context, identity of the parties and the context of the communications that the letters were not defamatory.

Appellant next argues that the lower court erred in holding that his claim in defamation against Joseph Gordon was insufficient as a matter of law. The letter complained of requested that appellant return books, keys and reimburse LOH for personal telephone calls. Appellant argues that these requests suggest that he is a thief. In light of the analysis above, we agree with the lower court that the letter bears no reasonable defamatory interpretation.

Appellant next alleges that the lower court erred in dismissing his action for outrageous conduct and intentional infliction of emotional distress. We hold that the count was properly dismissed. Recovery for intentional infliction of emotional distress will be allowed where there is conduct "so outrageous in character and so extreme in degree as to go beyond all possible bounds of decency and to be regarded as atrocious and utterly intolerable in a civilized society". . . .

The Court then cites cases as examples:
- **Altering medical records to impute criminal acts;**
- **Reckless diagnosis of fatal disease;**
- **Mishandling of a corpse.**

The publication of letters of 'no confidence', as a matter of law, does not rise to this level of atrocity.

Finally, appellant alleges that the lower court erred in dismissing his actions for conspiracy to defame and conspiracy to interfere with contractual relations. In light of our holding that the letters were incapable of any reasonable defamatory meaning, the action as to conspiracy to defame must fall. . . .

The order is affirmed in part, reversed in part and remanded for proceedings consistent with this opinion. Jurisdiction is relinquished.

The Court sends the case back for trial on the issue of conspiracy to interfere with Gordon's prospective contractual relations:

In the instant case, taking all facts pleaded in the complaint as true, appellant has alleged that the letters were written as the product of combined action of the physicians for the unlawful purpose of interfering with his prospective contractual relations. . . . [A]ppellant has alleged that appellees did not have the responsibility or legal function to review the professional abilities of other professional staff members under the medical staff constitution and by-laws. This allegation persuades us that the issue must go to trial.

DISSENT AND CONCURRENCE: CIRILLO, Judge:

I respectfully must disagree with the conclusion that the words contained in the letters of Drs. Arrow, Axelrod, Hartz, and Yunginger were incapable of a defamatory meaning.

Defendant Arrow's letter stated, in part:

At an official meeting of the Department of Internal Medicine, it was a unanimous decision upon the following matter; we are totally unhappy and would like to present a vote of no confidence in Dr. Ivan Gordon.

We all feel that we lack trust in the reporting of Dr. Gordon. We feel that the Pathology Department should be stronger as the institution grows.

The first paragraph of defendant Axelrod's letter read:

At the February meeting of the surgical staff the continual ongoing serious problem of the present junior pathologist was discussed in detail by my department. The department concludes that because of the difficulty of communication and the lack of confidence in Dr. Ivan Gordon's work, that [sic] we regretfully recommend to you that under no circumstances shall Dr. Ivan Gordon accede the [sic] chairmanship of the department of Pathology at the Lancaster Osteopathic Hospital, and we further feel that attempts at recruitment of a pathologist should be actively carried out by the institution.

Defendant Hartz's letter said:

At a department head meeting held Tuesday, March 4, 1980 we discussed the service provided by and the relationship with Dr. C. Ivan Gordon, Department of Pathology. A resolution of no confidence in the above individual was passed by a unanimous vote.

A fourth letter signed by defendants Arrow and Yunginger also expressed "no confidence" in Gordon's "attitude" and "performance."

I should think that no citation of authority beyond that provided by the majority is necessary to demonstrate that these imputations are capable of a defamatory meaning. . . .

The comment to section 573 elaborates:

The imputation must be of such a character as to disparage the other in his business, trade, profession or office or tend to harm him in it. . . . When peculiar skill or ability is necessary, an imputation that attributes a lack of skill or ability tends to harm the other in his business or profession.

Restatement (Second) of Torts § 573, comment (c) (1977).

If the court has any doubt that the communication is defamatory, then the issue must be given to the jury for them to determine whether the defamatory meaning was understood by the recipient. . . .

Without reading more into the letters than their plain wording imports, one could easily determine that: 1) Arrow's letter imputes that the internal medicine department did not trust Gordon's capability to report pathology department findings, and felt that Gordon's continued presence would therefore be inconsistent with a strong pathology department; 2) Axelrod's letter implies that Gordon was unfit to be chairman of the pathology department because the department of surgery "lack[ed] ... confidence in Dr. Ivan Gordon's work"; 3) the other two letters indicate that the members of two medical departments at the hospital had no confidence in Gordon's "service" and "performance." Surely these expressions can be understood to imply that Dr. Gordon's actual work performance showed him to be unfit to practice his business or calling as a pathologist at the hospital and lacking in the professional competence required for the chairmanship of the pathology department. So understood, the words clearly bore the potential to impair Gordon's "'reputation' in the popular sense; to diminish the esteem, respect, goodwill or *confidence*" in which his colleagues and employers held him.... In fact, Gordon alleges that the words had exactly such a damaging effect on his professional reputation, with the ultimate result that the Lancaster Osteopathic Hospital refused to renew his contract.

The majority holds that the "only reasonable interpretation of these letters is that they are expressions of opinion." ... Even if the only reasonable way to interpret the defendants' letters is as expressions of opinion, I think it obvious that the particular expressions used can be read reasonably to imply defamatory allegations of fact, namely Dr. Gordon's unreliable performance as a pathologist and deficiency in the objective qualifications needed in the position of department chairman.

Moreover, under any interpretation the letters do not consist entirely of opinion; they profess to report as *fact* that the collective members of various medical departments passed votes of no confidence in Dr. Gordon. The Doctor alleges that the letters were false, and accordingly we must treat this "fact" recited in the letters as false....

The mere susceptibility of a statement to an innocuous interpretation does not defeat a cause of action in libel. Especially in ruling on preliminary objections in the nature of a demurrer, the court should not decide that words are nondefamatory as a matter of law unless it is certain that a nondefamatory meaning is the *only* reasonable interpretation to be given to the words.

I cannot agree that the only rational interpretation of the defendants' letters is to view them as innocuous and nondefamatory expressions of opinion. Giving appellant the benefit of reasonable inferences from well-pleaded facts to which he is entitled on appeal from a demurrer. I find the letters to be *capable* of a defamatory meaning....

Query: Would Gordon really want this sort of support from the Court? After all, a finding that the hospital was not questioning the quality of his work is better for his record than a finding that the hospital fired him for incompetence!

Defamation: Case 2

CARL SAGAN, Plaintiff, v. APPLE COMPUTER, INC., Defendant

CV 94-2180 LGB (BRx)

UNITED STATES DISTRICT COURT FOR THE CENTRAL DISTRICT OF CALIFORNIA

874 F. Supp. 1072; 1994 U.S. Dist. LEXIS 20154

June 27, 1994, Decided
June 27, 1994, FILED

OPINION: BAIRD, Judge:

I. Background

On April 5, 1994, Carl Sagan ("Plaintiff") initiated this action against Apple Computer, Inc. ("Defendant")[.]

Plaintiff alleges that Defendant began using the name "Carl Sagan" in connection with a personal computer in 1993. After Defendant's use was allegedly publicized in computer periodicals and other publications, Plaintiff's attorneys demanded that Defendant cease use of the name. Plaintiff alleges that Defendant informed Plaintiff that it was using Plaintiff's name as a "code name" for a new personal computer, and that Defendant would cease use of the name. Plaintiff contends that in January of 1994, Defendant changed the "code name" to "Butt-Head Astronomer," which was published by Defendant and appeared in numerous newspapers and in other media.

Sagan alleges a number of things:

1. **Lanham Act violation (the federal law governing many trade practices)**
2. **Violation of California law**
3. **Unfair competition**
4. **Infringement of Sagan's right of publicity (a right that will be explored in detail in Chapter 11)**
5. **Invasion of privacy**
6. **Libel**
7. **The tort of intentional infliction of emotional distress**

The Court here decides to grant Apple's motion to dismiss claims six and seven.

A. Plaintiff's Sixth Claim for Libel

Defendant argues that the statement "Butt-Head Astronomer" cannot be the basis of a libel action because such a statement is an opinion which is nonactionable under the First Amendment....

The Supreme Court held in *Milkovich v. Lorain Journal Co.*, 497 U.S. 1, 111 L. Ed. 2d 1, 110 S. Ct. 2695 (1990), that *Gertz, supra*, did not "create a wholesale defamation exemption for anything that might be labeled 'opinion.'" *Milkovich*, 497 U.S. at 18. The Court recognized that expressions of opinion may often imply an assertion of objective fact. *Id.* Thus, the dispositive question in determining whether a statement of opinion can form the basis of a state libel action is "whether a reasonable factfinder could conclude that the statements imply an assertion [of fact]." *Id.* at 21.

In the Ninth Circuit, courts analyze the following conditions set forth in *Milkovich*:

(1) whether the defendant used figurative or hyperbolic language that would negate the impression that he was seriously maintaining an assertion of fact;
(2) whether the general tenor of the communication negated the assertion of fact; and
(3) whether the assertion is susceptible of being proved true or false.

Plaintiff's libel action is based on the allegation that Defendant changed the "code name" on its personal computer from "Carl Sagan" to "Butt-Head Astronomer" after Plaintiff had requested that Defendant cease use of Plaintiff's name. There can be no question that the use of the figurative term "Butt-Head" negates the impression that Defendant was seriously implying an assertion of fact. It strains reason to conclude that Defendant was attempting to criticize Plaintiff's reputation or competency as an astronomer. One does not seriously attack the expertise of a scientist using the undefined phrase "butt-head." Thus, the figurative language militates against implying an assertion of fact.

Furthermore, the tenor of any communication of the information, especially the phrase "Butt-Head Astronomer," would negate the impression that Defendant was implying an assertion of fact. The complaint states that Defendant changed the name of its personal computer from "Carl Sagan" to "Butt-Head Astronomer," and that "this change was published by Apple, and it appeared in numerous newspaper articles and in other media." Any reader exposed to such a publication would likely have knowledge of the context in which the language was used. A reader aware of the context would understand that Defendant was clearly attempting to retaliate in a humorous and satirical way against Plaintiff's reaction to Defendant's use of his name. A reasonable reader would further conclude that the use of the term "astronomer" did not imply that Plaintiff was a less than able astronomer, but that the word was a merely a means of identifying Plaintiff. Finally, a reasonable reader would conclude that the phrase "Butt-Head Astronomer" did not imply that Plaintiff was legally wrong in asking Defendant to cease using his name. After all, by ceasing use of Plaintiff's name, Defendant's actions spoke louder than words. Thus, the tenor of the communication militates against implying an assertion of fact.

Because a reasonable factfinder could not conclude that "Butt-Head Astronomer" implied that Plaintiff was a less than able astronomer or that Plaintiff was legally wrong in asking Defendant to cease using Plaintiff's name, the only remaining assertion is the bare statement that Plaintiff is a "Butt-Head Astronomer." Clearly this phrase cannot rest on a core of objective evidence. Plaintiff does not suggest any other assertions of objective fact that could be reasonably implied from the phrase.

Based on an analysis of the factors identified in *Unelko,* the Court has no reason to conclude that the statement made by Defendant implies an assertion of objective fact. *Milkovich,* 497 U.S. at 21. Therefore, the statement is protected under the First Amendment and cannot form the basis of a claim for libel.

Because the statement made by Defendant is not actionable under the First Amendment the Court hereby Orders that Defendant's motion to dismiss Plaintiff's sixth Claim for libel is Granted.

B. Plaintiff's Seventh Claim for Intentional Infliction of Emotional Distress

In *Hustler Magazine, Inc. v. Falwell,* 485 U.S. 46, 99 L. Ed. 2d 41, 108 S. Ct. 876 (1987), the Supreme Court held that public figures may not recover for the tort of intentional infliction of emotional distress without showing that the publication contains a false statement of fact made with actual malice. Furthermore, in *Ault v. Hustler Magazine, Inc.,* 860 F.2d 877, 880 (9th Cir. 1988), the Ninth Circuit held that the First Amendment prohibits a constitutionally privileged statement of opinion from forming the basis of a claim for intentional infliction of emotional distress. California substantive law is in accord.

Plaintiff cannot deny that he is a public figure. Furthermore, as discussed above, "Butt-Head Astronomer" is not, nor does it imply, a statement of fact capable of being proven true or false. Therefore, the statement is protected by the First Amendment and is not actionable under California law.

Accordingly, the Court hereby Orders that Defendant's motion to dismiss Plaintiff's Seventh Claim is Granted....

The Court permits the other causes of action to stand (but presumably the matter was subsequently either dropped or settled out of court).

Defamation: Case 3

SIDNEY BLUMENTHAL and JACQUELINE JORDAN BLUMENTHAL, Plaintiffs, v. MATT DRUDGE and AMERICA ONLINE, INC., Defendants.

Civil Action No. 97-1968 (PFL)

UNITED STATES DISTRICT COURT FOR THE DISTRICT OF COLUMBIA

992 F. Supp. 44; 1998 U.S. Dist. LEXIS 5606; 26 Media L. Rep. 1717; 12 Comm. Reg. (P & F) 367

April 22, 1998, Decided
April 22, 1998, Filed

OPINION: FRIEDMAN, Judge:

This is a defamation case revolving around a statement published on the Internet by defendant Matt Drudge. On August 10, 1997, the following was available to all having access to the Internet:

> The DRUDGE REPORT has learned that top GOP operatives who feel there is a double-standard of only reporting Republican shame believe they are holding an ace card: New White House recruit Sidney Blumenthal has a spousal abuse past that has been effectively covered up.
>
> The accusations are explosive.
>
> There are court records of Blumenthal's violence against his wife, one influential Republican, who demanded anonymity, tells the DRUDGE REPORT.
>
> If they begin to use [Don] Sipple and his problems against us, against the Republican Party . . . to show hypocrisy, Blumenthal would become fair game. Wasn't it Clinton who signed the Violence Against Women Act?
>
> There goes the budget deal honeymoon.
>
> One White House source, also requesting anonymity, says the Blumenthal wife-beating allegation is a pure fiction that has been created by Clinton enemies. [The First Lady] would not have brought him in if he had this in his background, assures the well-placed staffer. This story about Blumenthal has been in circulation for years.
>
> Last month President Clinton named Sidney Blumenthal an Assistant to the President as part of the Communications Team. He's brought in to work on communications strategy, special projects themeing – a newly created position.
>
> Every attempt to reach Blumenthal proved unsuccessful.

Currently before this Court are a motion for summary judgment filed by defendant America Online, Inc. ("AOL") and a motion to dismiss or transfer for lack of personal jurisdiction filed by defendant Matt Drudge. Upon consideration of the papers filed by the parties and the oral arguments of counsel, the Court concludes that AOL's motion should be granted and Drudge's motion should be denied.

I. Background

... Sidney Blumenthal works in the White House as an Assistant to the President of the United States. His first day of work as Assistant to the President was Monday, August 11, 1997, the day after the publication of the alleged defamatory statement. Jacqueline Jordan Blumenthal, Sidney Blumenthal's wife, also works in the White House as Director of the President's Commission On White House Fellowships.

... In early 1995, defendant Drudge created an electronic publication called the Drudge Report, a gossip column focusing on gossip from Hollywood and Washington, D.C. ...

Access to defendant Drudge's world wide web site is available at no cost to anyone who has access to the Internet at the Internet address of "www.drudgereport.com." ... By March 1995, the Drudge Report had 1,000 e-mail subscribers, and plaintiffs allege that by 1997 Drudge had 85,000 subscribers to his e-mail service. ...

In late May or early June of 1997, at approximately the time when the licensing agreement expired, defendant Drudge entered into a written license agreement with AOL. The agreement made the Drudge Report available to all members of AOL's service for a period of one year. In exchange, defendant Drudge received a flat monthly "royalty payment" of $ 3,000 from AOL. ... Under the licensing agreement, Drudge is to create, edit, update and "otherwise manage" the content of the Drudge Report, and AOL may "remove content that AOL reasonably determine[s] to violate AOL's then standard terms of service." Drudge transmits new editions of the Drudge Report by e-mailing them to AOL. AOL then posts the new editions on the AOL service. Drudge also has continued to distribute each new edition of the Drudge Report via e-mail and his own web site.

Late at night on the evening of Sunday, August 10, 1997 (Pacific Daylight Time), defendant Drudge wrote and transmitted the edition of the Drudge Report that contained the alleged defamatory statement about the Blumenthals. ...

After receiving a letter from plaintiffs' counsel on Monday, August 11, 1997, defendant Drudge retracted the story through a special edition of the Drudge Report posted on his web site and e-mailed to his subscribers. At approximately 2:00 a.m. on Tuesday, August 12, 1997, Drudge e-mailed the retraction to AOL which posted it on the AOL service. Defendant Drudge later publicly apologized to the Blumenthals.

II. AOL's Motion for Summary Judgment

The near instantaneous possibilities for the dissemination of information by millions of different information providers around the world to those with access to computers and thus to the Internet have created ever-increasing opportunities for the exchange of information and ideas in "cyberspace." This information revolution has also presented unprecedented challenges relating to rights of privacy and reputational rights of individuals, to the control of obscene and pornographic materials, and to competition among journalists and news organizations for instant news, rumors and other information that is communicated so quickly that it is too often unchecked and unverified. Needless to say, the legal rules that will govern this new medium are just beginning to take shape.

Communications Decency Act of 1996, Section 230

In February of 1996, Congress made an effort to deal with some of these challenges in enacting the Communications Decency Act of 1996. While various policy options were open to the Congress, it chose to "promote the continued development of the Internet and other interactive computer services and other interactive media" and "to preserve the vibrant and competitive free market" for such services, largely "unfettered by Federal or State regulation. . . . " 47 U.S.C. § 230(b)(1) and (2). Whether wisely or not, it made the legislative judgment to effectively immunize providers of interactive computer services from civil liability in tort with respect to material disseminated by them but created by others. In recognition of the speed with which information may be disseminated and the near impossibility of regulating information content, Congress decided not to treat providers of interactive computer services like other information providers such as newspaper magazines or television and radio stations, all of which may be held liable for publishing or distributing obscene or defamatory material written or prepared by others. While Congress could have made a different policy choice, it opted not to hold interactive computer services liable for their failure to edit, withhold or restrict access to offensive material disseminated through their medium.

Section 230(c) of the Communications Decency Act of 1996 provides:

> No provider or user of an interactive computer service shall be treated as the publisher or speaker of any information provided by another information content provider.

47 U.S.C. § 230(c)(1). The statute goes on to define the term "information content provider" as "any person or entity that is responsible, in whole or in part, for the creation or development of information provided through the Internet or any other interactive computer service." 47 U.S.C. § 230(e)(3). In view of this statutory language, plaintiffs' argument that the *Washington Post* would be liable if it had done what AOL did here – publish Drudge's story without doing anything whatsoever to edit, verify, or even read it (despite knowing what Drudge did for a living and how he did it)," . . . has been rendered irrelevant by Congress.

Plaintiffs concede that AOL is a "provider . . . of an interactive computer service" for purposes of Section 230, and that if AOL acted exclusively as a provider of an interactive computer service it may not be held liable for making the Drudge Report available to AOL subscribers. See 47 U.S.C. § 230(c)(1). They also concede that Drudge is an "information content provider" because he wrote the alleged defamatory material about the Blumenthals contained in the Drudge Report. While plaintiffs suggest that AOL is responsible along with Drudge because it had some role in writing or editing the material in the Drudge Report, they have provided no factual support for that assertion. Indeed, plaintiffs affirmatively state that "no person, other than Drudge himself, edited, checked, verified, or supervised the information that Drudge published in the Drudge Report." It also is apparent to the Court that there is no evidence to support the view originally taken by plaintiffs that Drudge is or was an employee or agent of AOL, and plaintiffs seem to have all but abandoned that argument.

AOL acknowledges both that Section 230(c)(1) would not immunize AOL with respect to any information AOL developed or created entirely by itself and that there are situations in which there may be two or more information content providers responsible for material disseminated on the Internet – joint authors, a lyricist and a composer, for example. While Section 230 does not preclude joint liability for the joint development of content, AOL maintains that there simply is no evidence here that AOL had any role in creating or developing any of the information in the Drudge Report. The Court agrees. It is undisputed that the Blumenthal story was written by Drudge without any substantive or editorial involvement by AOL. AOL was nothing more than a provider of an interactive computer service on which the Drudge Report was carried, and Congress has said quite clearly that such a provider shall not be treated as a "publisher or speaker" and therefore may not be held liable in tort. 47 U.S.C. § 230(c)(1).

As Chief Judge Wilkinson recently wrote for the Fourth Circuit:

> By its plain language, § 230 creates a federal immunity to any cause of action that would make service providers liable for information originating with a third-party user of the service. Specifically, § 230 precludes courts from entertaining claims that would place a computer service provider in a publisher's role. Thus, lawsuits seeking to hold a service provider liable for its exercise of a publisher's traditional editorial functions – such as deciding whether to publish, withdraw, postpone or alter content – are barred.
>
> The purpose of this statutory immunity is not difficult to discern. Congress recognized the threat that tort-based lawsuits pose to freedom of speech in the new and burgeoning Internet medium. The imposition of tort liability on service providers for the communications of others represented, for Congress, simply another form of intrusive government regulation of speech. Section 230 was enacted, in part, to maintain the robust nature of Internet communication and, accordingly, to keep government interference in the medium to a minimum.

* * *

> None of this means, of course, that the original culpable party who posts defamatory messages would escape accountability. While Congress acted to keep government regulation of the Internet to a minimum, it also found it to be the policy of the United States "to ensure vigorous enforcement of Federal criminal laws to deter and punish trafficking in obscenity, stalking, and harassment by means of computer." Id. § 230(b)(5). Congress made a policy choice, however, not to deter harmful online speech through the separate route of imposing tort liability on companies that serve as intermediaries for other parties' potentially injurious messages.

Zeran v. America Online, Inc., 129 F.3d 327, 330-31 (4th Cir. 1997). The court in *Zeran* has provided a complete answer to plaintiffs' primary argument, an answer grounded in the statutory language and intent of Section 230.

Plaintiffs make the additional argument, however, that Section 230 of the Communications Decency Act does not provide immunity to AOL in this case because Drudge was not just an anonymous person who sent a message over the Internet through AOL. He is a person with whom AOL contracted, whom AOL paid $ 3,000 a month – $ 36,000 a year, Drudge's sole, consistent source of income – and whom AOL promoted to its subscribers and potential subscribers as a reason to subscribe to AOL.

Furthermore, the license agreement between AOL and Drudge by its terms contemplates more than a passive role for AOL; in it, AOL reserves the "right to remove, or direct [Drudge] to remove, any content which, as reasonably determined by AOL . . . violates AOL's then-standard Terms of Service. . . . " By the terms of the agreement, AOL also is "entitled to require reasonable changes to . . . content, to the extent such content will, in AOL's good faith judgment, adversely affect operations of the AOL network."

In addition, shortly after it entered into the licensing agreement with Drudge, AOL issued a press release making clear the kind of material Drudge would provide to AOL subscribers – gossip and rumor – and urged potential subscribers to sign onto AOL in order to get the benefit of the Drudge Report. The press release was captioned: "AOL Hires Runaway Gossip Success Matt Drudge." It noted that "maverick gossip columnist Matt Drudge has teamed up with America Online," and stated: "Giving the Drudge Report a home on America Online (keyword: Drudge) opens up the floodgates to an audience ripe for Drudge's brand of reporting.... AOL has made Matt Drudge instantly accessible to members who crave instant gossip and news breaks." Why is this different, the Blumenthals suggest, from AOL advertising and promoting a new purveyor of child pornography or other offensive material? Why should AOL be permitted to tout someone as a gossip columnist or rumor monger who will make such rumors and gossip "instantly accessible" to AOL subscribers, and then claim immunity when that person, as might be anticipated, defames another?

If it were writing on a clean slate, this Court would agree with plaintiffs. AOL has certain editorial rights with respect to the content provided by Drudge and disseminated by AOL, including the right to require changes in content and to remove it; and it has affirmatively promoted Drudge as a new source of unverified instant gossip on AOL. Yet it takes no responsibility for any damage he may cause. AOL is not a passive conduit like the telephone company, a common carrier with no control and therefore no responsibility for what is said over the telephone wires. Because it has the right to exercise editorial control over those with whom it contracts and whose words it disseminates, it would seem only fair to hold AOL to the liability standards applied to a publisher or, at least, like a book store owner or library, to the liability standards applied to a distributor. But Congress has made a different policy choice by providing immunity even where the interactive service provider has an active, even aggressive role in making available content prepared by others. In some sort of tacit *quid pro quo* arrangement with the service provider community, Congress has conferred immunity from tort liability as an incentive to Internet service providers to self-police the Internet for obscenity and other offensive material, even where the self-policing is unsuccessful or not even attempted.

In Section 230(c)(2) of the Communications Decency Act, Congress provided:

No provider or user of an interactive computer service shall be held liable on account of –

(A) Any action voluntarily taken in good faith to restrict access to or availability of material that the provider or user considers to be obscene, lewd, lascivious, filthy, excessively violent, harassing, or otherwise objectionable, whether or not such material is constitutionally protected; or

(B) any action taken to enable or make available to information content providers or others the technical means to restrict access to material described in paragraph (1).

47 U.S.C. § 230(c)(2). As the Fourth Circuit stated in Zeran: "Congress enacted § 230 to remove... disincentives to self-regulation.... Fearing that the specter of liability would... deter service providers from blocking and screening offensive material.... § 230 forbids the imposition of publisher liability on a service provider for the exercise of its editorial and self-regulatory functions." *Zeran v. America Online, Inc.*, 129 F.3d at 331.

Previously, Internet Service Providers who tried to exercise control WERE liable, but those who did not were not, and Congress would prefer that ISPs try to exercise some control.

Any attempt to distinguish between "publisher" liability and notice-based "distributor" liability and to argue that Section 230 was only intended to immunize the former would be unavailing. Congress made no distinction between publishers and distributors in providing immunity from liability. As the Fourth Circuit has noted: "If computer service providers were subject to distributor liability, they would face potential liability each time they receive notice of a potentially defamatory statement – from any party, concerning any message," and such notice-based liability "would deter service providers from regulating the dissemination of offensive material over their own services" by confronting them with "ceaseless choices of suppressing controversial speech or sustaining prohibitive liability" exactly what Congress intended to insulate them from in Section 230. *Zeran v. America Online, Inc.*, 129 F.3d at 333. While it appears to this Court that AOL in this case has taken advantage of all the benefits conferred by Congress in the Communications Decency Act, and then some, without accepting any of the burdens that Congress intended, the statutory language is clear: AOL is immune from suit, and *the Court therefore must grant its motion for summary judgment. . . .*

≈

5. Third Party Liability

Introduction

There is a great deal of potential third party liability created by activities in cyberspace. Partially this is due to the difficulty in holding persons responsible for their actions on the Internet, either because of international jurisdiction issues, or simply because of an inability to find them due to their anonymity or sheer numbers. As a result, third parties such as service providers and systems operators are often targeted instead. Employers, as well, are often targets of liability for actions of their employees.

Cases involving third party liability have been brought in a number of legal areas, including defamation, copyright infringement, trademark infringement, and unfair competition. Defamation and copyright, however, have been the primary source of third party liability claims in cyberspace.

Third Party Liability for Defamation

Liability of third parties for defamation traditionally depends on whether the court sees the third party as a "publisher," "distributor," or "common carrier." A publisher is presumed to exercise control over the contents of what is published, and is therefore usually liable for those contents. A distributor is presumed not to have control over the contents of what is distributed and is therefore only potentially liable for those contents if the nature of the contents, and any alleged legal problems created by them, is brought to the distributor's attention and the distributor does nothing in response to notification. A common carrier is a business that serves all indiscriminately, and therefore has a duty to carry *all* content and is thus immune from liability for the content of what is carried or transmitted – for example, licensed entities such as telephone companies or the postal service.

In the 1990s, two highly publicized court decisions, which addressed the liability of Internet service providers for defamatory statements posted by users, illustrated the distinction between "publishers" and "distributors" and created the background for Congress's passage of Section 230 of the Communications Decency Act (the effect of which we saw in the *Blumenthal v. Drudge and AOL* case in Chapter 4).

In 1991, in the case of *Cubby v. Compuserve*, the District Court for the Southern District of New York held that Compuserve was *not* liable for defamatory statements posted by a user because Compuserve had no knowledge or reason to know of the content of the statements. Compuserve was therefore seen to be a "distributor" of the information. However, in 1995, in the very similar case of *Stratton Oakmont v. Prodigy*, a New York State court held that Prodigy *was* liable for defamatory statements posted by a user because Prodigy held itself out to be aware of, and in control of, the content it provided. Prodigy was therefore a "publisher."

The results of these two cases created a disincentive for Internet service providers to attempt to exercise control over the contents of the material appearing through their services. If they attempted to control content, they would be liable for that content if anything problematic slipped through (and everyone knew it was simply not feasible to block all problematic content). If, on the other hand, they made no effort to control content, they would not be liable. Congress wanted to *encourage* ISPs to attempt to control content. Section 230 of the Communications Decency Act (CDA) was the result. (Note that many people believe or have at least heard that the Supreme Court struck down the Communications Decency Act as being unconstitutional in the famous case of *Reno v. ACLU*, which will be discussed in Chapter 12. However, in the *Reno* case the Supreme Court struck down only two small sections of the CDA. The rest remains good law.)

Let's look at another case involving Section 230 of the CDA.

Third Party Liability: Case 1

KENNETH M. ZERAN, Plaintiff-Appellant, v. AMERICA ONLINE, INCORPORATED, Defendant-Appellee.

No. 97-1523

UNITED STATES COURT OF APPEALS FOR THE FOURTH CIRCUIT

129 F.3d 327; 1997 U.S. App. LEXIS 31791; 25 Media L. Rep. 2526; 10 Comm. Reg. (P & F) 456

October 2, 1997, Argued
November 12, 1997, Decided

OPINION: WILKINSON, Judge:

Kenneth Zeran brought this action against America Online, Inc. ("AOL"), arguing that AOL unreasonably delayed in removing defamatory messages posted by an unidentified third party, refused to post retractions of those messages, and failed to screen for similar postings thereafter. The district court granted judgment for AOL on the grounds that the Communications Decency Act of 1996 ("CDA") – 47 U.S.C. § 230 – bars Zeran's claims. Zeran appeals.... [W]e affirm the judgment of the district court.

I.

"The Internet is an international network of interconnected computers," currently used by approximately 40 million people worldwide. *Reno v. ACLU*, 521 U.S. 844, 138 L. Ed. 2d 874, 117 S. Ct. 2329, 2334 (1997). One of the many means by which individuals access the Internet is through an interactive computer service. These services offer not only a connection to the Internet as a whole, but also allow their subscribers to access information communicated and stored only on each computer service's individual proprietary network. AOL is just such an interactive computer service. Much of the information transmitted over its network originates with the company's millions of subscribers. They may transmit information privately via electronic mail, or they may communicate publicly by posting messages on AOL bulletin boards, where the messages may be read by any AOL subscriber.

... On April 25, 1995, an unidentified person posted a message on an AOL bulletin board advertising "Naughty Oklahoma T-Shirts." The posting described the sale of shirts featuring offensive and tasteless slogans related to the April 19, 1995, bombing of the Alfred P. Murrah Federal Building in Oklahoma City. Those interested in purchasing the shirts were instructed to call "Ken" at Zeran's home phone number in Seattle, Washington. As a result of this anonymously perpetrated prank, Zeran received a high volume of calls, comprised primarily of angry and derogatory messages, but also including death threats. Zeran could not change his phone number because he relied on its availability to the public in running his business out of his home. Later that day, Zeran called AOL and informed a company representative of his predicament. The employee assured Zeran that the posting would be removed from AOL's bulletin board but explained that as a matter of policy AOL would not post a retraction. The parties dispute the date that AOL removed this original posting from its bulletin board.

On April 26, the next day, an unknown person posted another message advertising additional shirts with new tasteless slogans related to the Oklahoma City bombing. Again, interested buyers were told to call Zeran's phone number, to ask for "Ken," and to "please call back if busy" due to high demand. The angry, threatening phone calls intensified. Over the next four days, an unidentified party continued to post messages on AOL's bulletin board, advertising additional items including bumper stickers and key chains with still more offensive slogans. During this time period, Zeran called AOL repeatedly and was told by company representatives that the individual account from which the messages were posted would soon be closed. Zeran also reported his case to Seattle FBI agents. By April 30, Zeran was receiving an abusive phone call approximately every two minutes.

Meanwhile, an announcer for Oklahoma City radio station KRXO received a copy of the first AOL posting. On May 1, the announcer related the message's contents on the air, attributed them to "Ken" at Zeran's phone number, and urged the listening audience to call the number. After this radio broadcast, Zeran was inundated with death threats and other violent calls from Oklahoma City residents. Over the next few days, Zeran talked to both KRXO and AOL representatives. He also spoke to his local police, who subsequently surveilled his home to protect his safety. By May 14, after an Oklahoma City newspaper published a story exposing the shirt advertisements as a hoax and after KRXO made an on-air apology, the number of calls to Zeran's residence finally subsided to fifteen per day.

Zeran first filed suit on January 4, 1996, against radio station KRXO in the United States District Court for the Western District of Oklahoma. On April 23, 1996, he filed this separate suit against AOL in the same court. Zeran did not bring any action against the party who posted the offensive messages.... AOL answered Zeran's complaint and interposed 47 U.S.C. § 230 as an affirmative defense. AOL then moved for judgment on the pleadings pursuant to Fed. R. Civ. P. 12(c). The district court granted AOL's motion, and Zeran filed this appeal.

II.

A.

Because § 230 was successfully advanced by AOL in the district court as a defense to Zeran's claims, we shall briefly examine its operation here. Zeran seeks to hold AOL liable for defamatory speech initiated by a third party. He argued to the district court that once he notified AOL of the unidentified third party's hoax, AOL had a duty to remove the defamatory posting promptly, to notify its subscribers of the message's false nature, and to effectively screen future defamatory material. Section 230 entered this litigation as an affirmative defense pled by AOL. The company claimed that Congress immunized interactive computer service providers from claims based on information posted by a third party.

The relevant portion of § 230 states: "No provider or user of an interactive computer service shall be treated as the publisher or speaker of any information provided by another information content provider." 47 U.S.C. § 230(c)(1). By its plain language, § 230 creates a federal immunity to any cause of action that would make service providers liable for information originating with a third-party user of the service. Specifically, § 230 precludes courts from entertaining claims that would place a computer service provider in a publisher's role. Thus, lawsuits seeking to hold a service provider liable for its exercise of a publisher's traditional editorial functions – such as deciding whether to publish, withdraw, postpone or alter content – are barred.

The purpose of this statutory immunity is not difficult to discern. Congress recognized the threat that tort-based lawsuits pose to freedom of speech in the new and burgeoning Internet medium. The imposition of tort liability on service providers for the communications of others represented, for Congress, simply another form of intrusive government regulation of speech. Section 230 was enacted, in part, to maintain the robust nature of Internet communication and, accordingly, to keep government interference in the medium to a minimum. In specific statutory findings, Congress recognized the Internet and interactive computer services as offering "a forum for a true diversity of political discourse, unique opportunities for cultural development, and myriad avenues for intellectual activity." *Id.* § 230(a)(3). It also found that the Internet and interactive computer services "have flourished, to the benefit of all Americans, *with a minimum of government regulation*." *Id.* § 230(a)(4) (emphasis added). Congress further stated that it is "the policy of the United States . . . to preserve the vibrant and competitive free market that presently exists for the Internet and other interactive computer services, *unfettered by Federal or State regulation*." *Id.* § 230(b)(2) (emphasis added).

None of this means, of course, that the original culpable party who posts defamatory messages would escape accountability. While Congress acted to keep government regulation of the Internet to a minimum, it also found it to be the policy of the United States "to ensure vigorous enforcement of Federal criminal laws to deter and punish trafficking in obscenity, stalking, and harassment by means of computer." *Id.* § 230(b)(5). Congress made a policy choice, however, not to deter harmful online speech through the separate route of imposing tort liability on companies that serve as intermediaries for other parties' potentially injurious messages.

Congress' purpose in providing the § 230 immunity was thus evident. Interactive computer services have millions of users. . . . The amount of information communicated via interactive computer services is therefore staggering. The specter of tort liability in an area of such prolific speech would have an obvious chilling effect. It would be impossible for service providers to screen each of their millions of postings for possible problems. Faced with potential liability for each message republished by their services, interactive computer service providers might choose to severely restrict the number and type of messages posted. Congress considered the weight of the speech interests implicated and chose to immunize service providers to avoid any such restrictive effect.

Another important purpose of § 230 was to encourage service providers to self-regulate the dissemination of offensive material over their services. In this respect, § 230 responded to a New York state court decision, *Stratton Oakmont v. Prodigy Servs. Co.*, 1995 N.Y. Misc. LEXIS 229, 1995 WL 323710 (N.Y. Sup. Ct. May 24, 1995). There, the plaintiffs sued Prodigy – an interactive computer service like AOL – for defamatory comments made by an unidentified party on one of Prodigy's bulletin boards. The court held Prodigy to the strict liability standard normally applied to original publishers of defamatory statements, rejecting Prodigy's claims that it should be held only to the lower "knowledge" standard usually reserved for distributors. The court reasoned that Prodigy acted more like an original publisher than a distributor both because it advertised its practice of controlling content on its service and because it actively screened and edited messages posted on its bulletin boards.

Congress enacted § 230 to remove the disincentives to self-regulation created by the *Stratton Oakmont* decision. Under that court's holding, computer service providers who regulated the dissemination of offensive material on their services risked subjecting themselves to liability, because such regulation cast the service provider in the role of a publisher. Fearing that the specter of liability would therefore deter service providers from blocking and screening offensive material, Congress enacted § 230's broad immunity "to remove disincentives for the development and utilization of blocking and filtering technologies that empower parents to restrict their children's access to objectionable or inappropriate online material." 47 U.S.C. § 230(b)(4). In line with this purpose, § 230 forbids the imposition of publisher liability on a service provider for the exercise of its editorial and self-regulatory functions.

B.

Zeran argues, however, that the § 230 immunity eliminates only publisher liability, leaving distributor liability intact. Publishers can be held liable for defamatory statements contained in their works even absent proof that they had specific knowledge of the statement's inclusion. According to Zeran, interactive computer service providers like AOL are normally considered instead to be distributors, like traditional news vendors or book sellers. Distributors cannot be held liable for defamatory statements contained in the materials they distribute unless it is proven at a minimum that they have actual knowledge of the defamatory statements upon which liability is predicated. . . .

Zeran contends that he provided AOL with sufficient notice of the defamatory statements appearing on the company's bulletin board. This notice is significant, says Zeran, because AOL could be held liable as a distributor only if it acquired knowledge of the defamatory statements' existence.

Because of the difference between these two forms of liability, Zeran contends that the term "distributor" carries a legally distinct meaning from the term "publisher." Accordingly, he asserts that Congress' use of only the term "publisher" in § 230 indicates a purpose to immunize service providers only from publisher liability. He argues that distributors are left unprotected by § 230 and, therefore, his suit should be permitted to proceed against AOL. We disagree. Assuming *arguendo* that Zeran has satisfied the requirements for imposition of distributor liability, this theory of liability is merely a subset, or a species, of publisher liability, and is therefore also foreclosed by § 230.

The terms "publisher" and "distributor" derive their legal significance from the context of defamation law. Although Zeran attempts to artfully plead his claims as ones of negligence, they are indistinguishable from a garden variety defamation action. Because the publication of a statement is a necessary element in a defamation action, only one who publishes can be subject to this form of tort liability. Publication does not only describe the choice by an author to include certain information. In addition, both the negligent communication of a defamatory statement and the failure to remove such a statement when first communicated by another party – each alleged by Zeran here under a negligence label – constitute publication. In fact, every repetition of a defamatory statement is considered a publication. Keeton et al., *supra*, § 113, at 799.

In this case, AOL is legally considered to be a publisher. "Every one who takes part in the publication . . . is charged with publication." *Id.* Even distributors are considered to be publishers for purposes of defamation law:

> Those who are in the business of making their facilities available to disseminate the writings composed, the speeches made, and the information gathered by others may also be regarded as participating to such an extent in making the books, newspapers, magazines, and information available to others as to be regarded as publishers. They are intentionally making the contents available to others, sometimes without knowing all of the contents – including the defamatory content – and sometimes without any opportunity to ascertain, in advance, that any defamatory matter was to be included in the matter published.

Id. at 803. AOL falls squarely within this traditional definition of a publisher and, therefore, is clearly protected by § 230's immunity.

Zeran contends that decisions like *Stratton Oakmont* and *Cubby, Inc. v. CompuServe Inc.*, 776 F. Supp. 135 (S.D.N.Y. 1991) recognize a legal distinction between publishers and distributors. He misapprehends, however, the significance of that distinction for the legal issue we consider here. It is undoubtedly true that mere conduits, or distributors, are subject to a different standard of liability. As explained above, distributors must at a minimum have knowledge of the existence of a defamatory statement as a prerequisite to liability. But this distinction signifies only that different standards of liability may be applied *within* the larger publisher category, depending on the specific type of publisher concerned. To the extent that decisions like *Stratton* and *Cubby* utilize the terms "publisher" and "distributor" separately, the decisions correctly describe two different standards of liability. *Stratton* and *Cubby* do not, however, suggest that distributors are not also a type of publisher for purposes of defamation law.

Zeran simply attaches too much importance to the presence of the distinct notice element in distributor liability. The simple fact of notice surely cannot transform one from an original publisher to a distributor in the eyes of the law. To the contrary, once a computer service provider receives notice of a potentially defamatory posting, it is thrust into the role of a traditional publisher. The computer service provider must decide whether to publish, edit, or withdraw the posting. In this respect, Zeran seeks to impose liability on AOL for assuming the role for which § 230 specifically proscribes liability – the publisher role.

. . . Zeran fails . . . to understand the practical implications of notice liability in the interactive computer service context. Liability upon notice would defeat the dual purposes advanced by § 230 of the CDA. Like the strict liability imposed by the *Stratton*

Oakmont court, liability upon notice reinforces service providers' incentives to restrict speech and abstain from self-regulation.

If computer service providers were subject to distributor liability, they would face potential liability each time they receive notice of a potentially defamatory statement – from any party, concerning any message. Each notification would require a careful yet rapid investigation of the circumstances surrounding the posted information, a legal judgment concerning the information's defamatory character, and an on-the-spot editorial decision whether to risk liability by allowing the continued publication of that information. Although this might be feasible for the traditional print publisher, the sheer number of postings on interactive computer services would create an impossible burden in the Internet context. Because service providers would be subject to liability only for the publication of information, and not for its removal, they would have a natural incentive simply to remove messages upon notification, whether the contents were defamatory or not. Thus, like strict liability, liability upon notice has a chilling effect on the freedom of Internet speech.

Similarly, notice-based liability would deter service providers from regulating the dissemination of offensive material over their own services. . . .

More generally, notice-based liability for interactive computer service providers would provide third parties with a no-cost means to create the basis for future lawsuits. Whenever one was displeased with the speech of another party conducted over an interactive computer service, the offended party could simply "notify" the relevant service provider, claiming the information to be legally defamatory. . . . Because the probable effects of distributor liability on the vigor of Internet speech and on service provider self-regulation are directly contrary to § 230's statutory purposes, we will not assume that Congress intended to leave liability upon notice intact. . . .

III.

The CDA was signed into law and became effective on February 8, 1996. Zeran did not file his complaint until April 23, 1996. Zeran contends that even if § 230 does bar the type of claim he brings here, it cannot be applied retroactively to bar an action arising from AOL's alleged misconduct prior to the CDA's enactment. We disagree. Section 230 applies by its plain terms to complaints brought after the CDA became effective. As noted in Part IIB, the statute provides, in part: "No cause of action may be brought and no liability may be imposed under any State or local law that is inconsistent with this section." 47 U.S.C. § 230(d)(3). . . .

. . . Here, Congress decided that free speech on the Internet and self-regulation of offensive speech were so important that § 230 should be given immediate, comprehensive effect.

. . . Zeran cannot point to any action he took in reliance on the law prior to § 230's enactment. Because § 230 has no untoward retroactive effect, even the presumption against statutory retroactivity absent an express directive from Congress is of no help to Zeran here.

Affirmed.

- **The Court says Section 230 of the CDA clearly expresses Congress's intent that it apply to all COMPLAINTS filed after the bill's effective date, regardless of when the behavior occurred.**

- So perhaps Zeran would have won on this point if he had filed before February 8, 1996.
- Note also that radio station KXRO is not immune from third party liability because Section 230 of the CDA immunizes only ISPs.
- Note also that the language of the Court in this case created some uncertainty regarding the scope of the immunity provided by Section 230. The Court says that it "plainly immunizes computer service providers like AOL from liability for *information* that originates with third parties." (My emphasis.) Was the Court suggesting that immunity extends to causes of action other than for defamation – perhaps copyright infringement, as one example? Some recent decisions have taken a more restrictive view of the immunity conferred by Section 230, limiting it to immunity from defamation.

A second treatment of the issue of third party liability for providing information in cyberspace comes from an unusual source, a 1959 United States Supreme Court case.

Third Party Liability: Case 2

SMITH v. CALIFORNIA

No. 9

SUPREME COURT OF THE UNITED STATES

361 U.S. 147; 80 S. Ct. 215; 4 L. Ed. 2d 205; 1959 U.S. LEXIS 1885; 14 Ohio Op. 2d 459

October 20, 1959, Argued
December 14, 1959, Decided

JUDGES: Warren, Black, Frankfurter, Douglas, Clark, Harlan, Brennan, Whittaker, Stewart

OPINION: BRENNAN, Justice:

So, this is a unanimous decision, with only Justice Harlan dissenting in part.

Appellant, the proprietor of a bookstore, was convicted in a California Municipal Court under a Los Angeles City ordinance which makes it unlawful "for any person to have in his possession any obscene or indecent writing, [or] book . . . in any place of business where . . . books . . . are sold or kept for sale."[1] The offense was defined by the Municipal Court, and by the Appellate Department of the Superior Court, which affirmed the Municipal Court judgment imposing a jail sentence on appellant, as consisting solely

---

[1] The ordinance is § 41.01.1 of the Municipal Code of the City of Los Angeles. It provides:

INDECENT WRITINGS, ETC. – POSSESSION PROHIBITED:

It shall be unlawful for any person to have in his possession any obscene or indecent writing, book, pamphlet, picture, photograph, drawing, figure, motion picture film, phonograph recording, wire recording or transcription of any kind in any of the following places:

1. In any school, school-grounds, public park or playground or in any public place, grounds, street or way within 300 yards of any school, park or playground;
2. In any place of business where ice-cream, soft drinks, candy, food, school supplies, magazines, books, pamphlets, papers, pictures or postcards are sold or kept for sale;
3. In any toilet or restroom open to the public;
4. In any poolroom or billiard parlor, or in any place where alcoholic liquor is sold or offered for sale to the public;
5. In any place where phonograph records, photographs, motion pictures, or transcriptions of any kind are made, used, maintained, sold or exhibited.

of the possession, in the appellant's bookstore, of a certain book found upon judicial investigation to be obscene. The definition included no element of scienter – knowledge by appellant of the contents of the book – and thus the ordinance was construed as imposing a "strict" or "absolute" criminal liability. The appellant made timely objection below that if the ordinance were so construed it would be in conflict with the Constitution of the United States. This contention, together with other contentions based on the Constitution, was rejected, and the case comes here on appeal.

Almost 30 years ago, Chief Justice Hughes declared for this Court: "It is no longer open to doubt that the liberty of the press, and of speech, is within the liberty safeguarded by the due process clause of the Fourteenth Amendment from invasion by state action. It was found impossible to conclude that this essential personal liberty of the citizen was left unprotected by the general guaranty of fundamental rights of person and property. . . . " It is too familiar for citation that such has been the doctrine of this Court, in respect of these freedoms, ever since. And it also requires no elaboration that the free publication and dissemination of books and other forms of the printed word furnish very familiar applications of these constitutionally protected freedoms. It is of course no matter that the dissemination takes place under commercial auspices. Certainly a retail bookseller plays a most significant role in the process of the distribution of books.

California here imposed a strict or absolute criminal responsibility on appellant not to have obscene books in his shop. "The existence of a *mens rea* is the rule of, rather than the exception to, the principles of Anglo-American criminal jurisprudence." Still, it is doubtless competent for the States to create strict criminal liabilities by defining criminal offenses without any element of scienter – though even where no freedom-of-expression question is involved, there is precedent in this Court that this power is not without limitations. But the question here is as to the validity of this ordinance's elimination of the scienter requirement – an elimination which may tend to work a substantial restriction on the freedom of speech and of the press. Our decisions furnish examples of legal devices and doctrines, in most applications consistent with the Constitution, which cannot be applied in settings where they have the collateral effect of inhibiting the freedom of expression, by making the individual the more reluctant to exercise it. . . . Very much to the point here, where the question is the elimination of the mental element in an offense, is this Court's holding in *Wieman v. Updegraff*, 344 U.S. 183. There an oath as to past freedom from membership in subversive organizations, exacted by a State as a qualification for public employment, was held to violate the Constitution in that it made no distinction between members who had, and those who had not, known of the organization's character. The Court said of the elimination of scienter in this context: "To thus inhibit individual freedom of movement is to stifle the flow of democratic expression and controversy at one of its chief sources."

These principles guide us to our decision here. We have held that obscene speech and writings are not protected by the constitutional guarantees of freedom of speech and the press. *Roth v. United States*, 354 U.S. 476.

For purposes of discussion, it is assumed that the lower courts correctly judged the book to be obscene.

But our holding in *Roth* does not recognize any state power to restrict the dissemination of books which are not obscene; and we think this ordinance's strict liability feature would tend seriously to have that effect, by penalizing booksellers, even though they had not the slightest notice of the character of the books they sold. The appellee and the court below analogize this strict liability penal ordinance to familiar forms of penal statutes which dispense with any element of knowledge on the part of the person charged, food and drug legislation being a principal example. We find the analogy instructive in our examination of the question before us. The usual rationale for such statutes is that the public interest in the purity of its food is so great as to warrant the imposition of the highest standard of care on distributors – in fact an absolute standard which will not hear the distributor's plea as to the amount of care he has used. His ignorance of the character of the food is irrelevant. There is no specific constitutional inhibition against making the distributors of food the strictest censors of their merchandise, but the constitutional guarantees of the freedom of speech and of the press stand in the way of imposing a similar requirement on the bookseller. By dispensing with any requirement of knowledge of the contents of the book on the part of the seller, the ordinance tends to impose a severe limitation on the public's access to constitutionally protected matter. For if the bookseller is criminally liable without knowledge of the contents, and the ordinance fulfills its purpose, he will tend to restrict the books he sells to those he has inspected; and thus the State will have imposed a restriction upon the distribution of constitutionally protected as well as obscene literature. It has been well observed of a statute construed as dispensing with any requirement of scienter that: "Every bookseller would be placed under an obligation to make himself aware of the contents of every book in his shop. It would be altogether unreasonable to demand so near an approach to omniscience." *The King v. Ewart*, 25 N. Z. L. R. 709, 729 (C. A.). And the bookseller's burden would become the public's burden, for by restricting him the public's access to reading matter would be restricted. If the contents of bookshops and periodical stands were restricted to material of which their proprietors had made an inspection, they might be depleted indeed.... The bookseller's self-censorship, compelled by the State, would be a censorship affecting the whole public, hardly less virulent for being privately administered. Through it, the distribution of all books, both obscene and not obscene, would be impeded.

It is argued that unless the scienter requirement is dispensed with, regulation of the distribution of obscene material will be ineffective, as booksellers will falsely disclaim knowledge of their books' contents or falsely deny reason to suspect their obscenity. We might observe that it has been some time now since the law viewed itself as impotent to explore the actual state of a man's mind....

We need not and most definitely do not pass today on what sort of mental element is requisite to a constitutionally permissible prosecution of a bookseller for carrying an obscene book in stock; whether honest mistake as to whether its contents in fact constituted obscenity need be an excuse; whether there might be circumstances under which the State constitutionally might require that a bookseller investigate further, or might put on him the burden of explaining why he did not, and what such circumstances might be. Doubtless any form of criminal obscenity statute applicable to a bookseller will induce some tendency to self-censorship and have some inhibitory effect on the dissemination of material not obscene, but we consider today only one which goes to the extent of eliminating all mental elements from the crime.

We have said: "The fundamental freedoms of speech and press have contributed greatly to the development and well-being of our free society and are indispensable to its continued growth. Ceaseless vigilance is the watchword to prevent their erosion by Congress or by the States. The door barring federal and state intrusion into this area cannot be left ajar; it must be kept tightly closed and opened only the slightest crack necessary to prevent encroachment upon more important interests." *Roth v. United States, supra*, at 488. This ordinance opens that door too far. The existence of the State's power to prevent the distribution of obscene matter does not mean that there can be no constitutional barrier to any form of practical exercise of that power.

Reversed

BLACK; FRANKFURTER; DOUGLAS; HARLAN (In Part) concur.

CONCURRENCE: BLACK, Justice:

. . . I concur in the judgment holding that ordinance unconstitutional, but not for the reasons given in the Court's opinion.

. . . The fact is, of course, that prison sentences for possession of "obscene" books will seriously burden freedom of the press whether punishment is imposed with or without knowledge of the obscenity. The Court's opinion correctly points out how little extra burden will be imposed on prosecutors by requiring proof that a bookseller was aware of a book's contents when he possessed it. And if the Constitution's requirement of knowledge is so easily met, the result of this case is that one particular bookseller gains his freedom, but the way is left open for state censorship and punishment of all other booksellers by merely adding a few new words to old censorship laws. Our constitutional safeguards for speech and press therefore gain little. Their victory, if any, is a Pyrrhic one.

That it is apparently intended to leave the way open for both federal and state governments to abridge speech and press (to the extent this Court approves) is also indicated by the following statements in the Court's opinion: "'The door barring federal and state intrusion into this area [freedom of speech and press] cannot be left ajar; it must be kept tightly closed and opened only the slightest crack necessary to prevent encroachment upon more important interests.' . . . This ordinance opens that door too far."

This statement raises a number of questions for me. What are the "more important" interests for the protection of which constitutional freedom of speech and press must be given second place? What is the standard by which one can determine when abridgment of speech and press goes "too far" and when it is slight enough to be constitutionally allowable? Is this momentous decision to be left to a majority of this Court on a case-by-case basis? What express provision or provisions of the Constitution put freedom of speech and press in this precarious position of subordination and insecurity?

Certainly the First Amendment's language leaves no room for inference that abridgments of speech and press can be made just because they are slight. That Amendment provides, in simple words, that "Congress shall make no law . . . abridging the freedom of speech, or of the press." I read "no law . . . abridging" to mean *no law abridging*. The First Amendment, which is the supreme law of the land, has thus fixed its own value on freedom of speech and press by putting these freedoms wholly "beyond the reach" of *federal* power to abridge. No other provision of the Constitution purports to dilute the scope of these unequivocal commands of the First Amendment. Consequently, I do not believe that any federal agencies, including Congress and this Court, have power or authority to subordinate speech and press to what they think are "more important interests." The contrary notion is, in my judgment, court-made not Constitution-made.

State intrusion or abridgment of freedom of speech and press raises a different question, since the First Amendment by its terms refers only to laws passed by Congress. But I adhere to our prior decisions holding that the Fourteenth Amendment made the First applicable to the States. It follows that I am for reversing this case because I believe that the Los Angeles ordinance sets up a censorship in violation of the First and Fourteenth Amendments.

If, as it seems, we are on the way to national censorship, I think it timely to suggest again that there are grave doubts in my mind as to the desirability or constitutionality of this Court's becoming a Supreme Board of Censors – reading books and viewing television performances to determine whether, if permitted, they might adversely affect the morals of the people throughout the many diversified local communities in this vast country. It is true that the ordinance here is on its face only applicable to "obscene or indecent writing." It is also true that this particular kind of censorship is considered by many to be "the obnoxious thing in its mildest and least repulsive form. . . . " But "illegitimate and unconstitutional practices get their first footing in that way. . . . It is the duty of courts to be watchful for the constitutional rights of the citizen, and against any stealthy encroachments thereon." *Boyd v. United States*, 116 U.S. 616, 635. While it is "obscenity and indecency" before us today, the experience of mankind – both ancient and modern – shows that this type of elastic phrase can, and most likely will, be synonymous with the political and maybe with the religious unorthodoxy of tomorrow.

Censorship is the deadly enemy of freedom and progress. The plain language of the Constitution forbids it. I protest against the Judiciary giving it a foothold here.

CONCURRENCE: FRANKFURTER, Justice:

. . . I am no friend of deciding a case beyond what the immediate controversy requires, particularly when the limits of constitutional power are at stake. On the other hand, a case before this Court is not just a case. Inevitably its disposition carries implications and gives directions beyond its particular facts. Were the Court holding that this kind of prosecution for obscenity requires proof of the guilty mind associated with the concept of crimes deemed infamous, that would be that and no further elucidation would be needed. But if the requirement of scienter in obscenity cases plays a role different from the normal role of *mens rea* in the definition of crime, a different problem confronts the Court. If, as I assume, the requirement of scienter in an obscenity prosecution like the one before us does not mean that the bookseller must have read the book or must substantially know its contents on the one hand, nor on the other that he can exculpate himself by studious avoidance of knowledge about its contents, then, I submit, invalidating an obscenity statute because a State dispenses altogether with the requirement of scienter does require some indication of the scope and quality of scienter that is required. It ought at least to be made clear, and not left for future litigation, that the Court's decision in its practical effect is not intended to nullify the conceded power of the State to prohibit booksellers from trafficking in obscene literature.

[T]he constitutional protection of non-obscene speech cannot absorb the constitutional power of the States to deal with obscenity. It would certainly wrong them to attribute to Jefferson or Madison a doctrinaire absolutism that would bar legal restriction against obscenity as a denial of free speech. We have not yet been told that all laws against defamation and against inciting crime by speech are unconstitutional as impermissible curbs upon unrestrictable utterance. We know this was not Jefferson's view, any more than it was the view of Holmes and Brandeis, JJ., the originating architects of our prevailing constitutional law protective of freedom of speech.

Accordingly, the proof of scienter that is required to make prosecutions for obscenity constitutional cannot be of a nature to nullify for all practical purposes the power of the

State to deal with obscenity. Out of regard for the State's interest, the Court suggests an unguiding, vague standard for establishing "awareness" by the bookseller of the contents of a challenged book in contradiction of his disclaimer of knowledge of its contents. A bookseller may, of course, be well aware of the nature of a book and its appeal without having opened its cover, or, in any true sense, having knowledge of the book. As a practical matter therefore the exercise of the constitutional right of a State to regulate obscenity will carry with it some hazard to the dissemination by a bookseller of non-obscene literature. Such difficulties or hazards are inherent in many domains of the law for the simple reason that law cannot avail itself of factors ascertained quantitatively or even wholly impersonally. . . .

There is no external measuring rod for obscenity. Neither, on the other hand, is its ascertainment a merely subjective reflection of the taste or moral outlook of individual jurors or individual judges. Since the law through its functionaries is "applying contemporary community standards" in determining what constitutes obscenity, *Roth v. United States*, 354 U.S. 476, 489, it surely must be deemed rational, and therefore relevant to the issue of obscenity, to allow light to be shed on what those "contemporary community standards" are. Their interpretation ought not to depend solely on the necessarily limited, hit-or-miss, subjective view of what they are believed to be by the individual juror or judge. It bears repetition that the determination of obscenity is for juror or judge not on the basis of his personal upbringing or restricted reflection or particular experience of life, but on the basis of "contemporary community standards." Can it be doubted that there is a great difference in what is to be deemed obscene in 1959 compared with what was deemed obscene in 1859? The difference derives from a shift in community feeling regarding what is to be deemed prurient or not prurient by reason of the effects attributable to this or that particular writing. Changes in the intellectual and moral climate of society, in part doubtless due to the views and findings of specialists, afford shifting foundations for the attribution. . . . Unless we disbelieve that the literary, psychological or moral standards of a community can be made fruitful and illuminating subjects of inquiry by those who give their life to such inquiries, it was violative of "due process" to exclude the constitutionally relevant evidence proffered in this case. . . . For the reasons I have indicated, I would make the right to introduce such evidence a requirement of due process in obscenity prosecutions.

CONCURRENCE: DOUGLAS, Justice:

I need not repeat here all I said in my dissent in *Roth v. United States*, 354 U.S. 476, 508, to underline my conviction that neither the author nor the distributor of this book can be punished under our Bill of Rights for publishing or distributing it. The notion that obscene publications or utterances were not included in free speech developed in this country much later than the adoption of the First Amendment, as the judicial and legislative developments in this country show. Our leading authorities on the subject have summarized the matter as follows:

> In the United States before the Civil War there were few reported decisions involving obscene literature. This of course is no indication that such literature was not in circulation at that time; the persistence of pornography is entirely too strong to warrant such an inference. Nor is it an indication that the people of the time were totally indifferent to the proprieties of the literature they read. In 1851 Nathaniel Hawthorne's *The Scarlet Letter* was bitterly attacked as an immoral book that degraded literature and encouraged social licentiousness. The lack of cases merely means that the

problem of obscene literature was not thought to be of sufficient importance to justify arousing the forces of the state to censorship. Lockhart and McClure, Literature, The Law of Obscenity, and the Constitution, 38 Minn. L. Rev. 295, 324-325.

Neither we nor legislatures have power, as I see it, to weigh the values of speech or utterance against silence. The only grounds for suppressing this book are very narrow. I have read it; and while it is repulsive to me, its publication or distribution can be constitutionally punished only on a showing not attempted here. My view was stated in the *Roth* case, at 514:

> Freedom of expression can be suppressed if, and to the extent that, it is so closely brigaded with illegal action as to be an inseparable part of it. As a people, we cannot afford to relax that standard. For the test that suppresses a cheap tract today can suppress a literary gem tomorrow. All it need do is to incite a lascivious thought or arouse a lustful desire. The list of books that judges or juries can place in that category is endless.

Yet my view is in the minority; and rather fluid tests of obscenity prevail which require judges to read condemned literature and pass judgment on it. This role of censor in which we find ourselves is not an edifying one. But since by the prevailing school of thought we must perform it, I see no harm, and perhaps some good, in the rule fashioned by the Court which requires a showing of *scienter*. For it recognizes implicitly that these First Amendment rights, by reason of the strict command in that Amendment – a command that carries over to the States by reason of the Due Process Clause of the Fourteenth Amendment – are preferred rights. What the Court does today may possibly provide some small degree of safeguard to booksellers by making those who patrol bookstalls proceed less high-handedly than has been their custom.

DISSENT AND CONCURRENCE: HARLAN, Justice:

The striking down of local legislation is always serious business for this Court. In my opinion in the *Roth* case, 354 U.S., at 503-508, I expressed the view that state power in the obscenity field has a wider scope than federal power. The question whether *scienter* is a constitutionally required element in a criminal obscenity statute is intimately related to the constitutional scope of the power to bar material as obscene, for the impact of such a requirement on effective prosecution may be one thing where the scope of the power to proscribe is broad and quite another where the scope is narrow. Proof of *scienter* may entail no great burden in the case of obviously obscene material; it may, however, become very difficult where the character of the material is more debatable. In my view then, the *scienter* question involves considerations of a different order depending on whether a state or a federal statute is involved. We have here a state ordinance, and on the meagre data before us I would not reach the question whether the absence of a *scienter* element renders the ordinance unconstitutional. I must say, however, that the generalities in the Court's opinion striking down the ordinance leave me unconvinced.

From the point of view of the free dissemination of constitutionally protected ideas, the Court invalidates the ordinance on the ground that its effect may be to induce booksellers to restrict their offerings of nonobscene literary merchandise through fear of prosecution for unwittingly having on their shelves an obscene publication. From the point of view of the State's interest in protecting its citizens against the dissemination of obscene material, the Court in effect says that proving the state of a man's mind is little more difficult than proving the state of his digestion, but also intimates that a relaxed standard of *mens rea* would satisfy constitutional requirements. This is for me too rough a balancing of the competing interests at stake. Such a balancing is unavoidably required in this kind of constitutional adjudication, notwithstanding that it arises in the domain of liberty of speech and press. A more critical appraisal of both sides of the constitutional balance, not possible on the meagre material before us, seems to me required before the ordinance can be struck down on this ground. For, as the concurring opinions of my Brothers BLACK and FRANKFURTER show, the conclusion that this ordinance, but not one embodying some element of *scienter*, is likely to restrict the dissemination of legitimate literature seems more dialectical than real.

I am also not persuaded that the ordinance in question was unconstitutionally applied in this instance merely because of the state court's refusal to admit expert testimony. I agree with my Brother FRANKFURTER that the trier of an obscenity case must take into account "contemporary community standards," *Roth v. United States*, 354 U.S. 476, 489. This means that, regardless of the elements of the offense under state law, the Fourteenth Amendment does not permit a conviction such as was obtained here unless the work complained of is found substantially to exceed the limits of candor set by contemporary community standards. The community cannot, where liberty of speech and press are at issue, condemn that which it generally tolerates. This being so, it follows that due process . . . requires a State to allow a litigant in some manner to introduce proof on this score. While a State is not debarred from regarding the trier of fact as the embodiment of community standards, competent to judge a challenged work against those standards, it is not privileged to rebuff *all* efforts to enlighten or persuade the trier.

However, I would not hold that any particular kind of evidence must be admitted, specifically, that the Constitution requires that oral opinion testimony by experts be heard. . . .

In my opinion this conviction is fatally defective in that the trial judge, as I read the record, turned aside *every* attempt by appellant to introduce evidence bearing on community standards. The exclusionary rulings were not limited to offered expert testimony. This had the effect of depriving appellant of the opportunity to offer any proof on a constitutionally relevant issue. On this ground I would reverse the judgment below, and remand the case for a new trial.

Why is this case important to cyberlaw?

- It is important because it states that it is constitutionally impermissible to hold a *distributor of information* strictly liable for the contents of what he distributes.
- That is, it is not constitutionally permissible to expect a distributor to be aware of the contents of everything distributed.
- "It would be altogether unreasonable to demand so near an approach to omniscience."
- Thus, as applied in the context of cyberspace, this case might be said to make unconstitutional any law that makes ISPs, universities, and so on strictly liable for the contents of what they "distribute" by virtue of their providing Internet access.

～

Third Party Liability for Copyright Infringement

A look at potential third party liability for copyright infringement will provide a useful background for the copyright material in Chapter 6.

There are three types of copyright infringement: direct, contributory, and vicarious. All three can potentially be used as the basis of liability by third party defendants, such as employers and systems operators.

Direct Infringement

Direct copyright infringers are those who actually make copies or infringe one of the other rights of the copyright holder. Direct infringers are *strictly* liable. That is, knowledge or intent is not required in order to establish liability. Even the "innocent infringer," someone who did not realize the material being copied was copyrighted, is liable if that person is a direct infringer. (However, the *damages* against an innocent infringer may be negligible or zero.) Can third parties like systems operators and ISPs be held liable as *direct* infringers when it is their clients who do the actual infringing?

The 1993 case of *Playboy v. Frena* (which will be discussed in detail further on in Chapter 6) seems to say that an electronic bulletin board (BBS) operator *can* be held liable as a direct infringer even when it is the clients who do the infringing. And the case does "say" this, but there is much between the lines in the decision. The circumstances of the case make it very obvious to the Court that Frena was lying and actually knew the copying was going on.

On the other hand, the 1995 case of *Religious Technology Center v. Netcom*, involving the Church of Scientology's efforts to hold an ISP liable for postings of copyrighted material by an ex-Church member, said the ISP was *not* liable as a direct infringer since it had taken no affirmative steps that resulted in the copying. The Court compared Netcom's role to that of someone who permits the public to use a copy machine. The Court expressly stated its disagreement with the *Frena* court – or at least with the somewhat misleading decision of that court, and said a rule that would make ISPs strictly liable as direct infringers made no sense and would amount to holding people liable for simply setting up and operating an essential element of the Internet.

Contributory Infringement

To establish contributory infringement by a defendant a plaintiff must show that the third party had knowledge of the infringing activity and that the third party caused or materially contributed to the infringing activity.

The knowledge element can be actual knowledge or "constructive" knowledge. That is, that the defendant knew or should have known of the infringing activity. In the *RTC v. Netcom* case the Court held that once the ISP was on notice of the infringing activity, its refusal to remove the allegedly infringing material *could* lead to liability for contributory infringement. However, this raises a problem: is an ISP supposed to believe every allegation of infringement that is made by some party? If not, is the ISP safe in relying on the assurances of the party accused of infringement? The Court held that an ISP must make some reasonable effort to determine the truth of the allegations. If the ISP cannot reasonably verify the alleged infringement (e.g., no copyright notice appears, or the alleged infringer claims the use is a protected "fair use," or no documentation is provided by the accuser), the ISP will not be liable for contributory infringement.

The requirement that the defendant have caused or materially contributed to the infringement can be satisfied either through direct participation or through contribution of materials or equipment that provides the means to infringe. Direct participation occurs when the third party's conduct is a material element in furthering the direct infringement. Examples include a system operator soliciting users to upload copyrighted video games to exchange with one another, or someone shipping infringing "pirate" CDs for a direct infringer, or providing a system for peer-to-peer sharing of copyrighted files and encouraging use of the system for that purpose.

Vicarious Liability

Establishing vicarious liability for copyright infringement requires a showing that the defendant had the right and ability to supervise the infringing activity – or at least control over the operation of the place where the infringement occurred, and a financial interest in the resulting infringement. Basically, the third party must have had the ability to stop the infringement. The *RTC v. Netcom* court decided that Netcom was *not* a vicarious infringer because it was paid a flat fee, and therefore derived no additional income as a result of any infringing activity.

6. Copyrights

Introduction

Article I, Section 8 of the U.S. Constitution is the source of copyright law. It says:

> The Congress shall have Power To ... promote the Progress of Science and useful Arts, by securing for limited Times to Authors and Inventors the exclusive Right to their respective Writings and Discoveries. ...

Note that the application of copyright law involves balancing the dual goals of, first, protecting intellectual property to provide an incentive for creators of new works and, second, generating "Progress" (i.e., permitting authors and inventors to build upon previous work).

Personal copyrights currently last for the life of the author plus seventy years; corporately owned copyrights last for ninety-five years (since corporations theoretically can "live" infinitely).

A copyright is created automatically in any original expression that is fixed in a tangible form – for example, in any original expression that is written or drawn on paper, or recorded on tape, or preserved on film, or saved to a disk. There is no longer a requirement that a copyright notice be posted on a copyrighted work. However, posting a notice that a work is copyrighted ("© 2009 by Jane Doe") prevents an infringer from asserting the "innocent infringer" defense, claiming that the infringer did not know the work was copyrighted. The "innocent infringer" would still be infringing, but the copyright holder might be unable to collect damages.

There is no requirement that a copyright be registered, but the copyright holder *must* register the copyright before filing an action for infringement. Furthermore, as will be discussed further later, not registering prior to an alleged act of infringement can affect the copyright holder's potential to recover statutory damages and attorney's fees.

A copyright holder gets not just the right to reproduce the copyrighted work (which is an important right in cyberspace since almost everything done online involves making a copy), but a bundle of other rights including:

- the right to create a derivative work based on the original (e.g., to make a film from a book or to translate a book into another language);
- the right to *public* distribution, performance, or display of the copyrighted work (which can be involved almost any time information is sent from one computer to another);

- the "attribution" right, that is, the right to claim the work as one's own; and
- the "integrity" right, that is, the right to prevent the use of the copyright holder's name as the creator of a modified or distorted version of the copyrighted work. (A good example is the case of *Gilliam v. ABC*, in which the Monty Python comedy team succeeded in preventing ABC from airing truncated, commercial-filled versions of the original Monty Python BBC shows, which ran an hour without commercials.)

As noted above, the first requirement of copyright is that the work be "original." *The* case defining this requirement is the 1991 U.S. Supreme Court decision commonly referred to simply as *Feist*.

Copyright: Case 1

FEIST PUBLICATIONS, INC. v. RURAL TELEPHONE SERVICE CO., INC.

No. 89-1909

SUPREME COURT OF THE UNITED STATES

499 U.S. 340; 111 S. Ct. 1282; 113 L. Ed. 2d 358; 1991 U.S. LEXIS 1856;
59 U.S.L.W. 4251; 18 U.S.P.Q.2D (BNA) 1275; Copy. L. Rep. (CCH) P26,702;
68 Rad. Reg. 2d (P & F) 1513; 18 Media L. Rep. 1889; 121 P.U.R.4th 1;
91 Cal. Daily Op. Service 2217; 91
Daily Journal DAR 3580

January 9, 1991, Argued
March 27, 1991, Decided

JUDGES: O'Connor, J., delivered the opinion of the Court, in which Rehnquist, C. J., and White, Marshall, Stevens, Scalia, Kennedy, and Souter, JJ., joined. Blackmun, J., concurred in the judgment.

OPINION: O'CONNOR, Justice:

This case requires us to clarify the extent of copyright protection available to telephone directory white pages.

This is a case about originality as a prerequisite for copyright.

I

Rural Telephone Service Company, Inc., is a certified public utility that provides telephone service to several communities in northwest Kansas. It is subject to a state regulation that requires all telephone companies operating in Kansas to issue annually an updated telephone directory. Accordingly, as a condition of its monopoly franchise, Rural publishes a typical telephone directory, consisting of white pages and yellow pages. The white pages list in alphabetical order the names of Rural's subscribers, together with their towns and telephone numbers. The yellow pages list Rural's business subscribers alphabetically by category and feature classified advertisements of various sizes. Rural distributes its directory free of charge to its subscribers, but earns revenue by selling yellow pages advertisements.

Feist Publications, Inc., is a publishing company that specializes in area-wide telephone directories. Unlike a typical directory, which covers only a particular calling area, Feist's area-wide directories cover a much larger geographical range, reducing the need to call directory assistance or consult multiple directories. The Feist directory that is the subject of this litigation covers 11 different telephone service areas in 15 counties and contains 46,878 white pages listings – compared to Rural's approximately 7,700 listings. Like Rural's directory, Feist's is distributed free of charge and includes both white pages and yellow pages. Feist and Rural compete vigorously for yellow pages advertising.

As the sole provider of telephone service in its service area, Rural obtains subscriber information quite easily. Persons desiring telephone service must apply to Rural and provide their names and addresses; Rural then assigns them a telephone number. Feist is not a telephone company, let alone one with monopoly status, and therefore lacks independent access to any subscriber information. To obtain white pages listings for its area-wide directory, Feist approached each of the 11 telephone companies operating in northwest Kansas and offered to pay for the right to use its white pages listings.

Of the 11 telephone companies, only Rural refused to license its listings to Feist. Rural's refusal created a problem for Feist, as omitting these listings would have left a gaping hole in its area-wide directory, rendering it less attractive to potential yellow pages advertisers. In a decision subsequent to that which we review here, the District Court determined that this was precisely the reason Rural refused to license its listings. The refusal was motivated by an unlawful purpose "to extend its monopoly in telephone service to a monopoly in yellow pages advertising." *Rural Telephone Service Co.* v. *Feist Publications, Inc.*, 737 F. Supp. 610, 622 (Kan. 1990).

Query: Do you think the Court's awareness of this earlier decision affected this one?

Unable to license Rural's white pages listings, Feist used them without Rural's consent. Feist began by removing several thousand listings that fell outside the geographic range of its area-wide directory, then hired personnel to investigate the 4,935 that remained. These employees verified the data reported by Rural and sought to obtain additional information. As a result, a typical Feist listing includes the individual's street address; most of Rural's listings do not. Notwithstanding these additions, however, 1,309 of the 46,878 listings in Feist's 1983 directory were identical to listings in Rural's 1982–1983 white pages. Four of these were fictitious listings that Rural had inserted into its directory to detect copying.

Rural sued for copyright infringement in the District Court for the District of Kansas taking the position that Feist, in compiling its own directory, could not use the information contained in Rural's white pages. Rural asserted that Feist's employees were obliged to travel door-to-door or conduct a telephone survey to discover the same information for themselves. Feist responded that such efforts were economically impractical and, in any event, unnecessary because the information copied was beyond the scope of copyright protection. The District Court granted summary judgment to Rural, explaining that "courts have consistently held that telephone directories are copyrightable" and citing a string of lower court decisions. In an unpublished opinion, the Court of Appeals for the Tenth Circuit affirmed "for substantially the reasons given by the district court."

II

A

This case concerns the interaction of two well-established propositions. The first is that facts are not copyrightable; the other, that compilations of facts generally are. Each of these propositions possesses an impeccable pedigree. . . .

There is an undeniable tension between these two propositions. Many compilations consist of nothing but raw data – *i.e.*, wholly factual information not accompanied by any original written expression. On what basis may one claim a copyright in such a work? Common sense tells us that 100 uncopyrightable facts do not magically change their status when gathered together in one place. Yet copyright law seems to contemplate that compilations that consist exclusively of facts are potentially within its scope.

The key to resolving the tension lies in understanding why facts are not copyrightable. The *sine qua non* of copyright is originality. To qualify for copyright protection, a work must be original to the author. Original, as the term is used in copyright, means only that the work was independently created by the author (as opposed to copied from other works), and that it possesses at least some minimal degree of creativity. To be sure, the requisite level of creativity is extremely low; even a slight amount will suffice. The vast majority of works make the grade quite easily, as they possess some creative spark, "no matter how crude, humble or obvious" it might be. Originality does not signify novelty; a work may be original even though it closely resembles other works so long as the similarity is fortuitous, not the result of copying. To illustrate, assume that two poets, each ignorant of the other, compose identical poems. Neither work is novel, yet both are original and, hence, copyrightable.

Originality is a constitutional requirement. The source of Congress' power to enact copyright laws is Article I, § 8, cl. 8, of the Constitution, which authorizes Congress to "secure for limited Times to Authors . . . the exclusive Right to their respective Writings." In two decisions from the late 19th century – *The Trade-Mark Cases*, 100 U.S. 82 (1879); and *Burrow-Giles Lithographic Co.* v. *Sarony*, 111 U.S. 53 (1884) – this Court defined the crucial terms "authors" and "writings." In so doing, the Court made it unmistakably clear that these terms presuppose a degree of originality.

. . . The originality requirement articulated in *The Trade-Mark Cases* and *Burrow-Giles* remains the touchstone of copyright protection today. "No one may claim originality as to facts." *Id.*, § 2.11[A], p. 2–157. This is because facts do not owe their origin to an act of authorship. The same is true of all facts – scientific, historical, biographical, and news of the day. "They may not be copyrighted and are part of the public domain available to every person."

Factual compilations, on the other hand, may possess the requisite originality. The compilation author typically chooses which facts to include, in what order to place them, and how to arrange the collected data so that they may be used effectively by readers. These choices as to selection and arrangement, so long as they are made independently by the compiler and entail a minimal degree of creativity, are sufficiently original that Congress may protect such compilations through the copyright laws. . . .

This protection is subject to an important limitation. The mere fact that a work is copyrighted does not mean that every element of the work may be protected. . . . Thus, if the compilation author clothes facts with an original collocation of words, he or she may be able to claim a copyright in this written expression. Others may copy the underlying facts from the publication, but not the precise words used to present them. . . . No matter how original the format, the facts themselves do not become original through association.

This inevitably means that the copyright in a factual compilation is thin. Notwithstanding a valid copyright, a subsequent compiler remains free to use the facts contained in another's publication to aid in preparing a competing work, so long as the competing work does not feature the same selection and arrangement. . . .

It may seem unfair that much of the fruit of the compiler's labor may be used by others without compensation. . . . [But t]he primary objective of copyright is not to reward the labor of authors, but "to promote the Progress of Science and useful Arts."

To this end, copyright assures authors the right to their original expression, but encourages others to build freely upon the ideas and information conveyed by a work. *Harper & Row, supra*, at 556–557. This principle, known as the idea/expression or fact/expression dichotomy, applies to all works of authorship. This, then, resolves the doctrinal tension: Copyright treats facts and factual compilations in a wholly consistent manner. Facts, whether alone or as part of a compilation, are not original and therefore may not be copyrighted. A factual compilation is eligible for copyright if it features an original selection or arrangement of facts, but the copyright is limited to the particular selection or arrangement. In no event may copyright extend to the facts themselves.

B

The Court then reviews the "sweat of the brow" theory and cases relying on it.

. . . The "sweat of the brow" doctrine had numerous flaws, the most glaring being that it extended copyright protection in a compilation beyond selection and arrangement – the compiler's original contributions – to the facts themselves. Under the doctrine, the only defense to infringement was independent creation. A subsequent compiler was "not entitled to take one word of information previously published," but rather had to "independently work out the matter for himself, so as to arrive at the same result from the same common sources of information." *Id.*, at 88–89 (internal quotations omitted). "Sweat of the brow" courts thereby eschewed the most fundamental axiom of copyright law – that no one may copyright facts or ideas.

Decisions of this Court applying the 1909 Act make clear that the statute did not permit the "sweat of the brow" approach. The best example is *International News Service v. Associated Press*, 248 U.S. 215 (1918). In that decision, the Court stated unambiguously that the 1909 Act conferred copyright protection only on those elements of a work that were original to the author. International News Service had conceded taking news reported by Associated Press and publishing it in its own newspapers. Recognizing that § 5 of the Act specifically mentioned "'periodicals, including newspapers,'" § 5(b), the Court acknowledged that news articles were copyrightable. *Id.*, at 234. It flatly rejected, however, the notion that the copyright in an article extended to the factual information it contained: "The news element – the information respecting current events contained in the literary production – is not the creation of the writer, but is a report of matters that ordinarily are *publici juris*; it is the history of the day."

SIDEBAR: Publici juris

In this context, this phrase means "owned by all."

C

The Court says the Sweat of the Brow theory leads to useless duplication of effort.

The Court then lays out the three elements required for a copyrightable compilation of facts or data:

... The purpose of the statutory definition is to emphasize that collections of facts are not copyrightable *per se....* The statute identifies three distinct elements and requires each to be met for a work to qualify as a copyrightable compilation: (1) the collection and assembly of pre-existing material, facts, or data; (2) the selection, coordination, or arrangement of those materials; and (3) the creation, by virtue of the particular selection, coordination, or arrangement, of an "original" work of authorship....

... The key to the statutory definition is the second requirement. It instructs courts that, in determining whether a fact-based work is an original work of authorship, they should focus on the manner in which the collected facts have been selected, coordinated, and arranged. This is a straightforward application of the originality requirement. Facts are never original, so the compilation author can claim originality, if at all, only in the way the facts are presented. To that end, the statute dictates that the principal focus should be on whether the selection, coordination, and arrangement are sufficiently original to merit protection.

... As discussed earlier, however, the originality requirement is not particularly stringent. A compiler may settle upon a selection or arrangement that others have used; novelty is not required. Originality requires only that the author make the selection or arrangement independently (*i.e.*, without copying that selection or arrangement from another work), and that it display some minimal level of creativity. Presumably, the vast majority of compilations will pass this test, but not all will. There remains a narrow category of works in which the creative spark is utterly lacking or so trivial as to be virtually nonexistent....

III

There is no doubt that Feist took from the white pages of Rural's directory a substantial amount of factual information. At a minimum, Feist copied the names, towns, and telephone numbers of 1,309 of Rural's subscribers. Not all copying, however, is copyright infringement. To establish infringement, two elements must be proven: (1) ownership of a valid copyright, and (2) copying of constituent elements of the work that are original. The first element is not at issue here; Feist appears to concede that Rural's directory, considered as a whole, is subject to a valid copyright because it contains some foreword text, as well as original material in its yellow pages advertisements.

The question is whether Rural has proved the second element. In other words, did Feist, by taking 1,309 names, towns, and telephone numbers from Rural's white pages, copy anything that was "original" to Rural? Certainly, the raw data does not satisfy the originality requirement. Rural may have been the first to discover and report the names, towns, and telephone numbers of its subscribers, but this data does not "'owe its origin'" to Rural. The originality requirement "rules out protecting ... names, addresses, and telephone numbers of which the plaintiff by no stretch of the imagination could be called the author."

The question that remains is whether Rural selected, coordinated, or arranged these uncopyrightable facts in an original way....

The selection, coordination, and arrangement of Rural's white pages do not satisfy the minimum constitutional standards for copyright protection. As mentioned at the outset, Rural's white pages are entirely typical. Persons desiring telephone service in Rural's service area fill out an application and Rural issues them a telephone number. In preparing its white pages, Rural simply takes the data provided by its subscribers and lists it alphabetically by surname. The end product is a garden-variety white pages directory, devoid of even the slightest trace of creativity.

Rural's selection of listings could not be more obvious: It publishes the most basic information – name, town, and telephone number – about each person who applies to it for telephone service. This is "selection" of a sort, but it lacks the modicum of creativity necessary to transform mere selection into copyrightable expression. Rural expended sufficient effort to make the white pages directory useful, but insufficient creativity to make it original.

We note in passing that the selection featured in Rural's white pages may also fail the originality requirement for another reason. Feist points out that Rural did not truly "select" to publish the names and telephone numbers of its subscribers; rather, it was required to do so by the Kansas Corporation Commission as part of its monopoly franchise. Accordingly, one could plausibly conclude that this selection was dictated by state law, not by Rural.

Nor can Rural claim originality in its coordination and arrangement of facts. The white pages do nothing more than list Rural's subscribers in alphabetical order. . . . It is not only unoriginal, it is practically inevitable. . . .

We conclude that the names, towns, and telephone numbers copied by Feist were not original to Rural and therefore were not protected by the copyright in Rural's combined white and yellow pages directory. As a constitutional matter, copyright protects only those constituent elements of a work that possess more than a *de minimis* quantum of creativity. Rural's white pages, limited to basic subscriber information and arranged alphabetically, fall short of the mark. . . .

SIDEBAR: *De minimis*

Refers to any small or trifling matter of which the law takes no note.

Because Rural's white pages lack the requisite originality, Feist's use of the listings cannot constitute infringement. This decision should not be construed as demeaning Rural's efforts in compiling its directory, but rather as making clear that copyright rewards originality, not effort. As this Court noted more than a century ago, "'great praise may be due to the plaintiffs for their industry and enterprise in publishing this paper, yet the law does not contemplate their being rewarded in this way.'" *Baker* v. *Selden*, 101 U.S., at 105.

The judgment of the Court of Appeals is Reversed.
Justice Blackmun concurs in the judgment.

∾

So to satisfy the "originality" requirement, a work must be the product of the author's own creative labor. However, compilations, or collected works, may be protected independently of the individual contents on the collected work. So, for example, an anthology of short stories may contain fifteen stories, each still copyrighted by their authors, but the editor of the collection of stories gets a copyright in the collection itself. However, as *Feist* illustrates, compilations are protected only if they have that "spark of creativity."

The requirement that the original expression be fixed in a tangible form is satisfied, according to the Copyright Act, if the expression is fixed in a tangible medium from which it can be perceived, reproduced, or otherwise communicated, either directly or with the aid of a machine or device – so, for example, original expression printed on paper, painted on canvas, or recorded on a disk.

Infringement of copyright consists of violating any of the "bundle" of rights exclusive to the copyright owner. The following case provides a nice example of infringement analysis.

Copyright: Case 2

PLAYBOY ENTERPRISES, INC., Plaintiff, v. GEORGE FRENA, d/b/a/ TECHS
WAREHOUSE BBS SYSTEMS AND CONSULTING, and MARK DYESS, Defendants.

Case No. 93-489-Civ-J-20

UNITED STATES DISTRICT COURT FOR THE MIDDLE DISTRICT OF FLORIDA,
JACKSONVILLE DIVISION

839 F. Supp. 1552; 1993 U.S. Dist. LEXIS 19165; 29 U.S.P.Q.2D (BNA) 1827;
Copy. L. Rep. (CCH) P27,228; 22 Media L. Rep. 1301

December 9, 1993, Decided
December 9, 1993, Filed

OPINION: SCHLESINGER, Judge:

Defendant George Frena operates a subscription computer bulletin board service, Techs Warehouse BBS ("BBS"), that distributed unauthorized copies of Plaintiff Playboy Enterprises, Inc.'s ("PEI") copyrighted photographs. BBS is accessible via telephone modem to customers. For a fee, or to those who purchase certain products from Defendant Frena, anyone with an appropriately equipped computer can log onto BBS. Once logged on subscribers may browse though different BBS directories to look at the pictures and customers may also download the high quality computerized copies of the photographs and then store the copied image from Frena's computer onto their home computer. Many of the images found on BBS include adult subject matter. One hundred and seventy of the images that were available on BBS were copies of photographs taken from PEI's copyrighted materials.

Subscribers can upload material onto the bulletin board so that any other subscriber, by accessing their computer, can see that material. Defendant Frena states in his Affidavit filed August 4, 1993, that he never uploaded any of PEI's photographs onto BBS and that subscribers to BBS uploaded the photographs. Defendant Frena states that as soon as he was served with a summons and made aware of this matter, he removed the photographs from BBS and has since that time monitored BBS to prevent additional photographs of PEI from being uploaded.

Frena tries to argue that he did not know about the presence of the photographs before being served with a summons. But note that later in the decision, the Court says that the names "Playboy" and "Playmate" appear in the file names themselves and should thus have been easily spotted by Frena.

Note also that the Court says that this text was deleted from the Playboy images and Frena's name, the BBS name, and its phone number were substituted.

I. Copyright Infringement

The Copyright Act of 1976 gives copyright owners control over most, if not all, activities of conceivable commercial value. The statute provides that:

> the owner of a copyright... has the exclusive rights to do and to authorize any of the following: (1) to reproduce the copyrighted work in copies...; (2) to prepare derivative works based upon the copyrighted work; (3) to distribute copies... of the copyrighted work to the public... and (5) in the case of... pictorial... works... to display the copyrighted work publicly.

Engaging in or authorizing any of these categories without the copyright owner's permission violates the exclusive rights of the copyright owner and constitutes infringement of the copyright.

To establish copyright infringement, PEI must show ownership of the copyright and "copying" by Defendant Frena.

There is no dispute that PEI owns the copyrights on the photographs in question. PEI owns copyright registrations for each of the 50 issues of Playboy publications that contain the photographs on BBS.

Next, PEI must demonstrate copying by Defendant Frena. Since direct evidence of copying is rarely available in a copyright infringement action, copying may be inferentially proven by showing that Defendant Frena had access to the allegedly infringed work, that the allegedly infringing work is substantially similar to the copyrighted work, and that one of the rights statutorily guaranteed to copyright owners is implicated by Frena's actions.

Access to the copyrighted work is not at issue. Access is essentially undeniable because every month PEI sells over 3.4 million copies of Playboy magazine throughout the United States.

Substantial similarity is also a non-issue in this case. Defendant Frena has admitted that every one of the accused images is substantially similar to the PEI copyrighted photograph from which the accused image was produced. Moreover, not only are the accused works substantially similar to the copyrighted work, but the infringing photographs are essentially exact copies. In many cases, the only difference is that PEI's written text appearing on the same page of the photograph has been removed from the infringing copy.

The next step is to determine whether Defendant Frena violated one of the rights statutorily guaranteed to copyright owners under 17 U.S.C. § 106.

Public distribution of a copyrighted work is a right reserved to the copyright owner, and usurpation of that right constitutes infringement. PEI's right under 17 U.S.C. § 106 (3) to distribute copies to the public has been implicated by Defendant Frena. There is no dispute that Defendant Frena supplied a product containing unauthorized copies of a copyrighted work. It does not matter that Defendant Frena claims he did not make the copies itself.

Furthermore, the "display" rights of PEI have been infringed upon by Defendant Frena. The concept of display is broad. It covers "the projection of an image on a screen or other surface by any method, the transmission of an image by electronic or other means, and the showing of an image on a cathode ray tube, or similar viewing apparatus connected with any sort of information storage and retrieval system." The display right precludes unauthorized transmission of the display from one place to another, for example, by a computer system.

"Display" covers any showing of a "copy" of the work, "either directly or by means of a film, slide, television image or any other device or process." However, in order for there to be copyright infringement, the display must be public. A "public display" is a display "at a place open to the public or . . . where a substantial number of persons outside of a normal circle of family and its social acquaintances is gathered." A place is "open to the public" in this sense even if access is limited to paying customers.

Defendant's display of PEI's copyrighted photographs to subscribers was a public display. Though limited to subscribers, the audience consisted of "a substantial number of persons outside of a normal circle of family and its social acquaintances."

Defendant Frena argues that the affirmative defense of fair use precludes a finding of copyright infringement.

This is a silly defense here.

"Fair use" describes "limited and useful forms of copying and distribution that are tolerated as exceptions to copyright protection."

The question of fair use constitutes a mixed issue of law and fact.

The Copyright Act mandates four nonexclusive factors which courts shall consider case by case in determining fair use. Section 107 does not attempt to define "fair use." It merely lists the factors to be considered in determining whether a use made of a work in a particular case is fair. Section 107 states:

> The fair use of a copyrighted work . . . for purposes such as criticism, comment, news reporting, teaching (including multiple copies for classroom use), scholarship or research, is not an infringement of copyright. In determining whether the use made of a work in any particular case is a fair use the factors to be considered shall include –
>
> (1) the purpose and character of the use, including whether such use is of a commercial nature or is for nonprofit educational purposes;
> (2) the nature of the copyrighted work;
> (3) the amount and substantiality of the portion used in relation to the copyrighted work as a whole; and
> (4) the effect of the use upon the potential market for or value of the copyrighted work.

17 U.S.C. § 107.

With respect to the first factor, "every commercial use of copyrighted material is presumptively an unfair exploitation of the monopoly privilege that belongs to the owner of the copyright . . . ," "so that "any commercial use tends to cut against a fair use defense."

Defendant Frena's use was clearly commercial. BBS was provided to those paying twenty-five dollars ($ 25) per month or to those who purchased products from Defendant Frena. One who distributes copyrighted material for profit is engaged in a commercial use even if the customers supplied with such material themselves use it for personal use.

Implicit in the presumption that every commercial use is presumptively unfair is "some meaningful likelihood that future market harm exists." It is clear that future market harm exists to PEI due to Frena's activities, as will be discussed in more detail under factor four.

The second factor is the "nature of the copyrighted work." "Copyright protection is narrower, and the corresponding application of fair use defense greater, in the case of factual works than in the case of works of fiction or fantasy." If a work is more appropriately characterized as entertainment, it is less likely that a claim of fair use will be accepted. The copyrighted works involved in this case are in the category of fantasy and entertainment. Therefore, the second factor works against Frena's fair use defense.

Regarding the third factor, the amount and substantiality of the portion of the copyrighted work used, the Supreme Court has directed a qualitative evaluation of the copying of the copyrighted work. That is, "a small degree of taking is sufficient to transgress fair use if the copying is the essential part of the copyrighted work."

There is no doubt that the photographs in Playboy magazine are an essential part of the copyrighted work. The Court is not implying that people do not read the articles in PEI's magazine. However, a major factor to PEI's success is the photographs in its magazine. By pirating the photographs for which PEI has become famous, Defendant Frena has taken a very important part of PEI's copyrighted publications.

The fourth factor, the "effect of the use upon the potential market for or value of the copyrighted work," is "undoubtedly the single most important element of fair use, since a proper application of fair use does not impair materially the marketability of the copied work." This factor poses the issue of "whether unrestricted and widespread conduct of the sort engaged in by the defendant (whether in fact engaged in by the defendant or others) would result in a substantially adverse impact on the potential market for or value of the plaintiff's present work." "Potential market means either an immediate or delayed market, and includes harm to derivative works."

Obviously, if this type of conduct became widespread, it would adversely affect the potential market for the copyrighted work. Such conduct would deny PEI considerable revenue to which it is entitled for the service it provides.

There is irrefutable evidence of direct copyright infringement in this case. It does not matter that Defendant Frena may have been unaware of the copyright infringement. Intent to infringe is not needed to find copyright infringement. Intent or knowledge is not an element of infringement, and thus even an innocent infringer is liable for infringement; rather, innocence is significant to a trial court when it fixes statutory damages, which is a remedy equitable in nature.

Frena argues that his commercial use was so insignificant as to justify holding for him under the principle of *de minimis non curat lex*.

De minimis non curat lex means that the copying is so insignificant a portion of the total work that it should be overlooked.

Presumably Frena wants to say the number of pictures he displayed is tiny compared to the number of pictures Playboy has published, but the problem is that each picture is separately copyrighted, and he used 100% of each picture that he displayed.

Another silly argument that the Court says is nonsense.

The Court disagrees. The detrimental market effects coupled with the commercial-use presumption negates the fair use defense. Defendant Frena infringed Plaintiff's copyrights. *The Court finds that the undisputed facts mandate partial summary judgment that Defendant Frena's unauthorized display and distribution of PEI's copyrighted material is copyright infringement under 17 U.S.C. § 501.*

This case became much talked about because of the idea that the Court expects BBS operators to *know* what is on their systems, which makes little practical sense.

- **In practice, however, the case has not had much influence on that aspect of the law.**
- **Given the facts of this particular case, do you think the decision was right or wrong?**
- **Do you agree that it is evident that the Court here really felt Frena was lying about not knowing the pictures were on the system?**

~

As the Court points out in the *Frena* case, the first requirement to prove copyright infringement is to establish ownership by the plaintiff of a valid copyright. This, of course, raises the question, Who *does* own a copyright? Generally, the answer is simple: the author of the copyrighted work owns the copyright. However, there are two situations in which a copyrighted work can be a "work for hire" and, by definition, ownership of the copyright belongs to the hiring party. The most common case in which a work is a "work for hire" arises when a copyrighted work is produced by an employee in the course of his or her employment. But what about "independent contractors" who are hired for some specialized task? The answer lies in the following case.

Copyright: Case 3

COMMUNITY FOR CREATIVE NON-VIOLENCE ET AL. v. REID

No. 88-293

SUPREME COURT OF THE UNITED STATES

490 U.S. 730; 109 S. Ct. 2166; 104 L. Ed. 2d 811; 1989 U.S. LEXIS 2727; 57 U.S.L.W. 4607; 10 U.S.P.Q.2D (BNA) 1985; Copy. L. Rep. (CCH) P26,425; 16 Media L. Rep. 1769

March 29, 1989, Argued
June 5, 1989, Decided

OPINION: MARSHALL, Justice:

In this case, an artist and the organization that hired him to produce a sculpture contest the ownership of the copyright in that work. To resolve this dispute, we must construe the "work made for hire" provisions of the Copyright Act of 1976 (Act or 1976 Act), 17 U. S. C. §§ 101 and 201(b), and in particular, the provision in § 101, which defines as a "work made for hire" a "work prepared by an employee within the scope of his or her employment" (hereinafter § 101(1)).

I

Petitioners are the Community for Creative Non-Violence (CCNV), a nonprofit unincorporated association dedicated to eliminating homelessness in America, and Mitch Snyder, a member and trustee of CCNV. In the fall of 1985, CCNV decided to participate in the annual Christmastime Pageant of Peace in Washington, D.C., by sponsoring a display to dramatize the plight of the homeless. As the District Court recounted:

> Snyder and fellow CCNV members conceived the idea for the nature of the display: a sculpture of a modern Nativity scene in which, in lieu of the traditional Holy Family, the two adult figures and the infant would appear as contemporary homeless people huddled on a streetside steam grate. The family was to be black (most of the homeless in Washington being black); the figures were to be life-sized, and the steam grate would be positioned atop a platform 'pedestal,' or base, within which special-effects equipment would be enclosed to emit simulated 'steam' through the grid to swirl about the figures. They also settled upon a title for the work – 'Third World America' – and a legend for the pedestal: 'and still there is no room at the inn.'

Snyder made inquiries to locate an artist to produce the sculpture. He was referred to respondent James Earl Reid, a Baltimore, Maryland, sculptor. In the course of two telephone calls, Reid agreed to sculpt the three human figures. CCNV agreed to make the steam grate and pedestal for the statue. Reid proposed that the work be cast in bronze, at a total cost of approximately $ 100,000 and taking six to eight months to complete. Snyder rejected that proposal because CCNV did not have sufficient funds, and because the statue had to be completed by December 12 to be included in the pageant. Reid then suggested, and Snyder agreed, that the sculpture would be made of a material known as "Design Cast 62," a synthetic substance that could meet CCNV's monetary and time constraints, could be tinted to resemble bronze, and could withstand the elements. The parties agreed that the project would cost no more than $ 15,000, not including Reid's services, which he offered to donate. The parties did not sign a written agreement. Neither party mentioned copyright.

These omissions, of course, were a mistake.

After Reid received an advance of $ 3,000, he made several sketches of figures in various poses. At Snyder's request, Reid sent CCNV a sketch of a proposed sculpture showing the family in a crechelike setting: the mother seated, cradling a baby in her lap; the father standing behind her, bending over her shoulder to touch the baby's foot. Reid testified that Snyder asked for the sketch to use in raising funds for the sculpture. Snyder testified that it was also for his approval. Reid sought a black family to serve as a model for the sculpture. Upon Snyder's suggestion, Reid visited a family living at CCNV's Washington shelter but decided that only their newly born child was a suitable model. While Reid was in Washington, Snyder took him to see homeless people living on the streets. Snyder pointed out that they tended to recline on steam grates, rather than sit or stand, in order to warm their bodies. From that time on, Reid's sketches contained only reclining figures.

Throughout November and the first two weeks of December 1985, Reid worked exclusively on the statue, assisted at various times by a dozen different people who were paid with funds provided in installments by CCNV. On a number of occasions, CCNV members visited Reid to check on his progress and to coordinate CCNV's construction of the base. CCNV rejected Reid's proposal to use suitcases or shopping bags to hold the family's personal belongings, insisting instead on a shopping cart. Reid and CCNV members did not discuss copyright ownership on any of these visits.

On December 24, 1985, 12 days after the agreed-upon date, Reid delivered the completed statue to Washington.

Note there is no litigation over the delay. These are nice folks – all of them it seems.

There it was joined to the steam grate and pedestal prepared by CCNV and placed on display near the site of the pageant. Snyder paid Reid the final installment of the $ 15,000. The statue remained on display for a month. In late January 1986, CCNV members returned it to Reid's studio in Baltimore for minor repairs. Several weeks later, Snyder began making plans to take the statue on a tour of several cities to raise money for the homeless. Reid objected, contending that the Design Cast 62 material was not strong enough to withstand the ambitious itinerary. He urged CCNV to cast the statue in bronze at a cost of $ 35,000, or to create a master mold at a cost of $ 5,000. Snyder declined to spend more of CCNV's money on the project.

In March 1986, Snyder asked Reid to return the sculpture. Reid refused. He then filed a certificate of copyright registration for "Third World America" in his name and announced plans to take the sculpture on a more modest tour than the one CCNV had proposed. Snyder, acting in his capacity as CCNV's trustee, immediately filed a competing certificate of copyright registration.

The District Court granted a preliminary injunction, ordering the sculpture's return. After a 2-day bench trial, the District Court declared that "Third World America" was a "work made for hire" under § 101 of the Copyright Act and that Snyder, as trustee for CCNV, was the exclusive owner of the copyright in the sculpture.

The Court of Appeals for the District of Columbia Circuit reversed and remanded, holding that Reid owned the copyright because "Third World America" was not a work for hire.

We granted certiorari to resolve a conflict among the Courts of Appeals over the proper construction of the "work made for hire" provisions of the Act.

II

A

The Copyright Act of 1976 provides that copyright ownership "vests initially in the author or authors of the work." As a general rule, the author is the party who actually creates the work, that is, the person who translates an idea into a fixed, tangible expression entitled to copyright protection. The Act carves out an important exception, however, for "works made for hire." If the work is for hire, "the employer or other person for whom the work was prepared is considered the author" and owns the copyright, unless there is a written agreement to the contrary. Classifying a work as "made for hire" determines not only the initial ownership of its copyright, but also the copyright's duration, and the owners' renewal rights, termination rights, and right to import certain goods bearing the copyright. The contours of the work for hire doctrine therefore carry profound significance for freelance creators – including artists, writers, photographers, designers, composers, and computer programmers – and for the publishing, advertising, music, and other industries which commission their works.

Section 101 of the 1976 Act provides that a work is "for hire" under two sets of circumstances:

(1) a work prepared by an employee within the scope of his or her employment; or
(2) a work specially ordered or commissioned for use as a contribution to a collective work, as a part of a motion picture or other audiovisual work, as a translation, as a supplementary work, as a compilation, as an instructional text, as a test, as answer material for a test, or as an atlas, if the parties expressly agree in a written instrument signed by them that the work shall be considered a work made for hire.

Petitioners do not claim that the statue satisfies the terms of § 101(2). Quite clearly, it does not. Sculpture does not fit within any of the nine categories of "specially ordered or commissioned" works enumerated in that subsection, and no written agreement between the parties establishes "Third World America" as a work for hire.

Note that there is also no signed written instrument governing the agreement.

The dispositive inquiry in this case therefore is whether "Third World America" is "a work prepared by an employee within the scope of his or her employment" under § 101(1). The Act does not define these terms. In the absence of such guidance, four interpretations have emerged. The first holds that a work is prepared by an employee whenever the hiring party retains the right to control the product.

This is what CCNV claims here.

This clashes with the language of the statute, which focuses on the relationship between the parties, not on who controls the product.

A second, and closely related, view is that a work is prepared by an employee under § 101(1) when the hiring party has actually wielded control with respect to the creation of a particular work.

To some extent CCNV claims this too.

A third view is that the term "employee" within § 101(1) carries its common-law agency law meaning.

This aligns with the statute's language.

This was the basis for the Court of Appeals' decision in this case.

Finally, respondent and numerous *amici curiae* contend that the term "employee" only refers to "formal, salaried" employees.

Reid argues this.

The Court finds it too restrictive.

The starting point for our interpretation of a statute is always its language. The Act nowhere defines the terms "employee" or "scope of employment." It is, however, well established that "[w]here Congress uses terms that have accumulated settled meaning under…the common law, a court must infer, unless the statute otherwise dictates, that Congress means to incorporate the established meaning of these terms." In the past, when Congress has used the term "employee" without defining it, we have concluded that Congress intended to describe the conventional master-servant relationship as understood by common-law agency doctrine. Nothing in the text of the work for hire provisions indicates that Congress used the words "employee" and "employment" to describe anything other than "'the conventional relation of employer and employee.'" On the contrary, Congress' intent to incorporate the agency law definition is suggested by § 101(1)'s use of the term, "scope of employment," a widely used term of art in agency law.

Section 101 plainly creates two distinct ways in which a work can be deemed for hire: one for works prepared by employees, the other for those specially ordered or commissioned works which fall within one of the nine enumerated categories and are the subject of a written agreement. The right to control the product test ignores this dichotomy by transforming into a work for hire under § 101(1) any "specially ordered or commissioned" work that is subject to the supervision and control of the hiring party. Because a party who hires a "specially ordered or commissioned" work by definition has a right to specify the characteristics of the product desired, at the time the commission is accepted, and frequently until it is completed, the right to control the product test would mean that many works that could satisfy § 101(2) would already have been deemed works for hire under § 101(1).

The actual control test, articulated by the Second Circuit in *Aldon Accessories*, fares only marginally better when measured against the language and structure of § 101. Section 101 clearly delineates between works prepared by an employee and commissioned works. Sound though other distinctions might be as a matter of copyright policy, there is no statutory support for an additional dichotomy between commissioned works that are actually controlled and supervised by the hiring party and those that are not.

We therefore conclude that the language and structure of § 101 of the Act do not support either the right to control the product or the actual control approaches. The structure of § 101 indicates that a work for hire can arise through one of two mutually exclusive means, one for employees and one for independent contractors, and ordinary canons of statutory interpretation indicate that the classification of a particular hired party should be made with reference to agency law.

To determine whether a work is for hire under the Act, a court first should ascertain, using principles of general common law of agency, whether the work was prepared by an employee or an independent contractor. After making this determination, the court can apply the appropriate subsection of § 101.

B

We turn, finally, to an application of § 101 to Reid's production of "Third World America." In determining whether a hired party is an employee under the general common law of agency, we consider the hiring party's right to control the manner and means by which the product is accomplished. Among the other factors relevant to this inquiry are the skill required; the source of the instrumentalities and tools; the location of the work; the duration of the relationship between the parties; whether the hiring party has the right to assign additional projects to the hired party; the extent of the hired party's discretion over when and how long to work; the method of payment; the hired party's role in hiring and paying assistants; whether the work is part of the regular business of the hiring party; whether the hiring party is in business; the provision of employee benefits; and the tax treatment of the hired party.

Examining the circumstances of this case in light of these factors, we agree with the Court of Appeals that Reid was not an employee of CCNV but an independent contractor. True, CCNV members directed enough of Reid's work to ensure that he produced a sculpture that met their specifications. But the extent of control the hiring party exercises over the details of the product is not dispositive. Indeed, all the other circumstances weigh heavily against finding an employment relationship. Reid is a sculptor, a skilled occupation. Reid supplied his own tools. He worked in his own studio in Baltimore, making daily supervision of his activities from Washington practicably impossible. Reid was retained for less than two months, a relatively short period of time. During and after this time, CCNV had no right to assign additional projects to Reid. Apart from the deadline for completing the sculpture, Reid had absolute freedom to decide when and how long to work. CCNV paid Reid $ 15,000, a sum dependent on "completion of a specific job, a method by which independent contractors are often compensated." Reid had total discretion in hiring and paying assistants. "Creating sculptures was hardly 'regular business' for CCNV." Indeed, CCNV is not a business at all. Finally, CCNV did not pay payroll or Social Security taxes, provide any employee benefits, or contribute to unemployment insurance or workers' compensation funds.

Because Reid was an independent contractor, whether "Third World America" is a work for hire depends on whether it satisfies the terms of § 101(2). This petitioners concede it cannot do. Thus, CCNV is not the author of "Third World America" by virtue of the work for hire provisions of the Act. However, as the Court of Appeals made clear, CCNV nevertheless may be a joint author of the sculpture if, on remand, the District Court determines that CCNV and Reid prepared the work "with the intention that their contributions be merged into inseparable or interdependent parts of a unitary whole." In that case, CCNV and Reid would be co-owners of the copyright in the work. See § 201(a).

For the aforestated reasons, we affirm the judgment of the Court of Appeals for the District of Columbia Circuit.

∾

So, here is a summary of "Who Owns the Copyright?"

- Generally the author owns it.
- BUT in certain circumstances a work may be a "work for hire" and owned by a hiring party.
- Copyright Act of 1976 § 101 provides two sets of circumstances in which something is a "work for hire":
    1. a work is prepared by an employee in the scope of employment (unless ee and er have agreed otherwise in advance)
    2. a work is *commissioned* from an "independent contractor" as:
        - contribution to a collective work
        - part of a motion picture or other audiovisual work
        - a translation

- a supplementary work
- a compilation
- instructional text
- a test
- answer material for a test
- an atlas

BUT ONLY IF the parties expressly agree in a *written instrument signed by them* that the work shall be considered "made for hire."

So, to analyze one of these problems:

- First ask if the work was prepared by an employee (EE) or an independent contractor (IC), according to general common law principles of "Agency Law" (common sense and the circumstances).
- You should look to (for example):
  - whether the hiring party has the right to control the manner and means by which the product is created
  - skill required
  - source of tools
  - location of work
  - duration of relationship
  - whether the hiring party has the right to assign additional projects
  - extent of hired party's discretion over work hours
  - hired party's role in hiring assistants
  - whether the work is part of the regular business of the hiring party
  - whether the hiring party is in business
  - employee benefits situation
  - tax withholding situation
  - etc.
- If, based on this analysis, you determine that the party is an IC, then ask if there is a written, signed agreement stating that the work is to be considered work made for hire.
- If there is no written agreement you can stop your analysis right there since the IC owns the copyright in the absence of such an agreement.
- If there is a written agreement, then see if the work fits into one of the nine specified categories listed above, in which work by an independent contractor can be a "work made for hire."
- If the work fits one of the categories and there is a written agreement stating it is work made for hire, the copyright belongs to the hiring party.
- How can you hire someone to create something that does not fall into one of the nine categories and to which you want to own the copyright? This is a common situation in the software world. Many companies – particularly smaller companies – frequently find themselves in need of someone with specialized expertise for a short time during the development of a new product. Clearly the company needing the services of this "consultant" will want to own the intellectual property associated with the consultant's services. The solution is to have the "consultant" author agree to *assign* the copyright to the hiring party as part of the written consulting agreement (contract) used to hire the specialist.

Remedies for Copyright Infringement

Both civil and criminal remedies are potentially applicable when copyright infringement occurs.

Civil remedies for the owner of the copyright include an injunction prohibiting continued infringement, impoundment of allegedly infringing copies (the Copyright Act says the court can order impoundment of all allegedly infringing copies at any time during a suit), destruction of infringing copies, and, of course, damages.

Two types of damages are available:

- *Actual Damages*, the plaintiff's actual losses plus the defendant's profits (to the extent that they are not the same thing), and
- *Statutory Damages* (at the option of copyright owner at any point during the suit).
  - There is no need to prove any actual loss for statutory damages.
  - The damage award can range from $500 to $20,000.
  - If the court feels the infringement is *willful* damages can be up to $100,000.
  - NOTE: Statutory damages are *not* available to a plaintiff unless the copyright was registered *prior* to the alleged infringing act, *or* within three months of the publication of the work if the infringement occurs after publication. For example:
    - An unknown rock group releases a CD of original music on January 1st and it is a smash hit.
    - No copyright has been registered.
    - On March 1st a bootlegger starts distributing hundreds of thousands of copies of the CD.
    - The copyright owner then registers and sues.
    - The copyright owner can *still* get statutory damages even though registration came *after* the alleged infringement because the registration was done during the three-month "grace period" afforded to the copyright owner.
- NOTE: In addition to actual and statutory damages, attorneys' fees can be awarded by the court to the prevailing party, but the plaintiff can get them only if the copyright was registered according to the same requirements as for statutory damages.

Criminal penalties for copyright infringement can be sought if certain requirements apply, such as whether the infringement was "willful," that is, if it was an intentional violation of a known legal duty. Therefore, the prosecution must be able to establish both *intent* and *knowledge*. Criminal penalties can be up to five years in prison plus $250,000 in fines if the infringement consisted of making ten or more copies of one or more works in a 180-day period with a retail value of over $2,500.

Defenses to Copyright Infringement

There are six basic defenses to an allegation of copyright infringement:

1. Implied license
2. Fair use
3. De minimis copying
4. The work is in the public domain

5. The first sale doctrine
6. The work is not copyrightable material

We devote the remainder of this chapter to an exploration of each of these defenses.

1. Implied License (resulting from conduct of owner)

It is true that an implied license may arise from an owner's conduct, but how "implied license" will work as a defense to copyright infringement in cyberspace is still a bit unclear.

One school of thought says that an implied license can arise by "necessity."

That is, if copying is required for others to make use of the material we present electronically in the way we intend them to use it, we can be said to have agreed to an implied license for that copying.

For example, it can be said that when we send e-mail we consent to an implied license for the e-mail to be copied, as this copying is necessary for the e-mail to pass through the network. Or if we put a photo on a website we consent to an implied license that it be copied on others' screens so it can be viewed.

An implied license may also arise through custom and usage. Some commentators suggest that various usages and customs on the Net have become so accepted that all users might be presumed to understand them and agree to them. For example, we should all be aware when sending e-mail that it is customary for recipients to forward it to others who they think might be interested in its contents.

Some people say that "if everyone does it, it must be okay" is a good defense to an infringement claim, and cite the *Sony v. Universal Studios* case as support. In *Sony*, Universal sued, alleging contributory infringement by Sony because Sony was providing the VCR equipment for use by potential copiers of films. The Supreme Court decided that copying by individuals for their own private use was "fair use" and found for Sony.

But *Sony* is really a pretty narrow decision, applying only to its own specific factual circumstances and covering only copying done by individuals for private use. Claiming that the case stands for the proposition that "if everybody does it, it must be okay" is exaggerating the result significantly.

Some owner conduct, such as placing a file on a server intended to provide material for downloading by others, is clearly a situation in which the owner has created an implied license for others to copy the work. But even when an implied license can be said to be created in various circumstances, keep in mind that the scope of the license is almost surely limited. For example, while we may implicitly license others to view the contents of our web page on their own systems, that does *not* necessarily mean that the license permits them to print the contents out, or copy them to their own disks, or make any other use of them.

How can you tell what the scope of the license is? *Probably* the best bet is to assume that the implied license is limited only to the things that *must* be done in order to achieve the ends the owner most likely intended. So, feel free to assume that the creator of a web page has licensed you to view the page, but be aware that that is probably all the owner has licensed you to do with the page's contents.

2. Fair Use

Fair use is always analyzed on a case-by-case basis. We have already seen an example of this analysis in the *Playboy v. Frena* case. There are four factors applied in the analysis:

- the purpose and character of the use (commercial or nonprofit; if the use is commercial, it is *presumed* not to be fair use – but presumptions can be overcome);
- the nature of the work (factual or fictitious);
- the amount and *substantiality* of the portion used; and
- the effect on the *potential* market for the work.

As applied in the *Frena* case, the Court said

- This was a commercial use,
- The nature of the work was fantasy and entertainment,
- Frena took 100% of each photo copied, and
- "If this type of thing goes on unchecked, there could be very big market effect."

Now let's look at a successful application of this defense.

Copyright: Case 4

SEGA ENTERPRISES LTD., a Japanese corporation, Plaintiff-Appellee,
v. ACCOLADE, INC., a California corporation, Defendant-Appellant.

No. 92-15655

UNITED STATES COURT OF APPEALS FOR THE NINTH CIRCUIT

1993 U.S. App. LEXIS 78; 93 Daily Journal DAR 304

July 20, 1992, Argued and Submitted, San Francisco, California
January 6, 1993, Filed

OPINION: REINHARDT, Judge:

This case presents several difficult questions of first impression involving our copyright and trademark laws. We are asked to determine, first, whether the Copyright Act permits persons who are neither copyright holders nor licensees to disassemble a copyrighted computer program in order to gain an understanding of the unprotected functional elements of the program. In light of the public policies underlying the Act, we conclude that, when the person seeking the understanding has a legitimate reason for doing so and when no other means of access to the unprotected elements exists, such disassembly is as a matter of law a fair use of the copyrighted work.

I. Background

Plaintiff-appellee **Sega** Enterprises, Ltd. ("**Sega**"), a Japanese corporation, and its subsidiary, **Sega** of America, develop and market video entertainment systems, including the "Genesis" console (distributed in Asia under the name "Mega-Drive") and video game cartridges. Defendant-appellant Accolade, Inc., is an independent developer, manufacturer, and marketer of computer entertainment software, including game cartridges that are compatible with the Genesis console, as well as game cartridges that are compatible with other computer systems.

Sega licenses its copyrighted computer code and its "**SEGA**" trademark to a number of independent developers of computer game software. Those licensees develop and sell Genesis-compatible video games in competition with **Sega.** Accolade is not and never has been a licensee of **Sega.** Prior to rendering its own games compatible with the Genesis console, Accolade explored the possibility of entering into a licensing agreement with **Sega**, but abandoned the effort because the agreement would have required that **Sega** be the exclusive manufacturer of all games produced by Accolade.

Accolade used a two-step process to render its video games compatible with the Genesis console. First, it "reverse engineered" **Sega's** video game programs in order to discover the requirements for compatibility with the Genesis console. As part of the reverse engineering process, Accolade transformed the machine-readable object code contained in commercially available copies of **Sega's** game cartridges into human-readable source code using a process called "disassembly" or "decompilation."[1]

Accolade purchased a Genesis console and three **Sega** game cartridges, wired a decompiler into the console circuitry, and generated printouts of the resulting source code. Accolade engineers studied and annotated the printouts in order to identify areas of commonality among the three game programs. They then loaded the disassembled code back into a computer, and experimented to discover the interface specifications for the Genesis console by modifying the programs and studying the results. At the end of the reverse engineering process, Accolade created a development manual that incorporated the information it had discovered about the requirements for a Genesis-compatible game. According to the Accolade employees who created the manual, the manual contained only functional descriptions of the interface requirements and did not include any of **Sega's** code.

In the second stage, Accolade created its own games for the Genesis. According to Accolade, at this stage it did not copy **Sega's** programs, but relied only on the information concerning interface specifications for the Genesis that was contained in its development manual. Accolade maintains that with the exception of the interface specifications, none of the code in its own games is derived in any way from its examination of **Sega's** code. In 1990, Accolade released "Ishido", a game which it had originally developed and released for use with the Macintosh and IBM personal computer systems, for use with the Genesis console.

With respect to **Sega's** copyright claim, the district court rejected Accolade's contention that intermediate copying of computer object code does not constitute infringement under the Copyright Act. It found that Accolade had disassembled **Sega's** code for a commercial purpose, and that **Sega** had likely lost sales of its games as a result of Accolade's copying. The court further found that there were alternatives to disassembly

[1] Computer programs are written in specialized alphanumeric languages, or "source code." In order to operate a computer, source code must be translated into computer readable form, or "object code." Object code uses only two symbols, 0 and 1, in combinations which represent the alphanumeric characters of the source code. A program written in source code is translated into object code using a computer program called an "assembler" or "compiler," and then imprinted onto a silicon chip for commercial distribution. Devices called "disassemblers" or "decompilers" can reverse this process by "reading" the electronic signals for "0" and "1" that are produced while the program is being run, storing the resulting object code in computer memory, and translating the object code into source code. Both assembly and disassembly devices are commercially available, and both types of devices are widely used within the software industry.

that Accolade could have used in order to study the functional requirements for Genesis compatibility. Accordingly, it also rejected Accolade's fair use defense to **Sega's** copyright infringement claim.

Based on its conclusion that **Sega** is likely to succeed on the merits of its claims for copyright and trademark infringement, on April 3, 1992, the district court enjoined Accolade from: (1) disassembling **Sega's** copyrighted code; (2) using or modifying **Sega's** copyrighted code; (3) developing, manufacturing, distributing, or selling Genesis-compatible games that were created in whole or in part by means that included disassembly; and (4) manufacturing, distributing, or selling any Genesis-compatible game that prompts the **Sega** Message. On April 9, 1992, in response to a request from **Sega**, the district court modified the preliminary injunction order to require the recall of Accolade's infringing games within ten business days.

On April 14, 1992, Accolade filed a motion in the district court for a stay of the preliminary injunction pending appeal. When the district court failed to rule on the motion for a stay by April 21, ten business days after the April 9 recall order, Accolade filed a motion for an emergency stay in this court pursuant to 9th Cir. R. 27-3, together with its notice of appeal. On April 23, we stayed the April 9 recall order. The April 3 preliminary injunction order remained in effect until August 28, when we ordered it dissolved and announced that this opinion would follow.

II. Standard of Review

In order to obtain a preliminary injunction, the movant must demonstrate "either a likelihood of success on the merits and the possibility of irreparable injury, or that serious questions going to the merits were raised and the balance of hardships tips sharply in its favor." We may reverse the district court's grant of a preliminary injunction to **Sega** if the district court abused its discretion, made an error of law, or based its decision on an erroneous legal standard or on clearly erroneous findings of fact.

III. Copyright Issues

Accolade raises four arguments in support of its position that disassembly of the object code in a copyrighted computer program does not constitute copyright infringement. First, it maintains that intermediate copying does not infringe the exclusive rights granted to copyright owners in section 106 of the Copyright Act unless the end product of the copying is substantially similar to the copyrighted work. Second, it argues that disassembly of object code in order to gain an understanding of the ideas and functional concepts embodied in the code is lawful under section 102(b) of the Act, which exempts ideas and functional concepts from copyright protection. Third, it suggests that disassembly is authorized by section 117 of the Act, which entitles the lawful owner of a copy of a computer program to load the program into a computer. Finally, Accolade contends that disassembly of object code in order to gain an understanding of the ideas and functional concepts embodied in the code is a fair use that is privileged by section 107 of the Act.

The Court shoots down the first three arguments:

– **Intermediate copying is infringement.**
– **Object code is protected.**
– **Accolade's use went far beyond what it needed to do to use the software.**

But the Court likes the fair use argument, which is what we are principally interested in here.

[Sections A, B, and C are omitted.]

D. Fair Use

Accolade contends, finally, that its disassembly of copyrighted object code as a necessary step in its examination of the unprotected ideas and functional concepts embodied in the code is a fair use that is privileged by section 107 of the Act. Because, in the case before us, disassembly is the only means of gaining access to those unprotected aspects of the program, and because Accolade has a legitimate interest in gaining such access (in order to determine how to make its cartridges compatible with the Genesis console), we agree with Accolade. Where there is good reason for studying or examining the unprotected aspects of a copyrighted computer program, disassembly for purposes of such study or examination constitutes a fair use.

Section 107 lists the factors to be considered in determining whether a particular use is a fair one. Those factors include:

(1) the purpose and character of the use, including whether such use is of a commercial nature or is for nonprofit educational purposes;
(2) the nature of the copyrighted work;
(3) the amount and substantiality of the portion used in relation to the copyrighted work as a whole; and
(4) the effect of the use upon the potential market for or value of the copyrighted work.

The statutory factors are not exclusive. Rather, the doctrine of fair use is in essence "an equitable rule of reason." Fair use is a mixed question of law and fact. "Where the district court has found facts sufficient to evaluate each of the statutory factors," an appellate court may resolve the fair use question as a matter of law.

(a)

With respect to the first statutory factor, we observe initially that the fact that copying is for a commercial purpose weighs against a finding of fair use. *Harper & Row*, 471 U.S. at 562. However, the presumption of unfairness that arises in such cases can be rebutted by the characteristics of a particular commercial use. Further "the commercial nature of a use is a matter of degree, not an absolute. . . . "

Sega argues that because Accolade copied its object code in order to produce a competing product, the *Harper & Row* presumption applies and precludes a finding of fair use. That analysis is far too simple and ignores a number of important considerations. We must consider other aspects of "the purpose and character of the use" as well. As we have noted, the use at issue was an intermediate one only and thus any commercial "exploitation" was indirect or derivative.

The declarations of Accolade's employees indicate, and the district court found, that Accolade copied **Sega's** software solely in order to discover the functional requirements for compatibility with the Genesis console – aspects of **Sega's** programs that are not protected by copyright. With respect to the video game programs contained in Accolade's game cartridges, there is no evidence in the record that Accolade sought to avoid performing its own creative work. Indeed, most of the games that Accolade released for use with the Genesis console were originally developed for other hardware systems. Moreover, with respect to the interface procedures for the Genesis console, Accolade did not seek to avoid paying a customarily charged fee for use of those procedures, nor did it simply copy **Sega's** code; rather, it wrote its own procedures based on what it had learned through disassembly. Taken together, these facts indicate that although Accolade's ultimate purpose was the release of Genesis-compatible games for sale, its direct purpose in copying **Sega's** code, and thus its direct use of the copyrighted material, was simply to study the functional requirements for Genesis compatibility so that it could modify existing games and make them usable with the Genesis console. Moreover, as we discuss below, no other method of studying those requirements was available to Accolade. On these facts, we conclude that Accolade copied **Sega's** code for a legitimate, essentially non-exploitative purpose, and that the commercial aspect of its use can best be described as of minimal significance.

We further note that we are free to consider the public benefit resulting from a particular use notwithstanding the fact that the alleged infringer may gain commercially. Public benefit need not be direct or tangible, but may arise because the challenged use serves a public interest. In the case before us, Accolade's identification of the functional requirements for Genesis compatibility has led to an increase in the number of independently designed video game programs offered for use with the Genesis console. It is precisely this growth in creative expression, based on the dissemination of other creative works and the unprotected ideas contained in those works, that the Copyright Act was intended to promote. The fact that Genesis-compatible video games are not scholarly works, but works offered for sale on the market, does not alter our judgment in this regard. We conclude that given the purpose and character of Accolade's use of **Sega's** video game programs, the presumption of unfairness has been overcome and the first statutory factor weighs in favor of Accolade.

(b)

As applied, the fourth statutory factor, effect on the potential market for the copyrighted work, bears a close relationship to the "purpose and character" inquiry in that it, too, accommodates the distinction between the copying of works in order to make independent creative expression possible and the simple exploitation of another's creative efforts. We must, of course, inquire whether, "if [the challenged use] should become widespread, it would adversely affect the potential market for the copyrighted work," by diminishing potential sales, interfering with marketability, or usurping the market. If the copying resulted in the latter effect, all other considerations might be irrelevant. The *Harper & Row* Court found a use that effectively usurped the market for the copyrighted work by supplanting that work to be dispositive. However, the same consequences do not and could not attach to a use which simply enables the copier to enter the market for works of the same type as the copied work.

Unlike the defendant in *Harper & Row*, which printed excerpts from President Ford's memoirs verbatim with the stated purpose of "scooping" a *Time* magazine review of the book, Accolade did not attempt to "scoop" **Sega's** release of any particular game or games, but sought only to become a legitimate competitor in the field of Genesis-compatible video games. Within that market, it is the characteristics of the game program as experienced by the user that determine the program's commercial success. As we have noted, there is nothing in the record that suggests that Accolade copied any of those elements.

By facilitating the entry of a new competitor, the first lawful one that is not a **Sega** licensee, Accolade's disassembly of **Sega's** software undoubtedly "affected" the market for Genesis-compatible games in an indirect fashion. We note, however, that while no consumer except the most avid devotee of President Ford's regime might be expected to buy more than one version of the President's memoirs, video game users typically purchase more than one game. There is no basis for assuming that Accolade's "Ishido" has significantly affected the market for **Sega's** "Altered Beast", since a consumer might easily purchase both; nor does it seem unlikely that a consumer particularly interested in sports might purchase both Accolade's "Mike Ditka Power Football" and **Sega's** "Joe Montana Football", particularly if the games are, as Accolade contends, not substantially similar. In any event, an attempt to monopolize the market by making it impossible for others to compete runs counter to the statutory purpose of promoting creative expression and cannot constitute a strong equitable basis for resisting the invocation of the fair use doctrine. Thus, we conclude that the fourth statutory factor weighs in Accolade's, not **Sega's**, favor, notwithstanding the minor economic loss **Sega** may suffer.

(c)

The second statutory factor, the nature of the copyrighted work, reflects the fact that not all copyrighted works are entitled to the same level of protection. The protection established by the Copyright Act for original works of authorship does not extend to the ideas underlying a work or to the functional or factual aspects of the work. 17 U.S.C. § 102(b). To the extent that a work is functional or factual, it may be copied, *Baker v. Selden*, 101 U.S. 99, 102-04, 25 L. Ed. 841 (1879), as may those expressive elements of the work that "must necessarily be used as incident to" expression of the underlying ideas, functional concepts, or facts. Works of fiction receive greater protection than works that have strong factual elements, such as historical or biographical works, or works that have strong functional elements, such as accounting textbooks. Works that are merely compilations of fact are copyrightable, but the copyright in such a work is "thin." *Feist Publications*, 111 S. Ct. at 1289.

Computer programs pose unique problems for the application of the "idea/expression distinction" that determines the extent of copyright protection. To the extent that there are many possible ways of accomplishing a given task or fulfilling a particular market demand, the programmer's choice of program structure and design may be highly creative and idiosyncratic. However, computer programs are, in essence, utilitarian articles – articles that accomplish tasks. As such, they contain many logical, structural, and visual display elements that are dictated by the function to be performed, by considerations of efficiency, or by external factors such as compatibility requirements and industry demands. In some circumstances, even the exact set of commands used by the programmer is deemed functional rather than creative for purposes of copyright. "When specific instructions, even though previously copyrighted, are the only and essential means of accomplishing a given task, their later use by another will not amount to infringement."

Because of the hybrid nature of computer programs, there is no settled standard for identifying what is protected expression and what is unprotected idea in a case involving the alleged infringement of a copyright in computer software. We are in wholehearted agreement with the Second Circuit's recent observation that "thus far, many of the decisions in this area reflect the courts' attempt to fit the proverbial square peg in a round hole." In 1986, the Third Circuit attempted to resolve the dilemma by suggesting that the idea or function of a computer program is the idea of the program as a whole, and "everything that is not necessary to that purpose or function [is] part of the expression of that idea." *Whelan Assoc., Inc. v. Jaslow Dental Laboratory, Inc.*, 797 F.2d 1222, 1236 (3d Cir. 1986). The *Whelan* rule, however, has been widely – and soundly – criticized as simplistic and overbroad. See *CAI, 23 U.S.P.Q. 2d at 1252* (citing cases, treatises, and articles). In reality, "a computer program's ultimate function or purpose is the composite result of interacting subroutines. Since each subroutine is itself a program, and thus, may be said to have its own 'idea,' *Whelan*'s general formulation . . . is descriptively inadequate." For example, the computer program at issue in the case before us, a video game program, contains at least two such subroutines – the subroutine that allows the user to interact with the video game and the subroutine that allows the game cartridge to interact with the console. Under a test that breaks down a computer program into its component subroutines and sub-subroutines and then identifies the idea or core functional element of each, such as the test recently adopted by the Second Circuit in *CAI*, 23 U.S.P.Q. 2d at 1252–53, many aspects of the program are not protected by copyright. In our view, in light of the essentially utilitarian nature of computer programs, the Second Circuit's approach is an appropriate one.

Sega argues that even if many elements of its video game programs are properly characterized as functional and therefore not protected by copyright, Accolade copied protected expression. **Sega** is correct. The record makes clear that disassembly is wholesale copying. Because computer programs are also unique among copyrighted works in the form in which they are distributed for public use, however, **Sega's** observation does not bring us much closer to a resolution of the dispute.

The unprotected aspects of most functional works are readily accessible to the human eye. The systems described in accounting textbooks or the basic structural concepts embodied in architectural plans, to give two examples, can be easily copied without also copying any of the protected, expressive aspects of the original works. Computer programs, however, are typically distributed for public use in object code form, embedded in a silicon chip or on a floppy disk. For that reason, humans often cannot gain access to the unprotected ideas and functional concepts contained in object code without disassembling that code – i.e., making copies.

Sega argues that the record does not establish that disassembly of its object code is the only available method for gaining access to the interface specifications for the Genesis console, and the district court agreed. An independent examination of the record reveals that **Sega** misstates its contents, and demonstrates that the district court committed clear error in this respect.

First, the record clearly establishes that humans cannot *read* object code. **Sega** makes much of Mike Lorenzen's statement that a reverse engineer can work directly from the zeros and ones of object code but "it's not as fun." In full, Lorenzen's statements establish only that the use of an *electronic* decompiler is not absolutely necessary. Trained programmers can disassemble object code by hand. Because even a trained programmer cannot possibly remember the millions of zeros and ones that make up a program, however, he must make a written or computerized copy of the disassembled code in order to keep track of his work. The relevant fact for purposes of **Sega's** copyright infringement claim and Accolade's fair use defense is that *translation* of a program from object code into source code cannot be accomplished without making copies of the code.

Second, the record provides no support for a conclusion that a viable alternative to disassembly exists. The district court found that Accolade could have avoided a copyright infringement claim by "peeling" the chips contained in **Sega's** games or in the Genesis console, as authorized by section 906 of the SCPA. Even **Sega's** amici agree that this finding was clear error. The declaration of Dr. Harry Tredennick, an expert witness for Accolade, establishes that chip peeling yields only a physical diagram of the *object code* embedded in a ROM chip. It does not obviate the need to translate object code into source code.

The district court also suggested that Accolade could have avoided a copyright infringement suit by programming in a "clean room". That finding too is clearly erroneous. A "clean room" is a procedure used in the computer industry in order to prevent direct copying of a competitor's code during the development of a competing product. Programmers in clean rooms are provided only with the functional specifications for the desired program. As Dr. Tredennick explained, the use of a clean room would not have avoided the need for disassembly because disassembly was necessary in order to discover the functional specifications for a Genesis-compatible game.

In summary, the record clearly establishes that disassembly of the object code in **Sega's** video game cartridges was necessary in order to understand the functional requirements for Genesis compatibility. The interface procedures for the Genesis console are distributed for public use only in object code form, and are not visible to the user during operation of the video game program. Because object code cannot be read by humans, it must be disassembled, either by hand or by machine. Disassembly of object code necessarily entails copying. Those facts dictate our analysis of the second statutory fair use factor. If disassembly of copyrighted object code is *per se* an unfair use, the owner of the copyright gains a *de facto* monopoly over the functional aspects of his work – aspects that were expressly denied copyright protection by Congress. In order to enjoy a lawful monopoly over the idea or functional principle underlying a work, the creator of the work must satisfy the more stringent standards imposed by the patent laws. **Sega** does not hold a patent on the Genesis console.

Because **Sega's** video game programs contain unprotected aspects that cannot be examined without copying, we afford them a lower degree of protection than more traditional literary works. In light of all the considerations discussed above, we conclude that the second statutory factor also weighs in favor of Accolade.

(d)

As to the third statutory factor, Accolade disassembled entire programs written by **Sega.** Accordingly, the third factor weighs against Accolade. The fact that an entire work was copied does not, however, preclude a finding a fair use. In fact, where the ultimate (as opposed to direct) use is as limited as it was here, the factor is of very little weight.

(e)

In summary, careful analysis of the purpose and characteristics of Accolade's use of **Sega's** video game programs, the nature of the computer programs involved, and the nature of the market for video game cartridges yields the conclusion that the first, second, and fourth statutory fair use factors weigh in favor of Accolade, while only the third weighs in favor of **Sega**, and even then only slightly. Accordingly, Accolade clearly has by far the better case on the fair use issue.

We are not unaware of the fact that to those used to considering copyright issues in more traditional contexts, our result may seem incongruous at first blush. To oversimplify, the record establishes that Accolade, a commercial competitor of **Sega**, engaged in wholesale copying of **Sega's** copyrighted code as a preliminary step in the development of a competing product. However, the key to this case is that we are dealing with computer software, a relatively unexplored area in the world of copyright law. We must avoid the temptation of trying to force "the proverbial square peg into a round hole."

In determining whether a challenged use of copyrighted material is fair, a court must keep in mind the public policy underlying the Copyright Act. "'The immediate effect of our copyright law is to secure a fair return for an "author's" creative labor. But the ultimate aim is, by this incentive, to stimulate artistic creativity for the general public good.'" When technological change has rendered an aspect or application of the Copyright Act ambiguous, "'the Copyright Act must be construed in light of this basic purpose.'" As discussed above, the fact that computer programs are distributed for public use in object code form often precludes public access to the ideas and functional concepts contained in those programs, and thus confers on the copyright owner a *de facto* monopoly over those ideas and functional concepts. That result defeats the fundamental purpose of the Copyright Act – to encourage the production of original works by protecting the expressive elements of those works while leaving the ideas, facts, and functional concepts in the public domain for others to build on.

Sega argues that the considerable time, effort, and money that went into development of the Genesis and Genesis-compatible video games militate against a finding of fair use. Borrowing from antitrust principles, **Sega** attempts to label Accolade a "free rider" on its product development efforts. In *Feist Publications*, however, the Court unequivocally rejected the "sweat of the brow" rationale for copyright protection. Under the Copyright Act, if a work is largely functional, it receives only weak protection. "This result is neither unfair nor unfortunate. It is the means by which copyright advances the progress of science and art." Here, while the work may not be largely functional, it incorporates functional elements which do not merit protection. The equitable considerations involved weigh on the side of public access. Accordingly, we reject **Sega's** argument.

(f)

We conclude that where disassembly is the only way to gain access to the ideas and functional elements embodied in a copyrighted computer program and where there is a legitimate reason for seeking such access, disassembly is a fair use of the copyrighted work, as a matter of law. Our conclusion does not, of course, insulate Accolade from a claim of copyright infringement with respect to its finished products. **Sega** has reserved the right to raise such a claim, and it may do so on remand.

⁓

Parody can be a form of fair use. The focus in an analysis of parody is on the "substantiality" of the copying. The key, however, in analyzing the question of substantiality of the copying is whether the defendant has taken more than necessary to achieve the allegedly fair use of the original work. For parody to be fair use, then, the question is whether the parodist has taken more than necessary of the original in order to create the parody.

Copyright: Case 5

WALT DISNEY PRODUCTIONS, Plaintiff-Appellee, v. The AIR PIRATES et al., Defendants-Appellants.

Nos. 75-3116, 75-3243

UNITED STATES COURT OF APPEALS, NINTH CIRCUIT

581 F.2d 751; 1978 U.S. App. LEXIS 9243; 199 U.S.P.Q. (BNA) 769; Copy. L. Rep. (CCH) P25,033

September 5, 1978

OPINION: CUMMINGS, Judge:

This case involves the admitted copying of plaintiff Walt Disney Productions' ("Disney") cartoon characters in defendants' adult "counter-culture" comic books. The present defendants are three individuals and two business entities operated by them. The complaint alleges that they infringed Disney copyrights. . . . Disney sought injunctive relief, destruction of infringing materials, damages, costs and attorney's fees.

The district court awarded Disney a temporary restraining order and subsequently granted its motion for a preliminary injunction.

According to plaintiff, defendants infringed Disney copyrights by copying the graphic depiction of over 17 characters. Two of the characters are represented as insects, and the others as animals endowed with human qualities. Each character has a recognizable image.

The individual defendants have participated in preparing and publishing two magazines of cartoons entitled "Air Pirates Funnies." The characters in defendants' magazines bear a marked similarity to those of plaintiff. The names given to defendants' characters are the same names used in plaintiff's copyrighted work. However, the themes of defendants' publications differ markedly from those of Disney. While Disney sought only to foster "an image of innocent delightfulness," defendants supposedly sought to convey an allegorical message of significance. Put politely by one commentator, the "Air Pirates" was "an 'underground' comic book which had placed several well-known Disney cartoon characters in incongruous settings where they engaged in activities clearly antithetical to the accepted Mickey Mouse world of scrubbed faces, bright smiles and happy endings." It centered around "a rather bawdy depiction of the Disney characters as active members of a free thinking, promiscuous, drug ingesting counterculture."

Three years after granting the preliminary injunction, the district court granted summary judgment for plaintiff because the issues were "purely legal and ripe for decision". The court concluded that defendants' challenged publications constituted trade(mark) infringements (concerning the Disney "Silly Symphony" trademark) and violated Disney's valid copyrights and that defendants were guilty of "unfair competition in the form of trade disparagement". We affirm as to copyright violation and reverse and remand as to the remainder.

I. Copyright Infringement

The issue that has attracted the most attention from the parties in this case is whether defendants' copies of the images of Disney's characters are infringements of Disney's copyright.

A. Copyrightability

In some instances Disney's copyrights cover a book and others an entire strip of several cartoon panels. The fact that its characters are not the separate subject of a copyright does not preclude their protection, however, because Section 3 of the then Copyright Act provided that Disney's copyrights included protection for "all the copyrightable component parts of the work copyrighted."

The essence of defendants' argument is that characters are never copyrightable and therefore cannot in any way constitute a copyrightable component part. That argument flies in the face of a series of cases dating back to 1914 that have held comic strip characters protectable under the old Copyright Act. See *Detective Comics, Inc. v. Bruns Publications Inc.*, 111 F.2d 432 (2d Cir. 1940); *Fleischer Studios v. Freundlich*, 73 F.2d 276 (2d Cir. 1934), certiorari denied, 294 U.S. 717, 55 S. Ct. 516, 79 L. Ed. 1250; *King Features Syndicate v. Fleischer*, 299 F. 533 (2d Cir. 1924); *Detective Comics, Inc. v. Fox Publications Inc.*, 46 F. Supp. 872 (S.D.N.Y.1942); *Hill v. Whalen & Martell*, Inc., 220 F. 359 (S.D.N.Y.1914);

But note that the appellate decisions are only by the 2nd Circuit, and the others are District Court decisions.

It is true that this Court's opinion in *Warner Brothers Pictures v. Columbia Broadcasting System*, 216 F.2d 945 (9th Cir. 1954), certiorari denied, 348 U.S. 971, 75 S. Ct. 532, 99 L. Ed. 756, lends some support to the position that characters ordinarily are not copyrightable. There the mystery writer Dashiell Hammett and his publisher entered into a 1930 contract with Warner Brothers giving the movie production company copyright and various other rights to a "certain story entitled Maltese Falcon" involving the fictional detective Sam Spade. In 1946, Hammett and other defendants used the Maltese Falcon characters in other writings, causing Warner Brothers to sue for copyright infringement and "unfair use and competition." After pointing out the sophisticated nature of the plaintiff, we construed the contracts between the parties and held:

> We are of the opinion that since the use of characters and character names are nowhere specifically mentioned in the agreements (including the assignment of copyright instrument), but that other items, including the title, 'The Maltese Falcon', and their use are specifically mentioned as being granted (to Warner Brothers), that the character rights with the names cannot be held to be within the grants, and that

under the doctrine of Ejusdem generis, general language cannot be held to include them.

SIDEBAR: Ejusdem generis

"Of the same kind, class, or nature." As applied to statutory construction, "where general words follow the enumeration of particular classes of things, the general words will be construed as applying only to things of the same general class as those enumerated." (From *Black's Law Dictionary*).

After so holding, Judge Stephens' opinion considered "whether it was ever intended by the copyright statute that characters with their names should be under its protection." In that context he concluded that such a restriction on Hammett's future use of a character was unreasonable, at least when the characters were merely vehicles for the story and did not "really constitute" the story being told. Judge Stephens' reasons for that conclusion provide an important indication of the applicability of that conclusion to comic book characters as opposed to literary characters. In reasoning that characters "are always limited and always fall into limited patterns," Judge Stephens recognized that it is difficult to delineate distinctively a literary character. When the author can add a visual image, however, the difficulty is reduced. Put another way, while many literary characters may embody little more than an unprotected idea, a comic book character, which has physical as well as conceptual qualities, is more likely to contain some unique elements of expression. Because comic book characters therefore are distinguishable from literary characters, the Warner Brothers language does not preclude protection of Disney's characters.

B. Infringement and Fair Use

Defendants do not contend that their admitted copying was not substantial enough to constitute an infringement, and it is plain that copying a comic book character's graphic image constitutes copying to an extent sufficient to justify a finding of infringement. Defendants instead claim that this infringement should be excused through the application of the fair use defense, since it purportedly is a parody of Disney's cartoons.

At least since this Court's controversial ruling in *Benny v. Loew's Inc.*, 239 F.2d 532 (9th Cir. 1956), affirmed by an equally divided Court, 356 U.S. 43, 78 S. Ct. 667, 2 L. Ed. 2d 583, the standards for applying the fair use defense in parody cases, like the standards for applying fair use in other contexts, have been a source of considerable attention and dispute. As a general matter, while some commentators have urged that the fair use defense depends only on whether the infringing work fills the demand for the original this Court and others have also consistently focused on the substantiality of the taking.

In inquiring into the substantiality of the taking, the district court read our *Benny* opinion to hold that any substantial copying by a defendant, combined with the fact that the portion copied constituted a substantial part of the defendant's work, automatically precluded the fair use defense. That such a strict reading of *Benny* was unjustified is indicated first by the fact that it would essentially make any fair use defense fruitless. If the substantiality of the taking necessary to satisfy the first half of that test is no different from the substantiality necessary to constitute an infringement, then the *Benny* test would be reduced to an absurdity, covering any infringement except those falling within the much-criticized and abandoned exception for cases in which the part copied was not a substantial part of the defendant's work. The language in *Benny* concerning the substantiality of copying can be given a reading much more in keeping with the context of that case and the established principles at the time of that case if the opinion is understood as setting a threshold that eliminates from the fair use defense copying that is virtually complete or almost verbatim. It was an established principle at the time of *Benny* that such verbatim copying precluded resort to the fair use defense. Moreover, the *Benny* facts presented a particularly appropriate instance to apply that settled principle. As the *Benny* district court found, Benny's "Autolight" tracked the parodied "Gas Light" in almost every respect: the locale and period, the setting, characters, story points, incidents, climax and much of the dialogue all were found to be identical. In this context, *Benny* should not be read as taking the drastic step of virtually turning the test for fair use into the test for infringement. To do otherwise would be to eliminate fair use as a defense except perhaps for those infringers who added an extra act at the end of their parody.

Thus *Benny* should stand only as a threshold test that eliminates near-verbatim copying. In the absence of near-verbatim copying, other courts have analyzed the substantiality of copying by a parodist by asking whether the parodist has appropriated a greater amount of the original work than is necessary to "recall or conjure up" the object of his satire.

In order to facilitate application of either the Benny threshold test or the Berlin test, it is important to determine what are the relevant parts of each work that are compared in analyzing similarity. Plaintiff assumes in its brief that the graphic depiction, or pictorial illustration, is separately copyrightable as a component part, so that a verbatim copy of the depiction alone would satisfy the *Benny* test. Defendants proceed on the assumption that comparing their characters with plaintiff's involves a comparison not only of the physical image but also of the character's personality, pattern of speech, abilities, and other traits. Apparently this issue has not been addressed previously, and neither position is without merit. On the one hand, since an illustration in a book or catalogue can be copyrighted separately it might follow that an illustration in a comic strip is entitled to the same protection by virtue of Section 3 of the former Copyright Act. On the other hand, to a different extent than in other illustrations, a cartoon character's image is intertwined with its personality and other traits, so that the "total concept and feel" of even the component part cannot be limited to the image itself.

We need not decide which of these views is correct, or whether this copying was so substantial to satisfy the *Benny* test, because it is our view that defendants took more than is allowed even under the Berlin test as applied to both the conceptual and physical aspects of the characters. In evaluating how much of a taking was necessary to recall or conjure up the original, it is first important to recognize that given the widespread public recognition of the major characters involved here, such as Mickey Mouse and Donald Duck, in comparison with other characters very little would have been necessary to place Mickey Mouse and his image in the minds of the readers. Second, when the medium involved is a comic book, a recognizable caricature is not difficult to draw, so that an alternative that involves less copying is more likely to be available than if a speech, for instance, is parodied. Also significant is the fact that the essence of this parody did not focus on how the characters looked, but rather parodied their personalities, their wholesomeness and their innocence. Thus arguably defendants' copying could have been justified as necessary more easily if they had paralleled closely (with a few significant twists) Disney characters and their actions in a manner that conjured up the particular elements of the innocence of the characters that were to be satirized. While greater license may be necessary under those circumstances, here the copying of the graphic image appears to have no other purpose than to track Disney's work as a whole as closely as possible.

Defendants' assertion that they copied no more than necessary appears to be based on an affidavit, which stated that "the humorous effect of parody is best achieved when at first glance the material appears convincingly to be the original, and upon closer examination is discovered to be quite something else". The short answer to this assertion, which would also justify substantially verbatim copying, is that when persons are parodying a copyrighted work, the constraints of the existing precedent do not permit them to take as much of a component part as they need to make the "best parody." Instead, their desire to make the "best parody" is balanced against the rights of the copyright owner in his original expressions. That balance has been struck at giving the parodist what is necessary to conjure up the original, and in the absence of a special need for accuracy that standard was exceeded here. By copying the images in their entirety, defendants took more than was necessary to place firmly in the reader's mind the parodied work and those specific attributes that are to be satirized.

Parodists don't get what they want, they get what they need.

While other factors in the fair use calculus may not be sufficient by themselves to preclude the fair use defense, this and other courts have accepted the traditional American rule that excessive copying precludes fair use.

∾

Let's continue to examine defenses to allegations of copyright infringement.

3. De Minimis Copying

This is similar to the third element of the Fair Use analysis (amount and substantiality).

The claim is that such a small *and insignificant* portion of the original was copied that it can and should be overlooked. However, sometimes, as with the Fair Use analysis, not much copying is needed in order to achieve a stated goal. The question is how important or significant the piece copied was in relation to the original.

4. Public Domain

If a work is in the public domain it can be used freely. One way in which a work falls into the public domain, of course, is if the copyright has expired. However, there are other ways in which works become part of the public domain.

Copyrights may be abandoned. At one time, the author of a copyrightable work that did not carry a notice of copyright was considered to have abandoned the copyright, placing the work in the public domain. There is no longer a requirement that a copyrighted work be labeled as such. Thus, lack of a copyright notice does not mean that a work is in the public domain. It is best to assume that a work is copyrighted unless there is reason to believe it is not. You might find such grounds in certain online communities. In the world of software development it is not uncommon for authors of software to abandon their copyrights by distributing their work as "freeware."

Works created by the federal government (or created as its works for hire) are in the public domain by law. Note, however, that this applies only to the *federal* government.

Note also that the federal government *may* hold copyrights that have been assigned to it or left to it in bequests or so on, so be careful. Publication by the government does not necessarily mean the work is not copyrighted. Copyright ownership of works created as a result of federal grants and contracts is governed by the terms of the grant or contract. The copyrights *may* be given to the individuals performing the work or may be considered uncopyrightable government works. The only time you can be sure a government work is in the public domain is if it was created by a government employee in the course of business, or if the work was created by an independent contractor for the government and there is a written agreement with the independent contractor that the work is a work for hire and it falls into one of the nine categories referred to in the *CCNV v. Reid* case.

There are some caveats regarding the public domain defense:

- A work in the public domain in one country may not be in another.
- A new work that is based on public domain material may itself be under copyright (such as a photo of an old painting).
- Copyrights can overlap. That is, a work in the public domain may be incorporating some other work that is still copyrighted, as will be illustrated in the next case.

Copyright: Case 6

LONE RANGER TELEVISION, INC., a corporation, Plaintiff-Appellee, v. PROGRAM RADIO CORPORATION, a California corporation,
JL PRODUCTIONS, INC., a business entity, and WESTON E. LEWIS, JR.
aka JIM LEWIS, Defendants-Appellants

No. 82-4690

UNITED STATES COURT OF APPEALS FOR THE NINTH CIRCUIT

740 F.2d 718; 1984 U.S. App. LEXIS 20149; 223 U.S.P.Q. (BNA) 112; Copy. L. Rep. (CCH) P25,691

March 13, 1984, Argued and Submitted
July 26, 1984

OPINION: WALLACE, Judge:

This appeal from summary judgment for federal copyright infringement and state law conversion requires us to return to the yesteryear of the Lone Ranger, and to the Copyright Act of 1909.

I

Around 1953, a Michigan company called The Lone Ranger, Incorporated owned several original scripts for radio plays about the Lone Ranger, a fictitious early Western hero. In part, this case involves twelve of those scripts. The company also owned three scripts of the first adventures of the Lone Ranger it planned to use for phonograph records. By 1954 the company held federal copyrights in all fifteen scripts. Meanwhile, it had recorded a production of each episode on magnetic tape. It first broadcast the radio plays in 1953 and 1954.

During 1954 The Lone Ranger, Incorporated transferred all rights in the tapes and the fifteen scripts to a California corporation with the same name. In 1962, the California company merged with the Wrather Corporation (Wrather). The rights to the scripts and tapes passed to Wrather, which later transferred them to a subsidiary, Lone Ranger Television, Incorporated (Lone Ranger TV). The copyrights in all fifteen scripts remained valid, either in their original term or by renewal.

Since at least 1960, the scripts' copyright owners have granted an exclusive license to lease Lone Ranger episodes for radio play. Since 1965, Charles Michelson, Incorporated has held this exclusive license. The scripts' copyright owners have also licensed various wholesalers and retailers to sell Lone Ranger records and cassette tapes for private home use. Both the tapes leased to radio stations and the recordings sold for home use contain a copyright notice.

In 1979, Jim Lewis, a former radio announcer, began unlicensed leasing of Lone Ranger episodes to radio stations. He bought reel-to-reel copies of the tapes from some collectors and re-mixed the recordings onto broadcast cartridges for radio play. The original tapes contained a copyright notice by The Lone Ranger, Incorporated at the end of each episode. Lewis's tapes reproduced this notice, although with disputed clarity.

Early in 1982 Lone Ranger TV sued Lewis and his two distribution companies, JL Productions and Program Radio Corporation (collectively Program Radio) in federal district court in California, claiming, among other things, infringement of its federal copyrights in the fifteen scripts and conversion of its intangible property rights in the tapes. As the company later made clear, its claimed rights in the tapes derived from California law. All the parties reside in California.

The district court permanently enjoined Program Radio from leasing the Lone Ranger tapes or otherwise infringing Lone Ranger TV's copyrights in the scripts.

II

In reviewing a summary judgment, we consider the evidence in the light most favorable to the losing party, and determine de novo whether there is any genuine issue of material fact and whether the winner is entitled to judgment as a matter of law. The scope of an injunction, even on summary judgment, lies in the district court's discretion, as does an award of attorney's fees against counsel under 28 U.S.C. § 1927 if supported by a not clearly erroneous finding of wrongful intent, recklessness, or bad faith. We address first, the summary judgment of injunctive relief and damages for federal copyright infringement; second, the summary judgment of damages for state law conversion of intangible property rights; and last, the award of partial attorney's fees against counsel under 28 U.S.C. § 1927.

III

The Copyright Act of 1909, Act of March 4, 1909, did not permit owners of copyrights in scripts to copyright separately any sound recordings produced from them. When the

1909 Act was repealed by the Copyright Act of 1976, protection of sound recordings of copyrighted scripts was not extended to those "fixed" for playing before 1972. Consequently, Lone Ranger TV has never registered any separate federal copyrights in the Lone Ranger tapes. Program Radio argues that, in the absence of such separate copyrights, duplication and distribution of the tapes cannot amount to a federal infringement. We disagree. Lone Ranger TV's valid copyrights in the underlying scripts secure to it, as Program Radio admits, the right to produce derivative works from them. Program Radio has infringed this right.

A.

Program Radio admits that Lone Ranger TV's licensed broadcasts, leases, and sales of recordings based on the scripts have not dedicated the scripts to the public domain for purposes of federal copyright protection. It continues to claim, however, that Lone Ranger TV has not properly recorded the transfers of title in the scripts' copyrights, and thus may not sue for their infringement. The district court found this defense meritless, and we agree. The record adequately shows original ownership of copyrights in the scripts by The Lone Ranger Incorporated of Michigan, a recorded transfer of those copyrights to The Lone Ranger Incorporated of California, and subsequent recorded transfers from The Lone Ranger Incorporated of California to Wrather, and from Wrather to Lone Ranger TV. No genuine issue of material fact exists as to the continued validity of Lone Ranger TV's copyrights in the scripts or its right to sue on them for infringement.

B.

Although Lone Ranger TV holds valid copyrights in the scripts, Program Radio correctly refused to consider the tapes produced by the copyright owners as "copies" of the scripts under the 1909 Act. However, the 1909 Act not only restricted to the copyright holder the right to copy an original writing, it also restricted to the holder the sole rights to prepare derivative works from a literary writing, and to "produce, or reproduce . . . in any manner or by any method whatsoever" a dramatic work. These provisions give the copyright holder an exclusive right to derivative productions from his copyrighted scripts. As one commentator distinguishes between such a derivative right and a right to copy: "It is that point at which the contribution of independent expression to an existing work effectively creates a new work for a different market." The Lone Ranger tapes meet this test: the contribution of independent expression by the actors, together with the contribution of independent expression by the special production methods of taping and editing for radio, effectively created a new work for a market different from both the market for printed scripts and the market for live dramas. Thus, although "an unlicensed use of [a] copyright is not an infringement unless it conflicts with one of the specific exclusive rights conferred by the copyright statute," the 1909 Act does confer a right with which Program Radio's unlicensed tapes of the scripts conflict.

In duplicating, remixing, and distributing the Lone Ranger tapes, Lewis in effect sought to manufacture and publish his own derivative work from the underlying scripts or make his own public production of the underlying scripts, just as if he had hired the actors, sound effects crew, and producers originally used for the tapes to do a second interpretation of the scripts for an audience.

Program Radio contends that the 1909 Act provided protections unique to musical compositions, but our leading film case shows that the principle of protecting derivative works also applies to the ubiquitous literary or dramatic work. *See Russell v. Price*, 612 F.2d 1123 (9th Cir. 1979), *cert. denied*, 446 U.S. 952, 64 L. Ed. 2d 809, 100 S. Ct. 2919 (1980) (*Russell*). There, the copyright owners of George Bernard Shaw's play "Pygmalion" sued a film distributor leasing, without their license, prints of the film "Pygmalion" derived from the play. We held that, although the film had passed into the public domain under the 1909 Act, the unauthorized leasing of prints of it infringed the underlying copyright in the play. We held: although the derivative work may enter the public domain, the matter contained therein which derives from a work still covered by statutory copyright is not dedicated to the public. The established doctrine prevents unauthorized copying or other infringing use of the underlying work or any part of that work contained in the derivative product so long as the underlying work itself remains copyrighted.

C.

As *Russell* makes clear, the protection of derivative rights extends beyond mere protection against unauthorized copying to include the right to "make other versions of, perform or exhibit the work." It makes no difference that the derivation may not satisfy certain requirements for statutory copyright registration itself. Instead, the principles of *Duchess Music* and *Russell* lead us to conclude that Program Radio infringed Lone Ranger TV's rights under sections 1(b), 1(d), and 7 of the 1909 Act to derivative productions of its copyrighted scripts. In view of the clear copyright notices at the end of the Lone Ranger tapes, the records of the copyrights and their transfer in the Copyright Office, and the other evidence presented in support of summary judgment, Program Radio's arguments of estoppel and unclean hands lack merit. *We affirm the district court's summary judgment of injunctive relief and statutory damages for federal copyright infringement.*

Therefore, be careful. You must watch for underlying copyrights in works.

∽

5. The First Sale Doctrine as a Defense to Infringement

This doctrine says that when the copyright owner transfers a particular copy, the copyright owner's right in *that* copy ends (but not his right to prohibit further copying of it). For example, if you buy a book you are permitted to sell or give your copy to another person. You are not infringing the copyright because you are not making a copy of the book. However, in the digital world of computers this can be a problem since "transferring a copy" usually does not mean transferring one discrete copy, but rather making another copy. So you are permitted to sell or give your copy of a piece of software that resides on your hard drive, but unless you delete the copy on your computer you will be infringing. At one time, it was proposed that the first sale doctrine should not apply to software. That is, that it would not be permissible to transfer ownership of a copy of a software program. Happily, that proposal died in the legislative process.

6. Non-Copyrightable Nature of a Work as Defense

Certain types of things are simply not copyrightable. Ideas are not copyrightable. Copyright protects the expression of an idea, but not the idea itself. So, while the novel *Jaws* is copyrightable, anyone is free to write another book based on the same general idea. Other things that are not copyrightable include facts (as we have seen in the *Feist* case), individual words, short phrases, titles, slogans, IP addresses and URLs. But be careful: there are other forms of intellectual property protection that might protect such things, such as trademarks. And remember that while facts themselves are not copyrightable, a *compilation* of facts may be if the organizational scheme has some minimal level of creativity.

Let's conclude the copyrights section with a look at some cases illustrating how copyright law has been applied in the context of digital data and works.

Copyright: Case 7

METRO-GOLDWYN-MAYER STUDIOS, INC., et al., Petitioners v. GROKSTER, LTD., et al.

No. 04-480

SUPREME COURT OF THE UNITED STATES

545 U.S. 913; 125 S. Ct. 2764; 162 L. Ed. 2d 781; 2005 U.S. LEXIS 5212; 75 U.S.P.Q.2D (BNA) 1001; 33 Media L. Rep. 1865; 18 Fla. L. Weekly Fed. S 547

March 29, 2005, Argued
June 27, 2005, Decided

JUDGES: Souter, J., delivered the opinion for a unanimous court. Ginsburg, J., filed a concurring opinion, in which Rehnquist, C. J., and Kennedy, J., joined. Breyer, J., filed a concurring opinion, in which Stevens and O'Connor, JJ., joined.

OPINION: SOUTER, Justice:

The question is under what circumstances the distributor of a product capable of both lawful and unlawful use is liable for acts of copyright infringement by third parties using the product. We hold that one who distributes a device with the object of promoting its use to infringe copyright, as shown by clear expression or other affirmative steps taken to foster infringement, is liable for the resulting acts of infringement by third parties.

I

A

Respondents, Grokster, Ltd., and StreamCast Networks, Inc., defendants in the trial court, distribute free software products that allow computer users to share electronic files through peer-to-peer networks, so called because users' computers communicate directly with each other, not through central servers.

Napster, on the other hand, required a central server.

Discovery during the litigation revealed the way the software worked, the business aims of each defendant company, and the predilections of the users.

Grokster and StreamCast use no servers to intercept the content of the search requests or to mediate the file transfers conducted by users of the software, there being no central point through which the substance of the communications passes in either direction.

Although Grokster and StreamCast do not therefore know when particular files are copied, a few searches using their software would show what is available on the networks the software reaches. MGM commissioned a statistician to conduct a systematic search, and his study showed that nearly 90% of the files available for download on the FastTrack system were copyrighted works. Grokster and StreamCast argue that potential noninfringing uses of their software are significant in kind, even if infrequent in practice.

But MGM's evidence gives reason to think that the vast majority of users' downloads are acts of infringement, and because well over 100 million copies of the software in question are known to have been downloaded, and billions of files are shared across the FastTrack and Gnutella networks each month, the probable scope of copyright infringement is staggering.

Grokster and StreamCast concede the infringement in most downloads, and it is uncontested that they are aware that users employ their software primarily to download copyrighted files, even if the decentralized FastTrack and Gnutella networks fail to reveal which files are being copied, and when.

Grokster and StreamCast are not, however, merely passive recipients of information about infringing use. The record is replete with evidence that from the moment Grokster and StreamCast began to distribute their free software, each one clearly voiced the objective that recipients use it to download copyrighted works, and each took active steps to encourage infringement.

After the notorious file-sharing service, Napster, was sued by copyright holders for facilitation of copyright infringement, StreamCast gave away a software program of a kind known as OpenNap, designed as compatible with the Napster program and open to Napster users for downloading files from other Napster and OpenNap users' computers. Evidence indicates that "[i]t was always [StreamCast's] intent to use [its OpenNap network] to be able to capture email addresses of [its] initial target market so that [it] could promote [its] StreamCast Morpheus interface to them"; indeed, the OpenNap program was engineered "'to leverage Napster's 50 million user base.'"

Internal company documents indicate that StreamCast hoped to attract large numbers of former Napster users if that company was shut down by court order or otherwise, and that StreamCast planned to be the next Napster. An internal e-mail from a company executive stated: "'We have put this network in place so that when Napster pulls the plug on their free service . . . or if the Court orders them shut down prior to that . . . we will be positioned to capture the flood of their 32 million users that will be actively looking for an alternative.'"

Thus, StreamCast developed promotional materials to market its service as the best Napster alternative. StreamCast even planned to flaunt the illegal uses of its software; when it launched the OpenNap network, the chief technology officer of the company averred that "[t]he goal is to get in trouble with the law and get sued. It's the best way to get in the new[s]."

In addition to this evidence of express promotion, marketing, and intent to promote further, the business models employed by Grokster and StreamCast confirm that their principal object was use of their software to download copyrighted works. Grokster and StreamCast receive no revenue from users, who obtain the software itself for nothing.

Instead, both companies generate income by selling advertising space, and they stream the advertising to Grokster and Morpheus users while they are employing the programs. As the number of users of each program increases, advertising opportunities become worth more. While there is doubtless some demand for free Shakespeare, the evidence shows that substantive volume is a function of free access to copyrighted work. Users seeking Top 40 songs, for example, or the latest release by Modest Mouse, are certain to be far more numerous than those seeking a free Decameron, and Grokster and StreamCast translated that demand into dollars.

Finally, there is no evidence that either company made an effort to filter copyrighted material from users' downloads or otherwise impede the sharing of copyrighted files.

B

After discovery, the parties on each side of the case cross-moved for summary judgment. The District Court held that those who used the Grokster and Morpheus software to download copyrighted media files directly infringed MGM's copyrights, a conclusion not contested on appeal, but the court nonetheless granted summary judgment in favor of Grokster and StreamCast as to any liability arising from distribution of the then current versions of their software. Distributing that software gave rise to no liability in the court's view, because its use did not provide the distributors with actual knowledge of specific acts of infringement.

The Court of Appeals affirmed. But the court read *Sony Corp. of America* v. *Universal City Studios, Inc.*, 464 U.S. 417, 78 L. Ed. 2d 574, 104 S. Ct. 774 (1984), as holding that distribution of a commercial product capable of substantial noninfringing uses could not give rise to contributory liability for infringement unless the distributor had actual knowledge of specific instances of infringement and failed to act on that knowledge. The fact that the software was capable of substantial noninfringing uses in the Ninth Circuit's view meant that Grokster and StreamCast were not liable, because they had no such actual knowledge, owing to the decentralized architecture of their software. The court also held that Grokster and StreamCast did not materially contribute to their users' infringement because it was the users themselves who searched for, retrieved, and stored the infringing files, with no involvement by the defendants beyond providing the software in the first place.

The Ninth Circuit also considered whether Grokster and StreamCast could be liable under a theory of vicarious infringement. The court held against liability because the defendants did not monitor or control the use of the software, had no agreed-upon right or current ability to supervise its use, and had no independent duty to police infringement. We granted certiorari.

II

A

MGM and many of the *amici* fault the Court of Appeals's holding for upsetting a sound balance between the respective values of supporting creative pursuits through copyright protection and promoting innovation in new communication technologies by limiting the incidence of liability for copyright infringement. The more artistic protection is favored, the more technological innovation may be discouraged; the administration of copyright law is an exercise in managing the tradeoff.

The tension between the two values is the subject of this case, with its claim that digital distribution of copyrighted material threatens copyright holders as never before, because every copy is identical to the original, copying is easy, and many people (especially the young) use file-sharing software to download copyrighted works. This very breadth of the software's use may well draw the public directly into the debate over copyright policy, and the indications are that the ease of copying songs or movies using software like Grokster's and Napster's is fostering disdain for copyright protection. As the case has been presented to us, these fears are said to be offset by the different concern that imposing liability, not only on infringers but on distributors of software based on its potential for unlawful use, could limit further development of beneficial technologies.

The argument for imposing indirect liability in this case is, however, a powerful one, given the number of infringing downloads that occur every day using StreamCast's and Grokster's software. When a widely shared service or product is used to commit infringement, it may be impossible to enforce rights in the protected work effectively against all direct infringers, the only practical alternative being to go against the distributor of the copying device for secondary liability on a theory of contributory or vicarious infringement.

One infringes contributorily by intentionally inducing or encouraging direct infringement, and infringes vicariously by profiting from direct infringement while declining to exercise a right to stop or limit it. Although "[t]he Copyright Act does not expressly render anyone liable for infringement committed by another," these doctrines of secondary liability emerged from common law principles and are well established in the law.

B

Despite the currency of these principles of secondary liability, this Court has dealt with secondary copyright infringement in only one recent case, and because MGM has tailored its principal claim to our opinion there, a look at our earlier holding is in order. In *Sony Corp.* v. *Universal City Studios, supra,* this Court addressed a claim that secondary liability for infringement can arise from the very distribution of a commercial product. There, the product, novel at the time, was what we know today as the videocassette recorder or VCR. Copyright holders sued Sony as the manufacturer, claiming it was contributorily liable for infringement that occurred when VCR owners taped copyrighted programs because it supplied the means used to infringe, and it had constructive knowledge that infringement would occur. At the trial on the merits, the evidence showed that the principal use of the VCR was for "'time-shifting,'" or taping a program for later viewing at a more convenient time, which the Court found to be a fair, not an infringing, use. There was no evidence that Sony had expressed an object of bringing about taping in violation of copyright or had taken active steps to increase its profits from unlawful taping. Although Sony's advertisements urged consumers to buy the VCR to "'record favorite shows'" or "'build a library'" of recorded programs, neither of these uses was necessarily infringing.

On those facts, with no evidence of stated or indicated intent to promote infringing uses, the only conceivable basis for imposing liability was on a theory of contributory infringement arising from its sale of VCRs to consumers with knowledge that some would use them to infringe. But because the VCR was "capable of commercially significant noninfringing uses," we held the manufacturer could not be faulted solely on the basis of its distribution.

This analysis reflected patent law's traditional staple article of commerce doctrine, now codified, that distribution of a component of a patented device will not violate the patent if it is suitable for use in other ways. The doctrine was devised to identify instances in which it may be presumed from distribution of an article in commerce that the distributor intended the article to be used to infringe another's patent, and so may justly be held liable for that infringement. "One who makes and sells articles which are only adapted to be used in a patented combination will be presumed to intend the natural consequences of his acts; he will be presumed to intend that they shall be used in the combination of the patent."

In sum, where an article is "good for nothing else" but infringement, there is no legitimate public interest in its unlicensed availability, and there is no injustice in presuming or imputing an intent to infringe. Conversely, the doctrine absolves the equivocal conduct of selling an item with substantial lawful as well as unlawful uses, and limits liability to instances of more acute fault than the mere understanding that some of one's products will be misused. It leaves breathing room for innovation and a vigorous commerce.

The parties and many of the *amici* in this case think the key to resolving it is the *Sony* rule and, in particular, what it means for a product to be "capable of commercially significant noninfringing uses." MGM advances the argument that granting summary judgment to Grokster and StreamCast as to their current activities gave too much weight to the value of innovative technology, and too little to the copyrights infringed by users of their software, given that 90% of works available on one of the networks was shown to be copyrighted. Assuming the remaining 10% to be its noninfringing use, MGM says this should not qualify as "substantial," and the Court should quantify *Sony* to the extent of holding that a product used "principally" for infringement does not qualify. As mentioned before, Grokster and StreamCast reply by citing evidence that their software can be used to reproduce public domain works, and they point to copyright holders who actually encourage copying. Even if infringement is the principal practice with their software today, they argue, the noninfringing uses are significant and will grow.

We agree with MGM that the Court of Appeals misapplied *Sony*, which it read as limiting secondary liability quite beyond the circumstances to which the case applied. The Ninth Circuit has read *Sony*'s limitation to mean that whenever a product is capable of substantial lawful use, the producer can never be held contributorily liable for third parties' infringing use of it; it read the rule as being this broad, even when an actual purpose to cause infringing use is shown by evidence independent of design and distribution of the product, unless the distributors had "specific knowledge of infringement at a time at which they contributed to the infringement, and failed to act upon that information."

This view of *Sony*, however, was error, converting the case from one about liability resting on imputed intent to one about liability on any theory. It is enough to note that the Ninth Circuit's judgment rested on an erroneous understanding of *Sony* and to leave further consideration of the *Sony* rule for a day when that may be required.

C

Sony's rule limits imputing culpable intent as a matter of law from the characteristics or uses of a distributed product. But nothing in *Sony* requires courts to ignore evidence of intent if there is such evidence, and the case was never meant to foreclose rules of fault-based liability derived from the common law.

The classic case of direct evidence of unlawful purpose occurs when one induces commission of infringement by another, or "entic[es] or persuad[es] another" to infringe, as by advertising. Thus at common law a copyright or patent defendant who "not only expected but invoked [infringing use] by advertisement" was liable for infringement "on principles recognized in every part of the law."

The rule on inducement of infringement as developed in the early cases is no different today. Evidence of "active steps . . . taken to encourage direct infringement," such as advertising an infringing use or instructing how to engage in an infringing use, shows an affirmative intent that the product be used to infringe, and a showing that infringement was encouraged overcomes the law's reluctance to find liability when a defendant merely sells a commercial product suitable for some lawful use.

We [hold] that one who distributes a device with the object of promoting its use to infringe copyright, as shown by clear expression or other affirmative steps taken to foster infringement, is liable for the resulting acts of infringement by third parties. We are, of course, mindful of the need to keep from trenching on regular commerce or discouraging the development of technologies with lawful and unlawful potential. Accordingly, just as *Sony* did not find intentional inducement despite the knowledge of the VCR manufacturer that its device could be used to infringe, mere knowledge of infringing potential or of actual infringing uses would not be enough here to subject a distributor to liability. The inducement rule, instead, premises liability on purposeful, culpable expression and conduct, and thus does nothing to compromise legitimate commerce or discourage innovation having a lawful promise.

III

A

The only apparent question about treating MGM's evidence as sufficient to withstand summary judgment under the theory of inducement goes to the need on MGM's part to adduce evidence that StreamCast and Grokster communicated an inducing message to their software users. The classic instance of inducement is by advertisement or solicitation that broadcasts a message designed to stimulate others to commit violations. MGM claims that such a message is shown here. It is undisputed that StreamCast beamed onto the computer screens of users of Napster-compatible programs ads urging the adoption of its OpenNap program, which was designed, as its name implied, to invite the custom of patrons of Napster, then under attack in the courts for facilitating massive infringement. Those who accepted StreamCast's OpenNap program were offered software to perform the same services, which a factfinder could conclude would readily have been understood in the Napster market as the ability to download copyrighted music files. Grokster distributed an electronic newsletter containing links to articles promoting its software's ability to access popular copyrighted music.

In StreamCast's case, of course, the evidence just described was supplemented by other unequivocal indications of unlawful purpose in the internal communications and advertising designs aimed at Napster users. Whether the messages were communicated is not to the point on this record. The function of the message in the theory of inducement is to prove by a defendant's own statements that his unlawful purpose disqualifies him from claiming protection (and incidentally to point to actual violators likely to be found among those who hear or read the message).

The unlawful objective is unmistakable.

B

In addition to intent to bring about infringement and distribution of a device suitable for infringing use, the inducement theory of course requires evidence of actual infringement by recipients of the device, the software in this case. As the account of the facts indicates, there is evidence of infringement on a gigantic scale, and there is no serious issue of the adequacy of MGM's showing on this point in order to survive the companies' summary judgment requests.

In sum, this case is significantly different from *Sony* and reliance on that case to rule in favor of StreamCast and Grokster was error. *Sony* dealt with a claim of liability based solely on distributing a product with alternative lawful and unlawful uses, with knowledge that some users would follow the unlawful course. The case struck a balance between the interests of protection and innovation by holding that the product's capability of substantial lawful employment should bar the imputation of fault and consequent secondary liability for the unlawful acts of others.

MGM's evidence in this case most obviously addresses a different basis of liability for distributing a product open to alternative uses. Here, evidence of the distributors' words and deeds going beyond distribution as such shows a purpose to cause and profit from third-party acts of copyright infringement. If liability for inducing infringement is ultimately found, it will not be on the basis of presuming or imputing fault, but from inferring a patently illegal objective from statements and actions showing what that objective was.

On remand, reconsideration of MGM's motion for summary judgment will be in order.

The judgment of the Court of Appeals is vacated, and the case is remanded for further proceedings consistent with this opinion.

It is so ordered.

GINSBURG; BREYER concur.

CONCURRENCE: GINSBURG, Justice:

I concur in the Court's decision, which vacates in full the judgment of the Court of Appeals for the Ninth Circuit and write separately to clarify why I conclude that the Court of Appeals misperceived, and hence misapplied, our holding in *Sony Corp. of America* v. *Universal City Studios, Inc.*, 464 U.S. 417, 78 L. Ed. 2d 574, 104 S. Ct. 774 (1984).

At bottom, however labeled, the question in this case is whether Grokster and Stream-Cast are liable for the direct infringing acts of others. Liability under our jurisprudence may be predicated on actively encouraging (or inducing) infringement through specific acts (as the Court's opinion develops) or on distributing a product distributees use to infringe copyrights, if the product is not capable of "substantial" or "commercially significant" noninfringing uses. While the two categories overlap, they capture different culpable behavior.

In *Sony*, 464 U.S. 417, 78 L. Ed. 2d 574, 104 S. Ct. 774, the Court considered Sony's liability for selling the Betamax video cassette recorder.

[T]o resolve the case, the Court explained, it had to determine "whether the Betamax is capable of commercially significant noninfringing uses." *Ibid.*

To answer that question, the Court considered whether "a significant number of [potential uses of the Betamax were] noninfringing." The Court homed in on one potential use – private, noncommercial time-shifting of television programs in the home (*i.e.*, recording a broadcast TV program for later personal viewing). Time-shifting was noninfringing, the Court concluded, because in some cases trial testimony showed it was authorized by the copyright holder and in others it qualified as legitimate fair use. Most purchasers used the Betamax principally to engage in time-shifting, a use that "plainly satisfie[d]" the Court's standard. Thus, there was no need in *Sony* to "give precise content to the question of how much [actual or potential] use is commercially significant." Further development was left for later days and cases.

This case differs markedly from *Sony*. Here, there has been no finding of any fair use and little beyond anecdotal evidence of noninfringing uses.

Even if the absolute number of noninfringing files copied using the Grokster and StreamCast software is large, it does not follow that the products are therefore put to substantial noninfringing uses and are thus immune from liability. The number of noninfringing copies may be reflective of, and dwarfed by, the huge total volume of files shared. Further, the District Court and the Court of Appeals did not sharply distinguish between uses of Grokster's and StreamCast's software products (which this case is about) and uses of peer-to-peer technology generally (which this case is not about).

On this record, the District Court should not have ruled dispositively on the contributory infringement charge by granting summary judgment to Grokster and StreamCast.

If, on remand, the case is not resolved on summary judgment in favor of MGM based on Grokster and StreamCast actively inducing infringement, the Court of Appeals, I would emphasize, should reconsider, on a fuller record, its interpretation of *Sony's* product distribution holding.

CONCURRENCE: BREYER, Justice:

I agree with the Court that the distributor of a dual-use technology may be liable for the infringing activities of third parties where he or she actively seeks to advance the infringement. I further agree that, in light of our holding today, we need not now "revisit" *Sony Corp. of America* v. *Universal City Studios, Inc.*, 464 U.S. 417, 78 L. Ed. 2d 574, 104 S. Ct. 774 (1984). Other Members of the Court, however, take up the *Sony* question: whether Grokster's product is "capable of 'substantial' or 'commercially significant' noninfringing uses." And they answer that question by stating that the Court of Appeals was wrong when it granted summary judgment on the issue in Grokster's favor. I write to explain why I disagree with them on this matter.

> **Be sure you understand that Justice Breyer and his fellow concurrers are NOT disagreeing with the ultimate outcome of this case. They agree that if there is inducement, a distributor of a potentially infringing product can be liable, but they disagree with the majority's interpretation of the meaning of the *Sony* case, believing that the majority's position amounts to a modification of the *Sony* rule.**

I

The Court's opinion in *Sony* and the record evidence (as described and analyzed in the many briefs before us) together convince me that the Court of Appeals' conclusion has adequate legal support.

A

I begin with *Sony*'s standard. In *Sony*, the Court considered the potential copyright liability of a company that did not itself illegally copy protected material, but rather sold a machine – a videocassette recorder (VCR) – that could be used to do so. A buyer could use that machine for *non* infringing purposes, such as recording for later viewing (sometimes called "'time-shifting,'") uncopyrighted television programs or copyrighted programs with a copyright holder's permission. The buyer could use the machine for infringing purposes as well, such as building libraries of taped copyrighted programs. Or, the buyer might use the machine to record copyrighted programs under circumstances in which the legal status of the act of recording was uncertain (*i.e.*, where the copying may, or may not, have constituted a "fair use"). Sony knew many customers would use its VCRs to engage in unauthorized copying and "'library-building.'" But that fact, said the Court, was insufficient to make Sony itself an infringer. And the Court ultimately held that Sony was not liable for its customers' acts of infringement.

In reaching this conclusion, the Court recognized the need for the law, in fixing *secondary* copyright liability, to "strike a balance between a copyright holder's legitimate demand for effective – not merely symbolic – protection of the statutory monopoly, and the rights of others freely to engage in substantially unrelated areas of commerce." The Court wrote that the sale of copying equipment, "like the sale of other articles of commerce, does not constitute contributory infringement if the product is widely used for legitimate, unobjectionable purposes. *Indeed, it need merely be capable of substantial noninfringing uses.*" The Court ultimately characterized the legal "question" in the particular case as "whether [Sony's VCR] is *capable of commercially significant noninfringing uses*" (while declining to give "precise content" to these terms). Ibid. (emphasis added).

It then applied this standard. The Court had before it a survey (commissioned by the District Court and then prepared by the respondents) showing that roughly 9% of all VCR recordings were of the type – namely, religious, educational, and sports programming – owned by producers and distributors testifying on Sony's behalf who did not object to time-shifting. (7.3% of all Sony VCR use is to record sports programs; representatives of the sports leagues do not object.)

The Court found that the magnitude of authorized programming was "significant," and it also noted the "significant potential for future authorized copying." The Court supported this conclusion by referencing the trial testimony of professional sports league officials and a religious broadcasting representative. It also discussed (1) a Los Angeles educational station affiliated with the Public Broadcasting Service that made many of its programs available for home taping, and (2) Mr. Rogers' Neighborhood, a widely watched children's program. On the basis of this testimony and other similar evidence, the Court determined that producers of this kind had authorized duplication of their copyrighted programs "in significant enough numbers to create a substantial market for a noninfringing use of the" VCR.

The Court, in using the key word "substantial," indicated that these circumstances alone constituted a sufficient basis for rejecting the imposition of secondary liability. Nonetheless, the Court buttressed its conclusion by finding separately that, in any event, unauthorized time-shifting often constituted not infringement, but "fair use."

B

When measured against *Sony's* underlying evidence and analysis, the evidence now before us shows that Grokster passes *Sony's* test – that is, whether the company's product is capable of substantial or commercially significant noninfringing uses. For one thing, petitioners' (hereinafter MGM) own expert declared that 75% of current files available on Grokster are infringing and 15% are "likely infringing." That leaves some number of files near 10% that apparently are noninfringing, a figure very similar to the 9% or so of authorized time-shifting uses of the VCR that the Court faced in *Sony*.

To be sure, in quantitative terms these uses account for only a small percentage of the total number of uses of Grokster's product. But the same was true in *Sony*, which characterized the relatively limited authorized copying market as "substantial."

Importantly, *Sony* also used the word "capable," asking whether the product is "capable of" substantial noninfringing uses. Its language and analysis suggest that a figure like 10%, if fixed for all time, might well prove insufficient, but that such a figure serves as an adequate foundation where there is a reasonable prospect of expanded legitimate uses over time.

Here the record reveals a significant future market for noninfringing uses of Grokster-type peer-to-peer software. Such software permits the exchange of any sort of digital file – whether that file does, or does not, contain copyrighted material. As more and more uncopyrighted information is stored in swappable form, it seems a likely inference that lawful peer-to-peer sharing will become increasingly prevalent.

And that is just what is happening. Such legitimate noninfringing uses are coming to include the swapping of: research information (the initial purpose of many peer-to-peer networks); public domain films (e.g., those owned by the Prelinger Archive); historical recordings and digital educational materials (e.g., those stored on the Internet Archive); digital photos (OurPictures, for example, is starting a P2P photo-swapping service); "shareware" and "freeware" (e.g., Linux and certain Windows software); secure licensed music and movie files (Intent MediaWorks, for example, protects licensed content sent across P2P networks); news broadcasts past and present (the BBC Creative Archive lets users "rip, mix and share the BBC"); user-created audio and video files (including "podcasts" that may be distributed through P2P software); and all manner of free "open content" works collected by Creative Commons (one can search for Creative Commons material on StreamCast).

Of course, Grokster itself may not want to develop these other noninfringing uses. But *Sony's* standard seeks to protect not the Groksters of this world (which in any event may well be liable under today's holding), but the development of technology more generally. And Grokster's desires in this respect are beside the point.

II

Instead, the real question is whether we should modify the Sony standard, as MGM requests, or interpret *Sony* more strictly, as I believe Justice Ginsburg's approach would do in practice. I would ask whether MGM has shown that *Sony* incorrectly balanced copyright and new-technology interests. In particular: (1) Has *Sony* (as I interpret it) worked to protect new technology? (2) If so, would modification or strict interpretation significantly weaken that protection? (3) If so, would new or necessary copyright-related benefits outweigh any such weakening?

A

The first question is the easiest to answer. *Sony's* rule, as I interpret it, has provided entrepreneurs with needed assurance that they will be shielded from copyright liability as they bring valuable new technologies to market.

> **Justice Breyer goes on to make a few pithy statements in support of his argument:**
> **Sony's rule is clear.**
> **Sony's rule is strongly technology protecting.**
> **Sony's rule is forward looking.**

Sony's rule is mindful of the limitations facing judges where matters of technology are concerned. Judges have no specialized technical ability to answer questions about present or future technological feasibility or commercial viability where technology professionals, engineers, and venture capitalists themselves may radically disagree and where answers may differ depending upon whether one focuses upon the time of product development or the time of distribution.

Given the nature of the *Sony* rule, it is not surprising that in the last 20 years, there have been relatively few contributory infringement suits – based on a product distribution theory – brought against technology providers (a small handful of federal appellate court cases and perhaps fewer than two dozen District Court cases in the last 20 years). I have found nothing in the briefs or the record that shows that *Sony* has failed to achieve its innovation-protecting objective.

B

The second, more difficult, question is whether a modified *Sony* rule (or a strict interpretation) would significantly weaken the law's ability to protect new technology. Justice Ginsburg's approach would require defendants to produce considerably more concrete evidence – more than was presented here – to earn Sony's shelter. That heavier evidentiary demand, and especially the more dramatic (case-by-case balancing) modifications that MGM and the Government seek, would, I believe, undercut the protection that *Sony* now offers.

C

The third question – whether a positive copyright impact would outweigh any technology-related loss – I find the most difficult of the three. I do not doubt that a more intrusive Sony test would generally provide greater revenue security for copyright holders. But it is harder to conclude that the gains on the copyright swings would exceed the losses on the technology roundabouts.

For one thing, the law disfavors equating the two different kinds of gain and loss; rather, it leans in favor of protecting technology. As Sony itself makes clear, the producer of a technology which permits unlawful copying does not himself engage in unlawful

copying – a fact that makes the attachment of copyright liability to the creation, production, or distribution of the technology an exceptional thing.

In any event, the evidence now available does not, in my view, make out a sufficiently
strong case for change.

Will an unmodified Sony lead to a significant diminution in the amount or quality
of creative work produced? Since copyright's basic objective is creation and its revenue
objectives but a means to that end, this is the underlying copyright question. And its
answer is far from clear.

Unauthorized copying likely diminishes industry revenue, though it is not clear by
how much.

The extent to which related production has actually and resultingly declined remains
uncertain, though there is good reason to believe that the decline, if any, is not substantial.

More importantly, copyright holders at least potentially have other tools available to
reduce piracy and to abate whatever threat it poses to creative production. As today's
opinion makes clear, a copyright holder may proceed against a technology provider where
a provable specific intent to infringe (of the kind the Court describes) is present.

In addition, a copyright holder has always had the legal authority to bring a traditional
infringement suit against one who wrongfully copies.

Further, copyright holders may develop new technological devices that will help curb
unlawful infringement. Some new technology, called "digital 'watermarking'" and "digital fingerprint[ing]," can encode within the file information about the author and the
copyright scope and date, which "fingerprints" can help to expose infringers.

At the same time, advances in technology have discouraged unlawful copying by
making lawful copying (e.g., downloading music with the copyright holder's permission)
cheaper and easier to achieve. Several services now sell music for less than $1 per song.
(Walmart.com, for example, charges $0.88 each.) Consequently, many consumers initially
attracted to the convenience and flexibility of services like Grokster are now migrating
to lawful paid services (services with copying permission) where they can enjoy at little
cost even greater convenience and flexibility without engaging in unlawful swapping.

Thus, lawful music downloading services – those that charge the customer for downloading music and pay royalties to the copyright holder – have continued to grow and to
produce substantial revenue.

Finally, as Sony recognized, the legislative option remains available. Courts are less
well suited than Congress to the task of "accommodat[ing] fully the varied permutations
of competing interests that are inevitably implicated by such new technology."

I do not know whether these developments and similar alternatives will prove sufficient, but I am reasonably certain that, given their existence, a strong demonstrated need
for modifying Sony (or for interpreting Sony's standard more strictly) has not yet been
shown. That fact, along with the added risks that modification (or strict interpretation)
would impose upon technological innovation, leads me to the conclusion that we should
maintain Sony, reading its standard as I have read it. As so read, it requires affirmance of
the Ninth Circuit's determination of the relevant aspects of the Sony question.

*For these reasons, I disagree with Justice Ginsburg, but I agree with the Court and join its
opinion.*

∿

The *Grokster* decision was widely misinterpreted by the media as meaning that peer-to-peer file sharing networks were inherently "illegal" because users of such networks can share copyrighted material. The case does not say that. What it says is that if a peer-to-peer network (or any other technological innovation) is *actively promoted* for infringing uses, then the creators of that technology can be held liable as contributory infringers. So long as there is no *inducement* to infringe, however, there is no problem with creating peer-to-peer networks.

Copyright: Case 8

NEW YORK TIMES COMPANY, INC., ET AL. v. JONATHAN TASINI, ET AL.

No. 00-201

SUPREME COURT OF THE UNITED STATES

533 U.S. 483; 121 S. Ct. 2381; 150 L. Ed. 2d 500; 2001 U.S. LEXIS 4667;
69 U.S.L.W. 4567; 59 U.S.P.Q.2D (BNA) 1001; 5 A.L.R. Fed. 2d 623;
29 Media L. Rep. 1865; 2001 Cal. Daily Op. Service 5260; 2001 Daily Journal
DAR 6435; 2001 Colo. J. C.A.R. 3509; 14 Fla. L. Weekly Fed. S 414

March 28, 2001, Argued
June 25, 2001, Decided

JUDGES: GINSBURG, J., delivered the opinion of the Court, in which REHNQUIST, C. J., and O'CONNOR, SCALIA, KENNEDY, SOUTER, and THOMAS, JJ., joined. STEVENS, J., filed a dissenting opinion, in which BREYER, J., joined.

OPINION: GINSBURG, Justice:

This copyright case concerns the rights of freelance authors and a presumptive privilege of their publishers. The litigation was initiated by six freelance authors and relates to articles they contributed to three print periodicals (two newspapers and one magazine). Under agreements with the periodicals' publishers, but without the freelancers' consent, two computer database companies placed copies of the freelancers' articles – along with all other articles from the periodicals in which the freelancers' work appeared – into three databases. Whether written by a freelancer or staff member, each article is presented to, and retrievable by, the user in isolation, clear of the context the original print publication presented.

The freelance authors' complaint alleged that their copyrights had been infringed by the inclusion of their articles in the databases. The publishers, in response, relied on the privilege of reproduction and distribution accorded them by § 201(c) of the Copyright Act, which provides:

> Copyright in each separate contribution to a collective work is distinct from copyright in the collective work as a whole, and vests initially in the author of the contribution. In the absence of an express transfer of the copyright or of any rights under it, the owner of copyright in the collective work is presumed to have acquired only the privilege of reproducing and distributing the contribution as part of that particular collective work, any revision of that collective work, and any later collective work in the same series. 17 U.S.C. § 201(c).

Specifically, the publishers maintained that, as copyright owners of collective works, *i.e.*, the original print publications, they had merely exercised "the privilege" § 201(c) accords them to "reproduce and distribute" the author's discretely copyrighted contribution.

In agreement with the Second Circuit, we hold that § 201(c) does not authorize the copying at issue here. The publishers are not sheltered by § 201(c), we conclude, because the databases reproduce and distribute articles standing alone and not in context, not "as part of that particular collective work" to which the author contributed, "as part of . . . any revision" thereof, or "as part of . . . any later collective work in the same series." Both the print publishers and the electronic publishers, we rule, have infringed the copyrights of the freelance authors.

I

A

Respondents Jonathan Tasini, Mary Kay Blakely, Barbara Garson, Margot Mifflin, Sonia Jaffe Robbins, and David S. Whitford are authors (Authors). Between 1990 and 1993, they wrote the 21 articles (Articles) on which this dispute centers. The Authors registered copyrights in each of the Articles. The Times, Newsday, and Time (Print Publishers) registered collective work copyrights in each periodical edition in which an Article originally appeared. The Print Publishers engaged the Authors as independent contractors (freelancers) under contracts that in no instance secured consent from an Author to placement of an Article in an electronic database.

At the time the Articles were published, all three Print Publishers had agreements with petitioner LEXIS/NEXIS (formerly Mead Data Central Corp.), owner and operator of NEXIS, a computerized database that stores information in a text-only format. NEXIS contains articles from hundreds of journals (newspapers and periodicals) spanning many years. The Print Publishers have licensed to LEXIS/NEXIS the text of articles appearing in the three periodicals. The licenses authorize LEXIS/NEXIS to copy and sell any portion of those texts.

Pursuant to the licensing agreements, the Print Publishers regularly provide LEXIS/ NEXIS with a batch of all the articles published in each periodical edition. The Print Publisher codes each article to facilitate computerized retrieval, then transmits it in a separate file. After further coding, LEXIS/NEXIS places the article in the central discs of its database.

Subscribers to NEXIS, accessing the system through a computer, may search for articles by author, subject, date, publication, headline, key term, words in text, or other criteria. The display of each article includes the print publication (*e.g.*, The New York Times), date (September 23, 1990), section (Magazine), initial page number (26), headline or title ("Remembering Jane"), and author (Mary Kay Blakely). Each article appears as a separate, isolated "story" – without any visible link to the other stories originally published in the same newspaper or magazine edition. NEXIS does not contain pictures or advertisements, and it does not reproduce the original print publication's formatting features such as headline size, page placement (*e.g.*, above or below the fold for newspapers), or location of continuation pages.

Like NEXIS, NYTO is a text-only system. Unlike NEXIS and NYTO, GPO is an image-based, rather than a text-based, system.

GPO is image-based rather than text-based. It presents each article exactly as it appeared on the printed pages, with photos, ads, etc.

B

On December 16, 1993, the Authors filed this civil action in the United States District Court for the Southern District of New York. After discovery, both sides moved for summary judgment.

The District Court granted summary judgment for the Publishers, holding that § 201(c) shielded the Database reproductions.

The Authors appealed, and the Second Circuit reversed. 206 F.3d 161 (1999). The Court of Appeals granted summary judgment for the Authors on the ground that the Databases were not among the collective works covered by § 201(c), and specifically, were not "revisions" of the periodicals in which the Articles first appeared.

We granted certiorari to determine whether the copying of the Authors' Articles in the Databases is privileged by 17 U.S.C. § 201(c). Like the Court of Appeals, we conclude that the § 201(c) privilege does not override the Authors' copyrights, for the Databases do not reproduce and distribute the Articles as part of a collective work privileged by § 201(c).

II

Under the Copyright Act, as amended in 1976, "copyright protection subsists . . . in original works of authorship fixed in any tangible medium of expression . . . from which they can be perceived, reproduced, or otherwise communicated." When, as in this case, a freelance author has contributed an article to a "collective work" such as a newspaper or magazine, see § 101 (defining "collective work"), the statute recognizes two distinct copyrighted works: "Copyright in *each separate contribution to a collective work* is distinct from copyright in *the collective work as a whole. . . .* " § 201(c) (emphasis added). Copyright in the separate contribution "vests initially in the author of the contribution" (here, the freelancer). Copyright in the collective work vests in the collective author (here, the newspaper or magazine publisher) and extends only to the creative material contributed by that author, not to "the preexisting material employed in the work," § 103(b).

Section 201(c) both describes and circumscribes the "privilege" a publisher acquires regarding an author's contribution to a collective work:

> In the absence of an express transfer of the copyright or of any rights under it, the owner of copyright in the collective work is presumed to have acquired *only* the privilege of reproducing and distributing the contribution as part of that particular collective work, any revision of that collective work, and any later collective work in the same series. (Emphasis added)

Essentially, § 201(c) adjusts a publisher's copyright in its collective work to accommodate a freelancer's copyright in her contribution. If there is demand for a freelance article standing alone or in a new collection, the Copyright Act allows the freelancer to benefit from that demand; after authorizing initial publication, the freelancer may also sell the article to others.

III

In the instant case, the Authors wrote several Articles and gave the Print Publishers permission to publish the Articles in certain newspapers and magazines. It is undisputed that the Authors hold copyrights and, therefore, exclusive rights in the Articles.[1]

Against the Authors' charge of infringement, the Publishers contend that reproduction and distribution of each Article by the Databases lie within the "privilege of reproducing and distributing the [Articles] as part of . . . [a] revision of that collective work" § 201(c). The Publishers' encompassing construction of the § 201(c) privilege is unacceptable, we conclude, for it would diminish the Authors' exclusive rights in the Articles.

In determining whether the Articles have been reproduced and distributed "as part of" a "revision" of the collective works in issue, we focus on the Articles as presented to, and perceptible by, the user of the Databases. In this case, the three Databases present articles to users clear of the context provided either by the original periodical editions or by any revision of those editions. [W]e cannot see how the Database perceptibly reproduces and distributes the article "as part of" either the original edition or a "revision" of that edition.

One might view the articles as parts of a new compendium – namely, the entirety of works in the Database. In that compendium, each edition of each periodical represents only a miniscule fraction of the ever-expanding Database. The Database no more constitutes a "revision" of each constituent edition than a 400-page novel quoting a sonnet in passing would represent a "revision" of that poem. "Revision" denotes a new "version," and a version is, in this setting, a "distinct form of something regarded by its creators or others as one work." The massive whole of the Database is not recognizable as a new version of its every small part.

Alternatively, one could view the Articles in the Databases "as part of" no larger work at all, but simply as individual articles presented individually. That each article bears marks of its origin in a particular periodical (less vivid marks in NEXIS and NYTO, more vivid marks in GPO) suggests the article was *previously* part of that periodical. But the markings do not mean the article is *currently* reproduced or distributed as part of the periodical. The Databases' reproduction and distribution of individual Articles – simply *as individual Articles* – would invade the core of the Authors' exclusive rights under § 106.

The Publishers press an analogy between the Databases, on the one hand, and microfilm and microfiche, on the other. We find the analogy wanting. Microforms typically contain continuous photographic reproductions of a periodical in the medium of miniaturized film. Accordingly, articles appear on the microforms, writ very small, in precisely the position in which the articles appeared in the newspaper. In the Databases, by contrast, the Articles appear disconnected from their original context.

---

[1] The Publishers do not claim that the Articles are "works made for hire." As to such works, the employer or person for whom a work was prepared is treated as the author. The Print Publishers, however, neither engaged the Authors to write the Articles as "employees" nor "commissioned" the Articles through "a written instrument signed by [both parties]" indicating that the Articles shall be considered "works made for hire."

Invoking the concept of "media neutrality," the Publishers urge that the "transfer of a work between media" does not "alter the character of" that work for copyright purposes. That is indeed true. But unlike the conversion of newsprint to microfilm, the transfer of articles to the Databases does not represent a mere conversion of intact periodicals (or revisions of periodicals) from one medium to another. The Databases offer users individual articles, not intact periodicals. In this case, media neutrality should protect the Authors' rights in the individual Articles to the extent those Articles are now presented individually, outside the collective work context, within the Databases' new media.

For the purpose at hand – determining whether the Authors' copyrights have been infringed – an analogy to an imaginary library may be instructive. Rather than maintaining intact editions of periodicals, the library would contain separate copies of each article. The library would store the folders containing the articles in a file room, indexed based on diverse criteria, and containing articles from vast numbers of editions. In response to patron requests, an inhumanly speedy librarian would search the room and provide copies of the articles matching patron-specified criteria.

Viewing this strange library, one could not, consistent with ordinary English usage, characterize the articles "as part of" a "revision" of the editions in which the articles first appeared.

The Publishers claim the protection of § 201(c) because users can manipulate the Databases to generate search results consisting entirely of articles from a particular periodical edition. By this logic, § 201(c) would cover the hypothetical library if, in response to a request, that library's expert staff assembled all of the articles from a particular periodical edition. However, the fact that a third party can manipulate a database to produce a noninfringing document does not mean the database is not infringing.

The Publishers finally invoke *Sony Corp. of America* v. *Universal City Studios, Inc.*, 464 U.S. 417, 78 L. Ed. 2d 574, 104 S. Ct. 774 (1984). That decision, however, does not genuinely aid their argument. *Sony* held that the "sale of copying equipment" does not constitute contributory infringement if the equipment is "capable of substantial noninfringing uses." The Publishers suggest that their Databases could be liable only under a theory of contributory infringement, based on end-user conduct, which the Authors did not plead. The Electronic Publishers, however, are not merely selling "equipment"; they are selling copies of the Articles. And, as we have explained, it is the copies themselves, without any manipulation by users, that fall outside the scope of the § 201(c) privilege.

IV

The Publishers warn that a ruling for the Authors will have "devastating" consequences. *Notwithstanding the dire predictions from some quarters* it hardly follows from today's decision that an injunction against the inclusion of these Articles in the Databases (much less all freelance articles in any databases) must issue. The parties (Authors and Publishers) may enter into an agreement allowing continued electronic reproduction of the Authors' works; they, and if necessary the courts and Congress, may draw on numerous models for distributing copyrighted works and remunerating authors for their distribution. In any event, speculation about future harms is no basis for this Court to shrink authorial rights Congress established in § 201(c). Agreeing with the Court of Appeals that the

Publishers are liable for infringement, we leave remedial issues open for initial airing and decision in the District Court.

We therefore affirm the judgment of the Court of Appeals.
It is so ordered.

STEVENS dissents.

DISSENT: STEVENS, Justice:

This case raises an issue of first impression concerning the meaning of the word "revision" as used in § 201(c) of the 1976 revision of the Copyright Act of 1909 (1976 Act). The first [question] is whether the electronic versions of the collective works created by the owners of the copyright in those works (Print Publishers or publishers) are "revisions" of those works within the meaning of 17 U.S.C. § 201(c). In my judgment they definitely are. The second is whether the aggregation by LEXIS/NEXIS and UMI (Electronic Databases) of the revisions with other editions of the same periodical or with other periodicals within a single database changes the equation. I think it does not. Finally, I will consider the implications of broader copyright policy for the issues presented in this case.

I

As the majority correctly observes, prior to 1976, an author's decision to publish her individual article as part of a collective work was a perilous one.

The majority is surely correct that the 1976 Act's new approach to collective works was an attempt to "'clarify and improve the . . . confused and frequently unfair legal situation'" that existed under the prior regime. It is also undoubtedly true that the drafters of the 1976 Act hoped to "enhance the author's position vis-a-vis the patron." It does not follow, however, that Congress' efforts to "preserve the author's copyright in a contribution," H. R. Rep. 122, can *only* be honored by a finding in favor of the respondent authors.

Indeed, the conclusion that the petitioners' actions were lawful is fully consistent with both of Congress' principal goals for collective works in the 1976 Act. First, neither the publication of the collective works by the Print Publishers, nor their transfer to the Electronic Databases had any impact on the legal status of the copyrights of the respondents' individual contributions. By virtue of the 1976 Act, respondents remain the owners of the copyright in their individual works.

Does this make sense?

Moreover, petitioners neither modified respondents' individual contributions nor, as I will show in Part II, published them in a "new anthology or an *entirely different magazine or other collective work.*"

II

Like the majority, I believe that the crucial inquiry is whether the article appears within the "context" of the original collective work. But this question simply raises the further issue of precisely how much "context" is enough.

The record indicates that what is sent from the New York Times to the Electronic Databases (with the exception of General Periodicals on Disc (GPO)) is simply a collection of ASCII text files representing the editorial content of the New York Times for a particular day. Each individual ASCII file contains the text of a single article as well as additional coding intended to help readers identify the context in which the article originally appeared and to facilitate database searches.

I see no compelling reason why a collection of files corresponding to a single edition of the New York Times, standing alone, cannot constitute a "revision" of that day's New York Times. After all, one of the hallmarks of copyright policy, as the majority recognizes, is the principle of media neutrality.

No one doubts that the New York Times has the right to reprint its issues in Braille, in a foreign language, or in microform, even though such revisions might look and feel quite different from the original. Such differences, however, would largely result from the different medium being employed. Similarly, the decision to convert the single collective work newspaper into a collection of individual ASCII files can be explained as little more than a decision that reflects the different nature of the electronic medium.

I think that a proper respect for media neutrality suggests that the New York Times, reproduced as a collection of individual ASCII files, should be treated as a "revision" of the original edition, as long as each article explicitly refers to the original collective work and as long as substantially the rest of the collective work is, at the same time, readily accessible to the reader of the individual file.

To see why an electronic version of the New York Times made up of a group of individual ACSCII article-files, standing alone, may be considered a § 201(c) revision, suppose that, instead of transmitting to NEXIS the articles making up a particular day's edition, the New York Times saves all of the individual files on a single floppy disk, labels that disk "New York Times, October 31, 2000," and sells copies of the disk to users as the electronic version of that day's New York Times. The disk reproduces the creative, editorial selection of that edition of the New York Times. The reader, after all, has at his finger tips substantially all of the relevant content of the October 31 edition of the collective work. Moreover, each individual article makes explicit reference to that selection by including tags that remind the reader that it is a part of the New York Times for October 31, 2000. Such a disk might well constitute "that particular collective work"; it would surely qualify as a "revision" of the original collective work. Yet all the features identified as essential by the majority and by the respondents would still be lacking. An individual looking at one of the articles contained on the disk would still see none of the original formatting context and would still be unable to flip the page.

Once one accepts the premise that a disk containing all the files from the October 31, 2000, New York Times can constitute a "revision," there is no reason to treat any differently the same set of files, stored in a folder on the hard disk of a computer at the New York Times. Thus, at least before it is republished by the Electronic Databases, the collection of files that the New York Times transmits to them constitutes a revision, in electronic form, of a particular edition of the New York Times.

III

The next question, then, is whether anything that the Electronic Databases do to the transmitted "revision" strips it of that status.

If my hypothetical October 31, 2000, floppy disk can be a revision, I do not see why the inclusion of other editions and other periodicals is any more significant than the placement of a single edition of the New York Times in a large public library or in a book store. Each individual file still reminds the reader that he is viewing "part of" a particular collective work. And the *entire* editorial content of that work still exists at the reader's fingertips.

It is true that, once the revision of the October 31, 2000, New York Times is surrounded by the additional content, it can be conceptualized as existing as part of an even larger collective work (*e.g.*, the entire NEXIS database). The question then becomes whether this ability to conceive of a revision of a collective work as existing within a larger "collective work" changes the status of the original revision. A microfilm of the New York Times for October 31, 2000, does not cease to be a revision of that individual collective work simply because it is stored on the same roll of film as other editions of the Times or on a library shelf containing hundreds of other microfilm periodicals. Similarly, the placement of our hypothetical electronic revision of the October 31, 2000, New York Times within a larger electronic database does nothing to alter either the nature of our original electronic revision or the relationship between that revision and the individual articles that exist as "part of" it.

Finally, the mere fact that an individual user may either view or print copies of individual articles stored on the Electronic Databases does not change the nature of the revisions contained within those databases. And to the extent that the user's decision to make a copy of a particular article violates the author's copyright in that article, such infringing third-party behavior should not be attributed to the database. See *Sony Corp. of America* v. *Universal City Studios, Inc.*, 464 U.S. 417, 434, 78 L. Ed. 2d 574, 104 S. Ct. 774 (1984).

In other words, in the Dissent's opinion the *Sony* analogy is a good one. Users can produce noninfringing versions from the databases and therefore the publishers should only be contributorily liable.

IV

The majority discounts the effect its decision will have on the availability of comprehensive digital databases, but I am not as confident. As petitioners' *amici* have persuasively argued, the difficulties of locating individual freelance authors and the potential of exposure to statutory damages may well have the effect of forcing electronic archives to purge freelance pieces from their databases.

Because it is likely that Congress did not consider the question raised by this case when drafting § 201(c), because I think the District Court's reading of that provision is reasonable and consistent with the statute's purposes, and because the principal goals of copyright policy are better served by that reading, I would reverse the judgment of the Court of Appeals. The majority is correct that we cannot know in advance the effects of today's decision on the comprehensiveness of electronic databases. We can be fairly certain, however, that it will provide little, if any, benefit to either authors or readers.

&

Since 1995, *The New York Times* requires authors to grant electronic rights to articles. Thus, despite the fact that this case reached the U.S. Supreme Court, its outcome has had little practical effect. However, the general question of how to determine if digital publication and use of collections of material are "revisions" of the earlier material is an interesting one that has proven troublesome to courts, who often seem to think that any involvement of computers or software in a work that would otherwise be considered a revision makes the work something new and different.

7. Trade Secrets

Introduction

A "trade secret" is information that is secret **and** has economic value by virtue of the fact that it is **kept** secret. Examples of the types of information that is commonly protected as trade secrets include customer lists, formulas for products, the contents of databases, and even software code itself.

One great advantage of using trade secrecy to protect intellectual property is that trade secrets can potentially last forever, unlike patents and copyrights. Patent protection now lasts for twenty years from the date the patent application is filed (although *design patents* expire fourteen years from the date the patent is issued); copyright protection, as we have seen in the previous chapter, now lasts for the life of the author plus seventy years or for a total of ninety-five years if the copyright is owned by a corporation.

Trade secrets do not require absolute secrecy. "Non-disclosure agreements" are used extensively to bar the recipients of trade secret information from disclosing the information. Non-disclosure agreements are simply another form of contract and, if properly executed, are binding on the individuals or entities agreeing to them.

Despite the fact that trade secrets do not require absolute secrecy, the owner of the trade secret must take reasonable steps to keep the secret in order to preserve the status of the information as a trade secret. That is, if the trade secret's owner is sufficiently careless in protecting the information, thus not taking precautions that make it reasonably clear that the information is a trade secret, the trade secret may be lost. For information in digital form, one clear indicator to the world at large that the protected information is a proprietary trade secret is encryption.

Note that the requirement that a trade secret have "economic value" by virtue of its being kept secret can be satisfied by almost any value. Even the "head start" that a company can expect to get over its competitors by forcing others to do the same start-up work is enough value.

The following case nicely illustrates the requirements of trade secrecy and how the courts apply the law on this topic.

Trade Secrets: Case 1

COCA-COLA BOTTLING COMPANY OF SHREVEPORT, INC., et al.,
Plaintiffs, v. The COCA-COLA COMPANY, a Delaware corporation, Defendant;
ALEXANDRIA COCA-COLA BOTTLING COMPANY, LTD., et al., Plaintiffs, v. The
COCA-COLA COMPANY, Defendant

Nos. 83-95 MMS, 83-120

UNITED STATES DISTRICT COURT FOR THE DISTRICT OF DELAWARE

107 F.R.D. 288; 1985 U.S. Dist. LEXIS 16644; 4 Fed. R. Serv. 3d (Callaghan) 1291;
227 U.S.P.Q. (BNA) 18

August 20, 1985

OPINION: SCHWARTZ, Judge:

The complete formula for Coca-Cola is one of the best-kept trade secrets in the world. Although most of the ingredients are public knowledge, the ingredient that gives Coca-Cola its distinctive taste is a secret combination of flavoring oils and ingredients known as "Merchandise 7X." The formula for Merchandise 7X has been tightly guarded since Coca-Cola was first invented and is known by only two persons within The Coca-Cola Company ("the Company"). The only written record of the secret formula is kept in a security vault at the Trust Company Bank in Atlanta, Georgia, which can only be opened upon a resolution from the Company's Board of Directors.

The impregnable barriers which the Company has erected to protect its valuable trade secret are now threatened by pretrial discovery requests in two connected cases before this Court. Plaintiffs in these lawsuits are bottlers of Coca-Cola products who seek declaratory, injunctive and monetary relief against the Company based upon allegations of breach of contract, violation of two 1921 Consent Decrees, trademark infringement, dilution of trademark value, and violation of federal antitrust laws, all of which allegedly occurred when the Company introduced diet Coke in 1982. Stripped to bare essentials, the plaintiffs' contention is that the Company is obligated to sell them the syrup used in the bottling of diet Coke under the terms of their existing contracts covering the syrup used in the bottling of Coca-Cola. The primary issue arising from this contention is whether the contractual term "Coca-Cola Bottler's Syrup" includes the syrup used to make diet Coke. Plaintiffs contend that in order to prevail on this issue, they need to discover the complete formula, including the secret ingredients, for Coca-Cola, as well as the complete formulae, also secret, for diet Coke and other Coca-Cola soft drinks. Accordingly, plaintiffs have filed a motion to compel production of the complete formulae under Fed. R. Civ. P. 37(a). Defendant, which has resisted disclosure of its secret formulae at every turn, contests the relevance of the complete formulae to the instant litigation and avers that disclosure of the secret formulae would cause great damage to the Company.

The issue squarely presented by plaintiffs' motion to compel is whether plaintiffs' need for the secret formulae outweighs defendant's need for protection of its trade secrets. In considering this dispute, I am well aware of the fact that disclosure of trade secrets in litigation, even with the use of an appropriate protective order, could "become by indirection the means of ruining an honest and profitable enterprise." Moreover, I am also aware that an order compelling disclosure of the Company's secret formulae could be a bludgeon in the hands of plaintiffs to force a favorable settlement. On the other hand, unless defendant is required to respond to plaintiffs' discovery, plaintiffs will be unable to learn whether defendant has done them a wrong. Except for a few privileged matters, nothing is sacred in civil litigation; even the legendary barriers erected by The Coca-Cola Company to keep its formulae from the world must fall if the formulae are needed to allow plaintiffs and the Court to determine the truth in these disputes.

I. Factual Background

Since the turn of the century, Coca-Cola has been produced in a two-stage process: the Company manufactures "Coca-Cola Bottler's Syrup" ("Bottler's Syrup") and sells it to bottlers, who add carbonated water to the syrup and place the resulting product in bottles and cans. In 1921, following litigation between bottler groups and the Company concerning their contracts for Bottler's Syrup, the Company entered into Consent Decrees which established certain contractual terms between the Company and its bottlers.

So the original contracts permitted the Company to pass along increases in sugar prices to bottlers.

Beginning in 1978, due to inflationary pressures and declining sales, the Company sought price relief from the existing price formula in its contracts with bottlers. After negotiations, most of the bottlers agreed to an amendment ("the 1978 Amendment") to their contracts in exchange for a clause requiring the Company to pass on any cost savings if the Company decided to substitute a lower cost sweetener for granulated sugar.

Now, the contracts, as amended for most bottlers, will pass along to the bottlers any savings incurred by using lower cost substitutes for sugar.

On July 8, 1982, the Company introduced diet Coke to the market with great fanfare. The name was chosen carefully and focused on the descriptive nature of the word "diet" and the tremendous market recognition of "Coke." The advertising emphasized the taste of the new cola and its relationship to Coke.

The ads for Diet Coke reassured customers about the similarity of its taste to regular Coke.

The public response to diet Coke has been phenomenal – in just three years, it has become the third largest selling soft drink in the United States and the best-selling diet soft drink in the world.

The introduction of diet Coke immediately gave rise to a dispute between Coke bottlers and the Company over what price bottlers must pay for diet Coke syrup. The Company took the position that diet Coke was not within the scope of the existing contracts, and a new contract term with flexible pricing would have to be developed. Many of the bottlers – both amended and unamended – believed that the Company was obligated to provide diet Coke under the terms of their existing Bottler's Contracts for Coca-Cola.

This dispute arose because the bottlers wanted Diet Coke syrup under the same terms as Coca-Cola Bottler's syrup, claiming that Diet Coke is just Coca-Cola with a substitute sweetener, presumably costing less than other sweeteners.

This dispute led to the filing of these lawsuits in early 1983.

Since that time, there have been two significant and widely-publicized changes in Coca-Cola. First, in April, 1985, the Company announced that it would stop producing

Coca-Cola under the existing formula ("old Coke") and immediately start producing "new" Coke, which, the Company proclaims, tastes even better than old Coke. According to the promotional materials that accompanied the announcement of new Coke, the formula for new Coke was derived from the research that led to the development of diet Coke. The secret ingredient in new Coke, called "7X-100," is different than the secret ingredient in old Coke, but it is still only known to a handful of individuals and is kept locked in a bank vault in Georgia.

The second significant change came when the Company, in response to consumer demand, announced in July, 1985, that it would bring back old Coke under the name "Coca-Cola Classic." The Company will now provide bottlers with two kinds of sugar-sweetened cola syrups – old Coke syrup, to be packaged as Coca-Cola Classic, and new Coke syrup. The Company has informed its bottlers that for the present, it will supply them with Coca-Cola Classic syrup under the terms of their contracts for Coca-Cola, but without prejudicing the Company's rights. As defendant's supplemental brief makes clear, the Company is ostensibly reserving the right to decide at a later time that the syrup for Coca-Cola Classic is not Coca-Cola Bottler's Syrup, even though the identical syrup was considered Coca-Cola Bottler's Syrup a few months ago. The merits of this remarkable position, however, are not before the Court at this time.

II. Plaintiffs' Motion to Compel

After extensive discovery, plaintiffs filed the instant motion that, in essence, seeks to compel the Company to produce the complete formulae, including secret ingredients, for Coca-Cola, diet Coke, caffeine free Coca-Cola, caffeine free diet Coke, TAB, and every experimental cola formula developed and tested by the Company for possible marketing under the Coca-Cola or Coke trademarks.

In support of their motion to compel, plaintiffs have contended that the secret formulae are relevant and necessary to prove their contentions and respond to defendant's argument that Coca-Cola and diet Coke are two different products. In response, the Company denies that the formulae are relevant and essential to resolve the central issues in these cases, and also contends that disclosure of these trade secrets is inappropriate at this stage of the litigation.

A. The Legal Standard Applicable to Discovery of Trade Secrets

It is well established that trade secrets are not absolutely privileged from discovery in litigation. In order to resist discovery of a trade secret, a party must first demonstrate by competent evidence that the information sought through discovery is a trade secret and that disclosure of the secret might be harmful. If this showing is made, "the burden shifts to the party seeking discovery to establish that the disclosure of trade secrets is relevant and necessary to the action." The level of necessity that must be shown is that the information must be necessary for the movant to prepare its case for trial, which includes proving its theories and rebutting its opponent's theories.

Once relevancy and need have been established, the Court must balance the need for the information against the injury that would ensue if disclosure is ordered. Because protective orders are available to limit the extent to which disclosure is made, the relevant injury to be weighed in the balance is not the injury that would be caused by public disclosure, but the injury that would result from disclosure under an appropriate protective order. In this regard, it is presumed that disclosure to a party who is not in competition with the holder of the trade secret will be less harmful than disclosure to a competitor.

The balance between the need for information and the need for protection against the injury caused by disclosure is tilted in favor of disclosure once relevance and necessity have been shown. As the Supreme Court has recognized, "orders forbidding any disclosure of trade secrets or confidential commercial information are rare." The reason for allowing the discovery of trade secrets whenever they are needed to advance the just adjudication of a lawsuit is simple: in the absence of an applicable privilege, "judicial inquiry should not be unduly hampered." As Judge Learned Hand stated in one of the earliest trade secret cases: "It is true that the result may be to compel the defendant to disclose [trade secrets], and that that may damage the defendant. . . . That is, however, an inevitable incident to any inquiry in such a case; unless the defendant may be made to answer, the plaintiff is deprived of its right to learn whether the defendant has done it a wrong."

B. The Coca-Cola Formulae Are Trade Secrets

First, the Court Asks Whether They Are Well-Kept Secrets

According to the Keller affidavit, the Company has taken every precaution to prevent disclosure of the formula for "Merchandise 7X," the secret ingredient in old Coke. The written version of the secret formula is kept in a security vault at the Trust Company Bank in Atlanta, and that vault can only be opened by a resolution from the Company's Board of Directors. It is the Company's policy that only two persons in the Company shall know the formula at any one time, and that only those persons may oversee the actual preparation of Merchandise 7X. The Company refuses to allow the identity of those persons to be disclosed or to allow those persons to fly on the same airplane at the same time. The same precautions are taken regarding the secret formulae of the Company's other cola drinks – diet Coke, caffeine free diet Coke, TAB, caffeine free TAB, and caffeine free Coca-Cola.

Second, the Court Asks Whether They Have Economic Value

The Keller affidavit further states that these secret formulae are highly valued assets of the Company and have never been disclosed to persons outside the Company. As an indication of the value the Company places on its secret formulae, Keller avers that the Company elected to forego producing Coca-Cola in India, a potential market of 550 million persons, because the Indian government required the Company to disclose the secret formula for Coca-Cola as a condition of doing business there. The affidavit concludes by stating that because of intense competition in the soft drink industry, the disclosure of any information reflecting the formulae or the Company's research and development would be extremely damaging to the Company.

Accordingly, I find that defendant's secret formulae are trade secrets and subject to the maximum protection that the law, as set forth above, allows.

C. Relevance and Necessity of the Formulae

Plaintiffs contend that discovery of these secret formulae is required because they are relevant and necessary to the presentation of plaintiffs' case.

How relevant and important to the litigation are the secret ingredients?

The plaintiffs say that Coca-Cola and Diet Coke are two versions of the same thing, with only the sweetener being different. The Company says they are different products.

Plaintiffs contend that the complete formulae for diet Coke and Coca-Cola would be relevant to rebut this defense by showing that the two colas share common attributes and that any differences between the two are insignificant and merely reflect attempts to achieve taste identity. With the introduction of new Coke, plaintiffs argue that because new Coke was derived in part from the secret formula for diet Coke, it may be true that new Coke is more like diet Coke than new Coke is like old Coke. In response, defendant argues that except for the difference in sweeteners, ingredient similarities and differences are not relevant to the determination of whether diet Coke and Coca-Cola are the same product. Instead, defendant relies upon the difference in taste,

This, after the Company advertised widely the allegedly similar taste!

different essential characteristics of the beverages, different consumer markets for the beverages, and different consumer perceptions of the beverages.

Defendant's response is unavailing. When this Court previously addressed the merits of this litigation in the context of a motion for preliminary injunction, the first issue addressed was whether Coke and diet Coke are two versions of the same product. Although the parties' contentions have evolved in the intervening two years, the issue of product identity remains a part of these lawsuits. Although defendant has attempted to define the issues so that the only relevant ingredient is the sweetener, all the ingredients are relevant to determine whether the two colas are the same product. In fact, the secret ingredients may be the most relevant ones because the secret ingredients are what gives these drinks their distinctive tastes.

Plaintiffs could use the secret formulae to prove one of several product identity theories. An analysis of the secret ingredients in diet Coke and old Coke might show that diet Coke was designed to taste as much like old Coke as a low calorie cola could, and that any differences in secret ingredients reflect defendant's attempts to achieve taste identity. Alternatively, plaintiffs might use the secret formulae for diet Coke, old Coke, and new Coke in the following way: The syrup for old Coke and new Coke have both been sold as Coca-Cola Bottler's Syrup by the Company. It has been publicly disclosed, however, that the formula for new Coke was derived from the research used for diet Coke. If plaintiffs, armed with the complete formulae, can show that diet Coke is very similar to new Coke, and that diet Coke is more like new Coke than new Coke is like old Coke, that fact could tend to show that diet Coke is within the range of syrups that have been sold as Coca-Cola Bottler's Syrup.

These examples, based only on speculation as to what plaintiffs might learn through discovery, illustrate that the complete formulae for diet Coke, old Coca-Cola, and new Coca-Cola are relevant to one of the primary issues in this litigation – product identity. The complete formulae, once known, will tend to make a disputed fact more (or less) likely: that, for purposes of this litigation, diet Coke syrup is Bottler's Syrup.

Finally, plaintiffs seek the formulae and test data for experimental colas which were developed and tested by the Company but never marketed. To the extent that plaintiffs seek the formulae and related information for *low-calorie* colas developed by the Company that were based on the Coke formula or were directly or indirectly related to the development of diet Coke, the information they seek is relevant. This information relates to the motivations and intent of the Company in its development of diet Coke, and may show whether, as defendant has contended through an expert, the Company could have made a diet cola that tastes more like regular Coke than does diet Coke. Comparison of the experimental low-calorie colas with diet Coke and regular Coke would show why the Company chose the diet Coke formula over other available alternatives. If the Company chose the formula most like Coke, that tends to show the Company's intent to have diet Coke taste just like Coke. In addition, plaintiffs have discovered that the Company tested a low-calorie cola in 1978, which bears on the intent and understanding of the Company in signing the 1978 Amendment. The formula of that cola is certainly relevant.

Necessity of Discovery of This Information

As in most disputes over the discoverability of trade secrets, the necessity of the discovery of the complete formulae follows logically from the determination that the formulae are relevant. Plaintiffs need the complete formulae in order to address the product identity issue by comparing the ingredients of the various soft drinks involved. Plaintiffs cannot respond to the assertions of defendant's experts that diet Coke and Coca-Cola are two products unless plaintiffs' experts can analyze the complete formulae and explain why the products are the same.

In addition, plaintiffs need the complete formulae in order to explore on cross-examination the bases for the opinions of Company witnesses that Coca-Cola and diet Coke are two separate products. Moreover, the formula information is not available from any other source, and no adequate substitute exists for this information. It follows that discovery of the complete formulae is necessary.

Need Balanced Against Harm

The final part of the test for discoverability of trade secrets is to balance the need for disclosure against the harm that would ensue from disclosure. The potential harm that would come from public disclosure of the formulae for old Coke, new Coke, diet Coke, and caffeine free Coke is great but virtually all of that harm can be eliminated with stringent protective orders and other safeguards. Because plaintiffs are Coca-Cola bottlers, they will have an incentive to keep the formulae secret. The likelihood of harm is less than if defendant's trade secrets were disclosed in litigation to competitors. The potential for harm from protected disclosure of the formulae for old Coke, new Coke, diet Coke, and caffeine free Coke is outweighed by the plaintiffs' need for the information.

In sum, the product identity issue is important in these two cases, and analyses of the complete formulae will be a significant part of the proof on that issue. Plaintiffs' need for this information outweighs the harm that disclosure under protective order would cause. Disclosure will be ordered.

IV. Conclusion

It has been held that defendant must disclose its complete formulae, including secret ingredients, for diet Coke, old Coke, new Coke, caffeine free Coke, and certain experimental low calorie colas. Given the proprietary nature of the formula information, however, a more stringent protective order than the one currently in effect is warranted to prevent public disclosure of the formulae. For example, it may be advisable to limit the disclosure of the formulae to plaintiffs' trial counsel and independent experts. *Because the parties have not addressed what additional protective measures would be satisfactory, the Court will not enter a new protective order at this time. Instead, the parties shall negotiate a protective order that both allows access to information and prevents disclosure of trade secrets. The parties shall submit that order within twenty days.*

~

In an online setting, creating valid non-disclosure agreements raises certain issues related to contract law. For example, in cyberspace, it is not as easy to establish the identity of the person "signing" a non-disclosure form, although digital signatures *should* satisfy evidentiary requirements. It might perhaps be possible to create a valid non-disclosure agreement online merely by asking a person to agree to the terms by "clicking" on a button on a web page.

While trade secrecy has its advantages as a form of intellectual property protection, it does not come without dangers, the chief of which is that trade secrets can be lost through:

- independent discovery of the secret by another person,
- reverse engineering of a product sold in the market, or
- unrestricted disclosure to people not under an obligation of confidentiality. Note that this unrestricted disclosure might be by *anyone*, not just by the secret's owner.

Thus, posting trade secret information on the Net to persons not under an obligation of confidentiality will destroy trade secret protection if people do not or should not know the information is a trade secret. The problem, of course, is that in cyberspace it is possible for someone to post to the Net anonymously, creating a "judgment proof" potential defendant.

If a product is *licensed*, rather than sold, and the license includes a confidentiality requirement and, perhaps, a prohibition on reverse engineering, trade secret protection is *not* waived. Thus, reverse engineering by the person who licensed the product does not destroy trade secret status for the information because that person is under an obligation of non-disclosure.

Once trade secret protection is lost the trade secret cannot be protected by patent, assuming it is patentable in the first place. The reason for this is that the underlying motive for all protection of intellectual property is a dual one. Article I § 8 of the U.S. Constitution gives Congress the power to "promote the Progress of Science and useful Arts, by securing for *limited* Times to Authors and Inventors the exclusive Right to their respective Writings and Discoveries." Courts have therefore held that granting patent protection to something that had already been protected as a trade secret would undermine the intent of the Constitution and Congress by unfairly extending the "limited time" for which the information should be protected. Besides, patents must be applied for within a year after the invention is first in public use, or on sale in the United States, or patented or disclosed in print anywhere else.

Given the limited life span of most patentable electronic or software products, why would anyone choose trade secret protection versus patent protection? Perhaps because with patented products or processes, "*new and useful improvements*" on a product can be separately patented themselves, and can then prevent the original patent owner from developing them. Trade secret information cannot be used as the basis of a patentable improvement on that information since obtaining a patent requires public disclosure of the patented material or process and that would make an improver guilty of misappropriation of the trade secret.

Acquiring information by improper means is called "misappropriation." The fact that the secret *could* have been discovered legitimately does not make improper acquisition permissible. Note that improper *use* of a trade secret, not merely disclosure, is also misappropriation. Only the trade secret's owner has the right to use the trade secret.

Thus, if a person uses a trade secret to develop some new product or process that is totally unrelated to the original trade secret, that is still misappropriation. Misappropriation of a trade secret makes a person liable to the trade secret's owner for damages, which are defined as the trade secret's owner's actual losses plus any profits by the misappropriator, to the extent the two things are different. If the court finds the misappropriation was "willful" penalties can be up to twice actual damages, plus attorney fees.

Courts attempt to protect trade secrets that might be revealed in the course of litigation in a number of ways. These include protective orders during discovery (as in the *Coca-Cola* case), in-camera hearings, sealing records of the litigation, and ordering all those participating not to disclose the trade secret without the court's approval.

Trade Secrets: Case 2

MAI SYSTEMS CORPORATION, a Delaware corporation, Plaintiff-Appellee, v. PEAK COMPUTER, INC., a California corporation; VINCENT CHIECHI, an individual; ERIC FRANCIS, an individual, Defendants-Appellants.

No. 92-55363, No. 93-55106

UNITED STATES COURT OF APPEALS FOR THE NINTH CIRCUIT

991 F.2d 511; 1993 U.S. App. LEXIS 7522; 26 U.S.P.Q.2D (BNA) 1458; Copy. L. Rep. (CCH) P27,096; 93 Cal. Daily Op. Service 2596; 93 Daily Journal DAR 4604

June 4, 1992, Argued, Submitted, Pasadena, California; February 24, 1993 *, Submitted

*The panel unanimously finds this case suitable for decision without oral argument. Fed. R. App. P. 34(a); Ninth Circuit Rule 3(f).

April 7, 1993, Filed

OPINION: BRUNETTI, Judge:

I. Facts

MAI Systems Corp., until recently, manufactured computers and designed software to run those computers. The company continues to service its computers and the software necessary to operate the computers. MAI software includes operating system software, which is necessary to run any other program on the computer.

Peak Computer, Inc. is a company organized in 1990 that maintains computer systems for its clients. Peak maintains MAI computers for more than one hundred clients in Southern California. This accounts for between fifty and seventy percent of Peak's business.

Peak's service of MAI computers includes routine maintenance and emergency repairs. Malfunctions often are related to the failure of circuit boards inside the computers, and it may be necessary for a Peak technician to operate the computer and its operating system software in order to service the machine.

In August, 1991, Eric Francis left his job as customer service manager at MAI and joined Peak. Three other MAI employees joined Peak a short time later. Some businesses that had been using MAI to service their computers switched to Peak after learning of Francis's move.

[Sections II– IV are omitted as they do not pertain to Trade Secret Misappropriation.]

V. Misappropriation of Trade Secrets

The district court granted summary judgment in favor of MAI on its misappropriation of trade secrets claims and issued a permanent injunction against Peak on these claims. The permanent injunction prohibits Peak from "misappropriating, using in any manner in their business, including advertising connected therewith, and/or disclosing to others MAI's trade secrets," including: (1) MAI Customer Database; (2) MAI Field Information Bulletins ("FIB"); and, (3) MAI software.

A. Customer Database

The Court asks first if the Database is a Trade Secret.

California has adopted the Uniform Trade Secrets Act ("UTSA") which codifies the basic principles of common law trade secret protection. To establish a violation under the UTSA, it must be shown that a defendant has been unjustly enriched by the improper appropriation, use or disclosure of a "trade secret."

Peak argues both that the MAI Customer Database is not a "trade secret," and that even if it is a trade secret, that Peak did not "misappropriate" it.

The UTSA defines a "trade secret" as:

information, including a formula, pattern, compilation, program, device, method, technique, or process, that:

(1) Derives independent economic value, actual or potential, from not being generally known to the public or to other persons who can obtain economic value from its disclosure or use; and
(2) Is the subject of efforts that are reasonable under the circumstances to maintain its secrecy.

MAI contends its Customer Database is a valuable collection of data assembled over many years that allows MAI to tailor its service contracts and pricing to the unique needs of its customers and constitutes a trade secret.

We agree that the Customer Database qualifies as a trade secret. The Customer Database has potential economic value because it allows a competitor like Peak to direct its sales efforts to those potential customers that are already using the MAI computer system. Further, MAI took reasonable steps to insure the secrecy to this information as required by the UTSA. MAI required its employees to sign confidentiality agreements respecting its trade secrets, including the Customer Database. Thus, under the UTSA, the MAI Customer Database constitutes a trade secret.

The Court then asks if Peak misappropriated the trade secret.

We also agree with MAI that the record before the district court on summary judgment establishes that Peak misappropriated the Customer Database.

"Misappropriation" is defined under the UTSA as:

(1) Acquisition of a trade secret of another by a person who knows or has reason to know that the trade secret was acquired by improper means; or
(2) Disclosure or use of a trade secret of another without express or implied consent by a person who:
  (A) Used improper means to acquire knowledge of the trade secret; or
  (B) At the time of disclosure or use, knew or had reason to know that his or her knowledge of the trade secret was: (i) Derived from or through a person who had utilized improper means to acquire it; (ii) Acquired under circumstances giving rise to a duty to maintain its secrecy or limit its use; or (iii) Derived from or through a person who owed a duty to the person seeking relief to maintain its secrecy or limit its use; or
  (C) Before a material change of his or her position knew or had reason to know that it was a trade secret and that knowledge of it had been acquired by accident or by mistake.

Peak contends that Francis never physically took any portion of MAI's customer database and that neither Francis nor anyone under his direction put information he had obtained from working at MAI in the Peak database. However, to find misappropriation under the UTSA, this need not be established.

Note that merely announcing that a particular employee has joined a competing firm is not "solicitation" and therefore not misappropriation. But here the Peak employee actually telephoned and visited customers to convince them to switch to Peak.

These actions constituted solicitation and misappropriation under the UTSA definition. We affirm the district court's grant of summary judgment in favor of MAI on its claim that Peak misappropriated its Customer Database and affirm the permanent injunction as it relates to this issue.

B. Field Information Bulletins

The Court next asks if the Field Information Bulletins are trade secrets.

MAI argues summary judgment was properly granted on its claim of misappropriation of the FIBs because the FIBs are a valuable trade secret of MAI and the evidence showed that the FIBs were being used by Peak to operate a business competing unfairly with MAI.

We agree that the FIBs constitute trade secrets. It is uncontroverted that they contain technical data developed by MAI to aid in the repair and servicing of MAI computers, and that MAI has taken reasonable steps to insure that the FIBs are not generally known to the public.

Did Peak misappropriate the secret?

However, whether Peak has misappropriated the FIBs remains a genuine issue of material fact. The only evidence introduced by MAI to establish Peak's use of the FIBs is Peak's advertisements claiming that "Peak's system specialists are specifically trained on the latest hardware releases on MAI Basic Four." MAI asserts that if Peak did not use FIBs that this claim would have to be false. However, Weiner and Boulanger testified in their depositions that they had never seen a FIB at Peak. Similarly, Boulanger, Robert Pratt and Michael McIntosh each testified that they did not have any FIB information when they left MAI. Weighing this evidence in the light most favorable to Peak, whether Peak used any of the FIBs remains a genuine issue of material fact, and the district court's grant of summary judgment on this claim of trade secret misappropriation is reversed and the permanent injunction is vacated as it relates to this issue.

> **Summary judgment is proper when no material issues of fact are in dispute. Here Peak says MAI would have had to use the FIBs to train its technicians maintaining MAI software; Peak denies this. Since this remains an issue of fact, Peak should have opportunity to take the question to a jury.**

C. Software

Is the software itself a trade secret?

MAI contends the district court properly granted summary judgment on its claim of misappropriation of software because its software constitutes valuable unpublished works that allow its machines to be maintained. MAI argues that Peak misappropriated the software by loading it into the RAM.

We recognize that computer software can qualify for trade secret protection under the UTSA. However, a plaintiff who seeks relief for misappropriation of trade secrets must identify the trade secrets and carry the burden of showing that they exist.

Here, while MAI asserts that it has trade secrets in its diagnostic software and operating system, and that its licensing agreements constitute reasonable efforts to maintain their secrecy, MAI does not specifically identify these trade secrets. Since the trade secrets are not specifically identified, we cannot determine whether Peak has misappropriated any trade secrets by running the MAI operating software and/or diagnostic software in maintaining MAI systems for its customers, and *we reverse the district court's grant of summary judgment in favor of MAI on its claim that Peak misappropriated trade secrets in its computer software and vacate the permanent injunction as it relates to this issue.*

> **So merely claiming that software *contains* trade secrets is not sufficiently specific to receive full protection under the law.**

8. Trademarks

Introduction

Products have trademarks. *Services* have service marks. The two will generally be referred to in this chapter generically as "trademarks," but it is important to be aware of the distinction.

Trademarks can be almost anything, including:

- Words or phrases
- Pictures and symbols (like the Nike "swoosh")
- Numerals and letters (MCI)
- Abbreviations and nicknames (Coke)
- Colors (Owens Corning has a trademark on the pink color of its fiberglass insulation)
- Sounds and music
- Domain names
- Smells (as is true of a particular scented yarn)
- Buildings themselves (the Photomat "huts" for example)

Trademarks are easy to acquire. Simply select a mark and then use it in commerce. Ownership does not begin until the mark is used in commerce. However, application for a registration with the Patent and Trademark Office (PTO) can be made (and protection can begin) under an "Intent to Use" application for six-month intervals up to a maximum of thirty-six months. At some point during that time, a "Statement of Use" must be filed with the PTO, establishing that the mark has actually been used in commerce.

"Use in commerce" begins at the time the public first has a chance to associate the goods with the mark. Usually, this is when the goods are shipped or the services are first performed. Use in *interstate* commerce is required for federal, as opposed to state, registration, but this is easily established. Simply having customers from out of state is sufficient, and when the commerce is on the Net that is almost always the case.

The owner of a trademark has the exclusive right to use the mark on particular kinds of goods or services, but only in a specific market. Thus, the owner of a trademark for a restaurant can prevent others in the same (or a related) business from using the mark, but cannot prevent someone from using the same mark for an unrelated product or service, such as, say, to identify a type of spark plug. The goal is to give consumers a reliable indicator of source (and quality).

Online use of marks today is ubiquitous. Commercial web pages advertise products and services that are identified by trademarks. Domain names often include trademarks, and can in fact be trademarks themselves.

Some trademarks are stronger (more protected) than others. There is a hierarchy of strength (in descending order):

- Fanciful marks, which are simply invented, are the most protected (such as *Exxon*);
- Arbitrary marks, which are words that have meaning but one that is not obviously related to the product (such as *Realistic* for a brand of radios or *Comet* for powdered cleanser);
- Suggestive marks, which suggest a feature of the product but require at least some imagination, thought, and perception to reach a conclusion as to the nature of the goods (such as *Nair* for a depilatory);
- Descriptive marks, which merely describe a feature of the product or service (such as *Compuquik* for a company making high-performance software, or *One Hour Photo*, for a photo development service).

Generic "common" names for the goods or services they identify are not protected as trademarks for those goods or services but may be used as marks for other types of goods or services. So, while *soap* could not be used as a mark for soap itself, it could be used as a mark for, perhaps, a restaurant (and would probably be classified as an arbitrary mark).

Descriptive marks can become protected if it can be proven that they have acquired a "secondary meaning" to the public, that is, that they have become closely associated with the particular product or service.

NOTE: Establishing use in commerce for "tangible goods" requires placing the mark directly on the goods. Thus, mere online advertising of tangible goods does not in itself generate a registerable trademark right (although advertising does satisfy requirements for service mark registration if the services have actually been performed). If software is distributed on a compact disk, the mark should appear on the disk itself – or at least the packaging. If a software product is distributed via download, the mark should be used to identify the product online and it is wise to encode the mark in the software itself.

In the United States (and in the United Kingdom) ownership of a mark does not require registration. Ownership, as noted above, vests in the first person who uses the mark in commerce on goods or services. However, registration is simple (it can be done online), reasonably inexpensive, and does provide some advantages. Filing an application for registration for a trademark gives the registrant a presumption of being the senior user nationwide as of the date the application is filed. The owner of a registered mark can also bring an infringement action in federal court and potentially be awarded treble damages, attorneys' fees, and even destruction of infringing goods.

When using a trademark, notice that it *is*, in fact, a trademark is not required. However, lack of notice may mean that the owner will not be awarded damages in an action for infringement. A trademark notice consists of the use of the "TM" superscript beside the mark (or "SM" for service marks). If the mark is registered these are replaced by the use of the ® symbol.

If a mark is used multiple times in the same advertisement or document, notice is not required to appear each time the mark is used. Providing notice the first time the mark appears is sufficient. So, on a website, providing notice the first time a visitor to the site sees the mark will be enough.

Trademark ownership rights may be lost if the mark becomes "generic." A product's once strong mark can become generic if it comes to be the term by which the general type of product to which it belongs is identified. The question is what does the consumer understand by the term. *Thermos* was once a trademark for a particular brand of insulated beverage container but is now commonly used to identify all such containers and has become a generic term. *Rollerblades* as a trademark for a brand of in-line roller skates may be in danger of losing its distinctiveness and becoming generic. No one calls a friend and suggests the friend bring along her "in-line skates" for the day. Even *Xerox* may have become generic. Some years ago, the company engaged in an extensive media advertising campaign to remind people that "it's not a xerox copy, it's a photo copy made on a *Xerox* brand copying machine." The effectiveness of the campaign is questionable as the term "xerox" now appears in many dictionaries as a word meaning "copy."

It is ironic that the strong association of a mark with the product in the mind of the public can lead to the loss of the mark. A trademark's owner *wants* the public to think of his or her brand of product when they hear or see the mark, but if the product becomes so dominant that all other similar products begin to be referred to by use of the mark, the trademark owner may lose it.

Trademarks can also be abandoned. This can occur through simply not renewing a mark's registration (which is required every ten years). Abandonment of a mark can also be inferred if the trademark owner discontinues use of the mark and has no intent to resume use, or if the trademark owner does not carefully control licensed use of the mark (so fast food franchises exercise very tight quality controls on their franchise holders).

When trademark infringement is alleged, the question is whether or not the alleged infringing use creates a likelihood of confusion regarding the source of the product or service. In analyzing this question courts generally look at a set of factors, most often called the "Polaroid factors" from a case involving the *Polaroid* company. The factors are:

1. strength of the allegedly infringed mark
2. similarity of the allegedly infringing mark
3. proximity of the products and services, both in terms of markets and geography
4. evidence of actual consumer confusion
5. defendant's good or bad faith in using the mark
6. quality of the defendant's product
7. sophistication of the buyers (how careful consumers are when buying this type of product)

The following four cases illustrate the principles of trademark law.

Trademarks: Case 1

Jordache Enterprises, Inc., Plaintiff-Appellant, v. Hogg Wyld, Ltd., Susan Duran, Marsha Stafford and Oink, Inc., Defendants-Appellees

No. 85-2254

UNITED STATES COURT OF APPEALS FOR THE TENTH CIRCUIT

828 F.2d 1482; 1987 U.S. App. LEXIS 12220; 4 U.S.P.Q.2D (BNA) 1216; 92 A.L.R.
Fed. 1

September 14, 1987, Filed

OPINION: TACHA, Judge:

This case, a trademark infringement action brought against a manufacturer that identifies its blue jeans for larger women with a smiling pig and the word "Lardashe" on the seat of the pants, reminds us that "you can't make a silk purse out of a sow's ear." Appellant Jordache Enterprises, Inc., alleges error in a district court decision finding no likelihood of confusion between the Jordache and Lardashe trademarks and finding no violation of New Mexico's antidilution statute. We affirm.

Appellant, a New York corporation formed by three immigrant brothers in 1978, is the fourth largest blue jeans manufacturer in the United States. It produces and markets all types of apparel for men, women, and children, the principal product being designer blue jeans. Most items are identified by one of appellant's several registered trademarks, including the word "Jordache" printed in block letters, the word "Jordache" printed in block letters and superimposed over a drawing of a horse's head, and a drawing of a horse's head alone. Some products are identified by the word "Jordache" written in script lettering, a mark which has not been registered.

An intensive advertising campaign has created great customer awareness of Jordache products. In 1984, for example, appellant spent about thirty million dollars annually on television, radio, newspaper, and magazine advertisements and other promotional efforts. The message of this advertising has been that Jordache jeans convey "the look of the good life." Jordache jeans are now sold in retail outlets throughout the world.

Appellant has licensed Shaker Sport to manufacture and market Jordache jeans for larger women. Shaker Sport has expended substantial resources in advertising these jeans, and it had sold between 33,000 and 60,000 pairs by 1985.

"Between 33,000 and 60,000 pairs"? How come they don't know the exact number?

Perhaps these people went to work for the U.S. Mint in the following year and are the ones mentioned in the *Mesaros* case who didn't know when exactly they had filled their last order for Statue of Liberty coins.

In 1984, appellees Marsha Stafford and Susan Duran formed Hogg Wyld, Ltd., now Oink, Inc., for the purpose of marketing designer blue jeans for larger women. In an operation conducted out of their homes in New Mexico, the two women designed a product, selected a manufacturer, and ultimately sold over 1,000 pairs of jeans. Sales were limited to specialty shops in several southwestern states and to acquaintances or others who heard of the product. The women have not directly advertised their jeans, although several retailers have done so.

The name of the Oink, Inc. blue jeans gave rise to this suit. Names suggested at one time or another for the jeans by Stafford, Duran, or others, included "Thunder Thighs," "Buffalo Buns," "Seambusters," "Rino Asirus," "Hippo Hoggers," "Vidal Sowsoon," and "Calvin Swine." Other names and marks were suggested as a take-off on Stafford's childhood nickname, "lardass." This nickname inspired ideas such as "Wiseashe" with a picture of an owl, "Dumbashe" with a picture of a donkey, "Horsesashe" with a picture of a horse, and "Helium Ash" with a picture of a balloon. The women decided to name their jeans "Lardashe."

Appellant first became aware of Lardashe jeans after an Albuquerque TV station broadcast a news segment, which was also broadcast nationally by NBC, highlighting the new product. Jordache brought suit against Stafford, Duran, and their corporation, alleging trademark infringement in violation of the Lanham Trademark Act, 15 U.S.C. §§ 1051-1127, the New Mexico Trademark Act, N.M. Stat. Ann. §§ 57-3-1 to -14 (1987), and common law. The district court, after a three-day bench trial, held that no trademark infringement had occurred on any of the alternative claims. *Jordache Enters. v. Hogg Wyld, Ltd.*, 625 F. Supp. 48 (D.N.M. 1985). Jordache now appeals to this court.

I.

The Lanham Act prohibits the unauthorized use of a reproduction, copy, or imitation of a registered trademark in a way that "is likely to cause confusion" with the registered mark. "Confusion occurs when consumers make an incorrect mental association between the involved commercial products or their producers." This court has identified several factors, originally set forth in Restatement of Torts § 729 (1938), that are relevant to whether there is a likelihood of confusion between two marks:

  (a) the degree of similarity between the designation and the trade-mark or trade name in
   (i) appearance;
   (ii) pronunciation of the words used;
   (iii) verbal translation of the pictures or designs involved;
   (iv) suggestion;
  (b) the intent of the actor in adopting the designation;
  (c) the relation in use and manner of marketing between the goods or services marketed by the actor and those marketed by the other;
  (d) the degree of care likely to be exercised by purchasers.

This list is not exhaustive. All of the factors are interrelated, and no one factor is dispositive. The party alleging infringement has the burden of proving likelihood of confusion.

The district court examined these factors and concluded that there is no likelihood of confusion between the Jordache trademark and the Lardashe trademark. Appellant contends that the district court erred as a matter of law in its consideration of several of the factors and that, in any event, the court's findings are clearly erroneous.

A.

The similarity between the marks in appearance, pronunciation of the words used, translation of the designs used, and suggestion or meaning is the first factor to consider in determining whether there is a likelihood of confusion.

Trademarks may be confusingly similar if they suggest the same idea or meaning. For example, this court has held that a trademark consisting of an overflowing stein with the words "Brew Nuts" conveys the same meaning as a trademark consisting of the words "Beer Nuts." *Beer Nuts II*, 805 F.2d at 926. The district court in the present case found that "the two marks suggest dissimilar images or concepts." Appellant alleges that the district court erred as a matter of law in its application of this factor by attributing a meaning of "class" or "style" to the Jordache mark. According to appellant, since the word "Jordache" has no inherent meaning, the district court necessarily must have relied upon a legally incorrect understanding of "suggestion" or "meaning" in order to find no similarity between the marks.

This argument mischaracterizes the findings of the district court. The court found the *words* "Jordache" and "Lardashe" similar, but not the horse and pig *designs*. The court did not find the word "Jordache" has an inherent meaning. Rather the "meaning" described by the court referred to the "relatively subtle and refined" horse design that is employed in the Jordache trademarks. The district court did not attach an improper "meaning" to the Jordache marks.

Our review of the evidence shows that the marks, and their suggested images, are obviously different. Many of the Jordache jeans are identified by a small brown patch with the word "Jordache" written in white in block letters with a gold horse's head superimposed over the lettering. In other instances, the patch is white with blue block lettering and no horse. Sometimes "Jordache" is written in script or only the horse's head is used. In contrast, the Lardashe jeans have a large, brightly colored pig head and two hooves, giving the appearance that a pig is peering over the back pocket. The word "Lardashe" is written in script beneath the pig's head, below which is an upside down embroidered heart. We agree with the district court that the "striking, brightly colored, and far from subtle" pig design is "humorous, or 'cute,' or facetious." Thus, while the similarity of the words used in the mark would support an inference of likelihood of confusion, we agree with the district court's finding that the striking dissimilarities in the designs used in the marks greatly outweigh any similarities.

B.

The intent of a party in selecting a trademark is another factor in determining whether there is a likelihood of confusion.

The "deliberate adoption of a similar mark may lead to an inference of intent to pass off goods as those of another which in turn supports a finding of likelihood of confusion." "The proper focus is whether defendant had the intent to derive benefit from the reputation or goodwill of plaintiff." A conscious choice of a mark similar to a mark already established in the marketplace usually supports a finding of a likelihood of confusion "because the court presumes that [the alleged infringer] 'can accomplish his purpose: that is, that the public will be deceived.'"

Given the unlimited number of possible names and symbols that could serve as a trademark, it is understandable that a court generally presumes one who chooses a mark similar to an existing mark intends to confuse the public. However, where a party chooses a mark as a parody of an existing mark, the intent is not necessarily to confuse the public but rather to amuse.

In one sense, a parody is an attempt "to derive benefit from the reputation" of the owner of the mark, if only because no parody could be made without the initial mark. The benefit to the one making the parody, however, arises from the humorous association, not from public confusion as to the source of the marks. A parody relies upon a difference from the original mark, presumably a humorous difference, in order to produce its desired effect.

As McCarthy writes, "No one likes to be the butt of a joke, not even a trademark. But the requirement of trademark law is that a likely confusion of source, sponsorship or affiliation must be proven, which is not the same thing as a 'right' not to be made fun of."

An intent to parody is not an intent to confuse the public.

The district court found the appellee's explanation for their adoption of the Lardashe mark not credible.[1] The court found that their real intent was to parody Jordache. 625 F. Supp. at 52. After examining the record, we hold the district court's findings are not clearly erroneous. We therefore reject appellant's challenge to the district court's refusal to infer a wrongful intent.

C.

Another factor to be considered in determining whether there is a likelihood of confusion is "the degree of care likely to be exercised by purchasers." *Beer Nuts II*, 805 F.2d at 925. The district court found that customers are likely to exercise a high degree of care in purchasing clothing that costs between fifteen and sixty dollars. The district court's finding of a high degree of care is not clearly erroneous.

D.

Obviously, the best evidence of a likelihood of confusion in the marketplace is actual confusion. *Standard Oil Co. v. Standard Oil Co.*, 252 F.2d 65, 74 (10th Cir. 1958). Appellant offered evidence that it believed showed actual confusion, but the district court did not find this evidence compelling. Appellant challenges the court's findings.

Paul Ornstein, Executive Vice President of Shaker Sports, testified that he was called by associates who asked whether Lardashe jeans were affiliated with Jordache. The district court ruled that this testimony was hearsay and that even if it was admissible, it was not

---

[1] Stafford and Duran testified at trial that they had not heard of Jordache jeans when they selected the Lardashe name. Stafford explained that "Lardashe" was meant to be a more polite version of "lardass," her childhood nickname. She testified to the meaning of "ashe" as an alternative spelling by saying that "if you'll look in your Bible, it's the goddess of fertility. It's the goddess of womanhood which I've known about for a long time and which meant quite a bit to me." Further testimony revealed that Stafford was referring to several goddesses, but was unable to locate any of them in the Bible. Finally, Stafford testified that the "e" at the end of "Lardashe" is meant to appear like a pig's tail when the word is written in script.

"In cases where defendant concocts an elaborately fantastic and strained scenario of how it 'coincidentally' hit upon its symbol, judges are not amused when asked to swallow fantastic fabrications about coincidental, unknowing usage." In one case, *Sears, Roebuck, & Co.*, the owner of the trademark "SEARS" for its Sears Financial Network sued an individual who had established a corporation called Sears Financial Services. The defendant explained how he had chosen that particular name: "Realizing that the Corporation needed a name, I began considering my options. I had long ago been smitten with a Miss Patricia Sears and, upon parting, promised to memorialize her through one of my endeavors. Remembering this promise, I named the company Sears Financial Services." *Sears, Roebuck & Co. v. Sears Fin. Network*, 576 F. Supp. 857, 863 (D.D.C. 1983). The court said that it had difficulty in accepting this story, and "it can thus be preliminarily inferred that the defendant's intent was to trade off the plaintiff's well-known name and mark SEARS."

Similarly, the district court in this case correctly looked beyond appellees' stated explanation in determining their true purpose in selecting the Lardashe mark. Indeed, Duran testified that the reason for rejection of "Horsesashe" with a picture of a horse's head as a possible mark was that the appellees wanted to stay away from Jordache's horse mark. This awareness of the Jordache mark belies Stafford's explanation for choosing "Lardashe" and supports the district court's finding that "Lardashe" was intended to be a parody.

evidence of actual confusion by consumers in the marketplace. We hold that Ornstein's testimony was admissible because it was offered to show the then existing state of mind of Ornstein's associates.

Although Ornstein's testimony was admissible, the district court correctly gave it little weight. McCarthy advises, "The better view would seem to be that while [customer] enquiry evidence is admissible and relevant, standing alone with no other evidence it is insufficient proof of actual confusion."

Appellant also offered a survey of seventy people contacted in the Student Union building on the University of New Mexico campus as evidence of actual confusion. The district court afforded little weight to this survey. We have acknowledged that public recognition surveys can be used to show actual confusion. However, the evidentiary value of such surveys depends on the relevance of the questions asked and the technical adequacy of the survey procedures.

In *Beer Nuts I*, this court observed:

In evaluating similarity, "it is axiomatic in trademark law that 'side-by-side' comparison is not the test." The marks "must be compared in the light of what occurs in the marketplace, not in the courtroom." "A prospective purchaser does not ordinarily carry a sample or specimen of the article he knows well enough to call by its trade name; he necessarily depends upon the mental picture of that which symbolizes origin and ownership of the thing desired." Therefore, the court must determine whether the alleged infringing mark will be confusing to the public when singly presented.

Jordache's survey relied upon a "side-by-side" comparison. After the survey participants were asked several preliminary questions, they were handed a pair of Lardashe jeans and a pair of Jordache jeans and told to examine them. The participants were then asked if they thought the jeans were produced by the same manufacturer. This type of "side-by-side" comparison bears little resemblance to the actual workings of the marketplace. The district court did not err in giving little weight to the survey results.

E.

Appellant argues that the allegedly inferior quality of Lardashe jeans compared to Jordache jeans supports a finding of likelihood of confusion, and that the district court erred in not considering the quality of the jeans. If there is a difference in quality between the jeans, the public is less likely to be confused. A showing that products are of dissimilar quality affords no support for a finding of a likelihood of confusion.

F.

The district court weighed all of the factors and concluded there is no likelihood of confusion between the Lardashe mark and the Jordache marks. We have examined the record, including the testimony of Becky Ingram concerning industry confusion and all of the other evidence appellant contends the district court overlooked. We hold the district court's finding of no likelihood of confusion is not clearly erroneous.

II.

Jordache also raises a claim under New Mexico's antidilution statute which provides:

> Likelihood of injury to business reputation or of dilution of the distinctive quality
> of a trademark or trade name . . . is a ground for injunctive relief notwithstanding
> the absence of competition between the parties or the absence of confusion as to
> the source of goods or services.

The Court also finds that there can be no dilution (impairment of quality perception to
public) because dilution requires a likelihood of confusion and that has not been established here. Furthermore, parody rules out dilution (since parody relies on understanding
that the products are not from the same source).

III.

"'If it had grown up,' she said to herself, 'it would have been a dreadfully ugly child; but
it makes rather a handsome pig, I think.'" L. Carroll, *Alice's Adventures in Wonderland*
78-79 (1892).

The judgment of the district court is affirmed.

Trademarks: Case 2

LUCASFILM LTD., Plaintiff, v. HIGH FRONTIER, ET AL., Defendants.
LUCASFILM LTD., Plaintiff, v. COMMITTEE FOR A STRONG,
PEACEFUL AMERICA, ET AL., Defendants

Nos. 85-3609, 85-3668

UNITED STATES DISTRICT COURT FOR THE DISTRICT OF COLUMBIA

622 F. Supp. 931; 1985 U.S. Dist. LEXIS 13432; 227 U.S.P.Q. (BNA) 967

November 26, 1985

OPINION: GESELL, Judge:

MEMORANDUM

Not so long ago, in a studio far, far away from the policymakers in Washington, D.C.,
George Lucas conceived of an imaginary galaxy where fantastic creatures and courageous
knights battled an evil empire with spaceships, "blaster" guns and light sabers. Plaintiff
Lucasfilms Ltd. marketed this imaginative fantasy in three enormously popular films,
the first of which was entitled "STAR WARS." STAR WARS has since become a strong
trademark owned by plaintiff and registered as a service mark under the Lanham Act.
Plaintiff has built on the national success of these movies and the goodwill associated
with STAR WARS by using the STAR WARS mark to merchandise dolls, toys, comic
books, cookies, paper cups, watches, candles and even bubble bath.

Meanwhile, in the real world of defense strategy and international politics, newspapers, politicians, scientists and spokesmen of allied and enemy nations have chosen to
characterize the Reagan Administration's Strategic Defense Initiative (SDI) as its "star
wars" program. SDI seeks to develop defenses against a nuclear attack with weapons

based in space somewhat reminiscent of those depicted in the STAR WARS movies. Some see SDI as a brilliant proposal full of promise. Others fear the idea will simply escalate the risk of nuclear war and frustrate efforts toward disarmament. An intense political debate is under way and still raging. Through persistent and prolific use in newspapers and magazines and over television and radio the phrase star wars has become a popular synonym for the SDI proposal.

The principal defendants are public interest groups aligned on opposite sides of this political controversy. Both have chosen to express their views through television messages which refer to SDI as star wars. Except for their viewpoints, defendants' television messages are similar; both focus on a child's response to space defenses against a nuclear attack. In addition, like many others, they sometimes refer to star wars in their literature as a catchy shorthand for SDI. Ironically, because of their opposing viewpoints, defendants are also engaged in a dispute between themselves as to whether star wars is an apt synonym for SDI, or should be replaced by more comforting phrases such as "Peace Shield" or "High Frontier."

Plaintiff disavows involvement in this political fray and wishes only to protect its business interest in the STAR WARS trademark. Plaintiff fears that associating STAR WARS with this political controversy will injure the valuable goodwill it has achieved by developing a mark associated with imaginary battles among fantastic creatures in distant worlds. Inevitably, the political debate identifies STAR WARS in some minds with devastation and death from uncontrollable nuclear escalation. Plaintiff urges this could detract from the public's present association of STAR WARS with humor and fantasy. The goodwill value of the trademark is particularly threatened by defendants' use of television advertisements that are attractive to young television viewers.

Plaintiff seeks to enjoin defendants' use of the phrase star wars alleging trademark infringement, unfair competition, misappropriation, disparagement and a number of other similar business torts. The proof presented at this stage leaves no doubt that STAR WARS is still a strong trademark and defendants' television messages injure the value of the mark in some minds. Nonetheless, while plaintiff admittedly faces this unfortunate series of circumstances, the Court has no authority to provide plaintiff relief.

Plaintiff has no property right in the use of words commonly found in the English language. It is well established that the property right conferred by a trademark is very limited:

A trademark is not property in the ordinary sense, but only a word or symbol indicating the origin of a commercial product. The owner of a mark acquires the right to prevent the goods to which the mark is applied from being confused with those of others and to prevent his own trade from being diverted to competitors through their use of misleading marks. There are no rights in a trademark beyond these. Thus plaintiff's trademark, STAR WARS, only protects him against those who seek to attach those words to products or services that compete with him in the marketplace, against those who dilute the value of his mark by engaging in a noncompeting trade or business but utilize the mark in connection with a disreputable or sleazy product or service, and, under some circumstances, even against those who injure his business by offering goods or services that disparage the goodwill value of STAR WARS.

This case fits none of these molds. The defendants have not affixed any trademark to any goods or services for sale. Indeed, they are not engaged in selling anything but ideas. They do not compete with plaintiff and are not engaged in creating any confusion or mistake that takes advantage of plaintiff's good will to further a trade or business. Defendants' television messages and literature merely attempt to persuade the public of their respective but conflicting viewpoints. In this sense, their use of the phrase star wars stands on the same footing as its use in books, newspapers, magazines, comics, news reports, editorials or public speeches as a shorthand reference to the SDI program. Thus it is not the type of use that the laws against trademark infringement and unfair competition are designed to restrict.

Nonetheless, plaintiff suggests that defendants' efforts to persuade the public of their viewpoint is a "service" within the meaning of the Lanham Act. Federal trademark laws, however, only prohibit unauthorized "use in commerce" of a trademark "in connection with the sale, offering for sale, distribution or advertisement of any goods or services" or affixing "a false designation of origin, or any false description or representation" to goods and services used in commerce. "Use in commerce" is defined as placing the mark on goods sold in commerce or using or displaying it in the sale or advertising of services rendered in commerce. Defendants' only activity is trying to communicate their ideas. Purveying points of view is not a service. Even if promoting of ideas was considered to be conducting an educational "service," television messages that are only used to express those ideas do not sell or advertise them. In this respect, defendants' activities are indistinguishable from those of a publisher or lecturer who uses the phrase star wars while attempting to educate others or promote a certain view.

Trademark law does not reach such uses. The purpose of trademark regulation is to prevent unfair competition and protect consumers from fraud and deception. Unfair competition and the other business torts invoked by plaintiff are similarly limited. These laws do not reach into the realm of public discourse to regulate the use of terms used outside the context of trade. Defendants' use of the phrase star wars to persuade the public of their viewpoint through television messages is not an infringing use.

Traditional trademark law supports the common sense conclusion that defendants' use of star wars under these circumstances cannot be enjoined. Defendants have not used the phrase as a title for their organization or propaganda campaign in a way that might create confusion among contributors or supporters.

When politicians, newspapers and the public generally use the phrase star wars for convenience, in parody or descriptively to further a communication of their views on SDI, plaintiff has no rights as owner of the mark to prevent this use of STAR WARS. Plaintiff is in the difficult position of objecting because what he has depicted as fantasy may be frightening when depicted as a potential reality. Plaintiff must be left to his own devices to maintain the strength of his trademark by making the differentiation clear and convincing.

Overlying this lawsuit is plaintiff's natural concern that if he does not seek legal remedies to protect his mark he will lose it. But the use of star wars in political propaganda, newspapers or noncommercial, non-trade references will not undermine plaintiff's exclusive property right to use it in connection with goods and services. The words "star" and "wars" were in the common domain before plaintiff established its service mark and plaintiff's efforts gave STAR WARS a special, secondary meaning. Now the phrase star wars has acquired a double meaning, but it has not become a generic term, that is a term associated with an entire class of goods or services. Plaintiff's right to prevent an infringing use of its mark remains intact.

It would be wholly unrealistic and unfair to allow the owner of a mark to interfere in the give-and-take of normal political discourse, particularly where such interference of things would be incomplete, selective and ineffective. Yet, it would be equally unrealistic and unfair to take from the lawful owner of a strong trademark his continued right to its commercial use because others, beyond his control and contemplating no harm to him, used the words of the trademark as part of an on-going international political debate.

The Court cannot venture beyond the property protections provided by the trademark laws and attempt to regulate the terms of public debate. As the dispute between plaintiff and the defendants and the dispute between the defendants in this case illustrate, labels can have great significance, in both business and politics. But courts have no role in overseeing the use of labels in the context presented by this case.

An appropriate order dismissing the complaints is filed concurrently with this Memorandum.

≈

Trademarks: Case 3

PLAYBOY ENTERPRISES, INC., Plaintiff-Appellant, v. NETSCAPE COMMUNICATIONS CORPORATION, Defendant-Appellee. **PLAYBOY** ENTERPRISES INTERNATIONAL, INC., Plaintiff-Appellant, v. EXCITE, INC., Defendant-Appellee.

No. 00-56648, No. 00-56662

UNITED STATES COURT OF APPEALS FOR THE NINTH CIRCUIT

354 F.3d 1020; 2004 U.S. App. LEXIS 442; 69 U.S.P.Q.2D (BNA) 1417

September 11, 2001, Argued and Submitted, Pasadena, California
January 14, 2004, Filed

OPINION: NELSON, Judge:

Playboy Enterprises International, Inc. (PEI) appeals from the district court's grant of summary judgment in favor of Netscape Communications Corporation and Excite, Inc. PEI sued defendants for trademark infringement and dilution.

I. Facts

PEI introduced evidence that the adult-oriented banner ads displayed on defendants' search results pages are often graphic in nature and are confusingly labeled or not labeled at all. In addition, the parties do not dispute that buttons on the banner ads say "click here." When a searcher complies, the search results page disappears, and the searcher finds him or herself at the advertiser's website. PEI presented uncontroverted evidence that defendants monitor "click rates," the ratio between the number of times searchers click on banner ads and the number of times the ads are shown. Defendants use click rate statistics to convince advertisers to renew their keyword contracts. The higher the click rate, the more successful they deem a banner ad.

PEI sued defendants, asserting that they were using PEI's marks in a manner that infringed upon and diluted them. The district court denied PEI's request for a preliminary injunction, and this court affirmed in an unpublished disposition. On remand, the parties filed cross-motions for summary judgment. The district court granted summary judgment in favor of defendants. We reverse.

[Section II. is omitted.]

III. Discussion

A. Trademark Infringement

1. Theory of Liability

Whether the defendants are directly or merely contributorily liable proves to be a tricky question. However, we need not decide that question here. We conclude that defendants are either directly or contributorily liable. Under either theory, PEI's case may proceed. Thus, we need not decide this issue.

2. PEI's Case for Trademark Infringement

The "core element of trademark infringement," the likelihood of confusion, lies at the center of this case. No dispute exists regarding the other requirements set forth by the statute: PEI clearly holds the marks in question and defendants used the marks in commerce without PEI's permission.

PEI's strongest argument for a likelihood of confusion is for a certain kind of confusion: initial interest confusion. Initial interest confusion is customer confusion that creates initial interest in a competitor's product. Although dispelled before an actual sale occurs, initial interest confusion impermissibly capitalizes on the goodwill associated with a mark and is therefore actionable trademark infringement.

PEI asserts that, by keying adult-oriented advertisements to PEI's trademarks, defendants actively create initial interest confusion in the following manner. Because banner advertisements appear immediately after users type in PEI's marks, PEI asserts that users are likely to be confused regarding the sponsorship of unlabeled banner advertisements. In addition, many of the advertisements instruct users to "click here." Because of their confusion, users may follow the instruction, believing they will be connected to a PEI site. Even if they realize "immediately upon accessing" the competitor's site that they have reached a site "wholly unrelated to" PEI's, the damage has been done: Through initial consumer confusion, the competitor "will still have gained a customer by appropriating the goodwill that [PEI] has developed in its [] mark."

PEI's theory strongly resembles the theory adopted by this court in *Brookfield Communications, Inc. v. West Coast Entertainment Corporation.*

In this case, PEI claims that defendants, in conjunction with advertisers, have misappropriated the goodwill of PEI's marks by leading Internet users to competitors' websites just as West Coast video misappropriated the goodwill of Brookfield's mark. Some consumers, initially seeking PEI's sites, may initially believe that unlabeled banner advertisements are links to PEI's sites or to sites affiliated with PEI. Once they follow the instructions to "click here," and they access the site, they may well realize that they are not at a PEI-sponsored site. However, they may be perfectly happy to remain on the competitor's site, just as the *Brookfield* court surmised that some searchers initially seeking Brookfield's site would happily remain on West Coast's site. The Internet user will have reached the site because of defendants' use of PEI's mark. Such use is actionable.

The Ninth Circuit employs an eight-factor test, originally set forth in *AMF Inc. v. Sleekcraft Boats*, to determine the likelihood of confusion. The eight factors are:

1. strength of the mark;
2. proximity of the goods;
3. similarity of the marks;
4. evidence of actual confusion;
5. marketing channels used;
6. type of goods and the degree of care likely to be exercised by the purchaser;
7. defendant's intent in selecting the mark; and
8. likelihood of expansion of the product lines.

In the Internet context, courts must be flexible in applying the factors, as some may not apply. Moreover, some factors are more important than others. For example, a showing of actual confusion among significant numbers of consumers provides strong support for the likelihood of confusion. For that reason, we turn first to an examination of factor four: evidence of actual confusion.

a. Factor four: Evidence of actual confusion. The expert study PEI introduced establishes a strong likelihood of initial interest confusion among consumers. Thus, factor four alone probably suffices to reverse the grant of summary judgment.

PEI's expert, Dr. Ford, concluded that a statistically significant number of Internet users searching for the terms "playboy" and "playmate" would think that PEI, or an affiliate, sponsored banner ads containing adult content that appear on the search results page. When study participants were shown search results for the term "playboy," 51% believed that PEI sponsored or was otherwise associated with the adult-content banner ad displayed.

Defendants criticize Dr. Ford's procedures and conclusions. They offer their own interpretations of his data, with significantly lower rates of confusion. Defendants may have valid criticism of Dr. Ford's methods and conclusions, and their critique may justify reducing the weight eventually afforded Dr. Ford's expert report. The district court's evidentiary ruling is not before us on appeal, however, and weighing admissible evidence at this stage is improper. Defendants' arguments prove the point that a genuine issue of material fact exists regarding actual confusion. The presence of Dr. Ford's criticized (but uncontradicted) report, with its strong conclusions that a high likelihood of initial interest confusion exists among consumers, thus generates a genuine issue of material fact on the actual confusion issue.

Because actual confusion is at the heart of the likelihood of confusion analysis, Dr. Ford's report alone probably precludes summary judgment. In the interest of being thorough, however, we will examine the other seven *Sleekcraft* factors. On balance, they also support PEI.

b. Factor one: Strength of the mark. PEI has established that strong secondary meanings for its descriptive marks exist, and that a genuine issue of material fact exists as to whether it created the secondary meanings. Thus, the first *Sleekcraft* factor favors PEI.

At this point, defendants concede that they use the marks for their secondary meanings. Thus, they concede that the marks have secondary meanings. Given that defendants themselves use the terms precisely because they believe that Internet searchers associate the terms with their secondary meanings, disputing the strength of the secondary meanings is somewhat farfetched. The only meaningful dispute is whether PEI created the strong secondary meanings associated with the mark.

PEI offered evidence, in the form of expert reports, tending to show that PEI did create the secondary meanings of "playboy" and "playmate." PEI's expert evidence countered the defendants' expert evidence to the contrary, and suffices to generate a genuine issue of material fact on this issue.

c. Factor two: Proximity of the goods. From an Internet searcher's perspective, the relevant "goods" are the links to the websites being sought and the goods or services available at those sites. The proximity between PEI's and its competitor's goods provides the reason Netscape keys PEI's marks to competitor's banner advertisements in the first place. Accordingly, this factor favors PEI as well.

d. Factor three: Similarity of the marks. No doubt exists regarding this factor. Aside from their lack of capitalization, their font, and the fact that defendants use the plural form of "playmate," the terms defendants use are identical to PEI's marks. Thus, they are certainly similar.

e. Factor five: Marketing channels used. This factor is equivocal. PEI and the advertisers use identical marketing channels: the Internet. More specifically, each of their sites appears on defendants' search results pages. Given the broad use of the Internet today, the same could be said for countless companies. Thus, this factor merits little weight.

f. Factor six: Type of goods and degree of consumer care expected. This factor favors PEI. Consumer care for inexpensive products is expected to be quite low. Low consumer care, in turn, increases the likelihood of confusion.

In addition to price, the content in question may affect consumer care as well. We presume that the average searcher seeking adult-oriented materials on the Internet is easily diverted from a specific product he or she is seeking if other options, particularly graphic ones, appear more quickly. Thus, the adult-oriented and graphic nature of the materials weighs in PEI's favor as well.

g. Factor seven: Defendants' intent in selecting the mark. This factor favors PEI somewhat. A defendant's intent to confuse constitutes probative evidence of likely confusion: Courts assume that the defendant's intentions were carried out successfully. In this case, the evidence does not definitively establish defendants' intent. At a minimum, however, it does suggest that defendants do nothing to prevent click-throughs that result from confusion. Moreover, they profit from such click-throughs.

h. Factor eight: Likelihood of expansion of product lines. Because the advertisers' goods and PEI's are already related, as discussed within factor two, this factor is irrelevant.

Having examined all of the *Sleekcraft* factors, we conclude that the majority favor PEI. Accordingly, we conclude that a genuine issue of material fact exists as to the substantial likelihood of confusion.

B. Trademark Dilution

We reverse the district court's grant of summary judgment on PEI's second cause of action, trademark dilution, and remand for further proceedings. We conclude that PEI has established that genuine issues of material fact exist regarding two of the three elements that the parties dispute: the famousness of the marks and defendants' commercial use of the mark.

1. Famousness of the Mark

The federal dilution statute provides eight factors courts may use, along with other relevant factors, "[i]n determining whether a mark is distinctive and famous." Those eight factors are:

(A) the degree of inherent or acquired distinctiveness of the mark;
(B) the duration and extent of use of the mark in connection with the goods or services with which the mark is used;
(C) the duration and extent of advertising and publicity of the mark;
(D) the geographical extent of the trading area in which the mark is used;
(E) the channels of trade for the goods or services with which the mark is used;
(F) the degree of recognition of the mark in the trading areas and channels of trade used by the marks' owner and the person against whom the injunction is sought;
(G) the nature and extent of use of the same or similar marks by third parties; and
(H) whether the mark was registered under the Act of March 3, 1881, or the Act of February 20, 1905, or on the principal register.

No grounds exist to contest factors (B), (C), (D), (E), and (H), all of which favor PEI. Defendants directly contest only factor (G): "the nature and extent of use of the same or similar marks by third parties." We conclude that PEI has established a genuine issue of material fact regarding factor (G). Accordingly, the first contested requirement of trademark dilution favors PEI for purposes of summary judgment.

Defendants introduced evidence that more than forty third-party trademark registrations exist for the terms "playboy" and "playmate," as well as evidence that hundreds of companies use the terms within their company names. Plaintiffs countered, however, by showing that: (a) many of the companies cited by defendants are active infringers whom PEI is diligently pursuing; (b) others are merely companies who have applied for similar marks but who have not yet received them; and (c) still others are listed several times. The remainder, PEI asserts, are in different fields or in localized areas and should not be counted, at least not when considering whether PEI's marks are famous within their market.

Thus, defendants introduced evidence of third-party use and PEI disputed the evidence with evidence of its own showing that defendants' list was substantially over-inclusive. A dispute of material fact thus exists as to the only factor relevant to the famousness of the marks that defendants contest. Accordingly, the first contested requirement of dilution favors PEI on summary judgment.

2. Defendants' Commercial Use of the Mark

Congress intended to limit only commercial speech, as opposed to political or other more closely protected speech, when it passed the dilution statute; thus, it included the requirement that the use be a commercial one. A successful argument that defendants make no commercial use of the marks, then, would be an argument that the speech associated with their actions was political, not commercial. Defendants do not make such an argument, and it would be difficult to do so in light of the clear evidence of the commercial nature of their enterprise. Accordingly, PEI has satisfied the second disputed requirement of dilution.

3. Dilution of Distinctive Quality of Marks

We conclude that the district court erred when it held, applying the standard then in force, that PEI had shown no likelihood of dilution. However, because the Supreme Court recently clarified the standard for withstanding summary judgment on dilution claims, we vacate the district court's decision on this point and remand with instructions to re-open discovery to allow the parties to introduce evidence that may satisfy, or undermine, the new standard.

IV. Conclusion

Genuine issues of material fact exist as to PEI's trademark infringement and dilution claims. Accordingly, we reverse the district court's grant of summary judgment in favor of defendants and remand for further proceedings.

Reversed and Remanded.

Marsha S. Berzon concurs.

CONCURRENCE: BERZON, Judge:

I concur in Judge Nelson's careful opinion in this case, as it is fully consistent with the applicable precedents. I write separately, however, to express concern that one of those precedents was wrongly decided and may one day, if not now, need to be reconsidered *en banc*.

I am struck by how analytically similar keyed advertisements are to the metatags found infringing in *Brookfield Communications v. West Coast Entertainment Corp.*, 174 F.3d 1036 (9th Cir. 1999).

As applied to this case, *Brookfield* might suggest that there could be a Lanham Act violation *even if* the banner advertisements were clearly labeled, either by the advertiser or by the search engine. I do not believe that to be so. So read, the metatag holding in *Brookfield* would expand the reach of initial interest confusion from situations in which a party is initially confused to situations in which a party is never confused. I do not think it is reasonable to find initial interest confusion when a consumer is never confused as to source or affiliation, but instead knows, or should know, from the outset that a product or web link is not related to that of the trademark holder because the list produced by the search engine so informs him.

Accordingly, I simply cannot understand the broad principle set forth in *Brookfield*. Even the main analogy given in *Brookfield* belies its conclusion. The Court gives an example of Blockbuster misdirecting customers from a competing video store, West Coast Video, by putting up a highway billboard sign giving directions to Blockbuster but telling customers that a West Coast Video store is located there. *Brookfield*, 174 F.3d at 1064. Even though customers who arrive at the Blockbuster realize that it is not West Coast Video, they were initially misled and confused.

But there was no similar misdirection in *Brookfield*, nor would there be similar misdirection in this case were the banner ads labeled or otherwise identified. The *Brookfield* defendant's website was described by the court as being accurately listed as westcoastvideo.com in the applicable search results. Consumers were free to choose the official moviebuff.com website and were not hijacked or misdirected elsewhere. I note that the billboard analogy has been widely criticized as inapplicable to the Internet situation, given both the fact that customers were not misdirected and the minimal inconvenience in directing one's web browser back to the original list of search results.

There will be time enough to address the continuing vitality of *Brookfield* should the labeled advertisement issue arise later. I wanted to flag the issue, however, as another case based on the metatag aspect of *Brookfield* was decided recently, *Horphag Research Ltd. v. Pellegrini*, 337 F.3d 1036 (9th Cir. 2003), so the issue is a recurring one. Should the question arise again, in this case or some other, this court needs to consider whether we want to continue to apply an insupportable rule.

Trademarks: Case 4

PANAVISION INTERNATIONAL, L.P., a Delaware Limited Partnership, Plaintiff-Appellee, v. DENNIS TOEPPEN; NETWORK SOLUTIONS, INC., a District of Columbia Corporation, Defendants-Appellants.

No. 97-55467

UNITED STATES COURT OF APPEALS FOR THE NINTH CIRCUIT

141 F.3d 1316; 1998 U.S. App. LEXIS 7557; 46 U.S.P.Q.2D (BNA) 1511; 98 Cal. Daily Op. Service 2846; 98 Daily Journal DAR 3929

March 3, 1998, Argued, Submitted, Pasadena, California
April 17, 1998, Filed

OPINION: THOMPSON, Judge:

Panavision accuses Dennis Toeppen of being a "cyber pirate" who steals valuable trademarks and establishes domain names on the Internet using these trademarks to sell the domain names to the rightful trademark owners.

The district court granted summary judgment in favor of Panavision, concluding that Toeppen's conduct violated the Federal Trademark Dilution Act of 1995, 15 U.S.C. § 1125(c), and the California Anti-dilution statute, California Business & Professions Code § 14330. *Panavision International, L.P. v. Toeppen*, 945 F. Supp. 1296, 1306 (C.D. Cal. 1996).

Toeppen appeals. He argues that the district court erred in granting summary judgment because his use of Panavision's trademarks on the Internet was not a commercial use and did not dilute those marks.

We conclude Panavision was entitled to summary judgment under the federal and state dilution statutes. Toeppen made commercial use of Panavision's trademarks and his conduct diluted those marks.

I. Background

The Internet is a worldwide network of computers that enables various individuals and organizations to share information.

Every web page has its own web site, which is its address, similar to a telephone number or street address. Every web site on the Internet has an identifier called a "domain name." The domain name often consists of a person's name or a company's name or trademark. For example, Pepsi has a web page with a web site domain name consisting of the company name, Pepsi, and .com, the "top level" domain designation: pepsi.com.

Domain names with the .com designation must be registered on the Internet with Network Solutions, Inc. ("NSI"). NSI registers names on a first-come, first-served basis for a $100 registration fee. NSI does not make a determination about a registrant's right to use a domain name. However, NSI does require an applicant to represent and warrant as an express condition of registering a domain name that (1) the applicant's statements are true and the applicant has the right to use the requested domain name; (2) the "use or registration of the domain name . . . does not interfere with or infringe the rights of any third party in any jurisdiction with respect to trademark, service mark, trade name, company name or any other intellectual property right"; and (3) the applicant is not seeking to use the domain name for any unlawful purpose, including unfair competition.

A domain name is the simplest way of locating a web site. If a computer user does not know a domain name, she can use an Internet "search engine." To do this, the user types in a key word search, and the search will locate all of the web sites containing the key word. Such key word searches can yield hundreds of web sites. To make it easier to find their web sites, individuals and companies prefer to have a recognizable domain name.

Panavision holds registered trademarks to the names "Panavision" and "Panaflex" in connection with motion picture camera equipment. Panavision promotes its trademarks through motion picture and television credits and other media advertising.

In December 1995, Panavision attempted to register a web site on the Internet with the domain name Panavision.com. It could not do that, however, because Toeppen had already established a web site using Panavision's trademark as his domain name. Toeppen's web page for this site displayed photographs of the City of Pana, Illinois.

On December 20, 1995, Panavision's counsel sent a letter from California to Toeppen in Illinois informing him that Panavision held a trademark in the name Panavision and telling him to stop using that trademark and the domain name Panavision.com. Toeppen responded by mail to Panavision in California, stating he had the right to use the name Panavision.com on the Internet as his domain name. Toeppen stated:

> If your attorney has advised you otherwise, he is trying to screw you. He wants to blaze new trails in the legal frontier at your expense. Why do you want to fund your attorney's purchase of a new boat (or whatever) when you can facilitate the acquisition of 'PanaVision.com' cheaply and simply instead?

Toeppen then offered to "settle the matter" if Panavision would pay him $13,000 in exchange for the domain name. Additionally, Toeppen stated that if Panavision agreed to his offer, he would not "acquire any other Internet addresses which are alleged by Panavision Corporation to be its property."

After Panavision refused Toeppen's demand, he registered Panavision's other trademark with NSI as the domain name Panaflex.com. Toeppen's web page for Panaflex.com simply displays the word "Hello."

Toeppen has registered domain names for various other companies including Delta Airlines, Neiman Marcus, Eddie Bauer, Lufthansa, and over 100 other marks. Toeppen has attempted to "sell" domain names for other trademarks such as intermatic.com to Intermatic, Inc. for $ 10,000 and americanstandard.com to American Standard, Inc. for $ 15,000.

Panavision filed this action against Toeppen in the District Court for the Central District of California. Panavision alleged claims for dilution of its trademark under the Federal Trademark Dilution Act of 1995, 15 U.S.C. § 1125(c), and under the California Anti-dilution statute, California Business and Professions Code § 14330. Panavision alleged that Toeppen was in the business of stealing trademarks, registering them as domain names on the Internet and then selling the domain names to the rightful trademark owners. The district court determined it had personal jurisdiction over Toeppen, and granted summary judgment in favor of Panavision on both its federal and state dilution claims. This appeal followed.

II. Discussion

[Section A, discussing jurisdictional issues, is omitted here.]

B. Trademark Dilution Claims

The Federal Trademark Dilution Act provides:

> The owner of a famous mark shall be entitled . . . to an injunction against another person's commercial use in commerce of a mark or trade name, if such use begins after the mark has become famous and causes dilution of the distinctive quality of the mark. . . .

The California Anti-dilution statute is similar. It prohibits dilution of "the distinctive quality" of a mark regardless of competition or the likelihood of confusion. The protection extends only to strong and well recognized marks. Panavision's state law dilution claim is subject to the same analysis as its federal claim.

In order to prove a violation of the Federal Trademark Dilution Act, a plaintiff must show that (1) the mark is famous; (2) the defendant is making a commercial use of the mark in commerce; (3) the defendant's use began after the mark became famous; and (4) the defendant's use of the mark dilutes the quality of the mark by diminishing the capacity of the mark to identify and distinguish goods and services.

Toeppen does not challenge the district court's determination that Panavision's trademark is famous, that his alleged use began after the mark became famous, or that the use was in commerce. Toeppen challenges the district court's determination that he made "commercial use" of the mark and that this use caused "dilution" in the quality of the mark.

1. Commercial Use

Toeppen argues that his use of Panavision's trademarks simply as his domain names cannot constitute a commercial use under the Act. Case law supports this argument.

Developing this argument, Toeppen contends that a domain name is simply an address used to locate a web page. He asserts that entering a domain name on a computer allows a user to access a web page, but a domain name is not associated with information on a web page. If a user were to type Panavision.com as a domain name, the computer screen would display Toeppen's web page with aerial views of Pana, Illinois. The screen would not provide any information about "Panavision," other than a "location window" which displays the domain name. Toeppen argues that a user who types in Panavision.com, but who sees no reference to the plaintiff Panavision on Toeppen's web page, is not likely to conclude the web page is related in any way to the plaintiff, Panavision.

Toeppen's argument misstates his use of the Panavision mark. His use is not as benign as he suggests. Toeppen's "business" is to register trademarks as domain names and then sell them to the rightful trademark owners. He "acts as a 'spoiler,' preventing Panavision and others from doing business on the Internet under their trademarked names unless they pay his fee." This is a commercial use.

As the district court found, Toeppen traded on the value of Panavision's marks. So long as he held the Internet registrations, he curtailed Panavision's exploitation of the value of its trademarks on the Internet, a value which Toeppen then used when he attempted to sell the Panavision.com domain name to Panavision.

In a nearly identical case involving Toeppen and Intermatic Inc., a federal district court in Illinois held that Toeppen's conduct violated the Federal Trademark Dilution Act. *Intermatic*, 947 F. Supp. 1227 at 1241. There, Intermatic sued Toeppen for registering its trademark on the Internet as Toeppen's domain name, intermatic.com. It was "conceded that one of Toeppen's intended uses for registering the Intermatic mark was to eventually sell it back to Intermatic or to some other party." The court found that "Toeppen's intention to arbitrage the 'intermatic.com' domain name constituted a commercial use."

Toeppen's reliance on *Holiday Inns, Inc. v. 800 Reservation, Inc.*, 86 F.3d 619 (6th Cir. 1996), *cert. denied*, 136 L. Ed. 2d 715, 117 S. Ct. 770 (1997) is misplaced. In *Holiday Inns*, the Sixth Circuit held that a company's use of the most commonly *misdialed* number for Holiday Inns' 1-800 reservation number was not trademark infringement.

Holiday Inns is distinguishable. There, the defendant did not use Holiday Inns' trademark. Rather, the defendant selected the most commonly misdialed telephone number for Holiday Inns and attempted to capitalize on consumer confusion.

A telephone number, moreover, is distinguishable from a domain name because a domain name is associated with a word or phrase. A domain name is similar to a "vanity number" that identifies its source. Using Holiday Inns as an example, when a customer dials the vanity number "1-800-Holiday," she expects to contact Holiday Inns because the number is associated with that company's trademark. A user would have the same expectation typing the domain name HolidayInns.com. The user would expect to retrieve Holiday Inns' web page.

Toeppen made a commercial use of Panavision's trademarks. It does not matter that he did not attach the marks to a product. Toeppen's commercial use was his attempt to sell the trademarks themselves. Under the Federal Trademark Dilution Act and the California Anti-dilution statute, this was sufficient commercial use.

2. Dilution

"Dilution" is defined as "the lessening of the capacity of a famous mark to identify and distinguish goods or services, regardless of the presence or absence of (1) competition between the owner of the famous mark and other parties, or (2) likelihood of confusion, mistake or deception."

Trademark dilution on the Internet was a matter of Congressional concern. Senator Patrick Leahy (D-Vt.) stated:

> It is my hope that this anti-dilution statute can help stem the use of deceptive Internet addresses taken by those who are choosing marks that are associated with the products and reputations of others.

To find dilution, a court need not rely on the traditional definitions such as "blurring" and "tarnishment." Indeed, in concluding that Toeppen's use of Panavision's trademarks diluted the marks, the district court noted that Toeppen's conduct varied from the two standard dilution theories of blurring and tarnishment. The court found that Toeppen's conduct diminished "the capacity of the Panavision marks to identify and distinguish Panavision's goods and services on the Internet."

Toeppen argues he is not diluting the capacity of the Panavision marks to identify goods or services. He contends that even though Panavision cannot use Panavision.com and Panaflex.com as its domain name addresses, it can still promote its goods and services on the Internet simply by using some other "address" and then creating its own web page using its trademarks.

We reject Toeppen's premise that a domain name is nothing more than an address. A significant purpose of a domain name is to identify the entity that owns the web site. "A customer who is unsure about a company's domain name will often guess that the domain name is also the company's name."

Using a company's name or trademark as a domain name is also the easiest way to locate that company's web site. Use of a "search engine" can turn up hundreds of web sites, and there is nothing equivalent to a phone book or directory assistance for the Internet.

Moreover, potential customers of Panavision will be discouraged if they cannot find its web page by typing in "Panavision.com," but instead are forced to wade through hundreds of web sites. This dilutes the value of Panavision's trademark. We echo the words of Judge Lechner, quoting Judge Wood: "Prospective users of plaintiff's services who mistakenly access defendant's web site may fail to continue to search for plaintiff's own home page, due to anger, frustration or the belief that plaintiff's home page does not exist."

Toeppen's use of Panavision.com also puts Panavision's name and reputation at his mercy.

We conclude that Toeppen's registration of Panavision's trademarks as his domain names on the Internet diluted those marks within the meaning of the Federal Trademark Dilution Act, 15 U.S.C. § 1125(c), and the California Anti-dilution statute, Cal.Bus. & Prof. Code § 14330.

III. Conclusion

We affirm the district court's summary judgment in favor of Panavision under the Federal Trademark Dilution Act, 15 U.S.C. § 1125(c), and the California Anti-dilution statute,

Cal.Bus. & Prof. Code § 14330. Toeppen made commercial use of Panavision's trademarks and his conduct diluted those marks.

Affirmed.

> There is now a federal statute making "cybersquatting" of domain names illegal. However, the statute requires proof that the alleged cybersquatter is holding the domain name for the purpose of selling it to an owner of the trademark contained in the domain name. This is difficult to establish and makes the statute equally difficult to enforce.

9. The Right of Privacy

Introduction

What do we mean by a "right of privacy"? Justice Cooley in 1888 defined it simply as a right to be left alone. Alternatively, it may be defined as a right to be anonymous. The two definitions are quite different but both are important, and the right to be anonymous is a form of privacy that has particularly significant implications in cyberspace.

In legal terms, our right of privacy amounts to a right to be free from government intrusion into certain areas of our lives and a right to be free from intrusion by other individuals into our "private" lives. The former is protected largely through Constitutional interpretation and a number of statutes; the latter is protected largely through the common law under tort principles.

Before 1890 no English or American court had ever granted relief based on such a claim as "invasion of privacy." However, in 1890 a *Harvard Law Review* article by Samuel Warren and Louis Brandeis examined a number of cases ostensibly decided on other grounds, and concluded that these decisions were actually based on a broader principle, a right of privacy. Warren and Brandeis claimed such a principle was in fact necessary to deal with what was seen as the growing problem of excesses of the press.

New York was the first state to confront this issue head on in the wake of the article. Several lower courts had held the existence of a right of privacy. The New York State Court of Appeals (which is, oddly, the State's highest court – the "Supreme Court" is the State's entry level court) got to review the matter in the case of *Roberson v. Rochester Folding Box Company* in 1902. In this case, the defendant had used a picture of an attractive young woman to advertise its flour without her consent. In a 4–3 decision, the Court of Appeals held that there was no legal precedent for such "right of privacy." Furthermore, the Court felt that recognizing a right of privacy was a poor idea because, first, the alleged harm was of a purely mental character and would thus be difficult to prove or disprove; second, recognizing a right of privacy would lead to a flood of litigation; third, there would be difficulty in distinguishing between "public" and "private" figures, whose protections under a right of privacy would differ; and finally because it might lead to undue restrictions on the freedom of the press.

A public outcry followed the decision and, in its next session, the New York State Legislature passed a law banning the use of a person's name or picture "for advertising purposes or for the purposes of trade" without the person's written consent. By the 1930s "virtually" all jurisdictions had recognized the Right of Privacy, either by statute or through the common law.

(The New York State Legislature's reaction to the *Roberson* decision is a wonderful example of the fact that many statutes are created because statutory bodies are dissatisfied with the position the judiciary takes on an issue.)

Common Law Right of Privacy: Four Torts

Just what is the common law Right of Privacy? (The tort-protected right.) Actually it is four different rights protected by four different tort causes of action. Thus, privacy is violated by any of the following:

1. Appropriation of Person's Name or Likeness for Defendant's Benefit

For this tort to be applicable, the plaintiff's *identity* must be used, not just his or her name. For example, using someone's name in a novel does not give that person a cause of action under this tort unless the person's actual identity is clear. Similarly, the coincidental use of a person's name for a company does not give the person a cause for damages. Also, since identity is the issue, there is no liability for using a picture of a plaintiff's house, car, dog, etc., without any indication of whose they are.

"News" use of a person's identity is okay. So, if a person is arrested, for example, he or she will have no legally based complaint if a newspaper reports that fact.

2. Unreasonable Intrusion (and note the word "unreasonable")

Unreasonable intrusion consists of intentional interference with another person's interest in solitude and seclusion, either as to his or her person or as to his or her private affairs. This can be intrusion upon physical solitude, such as invading a person's home, or intrusion upon a more intangible form of personal solitude. Examples of this are interception of personal e-mail, wiretapping, peeping toms, prying into a person's bank account information, and so on. Even persistent unwanted telephone calls can rise to the level of unreasonable intrusion. (It is an open question whether persistent unwanted e-mail might also satisfy this tort.)

The key is that there *must* be some sort of prying or intrusion. Whether there is or not is a very subjective "gut reaction" to the circumstances. Examples of situations in which the element of prying is lacking might be street noise disturbing a lecture, or someone to whom one owes money stopping by to ask for payment, or perhaps a student knocking on a faculty member's private office door to request the return of a paper.

The intrusion must be one that a "reasonable person" would find offensive. And, of course, the intrusion must be into something that is *private*, not, for example, statements on the public record.

Remember that we have no right to be "private" on a public street or in any other public place, so a photo taken of a person in a public place generally will not be grounds for a claim of unreasonable intrusion. However, even in a public place, some things are considered private. For example, in the 1950s and early 60s, a time when most women still wore skirts or dresses, many amusement parks installed grates in the sidewalks running through the park and when a woman walked across the grate a blast of wind would blow her skirt up in the air. This was ultimately considered to be an unreasonable intrusion upon a woman's privacy, despite the public setting of an amusement park.

Intrusion into private *information* can also be actionable, which is obviously an important notion in the intangible world of cyberspace. To determine if any given intrusion into private information is actionable, we consider the means used to obtain the information and the purpose of the defendant in obtaining the information. If the means used are "abnormal," such as e-mail packet sniffers or even standard wiretaps, then the intrusion is probably actionable regardless of the defendant's purpose in obtaining the information. Eavesdropping is an example of a means of obtaining information that is not "abnormal," since no device is used, and the defendants' purpose becomes an issue to be examined. News use of the information, if it is truly newsworthy, is acceptable.

3. Public Disclosure of Private Facts

It is important to remember that for this tort, unlike for the tort of defamation, an action will lie even if the facts disclosed are actual "facts," i.e., true.

The standard that applies is that the disclosure must be one that the court feels is "shocking" and that would be *highly* offensive to a reasonable person. So, for example, while a story in a local newspaper that someone has been married or a notice that someone has won a prize on a quiz show would not meet this standard, disclosures of intimate details of a person's private life probably would.

The disclosure does not have to be "public" in the usual sense of the word, meaning published in a newspaper or reported on television. As with defamation, the disclosure need only be to a third party, such as a person's employer or neighbor.

"Public figures" have more limited protection under this tort than the rest of us. A "public figure," as legally defined in the 1944 Florida case of *Cason v. Baskin*, is "a person who, by accomplishments, fame, or mode of living, or by adopting a profession or calling which gives the public a legitimate interest in his or her doings, affairs and character." In other words, a celebrity.

The rationale for giving public figures limited protection under this tort is that celebrities have sought publicity and can't complain when they get it. Their affairs are already matters of public interest and curiosity, and the press has a right to inform the public about the doings of celebrities. Perhaps most importantly, public figures are presumed to have the power to get media attention to refute anything said about them to which they object, unlike the rest of us. But note that there are people who become public figures who never intended to do so, such as Richard Jewell, the man falsely associated with the bombing at the 1996 Atlanta Olympics.

4. False Light in the Public Eye

This fourth and final privacy tort protects against publicity that places a person in a false light. The tort has its roots in the poet Lord Byron's successful enjoinment of distribution of a bad poem that was being falsely attributed to him in 1816. The tort arises in almost any situation in which someone is falsely said to have endorsed a cause, or whose picture is used to illustrate an article with which the person has an actual connection. So, for example, if a newspaper were to publish an article on taxi drivers who cheat their passengers and the article is accompanied by a photo of a taxi driver sitting in his cab, the paper had better be able to show that the particular driver in the photo is one who was involved in the cheating scandal.

The standard that applies for this tort is a simple one: the false light in which the plaintiff has been placed must be one that the reasonable person would consider objectionable.

The Constitutional Right of Privacy

Recall that the common law right of privacy protects us against intrusion by other individuals. Aside from a handful of statutes, our protection against intrusion upon our privacy by the federal government is largely based on the United States Constitution. The word "privacy" does not appear in the Constitution. Nonetheless, over the course of many years and many cases the Supreme Court has interpreted the Constitution to create such a right.

The Court has held that there are various types of privacy and the right is not absolute. For example:

- *Reynolds v. United States* (1878): The Court held that anti-polygamy laws are not an infringement of an individual's privacy rights.
- *Griswold v. Connecticut* (1965): A law against contraception is unconstitutional because it invades the "privacy of marriage."
- *Eisenstat v. Baird* (1972): Laws regulating contraceptive devices must treat married and unmarried people equally. (Thus, the Court identified a protection of an *individual* right of privacy.)
- *Roe v. Wade* (1973): The famous case in which the Court held that a woman has a right to choose to abort a pregnancy.
- *Bowers v. Hardwick* (1986): This is a case in which, perhaps, we see a shift in the pendulum's swing, which had been heavily in the direction of personal privacy. Here, the Court said that a law banning consensual sodomy is *not* unconstitutional.

Typically we think of certain decisions such as those about things like marriage or schooling as being "private." The Court's decisions over the years make it clear that is not always so. For example:

- *Singh v. Singh* (1990): The State *can* decide the level of consanguinity necessary to ban a marriage (i.e., where incest begins).
- *Loving v. Virginia* (1967): The State *cannot* ban interracial marriages.
- *Pierce v. Society of Sisters* (1925): States *cannot* insist that parents send their children to public schools.
- *Prince v. Massachusetts* (1944): A Jehovah's Witness sues to overturn a state child labor statute so her child can help sell "The Watchtower" at night. The Court held that laws for the benefit of minors are not subject to exception for parental religious beliefs.
- *Wisconsin v. Yoder* (1972): The Amish believe their children should not attend school beyond the eighth grade. The Court says States *cannot* compel students to attend school to age 16 if that is contrary to their parents' religious beliefs. (Justice William Douglas brilliantly dissented in this case that it was the rights of the *children* the Court should be considering, not the parents'. Suppose, for example, some Amish child harbored dreams of becoming a scientist but is forced to withdraw from school after grade eight. It is also interesting to speculate how this decision might have come out if the religious group in question had been, say, the Krishna set, rather than the benign seeming Amish.)

Our Constitutional right of privacy is largely protected via the Fourth Amendment, which prohibits unreasonable searches and seizures. It turns out that this right depends heavily on our expectations and how reasonable they are.

Let's review some of the Supreme Court's most influential decisions on the issue of privacy.

Privacy: Case 1

KATZ v. UNITED STATES

No. 35

SUPREME COURT OF THE UNITED STATES

389 U.S. 347; 88 S. Ct. 507; 19 L. Ed. 2d 576; 1967 U.S. LEXIS 2

October 17, 1967, Argued
December 18, 1967, Decided

JUDGES: Warren, Black, Douglas, Harlan, Brennan, Stewart, White, Fortas; Marshall took no part in the consideration or decision of the case.

OPINION: STEWART, Justice:

One of the interesting aspects of this case is that it is one of the first in which the Supreme Court grapples with the privacy of *intangible* property – that is, information.

The petitioner was convicted in the District Court for the Southern District of California under an eight-count indictment charging him with transmitting wagering information by telephone from Los Angeles to Miami and Boston, in violation of a federal statute. At trial the Government was permitted, over the petitioner's objection, to introduce evidence of the petitioner's end of telephone conversations, overheard by FBI agents who had attached an electronic listening and recording device to the outside of the public telephone booth from which he had placed his calls. In affirming his conviction, the Court of Appeals rejected the contention that the recordings had been obtained in violation of the Fourth Amendment, because "there was no physical entrance into the area occupied by [the petitioner]." We granted certiorari in order to consider the constitutional questions thus presented.

The petitioner has phrased those questions as follows:

A. Whether a public telephone booth is a constitutionally protected area so that evidence obtained by attaching an electronic listening recording device to the top of such a booth is obtained in violation of the right to privacy of the user of the booth.

B. Whether physical penetration of a constitutionally protected area is necessary before a search and seizure can be said to be violative of the Fourth Amendment to the United States Constitution.

We decline to adopt this formulation of the issues. In the first place, the correct solution of Fourth Amendment problems is not necessarily promoted by incantation of the phrase "constitutionally protected area." Secondly, the Fourth Amendment cannot be translated into a general constitutional "right to privacy." That Amendment protects individual privacy against certain kinds of governmental intrusion, but its protections go further, and often have nothing to do with privacy at all. Other provisions of the Constitution protect personal privacy from other forms of governmental invasion. But the protection of a person's *general* right to privacy – his right to be let alone by other people – is, like the protection of his property and of his very life, left largely to the law of the individual States.

Because of the misleading way the issues have been formulated, the parties have attached great significance to the characterization of the telephone booth from which the petitioner placed his calls. The petitioner has strenuously argued that the booth was a "constitutionally protected area." The Government has maintained with equal vigor that it was not. But this effort to decide whether or not a given "area," viewed in the abstract, is "constitutionally protected" deflects attention from the problem presented by this case. For the Fourth Amendment protects people, not places. What a person knowingly exposes to the public, even in his own home or office, is not a subject of Fourth Amendment protection. But what he seeks to preserve as private, even in an area accessible to the public, may be constitutionally protected.

The Government stresses the fact that the telephone booth from which the petitioner made his calls was constructed partly of glass, so that he was as visible after he entered it as he would have been if he had remained outside. But what he sought to exclude when he entered the booth was not the intruding eye – it was the uninvited ear. He did not shed his right to do so simply because he made his calls from a place where he might be seen. No less than an individual in a business office, in a friend's apartment, or in a taxicab, a person in a telephone booth may rely upon the protection of the Fourth Amendment. One who occupies it, shuts the door behind him, and pays the toll that permits him to place a call is surely entitled to assume that the words he utters into the mouthpiece will not be broadcast to the world. To read the Constitution more narrowly is to ignore the vital role that the public telephone has come to play in private communication.

The Government contends, however, that the activities of its agents in this case should not be tested by Fourth Amendment requirements, for the surveillance technique they employed involved no physical penetration of the telephone booth from which the petitioner placed his calls. It is true that the absence of such penetration was at one time thought to foreclose further Fourth Amendment inquiry, for that Amendment was thought to limit only searches and seizures of tangible property. But "the premise that property interests control the right of the Government to search and seize has been discredited." Indeed, we have expressly held that the Fourth Amendment governs not only the seizure of tangible items, but extends as well to the recording of oral statements, overheard without any "technical trespass under . . . local property law." Once this much is acknowledged, and once it is recognized that the Fourth Amendment protects people – and not simply "areas" – against unreasonable searches and seizures, it becomes clear that the reach of that Amendment cannot turn upon the presence or absence of a physical intrusion into any given enclosure.

The Government's activities in electronically listening to and recording the petitioner's words violated the privacy upon which he justifiably relied while using the telephone booth and thus constituted a "search and seizure" within the meaning of the Fourth Amendment. The fact that the electronic device employed to achieve that end did not happen to penetrate the wall of the booth can have no constitutional significance.

The question remaining for decision, then, is whether the search and seizure conducted in this case complied with constitutional standards. In that regard, the Government's position is that its agents acted in an entirely defensible manner: They did not begin their electronic surveillance until investigation of the petitioner's activities had established a strong probability that he was using the telephone in question to transmit gambling information to persons in other States, in violation of federal law. Moreover, the surveillance was limited, both in scope and in duration, to the specific purpose of establishing the contents of the petitioner's unlawful telephonic communications. The agents confined their surveillance to the brief periods during which he used the telephone booth, and they took great care to overhear only the conversations of the petitioner himself.

Accepting this account of the Government's actions as accurate, it is clear that this surveillance was so narrowly circumscribed that a duly authorized magistrate, properly notified of the need for such investigation, specifically informed of the basis on which it was to proceed, and clearly apprised of the precise intrusion it would entail, could constitutionally have authorized, with appropriate safeguards, the very limited search and seizure that the Government asserts in fact took place. Only last Term we sustained the validity of such an authorization, holding that, under sufficiently "precise and discriminate circumstances," a federal court may empower government agents to employ a concealed electronic device "for the narrow and particularized purpose of ascertaining the truth of the . . . allegations" of a "detailed factual affidavit alleging the commission of a specific criminal offense."

The Government urges that, because its agents relied upon the decisions in *Olmstead* and *Goldman*, and because they did no more here than they might properly have done with prior judicial sanction, we should retroactively validate their conduct. That we cannot do. It is apparent that the agents in this case acted with restraint. Yet the inescapable fact is that this restraint was imposed by the agents themselves, not by a judicial officer. Searches conducted without warrants have been held unlawful "notwithstanding facts unquestionably showing probable cause," for the Constitution requires "that the deliberate, impartial judgment of a judicial officer . . . be interposed between the citizen and the police. . . . " Over and again this Court has emphasized that the mandate of the [Fourth] Amendment requires adherence to judicial processes," and that searches conducted outside the judicial process, without prior approval by judge or magistrate, are *per se* unreasonable under the Fourth Amendment – subject only to a few specifically established and well-delineated exceptions.

It is difficult to imagine how any of those exceptions could ever apply to the sort of search and seizure involved in this case. Even electronic surveillance substantially contemporaneous with an individual's arrest could hardly be deemed an "incident" of that arrest. Nor could the use of electronic surveillance without prior authorization be justified on grounds of "hot pursuit." And, of course, the very nature of electronic surveillance precludes its use pursuant to the suspect's consent.

The Government does not question these basic principles. Rather, it urges the creation of a new exception to cover this case.[1] It argues that surveillance of a telephone booth should be exempted from the usual requirement of advance authorization by a magistrate upon a showing of probable cause. We cannot agree. Omission of such authorization "bypasses the safeguards provided by an objective predetermination of probable cause, and substitutes instead the far less reliable procedure of an after-the-event justification for the . . . search, too likely to be subtly influenced by the familiar shortcomings of hindsight judgment."

---

[1] Whether safeguards other than prior authorization by a magistrate would satisfy the Fourth Amendment in a situation involving the national security is a question not presented by this case.

And bypassing a neutral predetermination of the *scope* of a search leaves individuals secure from Fourth Amendment violations "only in the discretion of the police."

These considerations do not vanish when the search in question is transferred from the setting of a home, an office, or a hotel room to that of a telephone booth. Wherever a man may be, he is entitled to know that he will remain free from unreasonable searches and seizures. The government agents here ignored "the procedure of antecedent justification . . . that is central to the Fourth Amendment," a procedure that we hold to be a constitutional precondition of the kind of electronic surveillance involved in this case. Because the surveillance here failed to meet that condition, and because it led to the petitioner's conviction, the judgment must be reversed.

DOUGLAS; HARLAN; WHITE concur.

CONCURRENCE: DOUGLAS, Justice:

While I join the opinion of the Court, I feel compelled to reply to the separate concurring opinion of my Brother WHITE, which I view as a wholly unwarranted green light for the Executive Branch to resort to electronic eavesdropping without a warrant in cases which the Executive Branch itself labels "national security" matters.

Neither the President nor the Attorney General is a magistrate. In matters where they believe national security may be involved they are not detached, disinterested, and neutral as a court or magistrate must be. Under the separation of powers created by the Constitution, the Executive Branch is not supposed to be neutral and disinterested. Since spies and saboteurs are as entitled to the protection of the Fourth Amendment as suspected gamblers like petitioner, I cannot agree that where spies and saboteurs are involved adequate protection of Fourth Amendment rights is assured when the President and Attorney General assume both the position of adversary-and-prosecutor and disinterested, neutral magistrate.

CONCURRENCE: HARLAN, Justice:

I join the opinion of the Court, which I read to hold only (a) that an enclosed telephone booth is an area where, like a home, and unlike a field, a person has a constitutionally protected reasonable expectation of privacy; (b) that electronic as well as physical intrusion into a place that is in this sense private may constitute a violation of the Fourth Amendment; and (c) that the invasion of a constitutionally protected area by federal authorities is, as the Court has long held, presumptively unreasonable in the absence of a search warrant.

As the Court's opinion states, "the Fourth Amendment protects people, not places." The question, however, is what protection it affords to those people. Generally, as here, the answer to that question requires reference to a "place." My understanding of the rule that has emerged from prior decisions is that there is a twofold requirement, first that a person have exhibited an actual (subjective) expectation of privacy and, second, that the expectation be one that society is prepared to recognize as "reasonable." Thus a man's home is, for most purposes, a place where he expects privacy, but objects, activities, or statements that he exposes to the "plain view" of outsiders are not "protected" because no intention to keep them to himself has been exhibited. On the other hand, conversations in the open would not be protected against being overheard, for the expectation of privacy under the circumstances would be unreasonable.

The critical fact in this case is that "one who occupies it, shuts the door behind him, and pays the toll that permits him to place a call is surely entitled to assume" that his conversation is not being intercepted. The point is not that the booth is "accessible to the public" at other times, but that it is a temporarily private place whose momentary occupants' expectations of freedom from intrusion are recognized as reasonable.

Finally, I do not read the Court's opinion to declare that no interception of a conversation one-half of which occurs in a public telephone booth can be reasonable in the absence of a warrant. As elsewhere under the Fourth Amendment, warrants are the general rule, to which the legitimate needs of law enforcement may demand specific exceptions. It will be time enough to consider any such exceptions when an appropriate occasion presents itself, and I agree with the Court that this is not one.

CONCURRENCE: WHITE, Justice:

I agree that the official surveillance of petitioner's telephone conversations in a public booth must be subjected to the test of reasonableness under the Fourth Amendment and that on the record now before us the particular surveillance undertaken was unreasonable absent a warrant properly authorizing it. This application of the Fourth Amendment need not interfere with legitimate needs of law enforcement.

In joining the Court's opinion, I note the Court's acknowledgment that there are circumstances in which it is reasonable to search without a warrant. In this connection, in footnote [1] the Court points out that today's decision does not reach national security cases. Wiretapping to protect the security of the Nation has been authorized by successive Presidents. The present Administration would apparently save national security cases from restrictions against wiretapping. We should not require the warrant procedure and the magistrate's judgment if the President of the United States or his chief legal officer, the Attorney General, has considered the requirements of national security and authorized electronic surveillance as reasonable.

DISSENT: BLACK, Justice:

If I could agree with the Court that eavesdropping carried on by electronic means (equivalent to wiretapping) constitutes a "search" or "seizure," I would be happy to join the Court's opinion. For on that premise my Brother STEWART sets out methods in accord with the Fourth Amendment to guide States in the enactment and enforcement of laws passed to regulate wiretapping by government. In this respect today's opinion differs sharply from *Berger* v. *New York*, 388 U.S. 41, decided last Term, which held void on its face a New York statute authorizing wiretapping on warrants issued by magistrates on showings of probable cause. The *Berger* case also set up what appeared to be insuperable obstacles to the valid passage of such wiretapping laws by States. The Court's opinion in this case, however, removes the doubts about state power in this field and abates to a large extent the confusion and near-paralyzing effect of the *Berger* holding. Notwithstanding these good efforts of the Court, I am still unable to agree with its interpretation of the Fourth Amendment.

My basic objection is twofold: (1) I do not believe that the words of the Amendment will bear the meaning given them by today's decision, and (2) I do not believe that it is the proper role of this Court to rewrite the Amendment in order "to bring it into harmony with the times" and thus reach a result that many people believe to be desirable.

While I realize that an argument based on the meaning of words lacks the scope, and no doubt the appeal, of broad policy discussions and philosophical discourses on such nebulous subjects as privacy, for me the language of the Amendment is the crucial place to look in construing a written document such as our Constitution. The Fourth Amendment says that

> The right of the people to be secure in their persons, houses, papers, and effects, against unreasonable searches and seizures, shall not be violated, and no Warrants shall issue, but upon probable cause, supported by Oath or affirmation, and particularly describing the place to be searched, and the persons or things to be seized.

The first clause protects "persons, houses, papers, and effects, against unreasonable searches and seizures. . . . " These words connote the idea of tangible things with size, form, and weight, things capable of being searched, seized, or both. The second clause of the Amendment still further establishes its Framers' purpose to limit its protection to tangible things by providing that no warrants shall issue but those "particularly describing the place to be searched, and the persons or things to be seized." A conversation overheard by eavesdropping, whether by plain snooping or wiretapping, is not tangible and, under the normally accepted meanings of the words, can neither be searched nor seized. In addition the language of the second clause indicates that the Amendment refers not only to something tangible so it can be seized but to something already in existence so it can be described. How can one "describe" a future conversation, and, if one cannot, how can a magistrate issue a warrant to eavesdrop one in the future? It is argued that information showing what is expected to be said is sufficient to limit the boundaries of what later can be admitted into evidence; but does such general information really meet the specific language of the Amendment which says "particularly describing"? Rather than using language in a completely artificial way, I must conclude that the Fourth Amendment simply does not apply to eavesdropping.

Tapping telephone wires, of course, was an unknown possibility at the time the Fourth Amendment was adopted. But eavesdropping (and wiretapping is nothing more than eavesdropping by telephone) was "an ancient practice which at common law was condemned as a nuisance." There can be no doubt that the Framers were aware of this practice, and if they had desired to outlaw or restrict the use of evidence obtained by eavesdropping, I believe that they would have used the appropriate language to do so in the Fourth Amendment.

I do not deny that common sense requires and that this Court often has said that the Bill of Rights' safeguards should be given a liberal construction. This principle, however, does not justify construing the search and seizure amendment as applying to eavesdropping or the "seizure" of conversations. The Fourth Amendment was aimed directly at the abhorred practice of breaking in, ransacking and searching homes and other buildings and seizing people's personal belongings without warrants issued by magistrates. The Amendment deserves, and this Court has given it, a liberal construction in order to protect against warrantless searches of buildings and seizures of tangible personal effects. But until today this Court has refused to say that eavesdropping comes within the ambit of Fourth Amendment restrictions.

With this decision the Court has completed, I hope, its rewriting of the Fourth Amendment, which started only recently when the Court began referring incessantly to the Fourth Amendment not so much as a law against *unreasonable* searches and seizures as one to protect an individual's privacy. By clever word juggling the Court finds it plausible to argue that language aimed specifically at searches and seizures of things that can be searched and seized may, to protect privacy, be applied to eavesdropped evidence of conversations that can neither be searched nor seized. Few things happen to an individual that do not affect his privacy in one way or another. Thus, by arbitrarily substituting the Court's language, designed to protect privacy, for the Constitution's language, designed to protect against unreasonable searches and seizures, the Court has made the Fourth Amendment its vehicle for holding all laws violative of the Constitution which offend the Court's broadest concept of privacy.

The Fourth Amendment protects privacy only to the extent that it prohibits unreasonable searches and seizures of "persons, houses, papers, and effects." No general right is created by the Amendment so as to give this Court the unlimited power to hold unconstitutional everything which affects privacy. Certainly the Framers, well acquainted as they were with the excesses of governmental power, did not intend to grant this Court such omnipotent lawmaking authority as that. The history of governments proves that it is dangerous to freedom to repose such powers in courts.

For these reasons I respectfully dissent.

Thus, our right of privacy is violated when there is intrusion into something in which we have a "reasonable expectation of privacy." Katz had a reasonable expectation of privacy when he closed the door of the phone booth. This is cited by Justice Harlan as the critical fact in the case.

This case also tells us that there need not be a physical intrusion into the place that we assert is private, because the Fourth Amendment protects *people* not places. So it did not matter that the FBI overheard Katz's conversation by placing a bugging device on the *outside* of the phone booth.

Privacy: Case 2

CALIFORNIA v. GREENWOOD ET AL.

No. 86-684

SUPREME COURT OF THE UNITED STATES

486 U.S. 35; 108 S. Ct. 1625; 100 L. Ed. 2d 30; 1988 U.S. LEXIS 2279; 56 U.S.L.W. 4409

January 11, 1988, Argued
May 16, 1988, Decided

JUDGES: WHITE, J., delivered the opinion of the Court, in which REHNQUIST, C. J., and BLACKMUN, STEVENS, O'CONNOR, and SCALIA, JJ., joined. BRENNAN, J., filed a dissenting opinion, in which MARSHALL, J., joined, KENNEDY, J., took no part in the consideration or decision of the case.

OPINION: WHITE, Justice:

The issue here is whether the Fourth Amendment prohibits the warrantless search and seizure of garbage left for collection outside the curtilage of a home. We conclude, in accordance with the vast majority of lower courts that have addressed the issue, that it does not.

I

In early 1984, Investigator Jenny Stracner of the Laguna Beach Police Department received information indicating that respondent Greenwood might be engaged in narcotics trafficking. Stracner learned that a criminal suspect had informed a federal drug enforcement agent in February 1984 that a truck filled with illegal drugs was en route to the Laguna Beach address at which Greenwood resided. In addition, a neighbor complained of heavy vehicular traffic late at night in front of Greenwood's single-family home. The neighbor reported that the vehicles remained at Greenwood's house for only a few minutes.

Stracner sought to investigate this information by conducting a surveillance of Greenwood's home. She observed several vehicles make brief stops at the house during the late-night and early morning hours, and she followed a truck from the house to a residence that had previously been under investigation as a narcotics-trafficking location.

On April 6, 1984, Stracner asked the neighborhood's regular trash collector to pick up the plastic garbage bags that Greenwood had left on the curb in front of his house and to turn the bags over to her without mixing their contents with garbage from other houses. The trash collector cleaned his truck bin of other refuse, collected the garbage bags from the street in front of Greenwood's house, and turned the bags over to Stracner. The officer searched through the rubbish and found items indicative of narcotics use. She recited the information that she had gleaned from the trash search in an affidavit in support of a warrant to search Greenwood's home.

Police officers encountered both respondents at the house later that day when they arrived to execute the warrant. The police discovered quantities of cocaine and hashish during their search of the house. Respondents were arrested on felony narcotics charges. They subsequently posted bail.

The police continued to receive reports of many late-night visitors to the Greenwood house. On May 4, Investigator Robert Rahaeuser obtained Greenwood's garbage from the regular trash collector in the same manner as had Stracner. The garbage again contained evidence of narcotics use.

Rahaeuser secured another search warrant for Greenwood's home based on the information from the second trash search. The police found more narcotics and evidence of narcotics trafficking when they executed the warrant. Greenwood was again arrested.

The Superior Court dismissed the charges against respondents on the authority of *People* v. *Krivda*, 5 Cal. 3d 357, 486 P.2d 1262, 96 Cal. Rptr. 62 (1971), which held that warrantless trash searches violate the Fourth Amendment and the California Constitution. The court found that the police would not have had probable cause to search the Greenwood home without the evidence obtained from the trash searches.

The Court of Appeal affirmed. 182 Cal. App. 3d 729, 227 Cal. Rptr. 539 (1986). The court noted at the outset that the fruits of warrantless trash searches could no longer be suppressed if *Krivda* were based only on the California Constitution, because since 1982 the State has barred the suppression of evidence seized in violation of California law but not federal law. But *Krivda*, a decision binding on the Court of Appeal, also held that the fruits of warrantless trash searches were to be excluded under federal law. Hence, the Superior Court was correct in dismissing the charges against respondents.

The California Supreme Court denied the State's petition for review of the Court of Appeal's decision. We granted certiorari, 483 U.S. 1019, and now reverse.

II

The warrantless search and seizure of the garbage bags left at the curb outside the Greenwood house would violate the Fourth Amendment only if respondents manifested a subjective expectation of privacy in their garbage that society accepts as objectively reasonable. *Katz* v. *United States*, 389 U.S. 347, 361, 19 L. Ed. 2d 576, 88 S. Ct. 507 (1967) (Harlan, J., concurring). Respondents do not disagree with this standard.

They assert, however, that they had, and exhibited, an expectation of privacy with respect to the trash that was searched by the police: the trash, which was placed on the street for collection at a fixed time, was contained in opaque plastic bags, which the garbage collector was expected to pick up, mingle with the trash of others, and deposit at the garbage dump. The trash was only temporarily on the street, and there was little likelihood that it would be inspected by anyone.

It may well be that respondents did not expect that the contents of their garbage bags would become known to the police or other members of the public. An expectation of privacy does not give rise to Fourth Amendment protection, however, unless society is prepared to accept that expectation as objectively reasonable.

Here, we conclude that respondents exposed their garbage to the public sufficiently to defeat their claim to Fourth Amendment protection. It is common knowledge that plastic garbage bags left on or at the side of a public street are readily accessible to animals, children, scavengers, snoops, and other members of the public. Moreover, respondents placed their refuse at the curb for the express purpose of conveying it to a third party, the trash collector, who might himself have sorted through respondents' trash or permitted others, such as the police, to do so. Accordingly, having deposited their garbage "in an area particularly suited for public inspection and, in a manner of speaking, public consumption, for the express purpose of having strangers take it," respondents could have had no reasonable expectation of privacy in the inculpatory items that they discarded.

Furthermore, as we have held, the police cannot reasonably be expected to avert their eyes from evidence of criminal activity that could have been observed by any member of the public. Hence, "what a person knowingly exposes to the public, even in his own home or office, is not a subject of Fourth Amendment protection." *Katz* v. *United States*, *supra*, at 351. We held in *Smith* v. *Maryland*, 442 U.S. 735, 61 L. Ed. 2d 220, 99 S. Ct. 2577 (1979), for example, that the police did not violate the Fourth Amendment by causing a pen register to be installed at the telephone company's offices to record the telephone numbers dialed by a criminal suspect. An individual has no legitimate expectation of privacy in the numbers dialed on his telephone, we reasoned, because he voluntarily conveys those numbers to the telephone company when he uses the telephone. Again, we observed that "a person has no legitimate expectation of privacy in information he voluntarily turns over to third parties."

[Sections II–IV are omitted.]

V

The judgment of the California Court of Appeal is therefore reversed, and this case is remanded for further proceedings not inconsistent with this opinion.

It is so ordered.

DISSENT: BRENNAN, Justice:

Every week for two months, and at least once more a month later, the Laguna Beach police clawed through the trash that respondent Greenwood left in opaque, sealed bags on the curb outside his home. Complete strangers minutely scrutinized their bounty, undoubtedly dredging up intimate details of Greenwood's private life and habits. The intrusions proceeded without a warrant, and no court before or since has concluded that the police acted on probable cause to believe Greenwood was engaged in any criminal activity.

Scrutiny of another's trash is contrary to commonly accepted notions of civilized behavior. I suspect, therefore, that members of our society will be shocked to learn that the Court, the ultimate guarantor of liberty, deems unreasonable our expectation that the aspects of our private lives that are concealed safely in a trash bag will not become public.

I

The Framers of the Fourth Amendment understood that "unreasonable searches" of "paper[s] and effects" – no less than "unreasonable searches" of "person[s] and houses" – infringe privacy. As early as 1878, this Court acknowledged that the contents of "letters and sealed packages . . . in the mail are as fully guarded from examination and inspection . . . as if they were retained by the parties forwarding them in their own domiciles." In short, so long as a package is "closed against inspection," the Fourth Amendment protects its contents, "wherever they may be," and the police must obtain a warrant to search it just "as is required when papers are subjected to search in one's own household."

Our precedent, therefore, leaves no room to doubt that had respondents been carrying their personal effects in opaque, sealed plastic bags – identical to the ones they placed on the curb – their privacy would have been protected from warrantless police intrusion.

II

Respondents deserve no less protection just because Greenwood used the bags to discard rather than to transport his personal effects. Their contents are not inherently any less private, and Greenwood's decision to discard them, at least in the manner in which he did, does not diminish his expectation of privacy.

A trash bag, like any of the above-mentioned containers, "is a common repository for one's personal effects" and, even more than many of them, is "therefore . . . inevitably associated with the expectation of privacy." A single bag of trash testifies eloquently to the eating, reading, and recreational habits of the person who produced it. A search of trash, like a search of the bedroom, can relate intimate details about sexual practices, health, and personal hygiene. Like rifling through desk drawers or intercepting phone calls, rummaging through trash can divulge the target's financial and professional status, political affiliations and inclinations, private thoughts, personal relationships, and romantic interests. It cannot be doubted that a sealed trash bag harbors telling evidence of the "intimate activity associated with the 'sanctity of a man's home and the privacies of life,'" for which the Fourth Amendment is designed.

In evaluating the reasonableness of Greenwood's expectation that his sealed trash bags would not be invaded, the Court has held that we must look to "understandings that are recognized and permitted by society." Most of us, I believe, would be incensed to discover a meddler – whether a neighbor, a reporter, or a detective – scrutinizing our sealed trash containers to discover some detail of our personal lives. When a tabloid reporter examined then-Secretary of State Henry Kissinger's trash and published his findings, Kissinger was "really revolted" by the intrusion and his wife suffered "grave anguish." The public response roundly condemning the reporter demonstrates that society not only recognized those reactions as reasonable, but shared them as well. Commentators variously characterized his conduct as "a disgusting invasion of personal privacy."

That is not to deny that isolated intrusions into opaque, sealed trash containers occur. When, acting on their own, "animals, children, scavengers, snoops, [or] other members of the public," *actually* rummage through a bag of trash and expose its contents to plain view, "police cannot reasonably be expected to avert their eyes from evidence of criminal activity that could have been observed by any member of the public". That much follows from cases like *Jacobsen*, 466 U.S. at 117, 120, n. 17, which held that police may constitutionally inspect a package whose "integrity" a private carrier has *already* "compromised," because "the Fourth Amendment is implicated only if the authorities use information with respect to which the expectation of privacy has not *already* been frustrated". Faithful application of the warrant requirement does not require police to "avert their eyes from evidence of criminal activity that could have been observed by any member of the public." Rather, it only requires them to adhere to norms of privacy that members of the public plainly acknowledge.

The mere *possibility* that unwelcome meddlers *might* open and rummage through the containers does not negate the expectation of privacy in their contents any more than the possibility of a burglary negates an expectation of privacy in the home; or the possibility of a private intrusion negates an expectation of privacy in an unopened package; or the possibility that an operator will listen in on a telephone conversation negates an expectation of privacy in the words spoken on the telephone. "What a person . . . seeks to preserve as private, *even in an area accessible to the public,* may be constitutionally protected." *Katz*, 389 U.S. at 351-352. Nor is it dispositive that "respondents placed their refuse at the curb for the express purpose of conveying it to a third party, . . . who might himself have sorted through respondents' trash or permitted others, such as the police, to do so." In the first place, Greenwood can hardly be faulted for leaving trash on his curb when a county ordinance commanded him to do so, and prohibited him from disposing of it in any other way. Unlike in other circumstances where privacy is compromised, Greenwood could not "avoid exposing personal belongings . . . by simply leaving them at home." *O'Connor, supra,* at 725. More importantly, even the voluntary relinquishment of possession or control over an effect does not necessarily amount to a relinquishment of a privacy expectation in it. Were it otherwise, a letter or package would lose all Fourth Amendment protection when placed in a mailbox or other depository with the "express purpose" of entrusting it to the postal officer or a private carrier; those bailees are just as likely as trash collectors (and certainly have greater incentive) to "sor[t] through" the personal effects entrusted to them, "or permi[t] others, such as police to do so." Yet, it has been clear for at least 110 years that the possibility of such an intrusion does not justify a warrantless search by police in the first instance.

III

The American society with which I am familiar "chooses to dwell in reasonable security and freedom from surveillance," and is more dedicated to individual liberty and more sensitive to intrusions on the sanctity of the home than the Court is willing to acknowledge.

I dissent.

Note: Later, in *United States v. Scott* (1972), the Court extended this holding to a case in which the defendants had taken *extraordinary* measures to assure their privacy. They had shredded documents before placing them in the garbage but the IRS had reassembled them.

The facts are critical in most of these privacy cases. Slight changes might bring different outcomes.

Query:

What if the garbage collector were a private pick-up?

What if the bags were left at the front of the house instead of at the curb?

What if the defendants watched for the garbage collector and then brought the bags out?

What if the bags were deposited in a dumpster?

What if the bags were taken personally to the dump?

The *Greenwood* case underlines the fact that even though an individual may have a personal, subjective expectation of privacy, the expectation must also be one that society is willing to accept as being objectively reasonable. Here, the critical fact that will play a major role in later privacy rights analysis is that Greenwood left the garbage at the curb for the express purpose of conveying it to a third party. There can be no *objectively* reasonable expectation of privacy in anything (including information) voluntarily given to a third party.

Privacy: Case 3

DANNY LEE KYLLO v. UNITED STATES

No. 99-8508

SUPREME COURT OF THE UNITED STATES

533 U.S. 27; 121 S. Ct. 2038; 150 L. Ed. 2d 94; 2001 U.S. LEXIS 4487; 69 U.S.L.W. 4431; 2001 Cal. Daily Op. Service 4749; 2001 Daily Journal DAR 5879; 2001 Colo. J. C.A.R. 2926; 14 Fla. L. Weekly Fed. S 329

February 20, 2001, Argued
June 11, 2001, Decided

JUDGES: SCALIA, J., delivered the opinion of the Court, in which SOUTER, THOMAS, GINSBURG, and BREYER, JJ., joined. STEVENS, J., filed a dissenting opinion, in which REHNQUIST, C. J., and O'CONNOR and KENNEDY, JJ., joined.

OPINION: SCALIA, Justice:

This case presents the question whether the use of a thermal-imaging device aimed at a private home from a public street to detect relative amounts of heat within the home constitutes a "search" within the meaning of the Fourth Amendment.

I

In 1991 Agent William Elliott of the United States Department of the Interior came to suspect that marijuana was being grown in the home belonging to petitioner Danny Kyllo, part of a triplex on Rhododendron Drive in Florence, Oregon. Indoor marijuana growth typically requires high-intensity lamps. In order to determine whether an amount of heat was emanating from petitioner's home consistent with the use of such lamps, at 3:20 a.m. on January 16, 1992, Agent Elliott and Dan Haas used an Agema Thermovision 210 thermal imager to scan the triplex. Thermal imagers detect infrared radiation, which virtually all objects emit but which is not visible to the naked eye. The imager converts radiation into images based on relative warmth – black is cool, white is hot, shades of gray connote relative differences; in that respect, it operates somewhat like a video camera showing heat images. The scan of Kyllo's home took only a few minutes and was performed from the passenger seat of Agent Elliott's vehicle across the street from the front of the house and also from the street in back of the house. The scan showed that the roof over the garage and a side wall of petitioner's home were relatively hot compared to the rest of the home and substantially warmer than neighboring homes in the triplex. Agent Elliott concluded that petitioner was using halide lights to grow marijuana in his house, which indeed he was. Based on tips from informants, utility bills, and the thermal imaging, a Federal Magistrate Judge issued a warrant authorizing a search of petitioner's home, and the agents found an indoor growing operation involving more than 100 plants. Petitioner was indicted on one count of manufacturing marijuana, in violation of 21 U.S.C. § 841(a)(1). He unsuccessfully moved to suppress the evidence seized from his home and then entered a conditional guilty plea.

The Court of Appeals for the Ninth Circuit remanded the case for an evidentiary hearing regarding the intrusiveness of thermal imaging. On remand the District Court found that the Agema 210 "is a non-intrusive device which emits no rays or beams and shows a crude visual image of the heat being radiated from the outside of the house"; it "did not show any people or activity within the walls of the structure"; "the device used cannot penetrate walls or windows to reveal conversations or human activities"; and "no intimate details of the home were observed." Based on these findings, the District Court upheld the validity of the warrant that relied in part upon the thermal imaging, and reaffirmed its denial of the motion to suppress. A divided Court of Appeals initially reversed, but that opinion was withdrawn and the panel (after a change in composition) affirmed, with Judge Noonan dissenting. The court held that petitioner had shown no subjective expectation of privacy because he had made no attempt to conceal the heat escaping from his home, and even if he had, there was no objectively reasonable expectation of privacy because the imager "did not expose any intimate details of Kyllo's life," only "amorphous 'hot spots' on the roof and exterior wall." We granted certiorari.

II

"At the very core" of the Fourth Amendment "stands the right of a man to retreat into his own home and there be free from unreasonable governmental intrusion." With few exceptions, the question whether a warrantless search of a home is reasonable and hence constitutional must be answered no.

On the other hand, the antecedent question of whether or not a Fourth Amendment "search" has occurred is not so simple under our precedent. The permissibility of ordinary visual surveillance of a home used to be clear because, well into the 20th century, our Fourth Amendment jurisprudence was tied to common-law trespass. Visual surveillance was unquestionably lawful because "'the eye cannot by the laws of England be guilty of a trespass.'" We have since decoupled violation of a person's Fourth Amendment rights from trespassory violation of his property, but the lawfulness of warrantless visual surveillance of a home has still been preserved. As we observed in *California* v. *Ciraolo*, 476 U.S. 207, 213, 90 L. Ed. 2d 210, 106 S. Ct. 1809 (1986), "the Fourth Amendment protection of the home has never been extended to require law enforcement officers to shield their eyes when passing by a home on public thoroughfares."

One might think that the new validating rationale would be that examining the portion of a house that is in plain public view, while it is a "search" despite the absence of trespass, is not an "unreasonable" one under the Fourth Amendment. But in fact we have held that visual observation is no "search" at all – perhaps in order to preserve somewhat more intact our doctrine that warrantless searches are presumptively unconstitutional. In assessing when a search is not a search, we have applied somewhat in reverse the principle first enunciated in *Katz* v. *United States*, 389 U.S. 347, 19 L. Ed. 2d 576, 88 S. Ct. 507 (1967). We held that the Fourth Amendment protected Katz from the warrantless eavesdropping because he "justifiably relied" upon the privacy of the telephone booth. As Justice Harlan's oft-quoted concurrence described it, a Fourth Amendment search occurs when the government violates a subjective expectation of privacy that society recognizes as reasonable. We have subsequently applied this principle to hold that a Fourth Amendment search does *not* occur – even when the explicitly protected location of a *house* is concerned – unless "the individual manifested a subjective expectation of privacy in the object of the challenged search," and "society [is] willing to recognize that expectation as reasonable." We have applied this test in holding that it is not a search for the police to use a pen register at the phone company to determine what numbers were dialed in a private home, and we have applied the test on two different occasions in holding that aerial surveillance of private homes and surrounding areas does not constitute a search.

The present case involves officers on a public street engaged in more than naked-eye surveillance of a home. We have previously reserved judgment as to how much technological enhancement of ordinary perception from such a vantage point, if any, is too much. While we upheld enhanced aerial photography of an industrial complex in *Dow Chemical*, we noted that we found "it important that this is *not* an area immediately adjacent to a private home, where privacy expectations are most heightened" (emphasis in original).

III

It would be foolish to contend that the degree of privacy secured to citizens by the Fourth Amendment has been entirely unaffected by the advance of technology. For example, as the cases discussed above make clear, the technology enabling human flight has exposed to public view (and hence, we have said, to official observation) uncovered portions of the house and its curtilage that once were private. The question we confront today is what limits there are upon this power of technology to shrink the realm of guaranteed privacy.

The *Katz* test – whether the individual has an expectation of privacy that society is prepared to recognize as reasonable – has often been criticized as circular, and hence subjective and unpredictable. While it may be difficult to refine *Katz* when the search of areas such as telephone booths, automobiles, or even the curtilage and uncovered portions of residences are at issue, in the case of the search of the interior of homes – the prototypical and hence most commonly litigated area of protected privacy – there is a ready criterion, with roots deep in the common law, of the minimal expectation of privacy that *exists*, and that is acknowledged to be *reasonable*. To withdraw protection of this minimum expectation would be to permit police technology to erode the privacy guaranteed by the Fourth Amendment. We think that obtaining by sense-enhancing technology any information regarding the interior of the home that could not otherwise have been obtained without physical "intrusion into a constitutionally protected area," constitutes a search – at least where (as here) the technology in question is not in general public use.

Query: What about the *Katz* "people, not places" language?

This assures preservation of that degree of privacy against government that existed when the Fourth Amendment was adopted. On the basis of this criterion, the information obtained by the thermal imager in this case was the product of a search.

The Government maintains, however, that the thermal imaging must be upheld because it detected "only heat radiating from the external surface of the house." The dissent makes this its leading point, contending that there is a fundamental difference between what it calls "off-the-wall" observations and "through-the-wall surveillance." But just as a thermal imager captures only heat emanating from a house, so also a powerful directional microphone picks up only sound emanating from a house – and a satellite capable of scanning from many miles away would pick up only visible light emanating from a house. We rejected such a mechanical interpretation of the Fourth Amendment in *Katz*, where the eavesdropping device picked up only sound waves that reached the exterior of the phone booth. Reversing that approach would leave the homeowner at the mercy of advancing technology – including imaging technology that could discern all human activity in the home. While the technology used in the present case was relatively crude, the rule we adopt must take account of more sophisticated systems that are already in use or in development.[1] The dissent's reliance on the distinction between

[1] The ability to "see" through walls and other opaque barriers is a clear, and scientifically feasible, goal of law enforcement research and development. The National Law Enforcement and Corrections Technology Center, a program within the United States Department of Justice, features on its Internet Website projects that include a "Radar-Based Through-the-Wall Surveillance System," "Handheld Ultrasound Through the Wall Surveillance," and a "Radar Flashlight" that "will enable law officers to detect individuals through

"off-the-wall" and "through-the-wall" observation is entirely incompatible with the dissent's belief, which we discuss below, that thermal-imaging observations of the intimate details of a home are impermissible. The most sophisticated thermal imaging devices continue to measure heat "off-the-wall" rather than "through-the-wall"; the dissent's disapproval of those more sophisticated thermal-imaging devices is an acknowledgement that there is no substance to this distinction. As for the dissent's extraordinary assertion that anything learned through "an inference" cannot be a search, that would validate even the "through-the-wall" technologies that the dissent purports to disapprove. Surely the dissent does not believe that the through-the-wall radar or ultrasound technology produces an 8-by-10 Kodak glossy that needs no analysis (*i.e.*, the making of inferences). And, of course, the novel proposition that inference insulates a search is blatantly contrary to *United States* v. *Karo*, 468 U.S. 705, 82 L. Ed. 2d 530, 104 S. Ct. 3296 (1984), where the police "inferred" from the activation of a beeper that a certain can of ether was in the home. The police activity was held to be a search, and the search was held unlawful.

The Government also contends that the thermal imaging was constitutional because it did not "detect private activities occurring in private areas". It points out that in *Dow Chemical* we observed that the enhanced aerial photography did not reveal any "intimate details." *Dow Chemical*, however, involved enhanced aerial photography of an industrial complex, which does not share the Fourth Amendment sanctity of the home. The Fourth Amendment's protection of the home has never been tied to measurement of the quality or quantity of information obtained. In the home, our cases show, *all* details are intimate details, because the entire area is held safe from prying government eyes.

Limiting the prohibition of thermal imaging to "intimate details" would not only be wrong in principle; it would be impractical in application, failing to provide "a workable accommodation between the needs of law enforcement and the interests protected by the Fourth Amendment." To begin with, there is no necessary connection between the sophistication of the surveillance equipment and the "intimacy" of the details that it observes – which means that one cannot say (and the police cannot be assured) that use of the relatively crude equipment at issue here will always be lawful. The Agema Thermovision 210 might disclose, for example, at what hour each night the lady of the house takes her daily sauna and bath – a detail that many would consider "intimate"; and a much more sophisticated system might detect nothing more intimate than the fact that someone left a closet light on. We could not, in other words, develop a rule approving only that through-the-wall surveillance which identifies objects no smaller than 36 by 36 inches, but would have to develop a jurisprudence specifying which home activities are "intimate" and which are not. And even when (if ever) that jurisprudence were fully developed, no police officer would be able to know in *advance* whether his through-the-wall surveillance picks up "intimate" details – and thus would be unable to know in advance whether it is constitutional.

[T]he driving force of the dissent appears to be a distinction among different types of information – whether the "homeowner would even care if anybody noticed". The dissent offers no practical guidance for the application of this standard, and for reasons

interior building walls." www.nlectc.org/techproj/ (visited May 3, 2001). Some devices may emit low levels of radiation that travel "through-the-wall," but others, such as more sophisticated thermal imaging devices, are entirely passive, or "off-the-wall" as the dissent puts it.

already discussed, we believe there can be none. The people in their houses, as well as the police, deserve more precision.

"The Fourth Amendment is to be construed in the light of what was deemed an unreasonable search and seizure when it was adopted, and in a manner which will conserve public interests as well as the interests and rights of individual citizens." *Carroll v. United States*, 267 U.S. 132, 149, 69 L. Ed. 543, 45 S. Ct. 280 (1925).

Where, as here, the Government uses a device that is not in general public use, to explore details of the home that would previously have been unknowable without physical intrusion, the surveillance is a "search" and is presumptively unreasonable without a warrant.

Since we hold the Thermovision imaging to have been an unlawful search, it will remain for the District Court to determine whether, without the evidence it provided, the search warrant issued in this case was supported by probable cause – and if not, whether there is any other basis for supporting admission of the evidence that the search pursuant to the warrant produced.

The judgment of the Court of Appeals is reversed; the case is remanded for further proceedings consistent with this opinion.

It is so ordered.

DISSENT: STEVENS, Justice:

There is, in my judgment, a distinction of constitutional magnitude between "through-the-wall surveillance" that gives the observer or listener direct access to information in a private area, on the one hand, and the thought processes used to draw inferences from information in the public domain, on the other hand. I believe that the supposedly "bright-line" rule the Court has created in response to its concerns about future technological developments is unnecessary, unwise, and inconsistent with the Fourth Amendment.

I

There is no need for the Court to craft a new rule to decide this case, as it is controlled by established principles from our Fourth Amendment jurisprudence. One of those core principles, of course, is that "searches and seizures *inside a home* without a warrant are presumptively unreasonable." But it is equally well settled that searches and seizures of property in plain view are presumptively reasonable. Whether that property is residential or commercial, the basic principle is the same: "'What a person knowingly exposes to the public, even in his own home or office, is not a subject of Fourth Amendment protection.'" That is the principle implicated here.

> **But ponder the "knowingly" part. How does that factor into analyses involving new technologies? When can a person be said to "know" he or she is exposing information to new technologies?**

While the Court "takes the long view" and decides this case based largely on the potential of yet-to-be-developed technology that might allow "through-the-wall surveillance," this case involves nothing more than off-the-wall surveillance by law enforcement officers to gather information exposed to the general public from the outside of petitioner's home.

Indeed, the ordinary use of the senses might enable a neighbor or passerby to notice the heat emanating from a building, particularly if it is vented, as was the case here. Additionally, any member of the public might notice that one part of a house is warmer than another part or a nearby building if, for example, rainwater evaporates or snow melts at different rates across its surfaces.

Thus, the notion that heat emissions from the outside of a dwelling is a private matter implicating the protections of the Fourth Amendment (the text of which guarantees the right of people "to be secure *in* their ... houses" against unreasonable searches and seizures (emphasis added)) is not only unprecedented but also quite difficult to take seriously.

To be sure, the homeowner has a reasonable expectation of privacy concerning what takes place within the home, and the Fourth Amendment's protection against physical invasions of the home should apply to their functional equivalent. But the equipment in this case did not penetrate the walls of petitioner's home, and while it did pick up "details of the home" that were exposed to the public, it did not obtain "any information regarding the *interior* of the home". In the Court's own words, based on what the thermal imager "showed" regarding the outside of petitioner's home, the officers "concluded" that petitioner was engaging in illegal activity inside the home. It would be quite absurd to characterize their thought processes as "searches," regardless of whether they inferred (rightly) that petitioner was growing marijuana in his house, or (wrongly) that "the lady of the house [was taking] her daily sauna and bath." In either case, the only conclusions the officers reached concerning the interior of the home were at least as indirect as those that might have been inferred from the contents of discarded garbage, see *California* v. *Greenwood*, 486 U.S. 35, 100 L. Ed. 2d 30, 108 S. Ct. 1625 (1988).

> **Query: Is that a good analogy? Is the information gathered in this case truly akin to physical evidence not capable of any other interpretation – i.e., syringes and other drug paraphernalia?**

For the first time in its history, the Court assumes that an inference can amount to a Fourth Amendment violation.

[P]ublic officials should not have to avert their senses or their equipment from detecting emissions in the public domain such as excessive heat, traces of smoke, suspicious odors, odorless gases, airborne particulates, or radioactive emissions, any of which could identify hazards to the community. In my judgment, monitoring such emissions with "sense-enhancing technology," and drawing useful conclusions from such monitoring, is an entirely reasonable public service.

On the other hand, the countervailing privacy interest is at best trivial. [I]t does not seem to me that society will suffer from a rule requiring the rare homeowner who both intends to engage in uncommon activities that produce extraordinary amounts of heat, and wishes to conceal that production from outsiders, to make sure that the surrounding area is well insulated.

[T]he officers' conduct did not amount to a search and was perfectly reasonable.

II

The newly minted rule encompasses "obtaining [1] by sense-enhancing technology [2] any information regarding the interior of the home [3] that could not otherwise have been obtained without physical intrusion into a constitutionally protected area . . . [4] at least where (as here) the technology in question is not in general public use." As I have suggested, I would not erect a constitutional impediment to the use of sense-enhancing technology unless it provides its user with the functional equivalent of actual presence in the area being searched.

[H]ow much use is general public use is not even hinted at by the Court's opinion, which makes the somewhat doubtful assumption that the thermal imager used in this case does not satisfy that criterion.[2] In any event, putting aside its lack of clarity, this criterion is somewhat perverse because it seems likely that the threat to privacy will grow, rather than recede, as the use of intrusive equipment becomes more readily available.

It is clear, however, that the category of "sense-enhancing technology" covered by the new rule is far too broad. It would, for example, embrace potential mechanical substitutes for dogs trained to react when they sniff narcotics. But in *United States* v. *Place*, 462 U.S. 696, 707, 77 L. Ed. 2d 110, 103 S. Ct. 2637 (1983), we held that a dog sniff that "discloses only the presence or absence of narcotics" does "not constitute a 'search' within the meaning of the Fourth Amendment," and it must follow that sense-enhancing equipment that identifies nothing but illegal activity is not a search either. Nevertheless, the use of such a device would be unconstitutional under the Court's rule, as would the use of other new devices that might detect the odor of deadly bacteria or chemicals for making a new type of high explosive, even if the devices (like the dog sniffs) are "so limited in both the manner in which" they obtain information and "in the content of the information" they reveal.

The application of the Court's new rule to "any information regarding the interior of the home" is too sweeping in that information "regarding" the interior of a home apparently is not just information obtained through its walls, but also information concerning the outside of the building that could lead to (however many) inferences "regarding" what might be inside. Under that expansive view, I suppose, an officer using an infrared camera to observe a man silently entering the side door of a house at night carrying a pizza might conclude that its interior is now occupied by someone who likes pizza, and by doing so the officer would be guilty of conducting an unconstitutional "search" of the home.

The final requirement of the Court's new rule is that the information "could not otherwise have been obtained without physical intrusion into a constitutionally protected area."

The two reasons advanced by the Court as justifications for the adoption of its new rule are both unpersuasive. First, the Court suggests that its rule is compelled by our holding in *Katz*, because in that case, as in this, the surveillance consisted of nothing more than the monitoring of waves emanating from a private area into the public domain. Yet there are critical differences between the cases. In *Katz*, the electronic listening device

[2] The record describes a device that numbers close to a thousand manufactured units; that has a predecessor numbering in the neighborhood of 4,000 to 5,000 units; that competes with a similar product numbering from 5,000 to 6,000 units; and that is "readily available to the public" for commercial, personal, or law enforcement purposes, and is just an 800-number away from being rented from "half a dozen national companies" by anyone who wants one. Since, by virtue of the Court's new rule, the issue is one of first impression, perhaps it should order an evidentiary hearing to determine whether these facts suffice to establish "general public use."

attached to the outside of the phone booth allowed the officers to pick up the content of the conversation inside the booth, making them the functional equivalent of intruders because they gathered information that was otherwise available only to someone inside the private area; it would be as if, in this case, the thermal imager presented a view of the heat-generating activity inside petitioner's home. By contrast, the thermal imager here disclosed only the relative amounts of heat radiating from the house; it would be as if, in *Katz*, the listening device disclosed only the relative volume of sound leaving the booth, which presumably was discernible in the public domain.

> **Is this a useful analogy? Would the police have been able to infer anything from the volume of the conversation? They could, after all, SEE that Katz was talking on the phone.**

It is pure hyperbole for the Court to suggest that refusing to extend the holding of *Katz* to this case would leave the homeowner at the mercy of "technology that could discern all human activity in the home."

Second, the Court argues that the permissibility of "through-the-wall surveillance" cannot depend on a distinction between observing "intimate details" such as "the lady of the house [taking] her daily sauna and bath," and noticing only "the nonintimate rug on the vestibule floor" or "objects no smaller than 36 by 36 inches." This entire argument assumes, of course, that the thermal imager in this case could or did perform "through-the-wall surveillance" that could identify any detail "that would previously have been unknowable without physical intrusion." In fact, the device could not, and did not, enable its user to identify either the lady of the house, the rug on the vestibule floor, or anything else inside the house, whether smaller or larger than 36 by 36 inches.

III

Although the Court is properly and commendably concerned about the threats to privacy that may flow from advances in the technology available to the law enforcement profession, it has unfortunately failed to heed the tried and true counsel of judicial restraint. Instead of concentrating on the rather mundane issue that is actually presented by the case before it, the Court has endeavored to craft an all-encompassing rule for the future. It would be far wiser to give legislators an unimpeded opportunity to grapple with these emerging issues rather than to shackle them with prematurely devised constitutional constraints.

I respectfully dissent.

～

This chapter on privacy will conclude with a look at a few more cases. Two are Supreme Court cases in which the Court applies its reasonable expectation of privacy analysis in different factual settings. One case illustrates the application of one of the common law privacy right protections we discussed earlier: false light in the public eye. And finally, we will look at a case in which the Supreme Court addresses the question of whether we have a right of privacy that can be defined as a right to be anonymous.

Privacy: Case 4

SMITH v. MARYLAND

No. 78-5374

SUPREME COURT OF THE UNITED STATES

442 U.S. 735; 99 S. Ct. 2577; 61 L. Ed. 2d 220; 1979 U.S. LEXIS 134

March 28, 1979, Argued
June 20, 1979, Decided

JUDGES: BLACKMUN, J., delivered the opinion of the Court, in which BURGER, C. J., and WHITE, REHINQUIST, and STEVENS, JJ., joined. STEWART, J., and MARSHALL, J., filed dissenting opinions, in which BRENNAN, J., joined. POWELL, J., took no part in the consideration or decision of the case.

OPINION: BLACKMUN, Justice:

This case presents the question whether the installation and use of a pen register[1] constitutes a "search" within the meaning of the Fourth Amendment, made applicable to the States through the Fourteenth Amendment.

I

On March 5, 1976, in Baltimore, Md., Patricia McDonough was robbed. She gave the police a description of the robber and of a 1975 Monte Carlo automobile she had observed near the scene of the crime. After the robbery, McDonough began receiving threatening and obscene phone calls from a man identifying himself as the robber. On one occasion, the caller asked that she step out on her front porch; she did so, and saw the 1975 Monte Carlo she had earlier described to police moving slowly past her home. On March 16, police spotted a man who met McDonough's description driving a 1975 Monte Carlo in her neighborhood. By tracing the license plate number, police learned that the car was registered in the name of petitioner, Michael Lee Smith.

The next day, the telephone company, at police request, installed a pen register at its central offices to record the numbers dialed from the telephone at petitioner's home. The police did not get a warrant or court order before having the pen register installed. The register revealed that on March 17 a call was placed from petitioner's home to McDonough's phone. On the basis of this and other evidence, the police obtained a warrant to search petitioner's residence. The search revealed that a page in petitioner's phone book was turned down to the name and number of Patricia McDonough; the phone book was seized. Petitioner was arrested, and a six-man lineup was held on March 19. McDonough identified petitioner as the man who had robbed her.

Petitioner was indicted in the Criminal Court of Baltimore for robbery. By pretrial motion, he sought to suppress "all fruits derived from the pen register" on the ground that the police had failed to secure a warrant prior to its installation. The trial court denied the suppression motion, holding that the warrantless installation of the pen register did not

---

[1] "A pen register is a mechanical device that records the numbers dialed on a telephone by monitoring the electrical impulses caused when the dial on the telephone is released. It does not overhear oral communications and does not indicate whether calls are actually completed." *United States* v. *New York Tel. Co.*, 434 U.S. 159, 161 n. 1 (1977).

violate the Fourth Amendment. The pen register tape (evidencing the fact that a phone call had been made from petitioner's phone to McDonough's phone) and the phone book seized in the search of petitioner's residence were admitted into evidence against [petitioner]. Petitioner was convicted and was sentenced to six years. He appealed to the Maryland Court of Special Appeals, but the Court of Appeals of Maryland issued a writ of certiorari to the intermediate court in advance of its decision in order to consider whether the pen register evidence had been properly admitted at petitioner's trial.

The Court of Appeals affirmed the judgment of conviction, holding that "there is no constitutionally protected reasonable expectation of privacy in the numbers dialed into a telephone system and hence no search within the Fourth Amendment is implicated by the use of a pen register installed at the central offices of the telephone company." Because there was no "search," the court concluded, no warrant was needed. Three judges dissented, expressing the view that individuals do have a legitimate expectation of privacy regarding the phone numbers they dial from their homes; that the installation of a pen register thus constitutes a "search"; and that, in the absence of exigent circumstances, the failure of police to secure a warrant mandated that the pen register evidence here be excluded. Certiorari was granted in order to resolve indications of conflict in the decided cases as to the restrictions imposed by the Fourth Amendment on the use of pen registers.

II

A

The Fourth Amendment guarantees "[the] right of the people to be secure in their persons, houses, papers, and effects, against unreasonable searches and seizures." In determining whether a particular form of government-initiated electronic surveillance is a "search" within the meaning of the Fourth Amendment, our lodestar is *Katz* v. *United States*, 389 U.S. 347 (1967).

Consistently with *Katz*, this Court uniformly has held that the application of the Fourth Amendment depends on whether the person invoking its protection can claim a "justifiable," a "reasonable," or a "legitimate expectation of privacy" that has been invaded by government action. This inquiry, as Mr. Justice Harlan aptly noted in his *Katz* concurrence, normally embraces two discrete questions. The first is whether the individual, by his conduct, has "exhibited an actual (subjective) expectation of privacy," – whether, in the words of the *Katz* majority, the individual has shown that "he seeks to preserve [something] as private." The second question is whether the individual's subjective expectation of privacy is "one that society is prepared to recognize as 'reasonable,'" – whether, in the words of the *Katz* majority, the individual's expectation, viewed objectively, is "justifiable" under the circumstances.

B

In applying the *Katz* analysis to this case, it is important to begin by specifying precisely the nature of the state activity that is challenged. The activity here took the form of installing and using a pen register. Since the pen register was installed on telephone company property at the telephone company's central offices, petitioner obviously cannot claim that his "property" was invaded or that police intruded into a "constitutionally protected area." Petitioner's claim, rather, is that, notwithstanding the absence of a trespass, the State, as did the Government in *Katz*, infringed a "legitimate expectation of privacy" that petitioner held. Yet a pen register differs significantly from the listening device employed in *Katz*, for pen registers do not acquire the *contents* of communications.

Given a pen register's limited capabilities, therefore, petitioner's argument that its installation and use constituted a "search" necessarily rests upon a claim that he had a "legitimate expectation of privacy" regarding the numbers he dialed on his phone.

This claim must be rejected. First, we doubt that people in general entertain any actual expectation of privacy in the numbers they dial. All telephone users realize that they must "convey" phone numbers to the telephone company, since it is through telephone company switching equipment that their calls are completed. All subscribers realize, moreover, that the phone company has facilities for making permanent records of the numbers they dial, for they see a list of their long-distance (toll) calls on their monthly bills. In fact, pen registers and similar devices are routinely used by telephone companies "for the purposes of checking billing operations, detecting fraud, and preventing violations of law." Although most people may be oblivious to a pen register's esoteric functions, they presumably have some awareness of one common use: to aid in the identification of persons making annoying or obscene calls. Most phone books tell subscribers, on a page entitled "Consumer Information," that the company "can frequently help in identifying to the authorities the origin of unwelcome and troublesome calls." Although subjective expectations cannot be scientifically gauged, it is too much to believe that telephone subscribers, under these circumstances, harbor any general expectation that the numbers they dial will remain secret.

Petitioner argues, however, that, whatever the expectations of telephone users in general, he demonstrated an expectation of privacy by his own conduct here, since he "[used] the telephone *in his house* to the exclusion of all others." But the site of the call is immaterial for purposes of analysis in this case. Although petitioner's conduct may have been calculated to keep the *contents* of his conversation private, his conduct was not and could not have been calculated to preserve the privacy of the number he dialed. Regardless of his location, petitioner had to convey that number to the telephone company in precisely the same way if he wished to complete his call. The fact that he dialed the number on his home phone rather than on some other phone could make no conceivable difference, nor could any subscriber rationally think that it would.

Second, even if petitioner did harbor some subjective expectation that the phone numbers he dialed would remain private, this expectation is not "one that society is prepared to recognize as 'reasonable.'" *Katz* v. *United States*, 389 U.S., at 361. This Court consistently has held that a person has no legitimate expectation of privacy in information he voluntarily turns over to third parties. In *Miller*, for example, the Court held that a bank depositor has no "legitimate 'expectation of privacy'" in financial information "voluntarily conveyed to . . . banks and exposed to their employees in the ordinary course of business."

Because the depositor "assumed the risk" of disclosure, the Court held that it would be unreasonable for him to expect his financial records to remain private.

This analysis dictates that petitioner can claim no legitimate expectation of privacy here. [P]etitioner voluntarily conveyed to [the phone company] information that it had facilities for recording and that it was free to record. In these circumstances, petitioner assumed the risk that the information would be divulged to police.

We therefore conclude that petitioner in all probability entertained no actual expectation of privacy in the phone numbers he dialed, and that, even if he did, his expectation was not "legitimate." The installation and use of a pen register, consequently, was not a "search," and no warrant was required. The judgment of the Maryland Court of Appeals is affirmed.

It is so ordered.

DISSENT: STEWART, Justice:

I am not persuaded that the numbers dialed from a private telephone fall outside the constitutional protection of the Fourth and Fourteenth Amendments.

As the Court said in *United States* v. *United States District Court*, 407 U.S. 297, 313, "the broad and unsuspected governmental incursions into conversational privacy which electronic surveillance entails necessitate the application of Fourth Amendment safeguards."

Nevertheless, the Court today says that those safeguards do not extend to the numbers dialed from a private telephone, apparently because when a caller dials a number the digits may be recorded by the telephone company for billing purposes. But that observation no more than describes the basic nature of telephone calls. A telephone call simply cannot be made without the use of telephone company property and without payment to the company for the service.

The central question in this case is whether a person who makes telephone calls from his home is entitled to make a similar assumption about the numbers he dials. What the telephone company does or might do with those numbers is no more relevant to this inquiry than it would be in a case involving the conversation itself. It is simply not enough to say, after *Katz*, that there is no legitimate expectation of privacy in the numbers dialed because the caller assumes the risk that the telephone company will disclose them to the police.

I think that the numbers dialed from a private telephone – like the conversations that occur during a call – are within the constitutional protection recognized in *Katz*. It seems clear to me that information obtained by pen register surveillance of a private telephone is information in which the telephone subscriber has a legitimate expectation of privacy. The numbers dialed from a private telephone – although certainly more prosaic than the conversation itself – are not without "content." Most private telephone subscribers may have their own numbers listed in a publicly distributed directory, but I doubt there are any who would be happy to have broadcast to the world a list of the local or long distance numbers they have called. This is not because such a list might in some sense be incriminating, but because it easily could reveal the identities of the persons and the places called, and thus reveal the most intimate details of a person's life.

I respectfully dissent.

DISSENT: MARSHALL, Justice:

The Court concludes that because individuals have no actual or legitimate expectation of privacy in information they voluntarily relinquish to telephone companies, the use of pen registers by government agents is immune from Fourth Amendment scrutiny. Since I remain convinced that constitutional protections are not abrogated whenever a person apprises another of facts valuable in criminal investigations, I respectfully dissent.

[E]ven assuming, as I do not, that individuals "typically know" that a phone company monitors calls for internal reasons, it does not follow that they expect this information to be made available to the public in general or the government in particular. Privacy is not a discrete commodity, possessed absolutely or not at all. Those who disclose certain facts to a bank or phone company for a limited business purpose need not assume that this information will be released to other persons for other purposes.

[T]he Court determines that individuals who convey information to third parties have "assumed the risk" of disclosure to the government. This analysis is misconceived in two critical respects.

Implicit in the concept of assumption of risk is some notion of choice. At least in the third-party consensual surveillance cases, which first incorporated risk analysis into Fourth Amendment doctrine, the defendant presumably had exercised some discretion in deciding who should enjoy his confidential communications. By contrast here, unless a person is prepared to forgo use of what for many has become a personal or professional necessity, he cannot help but accept the risk of surveillance. It is idle to speak of "assuming" risks in contexts where, as a practical matter, individuals have no realistic alternative.

More fundamentally, to make risk analysis dispositive in assessing the reasonableness of privacy expectations would allow the government to define the scope of Fourth Amendment protections. For example, law enforcement officials, simply by announcing their intent to monitor the content of random samples of first-class mail or private phone conversations, could put the public on notice of the risks they would thereafter assume in such communications.

In my view, whether privacy expectations are legitimate within the meaning of *Katz* depends not on the risks an individual can be presumed to accept when imparting information to third parties, but on the risks he should be forced to assume in a free and open society.

The use of pen registers, I believe, constitutes an extensive intrusion. To hold otherwise ignores the vital role telephonic communication plays in our personal and professional relationships, see *Katz* v. *United States*, 389 U.S., at 352, as well as the First and Fourth Amendment interests implicated by unfettered official surveillance. Particularly given the Government's previous reliance on warrantless telephonic surveillance to trace reporters' sources and monitor protected political activity, I am unwilling to insulate use of pen registers from independent judicial review.

Just as one who enters a public telephone booth is "entitled to assume that the words he utters into the mouthpiece will not be broadcast to the world," *Katz* v. *United States, supra*, at 352, so too, he should be entitled to assume that the numbers he dials in the privacy of his home will be recorded, if at all, solely for the phone company's business purposes. Accordingly, I would require law enforcement officials to obtain a warrant before they enlist telephone companies to secure information otherwise beyond the government's reach.

Note that EVERYONE cites *Katz* here, and yet the Justices disagree as to the meaning of the case.

So, there is no legitimate expectation of privacy in telephone numbers called and pen registers do not trigger any Fourth Amendment claims. What if the calls were made from and to an unlisted number? Does that person have a reasonable expectation of privacy? A Wyoming court said the same rule applies in such a situation.

Any telephone user assumes the risk that the telephone can and will reveal to the phone company the numbers dialed. Thus, warrantless seizure of records of incoming and outgoing calls is not a violation of the Fourth Amendment.

Note that the Legislature has acted on this front. The Electronic Communications Privacy Act requires court authorization for governmental use of pen registers. This was a response to *Smith v. Maryland*. Thus, there is no Fourth Amendment claim if the police use a pen register, but there may be an ECPA violation.

How does this decision apply to cyberspace?

Can the government, without warrant, use records of the recipients of e-mail? Can it monitor hits on web pages?

Note again that these problems always arise when authorities do something without a warrant. Sometimes they might not have been able to get one at that point, but more often they simply do not bother obtaining a warrant, usually because they don't think they need one.

If the police have a warrant it doesn't matter what an individual's expectations are. A warrant, by definition, indicates that a judicial decision has been made that the government's need for the information or the search outweighs an individual's right of privacy.

A major theme in the debate over communications privacy is whether the need to protect personal privacy interests is strong enough to override criminal law enforcement interests.

Privacy: Case 5

UNITED STATES OF AMERICA, Plaintiff-Appellant, v. KEVIN L. POULSEN, et al., Defendant-Appellee.

No. 94-10020

UNITED STATES COURT OF APPEALS FOR THE NINTH CIRCUIT

41 F.3d 1330; 1994 U.S. App. LEXIS 34238; 94 Cal. Daily Op. Service 9349; 94 Daily Journal DAR 17306

November 17, 1994, Argued, Submitted, San Francisco, California
December 8, 1994, Filed

OPINION: ALARCON, Judge:

This is another case about the expectation of privacy and when it is or is not unreasonable. In this instance the issue is whether a lien on the contents of a rental unit is sufficient to extinguish the renter's legitimate expectation of privacy.

I.

Pertinent Facts and Procedural History

On April 28, 1987, Poulsen entered into a rental agreement for a storage unit with Menlo. Poulsen signed the rental agreement using the alias "John Anderson."

On January 8, 1988, the rent on the Anderson unit was 71 days in arrears; Poulsen owed Menlo $ 155.50. On that date, Menlo mailed a preliminary lien notice to John Anderson at the false address that Poulsen had provided on the rental agreement. The preliminary lien notice indicated the amount that was owed, and contained the following warning:

> If this sum is not paid in full within 14 days from the date of this notice your right to use the storage space and/or facility will terminate, you will be denied access, and an owner's lien on any stored property will be imposed.

This notice was returned to Menlo as undeliverable. On February 2, 1988, more than fourteen days after the date of the notice, Poulsen went to Menlo. He paid $ 70.00 towards the balance of the overdue rent on his storage unit. At that time, Poulsen provided Menlo with a second false address. A Menlo employee made a notation in Menlo's files that indicated the amount that Poulsen had paid, the amount that he still owed, and that he "wanted to know about access." That same day, Menlo mailed a second preliminary lien notice to the new address provided by Poulsen. This notice was returned to Menlo as undeliverable.

On February 8, 1988, Larry Tyson, the manager of Menlo, entered the Anderson unit to remove its contents. Tyson saw "a large amount of telecommunications equipment and manuals [that] apparently belonged to [PacBell]." Tyson transferred all of the property from the Anderson unit to one that was under his exclusive control ("Tyson's unit"). Thereafter, he called the Redwood City Police Department to inform them that he believed he had found stolen property in the Anderson unit. A Redwood City Police dispatcher called PacBell to request that a PacBell representative be sent to Menlo to examine the property that Tyson had found in the Anderson unit.

The following day, a Redwood City Police officer and John Von Brauch, a special investigator for PacBell, went to Menlo to view the property taken from the Anderson unit. Von Brauch testified that when he examined the property in Tyson's unit, he was acting solely in the interests of PacBell. When Von Brauch entered the Tyson unit, he observed numerous items that he believed had been stolen from PacBell. Specifically, Von Brauch saw a coin-operated telephone, computer manuals that contained proprietary PacBell information, PacBell identification badges, PacBell test equipment, and large reel-to-reel computer tapes.

With Tyson's consent, Von Brauch took some of the reel-to-reel computer tapes to PacBell. Von Brauch was unsuccessful in accessing the information on these tapes because the tapes were formatted in the UNIX operating system. PacBell does not use UNIX on its computers.

On February 12, 1988, Tyson called [the] Detective to report that Poulsen was at Menlo. Detective Neal arrested Poulsen. After Poulsen was advised of his *Miranda* rights, he consented to a search of his apartment. There, the police discovered additional computer tapes and PacBell equipment. Later that same day, Von Brauch gave the reel-to-reel computer tapes that he had taken from Tyson's unit to Detective Neal.

While Detective Neal was questioning Poulsen, he learned that Poulsen had been employed by the Stanford Research Institute ("SRI"). Detective Neal contacted the Federal Bureau of Investigation ("FBI"). An FBI agent asked SRI to inspect the reel-to-reel computer tapes that had been taken from the Anderson unit by Tyson. SRI reviewed the computer tapes and informed the FBI that the tapes were theirs, but contained nothing of "evidentiary value." SRI returned the tapes to Detective Neal.

Von Brauch requested permission to borrow the tapes to make another attempt to determine whether the tapes contained PacBell proprietary information. On March 18, 1988, representatives of PacBell were successful in accessing some of the tapes. The tapes contained "Air Tasking Orders." These orders list targets that the United States Air Force will attack in the event of hostilities.

On October 6, 1993, Poulsen filed a motion to suppress the evidence that was seized from his storage unit at Menlo and from his apartment. On December 7, 1993, the district court denied Poulsen's motion to suppress. Poulsen filed a motion for reconsideration. On January 3, 1994, the district court suppressed the computer tapes that had been seized by Tyson from the Anderson unit. The Government filed a timely appeal from this order.

II.

Jurisdiction to Review the Government's Appeal

The Court analyzes its jurisdictional rights and decides it has jurisdiction to review the suppression order because the three requirements have been met:

- **Poulsen has not yet been placed in jeopardy (in a jury trial jeopardy attaches when the jury is sworn in; in a "bench trial," (i.e., a trial without a jury), jeopardy attaches when the first witness is sworn in).**
- **The appeal is not taken for the purpose of delaying the proceedings.**
- **The suppressed evidence is substantial proof of a fact material to the proceedings (here, the espionage charge).**

III.

A Renter Does not have a Legitimate Expectation of Privacy in the Contents of a Rental Unit if the Rent is not Paid

We review de novo the question whether a defendant has asserted a valid Fourth Amendment violation.

The only search at issue in this appeal concerns the contents of the computer tapes that Tyson found in the Anderson unit. It is undisputed that when Tyson entered the Anderson unit and removed all of its contents, he was not acting as a police agent. Thus, Tyson's conduct in removing the items he found in the Anderson unit did not implicate Poulsen's Fourth Amendment rights.

The Government argues that after January 22, 1988, Poulsen did not have a legitimate expectation of privacy in the contents of the Anderson unit because Menlo had a lien on that property based upon paragraph 17 of the rental agreement, and the sections of the California Business and Professions Code that relate to self-storage rental facilities.

Paragraph 17 of the rental agreement provides as follows:

LIENS: Occupant's stored property will be subject to a claim of lien for unpaid rent and other charges and may be sold to satisfy the lien if the rent or other charges due remain unpaid for fourteen (14) consecutive days. This lien and its enforcement are authorized by Chapter 10 (commencing with Section 21700) of the California Business and Professions Code.

§ 21705 provides, in pertinent part:

If a notice has been sent, as required by Section 21703, and the total sum due has not been paid as of the date specified in the preliminary lien notice, the lien imposed by this chapter attaches as of that date, and the owner may deny an occupant access to the space, enter the space, and remove any property found therein to a place of safe keeping.

It is clear from the express language of the rental agreement that Menlo had a right to assert a lien on Poulsen's property at the time Tyson entered the Anderson unit and removed its contents to the Tyson unit, because at that time, Poulsen's rent was more than 14 days overdue. Additionally, because Poulsen failed to pay the total sum due within 14 days after the date that the first preliminary lien notice was mailed, Menlo had a lien on the contents of the Anderson unit, pursuant to section 21705 of the California Business and Professions Code.

Poulsen asserts that Menlo's lien was not valid because he made a partial payment of $ 70.00 on February 2, 1988. Poulsen has failed to cite any authority for the proposition that a partial payment prevents the enforcement of a lien pursuant to section 21705.

Poulsen also contends that the second preliminary lien notice altered the terms of the rental agreement by extending the date for payment of the total amount owed until February 16, 1988. To prove that the terms of the contract were modified by the second preliminary lien notice, Poulsen must demonstrate that Menlo intended to modify the terms of the contract.

[T]he undisputed evidence shows that Menlo did not intend to modify Poulsen's contractual obligation to pay the balance of the rental payments on or before January 22, 1988.

Poulsen maintains that he detrimentally relied on the second preliminary lien notice. Poulsen has failed to demonstrate that he was aware of the contents of the second preliminary lien notice. The record shows that the second preliminary lien notice was returned as undeliverable.

The question whether a lien on the contents of a rental unit is sufficient to extinguish the renter's legitimate expectation of privacy is an issue of first impression in this circuit. There are analogous cases, however, which hold that after the expiration of a rental period, the renter does not have standing to assert a Fourth Amendment violation concerning property left in the unit.

The Second Circuit's decision in *United States v. Rahme*, 813 F.2d 31 (2d Cir. 1987), closely parallels the question presented in this matter. In *Rahme*, a hotel clerk allowed police officers to search luggage and a briefcase that were left in a guest's room after the guest had failed to pay his rent and the rental period had expired.

The court held in *Rahme* that once a hotel "properly takes possession of the luggage, the guest no longer has the right to control access to it and can have no legitimate expectation of privacy in it."

Similarly, in this case, on January 22, 1988, Menlo had a lien on the contents of Poulsen's storage unit based upon the express terms of the rental agreement between the parties and sections 21702, 21703 and 21705 of the California Business and Professions Code. As of that date, Poulsen lost the right of access to his unit and its contents. Thus, Poulsen could no longer have a legitimate expectation of privacy in the contents of his storage unit.

IV.

Conclusion

Because Poulsen failed to pay the total amount of the unpaid rent prior to January 22, 1988, he did not have a legitimate expectation of privacy in the contents of his storage unit after that date. Therefore, Poulsen has failed to demonstrate that he has standing to assert a Fourth Amendment violation regarding the search of the contents of the tapes that were found by Tyson in the Anderson unit. *Accordingly, the district court's January 3, 1994 order granting suppression of the tapes is Reversed.*

> **Query: Do we have a reasonable expectation of privacy in the contents of a computer account held by an ISP if we default on the "rent" for that account?**

Privacy: Case 6

Teresa Parnell, Plaintiff, v. Booth Newspapers, Inc., Defendant

File No. G 82-722

UNITED STATES DISTRICT COURT FOR THE WESTERN DISTRICT OF MICHIGAN, SOUTHERN DIVISION

572 F. Supp. 909; 1983 U.S. Dist. LEXIS 19635

January 31, 1983

OPINION: ENSLEN, Judge:

Plaintiff in this diversity action alleges that photographs of her were published in connection with two newspaper articles on the subject of prostitution in Muskegon Heights, Michigan. The articles and accompanying photographs appeared on page 1B of the September 20, 1981 edition of *The Muskegon Chronicle*, a newspaper owned and published by Defendant. Plaintiff claims that as a result of the publication, in which she was allegedly recognizable to relatives, friends and acquaintances, she was falsely imputed to be a prostitute, and has consequently suffered damages. Specifically, Plaintiff's Complaint alleges four counts of liability against Defendant: defamation, negligent infliction of emotional distress, intentional infliction of emotional distress, and invasion of privacy.

> **We'll focus on the invasion of privacy aspect (Part IV) of the case.**

IV. Invasion of Privacy

Plaintiff alleges in Count IV of her Complaint that the use of her photograph was unreasonable and a serious interference with her right to privacy in that the publication portrayed Plaintiff in a "false light," and was an appropriation of her likeness without Plaintiff's permission. Plaintiff alleges that as the result of this invasion of her privacy she suffered emotional distress, loss of enjoyment of life, anxiety, emotional illness, embarrassment, and loss of reputation. Count IV also incorporates allegations of Count I.

Defendant moves for summary judgment on this Count, arguing that (1) since Plaintiff is not recognizable, there can be no claim for invasion of privacy; (2) the publication is not actionable because Plaintiff left herself open to the public eye; and (3) Plaintiff is required to make a showing of actual malice, and has failed to do so.

The tort of invasion of privacy is clearly recognized by the Michigan courts. *Beaumount v. Brown*, 401 Mich 80, 95, 257 NW 2d 522 (1977). Prosser describes four types of invasion of privacy: (1) the appropriation for the defendant's benefit or advantages, of the plaintiff's name or likeness; (2) intrusion upon the plaintiff's physical solitude or seclusion; (3) disclosure of private information; and (4) publicity which places plaintiff in a false light in the public eye. Prosser, *Torts*, (4th ed.) § 117, pp. 804–812. Because Plaintiff has chosen in her brief to rest only upon "false light" invasion of privacy, the Court will address only that aspect of the tort.

Since recognition of the Plaintiff is an inherent element of a false light invasion of privacy claim, Defendant's motion cannot be granted on this ground because it presents a contested fact issue. Defendant next argues that it cannot be held liable for what Plaintiff chose to expose to the public eye. Defendant relies upon *Fry v. Ionia Sentinel-Standard*, *supra*, for that proposition. However, that case involved a claim grounded on the public disclosure of embarrassing private facts, and was not a "false light" claim. As Plaintiff observes, the use of the photographs of Plaintiff in the present case is alleged as a classical false light case. The Restatement of Torts (2d) § 652E uses the following illustration to describe the "false light" aspect of invasion of privacy:

A is a taxi driver in the city of Washington. B newspaper publishes an article on the practices of Washington taxi drivers in cheating the public on fares, and makes use of A's photograph to illustrate the article, with the implication that he is one of the drivers who engaged in these practices. A never has done so. B is subject to liability to A for both libel and invasion of privacy.

It is conceded for the purpose of this motion that the implication of the publication was that Plaintiff was soliciting for prostitution; the truth of the publication has been contested by Plaintiff in her affidavit, and presents a jury question. The fact that Plaintiff's photograph was taken in public does not preclude her false light claim.

Defendant argues that regardless of whether Plaintiff may have been put in a false light, a qualified privilege protects the publication and requires Plaintiff to show actual knowledge of falsity of the publication or a reckless disregard for the truth. Defendant relies upon the United States Supreme Court case of *Time, Inc. v. Hill*, 385 U.S. 374, 87 S. Ct. 534, 17 L. Ed. 2d 456 (1966). In that case the Supreme Court held that a qualified privilege attached to a review of a play which stated that the play was a reenactment of the experience of the plaintiffs, who had some years before been held hostage by escaped convicts. The court found the claim analogous to the defamation claim in *New York Times v. Sullivan*, *supra*, and applied the *New York Times* "actual malice" standard of fault. The Court reasoned that the actual malice standard should apply, since the review was of public interest; the court also noted that plaintiffs were public figures, although involuntarily so. In the later case of *Gertz v. Welch*, *supra*, the Supreme Court restricted its actual malice test in the area of defamation law to those cases which involved public figures or public officials. In reaching that holding, the court rejected a "public interest" test for determining the applicability of the actual malice standard of fault. The effect of *Gertz v. Welch* on the holding of *Time, Inc. v. Hill*, as it applies to private individuals suing under a false light theory for invasion of privacy, has not been resolved by the Supreme Court.

According to the Restatement (2d) Torts, § 652G, the rules on conditional privileges to publish defamatory matter apply equally to the publication of matter which constitutes an invasion of privacy. Because in this case, contested fact issues preclude a finding at this time of whether or not the scope of a public interest qualified privilege has been exceeded by Defendant, the standard of fault by which Defendant's conduct will be judged, is as yet unresolved. Defendant's Motion for Summary Judgment on this ground is therefore denied.

V. Conclusion

For the reasons discussed in this Opinion, the cross-Motions for Summary Judgment by Defendant and Plaintiff, are denied.

Order

In accordance with the Opinion issued January 31, 1983 in the above entitled action, the cross-Motions for Summary Judgment by Defendant and Plaintiff are Denied.

Privacy: Case 7

JOSEPH MCINTYRE, EXECUTOR OF ESTATE OF MARGARET MCINTYRE, DECEASED, PETITIONER v. OHIO ELECTIONS COMMISSION

No. 93-986

SUPREME COURT OF THE UNITED STATES

514 U.S. 334; 115 S. Ct. 1511; 131 L. Ed. 2d 426; 1995 U.S. LEXIS 2847; 63 U.S.L.W. 4279; 23 Media L. Rep. 1577; 95 Cal. Daily Op. Service 2853; 95 Daily Journal DAR 4972; 8 Fla. L. Weekly Fed. S 721

October 12, 1994, Argued
April 19, 1995, Decided

JUDGES: STEVENS, J., delivered the opinion of the Court, in which O'CONNOR, KENNEDY, SOUTER, GINSBURG, and BREYER, JJ., joined. GINSBURG, J., filed a concurring opinion, THOMAS, J., filed an opinion concurring in the judgment. SCALIA, J., filed a dissenting opinion, in which REHNQUIST, C. J., joins.

OPINION: STEVENS, Justice:

The question presented is whether an Ohio statute that prohibits the distribution of anonymous campaign literature is a "law . . . abridging the freedom of speech" within the meaning of the First Amendment.

I

On April 27, 1988, Margaret McIntyre distributed leaflets to persons attending a public meeting at the Blendon Middle School in Westerville, Ohio. At this meeting, the superintendent of schools planned to discuss an imminent referendum on a proposed school tax levy. The leaflets expressed Mrs. McIntyre's opposition to the levy. There is no suggestion that the text of her message was false, misleading, or libelous. She had composed and printed it on her home computer and had paid a professional printer to make additional copies. Some of the handbills identified her as the author; others merely purported to express the views of "CONCERNED PARENTS AND TAX PAYERS." Except for the help provided by her son and a friend, who placed some of the leaflets on car windshields in the school parking lot, Mrs. McIntyre acted independently.

While Mrs. McIntyre distributed her handbills, an official of the school district, who supported the tax proposal, advised her that the unsigned leaflets did not conform to the Ohio election laws. Undeterred, Mrs. McIntyre appeared at another meeting on the next evening and handed out more of the handbills.

The proposed school levy was defeated at the next two elections, but it finally passed on its third try in November 1988. Five months later, the same school official filed a complaint with the Ohio Elections Commission charging that Mrs. McIntyre's distribution of unsigned leaflets violated § 3599.09(A) of the Ohio Code. The commission agreed and imposed a fine of $ 100.

Mrs. McIntyre could have paid the fine at this point but she decided to sue.

The Franklin County Court of Common Pleas reversed. Finding that Mrs. McIntyre did not "mislead the public nor act in a surreptitious manner," the court concluded that the statute was unconstitutional as applied to her conduct.

And now the State could have quit. But the State appealed.

The Ohio Court of Appeals, by a divided vote, reinstated the fine. The dissenting judge thought that *Talley* v. *California,* 362 U.S. 60, 4 L. Ed. 2d 559, 80 S. Ct. 536 (1960), in which we invalidated a city ordinance prohibiting all anonymous leafletting, compelled the Ohio court to adopt a narrowing construction of the statute to save its constitutionality.

The Ohio Supreme Court affirmed by a divided vote. The majority distinguished Mrs. McIntyre's case from *Talley* on the ground that § 3599.09(A) "has as its purpose the identification of persons who distribute materials containing false statements." The Ohio court believed that such a law should be upheld if the burdens imposed on the First Amendment rights of voters are "'*reasonable*'" and "'*nondiscriminatory.*'" Under that standard, the majority concluded that the statute was plainly valid:

> The minor requirement imposed by R.C. 3599.09 that those persons producing campaign literature identify themselves as the source thereof neither impacts the content of their message nor significantly burdens their ability to have it disseminated. This burden is more than counterbalanced by the state interest in providing the voters to whom the message is directed with a mechanism by which they may better evaluate its validity. Moreover, the law serves to identify those who engage in fraud, libel or false advertising. Not only are such interests sufficient to overcome the minor burden placed upon such persons, these interests were specifically acknowledged in *First Nat. Bank of Boston* v. *Bellotti,* 435 U.S. 765, 98 S. Ct. 1407, 55 L. Ed. 2d 707 (1978), to be regulations of the sort which would survive constitutional scrutiny.

In dissent, Justice Wright argued that the statute should be tested under a more severe standard because of its significant effect "on the ability of individual citizens to freely express their views in writing on political issues." He concluded that § 3599.09(A) "is not narrowly tailored to serve a compelling state interest and is, therefore, unconstitutional as applied to McIntyre."

Mrs. McIntyre passed away during the pendency of this litigation. Even though the amount in controversy is only $ 100, petitioner, as the executor of her estate, has pursued her claim in this Court.

Our grant of certiorari, 510 U.S. 1108 (1994), reflects our agreement with his appraisal of the importance of the question presented.

II

Ohio maintains that the statute under review is a reasonable regulation of the electoral process. The State does not suggest that all anonymous publications are pernicious or that a statute totally excluding them from the marketplace of ideas would be valid. This is a wise (albeit implicit) concession, for the anonymity of an author is not ordinarily a sufficient reason to exclude her work product from the protections of the First Amendment.

"Anonymous pamphlets, leaflets, brochures and even books have played an important role in the progress of mankind." *Talley* v. *California*, 362 U.S. at 64. Great works of literature have frequently been produced by authors writing under assumed names.[1] Despite readers' curiosity and the public's interest in identifying the creator of a work of art, an author generally is free to decide whether or not to disclose his or her true identity. The decision in favor of anonymity may be motivated by fear of economic or official retaliation, by concern about social ostracism, or merely by a desire to preserve as much of one's privacy as possible. Whatever the motivation may be, at least in the field of literary endeavor, the interest in having anonymous works enter the marketplace of ideas unquestionably outweighs any public interest in requiring disclosure as a condition of entry. Accordingly, an author's decision to remain anonymous, like other decisions concerning omissions or additions to the content of a publication, is an aspect of the freedom of speech protected by the First Amendment.

The freedom to publish anonymously extends beyond the literary realm. In *Talley*, the Court held that the First Amendment protects the distribution of unsigned handbills urging readers to boycott certain Los Angeles merchants who were allegedly engaging in discriminatory employment practices. Writing for the Court, Justice Black noted that "persecuted groups and sects from time to time throughout history have been able to criticize oppressive practices and laws either anonymously or not at all." Justice Black recalled England's abusive press licensing laws and seditious libel prosecutions, and he reminded us that even the arguments favoring the ratification of the Constitution advanced in the Federalist Papers were published under fictitious names. On occasion, quite apart from any threat of persecution, an advocate may believe her ideas will be more persuasive if her readers are unaware of her identity. Anonymity thereby provides a way for a writer who may be personally unpopular to ensure that readers will not prejudge her message simply because they do not like its proponent. Thus, even in the field of political rhetoric, where "the identity of the speaker is an important component of many attempts to persuade," the most effective advocates have sometimes opted for anonymity. The specific holding in *Talley* related to advocacy of an economic boycott,

---

[1] American names such as Mark Twain (Samuel Langhorne Clemens) and O. Henry (William Sydney Porter) come readily to mind. Benjamin Franklin employed numerous different pseudonyms.

but the Court's reasoning embraced a respected tradition of anonymity in the advocacy of political causes.[2] This tradition is perhaps best exemplified by the secret ballot, the hard-won right to vote one's conscience without fear of retaliation.

III

California had defended the Los Angeles ordinance at issue in *Talley* as a law "aimed at providing a way to identify those responsible for fraud, false advertising and libel." We rejected that argument because nothing in the text or legislative history of the ordinance limited its application to those evils. The Ohio statute likewise contains no language limiting its application to fraudulent, false, or libelous statements; to the extent, therefore, that Ohio seeks to justify § 3599.09(A) as a means to prevent the dissemination of untruths, its defense must fail for the same reason given in *Talley*.

Ohio's statute does, however, contain a different limitation: It applies only to unsigned documents designed to influence voters in an election. In contrast, the Los Angeles ordinance prohibited all anonymous handbilling "in any place under any circumstances." For that reason, Ohio correctly argues that *Talley* does not necessarily control the disposition of this case. We must, therefore, decide whether and to what extent the First Amendment's protection of anonymity encompasses documents intended to influence the electoral process.

The "ordinary litigation" test does not apply here.

The Ohio statute is not a regulation of the mechanics of the electoral process: it is a regulation of pure speech, a limitation on political expression.

Indeed, as we have explained on many prior occasions, the category of speech regulated by the Ohio statute occupies the core of the protection afforded by the First Amendment:

> Discussion of public issues and debate on the qualifications of candidates are integral to the operation of the system of government established by our Constitution. The First Amendment affords the broadest protection to such political expression in order 'to assure [the] unfettered interchange of ideas for the bringing about of political and social changes desired by the people.' In a republic where the people are sovereign, the ability of the citizenry to make informed choices among candidates for office is essential, for the identities of those who are elected will inevitably shape the course that we follow as a nation.

Of course, core political speech need not center on a candidate for office. Indeed, the speech in which Mrs. McIntyre engaged – handing out leaflets in the advocacy of a politically controversial viewpoint – is the essence of First Amendment expression. That this advocacy occurred in the heat of a controversial referendum vote only strengthens the protection afforded to Mrs. McIntyre's expression: Urgent, important, and effective speech can be no less protected than impotent speech, lest the right to speak be relegated to those instances when it is least needed. No form of speech is entitled to greater constitutional protection than Mrs. McIntyre's.

[2] That tradition is most famously embodied in the Federalist Papers, authored by James Madison, Alexander Hamilton, and John Jay, but signed "Publius."

Therefore in reviewing the statute we must apply strict scrutiny. That is, the statute must be narrowly tailored to serve a compelling interest.

When a law burdens core political speech, we apply "exacting scrutiny," and we uphold the restriction only if it is narrowly tailored to serve an overriding state interest. Our precedents thus make abundantly clear that the Ohio Supreme Court applied a significantly more lenient standard than is appropriate in a case of this kind.

IV

Nevertheless, the State argues that, even under the strictest standard of review, the disclosure requirement in § 3599.09(A) is justified by two important and legitimate state interests. Ohio judges its interest in preventing fraudulent and libelous statements and its interest in providing the electorate with relevant information to be sufficiently compelling to justify the anonymous speech ban. These two interests necessarily overlap to some extent, but it is useful to discuss them separately.

Insofar as the interest in informing the electorate means nothing more than the provision of additional information that may either buttress or undermine the argument in a document, we think the identity of the speaker is no different from other components of the document's content that the author is free to include or exclude. Moreover, in the case of a handbill written by a private citizen who is not known to the recipient, the name and address of the author add little, if anything, to the reader's ability to evaluate the document's message. Thus, Ohio's informational interest is plainly insufficient to support the constitutionality of its disclosure requirement.

The state interest in preventing fraud and libel stands on a different footing. We agree with Ohio's submission that this interest carries special weight during election campaigns when false statements, if credited, may have serious adverse consequences for the public at large. Ohio does not, however, rely solely on § 3599.09(A) to protect that interest. Its Election Code includes detailed and specific prohibitions against making or disseminating false statements during political campaigns.

As this case demonstrates, the prohibition encompasses documents that are not even arguably false or misleading. Moreover, as this case also demonstrates, the absence of the author's name on a document does not necessarily protect either that person or a distributor of a forbidden document from being held responsible for compliance with the Election Code. Nor has the State explained why it can more easily enforce the direct bans on disseminating false documents against anonymous authors and distributors than against wrongdoers who might use false names and addresses in an attempt to avoid detection. We recognize that a State's enforcement interest might justify a more limited identification requirement, but Ohio has shown scant cause for inhibiting the leafletting at issue here.

VI

Under our Constitution, anonymous pamphleteering is not a pernicious, fraudulent practice, but an honorable tradition of advocacy and of dissent. Anonymity is a shield from the tyranny of the majority. It thus exemplifies the purpose behind the Bill of Rights, and of the First Amendment in particular: to protect unpopular individuals from retaliation – and their ideas from suppression – at the hand of an intolerant society. The right to remain anonymous may be abused when it shields fraudulent conduct. But political speech by its nature will sometimes have unpalatable consequences, and, in general, our society accords greater weight to the value of free speech than to the dangers of its misuse. Ohio has not shown that its interest in preventing the misuse of anonymous election-related speech justifies a prohibition of all uses of that speech. The State may, and does, punish fraud directly. But it cannot seek to punish fraud indirectly by indiscriminately outlawing a category of speech, based on its content, with no necessary relationship to the danger sought to be prevented. One would be hard pressed to think of a better example of the pitfalls of Ohio's blunderbuss approach than the facts of the case before us.

The judgment of the Ohio Supreme Court is reversed.

It is so ordered.

GINSBURG; THOMAS concur.

CONCURRENCE: GINSBURG, Justice:

The dissent is stirring in its appreciation of democratic values. But I do not see the Court's opinion as unguided by "bedrock principle," tradition, or our case law.

In for a calf is not always in for a cow. The Court's decision finds unnecessary, overintrusive, and inconsistent with American ideals the State's imposition of a fine on an individual leafleteer who, within her local community, spoke her mind, but sometimes not her name. We do not thereby hold that the State may not in other, larger circumstances require the speaker to disclose its interest by disclosing its identity. Appropriately leaving open matters not presented by McIntyre's handbills, the Court recognizes that a State's interest in protecting an election process "might justify a more limited identification requirement." But the Court has convincingly explained why Ohio lacks "cause for inhibiting the leafletting at issue here."

CONCURRENCE: THOMAS, Justice:

I agree with the majority's conclusion that Ohio's election law is inconsistent with the First Amendment. I would apply, however, a different methodology to this case. Instead of asking whether "an honorable tradition" of anonymous speech has existed throughout American history, or what the "value" of anonymous speech might be, we should determine whether the phrase "freedom of speech, or of the press," as originally understood, protected anonymous political leafletting. I believe that it did.

[Sections I–III are omitted.]

IV

This evidence leads me to agree with the majority's result, but not its reasoning. The majority fails to seek the original understanding of the First Amendment, and instead attempts to answer the question in this case by resorting to three approaches. First, the majority recalls the historical practice of anonymous writing from Shakespeare's works to the Federalist Papers to Mark Twain. Second, it finds that anonymous speech has an expressive value both to the speaker and to society that outweighs public interest in disclosure. Third, it finds that § 3599.09(A) cannot survive strict scrutiny because it is a "content-based" restriction on speech.

I cannot join the majority's analysis because it deviates from our settled approach to interpreting the Constitution and because it superimposes its modern theories concerning expression upon the constitutional text. Whether "great works of literature" – by Voltaire or George Eliot – have been published anonymously should be irrelevant to our analysis, because it sheds no light on what the phrases "free speech" or "free press" meant to the people who drafted and ratified the First Amendment. Similarly, whether certain types of expression have "value" today has little significance; what *is* important is whether the Framers in 1791 believed anonymous speech sufficiently valuable to deserve the protection of the Bill of Rights. And although the majority faithfully follows our approach to "content-based" speech regulations, we need not undertake this analysis when the original understanding provides the answer.

While, like JUSTICE SCALIA, I am loath to overturn a century of practice shared by almost all of the States, I believe the historical evidence from the framing outweighs recent tradition. When interpreting other provisions of the Constitution, this Court has believed itself bound by the text of the Constitution and by the intent of those who drafted and ratified it. It should hold itself to no less a standard when interpreting the Speech and Press Clauses. After reviewing the weight of the historical evidence, it seems that the Framers understood the First Amendment to protect an author's right to express his thoughts on political candidates or issues in an anonymous fashion. Because the majority has adopted an analysis that is largely unconnected to the Constitution's text and history, I concur only in the judgment.

DISSENT: SCALIA, Justice:

At a time when both political branches of Government and both political parties reflect a popular desire to leave more decisionmaking authority to the States, today's decision moves in the opposite direction, adding to the legacy of inflexible central mandates (irrevocable even by Congress) imposed by this Court's constitutional jurisprudence. In an opinion which reads as though it is addressing some peculiar law like the Los Angeles municipal ordinance at issue in *Talley* v. *California*, 362 U.S. 60, 4 L. Ed. 2d 559, 80 S. Ct. 536 (1960), the Court invalidates a species of protection for the election process that exists, in a variety of forms, in every State except California, and that has a pedigree dating back to the end of the 19th century. Preferring the views of the English utilitarian philosopher John Stuart Mill to the considered judgment of the American people's elected representatives from coast to coast, the Court discovers a hitherto unknown right-to-be-unknown while engaging in electoral politics.

I dissent from this imposition of free-speech imperatives that are demonstrably not those of the American people today, and that there is inadequate reason to believe were those of the society that begat the First Amendment or the Fourteenth.

I

The question posed by the present case is not the easiest sort to answer for those who adhere to the Court's (and the society's) traditional view that the Constitution bears its original meaning and is unchanging. Under that view, "on every question of construction, [we should] carry ourselves back to the time when the Constitution was adopted; recollect the spirit manifested in the debates; and instead of trying [to find] what meaning may be squeezed out of the text, or invented against it, conform to the probable one in which it was passed."

Anonymous electioneering was not prohibited by law in 1791 or in 1868. In fact, it was widely practiced at the earlier date, an understandable legacy of the revolutionary era in which political dissent could produce governmental reprisal. But to prove that anonymous electioneering was used frequently is not to establish that it is a constitutional right.

Evidence that anonymous electioneering was regarded as a constitutional right is sparse, and as far as I am aware evidence that it was *generally* regarded as such is nonexistent.

[T]he sum total of the historical evidence marshaled by the concurrence for the principle of *constitutional entitlement* to anonymous electioneering is partisan claims in the debate on ratification (which was *almost* like an election) that a viewpoint-based restriction on anonymity by newspaper editors violates freedom of speech. This absence of historical testimony concerning the point before us is hardly remarkable. The issue of a governmental prohibition upon anonymous electioneering in particular (as opposed to a government prohibition upon anonymous publication in general) simply never arose.

What we have, then, is the most difficult case for determining the meaning of the Constitution. No accepted existence of governmental restrictions of the sort at issue here demonstrates their constitutionality, but neither can their nonexistence clearly be attributed to constitutional objections. In such a case, constitutional adjudication nec-essarily involves not just history but judgment: judgment as to whether the government action under challenge is consonant with the concept of the protected freedom (in this case, the freedom of speech and of the press) that existed when the constitutional pro-tection was accorded. In the present case, *absent other indication*, I would be inclined to agree with the concurrence that a society which used anonymous political debate so regularly would not regard as constitutional even moderate restrictions made to improve the election process.

But there *is* other indication, of the most weighty sort: the widespread and long-standing traditions of our people. Principles of liberty fundamental enough to have been embodied within constitutional guarantees are not readily erased from the Nation's consciousness. A governmental practice that has become general throughout the United States, and particularly one that has the validation of long, accepted usage, bears a strong presumption of constitutionality.

And that is what we have before us here. Ohio Rev. Code Ann. § 3599.09(A) (1988) was enacted by the General Assembly of the State of Ohio almost 80 years ago. Even at the time of its adoption, there was nothing unique or extraordinary about it. Such a universal and long-established American legislative practice must be given precedence, I think, over historical and academic speculation regarding a restriction that assuredly does not go to the heart of free speech.

II

The foregoing analysis suffices to decide this case for me. Where the meaning of a constitutional text (such as "the freedom of speech") is unclear, the widespread and long-accepted practices of the American people are the best indication of what funda-mental beliefs it was intended to enshrine. Even if I were to close my eyes to practice, however, and were to be guided exclusively by deductive analysis from our case law, I would reach the same result.

The Court's unprecedented protection for anonymous speech does not even have the virtue of establishing a clear (albeit erroneous) rule of law. For after having announced that this statute, because it "burdens core political speech," requires "'exacting scrutiny'" and must be "narrowly tailored to serve an overriding state interest," (ordinarily the kiss of death), the opinion goes on to proclaim soothingly (and unhelpfully) that "a State's enforcement interest might justify a more limited identification requirement." Perhaps, then, not *all* the state statutes I have alluded to are invalid, but just *some* of them; or indeed maybe *all* of them remain valid in "larger circumstances"! It may take decades to work out the shape of this newly expanded right-to-speak-incognito, even in the elections field. And in other areas, of course, a whole new boutique of wonderful First Amendment litigation opens its doors.

Here, Justice Scalia asks some good questions:

Must a parade permit, for example, be issued to a group that refuses to provide its identity, or that agrees to do so only under assurance that the identity will not be made public? Must a municipally owned theater that is leased for private productions book anonymously sponsored presentations? Must a government periodical that has a "letters to the editor" column disavow the policy that most newspapers have against the publication of anonymous letters? The silliness that follows upon a generalized right to anonymous speech has no end.

I do not know where the Court derives its perception that "anonymous pamphleteering is not a pernicious, fraudulent practice, but an honorable tradition of advocacy and of dissent." I can imagine no reason why an anonymous leaflet is any more honorable, as a general matter, than an anonymous phone call or an anonymous letter. It facilitates wrong by eliminating accountability, which is ordinarily the very purpose of the anonymity. There are of course exceptions, and where anonymity is needed to avoid "threats, harassment, or reprisals" the First Amendment will require an exemption from the Ohio law. But to strike down the Ohio law in its general application – and similar laws of 49 other States and the Federal Government – on the ground that all anonymous communication is in our society traditionally sacrosanct, seems to me a distortion of the past that will lead to a coarsening of the future.

I respectfully dissent.

∾

There are many practical problems arising from the anonymity available on the Net. These include things like infringement of intellectual property rights, fraudulent electronic commerce, harassment, defamation, and crime.

We will surely see a battle over online anonymity in the coming years.

10. E-Mail

Introduction

The question of e-mail privacy tends to arise most frequently in the workplace setting, and that is where we will look at it. We will concentrate primarily on issues related to employer monitoring of e-mail.

The first question, then, is what level of privacy in general can employees expect?

E-Mail: Case 1

O'CONNOR ET AL. v. ORTEGA

No. 85-530

SUPREME COURT OF THE UNITED STATES

480 U.S. 709; 107 S. Ct. 1492; 94 L. Ed. 2d 714; 1987 U.S. LEXIS 1507; 55 U.S.L.W. 4405; 42 Empl. Prac. Dec. (CCH) P36,891; 1 I.E.R. Cas. (BNA) 1617

October 15, 1986, Argued
March 31, 1987, Decided

JUDGES: O'CONNOR, J., announced the judgment of the Court and delivered an opinion in which REHNQUIST, C. J., and WHITE and POWELL, JJ., joined. SCALIA, J., filed an opinion concurring in the judgment. BLACKMUN, J., filed a dissenting opinion, in which BRENNAN, MARSHALL, and STEVENS, JJ., joined.

OPINION: O'CONNOR, Justice:

This is a 5–4 USSC decision that addresses the question of what sort of expectation of privacy an employee has.

This suit under 42 U. S. C. § 1983 presents two issues concerning the Fourth Amendment rights of public employees. First, we must determine whether the respondent, a public employee, had a reasonable expectation of privacy in his office, desk, and file cabinets at his place of work. Second, we must address the appropriate Fourth Amendment standard for a search conducted by a public employer in areas in which a public employee is found to have a reasonable expectation of privacy.

I

Dr. Magno Ortega, a physician and psychiatrist, held the position of Chief of Professional Education at Napa State Hospital (Hospital) for 17 years, until his dismissal from that position in 1981. As Chief of Professional Education, Dr. Ortega had primary responsibility for training young physicians in psychiatric residency programs.

In July 1981, Hospital officials, including Dr. Dennis O'Connor, the Executive Director of the Hospital, became concerned about possible improprieties in Dr. Ortega's management of the residency program. In particular, the Hospital officials were concerned with Dr. Ortega's acquisition of an Apple II computer for use in the residency program. The officials thought that Dr. Ortega may have misled Dr. O'Connor into believing that the computer had been donated, when in fact the computer had been financed by the possibly coerced contributions of residents. Additionally, the Hospital officials were concerned with charges that Dr. Ortega had sexually harassed two female Hospital employees, and had taken inappropriate disciplinary action against a resident.

On July 30, 1981, Dr. O'Connor requested that Dr. Ortega take paid administrative leave during an investigation of these charges. At Dr. Ortega's request, Dr. O'Connor agreed to allow Dr. Ortega to take two weeks' vacation instead of administrative leave. Dr. Ortega, however, was requested to stay off Hospital grounds for the duration of the investigation. On August 14, 1981, Dr. O'Connor informed Dr. Ortega that the investigation had not yet been completed, and that he was being placed on paid administrative leave. Dr. Ortega remained on administrative leave until the Hospital terminated his employment on September 22, 1981.

Dr. O'Connor selected several Hospital personnel to conduct the investigation, including an accountant, a physician, and a Hospital security officer. Richard Friday, the Hospital Administrator, led this "investigative team." At some point during the investigation, Mr. Friday made the decision to enter Dr. Ortega's office. The specific reason for the entry into Dr. Ortega's office is unclear from the record. The petitioners claim that the search was conducted to secure state property. Initially, petitioners contended that such a search was pursuant to a Hospital policy of conducting a routine inventory of state property in the office of a terminated employee. At the time of the search, however, the Hospital had not yet terminated Dr. Ortega's employment; Dr. Ortega was still on administrative leave. Apparently, there was no policy of inventorying the offices of those on administrative leave. Before the search had been initiated, however, petitioners had become aware that Dr. Ortega had taken the computer to his home. Dr. Ortega contends that the purpose of the search was to secure evidence for use against him in administrative disciplinary proceedings.

The resulting search of Dr. Ortega's office was quite thorough. The investigators entered the office a number of times and seized several items from Dr. Ortega's desk and file cabinets, including a Valentine's Day card, a photograph, and a book of poetry all sent to Dr. Ortega by a former resident physician. These items were later used in a proceeding before a hearing officer of the California State Personnel Board to impeach the credibility of the former resident, who testified on Dr. Ortega's behalf. The investigators also seized billing documentation of one of Dr. Ortega's private patients under the California Medicaid program. The investigators did not otherwise separate Dr. Ortega's property from state property because, as one investigator testified, "[trying] to sort State from non-State, it was too much to do, so I gave it up and boxed it up." Thus, no formal inventory of the property in the office was ever made. Instead, all the papers in Dr. Ortega's office were merely placed in boxes, and put in storage for Dr. Ortega to retrieve.

Dr. Ortega commenced this action against petitioners in Federal District Court under 42 U. S. C. § 1983, alleging that the search of his office violated the Fourth Amendment. On cross-motions for summary judgment, the District Court granted petitioners' motion for summary judgment. The District Court concluded that the search was proper because there was a need to secure state property in the office. The Court of Appeals for the Ninth Circuit affirmed in part and reversed in part, concluding that Dr. Ortega had a reasonable expectation of privacy in his office. While the Hospital had a procedure for office inventories, these inventories were reserved for employees who were departing or were terminated. The Court of Appeals also concluded – albeit without explanation – that the search violated the Fourth Amendment. The Court of Appeals held that the record justified a grant of partial summary judgment for Dr. Ortega on the issue of liability for an unlawful search, and it remanded the case to the District Court for a determination of damages.

We granted certiorari, 474 U.S. 1018 (1985), and now reverse and remand.

II

The strictures of the Fourth Amendment, applied to the States through the Fourteenth Amendment, have been applied to the conduct of governmental officials in various civil activities. Searches and seizures by government employers or supervisors of the private property of their employees are subject to the restraints of the Fourth Amendment.

The Fourth Amendment protects the "right of the people to be secure in their persons, houses, papers, and effects, against unreasonable searches and seizures. . . . " Our cases establish that Dr. Ortega's Fourth Amendment rights are implicated only if the conduct of the Hospital officials at issue in this case infringed "an expectation of privacy that society is prepared to consider reasonable."

Because the reasonableness of an expectation of privacy, as well as the appropriate standard for a search, is understood to differ according to context, it is essential first to delineate the boundaries of the workplace context. The workplace includes those areas and items that are related to work and are generally within the employer's control. At a hospital, for example, the hallways, cafeteria, offices, desks, and file cabinets, among other areas, are all part of the workplace. These areas remain part of the workplace context even if the employee has placed personal items in them, such as a photograph placed in a desk or a letter posted on an employee bulletin board.

Not everything that passes through the confines of the business address can be considered part of the workplace context, however. An employee may bring closed luggage to the office prior to leaving on a trip, or a handbag or briefcase each workday. While whatever expectation of privacy the employee has in the existence and the outward appearance of the luggage is affected by its presence in the workplace, the employee's expectation of privacy in the *contents* of the luggage is not affected in the same way. The appropriate standard for a workplace search does not necessarily apply to a piece of closed personal luggage, a handbag, or a briefcase that happens to be within the employer's business address.

Given the societal expectations of privacy in one's place of work expressed in both *Oliver* and *Mancusi*, we reject the contention made by the Solicitor General and petitioners that public employees can never have a reasonable expectation of privacy in their place of work. Individuals do not lose Fourth Amendment rights merely because they work for the government instead of a private employer. The operational realities of the workplace, however, may make *some* employees' expectations of privacy unreasonable when an intrusion is by a supervisor rather than a law enforcement official. Public employees' expectations of privacy in their offices, desks, and file cabinets, like similar expectations of employees in the private sector, may be reduced by virtue of actual office practices and procedures, or by legitimate regulation. The employee's expectation of privacy must be assessed in the context of the employment relation. An office is seldom a private enclave free from entry by supervisors, other employees, and business and personal invitees. Simply put, it is the nature of government offices that others – such as fellow employees, supervisors, consensual visitors, and the general public – may have frequent access to an individual's office. Given the great variety of work environments in the public sector, the question whether an employee has a reasonable expectation of privacy must be addressed on a case-by-case basis.

The Court of Appeals concluded that Dr. Ortega had a reasonable expectation of privacy in his office, and five Members of this Court agree with that determination. Because the record does not reveal the extent to which Hospital officials may have had work-related reasons to enter Dr. Ortega's office, we think the Court of Appeals should have remanded the matter to the District Court for its further determination. But regardless of any legitimate right of access the Hospital staff may have had to the office as such, we recognize that the undisputed evidence suggests that Dr. Ortega had a reasonable expectation of privacy in his desk and file cabinets. The undisputed evidence discloses that Dr. Ortega did not share his desk or file cabinets with any other employees. Dr. Ortega had occupied the office for 17 years and he kept materials in his office, which included personal correspondence, medical files, correspondence from private patients unconnected to the Hospital, personal financial records, teaching aids and notes, and personal gifts and mementos. The files on physicians in residency training were kept outside Dr. Ortega's office. Finally, we note that there was no evidence that the Hospital had established any reasonable regulation or policy discouraging employees such as Dr. Ortega from storing personal papers and effects in their desks or file cabinets, although the absence of such a policy does not create an expectation of privacy where it would not otherwise exist.

On the basis of this undisputed evidence, we accept the conclusion of the Court of Appeals that Dr. Ortega had a reasonable expectation of privacy at least in his desk and file cabinets.

III

BUT, even though Dr. Ortega had a reasonable expectation of privacy in his office, was the search itself "unreasonable"? Remember that the Fourth Amendment protects us only from *unreasonable* searches and seizures.

In the case of searches conducted by a public employer, we must balance the invasion of the employees' legitimate expectations of privacy against the government's need for supervision, control, and the efficient operation of the workplace.

There is surprisingly little case law on the appropriate Fourth Amendment standard of reasonableness for a public employer's work-related search of its employee's offices, desks, or file cabinets. Generally, however, the lower courts have held that any "work-related" search by an employer satisfies the Fourth Amendment reasonableness requirement.

The legitimate privacy interests of public employees in the private objects they bring to the workplace may be substantial. Against these privacy interests, however, must be balanced the realities of the workplace, which strongly suggest that a warrant requirement would be unworkable. While police, and even administrative enforcement personnel, conduct searches for the primary purpose of obtaining evidence for use in criminal or other enforcement proceedings, employers most frequently need to enter the offices and desks of their employees for legitimate work-related reasons wholly unrelated to illegal conduct. Employers and supervisors are focused primarily on the need to complete the government agency's work in a prompt and efficient manner.

In our view, requiring an employer to obtain a warrant whenever the employer wished to enter an employee's office, desk, or file cabinets for a work-related purpose would seriously disrupt the routine conduct of business and would be unduly burdensome.

Whether probable cause is an inappropriate standard for public employer searches of their employees' offices presents a more difficult issue. We have concluded, for example, that the appropriate standard for administrative searches is not probable cause in its traditional meaning. Instead, an administrative warrant can be obtained if there is a showing that reasonable legislative or administrative standards for conducting an inspection are satisfied.

As an initial matter, it is important to recognize the plethora of contexts in which employers will have an occasion to intrude to some extent on an employee's expectation of privacy. Because the parties in this case have alleged that the search was either a non-investigatory work-related intrusion or an investigatory search for evidence of suspected work-related employee misfeasance, we undertake to determine the appropriate Fourth Amendment standard of reasonableness *only* for these two types of employer intrusions and leave for another day inquiry into other circumstances.

The governmental interest justifying work-related intrusions by public employers is the efficient and proper operation of the workplace. To ensure the efficient and proper operation of the agency, therefore, public employers must be given wide latitude to enter employee offices for work-related, noninvestigatory reasons.

We come to a similar conclusion for searches conducted pursuant to an investigation of work-related employee misconduct. Even when employers conduct an investigation, they have an interest substantially different from "the normal need for law enforcement." Public employers have an interest in ensuring that their agencies operate in an effective and efficient manner, and the work of these agencies inevitably suffers from the inefficiency, incompetence, mismanagement, or other work-related misfeasance of its employees.

Balanced against the substantial government interests in the efficient and proper operation of the workplace are the privacy interests of government employees in their place of work which, while not insubstantial, are far less than those found at home or in some other contexts. Government offices are provided to employees for the sole purpose of facilitating the work of an agency. The employee may avoid exposing personal belongings at work by simply leaving them at home.

In sum, we conclude that the "special needs, beyond the normal need for law enforcement make the . . . probable-cause requirement impracticable," for legitimate work-related, noninvestigatory intrusions as well as investigations of work-related misconduct. A standard of reasonableness will neither unduly burden the efforts of government employers to ensure the efficient and proper operation of the workplace, nor authorize arbitrary intrusions upon the privacy of public employees. We hold, therefore, that public employer intrusions on the constitutionally protected privacy interests of government employees for noninvestigatory, work-related purposes, as well as for investigations of work-related misconduct, should be judged by the standard of reasonableness under all the circumstances. Under this reasonableness standard, both the inception and the scope of the intrusion must be reasonable.

Ordinarily, a search of an employee's office by a supervisor will be "justified at its inception" when there are reasonable grounds for suspecting that the search will turn up evidence that the employee is guilty of work-related misconduct, or that the search is necessary for a noninvestigatory work-related purpose such as to retrieve a needed file.

Query: Doesn't this sound a bit like "probable cause"?

Because petitioners had an "individualized suspicion" of misconduct by Dr. Ortega, we need not decide whether individualized suspicion is an essential element of the standard of reasonableness that we adopt today. The search will be permissible in its scope when "the measures adopted are reasonably related to the objectives of the search and not excessively intrusive in light of . . . the nature of the [misconduct]."

IV

We believe that both the District Court and the Court of Appeals were in error because summary judgment was inappropriate. The parties were in dispute about the actual justification for the search, and the record was inadequate for a determination on motion for summary judgment of the reasonableness of the search and seizure.

In their motion for summary judgment in the District Court, petitioners alleged that this search to secure property was reasonable as "part of the established hospital policy to inventory property within offices of departing, terminated or separated employees." At the time of the search, however, Dr. Ortega had not been terminated, but rather was still on administrative leave, and the record does not reflect whether the Hospital had a policy of inventorying the property of investigated employees. Respondent, moreover, has consistently rejected petitioners' characterization of the search as motivated by a need to secure state property. Instead, Dr. Ortega has contended that the intrusion was an investigatory search whose purpose was simply to discover evidence that would be of use in administrative proceedings.

On remand, therefore, the District Court must determine the justification for the search and seizure, and evaluate the reasonableness of both the inception of the search and its scope.

CONCURRENCE: SCALIA, Justice:

Although I share the judgment that this case must be reversed and remanded, I disagree with the reason for the reversal given by the plurality opinion, and with the standard it prescribes for the Fourth Amendment inquiry.

To address the latter point first: The plurality opinion instructs the lower courts that existence of Fourth Amendment protection for a public employee's business office is to be assessed "on a case-by-case basis," in light of whether the office is "so open to fellow employees or the public that no expectation of privacy is reasonable." No clue is provided as to how open "so open" must be; much less is it suggested how police officers are to gather the facts necessary for this refined inquiry. I object to the formulation of a standard so devoid of content that it produces rather than eliminates uncertainty in this field.

Whatever the plurality's standard means, however, it must be wrong if it leads to the conclusion on the present facts that if Hospital officials had extensive "work-related reasons to enter Dr. Ortega's office" no Fourth Amendment protection existed. It is privacy that is protected by the Fourth Amendment, not solitude. A man enjoys Fourth Amendment protection in his home, for example, even though his wife and children have the run of the place – and indeed, even though his landlord has the right to conduct unannounced inspections at any time. Similarly, in my view, one's personal office is constitutionally protected against warrantless intrusions by the police, even though employer and co-workers are not excluded. There is no reason why this determination that a legitimate expectation of privacy exists should be affected by the fact that the government, rather than a private entity, is the employer. Constitutional protection against *unreasonable* searches by the government does not disappear merely because the government has the right to make reasonable intrusions in its capacity as employer.

I cannot agree, moreover, with the plurality's view that the reasonableness of the expectation of privacy (and thus the existence of Fourth Amendment protection) changes "when an intrusion is by a supervisor rather than a law enforcement official." The identity of the searcher (police v. employer) is relevant not to whether Fourth Amendment protections apply, but only to whether the search of a protected area is reasonable.

I would hold, therefore, that the offices of government employees, and *a fortiori* the drawers and files within those offices, are covered by Fourth Amendment protections as a general matter. (The qualifier is necessary to cover such unusual situations as that in which the office is subject to unrestricted public access, so that it is "[exposed] to the public" and therefore "not a subject of Fourth Amendment protection.")

The case turns, therefore, on whether the Fourth Amendment was violated – *i.e.*, whether the governmental intrusion was reasonable. It is here that the government's status as employer, and the employment-related character of the search, become relevant. While as a general rule warrantless searches are *per se* unreasonable, we have recognized exceptions when "special needs, beyond the normal need for law enforcement, make the warrant and probable-cause requirement impracticable. . . . " Such "special needs" are present in the context of government employment. The government, like any other employer, needs frequent and convenient access to its desks, offices, and file cabinets for work-related purposes. I would hold that government searches to retrieve work-related materials or to investigate violations of workplace rules – searches of the sort that are regarded as reasonable and normal in the private-employer context – do not violate the Fourth Amendment.

Does this mean that Justice Scalia is essentially saying that since the Fourth Amendment doesn't apply to private employers, the same standard should be extended to public employers? That is, is he arguing in a backhanded sort of way that *all* searches by public employers should be acceptable under the Amendment?

Because the conflicting and incomplete evidence in the present case could not conceivably support summary judgment that the search did not have such a validating purpose, I agree with the plurality that the decision must be reversed and remanded.

DISSENT: BLACKMUN, Justice:

The facts of this case are simple and straightforward. Dr. Ortega had an expectation of privacy in his office, desk, and file cabinets, which were the target of a search by petitioners that can be characterized only as investigatory in nature. Because there was no "special need," to dispense with the warrant and probable-cause requirements of the Fourth Amendment, I would evaluate the search by applying this traditional standard. Under that standard, this search clearly violated Dr. Ortega's Fourth Amendment rights.

The problems in the plurality's opinion all arise from its failure or unwillingness to realize that the facts here are clear. The plurality, however, discovers what it feels is a factual dispute: the plurality is not certain whether the search was routine or investigatory. Accordingly, it concludes that a remand is the appropriate course of action. Despite the remand, the plurality assumes it must announce a standard concerning the reasonableness of a public employer's search of the workplace. Because the plurality treats the facts as in dispute, it formulates this standard at a distance from the situation presented by this case.

This does not seem to me to be the way to undertake Fourth Amendment analysis, especially in an area with which the Court is relatively unfamiliar. Because this analysis, when conducted properly, is always fact specific to an extent, it is inappropriate that the plurality's formulation of a standard does not arise from a sustained consideration of a particular factual situation. Moreover, given that *any* standard ultimately rests on judgments about factual situations, it is apparent that the plurality has assumed the existence of hypothetical facts from which its standard follows. These "assumed" facts are weighted in favor of the public employer, and, as a result, the standard that emerges makes reasonable almost any workplace search by a public employer.

The search stemmed neither from a Hospital policy nor from a practice of routine entrances into Dr. Ortega's office. It was plainly exceptional and investigatory in nature. Accordingly, there is no significant factual dispute in this case.

[Part I is omitted.]

II

With respect to the plurality's general comments, I am in complete agreement with its observation that "[individuals] do not lose Fourth Amendment rights merely because they work for the government instead of a private employer." Moreover, I would go along with the plurality's observation that, in certain situations, the "operational realities" of the workplace may remove some expectation of privacy on the part of the employee. However, I am disturbed by the plurality's suggestion, that routine entries by visitors might completely remove this expectation.

The common understanding of an office is that it is a place where a worker receives an occasional business-related visitor. Thus, when the office has received traditional Fourth Amendment protection in our cases, it has been with the understanding that such routine visits occur there.

Moreover, as the plurality appears to recognize, the precise extent of an employee's expectation of privacy often turns on the nature of the search. This observation is in accordance with the principle that the Fourth Amendment may protect an individual's expectation of privacy in one context, even though this expectation may be unreasonable in another. Thus, although an employee might well have no reasonable expectation of privacy with respect to an occasional visit by a fellow employee, he would have such an expectation as to an afterhours search of his locked office by an investigative team seeking materials to be used against him at a termination proceeding.

Finally and most importantly, the reality of work in modern time, whether done by public or private employees, reveals why a public employee's expectation of privacy in the workplace should be carefully safeguarded and not lightly set aside. It is, unfortunately, all too true that the workplace has become another home for most working Americans. Many employees spend the better part of their days and much of their evenings at work. Consequently, an employee's private life must intersect with the workplace, for example, when the employee takes advantage of work or lunch breaks to make personal telephone calls, to attend to personal business, or to receive personal visitors in the office. As a result, the tidy distinctions between the workplace and professional affairs, on the one hand, and personal possessions and private activities, on the other, do not exist in reality.

And how about telecommuters today?

Dr. Ortega clearly had an expectation of privacy in his office, desk, and file cabinets, particularly with respect to the type of investigatory search involved here.

III

A

At the outset of its analysis, the plurality observes that an appropriate standard of reasonableness to be applied to a public employer's search of the employee's workplace is arrived at from "balancing" the privacy interests of the employee against the public employer's interests justifying the intrusion. Under traditional Fourth Amendment jurisprudence, however, courts abandon the warrant and probable-cause requirements, which constitute the standard of reasonableness for a government search that the Framers established, "[only] in those exceptional circumstances in which special needs, beyond the normal need for law enforcement, make the warrant and probable-cause requirement impracticable. . . . " In sum, only when the practical realities of a particular situation suggest that a government official cannot obtain a warrant based upon probable cause without sacrificing the ultimate goals to which a search would contribute, does the Court turn to a "balancing" test to formulate a standard of reasonableness for this context.

[G]iven the facts of this case, no "special need" exists here to justify dispensing with the warrant and probable-cause requirements. As observed above, the facts suggest that this was an investigatory search undertaken to obtain evidence of charges of mismanagement at a time when Dr. Ortega was on administrative leave and not permitted to enter the Hospital's grounds. There was no special practical need that might have justified dispensing with the warrant and probable-cause requirements. Without sacrificing their ultimate goal of maintaining an effective institution devoted to training and healing, to which the disciplining of Hospital employees contributed, petitioners could have taken any evidence of Dr. Ortega's alleged improprieties to a magistrate in order to obtain a warrant.

Furthermore, this seems to be exactly the kind of situation where a neutral magistrate's involvement would have been helpful in curtailing the infringement upon Dr. Ortega's privacy. Petitioners would have been forced to articulate their exact reasons for the search and to specify the items in Dr. Ortega's office they sought, which would have prevented the general rummaging through the doctor's office, desk, and file cabinets. Thus, because no "special need" in this case demanded that the traditional warrant and probable-cause requirements be dispensed with, petitioners' failure to conduct the search in accordance with the traditional standard of reasonableness should end the analysis, and the judgment of the Court of Appeals should be affirmed.

B

A careful balancing with respect to the warrant requirement is absent from the plurality's opinion, an absence that is inevitable in light of the gulf between the plurality's analysis and any concrete factual setting. It is certainly correct that a public employer cannot be expected to obtain a warrant for every routine entry into an employee's workplace. This situation, however, should not justify dispensing with a warrant in *all* searches by the employer. The warrant requirement is perfectly suited for many work-related searches, including the instant one. In sum, the plurality's general result is preordained because, cut off from a particular factual setting, it cannot make the necessary distinctions among types of searches, or formulate an alternative to the warrant requirement that derives from a precise weighing of competing interests.

IV

By ignoring the specific facts of this case, and by announcing in the abstract a standard as to the reasonableness of an employer's workplace searches, the plurality undermines not only the Fourth Amendment rights of public employees but also any further analysis of the constitutionality of public employer searches.

I respectfully dissent.

In 1998, seventeen years and several trials after the event that triggered this litigation, Dr. Ortega ultimately prevailed in the Ninth Circuit Court of Appeals and was awarded damages. Nonetheless, this Supreme Court case remains important for its discussion and holdings regarding the general question of employee privacy rights.

Personal e-mail – that is to say, non-workplace e-mail – is protected from unauthorized interception by the Electronic Communications Privacy Act (ECPA). The ECPA applies to individuals as well as the government. But what, exactly, *is* an interception? To answer that question, we have to look at the following case.

E-Mail: Case 2

STEVE JACKSON GAMES, INCORPORATED, et al., Plaintiffs-Appellants, v. UNITED STATES SECRET SERVICE, et al., Defendants, United States Secret Service and United States of America, Defendants-Appellees.

No. 93-8661.

UNITED STATES COURT OF APPEALS FOR THE FIFTH CIRCUIT

36 F.3d 457; 1994 U.S. App. LEXIS 30323

October 31, 1994, Decided

OPINION: BARKSDALE, Judge:

The narrow issue before us is whether the seizure of a computer, used to operate an electronic bulletin board system, and containing private electronic mail which had been sent to (stored on) the bulletin board, but not read (retrieved) by the intended recipients, constitutes an unlawful intercept under the Federal Wiretap Act, 18 U.S.C. § 2510, et seq., as amended by Title I of the Electronic Communications Privacy Act of 1986, Pub.L. No. 99-508, Title I, 100 Stat. 1848 (1986). We hold that it is not, and therefore AFFIRM.

I.

The district court's findings of fact are not in dispute. Appellant Steve Jackson Games, Incorporated (SJG), publishes books, magazines, role-playing games, and related products. Starting in the mid-1980s, SJG operated an electronic bulletin board system, called "Illuminati" (BBS), from one of its computers. SJG used the BBS to post public information about its business, games, publications, and the role-playing hobby; to facilitate play-testing of games being developed; and to communicate with its customers and free-lance writers by electronic mail (E-mail).

Central to the issue before us, the BBS also offered customers the ability to send and receive private E-mail. Private E-mail was stored on the BBS computer's hard disk drive temporarily, until the addressees "called" the BBS (using their computers and modems) and read their mail. After reading their E-mail, the recipients could choose to either store it on the BBS computer's hard drive or delete it. In February 1990, there were 365 BBS users. Among other uses, appellants Steve Jackson, Elizabeth McCoy, William Milliken, and Steffan O'Sullivan used the BBS for communication by private E-mail.

In October 1988, Henry Kluepfel, Director of Network Security Technology (an affiliate Bell Company), began investigating the unauthorized duplication and distribution of a computerized text file, containing information about Bell's emergency call system. In July 1989, Kluepfel informed Secret Service Agent Foley and an Assistant United States Attorney in Chicago about the unauthorized distribution. In early February 1990, Kluepfel learned that the document was available on the "Phoenix Project" computer bulletin board, which was operated by Loyd Blankenship in Austin, Texas; that Blankenship was an SJG employee; and that, as a co-systems operator of the BBS, Blankenship had the ability to review and, perhaps, delete any data on the BBS.

On February 28, 1990, Agent Foley applied for a warrant to search SJG's premises and Blankenship's residence for evidence of violations of 18 U.S.C. §§ 1030 (proscribes interstate transportation of computer access information) and 2314 (proscribes interstate transportation of stolen property). A search warrant for SJG was issued that same day, authorizing the seizure of, *inter alia*, computer hardware . . . and computer software . . . and . . . documents relating to the use of the computer system, . . . and financial documents and licensing documentation relative to the computer programs and equipment at . . . [SJG] . . . which constitute evidence . . . of federal crimes. . . . This warrant is for the seizure of the above described computer and computer data and for the authorization to read information stored and contained on the above described computer and computer data.

The next day, March 1, the warrant was executed by the Secret Service, including Agents Foley and Golden. Among the items seized was the computer which operated the BBS. At the time of the seizure, 162 items of unread, private E-mail were stored on the BBS, including items addressed to the individual appellants. Despite the Secret

Service's denial, the district court found that Secret Service personnel or delegates read and deleted the private E-mail stored on the BBS.

Appellants filed suit in May 1991 against, among others, the Secret Service and the United States, claiming, *inter alia*, violations of the Privacy Protection Act, 42 U.S.C. § 2000aa, *et seq.*; the Federal Wiretap Act, as amended by Title I of the Electronic Communications Privacy Act (ECPA), 18 U.S.C. §§ 2510-2521 (proscribes, *inter alia*, the intentional interception of electronic communications); and Title II of the ECPA, 18 U.S.C. §§ 2701-2711 (proscribes, *inter alia*, intentional access, without authorization, to stored electronic communications).

The district court held that the Secret Service violated the Privacy Protection Act, and awarded actual damages of $ 51,040 to SJG; and that it violated Title II of the ECPA by seizing stored electronic communications without complying with the statutory provisions, and awarded the statutory damages of $ 1,000 to each of the individual appellants. And, it awarded appellants $ 195,000 in attorneys' fees and approximately $ 57,000 in costs. But, it held that the Secret Service did not "intercept" the E-mail in violation of Title I of the ECPA, 18 U.S.C. § 2511(1)(a), because its acquisition of the contents of the electronic communications was not contemporaneous with the transmission of those communications.

II.

As stated, the sole issue is a very narrow one: whether the seizure of a computer on which is stored private E-mail that has been sent to an electronic bulletin board, but not yet read (retrieved) by the recipients, constitutes an "intercept" proscribed by 18 U.S.C. § 2511(1)(a).

Section 2511 was enacted in 1968 as part of Title III of the Omnibus Crime Control and Safe Streets Act of 1968, often referred to as the Federal Wiretap Act. Prior to the 1986 amendment by Title I of the ECPA, it covered only wire and oral communications. Title I of the ECPA extended that coverage to electronic communications.[1] In relevant part, § 2511(1)(a) proscribes "intentionally intercepting . . . any wire, oral, or electronic communication," unless the intercept is authorized by court order or by other exceptions not relevant here.

The Act defines "intercept" as "the aural or other acquisition of the contents of any wire, electronic, or oral communication through the use of any electronic, mechanical, or other device." The district court, relying on our court's interpretation of intercept in *United States v. Turk*, 526 F.2d 654 (5th Cir.), *cert. denied*, 429 U.S. 823, 97 S. Ct. 74, 50 L. Ed. 2d 84 (1976), held that the Secret Service did not intercept the communications, because its acquisition of the contents of those communications was not contemporaneous

---

[1] An "electronic communication" is defined as:

any transfer of signs, signals, writing, images, sounds, data, or intelligence of any nature transmitted in whole or in part by a wire, radio, electromagnetic, photoelectronic or photooptical system that affects interstate or foreign commerce, but does not include –

  (A) the radio portion of a cordless telephone communication that is transmitted between the cordless telephone handset and the base unit;
  (B) any wire or oral communication;
  (C) any communication made through a tone-only paging device; or
  (D) any communication from a tracking device (as defined in section 3117 of this title). . . .

with their transmission. In *Turk*, the government seized from a suspect's vehicle an audio tape of a prior conversation between the suspect and Turk. (Restated, when the conversation took place, it was not recorded contemporaneously by the government.) Our court held that replaying the previously recorded conversation was not an "intercept," because an intercept "requires participation by the one charged with an 'interception' in the contemporaneous acquisition of the communication through the use of the device."

Appellants agree with *Turk*'s holding, but contend that it is not applicable, because it "says nothing about government action that both *acquires* the communication prior to its delivery, and *prevents* that delivery." (Emphasis by appellants.) Along that line, appellants note correctly that *Turk*'s interpretation of "intercept" predates the ECPA, and assert, in essence, that the information stored on the BBS could still be "intercepted" under the Act, even though it was not in transit. They maintain that to hold otherwise does violence to Congress' purpose in enacting the ECPA, to include providing protection for E-mail and bulletin boards. For the most part, appellants fail to even discuss the pertinent provisions of the Act, much less address their application. Instead, they point simply to Congress' intent in enacting the ECPA and appeal to logic (i.e., to seize something before it is received is to intercept it).

But, obviously, the language of the Act controls. In that regard, appellees counter that "Title II, not Title I, . . . governs the seizure of stored electronic communications such as unread e-mail messages," and note that appellants have recovered damages under Title II. Understanding the Act requires understanding and applying its many technical terms as defined by the Act, as well as engaging in painstaking, methodical analysis. As appellees note, the issue is not whether E-mail can be "intercepted"; it can. Instead, at issue is what constitutes an "intercept."

Prior to the 1986 amendment by the ECPA, the Wiretap Act defined "intercept" as the "aural acquisition" of the contents of wire or oral communications through the use of a device. The ECPA amended this definition to include the "aural *or other* acquisition of the contents of . . . wire, *electronic*, or oral communications. . . . " The significance of the addition of the words "or other" in the 1986 amendment to the definition of "intercept" becomes clear when the definitions of "aural" and "electronic communication" are examined; electronic communications (which include the non-voice portions of wire communications), as defined by the Act, cannot be acquired aurally.

Webster's Third New International Dictionary (1986) defines "aural" as "of or relating to the ear" or "of or relating to the sense of hearing." And, the Act defines "aural transfer" as "a transfer containing the human voice at any point between and including the point of origin and the point of reception." This definition is extremely important for purposes of understanding the definition of a "wire communication," which is defined by the Act as any aural transfer made in whole or in part through the use of facilities for the transmission of communications by the aid of wire, cable, or other like connection between the point of origin and the point of reception (including the use of such connection in a switching station) . . . *and such term includes any electronic storage of such communication.*

In contrast, as noted, an "electronic communication" is defined as "any *transfer* of signs, signals, writing, images, sounds, data, or intelligence of any nature transmitted in whole or in part by a wire, radio, electromagnetic, photoelectronic or photooptical system . . . but does not include . . . any wire or oral communication. . . . "

Critical to the issue before us is the fact that, unlike the definition of "wire communication," *the definition of "electronic communication" does not include electronic storage of such communications.* "Electronic storage" is defined as

(A) any *temporary*, intermediate *storage* of a wire or *electronic communication incidental to the electronic transmission thereof;* and
(B) any storage of such communication by an electronic communication service for purposes of backup protection of such communication. . . .

The E-mail in issue was in "electronic storage." Congress' use of the word "transfer" in the definition of "electronic communication," and its omission in that definition of the phrase "any electronic storage of such communication" (part of the definition of "wire communication") reflects that Congress did not intend for "intercept" to apply to "electronic communications" when those communications are in "electronic storage."

The Court notes that the Congressional intent to differentiate *electronic* from other types of communications can also be inferred from the fact that the law requires only a search warrant to access contents of stored *electronic* communications, while a court order is required to access stored *wire* communications.

Our conclusion is reinforced further by consideration of the fact that Title II of the ECPA clearly applies to the conduct of the Secret Service in this case. Needless to say, when construing a statute, we do not confine our interpretation to the one portion at issue but, instead, consider the statute as a whole.

Title II generally proscribes unauthorized access to stored wire or electronic communications. Section 2701(a) provides:

Except as provided in subsection (c) of this section whoever –

(1) intentionally accesses without authorization a facility through which an electronic communication service is provided; or
(2) intentionally exceeds an authorization to access that facility;

As stated, the district court found that the Secret Service violated § 2701 when it intentionally accessed without authorization a facility [the computer] through which an electronic communication service [the BBS] is provided . . . and thereby obtained [and] prevented authorized access [by appellants] to an . . . electronic communication while it is in electronic storage in such system.

The Secret Service does not challenge this ruling. We find no indication in either the Act or its legislative history that Congress intended for conduct that is clearly prohibited by Title II to furnish the basis for a civil remedy under Title I as well.

In other words, it is unlikely that Congress intended to permit civil remedies under both sections for the same conduct, and that's why there are two different sections. That is, something that can be "intercepted" is not in storage, and vice versa.

Again, the Court notes the different treatment accorded by Congress to "interceptions" as opposed to disclosures of stored electronic communications:

– Contents of electronic communications that have been in storage for fewer than 180 days can be accessed by warrant, but

- *interception* by law officers requires a court order.
- This is because interception necessarily will involve accessing and viewing lots of things that have no bearing on the case, while stored material may be examined in ways that will minimize the need to look at innocent material.

In light of the substantial differences between the statutory procedures and requirements for obtaining authorization to intercept electronic communications, on the one hand, and to gain access to the contents of stored electronic communications, on the other, it is most unlikely that Congress intended to require law enforcement officers to satisfy the more stringent requirements for an intercept in order to gain access to the contents of stored electronic communications.

III.

For the foregoing reasons, the judgment is Affirmed.

Thus, the Secret Service's viewing of stored e-mail was unauthorized seizure of stored communications, but not an "interception" of the e-mail because the acquisition of its contents was not contemporaneous with the transmission of the contents.

～

Applying the ECPA

The ECPA also says systems operators (sysops) cannot divulge contents of any messages on their systems unless the communication is sent to them or their agents.

But there are exceptions. Sysops can divulge message contents if:

1. the sysop is authorized to do so by other parts of ECPA, or
2. the sysop has the consent of the addressee, or
3. divulgence is necessary to forward the communication properly, or
4. a message is inadvertently read by sysop and the message appears to pertain to the commission of a crime.

The ECPA provides for penalties of fines and/or up to five years in prison. The ECPA also provides for civil suits by an injured party.

Additionally, the ECPA criminalizes unauthorized access and access beyond the appropriate level of privileges to computer systems and provides remedies for these offenses of fines and up to one year in prison. Civil suits by injured parties are also available for parties injured by these offenses.

The language of the ECPA specifies that the law is applicable to private parties, including employers, in addition to being applicable to the government. However, two exceptions built into the statute apparently authorize employer monitoring of e-mail (although for public employers, this is only permissible within Constitutional limits).

1. **Prior consent exception.**
   - If one of the parties to the communication has consented to the monitoring, it is okay.
   - Employee consent can be explicit, such as signing a document, or also implied from circumstances. Online, this might take the form of a message that appears

on an employee's screen every time he or she logs in. However, implied consent has been construed narrowly by the judiciary.

2. **Business Use Exception**
   - The entity that provides the electronic communication service is authorized to intercept messages.
   - This exception does not limit the degree or method of employee monitoring, nor does it require notice.
   - BUT: monitoring must be within the ordinary course of the employer's business, and the subject matter of the intercepted messages must be one in which the employer has a legal interest.
   - Generally, courts have allowed employer monitoring when the subject matter of the communications is business-related.
   - BUT "ordinary course of business" does not mean the employer may monitor anything the employer is curious about.
   - Monitoring messages about business topics is okay, including messages that are critical of supervisors.

Query: How does the employer know the subject of a message prior to monitoring?

The ECPA probably does not prohibit an employer from monitoring e-mail between employees and third parties who are not employees since the statute says monitoring or interception is permissible so long as *one* of the parties to the communication consents to the monitoring.

It is also worth noting that the ECPA provides even broader exceptions for employer access to *stored* communications, rather than those in transit, and information in storage is most commonly what an employer will be looking at.

Virtually all states also have laws addressing unauthorized access to stored messages and their interception. Some states provide even more protection than the ECPA. Some do not have a prior consent exception, for example, and some require that *all* parties to a communication consent to monitoring before monitoring can take place.

Note once again that while an employee of a private employer has protection under the ECPA, the employee *cannot* claim a Fourth Amendment violation. All Constitutional claims require government, not private, action.

Even when an employee may be able to assert a Fourth Amendment claim against a public employer, the courts have given employers great latitude. California, for example, has explicitly recognized a state constitutional right to privacy for private, as well, as public employees, but the California courts seem not to enforce this protection. They make it very hard for the employee to establish that a reasonable expectation of privacy existed in the first place, so therefore even though the employee's privacy *would* be protected under constitutional principles, it isn't.

The varying laws in the states create the usual problem in using the Net if you are a business with employees in multiple jurisdictions. Note also that even when employer monitoring is permitted, the employer might be in trouble if the information obtained is improperly used. Disciplinary actions based on the private life of an employee can also be improper. Under federal (and most state) law, employees cannot be fired for engaging in external, legal, leisure activities.

Employers are usually liable for the actions of their employees done within the scope of the employment relationship. So, under the principles of agency law, employers can be sued for employee violations of intellectual property rights, defamation, harassment, and committing the company.

E-mail sexual harassment cases are becoming more and more common. Protection for the employer lies in enforcing an e-mail policy that emphasizes prohibitions of all harassment. An employer is not *required* to monitor for sexual harassment, but the employer must respond quickly to any allegations.

E-mail can be used as evidence in court and can be obtained via the usual pre-trial process of discovery. Attempts to destroy e-mail as evidence can result in the same sort of sanctions used against those who try to destroy any other type of evidence (criminal charges, preclusion, and so on.)

People tend to think e-mail is transitory, like phone conversations, but it is in fact kept around for a long time. For example, e-mail back-up tapes helped sink Oliver North after he tried to erase messages related to the Iran-Contra Affair.

A proper e-mail policy is important to businesses. The policy should make it clear that the e-mail system is for business purposes. A total ban on private e-mail is unlikely to work, given the nature of the modern workplace and modern life. Think of telephones again. There is probably no one who has never used an office phone to call home for some reason. It is probably better for an employer to permit some limited personal use but to make it clear that the employer has a right to monitor if business-related circumstances justify it. These might include, for example, evaluations of employee productivity, investigations of employee misconduct, or sexual harassment.

11. The Right of Publicity

Introduction

The "Right of Publicity" is a fascinating legal topic. The cases on this issue tend to be extremely entertaining because the right of publicity is available only to those whose identities have publicity value – that is, the famous.

The "right of privacy" and the "right of publicity" are different. The right of privacy primarily prevents intrusion into a person's "private" life; financial loss is irrelevant to an individual's ability to sue. The right of publicity protects against financial loss through appropriation of a person's identity.

The right of publicity is protected in a minority of states. Sometimes it is protected through the common law. In some states it is protected by statute. While not every state explicitly recognizes the right of publicity, similar – although not identical – protections can be obtained in all states via the Lanham Act, the federal law that governs trade practices and, among other things, prohibits false endorsements. Note that, as usual, caution must be exercised in assessing possibilities regarding recovery under the right of privacy in cyberspace because of the borderless nature of the Net. To be on the safe side, abide by the laws as applied in the most restrictive jurisdiction.

The right of publicity is not absolute. There are First Amendment exceptions for use of a person's name or likeness (or identity) for the purposes of news reporting, political commentary, satire, or parody. The question is one of balancing a person's right of publicity against the need for free expression.

In most states that recognize the right of publicity the right continues after death and can be enforced by a deceased party's estate. The length of time the right survives varies from jurisdiction to jurisdiction.

The right of publicity has been given an interpretation that is much broader than that originally provided against commercial loss by use of a famous person's likeness or name. Brief descriptions of a few cases will illustrate the development of the right of publicity.

Bi-Rite Enterprises, Inc. v. Buttonmaster (1983)

- The plaintiff is a licensed seller of posters, buttons, patches, etc. of rock stars at concerts.
- Other plaintiffs are the rock groups whose rights of publicity are allegedly being infringed. These include Judas Priest, Devo, Styx, Iron Maiden, Neil Young, Pat Benatar, and others.
- The defendant is an unlicensed seller of buttons bearing pictures of the stars.

- The plaintiffs assert several claims, but the only one that the Court finds viable is a right of publicity claim.
- The reason it works here is that it gives persons the right to control the commercial use of their names and likenesses.
- The test for right of publicity cases is that the plaintiff must prove:
  - that his or her name or likeness has publicity value,
  - that he or she has "exploited" that value, and
  - that the defendant has appropriated that right.
- Here, the plaintiffs win.

Buttonmaster is a classic right of publicity case and nicely illustrates the elements that a plaintiff must prove in order to establish a violation of that right.

Carson v. Here's Johnny Portable Toilets (1983)

- Johnny Carson sues a company that is advertising with the slogan, "Here's Johnny! The world's foremost commodian."
- Note the defendant is not using Carson's full name or likeness.
- The Court says the right of publicity protects *more* than just a person's name or likeness.
- It protects *identity*.
- Therefore use of a phrase associated with a celebrity to evoke his or her identity is also protected.

Allen v. National Video, Inc. (1985)

- Woody Allen sues over the use of a "lookalike" of him in a commercial for a video rental store.
- "Woody" appears as a satisfied customer renting tapes.
- Is the use of a lookalike different from use of the person's "likeness"?
- Allen chooses here to pursue this claim via the Lanham Act § 43(a), which bans false endorsements (i.e., misrepresentations) rather than via his right of publicity. He probably did this because in some circumstances the Lanham Act provides avenues for broader claims than does the right of publicity.
- So this case gets analyzed pretty much like a trademark case, with Allen's likeness being the trademark.
- The question, as in any trademark infringement analysis, is whether there is a likelihood of confusion for consumers.
- The "mark" is considered strong here because Allen's name and likeness are well-known to the public and "he has built up a considerable investment in his unique, positive image," (which was true in 1983, although it is probably less true now).
- Regarding similarity of the marks, while the lookalike cannot be said to be identical in appearance, he is very close.
- Proximity of services or goods? Allen does not own a video store chain, but he is in the movie business, whose products the defendant rents out. They both serve the same audience, then, and can be said to share the same market.
- Evidence of actual confusion? Woody has submitted a consumer survey, which the Court finds unhelpful, but notes that no evidence of actual confusion is actually required.
- (Note that *some* other decisions regarding § 43(a) in other jurisdictions say that evidence of actual confusion *is* required.)

- Given the close resemblance of the lookalike, even a pretty sophisticated consumer might be fooled.
- The defendants admit they created the ad intentionally to evoke an association with Woody Allen and must therefore have been aware of a risk of confusion. (That is, they acted in bad faith. This was not intended to be a parody.)
- The court finds a likelihood of confusion and finds for Allen.
- NOTE: It's likely Allen would also have won had he chosen to pursue a right of publicity action. His likeness has publicity value; he has obviously exploited that value; and the defendants are appropriating his right to exploit the value of his likeness.

So the definition of "identity" has now been expanded from name and likeness to phrases associated with a celebrity or to a "lookalike" of a celebrity. What about "soundalikes"?

Midler v. Ford Motor Company (1988)

- Ford decides it wants to run a "Yuppie Ad Campaign" and wants to use nineteen hits of the 1970s as background music for the commercials.
- Ford is unable to get the original stars in ten of the cases.
- So Ford decides to use "soundalikes."
- Bette Midler sues over a soundalike's performance of her hit song, "Do You Wanna Dance?"
- Unlike Woody Allen, she decides to sue via her right of publicity.
- Note that the defendant has not used her name or likeness.
- BUT the court says the right of publicity protects against misappropriation of a person's identity, even if that consists of imitating a distinctive voice.
- Note that the Court does not say that the song in this case was like the "Here's Johnny" phrase in the *Carson* case. Why not? How do the two things differ?
  - The *Carson* case involves a short phrase closely associated with him and him alone.
  - The song in the *Midler* case could legitimately be sung by anyone. (For example, would Bette have had a case if Ford had chosen Luciano Pavarotti to sing it?)
  - (In fact, of course, Midler's 1973 version, although popular, was itself a cover of a 1958 hit by Bobby Freeman, which was also a hit for Del Shannon in 1964, The Beach Boys in 1965, and The Mamas and The Papas in 1968.)
- So it is the identifiability of the *voice* that is the key here.
- In that sense, it is more like the *Allen* case than the *Carson* case.
- But could Midler have won via the Lanham Act theory of false endorsement too? Probably not. It is not clear that people viewing the commercial would assume from her singing the song that she endorsed the product. More likely they'd assume she had been well paid.
- Note that Nancy Sinatra sued Goodyear in 1970 under the Lanham Act alleging "unfair competition" for its use of her hit, "These Boots Are Made For Walkin'." But she lost even though the claim is more like Carson's case than Midler's. (That is, it was not a soundalike case, but rather one in which she claimed the song was so closely associated with her that the company was trading on her identity.) The problem for her was that she didn't write the song and Goodyear had a license to use it. Just because she had a big hit with the song did not mean that the copyright owners no longer had a right to use it.

So the *Midler* case expands the definition of "identity" even further, to cover the use of a soundalike of a celebrity's voice. The following case illustrates the expansion of this definition even further. The dissents in this case are particularly interesting as they emphasize the dangers in overprotection of intellectual property.

Right of Publicity: Case 1

VANNA WHITE, Plaintiff-Appellant, v. SAMSUNG ELECTRONICS AMERICA, INC., a New York corporation, and DAVID DEUTSCH ASSOCIATES, INC., a New York corporation, Defendants-Appellees.

No. 90-55840

UNITED STATES COURT OF APPEALS FOR THE NINTH CIRCUIT

971 F.2d 1395; 1992 U.S. App. LEXIS 17205; 23 U.S.P.Q.2D (BNA) 1583; 20 Media L. Rep. 1457; 92 Cal. Daily Op. Service 6578; 92 Daily Journal DAR 10519

June 7, 1991, Argued and Submitted, Pasadena, California
July 29, 1992, Filed

OPINION: GOODWIN, Judge:

This case involves a promotional "fame and fortune" dispute. In running a particular advertisement without Vanna White's permission, defendants Samsung Electronics America, Inc. (Samsung) and David Deutsch Associates, Inc. (Deutsch) attempted to capitalize on White's fame to enhance their fortune. White sued, alleging infringement of various intellectual property rights, but the district court granted summary judgment in favor of the defendants. We affirm in part, reverse in part, and remand.

Plaintiff Vanna White is the hostess of "Wheel of Fortune," one of the most popular game shows in television history. An estimated forty million people watch the program daily. Capitalizing on the fame which her participation in the show has bestowed on her, White markets her identity to various advertisers.

The dispute in this case arose out of a series of advertisements prepared for Samsung by Deutsch. The series ran in at least half a dozen publications with widespread, and in some cases national, circulation. Each of the advertisements in the series followed the same theme. Each depicted a current item from popular culture and a Samsung electronic product. Each was set in the twenty-first century and conveyed the message that the Samsung product would still be in use by that time. By hypothesizing outrageous future outcomes for the cultural items, the ads created humorous effects. For example, one lampooned current popular notions of an unhealthy diet by depicting a raw steak with the caption: "Revealed to be health food. 2010 A.D." Another depicted irreverent "news"-show host Morton Downey Jr. in front of an American flag with the caption: "Presidential candidate. 2008 A.D."

The advertisement which prompted the current dispute was for Samsung videocassette recorders (VCRs). The ad depicted a robot, dressed in a wig, gown, and jewelry which Deutsch consciously selected to resemble White's hair and dress. The robot was posed next to a game board which is instantly recognizable as the Wheel of Fortune game show set, in a stance for which White is famous. The caption of the ad read: "Longest-running game show. 2012 A.D." Defendants referred to the ad as the "Vanna White" ad.

Unlike the other celebrities used in the campaign, White neither consented to the ads nor was she paid.

Following the circulation of the robot ad, White sued Samsung and Deutsch in federal district court under: (1) California Civil Code § 3344; (2) the California common law right of publicity; and (3) § 43(a) of the Lanham Act, 15 U.S.C. § 1125(a). The district court granted summary judgment against White on each of her claims. White now appeals.

II. Right of Publicity

White argues that the district court erred in granting summary judgment to defendants on White's common law right of publicity claim. In *Eastwood v. Superior Court*, 149 Cal. App. 3d 409, 198 Cal. Rptr. 342 (1983), the California court of appeal stated that the common law right of publicity cause of action "may be pleaded by alleging (1) the defendant's use of the plaintiff's identity; (2) the appropriation of plaintiff's name or likeness to defendant's advantage, commercially or otherwise; (3) lack of consent; and (4) resulting injury." The district court dismissed White's claim for failure to satisfy *Eastwood*'s second prong, reasoning that defendants had not appropriated White's "name or likeness" with their robot ad. We agree that the robot ad did not make use of White's name or likeness. However, the common law right of publicity is not so confined.

The *Eastwood* court did not hold that the right of publicity cause of action could be pleaded only by alleging an appropriation of name or likeness. *Eastwood* involved an unauthorized use of photographs of Clint Eastwood and of his name. Accordingly, the *Eastwood* court had no occasion to consider the extent beyond the use of name or likeness to which the right of publicity reaches. That court held only that the right of publicity cause of action "may be" pleaded by alleging, *inter alia*, appropriation of name or likeness, not that the action may be pleaded *only* in those terms.

The "name or likeness" formulation referred to in *Eastwood* originated not as an element of the right of publicity cause of action, but as a description of the types of cases in which the cause of action had been recognized. The source of this formulation is Prosser, *Privacy*, 48 Cal.L.Rev. 383, 401-07 (1960).

Even though Prosser focused on appropriations of name or likeness in discussing the right of publicity, he noted that "it is not impossible that there might be appropriation of the plaintiff's identity, as by impersonation, without the use of either his name or his likeness, and that this would be an invasion of his right of privacy."

In *Midler*, this court held that, even though the defendants had not used Midler's name or likeness, Midler had stated a claim for violation of her California common law right of publicity because "the defendants . . . for their own profit in selling their product did appropriate part of her identity" by using a Midler sound-alike.

In *Carson v. Here's Johnny Portable Toilets, Inc.*, 698 F.2d 831 (6th Cir. 1983), the defendant had marketed portable toilets under the brand name "Here's Johnny" – Johnny Carson's signature "Tonight Show" introduction – without Carson's permission. The district court had dismissed Carson's Michigan common law right of publicity claim because the defendants had not used Carson's "name or likeness." In reversing the district court, the sixth circuit found "the district court's conception of the right of publicity . . . too narrow" and held that the right was implicated because the defendant had appropriated Carson's identity by using, *inter alia*, the phrase "Here's Johnny."

These cases teach not only that the common law right of publicity reaches means of appropriation other than name or likeness, but that the specific means of appropriation are relevant only for determining whether the defendant has in fact appropriated the plaintiff's identity. The right of publicity does not require that appropriations of identity be accomplished through particular means to be actionable. It is noteworthy that the *Midler* and *Carson* defendants not only avoided using the plaintiff's name or likeness, but they also avoided appropriating the celebrity's voice, signature, and photograph.

Viewed separately, the individual aspects of the advertisement in the present case say little. Viewed together, they leave little doubt about the celebrity the ad is meant to depict. The female-shaped robot is wearing a long gown, blond wig, and large jewelry. Vanna White dresses exactly like this at times, but so do many other women. The robot is in the process of turning a block letter on a game-board. Vanna White dresses like this while turning letters on a game-board but perhaps similarly attired Scrabble-playing women do this as well. The robot is standing on what looks to be the Wheel of Fortune game show set. Vanna White dresses like this, turns letters, and does this on the Wheel of Fortune game show. She is the only one. Indeed, defendants themselves referred to their ad as the "Vanna White" ad. We are not surprised.

The law protects the celebrity's sole right to exploit this value whether the celebrity has achieved her fame out of rare ability, dumb luck, or a combination thereof. We decline Samsung and Deutch's invitation to permit the evisceration of the common law right of publicity through means as facile as those in this case. Because White has alleged facts showing that Samsung and Deutsch had appropriated her identity, the district court erred by rejecting, on summary judgment, White's common law right of publicity claim.

III. The Lanham Act

Application of the *Sleekcraft* factors to this case indicates that the district court erred in rejecting White's Lanham Act claim at the summary judgment stage. In so concluding, we emphasize two facts, however. First, construing the motion papers in White's favor, as we must, we hold only that White has raised a genuine issue of material fact concerning a likelihood of confusion as to her endorsement. Whether White's Lanham Act claim should succeed is a matter for the jury. Second, we stress that we reach this conclusion in light of the peculiar facts of this case. In particular, we note that the robot ad identifies White and was part of a series of ads in which other celebrities participated and were paid for their endorsement of Samsung's products.

IV. The Parody Defense

In defense, defendants cite a number of cases for the proposition that their robot ad constituted protected speech. The only cases they cite which are even remotely relevant to this case are *Hustler Magazine v. Falwell*, 485 U.S. 46, 99 L. Ed. 2d 41, 108 S. Ct. 876 (1988) and *L.L. Bean, Inc. v. Drake Publishers, Inc.*, 811 F.2d 26 (1st Cir. 1987). Those cases involved parodies of advertisements run for the purpose of poking fun at Jerry Falwell and L.L. Bean, respectively. This case involves a true advertisement run for the purpose of selling Samsung VCRs. The ad's spoof of Vanna White and Wheel of Fortune is subservient and only tangentially related to the ad's primary message: "buy Samsung VCRs." Defendants' parody arguments are better addressed to non-commercial parodies.

The difference between a "parody" and a "knock-off" is the difference between fun and profit.

> But what about *Jordache v. Hogg Wyld*? What about the *National Lampoon*? *Mad Magazine*? And so on. There are plenty of parodies that are created for commercial purposes.

V. Conclusion

In remanding this case, we hold only that White has pleaded claims which can go to the jury for its decision.

Affirmed in part, Reversed in part, and Remanded.

ALARCON dissents in part and concurs in part.

DISSENT: ALARCON, Judge:

I concur in the majority's conclusions on the right to privacy. I respectfully dissent from its holdings on the right to publicity and the Lanham Act claims.

II.

Right to Publicity

I must dissent from the majority's holding on Vanna White's right to publicity claim. The district court found that, since the television commercial did not show a "likeness" of Vanna White, Samsung did not improperly use the plaintiff's identity. The majority asserts that the use of a likeness is not required under California common law. According to the majority, recovery is authorized if there is an appropriation of one's "identity." I cannot find any holding of a California court that supports this conclusion. Furthermore, the record does not support the majority's finding that Vanna White's "identity" was appropriated.

All of the California cases that my research has disclosed hold that a cause of action for appropriation of the right to publicity requires proof of the appropriation of a name or likeness.

Notwithstanding the fact that California case law clearly limits the test of the right to publicity to name and likeness, the majority concludes that "the common law right of publicity is not so confined."

The majority states that the case law has borne out Dean Prosser's insight that the right to publicity is not limited to name or likeness. As noted above, however, the courts of California have never found an infringement on the right to publicity without the use of the plaintiff's name or likeness.

In this case, it is clear that a metal robot and not the plaintiff, Vanna White, is depicted in the television commercial. The record does not show an appropriation of Vanna White's identity.

In *Midler v. Ford Motor Co.*, 849 F.2d 460 (9th Cir. 1988), a singer who had been instructed to sound as much like Bette Midler as possible, sang a song in a radio commercial made famous by Bette Midler. A number of persons told Bette Midler that they thought that she had made the commercial. Aside from the voice, there was no information in the commercial from which the singer could be identified. We noted that "the human voice is one of the most palpable ways identity is manifested." We held that, "to impersonate her voice is to pirate her identity," and concluded that Midler had raised a question of fact as to the misappropriation of her identity.

The common theme in these federal cases is that identifying characteristics unique to the plaintiffs were used in a context in which they were the only information as to the identity of the individual. The commercial advertisements in each case showed attributes of the plaintiff's identities which made it appear that the plaintiff was the person identified in the commercial.

The case before this court is distinguishable from the factual showing made in *Motschenbacher, Midler,* and *Carson.* It is patently clear to anyone viewing the television commercial that Vanna White was not being depicted. No reasonable juror could confuse a metal robot with Vanna White.

The majority contends that "the individual aspects of the advertisement . . . viewed together leave little doubt about the celebrity the ad is meant to depict." In reaching this conclusion, the majority confuses Vanna White, the person, with the role she has assumed as the current hostess on the "Wheel of Fortune" television game show. A recognition of the distinction between a performer and the part he or she plays is essential for a proper analysis of the facts of this case. As is discussed below, those things which Vanna White claims identify her are not unique to her. They are, instead, attributes of the *role* she plays. The representation of those attributes, therefore, does not constitute a representation of Vanna White.

Vanna White is a one-role celebrity. She is famous solely for appearing as the hostess on the "Wheel of Fortune" television show. There is nothing unique about Vanna White or the attributes which she claims identify her. Although she appears to be an attractive woman, her face and figure are no more distinctive than that of other equally comely women. She performs her role as hostess on "Wheel of Fortune" in a simple and straight-forward manner. Her work does not require her to display whatever artistic talent she may possess.

The majority appears to argue that because Samsung created a robot with the physical proportions of an attractive woman, posed it gracefully, dressed it in a blond wig, an evening gown, and jewelry, and placed it on a set that resembles the Wheel of Fortune layout, it thereby appropriated Vanna White's identity. But an attractive appearance, a graceful pose, blond hair, an evening gown, and jewelry are attributes shared by many women, especially in Southern California.

The only characteristic in the television commercial that is not common to many female performers or celebrities is the imitation of the "Wheel of Fortune" set. This set is the only thing which might possibly lead a viewer to think of Vanna White. The Wheel of Fortune set, however, is not an attribute of Vanna White's identity. It is an identifying characteristic of a television game show, a prop with which Vanna White interacts in her role as the current hostess.

The record shows that Samsung recognized the market value of Vanna White's identity. No doubt the advertisement would have been more effective if Vanna White had appeared in it. But the fact that Samsung recognized Vanna White's value as a celebrity does not necessarily mean that it appropriated her identity. I quite agree that anyone seeing the television commercial would be reminded of Vanna White. *Any* performance by another female celebrity as a game-show hostess, however, will also remind the viewer of Vanna

White because Vanna White's celebrity is so closely associated with the role. But the fact that an actor or actress became famous for playing a particular role has, until now, never been sufficient to give the performer a proprietary interest in it. I cannot agree with the majority that the California courts, which have consistently taken a narrow view of the right to publicity, would extend law to these unique facts.

III.

The Lanham Act

Vanna White's Lanham Act claim is easily resolved by applying the proper legal standard. Vanna White seeks damages for violation of section 43(a) of the Lanham Act. To succeed, Vanna White must prove actual deception of the consuming public. Vanna White offered no evidence that any portion of the consuming public was deceived. The district court was correct in granting summary judgment on Vanna White's Lanham Act claim.

"There is no issue for trial unless there is sufficient evidence favoring the nonmoving party for a jury to return a verdict for that party." Vanna White has presented no evidence of actual deception. Thus, she has failed to raise a genuine issue of material fact that would support her Lanham Act claim.

IV.

Samsung's First Amendment Defense

The majority's attempt to distinguish this case from *Hustler Magazine v. Falwell*, 485 U.S. 46, 99 L. Ed. 2d 41, 108 S. Ct. 876 (1988), and *L.L. Bean, Inc. v. Drake Publishers, Inc.*, 811 F.2d 26 (1st Cir. 1987), is unpersuasive. The majority notes that the parodies in those cases were made for the purpose of poking fun at the Reverend Jerry Falwell and L.L. Bean. But the majority fails to consider that the defendants in those cases were making fun of the Reverend Jerry Falwell and L.L. Bean for the purely commercial purpose of selling soft-core pornographic magazines.

Generally, a parody does not constitute an infringement on the original work if it takes no more than is necessary to "conjure up" the original. *Walt Disney Prods. v. Air Pirates*, 581 F.2d 751, 756 (9th Cir. 1978). The majority has failed to consider these factors properly in deciding that Vanna White may bring an action for damages solely because of the popularity of the game show, Wheel of Fortune.

The effect of the majority's holding on expressive conduct is difficult to estimate. The majority's position seems to allow any famous person or entity to bring suit based on any commercial advertisement that depicts a character or role performed by the plaintiff. Under the majority's view of the law, Gene Autry could have brought an action for damages against all other singing cowboys. Clint Eastwood would be able to sue anyone who plays a tall, soft-spoken cowboy, unless, of course, Jimmy Stewart had not previously enjoined Clint Eastwood. Johnny Weismuller would have been able to sue each actor who played the role of Tarzan. Sylvester Stallone could sue actors who play blue-collar boxers. Chuck Norris could sue all karate experts who display their skills in motion pictures. Arnold Schwarzenegger could sue body builders who are compensated for appearing in public.

Direct competitive advertising could also be affected. Will BMW, which advertises its automobiles as "the ultimate driving machine," be able to maintain an action against Toyota for advertising one of its cars as "the ultimate saving machine"? Can Coca Cola sue Pepsi because it depicted a bottle of Coca Cola in its televised "taste test"? Indeed, any advertisement which shows a competitor's product, or any recognizable brand name, would appear to be liable for damages under the majority's view of the applicable law. Under the majority's analysis, even the depiction of an obvious facsimile of a competitor's product may provide sufficient basis for the maintenance of an action for damages.

V.

Conclusion

The protection of intellectual property presents the courts with the necessity of balancing competing interests. On the one hand, we wish to protect and reward the work and investment of those who create intellectual property. In so doing, however, we must prevent the creation of a monopoly that would inhibit the creative expressions of others. We have traditionally balanced those interests by allowing the copying of an idea, but protecting a unique expression of it. Samsung clearly used the idea of a glamorous female game show hostess. Just as clearly, it avoided appropriating Vanna White's expression of that role. Samsung did not use a likeness of her. The performer in the television commercial is unmistakably a lifeless robot. Vanna White has presented no evidence that any consumer confused the robot with her identity. Indeed, no reasonable consumer could confuse the robot with Vanna White or believe that, because the robot appeared in the advertisement, Vanna White endorsed Samsung's product.

I would affirm the district court's judgment in all respects.

Samsung petitioned for a rehearing and a rehearing en banc (by all the judges of the Circuit), which a panel of the Circuit court judges can grant. The panel rejected the petition for rehearing. Alarcon, who wrote the dissent, was on the panel considering rehearing and voted, of course, for a rehearing en banc. Since Alarcon had voted to recommend an en banc hearing, all the judges had to vote on whether to hear the case en banc. A majority voted not to rehear the case.

Three judges, however, wrote a dissent on the denial of a rehearing en banc.

DISSENT: KOZINSKI, Judge:

I

Saddam Hussein wants to keep advertisers from using his picture in unflattering contexts. Clint Eastwood doesn't want tabloids to write about him. Rudolf Valentino's heirs want to control his film biography. The Girl Scouts don't want their image soiled by association with certain activities. George Lucas wants to keep Strategic Defense Initiative fans from calling it "Star Wars." Pepsico doesn't want singers to use the word "Pepsi" in their songs. Guy Lombardo wants an exclusive property right to ads that show big bands playing on New Year's Eve. Uri Geller thinks he should be paid for ads showing psychics bending metal through telekinesis. Paul Prudhomme, that household name, thinks the same about ads featuring corpulent bearded chefs. And scads of copyright holders see purple when their creations are made fun of.

The Court here is referring to actual cases.

Something very dangerous is going on here. Private property, including intellectual property, is essential to our way of life. It provides an incentive for investment and innovation; it stimulates the flourishing of our culture; it protects the moral entitlements of people to the fruits of their labors. But reducing too much to private property can be bad medicine. Private land, for instance, is far more useful if separated from other private land by public streets, roads and highways. Public parks, utility rights-of-way and sewers reduce the amount of land in private hands, but vastly enhance the value of the property that remains.

So too it is with intellectual property. Overprotecting intellectual property is as harmful as underprotecting it. Creativity is impossible without a rich public domain. Nothing today, likely nothing since we tamed fire, is genuinely new: Culture, like science and technology, grows by accretion, each new creator building on the works of those who came before. Overprotection stifles the very creative forces it's supposed to nurture.

The panel's opinion is a classic case of overprotection. Concerned about what it sees as a wrong done to Vanna White, the panel majority erects a property right of remarkable and dangerous breadth: Under the majority's opinion, it's now a tort for advertisers to *remind* the public of a celebrity. Not to use a celebrity's name, voice, signature or likeness; not to imply the celebrity endorses a product; but simply to evoke the celebrity's image in the public's mind. This Orwellian notion withdraws far more from the public domain than prudence and common sense allow. It conflicts with the Copyright Act and the Copyright Clause. It raises serious First Amendment problems. It's bad law, and it deserves a long, hard second look.

[Section II is omitted.]

III

Intellectual property rights aren't like some constitutional rights, absolute guarantees protected against all kinds of interference, subtle as well as blatant. They cast no penumbras, emit no emanations: The very point of intellectual property laws is that they protect only against certain specific kinds of appropriation. I can't publish unauthorized copies of, say, *Presumed Innocent*; I can't make a movie out of it. But I'm perfectly free to write a book about an idealistic young prosecutor on trial for a crime he didn't commit. So what if I got the idea from *Presumed Innocent*? So what if it reminds readers of the original? Have I "eviscerated" Scott Turow's intellectual property rights? Certainly not. All creators draw in part on the work of those who came before, referring to it, building on it, poking fun at it; we call this creativity, not piracy.

Think of *Moby Dick* and *Jaws*, *War and Peace* and *Gone with the Wind*. . . .

The majority isn't, in fact, preventing the "evisceration" of Vanna White's existing rights; it's creating a new and much broader property right, a right unknown in California law. It's replacing the existing balance between the interests of the celebrity and those of the public by a different balance, one substantially more favorable to the celebrity. Instead of having an exclusive right in her name, likeness, signature or voice, every famous person now has an exclusive right to *anything that reminds the viewer of her*. After all, that's all Samsung did: It used an inanimate object to remind people of White, to "evoke [her identity]."

Consider how sweeping this new right is. What is it about the ad that makes people think of White? It's not the robot's wig, clothes or jewelry; there must be ten million blond women (many of them quasi-famous) who wear dresses and jewelry like White's. It's that the robot is posed near the "Wheel of Fortune" game board. Remove the game board from the ad, and no one would think of Vanna White.

Intellectual property rights aren't free: They're imposed at the expense of future creators and of the public at large. Where would we be if Charles Lindbergh had an exclusive right in the concept of a heroic solo aviator? If Arthur Conan Doyle had gotten a copyright in the idea of the detective story, or Albert Einstein had patented the theory of relativity? If every author and celebrity had been given the right to keep people from mocking them or their work? Surely this would have made the world poorer, not richer, culturally as well as economically.

This is why intellectual property law is full of careful balances between what's set aside for the owner and what's left in the public domain for the rest of us: The relatively short life of patents; the longer, but finite, life of copyrights; copyright's idea-expression dichotomy; the fair use doctrine; the prohibition on copyrighting facts; the compulsory license of television broadcasts and musical compositions; federal preemption of overbroad state intellectual property laws; the nominative use doctrine in trademark law; the right to make soundalike recordings. All of these diminish an intellectual property owner's rights. All let the public use something created by someone else. But all are necessary to maintain a free environment in which creative genius can flourish.

The intellectual property right created by the panel here has none of these essential limitations: No fair use exception; no right to parody; no idea-expression dichotomy. It impoverishes the public domain, to the detriment of future creators and the public at large. Instead of well-defined, limited characteristics such as name, likeness or voice, advertisers will now have to cope with vague claims of "appropriation of identity," claims often made by people with a wholly exaggerated sense of their own fame and significance.

To paraphrase only slightly *Feist Publications, Inc. v. Rural Telephone Service Co.*, 113 L. Ed. 2d 358, 111 S. Ct. 1282, 1289-90 (1991), it may seem unfair that much of the fruit of a creator's labor may be used by others without compensation. But this is not some unforeseen byproduct of our intellectual property system; it is the system's very essence.

[Sections IV-VI are omitted.]

VII

For better or worse, we are the Court of Appeals for the Hollywood Circuit. Millions of people toil in the shadow of the law we make, and much of their livelihood is made possible by the existence of intellectual property rights. But much of their livelihood – and much of the vibrancy of our culture – also depends on the existence of other intangible rights: The right to draw ideas from a rich and varied public domain, and the right to mock, for profit as well as fun, the cultural icons of our time.

In the name of avoiding the "evisceration" of a celebrity's rights in her image, the majority diminishes the rights of copyright holders and the public at large. In the name of fostering creativity, the majority suppresses it. Vanna White and those like her have been given something they never had before, and they've been given it at our expense. I cannot agree.

The somewhat apocalyptic ramifications of this decision foreseen by the dissenters have not actually come to pass. However, their cogent discussion illuminates the tension in the right of publicity – and in intellectual property law in general – between the need to protect the rights of the individual versus the need to promote progress by not overprotecting those rights.

12. Constitutional Law

A Constitutional Law Primer and How the First Amendment Fits In

We will focus here largely on First Amendment issues, although we deal with other constitutional issues, such as the Fourth Amendment obviously, in Chapters 9 and 10. Remember that the First Amendment applies only to federal (and state) *government* restrictions on free speech. It does not apply to restriction on speech by private employers, sysops, or access providers. For example, if AOL refuses to post e-mail critical of its policies that is *not* a constitutional problem.

Freedom of speech is a fundamental right and as such gets the "strict scrutiny" standard of review. Here is a summary of the standards and what they mean.

Strict Scrutiny

This is the highest standard of review. If the constitutionality of a law is challenged and this standard applies, the government has the burden of proving that the law is *necessary* for a *compelling* state interest. This is the standard used in reviewing laws involving "suspect classifications" and fundamental rights.

"Suspect classifications" refer to things like race or ethnicity, for example, so laws classifying people based on such criteria will be reviewed under strict scrutiny. While the burden of meeting the strict scrutiny standard is on the government, the plaintiff or plaintiffs (those challenging the constitutionality of the law) must demonstrate that the law in question has a discriminatory *purpose*, not merely a discriminatory impact.

The strict scrutiny standard also applies to:

- Affirmative action issues. Laws regarding affirmative action issues are usually upheld when the purpose of the law is to correct past *identifiable* discrimination, not merely some general societal discrimination. If the purpose of the law is to address the latter, it will usually be struck down.
- Alienage issues (requirement of citizenship). Citizenship cannot be required for private or government employment benefits. Citizenship *can* be a requirement for government policy-making or law enforcement positions.

Laws involving fundamental rights, which will be listed and examined separately below, get strict scrutiny under both the Due Process and Equal Protection clauses of the

Constitution. A law that denies a fundamental right to some persons but not to others is an Equal Protection problem; a law that denies a fundamental right to everyone violates the Due Process clause.

Intermediate Scrutiny

The standard the government must meet under intermediate scrutiny is that the law in question is *substantially related* to an *important* government interest.

This standard applies to laws involving "quasi-suspect classifications," which include classifications by, for example, gender. Most laws that classify people by gender are struck down. For example, the government cannot support an all-female nursing school. All gender-based employment benefits will be struck down. However, having a male-only draft was considered permissible because of the important government interest in preparing combat troops.

Rational Relationship Review

This is the standard used in reviewing laws related to all other classifications. The standard is that the law in question must be *rationally related* to a *legitimate* state objective. This is an easy test from the government's perspective. Furthermore, the burden under rational relationship is on those *challenging* the constitutionality of a law to prove that the law is *not* rationally related to a legitimate state interest.

So what are these fundamental rights that warrant strict scrutiny?

1. Privacy. This includes a number of rights, some of which have already come up in Chapter 9 on this topic. Some examples:

- Marriage and its dissolution. These rights are fundamental at their core (but not every law *regulating* marriage is subject to strict scrutiny – requirements for blood tests, or for the parties to be of a certain age, for example).
- Contraceptives. Buying contraceptives is considered a fundamental privacy right, but using them may not be (i.e., the government can regulate sexual activity).
- Abortion. A woman has a right to terminate a pregnancy prior to viability of the fetus. However, procedural laws (such as laws requiring waiting periods prior to the decision, for example) are acceptable unless the laws unduly burden the woman's right to opt for an abortion. Laws requiring informed consent by the woman are similarly acceptable. Even laws requiring parental or spousal notification are constitutional, but *not* laws requiring parental or spousal *consent.* The government is not required to pay for abortions and can even prohibit them in government-funded public hospitals.
- Possession of obscene material. There is a right to read or enjoy obscenity in the privacy of the home, but not to transport it, import it, or sell it. (This does not apply to child pornography, the mere possession of which is illegal.)
- Family relationships. Parents have a right to raise their children as the parents wish (within certain bounds, as discussed previously). Generally, there is a right to live with close relatives (i.e., zoning laws regarding maximum number of occupants do not apply to close relatives).

2. The right to vote. The Fourteenth and Fifteenth Amendments protect against race discrimination by the states; the Fourteenth Amendment also prohibits malapportionment of electoral districts.

The single most important concept is the Equal Protection right of one person, one vote. Electoral districts must be roughly equal in population if representatives are elected by district. "Gerrymandering" (drawing the boundaries of electoral districts to skew the distribution of voters) is unconstitutional if done with the *purpose* of reducing minority power. On the other hand, gerrymandering in *favor* of minorities is required by the Voting Rights Act. However, in no case can districts be *too* unnatural. *Political* gerrymandering (i.e., drawing district lines to give majority power to a particular political party) can in theory violate the Fourteenth Amendment, but there have been no cases on this issue.

3. Interstate travel. This is the right to move one's residence from one state to another. Problems arise with laws regarding long-term residency requirements for certain benefits, such as in-state tuition, welfare benefits, voting, etc. Generally a residency requirement of more than one year is too long, except for in-state tuition and the right to divorce.

Perhaps the fundamental right most often at the center of constitutional controversy is the right of free speech. First Amendment law is a well developed specialized area of constitutional law, with its own internal requirements and standards of review. Whether, and if so how, speech may be regulated by the government depends on the nature of the regulation and on a number of other factors.

There are two basic concepts that must be grasped before delving into First Amendment law in detail: "vagueness" and "overbreadth." A law that gives no clear notice of what the law prohibits is unconstitutional and void for vagueness; a law that burdens substantially more protected speech than is necessary to achieve the government's compelling interest is unconstitutionally overbroad.

Note: The right of free speech is also a right *not* to speak. That is, laws cannot require a person to endorse a symbol or slogan with which he or she does not agree.

Regulating Speech

Speech *can* be regulated. How speech can be regulated depends on whether the regulation is *content-neutral* or *content-based*.

Content-neutral Regulation of Speech

A law regulating speech is content-neutral if it is not based, or targeted at, the content of the speech – in other words on what is being said. If a speech regulation is content-neutral, the government can regulate the time, place, or manner of speech. Such regulations are very common and are usually upheld as constitutional if challenged.

However, there are three requirements for content-neutral speech regulations to be constitutional:

- The regulation must be content-neutral on its face and must be applied even-handedly. That is, there cannot be executive discretion to pick and choose among speakers because speakers might be chosen based on the content of their speech.

- The regulation must allow substantial opportunities for the speech to take place at other times and places.
- The regulation must be *narrowly tailored to serve a significant state interest*. A "significant" state interest is something less than a "compelling" interest.

Content-based Regulation

A law regulating speech is content-based if the regulation is based on what is being said. Such regulations are usually unconstitutional. The standard is that the regulation must serve a *compelling* government interest. There are, however, some categories of speech that are exceptions and can be regulated based on content.

- Incitement, if the incitement is *intended* to incite *immediate* violence. For example, inciting a lynch mob.
- Fighting words (hate speech), if the speech is so assaultive as to be a trigger to violence. However, while theoretically this type of speech is not protected speech, all "fighting words" statutes have failed to pass constitutional muster because of vagueness or overbreadth.
- Obscenity, if it is patently offensive to the average person in the community, is judged by the correct standards, and lacks serious value (artistic merit). This topic will be discussed in detail in the next chapter.
- Child pornography.
- Defamation, which is generally regulated as a tort.
- Commercial speech, which cannot be regulated if it is truthful and informative, but can be prohibited if it is misleading, pertains to an illegal product, or if the regulation directly advances a *substantial* (i.e., less than "compelling") state interest. Regulations on advertising of cigarettes, alcohol, and gambling are good examples of regulations that serve a substantial state interest.

The Doctrine of the Public Forum

True public fora are those places that traditionally have been used for speech expression. Examples include public streets, public parks, and public sidewalks around public buildings. In a public forum only content-neutral time and manner regulation of protected speech is permitted. In a non-public forum speech can be regulated in *any* reasonable way. Content-based speech regulation is often permissible, for example, in a public school.

A "limited" public forum is an area that the government *chooses* to make a public forum. These are very rare, and arguments alleging this, particularly if the limited public forum is alleged to exist as a result of how the place is used, almost always fail. For example, Grand Central Station in New York City was claimed to be a limited public forum because of the variety and frequency of speech activity that the government permitted to take place there, but the courts disagreed.

Regulating Speech by Government Employees

Generally, government employees have free speech rights. They cannot be hired or fired based on political party, political philosophy, or acts of expression. However, they *can* be fired for incompetence or for not doing their jobs. So if the firing of a government employee is in some way related to an act of expression, the question is whether the act of expression in some way interfered with the employee's job. These rules do not apply to high-ranking appointments in policy roles, which are frequently made based on considerations such as political affiliation.

The Analogy Game

How should or will online speech be regulated? It may depend on which analogy is applied to the Net and its activities.

Is the Net a form of broadcasting? Broadcasters are more regulated than publishers. They are required to air "replies" to editorials. Certain forms of advertising are regulated, or even prohibited, in the broadcast medium (for example, ads for cigarettes). But broadcasters are licensed, and the licenses come with strings attached. Furthermore, broadcasting is seen as a "uniquely pervasive" medium, and one that is easily accessible to children.

Is the Net like a vast adult bookstore? Adult bookstores and theaters are less regulated than broadcasting because they are *not* a pervasive medium. Those who do not wish to see the material they offer need simply not go there.

Is the Net like a telephone system? Telephone systems are also less regulated than broadcasting media. Telephones are considered less intrusive than broadcasting, and when used for "adults only" purposes, such as "Dial-a-porn" services, fees and some sort of age verification can be required.

Which medium, for example, does a web page most resemble? Is it like broadcasting? Perhaps not. It does require some affirmative steps to access information, it is not a licensed medium, and it is not a scarce commodity like broadcast bands.

The issue of how, or even if, speech in cyberspace should be regulated is still far from settled.

The following cases illustrate some of the basic principles of First Amendment law and give some examples of how the constitutional text has been applied so far in the context of cyberspace.

Constitutional Law: Case 1

WARD ET AL. v. ROCK AGAINST RACISM

No. 88-226

SUPREME COURT OF THE UNITED STATES

491 U.S. 781; 109 S. Ct. 2746; 105 L. Ed. 2d 661; 1989 U.S. LEXIS 3129; 57 U.S.L.W. 4879

February 27, 1989, Argued
June 22, 1989, Decided

JUDGES: Kennedy, J., delivered the opinion of the Court, in which Rehnquist, C. J., and White, O'Connor, and Scalia, JJ., joined. Blackmun, J., concurred in the result. Marshall, J., filed a dissenting opinion, in which Brennan and Stevens, JJ., joined.

OPINION: KENNEDY, Justice:

In the southeast portion of New York City's Central Park, about 10 blocks upward from the park's beginning point at 59th Street, there is an amphitheater and stage structure known as the Naumberg Acoustic Bandshell. The bandshell faces west across the remaining width of the park. In close proximity to the bandshell, and lying within the directional path of its sound, is a grassy open area called the Sheep Meadow. The city has designated the Sheep Meadow as a quiet area for passive recreations like reclining, walking, and reading. Just beyond the park, and also within the potential sound range of the bandshell, are the apartments and residences of Central Park West.

This case arises from the city's attempt to regulate the volume of amplified music at the bandshell so the performances are satisfactory to the audience without intruding upon those who use the Sheep Meadow or live on Central Park West and in its vicinity.

The city's regulation requires bandshell performers to use sound-amplification equipment and a sound technician provided by the city. The challenge to this volume control technique comes from the sponsor of a rock concert. The trial court sustained the noise control measures, but the Court of Appeals for the Second Circuit reversed. We granted certiorari to resolve the important First Amendment issues presented by the case.

I

Rock Against Racism, respondent in this case, is an unincorporated association which, in its own words, is "dedicated to the espousal and promotion of antiracist views." Each year from 1979 through 1986, RAR has sponsored a program of speeches and rock music at the bandshell. RAR has furnished the sound equipment and sound technician used by the various performing groups at these annual events.

Over the years, the city received numerous complaints about excessive sound amplification at respondent's concerts from park users and residents of areas adjacent to the park. On some occasions RAR was less than cooperative when city officials asked that the volume be reduced; at one concert, police felt compelled to cut off the power to the sound system, an action that caused the audience to become unruly and hostile.

Before the 1984 concert, city officials met with RAR representatives to discuss the problem of excessive noise. It was decided that the city would monitor sound levels at the edge of the concert ground, and would revoke respondent's event permit if specific volume limits were exceeded. Sound levels at the concert did exceed acceptable levels for sustained periods of time, despite repeated warnings and requests that the volume be lowered. Two citations for excessive volume were issued to respondent during the concert. When the power was eventually shut off, the audience became abusive and disruptive.

The following year, when respondent sought permission to hold its upcoming concert at the bandshell, the city declined to grant an event permit, citing its problems with noise and crowd control at RAR's previous concerts. The city suggested some other city-owned facilities as alternative sites for the concert. RAR declined the invitation and filed suit in United States District Court against the city, its mayor, and various police and parks department officials, seeking an injunction directing issuance of an event permit. After respondent agreed to abide by all applicable regulations, the parties reached agreement and a permit was issued.

The city then undertook the development of comprehensive Parks Department Use Guidelines. In researching the guidelines, the city discovered that occasionally the problem at the bandshell was in fact too *little* volume.

The city considered several solutions:

- **a fixed decibel limit for all performers (rejected);**
- **using a city technician to run private equipment (rejected);**

- **provide city equipment and retain an independent, experienced sound technician for all bandshell events (adopted).**

The Use Guidelines were promulgated on March 21, 1986. After learning that it would be expected to comply with the guidelines at its upcoming annual concert in May 1986, respondent returned to the District Court and filed a motion for an injunction against the enforcement of certain aspects of the guidelines. The District Court preliminarily enjoined enforcement of the sound-amplification rule on May 1, 1986. Under the protection of the injunction, and alone among users of the bandshell in the 1986 season, RAR was permitted to use its own sound equipment and technician, just as it had done in prior years. RAR's 1986 concert again generated complaints about excessive noise from park users and nearby residents.

After the concert, respondent amended its complaint to seek damages and a declaratory judgment striking down the guidelines as facially invalid.

Instead, the Court upheld the guidelines:

- **It cited the fact that the city's sound technician does all he can to accommodate the sponsor's desires about the quality of the sound.**
- **It also noted that the city's regulation leaves control of the "mix" in the hands of RAR.**

The Court of Appeals reversed. After recognizing that "[c]ontent neutral time, place and manner regulations are permissible so long as they are narrowly tailored to serve a substantial government interest and do not unreasonably limit alternative avenues of expression," the court added the proviso that "the method and extent of such regulation must be reasonable, that is, it must be the least intrusive upon the freedom of expression as is reasonably necessary to achieve a legitimate purpose of the regulation."

The Court of Appeals found that there were less intrusive means to achieving the city's goals. For example:

- **direct the performers to keep sound below maximum levels;**
- **install a "volume-limiting" device;**
- **pull the plug.**

The Court of Appeals was either unaware of what had already been tried or simply did not understand the case.

We granted certiorari to clarify the legal standard applicable to governmental regulation of the time, place, or manner of protected speech. Because the Court of Appeals erred in requiring the city to prove that its regulation was the least intrusive means of furthering its legitimate governmental interests, and because the ordinance is valid on its face, we now reverse.

II

Music, as a form of expression and communication, is protected under the First Amendment.

We need not here discuss whether a municipality which owns a bandstand or stage facility may exercise, in some circumstances, a proprietary right to select performances and control their quality. Though it did demonstrate its own interest in the effort to insure high quality performances by providing the equipment in question, the city justifies its guideline as a regulatory measure to limit and control noise. Here the bandshell was open, apparently, to all performers; and we decide the case as one in which the bandshell is a public forum for performances in which the government's right to regulate expression is subject to the protections of the First Amendment. Our cases make clear, however, that even in a public forum the government may impose reasonable restrictions on the time, place, or manner of protected speech, provided the restrictions "are justified without reference to the content of the regulated speech, that they are narrowly tailored to serve a significant governmental interest, and that they leave open ample alternative channels for communication of the information." We consider these requirements in turn.

A

The principal inquiry in determining content neutrality, in speech cases generally and in time, place, or manner cases in particular, is whether the government has adopted a regulation of speech because of disagreement with the message it conveys. The government's purpose is the controlling consideration. A regulation that serves purposes unrelated to the content of expression is deemed neutral, even if it has an incidental effect on some speakers or messages but not others. Government regulation of expressive activity is content neutral so long as it is "*justified* without reference to the content of the regulated speech."

The principal justification for the sound-amplification guideline is the city's desire to control noise levels at bandshell events, in order to retain the character of the Sheep Meadow and its more sedate activities, and to avoid undue intrusion into residential areas and other areas of the park. This justification for the guideline "ha[s] nothing to do with content," and it satisfies the requirement that time, place, or manner regulations be content neutral.

The only other justification offered below was the city's interest in "ensur[ing] the quality of sound at Bandshell events." Respondent urges that this justification is not content neutral because it is based upon the quality, and thus the content, of the speech being regulated. In respondent's view, the city is seeking to assert artistic control over performers at the bandshell by enforcing a bureaucratically determined, valueladen conception of good sound. That all performers who have used the city's sound equipment have been completely satisfied is of no moment, respondent argues, because "[t]he First Amendment does not permit and cannot tolerate state control of artistic expression merely because the State claims that [its] efforts will lead to 'top-quality' results."

While respondent's arguments that the government may not interfere with artistic judgment may have much force in other contexts, they are inapplicable to the facts of this case. The city has disclaimed in express terms any interest in imposing its own view of appropriate sound mix on performers. To the contrary, as the District Court found, the city requires its sound technician to defer to the wishes of event sponsors concerning sound mix.

The city's guideline states that its goals are to "provide the best sound for all events" and to "insure appropriate sound quality balanced with respect for nearby residential neighbors and the mayorally decreed quiet zone of [the] Sheep Meadow." While these standards are undoubtedly flexible, and the officials implementing them will exercise considerable discretion, perfect clarity and precise guidance have never been required even of regulations that restrict expressive activity.

B

The city's regulation is also "narrowly tailored to serve a significant governmental interest." Despite respondent's protestations to the contrary, it can no longer be doubted that government "ha[s] a substantial interest in protecting its citizens from unwelcome noise." This interest is perhaps at its greatest when government seeks to protect "'the well-being, tranquility, and privacy of the home,'" but it is by no means limited to that context, for the government may act to protect even such traditional public forums as city streets and parks from excessive noise.

We think it also apparent that the city's interest in ensuring the sufficiency of sound amplification at bandshell events is a substantial one. The record indicates that inadequate sound amplification has had an adverse affect on the ability of some audiences to hear and enjoy performances at the bandshell. The city enjoys a substantial interest in ensuring the ability of its citizens to enjoy whatever benefits the city parks have to offer, from amplified music to silent meditation.

This is a good example of a "substantial" interest versus a "compelling" interest.

The Court of Appeals erred in sifting through all the available or imagined alternative means of regulating sound volume in order to determine whether the city's solution was "the least intrusive means" of achieving the desired end. This "less-restrictive-alternative analysis has never been a part of the inquiry into the validity of a time, place, and manner regulation."

Lest any confusion on the point remain, we reaffirm today that a regulation of the time, place, or manner of protected speech must be narrowly tailored to serve the government's legitimate, content-neutral interests but that it need not be the least restrictive or least intrusive means of doing so. Rather, the requirement of narrow tailoring is satisfied "so long as the . . . regulation promotes a substantial government interest that would be achieved less effectively absent the regulation." So long as the means chosen are not substantially broader than necessary to achieve the government's interest the regulation will not be invalid simply because a court concludes that the government's interest could be adequately served by some less-speech-restrictive alternative.

It is undeniable that the city's substantial interest in limiting sound volume is served in a direct and effective way by the requirement that the city's sound technician control the mixing board during performances. Absent this requirement, the city's interest would have been served less well, as is evidenced by the complaints about excessive volume generated by respondent's past concerts. The alternative regulatory methods hypothesized by the Court of Appeals reflect nothing more than a disagreement with the city over how much control of volume is appropriate or how that level of control is to be achieved. The Court of Appeals erred in failing to defer to the city's reasonable determination that its interest in controlling volume would be best served by requiring bandshell performers to utilize the city's sound technician.

C

The final requirement, that the guideline leave open ample alternative channels of communication, is easily met. Indeed, in this respect the guideline is far less restrictive than regulations we have upheld in other cases, for it does not attempt to ban any particular manner or type of expression at a given place or time. Rather, the guideline continues to permit expressive activity in the bandshell, and has no effect on the quantity or content of that expression beyond regulating the extent of amplification. That the city's limitations on volume may reduce to some degree the potential audience for respondent's speech is of no consequence, for there has been no showing that the remaining avenues of communication are inadequate.

III

The city's sound-amplification guideline is narrowly tailored to serve the substantial and content-neutral governmental interests of avoiding excessive sound volume and providing sufficient amplification within the bandshell concert ground, and the guideline leaves open ample channels of communication. Accordingly, it is valid under the First Amendment as a reasonable regulation of the place and manner of expression. *The judgment of the Court of Appeals is Reversed.*

JUSTICE BLACKMUN concurs in the result.

DISSENT: MARSHALL, Justice:

Until today, a key safeguard of free speech has been government's obligation to adopt the least intrusive restriction necessary to achieve its goals. By abandoning the requirement that time, place, and manner regulations must be narrowly tailored, the majority replaces constitutional scrutiny with mandatory deference. The majority's willingness to give government officials a free hand in achieving their policy ends extends so far as to permit, in this case, government control of speech in advance of its dissemination. Because New York City's Use Guidelines (Guidelines) are not narrowly tailored to serve its interest in regulating loud noise, and because they constitute an impermissible prior restraint, I dissent.

I

The Guidelines indisputably are content neutral as they apply to all bandshell users irrespective of the message of their music. They also serve government's significant interest in limiting loud noise in public places by giving the city exclusive control of all sound equipment.

My complaint is with the majority's serious distortion of the narrow tailoring requirement. Our cases have not, as the majority asserts, "clearly" rejected a less-restrictive-alternative test. On the contrary, just last Term, we held that a statute is narrowly tailored only "if it targets and eliminates no more than the exact source of the 'evil' it seeks to remedy." While there is language in a few opinions which, taken out of context, supports the majority's position, in practice, the Court has interpreted the narrow tailoring requirement to mandate an examination of alternative methods of serving the asserted governmental interest and a determination whether the greater efficacy of the challenged regulation outweighs the increased burden it places on protected speech.

The Court's past concern for the extent to which a regulation burdens speech more than would a satisfactory alternative is noticeably absent from today's decision. The majority requires only that government show that its interest cannot be served as effectively without the challenged restriction. It will be enough, therefore, that the challenged regulation advances the government's interest only in the slightest, for any differential burden on speech that results does not enter the calculus.

Had the majority not abandoned the narrow tailoring requirement, the Guidelines could not possibly survive constitutional scrutiny. Government's interest in avoiding loud sounds cannot justify giving government total control over sound equipment, any more than its interest in avoiding litter could justify a ban on handbill distribution. In both cases, government's legitimate goals can be effectively and less intrusively served by directly punishing the evil – the persons responsible for excessive sounds and the persons who litter. Indeed, the city concedes that it has an ordinance generally limiting noise but has chosen not to enforce it.

Why not? Perhaps the penalty is only a fine? Perhaps there would be too many violations?

II

The majority's conclusion that the city's exclusive control of sound equipment is constitutional is deeply troubling for another reason. It places the Court's *imprimatur* on a quintessential prior restraint, incompatible with fundamental First Amendment values. Here, the city controls the volume and mix of sound through its monopoly on sound equipment. [T]he government's exclusive control of the means of communication enables public officials to censor speech in advance of its expression.

The majority's implication that government control of sound equipment is not a prior restraint because city officials do not "enjoy unguided discretion to deny the right to speak altogether," is startling.

As a system of prior restraint, the Guidelines are presumptively invalid. They may be constitutional only if accompanied by the procedural safeguards necessary "to obviate the dangers of a censorship system." The city must establish neutral criteria embodied in "narrowly drawn, reasonable and definite standards," in order to ensure that discretion is not exercised based on the content of speech. Moreover, there must be "an almost immediate judicial determination" that the restricted material was unprotected by the First Amendment.

The Guidelines contain neither of these procedural safeguards.

[A] presumption that city officials will act in good faith and adhere to standards absent from a regulation's face is "the very presumption that the doctrine forbidding unbridled discretion disallows."

Second, even if there were narrowly drawn guidelines limiting the city's discretion, the Guidelines would be fundamentally flawed. For the requirement that there be detailed standards is of value only so far as there is a judicial mechanism to enforce them. Here, that necessary safeguard is absent. With neither prompt judicial review nor detailed and neutral standards fettering the city's discretion to restrict protected speech, the Guidelines constitute a quintessential, and unconstitutional, prior restraint.

III

Today's decision has significance far beyond the world of rock music. Government no longer need balance the effectiveness of regulation with the burdens on free speech. After today, government need only assert that it is most effective to control speech in advance of its expression. Because such a result eviscerates the First Amendment, *I dissent.*

Dramatic, but was there any evisceration?

New York is a noisy town. Sitting in the Sheep Meadow on a summer afternoon, you can clearly hear the traffic noise, cars honking horns, sirens screaming, jackhammers drilling all around the park.

The issue then, is not whether noise is acceptable, but what KIND of noise is acceptable.

In the 1960s, a summer rock concert series was held in Central Park in a small stadium near Wollman Skating rink. There was plenty of noise from groups like the Byrds, Buffalo Springfield, and Jefferson Airplane. Maybe this was okay because the concerts were not free? Or because they were at night and no one was using the Sheep Meadow? Certainly the neighbors on Fifth Avenue could hear the music loud and clear.

There are often very loud and heavily publicized concerts held IN the Sheep Meadow: Simon and Garfunkel, the traditional Fourth of July concert with the 1812 Overture, fireworks, and cannons. Why are these okay?

Perhaps it is because there are not many of these 'loud and heavily publicized' concerts and they are VERY popular....

Almost anyone can get a permit to perform at the bandshell, and so it is frequently used and often by groups that, by most accounts, are lousy....

But doesn't this mean that regulating the bandshell volume is content-based?

A better way for RAR to have framed its argument would have been to argue that *Central Park* **is a public forum, not just the bandshell. If the argument had been framed in that way, RAR would have been able to raise the issue of other, even louder, concerts being held in the park.**

Constitutional Law: Case 2

FEDERAL COMMUNICATIONS COMMISSION v. PACIFICA FOUNDATION ET AL.

No. 77-528

SUPREME COURT OF THE UNITED STATES

438 U.S. 726; 98 S. Ct. 3026; 57 L. Ed. 2d 1073; 1978 U.S. LEXIS 135; 43 Rad. Reg. 2d (P & F) 493; 3 Media L. Rep. 2553

April 18, 1978, Argued July 3, 1978, Decided

JUDGES: STEVENS, J., announced the Court's judgment and delivered an opinion of the Court with respect to Parts I-III and IV-C, in which BURGER, C. J., and REHNQUIST, J., joined, and in all but Parts IV-A and IV-B of which BLACKMUN and POWELL, JJ., joined, and an opinion as to Parts IV-A and IV-B, in which BURGER, C. J., and REHNQUIST, J., joined. POWELL, J., filed an opinion concurring in part and concurring in the judgment, in which BLACKMUN, J., joined,. BRENNAN, J., filed a dissenting opinion, in which MARSHALL, J., joined. STEWART, J., filed a dissenting opinion, in which BRENNAN, WHITE, and MARSHALL, JJ., joined.

OPINION: STEVENS, Justice:

This case requires that we decide whether the Federal Communications Commission has any power to regulate a radio broadcast that is indecent but not obscene.

A satiric humorist named George Carlin recorded a 12-minute monologue entitled "Filthy Words" before a live audience in a California theater. He began by referring to his thoughts about "the words you couldn't say on the public, ah, airwaves, um, the ones you definitely wouldn't say, ever." He proceeded to list those words and repeat them over and over again in a variety of colloquialisms. The transcript of the recording indicates frequent laughter from the audience.

At about 2 o'clock in the afternoon on Tuesday, October 30, 1973, a New York radio station, owned by respondent Pacifica Foundation, broadcast the "Filthy Words" monologue. A few weeks later a man, who stated that he had heard the broadcast while driving with his young son, wrote a letter complaining to the Commission. He stated that, although he could perhaps understand the "record's being sold for private use, I certainly cannot understand the broadcast of same over the air that, supposedly, you control."

The complaint was forwarded to the station for comment. In its response, Pacifica explained that the monologue had been played during a program about contemporary society's attitude toward language and that, immediately before its broadcast, listeners had been advised that it included "sensitive language which might be regarded as offensive to some." Pacifica characterized George Carlin as "a significant social satirist" who "like Twain and Sahl before him, examines the language of ordinary people. . . . Carlin is not mouthing obscenities, he is merely using words to satirize as harmless and essentially silly our attitudes towards those words." Pacifica stated that it was not aware of any other complaints about the broadcast.

On February 21, 1975, the Commission issued a declaratory order granting the complaint and holding that Pacifica "could have been the subject of administrative sanctions." The Commission did not impose formal sanctions, but it did state that the order would be "associated with the station's license file, and in the event that subsequent complaints are received, the Commission will then decide whether it should utilize any of the available sanctions it has been granted by Congress."

The FCC has the power to revoke licenses, to issue cease and desist orders, to impose fines, to deny renewals of licenses, or to grant only a short term renewal.

In its memorandum opinion the Commission stated that it intended to "clarify the standards which will be utilized in considering" the growing number of complaints about indecent speech on the airwaves. Advancing several reasons for treating broadcast speech differently from other forms of expression, the Commission found a power to regulate indecent broadcasting in two statutes: 18 U. S. C. § 1464 (1976 ed.), which forbids the use of "any obscene, indecent, or profane language by means of radio communications," and 47 U. S. C. § 303 (g), which requires the Commission to "encourage the larger and more effective use of radio in the public interest."

The FCC says broadcasting requires special treatment because of four considerations:

- **Children have access to radios and in many cases are unsupervised by parents.**
- **Radio receivers are in the home, a place where people's privacy interest is entitled to extra deference (Query: how does this square with the *Katz* "people not places" idea?).**
- **Unconsenting adults may tune in to a station without any warning that offensive language is being or will be broadcast.**
- **There is a scarcity of spectrum space, the use of which the government therefore licenses in the public interest.**

The Commission characterized the language used in the Carlin monologue as "patently offensive," though not necessarily obscene, and expressed the opinion that it should be regulated by principles analogous to those found in the law of nuisance where the "law generally speaks to *channeling* behavior more than actually prohibiting it. . . . [The] concept of 'indecent' is intimately connected with the exposure of children to language that describes, in terms patently offensive as measured by contemporary community standards for the broadcast medium, sexual or excretory activities and organs, at times of the day when there is a reasonable risk that children may be in the audience."

Query: What might New York "community standards" be?

This suggests that broadcasts may be appropriate at night although indecent during the day.

Applying these considerations to the language used in the monologue as broadcast by respondent, the Commission concluded that certain words depicted sexual and excretory activities in a patently offensive manner, noted that they "were broadcast at a time when children were undoubtedly in the audience (i.e., in the early afternoon)," and that the prerecorded language, with these offensive words "repeated over and over," was "deliberately broadcast." In summary, the Commission stated: "We therefore hold that the language as broadcast was indecent and prohibited by 18 U. S. C. [§] 1464."

The Commission noted that its "declaratory order was issued in a specific factual context," and declined to comment on various hypothetical situations.

The Court of Appeals reversed the FCC order.

Judge Tamm concluded that the order represented censorship and was expressly prohibited by § 326 of the Communications Act. Alternatively, Judge Tamm read the Commission opinion as the functional equivalent of a rule and concluded that it was "overbroad." Chief Judge Bazelon's concurrence rested on the Constitution. He was persuaded that § 326's prohibition against censorship is inapplicable to broadcasts forbidden by § 1464. However, he concluded that § 1464 must be narrowly construed to cover only language that is obscene or otherwise unprotected by the First Amendment. Judge Leventhal, in dissent, stated that the only issue was whether the Commission could regulate the language *"as broadcast."* Emphasizing the interest in protecting children, not only from exposure to indecent language, but also from exposure to the idea that such language has official approval, he concluded that the Commission had correctly condemned the daytime broadcast as indecent.

The Supreme Court must now decide:

   I what the scope of judicial review in this case encompasses;
  II whether the FCC ruling was a form of censorship;
 III whether the broadcast was "indecent" within the meaning of § 1464;
 IV whether the order violates the First Amendment.

I

The general statements in the Commission's memorandum opinion do not change the character of its order. Its action did not purport to engage in formal rulemaking or in the promulgation of any regulations. The order "was issued in a specific factual context"; questions concerning possible action in other contexts were expressly reserved for the future. The specific holding was carefully confined to the monologue "as broadcast."

Accordingly, the focus of our review must be on the Commission's determination that the Carlin monologue was indecent as broadcast.

The reason this determination about scope is critical will become clear later.

II

The relevant statutory questions are whether the Commission's action is forbidden "censorship" within the meaning of 47 U. S. C. § 326 and whether speech that concededly is not obscene may be restricted as "indecent" under the authority of 18 U. S. C. § 1464 (1976 ed.). The questions are not unrelated, for the two statutory provisions have a common origin. Nevertheless, we analyze them separately.

Section 29 of the Radio Act of 1927 provided:

> Nothing in this Act shall be understood or construed to give the licensing authority the power of censorship over the radio communications or signals transmitted by any radio station, and no regulation or condition shall be promulgated or fixed by the licensing authority which shall interfere with the right of free speech by means of radio communications. No person within the jurisdiction of the United States shall utter any obscene, indecent, or profane language by means of radio communication. 44 Stat. 1172.

The prohibition against censorship unequivocally denies the Commission any power to edit proposed broadcasts in advance and to excise material considered inappropriate for the airwaves. The prohibition, however, has never been construed to deny the Commission the power to review the content of completed broadcasts in the performance of its regulatory duties.

A single section of the 1927 Act is the source of both the anticensorship provision and the Commission's authority to impose sanctions for the broadcast of indecent or obscene language. Quite plainly, Congress intended to give meaning to both provisions.

Respect for that intent requires that the censorship language be read as inapplicable to the prohibition on broadcasting obscene, indecent, or profane language.

That is, that the FCC may not "censor" content by previewing it, but CAN take such things into account when considering license renewals.

In 1948, when the Criminal Code was revised to include provisions that had previously been located in other Titles of the United States Code, the prohibition against obscene, indecent, and profane broadcasts was removed from the Communications Act and re-enacted as § 1464 of Title 18. That rearrangement of the Code cannot reasonably be interpreted as having been intended to change the meaning of the anticensorship provision.

We conclude, therefore, that § 326 does not limit the Commission's authority to impose sanctions on licensees who engage in obscene, indecent, or profane broadcasting.

The FCC's ruling is not a form of censorship.

III

The only other statutory question presented by this case is whether the afternoon broadcast of the "Filthy Words" monologue was indecent within the meaning of § 1464. Pacifica's claim that the broadcast was not indecent within the meaning of the statute rests entirely on the absence of prurient appeal.

The plain language of the statute does not support Pacifica's argument. The words "obscene, indecent, or profane" are written in the disjunctive, implying that each has a separate meaning. Prurient appeal is an element of the obscene, but the normal definition of "indecent" merely refers to nonconformance with accepted standards of morality.

Pacifica argues, however, that this Court has construed the term "indecent" in related statutes to mean "obscene," as that term was defined in *Miller* v. *California*, 413 U.S. 15. Pacifica relies most heavily on the construction this Court gave to 18 U. S. C. § 1461 in *Hamling* v. *United States*, 418 U.S. 87. *Hamling* rejected a vagueness attack on § 1461, which forbids the mailing of "obscene, lewd, lascivious, indecent, filthy or vile" material. In holding that the statute's coverage is limited to obscenity, the Court followed the lead of Mr. Justice Harlan in *Manual Enterprises, Inc.* v. *Day*, 370 U.S. 478. In that case, Mr. Justice Harlan recognized that § 1461 contained a variety of words with many shades of meaning. Nonetheless, he thought that the phrase "obscene, lewd, lascivious, indecent, filthy or vile," taken as a whole, was clearly limited to the obscene, a reading well grounded in prior judicial constructions: "[The] statute since its inception has always been taken as aimed at obnoxiously debasing portrayals of sex." In *Hamling* the Court agreed with Mr. Justice Harlan that § 1461 was meant only to regulate obscenity in the mails; by reading into it the limits set by *Miller* v. *California, supra*, the Court adopted a construction which assured the statute's constitutionality.

The reasons supporting *Hamling*'s construction of § 1461 do not apply to § 1464. Although the history of the former revealed a primary concern with the prurient, the Commission has long interpreted § 1464 as encompassing more than the obscene.[1] The

---

[1] "'[While] a nudist magazine may be within the protection of the First Amendment... the televising of nudes might well raise a serious question of programming contrary to 18 U. S. C. § 1464.... Similarly, regardless of whether the "4-letter words" and sexual description, set forth in *"Lady Chatterly's Lover,"* (when considered in the context of the whole book) make the book obscene for mailability purposes, the

former statute deals primarily with printed matter enclosed in sealed envelopes mailed from one individual to another; the latter deals with the content of public broadcasts. It is unrealistic to assume that Congress intended to impose precisely the same limitations on the dissemination of patently offensive matter by such different means.

Because neither our prior decisions nor the language or history of § 1464 supports the conclusion that prurient appeal is an essential component of indecent language, we reject Pacifica's construction of the statute. When that construction is put to one side, there is no basis for disagreeing with the Commission's conclusion that indecent language was used in this broadcast.

IV

Pacifica makes two constitutional attacks on the Commission's order. First, it argues that the Commission's construction of the statutory language broadly encompasses so much constitutionally protected speech that reversal is required even if Pacifica's broadcast of the "Filthy Words" monologue is not itself protected by the First Amendment. Second, Pacifica argues that inasmuch as the recording is not obscene, the Constitution forbids any abridgment of the right to broadcast it on the radio.

A

The first argument fails because our review is limited to the question whether the Commission has the authority to proscribe this particular broadcast.

Now that first determination about scope is important!

As the Commission itself emphasized, its order was "issued in a specific factual context." That approach is appropriate for courts as well as the Commission when regulation of indecency is at stake, for indecency is largely a function of context – it cannot be adequately judged in the abstract.

It is true that the Commission's order may lead some broadcasters to censor them-selves. At most, however, the Commission's definition of indecency will deter only the broadcasting of patently offensive references to excretory and sexual organs and activities. While some of these references may be protected, they surely lie at the periphery of First Amendment concern.

B

When the issue is narrowed to the facts of this case, the question is whether the First Amendment denies government any power to restrict the public broadcast of indecent language in any circumstances.[2] For if the government has any such power, this was an appropriate occasion for its exercise.

---

utterance of such words or the depiction of such sexual activity on radio or TV would raise similar public interest and section 1464 questions.'"

[2] Pacifica's position would, of course, deprive the Commission of any power to regulate erotic telecasts unless they were obscene under *Miller* v. *California*, 413 U.S. 15. Anything that could be sold at a newsstand for private examination could be publicly displayed on television. We are assured by Pacifica that the free play of market forces will discourage indecent programming. "Smut may," as Judge Leventhal put it, "drive itself from the market and confound Gresham." The prosperity of those who traffic in pornographic literature and films would appear to justify skepticism.

The words of the Carlin monologue are unquestionably "speech" within the meaning of the First Amendment. It is equally clear that the Commission's objections to the broadcast were based in part on its content. The order must therefore fall if, as Pacifica argues, the First Amendment prohibits all governmental regulation that depends on the content of speech. Our past cases demonstrate, however, that no such absolute rule is mandated by the Constitution.

The classic exposition of the proposition that both the content and the context of speech are critical elements of First Amendment analysis is Mr. Justice Holmes' statement for the Court in *Schenck v. United States*, 249 U.S. 47, 52:

We admit that in many places and in ordinary times the defendants in saying all that was said in the circular would have been within their constitutional rights. But the character of every act depends upon the circumstances in which it is done.... The most stringent protection of free speech would not protect a man in falsely shouting fire in a theatre and causing a panic. It does not even protect a man from an injunction against uttering words that may have all the effect of force.... The question in every case is whether the words used are used in such circumstances and are of such a nature as to create a clear and present danger that they will bring about the substantive evils that Congress has a right to prevent.

Think about this statement when considering the cyberspace First Amendment arguments in *Reno*, Case Number 3.

The question in this case is whether a broadcast of patently offensive words dealing with sex and excretion may be regulated because of its content. If there were any reason to believe that the Commission's characterization of the Carlin monologue as offensive could be traced to its political content – or even to the fact that it satirized contemporary attitudes about four-letter words – First Amendment protection might be required. But that is simply not this case. These words offend for the same reasons that obscenity offends. Their place in the hierarchy of First Amendment values was aptly sketched by Mr. Justice Murphy when he said: "[Such] utterances are no essential part of any exposition of ideas, and are of such slight social value as a step to truth that any benefit that may be derived from them is clearly outweighed by the social interest in order and morality."

Although these words ordinarily lack literary, political, or scientific value, they are not entirely outside the protection of the First Amendment. Nonetheless, the constitutional protection accorded to a communication containing such patently offensive sexual and excretory language need not be the same in every context.

In this case it is undisputed that the content of Pacifica's broadcast was "vulgar," "offensive," and "shocking." Because content of that character is not entitled to absolute constitutional protection under all circumstances, we must consider its context in order to determine whether the Commission's action was constitutionally permissible.

C

We have long recognized that each medium of expression presents special First Amendment problems. [A]lthough the First Amendment protects newspaper publishers from being required to print the replies of those whom they criticize, it affords no such protection to broadcasters; on the contrary, they must give free time to the victims of their criticism.

The reasons for these distinctions are complex, but two have relevance to the present case. First, the broadcast media have established a uniquely pervasive presence in the lives of all Americans. Patently offensive, indecent material presented over the airwaves confronts the citizen, not only in public, but also in the privacy of the home, where the individual's right to be left alone plainly outweighs the First Amendment rights of an intruder. Because the broadcast audience is constantly tuning in and out, prior warnings cannot completely protect the listener or viewer from unexpected program content. To say that one may avoid further offense by turning off the radio when he hears indecent language is like saying that the remedy for an assault is to run away after the first blow. One may hang up on an indecent phone call, but that option does not give the caller a constitutional immunity or avoid a harm that has already taken place.

Second, broadcasting is uniquely accessible to children, even those too young to read. Although Cohen's written message might have been incomprehensible to a first grader, Pacifica's broadcast could have enlarged a child's vocabulary in an instant.

It is appropriate, in conclusion, to emphasize the narrowness of our holding. This case does not involve a two-way radio conversation between a cab driver and a dispatcher, or a telecast of an Elizabethan comedy. We have not decided that an occasional expletive in either setting would justify any sanction or, indeed, that this broadcast would justify a criminal prosecution. The Commission's decision rested entirely on a nuisance rationale under which context is all-important. The concept requires consideration of a host of variables. The time of day was emphasized by the Commission. The content of the program in which the language is used will also affect the composition of the audience, and differences between radio, television, and perhaps closed-circuit transmissions, may also be relevant. As Mr. Justice Sutherland wrote, a "nuisance may be merely a right thing in the wrong place, – like a pig in the parlor instead of the barnyard." We simply hold that when the Commission finds that a pig has entered the parlor, the exercise of its regulatory power does not depend on proof that the pig is obscene.

The judgment of the Court of Appeals is reversed.

It is so ordered.

POWELL concurs in part.

CONCUR: POWELL, Justice:

[M]y views are generally in accord with what is said in Part IV-C of MR. JUSTICE STEVENS' opinion. I therefore join that portion of his opinion. I do not join Part IV-B, however, because I do not subscribe to the theory that the Justices of this Court are free generally to decide on the basis of its content which speech protected by the First Amendment is most "valuable" and hence deserving of the most protection, and which is less "valuable" and hence deserving of less protection. In my view, the result in this case does not turn on whether Carlin's monologue, viewed as a whole, or the words that constitute it, have more or less "value" than a candidate's campaign speech. This is a judgment for each person to make, not one for the judges to impose upon him.

The result turns instead on the unique characteristics of the broadcast media, combined with society's right to protect its children from speech generally agreed to be inappropriate for their years, and with the interest of unwilling adults in not being assaulted by such offensive speech in their homes.

Moreover, I doubt whether today's decision will prevent any adult who wishes to receive Carlin's message in Carlin's own words from doing so, and from making for himself a value judgment as to the merit of the message and words. Cf. *id.*, at 77–79 (POWELL, J., concurring). These are the grounds upon which I join the judgment of the Court as to Part IV.

DISSENT: BRENNAN, Justice:

I agree with MR. JUSTICE STEWART that, under *Hamling* v. *United States*, 418 U.S. 87 (1974), and *United States* v. *12 200-ft. Reels of Film*, 413 U.S. 123 (1973), the word "indecent" in 18 U. S. C. § 1464 (1976 ed.) must be construed to prohibit only obscene speech. I would, therefore, normally refrain from expressing my views on any constitutional issues implicated in this case. However, I find the Court's misapplication of fundamental First Amendment principles so patent, and its attempt to impose *its* notions of propriety on the whole of the American people so misguided, that I am unable to remain silent.

I

For the second time in two years the Court refuses to embrace the notion, completely antithetical to basic First Amendment values, that the degree of protection the First Amendment affords protected speech varies with the social value ascribed to that speech by five Members of this Court. Moreover, as do all parties, all Members of the Court agree that the Carlin monologue aired by Station WBAI does not fall within one of the categories of speech, such as "fighting words," or obscenity, that is totally without First Amendment protection. This conclusion, of course, is compelled by our cases expressly holding that communications containing some of the words found condemnable here are fully protected by the First Amendment in other contexts. Yet despite the Court's refusal to create a sliding scale of First Amendment protection calibrated to this Court's perception of the worth of a communication's content, and despite our unanimous agreement that the Carlin monologue is protected speech, a majority of the Court nevertheless finds that, on the facts of this case, the FCC is not constitutionally barred from imposing sanctions on Pacifica for its airing of the Carlin monologue. This majority apparently believes that the FCC's disapproval of Pacifica's afternoon broadcast of Carlin's "Dirty Words" recording is a permissible time, place, and manner regulation. Both the opinion of my Brother STEVENS and the opinion of my Brother POWELL rely principally on two factors in reaching this conclusion: (1) the capacity of a radio broadcast to intrude into the unwilling listener's home, and (2) the presence of children in the listening audience. Dispassionate analysis, removed from individual notions as to what is proper and what is not, starkly reveals that these justifications, whether individually or together, simply do not support even the professedly moderate degree of governmental homogenization of radio communications – if, indeed, such homogenization can ever be moderate given the pre-eminent status of the right of free speech in our constitutional scheme – that the Court today permits.

A

Without question, the privacy interests of an individual in his home are substantial and deserving of significant protection. In finding these interests sufficient to justify the content regulation of protected speech, however, the Court commits two errors. First, it misconceives the nature of the privacy interests involved where an individual voluntarily chooses to admit radio communications into his home. Second, it ignores the constitutionally protected interests of both those who wish to transmit and those who desire to receive broadcasts that many – including the FCC and this Court – might find offensive.

I believe that an individual's actions in switching on and listening to communications transmitted over the public airways and directed to the public at large do not implicate fundamental privacy interests, even when engaged in within the home. Instead, because the radio is undeniably a public medium, these actions are more properly viewed as a decision to take part, if only as a listener, in an ongoing public discourse.

Even if an individual who voluntarily opens his home to radio communications retains privacy interests of sufficient moment to justify a ban on protected speech if those interests are "invaded in an essentially intolerable manner," the very fact that those interests are threatened only by a radio broadcast precludes any intolerable invasion of privacy; for unlike other intrusive modes of communication, such as sound trucks, "[the] radio can be turned off," and with a minimum of effort.

The Court's balance, of necessity, fails to accord proper weight to the interests of listeners who wish to hear broadcasts the FCC deems offensive. It permits majoritarian tastes completely to preclude a protected message from entering the homes of a receptive, unoffended minority. [T]he visage of the censor is all too discernible here.

B

Although the government unquestionably has a special interest in the well-being of children and consequently "can adopt more stringent controls on communicative materials available to youths than on those available to adults," the Court has accounted for this societal interest by adopting a "variable obscenity" standard that permits the prurient appeal of material available to children to be assessed in terms of the sexual interests of minors. [W]e have made it abundantly clear that "under any test of obscenity as to minors . . . to be obscene 'such expression must be, in some significant way, erotic.'"

Because the Carlin monologue is obviously not an erotic appeal to the prurient interests of children, the Court, for the first time, allows the government to prevent minors from gaining access to materials that are not obscene, and are therefore protected, as to them.

Where, as here, the government may not prevent the exposure of minors to the suppressed material, the principle of *Butler* applies *a fortiori*. The opinion of my Brother POWELL acknowledges that there lurks in today's decision a potential for "'[reducing] the adult population . . . to [hearing] only what is fit for children,'" but expresses faith that the FCC will vigilantly prevent this potential from ever becoming a reality. I am far less certain than my Brother POWELL that such faith in the Commission is warranted; and even if I shared it, I could not so easily shirk the responsibility assumed by each Member of this Court jealously to guard against encroachments on First Amendment freedoms.

C

As demonstrated above, neither of the factors relied on by both the opinion of my Brother POWELL and the opinion of my Brother STEVENS – the intrusive nature of radio and the presence of children in the listening audience – can, when taken on its own terms, support the FCC's disapproval of the Carlin monologue. These two asserted justifications are further plagued by a common failing: the lack of principled limits on their use as a basis for FCC censorship. No such limits come readily to mind, and neither of the opinions constituting the Court serve to clarify the extent to which the FCC may assert the privacy and children-in-the-audience rationales as justification for expunging from the airways protected communications the Commission finds offensive. Taken to their logical extreme, these rationales would support the cleansing of public radio of any "four-letter words" whatsoever, regardless of their context. The rationales could justify the banning from radio of a myriad of literary works, novels, poems, and plays by the likes of Shakespeare, Joyce, Hemingway, Ben Jonson, Henry Fielding, Robert Burns, and Chaucer;

"Banning"? How can one "ban" *a posteriori*? But a good point nonetheless.

they could support the suppression of a good deal of political speech, such as the Nixon tapes; and they could even provide the basis for imposing sanctions for the broadcast of certain portions of the Bible.

I would place the responsibility and the right to weed worthless and offensive communications from the public airways where it belongs and where, until today, it resided: in a public free to choose those communications worthy of its attention from a marketplace unsullied by the censor's hand.

II

My Brother STEVENS, in reaching a result apologetically described as narrow, takes comfort in his observation that "[a] requirement that indecent language be avoided will have its primary effect on the form, rather than the content, of serious communication," and finds solace in his conviction that "[there] are few, if any, thoughts that cannot be expressed by the use of less offensive language." The idea that the content of a message and its potential impact on any who might receive it can be divorced from the words that are the vehicle for its expression is transparently fallacious.

III

[T]here runs throughout the opinions of my Brothers POWELL and STEVENS another vein I find equally disturbing: a depressing inability to appreciate that in our land of cultural pluralism, there are many who think, act, and talk differently from the Members of this Court, and who do not share their fragile sensibilities.

It is only an acute ethnocentric myopia that enables the Court to approve the censorship of communications solely because of the words they contain.

Today's decision will thus have its greatest impact on broadcasters desiring to reach, and listening audiences composed of, persons who do not share the Court's view as to which words or expressions are acceptable and who, for a variety of reasons, including a conscious desire to flout majoritarian conventions, express themselves using words that may be regarded as offensive by those from different socio-economic backgrounds.

Pacifica, in response to an FCC inquiry about its broadcast of Carlin's satire on "'the words you couldn't say on the public . . . airways,'" explained that "Carlin is not mouthing obscenities, he is merely using words to satirize as harmless and essentially silly our attitudes towards those words." In confirming Carlin's prescience as a social commentator by the result it reaches today, the Court evidences an attitude toward the "seven dirty words" that many others besides Mr. Carlin and Pacifica might describe as "silly." Whether today's decision will similarly prove "harmless" remains to be seen. One can only hope that it will.

DISSENT: STEWART, Justice:

The statute pursuant to which the Commission acted, 18 U. S. C. § 1464 (1976 ed.), makes it a federal offense to utter "any obscene, indecent, or profane language by means of radio communication." The Commission held, and the Court today agrees, that "indecent" is a broader concept than "obscene" as the latter term was defined in *Miller* v. *California*, 413 U.S. 15, because language can be "indecent" although it has social, political, or artistic value and lacks prurient appeal. But this construction of § 1464, while perhaps plausible, is by no means compelled. To the contrary, I think that "indecent" should properly be read as meaning no more than "obscene." Since the Carlin monologue concededly was not "obscene," I believe that the Commission lacked statutory authority to ban it. Under this construction of the statute, it is unnecessary to address the difficult and important issue of the Commission's constitutional power to prohibit speech that would be constitutionally protected outside the context of electronic broadcasting.

I would affirm the judgment of the Court of Appeals.

Constitutional Law: Case 3

JANET RENO, ATTORNEY GENERAL OF THE UNITED STATES, ET AL.,
APPELLANTS v. AMERICAN CIVIL LIBERTIES UNION ET AL.

No. 96-511

SUPREME COURT OF THE UNITED STATES

521 U.S. 844; 117 S. Ct. 2329; 138 L. Ed. 2d 874; 1997 U.S. LEXIS 4037; 65 U.S.L.W. 4715; 25 Media L. Rep. 1833; 97 Cal. Daily Op. Service 4998; 97 Daily Journal DAR 8133; 11 Fla. L. Weekly Fed. S 211

March 19, 1997, Argued
June 26, 1997, Decided

JUDGES: STEVENS, J., delivered the opinion of the Court, in which SCALIA, KENNEDY, SOUTER, THOMAS, GINSBURG, and BREYER, JJ., joined. O'CONNOR, J., filed an opinion concurring in the judgment in part and dissenting in part, in which REHNQUIST, C. J., joined.

OPINION: STEVENS, Justice:

This is the first Supreme Court decision on how (and whether) speech may be regulated on the Net.

At issue is the constitutionality of two statutory provisions enacted to protect minors from "indecent" and "patently offensive" communications on the Internet. Notwithstanding the legitimacy and importance of the congressional goal of protecting children from harmful materials, we agree with the three-judge District Court that the statute abridges "the freedom of speech" protected by the First Amendment.

I

The Internet

The Internet is "a unique and wholly new medium of worldwide human communication."

The Internet has experienced "extraordinary growth." The number of "host" computers – those that store information and relay communications – increased from about 300 in 1981 to approximately 9,400,000 by the time of the trial in 1996. Roughly 60% of these hosts are located in the United States. About 40 million people used the Internet at the time of trial, a number that is expected to mushroom to 200 million by 1999.

Anyone with access to the Internet may take advantage of a wide variety of communication and information retrieval methods. These methods are constantly evolving and difficult to categorize precisely. But, as presently constituted, those most relevant to this case are electronic mail ("e-mail"), automatic mailing list services ("mail exploders," sometimes referred to as "listservs"), "newsgroups," "chat rooms," and the "World Wide Web." All of these methods can be used to transmit text; most can transmit sound, pictures, and moving video images. Taken together, these tools constitute a unique medium – known to its users as "cyberspace" – located in no particular geographical location but available to anyone, anywhere in the world, with access to the Internet.

Navigating the Web is relatively straightforward. A user may either type the address of a known page or enter one or more keywords into a commercial "search engine" in an effort to locate sites on a subject of interest.

The Court is addressing the ease with which offensive materials may be obtained.

It then attempts to use an analogy to capture the nature of the Web:

Access to most Web pages is freely available, but some allow access only to those who have purchased the right from a commercial provider. The Web is thus comparable, from the readers' viewpoint, to both a vast library including millions of readily available and indexed publications and a sprawling mall offering goods and services.

From the publishers' point of view, it constitutes a vast platform from which to address and hear from a world-wide audience of millions of readers, viewers, researchers, and buyers. Any person or organization with a computer connected to the Internet can "publish" information. Publishers include government agencies, educational institutions, commercial entities, advocacy groups, and individuals.

Sexually Explicit Material

Sexually explicit material on the Internet includes text, pictures, and chat and "extends from the modestly titillating to the hardest-core." These files are created, named, and posted in the same manner as material that is not sexually explicit, and may be accessed either deliberately or unintentionally during the course of an imprecise search.

It seems the Court is setting up for another 'Net as radio' framing of the issue.

"Once a provider posts its content on the Internet, it cannot prevent that content from entering any community."

That is, what is intended to be seen in Baltimore and New York is also available to Mobile or Beijing.

Some of the communications over the Internet that originate in foreign countries are also sexually explicit.

The Court thus raises, without addressing it, the international problems of the Communications Decency Act (CDA).

It then directly assesses the 'Net as broadcast medium' analogy.

Though such material is widely available, users seldom encounter such content accidentally. " . . . Almost all sexually explicit images are preceded by warnings as to the content." For that reason, the "odds are slim" that a user would enter a sexually explicit site by accident. Unlike communications received by radio or television, "the receipt of information on the Internet requires a series of affirmative steps more deliberate and directed than merely turning a dial. A child requires some sophistication and some ability to read to retrieve material and thereby to use the Internet unattended."

Systems have been developed to help parents control the material that may be available on a home computer with Internet access. A system may either limit a computer's access to an approved list of sources that have been identified as containing no adult material, it may block designated inappropriate sites, or it may attempt to block messages containing identifiable objectionable features. "Although parental control software currently can screen for certain suggestive words or for known sexually explicit sites, it cannot now screen for sexually explicit images." Nevertheless, the evidence indicates that "a reasonably effective method by which parents can prevent their children from accessing sexually explicit and other material which parents may believe is inappropriate for their children will soon be available."

Age Verification

The District Court categorically determined that there "is no effective way to determine the identity or the age of a user who is accessing material through e-mail, mail exploders, newsgroups or chat rooms."
[I]t found:

> Even if credit card verification or adult password verification were implemented, the Government presented no testimony as to how such systems could ensure that the user of the password or credit card is in fact over 18. The burdens imposed by credit card verification and adult password verification systems make them effectively unavailable to a substantial number of Internet content providers.

II

The Telecommunications Act of 1996 was an unusually important legislative enactment. [I]ts primary purpose was to reduce regulation and encourage "the rapid deployment of new telecommunications technologies." The major components of the statute have nothing to do with the Internet; they were designed to promote competition in the local telephone service market, the multichannel video market, and the market for over-the-air broadcasting. The Act includes seven Titles, six of which are the product of extensive committee hearings and the subject of discussion in Reports prepared by Committees of the Senate and the House of Representatives. By contrast, Title V – known as the "Communications Decency Act of 1996" (CDA) – contains provisions that were either added in executive committee after the hearings were concluded or as amendments offered during floor debate on the legislation. An amendment offered in the Senate was the source of the two statutory provisions challenged in this case. They are informally described as the "indecent transmission" provision and the "patently offensive display" provision.

The first, 47 U.S.C. A. § 223(a) (Supp. 1997), prohibits the knowing transmission of obscene or indecent messages to any recipient under 18 years of age. It provides in pertinent part:

(a) Whoever –
(1) in interstate or foreign communications –
(B) by means of a telecommunications device knowingly –
(i) makes, creates, or solicits, and
(ii) initiates the transmission of,
any comment, request, suggestion, proposal, image, or other communication which is obscene or indecent, knowing that the recipient of the communication is under 18 years of age, regardless of whether the maker of such communication placed the call or initiated the communication;
(2) knowingly permits any telecommunications facility under his control to be used for any activity prohibited by paragraph (1) with the intent that it be used for such activity, "shall be fined under Title 18, or imprisoned not more than two years, or both.

The second provision, § 223(d), prohibits the knowing sending or displaying of patently offensive messages in a manner that is available to a person under 18 years of age. It provides:

(d) Whoever –
(1) in interstate or foreign communications knowingly –
(A) uses an interactive computer service to send to a specific person or persons under 18 years of age, or
(B) uses any interactive computer service to display in a manner available to a person under 18 years of age,
any comment, request, suggestion, proposal, image, or other communication that, in context, depicts or describes, in terms patently offensive as measured by contemporary community standards, sexual or excretory activities or organs, regardless of whether the user of such service placed the call or initiated the communication; or
(2) knowingly permits any telecommunications facility under such person's control to be used for an activity prohibited by paragraph (1) with the intent that it be used for such activity,
shall be fined under Title 18, or imprisoned not more than two years, or both.

The breadth of these prohibitions is qualified by two affirmative defenses. One covers those who take "good faith, reasonable, effective, and appropriate actions" to restrict access by minors to the prohibited communications. § 223(e)(5)(A). The other covers those who restrict access to covered material by requiring certain designated forms of age proof, such as a verified credit card or an adult identification number or code. § 223(e)(5)(B).

III

On February 8, 1996, immediately after the President signed the statute, 20 plaintiffs filed suit against the Attorney General of the United States and the Department of Justice challenging the constitutionality of §§ 223(a)(1) and 223(d). A week later, based on his conclusion that the term "indecent" was too vague to provide the basis for a criminal prosecution, District Judge Buckwalter entered a temporary restraining order against enforcement of § 223(a)(1)(B)(ii) insofar as it applies to indecent communications. A second suit was then filed by 27 additional plaintiffs, the two cases were consolidated, and a three-judge District Court was convened pursuant to § 561 of the Act. After an evidentiary hearing, that Court entered a preliminary injunction against enforcement of both of the challenged provisions. Each of the three judges wrote a separate opinion, but their judgment was unanimous.

Chief Judge Sloviter doubted the strength of the Government's interest in regulating "the vast range of online material covered or potentially covered by the CDA," but acknowledged that the interest was "compelling" with respect to some of that material. She concluded, nonetheless, that the statute "sweeps more broadly than necessary and thereby chills the expression of adults" and that the terms "patently offensive" and "indecent" were "inherently vague." She also determined that the affirmative defenses were not "technologically or economically feasible for most providers," specifically considering and rejecting an argument that providers could avoid liability by "tagging" their material in a manner that would allow potential readers to screen out unwanted transmissions. Chief Judge Sloviter also rejected the Government's suggestion that the scope of the statute could be narrowed by construing it to apply only to commercial pornographers.

Judge Buckwalter concluded that the word "indecent" in § 223(a)(1)(B) and the terms "patently offensive" and "in context" in § 223(d)(1) were so vague that criminal enforcement of either section would violate the "fundamental constitutional principle" of "simple fairness," and the specific protections of the First and Fifth Amendments. He found no statutory basis for the Government's argument that the challenged provisions would be applied only to "pornographic" materials, noting that, unlike obscenity, "indecency has *not* been defined to exclude works of serious literary, artistic, political or scientific value." Moreover, the Government's claim that the work must be considered patently offensive "in context" was itself vague because the relevant context might "refer to, among other things, the nature of the communication as a whole, the time of day it was conveyed, the medium used, the identity of the speaker, or whether or not it is accompanied by appropriate warnings". He believed that the unique nature of the Internet aggravated the vagueness of the statute.

Judge Dalzell's review of "the special attributes of Internet communication" disclosed by the evidence convinced him that the First Amendment denies Congress the power to regulate the content of protected speech on the Internet. His opinion explained at length why he believed the Act would abridge significant protected speech, particularly by noncommercial speakers, while "perversely, commercial pornographers would remain relatively unaffected." He construed our cases as requiring a "medium-specific" approach to the analysis of the regulation of mass communication, and concluded that the Internet – as "the most participatory form of mass speech yet developed" – is entitled to "the highest protection from governmental intrusion."

The judgment of the District Court enjoins the Government from enforcing the prohibitions in § 223(a)(1)(B) insofar as they relate to "indecent" communications, but expressly preserves the Government's right to investigate and prosecute the obscenity or child pornography activities prohibited therein.

In its appeal, the Government argues that the District Court erred in holding that the CDA violated both the First Amendment because it is overbroad and the Fifth Amendment because it is vague. While we discuss the vagueness of the CDA because of its relevance to the First Amendment overbreadth inquiry, we conclude that the judgment should be affirmed without reaching the Fifth Amendment issue.

IV

In arguing for reversal, the Government contends that the CDA is plainly constitutional under three of our prior decisions: (1) Ginsberg v. New York, 390 U.S. 629, 20 L. Ed. 2d 195, 88 S. Ct. 1274 (1968); (2) FCC v. Pacifica Foundation, 438 U.S. 726, 57 L. Ed. 2d 1073, 98 S. Ct. 3026 (1978); and (3) Renton v. Playtime Theatres, Inc., 475 U.S. 41, 89 L. Ed. 2d 29, 106 S. Ct. 925 (1986). A close look at these cases, however, raises – rather than relieves – doubts concerning the constitutionality of the CDA.

In Ginsberg, we upheld the constitutionality of a New York statute that prohibited selling to minors under 17 years of age material that was considered obscene as to them even if not obscene as to adults. In rejecting that contention, we relied not only on the State's independent interest in the well-being of its youth, but also on our consistent recognition of the principle that "the parents' claim to authority in their own household to direct the rearing of their children is basic in the structure of our society."

In four important respects, the statute upheld in Ginsberg was narrower than the CDA. First, we noted in Ginsberg that "the prohibition against sales to minors does not bar parents who so desire from purchasing the magazines for their children." Id., at 639. Under the CDA, by contrast, neither the parents' consent – nor even their participation – in the communication would avoid the application of the statute.[32] Second, the New York statute applied only to commercial transactions, id., at 647, whereas the CDA contains no such limitation. Third, the New York statute cabined its definition of material that is harmful to minors with the requirement that it be "utterly without redeeming social importance for minors." Id., at 646. The CDA fails to provide us with any definition of the term "indecent" as used in § 223(a)(1) and, importantly, omits any requirement that the "patently offensive" material covered by § 223(d) lack serious literary, artistic, political, or scientific value. Fourth, the New York statute defined a minor as a person under the age of 17, whereas the CDA, in applying to all those under 18 years, includes an additional year of those nearest majority.

In Pacifica, we upheld a declaratory order of the Federal Communications Commission, holding that the broadcast of a recording of a 12-minute monologue entitled "Filthy

Words" that had previously been delivered to a live audience "could have been the subject of administrative sanctions." [T]he plurality stated that the First Amendment does not prohibit all governmental regulation that depends on the content of speech. Accordingly, the availability of constitutional protection for a vulgar and offensive monologue that was not obscene depended on the context of the broadcast. [T]he Court concluded that the ease with which children may obtain access to broadcasts, "coupled with the concerns recognized in *Ginsberg*," justified special treatment of indecent broadcasting.

As with the New York statute at issue in *Ginsberg*, there are significant differences between the order upheld in *Pacifica* and the CDA. First, the order in *Pacifica*, issued by an agency that had been regulating radio stations for decades, targeted a specific broadcast that represented a rather dramatic departure from traditional program content in order to designate when – rather than whether – it would be permissible to air such a program in that particular medium. The CDA's broad categorical prohibitions are not limited to particular times and are not dependent on any evaluation by an agency familiar with the unique characteristics of the Internet. Second, unlike the CDA, the Commission's declaratory order was not punitive; we expressly refused to decide whether the indecent broadcast "would justify a criminal prosecution." *Id.*, at 750. Finally, the Commission's order applied to a medium which as a matter of history had "received the most limited First Amendment protection," *id.*, at 748, in large part because warnings could not adequately protect the listener from unexpected program content. The Internet, however, has no comparable history. Moreover, the District Court found that the risk of encountering indecent material by accident is remote because a series of affirmative steps is required to access specific material.

In *Renton*, we upheld a zoning ordinance that kept adult movie theatres out of residential neighborhoods. The ordinance was aimed, not at the content of the films shown in the theaters, but rather at the "secondary effects" – such as crime and deteriorating property values – that these theaters fostered: "'It is the secondary effect which these zoning ordinances attempt to avoid, not the dissemination of "offensive" speech.'" According to the Government, the CDA is constitutional because it constitutes a sort of "cyberzoning" on the Internet. But the CDA applies broadly to the entire universe of cyberspace. And the purpose of the CDA is to protect children from the primary effects of "indecent" and "patently offensive" speech, rather than any "secondary" effect of such speech. Thus, the CDA is a content-based blanket restriction on speech, and, as such, cannot be "properly analyzed as a form of time, place, and manner regulation."

These precedents, then, surely do not require us to uphold the CDA and are fully consistent with the application of the most stringent review of its provisions.

V

In *Southeastern Promotions, Ltd.* v. *Conrad*, 420 U.S. 546, 557, 43 L. Ed. 2d 448, 95 S. Ct. 1239 (1975), we observed that "each medium of expression . . . may present its own problems." Thus, some of our cases have recognized special justifications for regulation of the broadcast media that are not applicable to other speakers. In these cases, the Court relied on the history of extensive government regulation of the broadcast medium; the scarcity of available frequencies at its inception; and its "invasive" nature.

Those factors are not present in cyberspace. [T]he Internet is not as "invasive" as radio or television. The District Court specifically found that "communications over the Internet do not 'invade' an individual's home or appear on one's computer screen unbidden. Users seldom encounter content 'by accident.'"

In another example of this medium-specific approach, 'Dial-a-porn' is more protected than broadcasting too. The Court cites _Sable_, in which it held that a federal law prohibiting "obscene and indecent telephone messages" was unconstitutional with regards to the indecent part because the telephone medium is very different from broadcasting: an affirmative act is required to get the material.

Finally, unlike the conditions that prevailed when Congress first authorized regulation of the broadcast spectrum, the Internet can hardly be considered a "scarce" expressive commodity. It provides relatively unlimited, low-cost capacity for communication of all kinds. As the District Court found, "the content on the Internet is as diverse as human thought." We agree with its conclusion that our cases provide no basis for qualifying the level of First Amendment scrutiny that should be applied to this medium.

VI

Regardless of whether the CDA is so vague that it violates the Fifth Amendment, the many ambiguities concerning the scope of its coverage render it problematic for purposes of the First Amendment. For instance, each of the two parts of the CDA uses a different linguistic form. The first uses the word "indecent," while the second speaks of material that "in context, depicts or describes, in terms patently offensive as measured by contemporary community standards, sexual or excretory activities or organs." Given the absence of a definition of either term, this difference in language will provoke uncertainty among speakers about how the two standards relate to each other and just what they mean. Could a speaker confidently assume that a serious discussion about birth control practices, homosexuality, the First Amendment issues raised by the Appendix to our _Pacifica_ opinion, or the consequences of prison rape would not violate the CDA? This uncertainty undermines the likelihood that the CDA has been carefully tailored to the congressional goal of protecting minors from potentially harmful materials.

The vagueness of the CDA is a matter of special concern for two reasons. First, the CDA is a content-based regulation of speech. The vagueness of such a regulation raises special First Amendment concerns because of its obvious chilling effect on free speech. Second, the CDA is a criminal statute. In addition to the opprobrium and stigma of a criminal conviction, the CDA threatens violators with penalties including up to two years in prison for each act of violation. The severity of criminal sanctions may well cause speakers to remain silent rather than communicate even arguably unlawful words, ideas, and images.

The Government argues that the statute is no more vague than the obscenity standard this Court established in _Miller_ v. _California_, 413 U.S. 15, 37 L. Ed. 2d 419, 93 S. Ct. 2607 (1973).

Doesn't this sound like a good argument?

Why is the Court willing to permit regulation of "obscene" speech, when a person can't know what is obscene until a court has said it is obscene, but is not willing to permit regulation of "indecent" speech?

But that is not so. In *Miller*, this Court reviewed a criminal conviction against a commercial vendor who mailed brochures containing pictures of sexually explicit activities to individuals who had not requested such materials. Having struggled for some time to establish a definition of obscenity, we set forth in *Miller* the test for obscenity that controls to this day:

> (a) whether the average person, applying contemporary community standards would find that the work, taken as a whole, appeals to the prurient interest; (b) whether the work depicts or describes, in a patently offensive way, sexual conduct specifically defined by the applicable state law; and (c) whether the work, taken as a whole, lacks serious literary, artistic, political, or scientific value.

Because the CDA's "patently offensive" standard (and, we assume *arguendo*, its synonymous "indecent" standard) is one part of the three-prong *Miller* test, the Government reasons, it cannot be unconstitutionally vague.

The Government's assertion is incorrect as a matter of fact. The second prong of the *Miller* test – the purportedly analogous standard – contains a critical requirement that is omitted from the CDA: that the proscribed material be "specifically defined by the applicable state law." This requirement reduces the vagueness inherent in the open-ended term "patently offensive" as used in the CDA. Moreover, the *Miller* definition is limited to "sexual conduct," whereas the CDA extends also to include (1) "excretory activities" as well as (2) "organs" of both a sexual and excretory nature.

In contrast to *Miller* and our other previous cases, the CDA thus presents a greater threat of censoring speech that, in fact, falls outside the statute's scope.

> **Query: Does this suggest that if the statute were rewritten to use language like the *Miller* obscenity test, the CDA might be constitutional?**

Given the vague contours of the coverage of the statute, it unquestionably silences some speakers whose messages would be entitled to constitutional protection. That danger provides further reason for insisting that the statute not be overly broad. The CDA's burden on protected speech cannot be justified if it could be avoided by a more carefully drafted statute.

VII

We are persuaded that the CDA lacks the precision that the First Amendment requires when a statute regulates the content of speech. In order to deny minors access to potentially harmful speech, the CDA effectively suppresses a large amount of speech that adults have a constitutional right to receive and to address to one another. That burden on adult speech is unacceptable if less restrictive alternatives would be at least as effective in achieving the legitimate purpose that the statute was enacted to serve.

In evaluating the free speech rights of adults, we have made it perfectly clear that "sexual expression which is indecent but not obscene is protected by the First Amendment." *Sable*, 492 U.S. at 126. Indeed, *Pacifica* itself admonished that "the fact that society may find speech offensive is not a sufficient reason for suppressing it."

It is true that we have repeatedly recognized the governmental interest in protecting children from harmful materials. But that interest does not justify an unnecessarily broad suppression of speech addressed to adults. As we have explained, the Government may not "reduce the adult population . . . to . . . only what is fit for children." "Regardless of the strength of the government's interest" in protecting children, "the level of discourse reaching a mailbox simply cannot be limited to that which would be suitable for a sandbox."

In arguing that the CDA does not so diminish adult communication, the Government relies on the incorrect factual premise that prohibiting a transmission whenever it is known that one of its recipients is a minor would not interfere with adult-to-adult communication. The findings of the District Court make clear that this premise is untenable. Knowledge that, for instance, one or more members of a 100-person chat group will be minor – and therefore that it would be a crime to send the group an indecent message – would surely burden communication among adults.

The breadth of the CDA's coverage is wholly unprecedented. The general, undefined terms "indecent" and "patently offensive" cover large amounts of nonpornographic material with serious educational or other value. Moreover, the "community standards" criterion as applied to the Internet means that any communication available to a nation-wide audience will be judged by the standards of the community most likely to be offended by the message.

> **Query: Isn't this a problem for obscenity too, since, as will be discussed further in Chapter 13, it is defined by "contemporary community standards"?**

Under the CDA, a parent allowing her 17-year-old to use the family computer to obtain information on the Internet that she, in her parental judgment, deems appropriate could face a lengthy prison term. Similarly, a parent who sent his 17-year-old college freshman information on birth control via e-mail could be incarcerated even though neither he, his child, nor anyone in their home community, found the material "indecent" or "patently offensive," if the college town's community thought otherwise.

VIII

In an attempt to curtail the CDA's facial overbreadth, the Government advances three additional arguments for sustaining the Act's affirmative prohibitions: (1) that the CDA is constitutional because it leaves open ample "alternative channels" of communication; (2) that the plain meaning of the Act's "knowledge" and "specific person" requirement significantly restricts its permissible applications; and (3) that the Act's prohibitions are "almost always" limited to material lacking redeeming social value.

[T]he CDA regulates speech on the basis of its content. A "time, place, and manner" analysis is therefore inapplicable. The Government's position is equivalent to arguing that a statute could ban leaflets on certain subjects as long as individuals are free to publish books. In invalidating a number of laws that banned leafletting on the streets *regardless of* their content – we explained that "one is not to have the exercise of his liberty of expression in appropriate places abridged on the plea that it may be exercised in some other place." Because both sections prohibit the dissemination of indecent messages only to persons known to be under 18, the Government argues, it does not require transmitters to "refrain from communicating indecent material to adults; they need only refrain from disseminating such materials to persons they know to be under 18." This argument ignores the fact that most Internet fora – including chat rooms, newsgroups, mail exploders, and the Web – are open to all comers. The Government's assertion that the knowledge requirement somehow protects the communications of adults is therefore untenable. Even the strongest reading of the "specific person" requirement of § 223(d) cannot save the statute. It would confer broad powers of censorship, in the form of a "heckler's veto," upon any opponent of indecent speech who might simply log on and inform the would-be discoursers that his 17-year-old child – a "specific person . . . under 18 years of age," would be present.

Finally, we find no textual support for the Government's submission that material having scientific, educational, or other redeeming social value will necessarily fall outside the CDA's "patently offensive" and "indecent" prohibitions.

IX

The Government's three remaining arguments focus on the defenses provided in § 223(e)(5). First, relying on the "good faith, reasonable, effective, and appropriate actions" provision, the Government suggests that "tagging" provides a defense that saves the constitutionality of the Act. The suggestion assumes that transmitters may encode their indecent communications in a way that would indicate their contents, thus permitting recipients to block their reception with appropriate software. It is the requirement that the good faith action must be "effective" that makes this defense illusory. The Government recognizes that its proposed screening software does not currently exist. Even if it did, there is no way to know whether a potential recipient will actually block the encoded material. Without the impossible knowledge that every guardian in America is screening for the "tag," the transmitter could not reasonably rely on its action to be "effective."

For its second and third arguments concerning defenses – which we can consider together – the Government relies on the latter half of § 223(e)(5), which applies when the transmitter has restricted access by requiring use of a verified credit card or adult identification. Such verification is not only technologically available but actually is used by commercial providers of sexually explicit material. These providers, therefore, would be protected by the defense. Under the findings of the District Court, however, it is not economically feasible for most noncommercial speakers to employ such verification. Accordingly, this defense would not significantly narrow the statute's burden on noncommercial speech. Given that the risk of criminal sanctions "hovers over each content provider, like the proverbial sword of Damocles," the District Court correctly refused to rely on unproven future technology to save the statute.

We agree with the District Court's conclusion that the CDA places an unacceptably heavy burden on protected speech, and that the defenses do not constitute the sort of "narrow tailoring" that will save an otherwise patently invalid unconstitutional provision. In Sable, 492 U.S. at 127, we remarked that the speech restriction at issue there amounted to "'burning the house to roast the pig.'" The CDA, casting a far darker shadow over free speech, threatens to torch a large segment of the Internet community.

[Part X is omitted.]

XI

In this Court, though not in the District Court, the Government asserts that – in addition to its interest in protecting children – its "equally significant" interest in fostering the growth of the Internet provides an independent basis for upholding the constitutionality of the CDA. The Government apparently assumes that the unregulated availability of "indecent" and "patently offensive" material on the Internet is driving countless citizens away from the medium because of the risk of exposing themselves or their children to harmful material.

We find this argument singularly unpersuasive. The dramatic expansion of this new marketplace of ideas contradicts the factual basis of this contention.

For the foregoing reasons, the judgment of the district court is affirmed.

It is so ordered.

O'CONNOR concurs in part and dissents in part.

DISSENT: O'CONNOR, Justice:

I write separately to explain why I view the Communications Decency Act of 1996 (CDA) as little more than an attempt by Congress to create "adult zones" on the Internet.

I

Our cases make clear that a "zoning" law is valid only if adults are still able to obtain the regulated speech. If they cannot, the law does more than simply keep children away from speech they have no right to obtain – it interferes with the rights of adults to obtain constitutionally protected speech and effectively "reduces the adult population... to reading only what is fit for children." The First Amendment does not tolerate such interference. The Court in *Ginsberg* concluded that the New York law created a constitutionally adequate adult zone simply because, on its face, it denied access only to minors. A minor can see an adult dance show only if he enters an establishment that provides such entertainment. And should he attempt to do so, the minor will not be able to conceal completely his identity (or, consequently, his age). Thus, the twin characteristics of geography and identity enable the establishment's proprietor to prevent children from entering the establishment, but to let adults inside.

The electronic world is fundamentally different. Because it is no more than the interconnection of electronic pathways, cyberspace allows speakers and listeners to mask their identities. Cyberspace undeniably reflects some form of geography; chat rooms and Web sites, for example, exist at fixed "locations" on the Internet. Since users can transmit and receive messages on the Internet without revealing anything about their identities or ages, however, it is not currently possible to exclude persons from accessing certain messages on the basis of their identity.

Cyberspace differs from the physical world in another basic way: Cyberspace is malleable. Thus, it is possible to construct barriers in cyberspace and use them to screen for identity, making cyberspace more like the physical world and, consequently, more amenable to zoning laws.

Although gateway technology has been available on the World Wide Web for some time now, it is not available to *all* Web speakers, and is just now becoming technologically feasible for chat rooms and USENET newsgroups. Gateway technology is not ubiquitous in cyberspace, and because without it "there is no means of age verification," cyberspace still remains largely unzoned – and unzoneable.

Although the prospects for the eventual zoning of the Internet appear promising, I agree with the Court that we must evaluate the constitutionality of the CDA as it applies to the Internet as it exists today. Given the present state of cyberspace, I agree with the

Court that the "display" provision cannot pass muster. Thus, the only way for a speaker to avoid liability under the CDA is to refrain completely from using indecent speech. As a result, the "display" provision cannot withstand scrutiny.

The "indecency transmission" and "specific person" provisions present a closer issue, for they are not unconstitutional in all of their applications. As discussed above, the "indecency transmission" provision makes it a crime to transmit knowingly an indecent message to a person the sender knows is under 18 years of age. The "specific person" provision proscribes the same conduct, although it does not as explicitly require the sender to know that the intended recipient of his indecent message is a minor. Appellant urges the Court to construe the provision to impose such a knowledge requirement and I would do so.

So construed, both provisions are constitutional as applied to a conversation involving only an adult and one or more minors – *e.g.*, when an adult speaker sends an e-mail knowing the addressee is a minor, or when an adult and minor converse by themselves or with other minors in a chat room. In this context, these provisions are no different from the law we sustained in *Ginsberg*. Restricting what the adult may say to the minors in no way restricts the adult's ability to communicate with other adults. The relevant universe contains only one adult, and the adult in that universe has the power to refrain from using indecent speech and consequently to keep all such speech within the room in an "adult" zone.

The analogy to *Ginsberg* breaks down, however, when more than one adult is a party to the conversation. The CDA is akin to a law that makes it a crime for a bookstore owner to sell pornographic magazines to anyone once a minor enters his store. Even assuming such a law might be constitutional in the physical world as a reasonable alternative to excluding minors completely from the store, the absence of any means of excluding minors from chat rooms in cyberspace restricts the rights of adults to engage in indecent speech in those rooms. The "indecency transmission" and "specific person" provisions share this defect.

But these two provisions do not infringe on adults' speech in *all* situations. And as discussed below, I do not find that the provisions are overbroad in the sense that they restrict minors' access to a substantial amount of speech that minors have the right to read and view. Accordingly, the CDA can be applied constitutionally in some situations. I agree with the Court that the provisions are overbroad in that they cover any and all communications between adults and minors, regardless of how many adults might be part of the audience to the communication.

This conclusion does not end the matter, however. Where, as here, "the parties challenging the statute are those who desire to engage in protected speech that the overbroad statute purports to punish . . . the statute may forthwith be declared invalid to the extent that it reaches too far, but otherwise left intact." I would therefore sustain the "indecency transmission" and "specific person" provisions to the extent they apply to the transmission of Internet communications where the party initiating the communication knows that all of the recipients are minors.

II

Whether the CDA substantially interferes with the First Amendment rights of minors, and thereby runs afoul of the second characteristic of valid zoning laws, presents a closer question.

The Court neither "accepts nor rejects" the argument that the CDA is facially overbroad because it substantially interferes with the First Amendment rights of minors. I would reject it. Because the CDA denies minors the right to obtain material that is "patently offensive" – even if it has some redeeming value for minors and even if it does not appeal to their prurient interests – Congress' rejection of the *Ginsberg* "harmful to minors" standard means that the CDA could ban some speech that is "indecent" (*i.e.*, "patently offensive") but that is not obscene as to minors.

I do not deny this possibility, but it is not enough for a plaintiff to show "some" overbreadth. Our cases require a proof of "real" and "substantial" overbreadth, and appellees have not carried their burden in this case. That the CDA might deny minors the right to obtain material that has some "value," is largely beside the point. While discussions about prison rape or nude art may have some redeeming education value for *adults*, they do not necessarily have any such value for *minors*, and under *Ginsberg*, minors only have a First Amendment right to obtain patently offensive material that has "redeeming social importance *for minors*." Accordingly, in my view, the CDA does not burden a substantial amount of minors' constitutionally protected speech.

Thus, the constitutionality of the CDA as a zoning law hinges on the extent to which it substantially interferes with the First Amendment rights of adults. Because the rights of adults are infringed only by the "display" provision and by the "indecency transmission" and "specific person" provisions as applied to communications involving more than one adult, I would invalidate the CDA only to that extent. Insofar as the "indecency transmission" and "specific person" provisions prohibit the use of indecent speech in communications between an adult and one or more minors, however, they can and should be sustained. The Court reaches a contrary conclusion, and from that holding I respectfully dissent.

Constitutional Law: Case 4

UNITED STATES, et al., Appellants v. AMERICAN LIBRARY ASSOCIATION, INC., et al.

No. 02-361

SUPREME COURT OF THE UNITED STATES

539 U.S. 194; 123 S. Ct. 2297; 156 L. Ed. 2d 221; 2003 U.S. LEXIS 4799; 71 U.S.L.W. 4465; 2003 Cal. Daily Op. Service 5397; 16 Fla. L. Weekly Fed. S 415

March 5, 2003, Argued
June 23, 2003, Decided

JUDGES: Rehnquist, C. J., announced the judgment of the Court and delivered an opinion, in which O'Connor, Scalia, and Thomas, JJ., joined. Kennedy, J., and Breyer, J., filed opinions concurring in the judgment. Stevens, J., filed a dissenting opinion. Souter, J., filed a dissenting opinion, in which Ginsburg, J., joined.

OPINION: REHNQUIST, Chief Justice:

Can Congress regulate Internet access to certain speech in public libraries?

To address the problems associated with the availability of Internet pornography in public libraries, Congress enacted the Children's Internet Protection Act (CIPA), 114 Stat. 2763A-335. Under CIPA, a public library may not receive federal assistance to provide

Internet access unless it installs software to block images that constitute obscenity or child pornography, and to prevent minors from obtaining access to material that is harmful to them. The District Court held these provisions facially invalid on the ground that they induce public libraries to violate patrons' First Amendment rights. We now reverse.

To help public libraries provide their patrons with Internet access, Congress offers two forms of federal assistance. First, the E-rate program entitles qualifying libraries to buy Internet access at a discount. [T]he Institute of Museum and Library Services makes grants to state library administrative agencies. By 2000, 95% of the Nation's libraries provided public Internet access.

By connecting to the Internet, public libraries provide patrons with a vast amount of valuable information. But there is also an enormous amount of pornography on the Internet, much of which is easily obtained. The accessibility of this material has created serious problems for libraries, which have found that patrons of all ages, including minors, regularly search for online pornography. Some patrons also expose others to pornographic images by leaving them displayed on Internet terminals or printed at library printers.

Upon discovering these problems, Congress became concerned that the E-rate and LSTA programs were facilitating access to illegal and harmful pornography.

But Congress also learned that filtering software that blocks access to pornographic Web sites could provide a reasonably effective way to prevent such uses of library resources. By 2000, before Congress enacted CIPA, almost 17% of public libraries used such software on at least some of their Internet terminals, and 7% had filters on all of them.

Responding to this information, Congress enacted CIPA. It provides that a library may not receive E-rate or LSTA assistance unless it has "a policy of Internet safety for minors that includes the operation of a technology protection measure . . . that protects against access" by all persons to "visual depictions" that constitute "obscenity" or "child pornography," and that protects against access by minors to "visual depictions" that are "harmful to minors." The statute defines a "technology protection measure" as "a specific technology that blocks or filters Internet access to material covered by" CIPA. § 254(h)(7)(I). CIPA also permits the library to "disable" the filter "to enable access for bona fide research or other lawful purposes." Under the E-rate program, disabling is permitted "during use by an adult." Under the LSTA program, disabling is permitted during use by any person.

Appellees sued the United States and the Government agencies and officials responsible for administering the E-rate and LSTA programs in District Court, challenging the constitutionality of CIPA's filtering provisions.

[T]he District Court ruled that CIPA was facially unconstitutional and enjoined the relevant agencies and officials from withholding federal assistance for failure to comply with CIPA. The District Court held that Congress had exceeded its authority under the Spending Clause, U.S. Const., Art. I, § 8, cl. 1, because, in the court's view, "any public library that complies with CIPA's conditions will necessarily violate the First Amendment." Reasoning that "the provision of Internet access within a public library . . . is for use by the public . . . for expressive activity," the court analyzed such access as a "designated public forum." The District Court also likened Internet access in libraries to "traditional public fora . . . such as sidewalks and parks" because it "promotes First Amendment values in an analogous manner."

Based on both of these grounds, the court held that the filtering software contemplated by CIPA was a content-based restriction on access to a public forum, and was therefore subject to strict scrutiny. Applying this standard, the District Court held that, although the Government has a compelling interest "in preventing the dissemination of obscenity, child pornography, or, in the case of minors, material harmful to minors," the use of software filters is not narrowly tailored to further those interests. We now reverse.

Congress has wide latitude to attach conditions to the receipt of federal assistance in order to further its policy objectives. But Congress may not "induce" the recipient "to engage in activities that would themselves be unconstitutional." To determine whether libraries would violate the First Amendment by employing the filtering software that CIPA requires, we must first examine the role of libraries in our society.

Public libraries pursue the worthy missions of facilitating learning and cultural enrichment. To fulfill their traditional missions, public libraries must have broad discretion to decide what material to provide to their patrons. Although they seek to provide a wide array of information, their goal has never been to provide "universal coverage." [L]ibraries collect only those materials deemed to have "requisite and appropriate quality."

We have held that the government has broad discretion to make content-based judgments in deciding what private speech to make available to the public.

The principles underlying *Forbes* and *Finley* also apply to a public library's exercise of judgment in selecting the material it provides to its patrons. [F]orum analysis and heightened judicial scrutiny are incompatible with the discretion that public libraries must have to fulfill their traditional missions. Public library staffs necessarily consider content in making collection decisions and enjoy broad discretion in making them.

The public forum principles on which the District Court relied are out of place in the context of this case. Internet access in public libraries is neither a "traditional" nor a "designated" public forum.

First, this resource – which did not exist until quite recently – has not "immemorially been held in trust for the use of the public and, time out of mind,... been used for purposes of assembly, communication of thoughts between citizens, and discussing public questions."

Nor does Internet access in a public library satisfy our definition of a "designated public forum." To create such a forum, the government must make an affirmative choice to open up its property for use as a public forum. "The government does not create a public forum by inaction or by permitting limited discourse, but only by intentionally opening a non-traditional forum for public discourse."

A public library does not acquire Internet terminals in order to create a public forum for Web publishers to express themselves, any more than it collects books in order to provide a public forum for the authors of books to speak. It provides Internet access, not to "encourage a diversity of views from private speakers," but for the same reasons it offers other library resources: to facilitate research, learning, and recreational pursuits by furnishing materials of requisite and appropriate quality.

The District Court disagreed because, whereas a library reviews and affirmatively chooses to acquire every book in its collection, it does not review every Web site that it makes available. Based on this distinction, the court reasoned that a public library enjoys less discretion in deciding which Internet materials to make available than in making book selections. We do not find this distinction constitutionally relevant.

A library's failure to make quality-based judgments about all the material it furnishes from the Web does not somehow taint the judgments it does make. Most libraries already exclude pornography from their print collections because they deem it inappropriate for inclusion. We do not subject these decisions to heightened scrutiny; it would make little sense to treat libraries' judgments to block online pornography any differently, when these judgments are made for just the same reason.

Moreover, because of the vast quantity of material on the Internet and the rapid pace at which it changes, libraries cannot possibly segregate, item by item, all the Internet material that is appropriate for inclusion from all that is not.

Like the District Court, the dissents fault the tendency of filtering software to "overblock" – that is, to erroneously block access to constitutionally protected speech that falls outside the categories that software users intend to block.

Assuming that such erroneous blocking presents constitutional difficulties, any such concerns are dispelled by the ease with which patrons may have the filtering software disabled. When a patron encounters a blocked site, he need only ask a librarian to unblock it or (at least in the case of adults) disable the filter.

Appellees urge us to affirm the District Court's judgment on the alternative ground that CIPA imposes an unconstitutional condition on the receipt of federal assistance. Under this doctrine, "the government 'may not deny a benefit to a person on a basis that infringes his constitutionally protected . . . freedom of speech' even if he has no entitlement to that benefit." Appellees argue that CIPA imposes an unconstitutional condition on libraries that receive E-rate and LSTA subsidies by requiring them, as a condition on their receipt of federal funds, to surrender their First Amendment right to provide the public with access to constitutionally protected speech. The Government counters that this claim fails because Government entities do not have First Amendment rights.

We need not decide this question because, even assuming that appellees may assert an "unconstitutional conditions" claim, this claim would fail on the merits. Within broad limits, "when the Government appropriates public funds to establish a program it is entitled to define the limits of that program."

The E-rate and LSTA programs were intended to help public libraries fulfill their traditional role of obtaining material of requisite and appropriate quality for educational and informational purposes. Congress may certainly insist that these "public funds be spent for the purposes for which they were authorized."

CIPA does not "penalize" libraries that choose not to install such software, or deny them the right to provide their patrons with unfiltered Internet access. Rather, CIPA simply reflects Congress' decision not to subsidize their doing so. To the extent that libraries wish to offer unfiltered access, they are free to do so without federal assistance.

Because public libraries' use of Internet filtering software does not violate their patrons' First Amendment rights, CIPA does not induce libraries to violate the Constitution, and is a valid exercise of Congress' spending power. Nor does CIPA impose an unconstitutional condition on public libraries. *Therefore, the judgment of the District Court for the Eastern District of Pennsylvania is reversed.*

CONCURRENCE: KENNEDY, Justice:

If, on the request of an adult user, a librarian will unblock filtered material or disable the Internet software filter without significant delay, there is little to this case.

If some libraries do not have the capacity to unblock specific Web sites or to disable the filter or if it is shown that an adult user's election to view constitutionally protected Internet material is burdened in some other substantial way, that would be the subject for an as-applied challenge, not the facial challenge made in this case.

There are, of course, substantial Government interests at stake here. The interest in protecting young library users from material inappropriate for minors is legitimate, and even compelling, as all Members of the Court appear to agree. Given this interest, and the failure to show that the ability of adult library users to have access to the material is burdened in any significant degree, the statute is not unconstitutional on its face. *For these reasons, I concur in the judgment of the Court.*

CONCURRENCE: BREYER, Justice:

In ascertaining whether the statutory provisions are constitutional, I would apply a form of heightened scrutiny, examining the statutory requirements in question with special care. The Act directly restricts the public's receipt of information. And it does so through limitations imposed by outside bodies (here Congress) upon two critically important sources of information – the Internet as accessed via public libraries. For that reason, we should not examine the statute's constitutionality as if it raised no special First Amendment concern – as if, like tax or economic regulation, the First Amendment demanded only a "rational basis" for imposing a restriction. Nor should we accept the Government's suggestion that a presumption in favor of the statute's constitutionality applies.

At the same time, in my view, the First Amendment does not here demand application of the most limiting constitutional approach – that of "strict scrutiny." The statutory restriction in question is, in essence, a kind of "selection" restriction (a kind of editing). It affects the kinds and amount of materials that the library can present to its patrons. And libraries often properly engage in the selection of materials, either as a matter of necessity (*i.e.,* due to the scarcity of resources) or by design (*i.e.,* in accordance with collection development policies). "[S]trict scrutiny" implies too limiting and rigid a test for me to believe that the First Amendment requires it in this context.

Instead, I would examine the constitutionality of the Act's restrictions here as the Court has examined speech-related restrictions in other contexts where circumstances call for heightened, but not "strict," scrutiny. Typically the key question in such instances is one of proper fit.

In such cases the Court has asked whether the harm to speech-related interests is disproportionate in light of both the justifications and the potential alternatives. It has considered the legitimacy of the statute's objective, the extent to which the statute will tend to achieve that objective, whether there are other, less restrictive ways of achieving that objective, and ultimately whether the statute works speech-related harm that, in relation to that objective, is out of proportion.

The Act's restrictions satisfy these constitutional demands. The Act seeks to restrict access to obscenity, child pornography, and, in respect to access by minors, material that is comparably harmful. These objectives are "legitimate," and indeed often "compelling." Due to present technological limitations, however, the software filters both "overblock," screening out some perfectly legitimate material, and "underblock," allowing some obscene material to escape detection by the filter. But no one has presented any clearly superior or better fitting alternatives.

Given the comparatively small burden that the Act imposes upon the library patron seeking legitimate Internet materials, I cannot say that any speech-related harm that the Act may cause is disproportionate when considered in relation to the Act's legitimate objectives. I therefore agree with the plurality that the statute does not violate the First Amendment, and I concur in the judgment.

DISSENT: STEVENS, Justice:

"To fulfill their traditional missions, public libraries must have broad discretion to decide what material to provide their patrons." Accordingly, I agree with the plurality that it is neither inappropriate nor unconstitutional for a local library to experiment with filtering software as a means of curtailing children's access to Internet Web sites displaying sexually explicit images. I also agree with the plurality that the 7% of public libraries that decided to use such software on *all* of their Internet terminals in 2000 did not act unlawfully. Whether it is constitutional for the Congress of the United States to impose that requirement on the other 93%, however, raises a vastly different question. Rather than allowing local decisionmakers to tailor their responses to local problems, the Children's Internet Protection Act (CIPA) operates as a blunt nationwide restraint on adult access to "an enormous amount of valuable information" that individual librarians cannot possibly review. Most of that information is constitutionally protected speech. In my view, this restraint is unconstitutional.

I

The unchallenged findings of fact made by the District Court reveal fundamental defects in the filtering software that is now available or that will be available in the foreseeable future.

Given the quantity and ever-changing character of Web sites offering free sexually explicit material, it is inevitable that a substantial amount of such material will never be blocked. Because of this "underblocking," the statute will provide parents with a false sense of security without really solving the problem that motivated its enactment. Conversely, the software's reliance on words to identify undesirable sites necessarily results in the blocking of thousands of pages that "contain content that is completely innocuous for both adults and minors, and that no rational person could conclude matches the filtering companies' category definitions, such as 'pornography' or 'sex.'" In my judgment, a statutory blunderbuss that mandates this vast amount of "overblocking" abridges the freedom of speech protected by the First Amendment.

Although CIPA does not permit any experimentation, the District Court expressly found that a variety of alternatives less restrictive are available at the local level.

Those findings are consistent with scholarly comment on the issue arguing that local decisions tailored to local circumstances are more appropriate than a mandate from Congress. The plurality does not reject any of those findings. Instead, "assuming that such erroneous blocking presents constitutional difficulties," it relies on the Solicitor General's assurance that the statute permits individual librarians to disable filtering mechanisms whenever a patron so requests. In my judgment, that assurance does not cure the constitutional infirmity in the statute.

Until a blocked site or group of sites is unblocked, a patron is unlikely to know what is being hidden and therefore whether there is any point in asking for the filter to be removed.

II

The plurality incorrectly argues that the statute does not impose "an unconstitutional condition on public libraries." On the contrary, it impermissibly conditions the receipt of Government funding on the restriction of significant First Amendment rights.

As the plurality recognizes, we have always assumed that libraries have discretion when making decisions regarding what to include in, and exclude from, their collections. Given our Nation's deep commitment "to safeguarding academic freedom" and to the "robust exchange of ideas," a library's exercise of judgment with respect to its collection is entitled to First Amendment protection.

A federal statute penalizing a library for failing to install filtering software on every one of its Internet-accessible computers would unquestionably violate that Amendment.

I think it equally clear that the First Amendment protects libraries from being denied funds for refusing to comply with an identical rule.

[T]he Government does not merely seek to control a library's discretion with respect to computers purchased with Government funds or those computers with Government-discounted Internet access. CIPA requires libraries to install filtering software on *every* computer with Internet access if the library receives *any* discount from the E-rate program or *any* funds from the LSTA program.

This Court should not permit federal funds to be used to enforce this kind of broad restriction of First Amendment rights, particularly when such a restriction is unnecessary to accomplish Congress' stated goal. The abridgment of speech is equally obnoxious whether a rule like this one is enforced by a threat of penalties or by a threat to withhold a benefit.

I would affirm the judgment of the District Court.

DISSENT: SOUTER, Justice:

I agree in the main with Justice Stevens that the blocking requirements of the Children's Internet Protection Act impose an unconstitutional condition on the Government's subsidies to local libraries for providing access to the Internet. I also agree with the library appellees on a further reason to hold the blocking rule invalid in the exercise of the spending power under Article I, § 8: the rule mandates action by recipient libraries that would violate the First Amendment's guarantee of free speech if the libraries took that action entirely on their own. I respectfully dissent on this further ground.

I

Like the other Members of the Court, I have no doubt about the legitimacy of governmental efforts to put a barrier between child patrons of public libraries and the raw offerings on the Internet otherwise available to them there, and if the only First Amendment interests raised here were those of children, I would uphold application of the Act.

Nor would I dissent if I agreed with the majority of my colleagues that an adult library patron could, consistently with the Act, obtain an unblocked terminal simply for the asking. But the Federal Communications Commission, in its order implementing the Act, pointedly declined to set a federal policy on when unblocking by local libraries would be appropriate under the statute. Moreover, the District Court expressly found that "unblocking may take days, and may be unavailable, especially in branch libraries, which are often less well staffed than main libraries."

In any event, we are here to review a statute, and the unblocking provisions simply cannot be construed, even for constitutional avoidance purposes, to say that a library must unblock upon adult request, no conditions imposed and no questions asked. First, the statute says only that a library "may" unblock, not that it must.

We therefore have to take the statute on the understanding that adults will be denied access to a substantial amount of nonobscene material harmful to children but lawful for adult examination, and a substantial quantity of text and pictures harmful to no one.

We likewise have to examine the statute on the understanding that the restrictions on adult Internet access have no justification in the object of protecting children. Children could be restricted to blocked terminals, leaving other unblocked terminals in areas restricted to adults and screened from casual glances. And of course the statute could simply have provided for unblocking at adult request, with no questions asked. The statute could, in other words, have protected children without blocking access for adults or subjecting adults to anything more than minimal inconvenience, just the way (the record shows) many librarians had been dealing with obscenity and indecency before imposition of the federal conditions.

The question for me, then, is whether a local library could itself constitutionally impose these restrictions on the content otherwise available to an adult patron through an Internet connection, at a library terminal provided for public use. The answer is no. A library that chose to block an adult's Internet access to material harmful to children (and whatever else the undiscriminating filter might interrupt) would be imposing a content-based restriction on communication of material in the library's control that an adult could otherwise lawfully see. This would simply be censorship.

II

The Court's plurality does not treat blocking affecting adults as censorship, but chooses to describe a library's act in filtering content as simply an instance of the kind of selection from available material that every library (save, perhaps, the Library of Congress) must perform. But this position does not hold up.

A

Public libraries are indeed selective in what they acquire to place in their stacks, as they must be.

At every significant point, however, the Internet blocking here defies comparison to the process of acquisition. Whereas traditional scarcity of money and space require a library to make choices about what to acquire, and the choice to be made is whether or not to spend the money to acquire something, blocking is the subject of a choice made after the money for Internet access has been spent or committed. In the instance of the Internet, what the library acquires is electronic access, and the choice to block is a choice to limit access that has already been acquired. The proper analogy therefore is not to passing up a book that might have been bought; it is either to buying a book and then keeping it from adults lacking an acceptable "purpose," or to buying an encyclopedia and then cutting out pages with anything thought to be unsuitable for all adults.

B

The plurality thus argues, in effect, that the traditional responsibility of public libraries has called for denying adult access to certain books, or bowdlerizing the content of what the libraries let adults see. But, in fact, the plurality's conception of a public library's mission has been rejected by the libraries themselves. And no library that chose to block adult access in the way mandated by the Act could claim that the history of public library practice in this country furnished an implicit gloss on First Amendment standards, allowing for blocking out anything unsuitable for adults.

Institutional history of public libraries in America discloses an evolution toward a general rule, now firmly rooted, that any adult entitled to use the library has access to any of its holdings.

C

Thus, there is no preacquisition scarcity rationale to save library Internet blocking from treatment as censorship, and no support for it in the historical development of library practice. To these two reasons to treat blocking differently from a decision declining to buy a book, a third must be added. Quite simply, we can smell a rat when a library blocks material already in its control, just as we do when a library removes books from its shelves for reasons having nothing to do with wear and tear, obsolescence, or lack of demand. Content-based blocking and removal tell us something that mere absence from the shelves does not.

After a library has acquired material in the first place, the variety of possible reasons that might legitimately support an initial rejection are no longer in play. Removal of books or selective blocking by controversial subject matter is not a function of limited resources and less likely than a selection decision to reflect an assessment of esthetic or scholarly merit.

III

There is no good reason, then, to treat blocking of adult enquiry as anything different from the censorship it presumptively is. For this reason, I would hold in accordance with conventional strict scrutiny that a library's practice of blocking would violate an adult patron's First and Fourteenth Amendment right to be free of Internet censorship, when unjustified (as here) by any legitimate interest in screening children from harmful material. On that ground, the Act's blocking requirement in its current breadth calls for unconstitutional action by a library recipient, and is itself unconstitutional.

Constitutional Law: Case 5

JOHN D. ASHCROFT, ATTORNEY GENERAL, Petitioner v. AMERICAN CIVIL
LIBERTIES UNION et al.

No. 03-218

SUPREME COURT OF THE UNITED STATES

542 U.S. 656; 124 S. Ct. 2783; 159 L. Ed. 2d 690; 2004 U.S. LEXIS 4762; 72 U.S.L.W.
4649; 32 Media L. Rep. 1865; 2004 Fla. L. Weekly Fed. S 507

March 2, 2004, Argued
June 29, 2004, Decided

JUDGES: Kennedy, J., delivered the opinion of the Court, in which Stevens, Souter,
Thomas, and Ginsburg, JJ., joined. Stevens, J., filed a concurring opinion, in which
Ginsburg, J., joined. Scalia, J., filed a dissenting opinion. Breyer, J., filed a dissenting
opinion, in which Rehnquist, C. J., and O'Connor, J., joined.

OPINION: KENNEDY, Justice:

**After the *Reno* decision, Congress tried again to craft a law, the Child Online
Protection Act (COPA), that would address the shortcomings of the CDA. Not
surprisingly, the Supreme Court was called upon to revisit the issues.**

I

A

COPA is the second attempt by Congress to make the Internet safe for minors by criminalizing certain Internet speech. The first attempt was the Communications Decency Act
of 1996, Pub L 104-104, § 502, 110 Stat 133, 47 U.S.C. § 223 (1994 ed., Supp. II) [47 USCS
§ 223]. The Court held the CDA unconstitutional because it was not narrowly tailored
to serve a compelling governmental interest and because less restrictive alternatives were
available.

In response to the Court's decision in *Reno*, Congress passed COPA. COPA imposes
criminal penalties of a $50,000 fine and six months in prison for the knowing posting,
for "commercial purposes," of World Wide Web content that is "harmful to minors."
§ 231(a)(1). Material that is "harmful to minors" is defined as:

any communication, picture, image, graphic image file, article, recording, writing,
or other matter of any kind that is obscene or that –

(A) the average person, applying contemporary community standards, would find,
taking the material as a whole and with respect to minors, is designed to appeal to,
or is designed to pander to, the prurient interest;

(B) depicts, describes, or represents, in a manner patently offensive with respect to
minors, an actual or simulated sexual act or sexual contact, an actual or simulated
normal or perverted sexual act, or a lewd exhibition of the genitals or post-pubescent
female breast; and

(C) taken as a whole, lacks serious literary, artistic, political, or scientific value for minors." § 231(e)(6).

Minors" are defined as "any person under 17 years of age." § 231(e)(7). A person acts for "commercial purposes only if such person is engaged in the business of making such communications." "Engaged in the business," in turn,

"means that the person who makes a communication, or offers to make a communication, by means of the World Wide Web, that includes any material that is harmful to minors, devotes time, attention, or labor to such activities, as a regular course of such person's trade or business, with the objective of earning a profit as a result of such activities (although it is not necessary that the person make a profit or that the making or offering to make such communications be the person's sole or principal business or source of income). § 231(e)(2).

While the statute labels all speech that falls within these definitions as criminal speech, it also provides an affirmative defense to those who employ specified means to prevent minors from gaining access to the prohibited materials on their Web site. A person may escape conviction under the statute by demonstrating that he

has restricted access by minors to material that is harmful to minors –

(A) by requiring use of a credit card, debit account, adult access code, or adult personal identification number;

(B) by accepting a digital certificate that verifies age, or

(C) by any other reasonable measures that are feasible under available technology. § 231(c)(1).

B

Respondents sought a preliminary injunction against enforcement of the statute. The court concluded that respondents were likely to prevail on their argument that there were less restrictive alternatives to the statute. In particular, it noted that "[t]he record before the Court reveals that blocking or filtering technology may be at least as successful as COPA would be in restricting minors' access to harmful material online without imposing the burden on constitutionally protected speech that COPA imposes on adult users or Web site operators".

   The Court of Appeals affirmed the preliminary injunction, but on a different ground. The court concluded that the "community standards" language in COPA by itself rendered the statute unconstitutionally overbroad. We granted certiorari and reversed, holding that the community-standards language did not, standing alone, make the statute unconstitutionally overbroad. We emphasized, however, that our decision was limited to that narrow issue. We remanded the case to the Court of Appeals to reconsider whether the District Court had been correct to grant the preliminary injunction. On remand, the Court of Appeals again affirmed the District Court. The Court of Appeals concluded that the statute was not narrowly tailored to serve a compelling Government interest, was overbroad, and was not the least restrictive means available for the Government to serve the interest of preventing minors from using the Internet to gain access to materials that are harmful to them.

II

A

Because we affirm the District Court's decision to grant the preliminary injunction for the reasons relied on by the District Court, we decline to consider the correctness of the other arguments relied on by the Court of Appeals.

The District Court, in deciding to grant the preliminary injunction, concentrated primarily on the argument that there are plausible, less restrictive alternatives to COPA. A statute that "effectively suppresses a large amount of speech that adults have a constitutional right to receive and to address to one another . . . is unacceptable if less restrictive alternatives would be at least as effective in achieving the legitimate purpose that the statute was enacted to serve." When plaintiffs challenge a content-based speech restriction, the burden is on the Government to prove that the proposed alternatives will not be as effective as the challenged statute.

In considering this question, a court assumes that certain protected speech may be regulated, and then asks what is the least restrictive alternative that can be used to achieve that goal. The purpose of the test is to ensure that speech is restricted no further than necessary to achieve the goal, for it is important to assure that legitimate speech is not chilled or punished.

As the Government bears the burden of proof on the ultimate question of COPA's constitutionality, respondents must be deemed likely to prevail unless the Government has shown that respondents' proposed less restrictive alternatives are less effective than COPA. Applying that analysis, the District Court concluded that respondents were likely to prevail. That conclusion was not an abuse of discretion, because on this record there are a number of plausible, less restrictive alternatives to the statute.

The primary alternative considered by the District Court was blocking and filtering software.

Filters are less restrictive than COPA. They impose selective restrictions on speech at the receiving end, not universal restrictions at the source. Under a filtering regime, adults without children may gain access to speech they have a right to see without having to identify themselves or provide their credit card information. Even adults with children may obtain access to the same speech on the same terms simply by turning off the filter on their home computers. Above all, promoting the use of filters does not condemn as criminal any category of speech, and so the potential chilling effect is eliminated, or at least much diminished. All of these things are true, moreover, regardless of how broadly or narrowly the definitions in COPA are construed.

Filters also may well be more effective than COPA. [A] filter can prevent minors from seeing all pornography, not just pornography posted to the Web from America. It is not an answer to say that COPA reaches some amount of materials that are harmful to minors; the question is whether it would reach more of them than less restrictive alternatives. In addition, the District Court found that verification systems may be subject to evasion and circumvention, for example by minors who have their own credit cards. Finally, filters also may be more effective because they can be applied to all forms of Internet communication, including e-mail, not just communications available via the World Wide Web.

Filtering software, of course, is not a perfect solution to the problem of children gaining access to harmful-to-minors materials. It may block some materials that are not harmful to minors and fail to catch some that are. Whatever the deficiencies of filters, however, the Government failed to introduce specific evidence proving that existing technologies are less effective than the restrictions in COPA.

One argument to the contrary is worth mentioning – the argument that filtering software is not an available alternative because Congress may not require it to be used. That argument carries little weight, because Congress undoubtedly may act to encourage the use of filters. We have held that Congress can give strong incentives to schools and libraries to use them. It could also take steps to promote their development by industry, and their use by parents. It is incorrect, for that reason, to say that filters are part of the current regulatory status quo. The need for parental cooperation does not automatically disqualify a proposed less restrictive alternative.

"The starch in our constitutional standards cannot be sacrificed to accommodate the enforcement choices of the Government."

B

There are also important practical reasons to let the injunction stand pending a full trial on the merits. First, the potential harms from reversing the injunction outweigh those of leaving it in place by mistake. Where a prosecution is a likely possibility, yet only an affirmative defense is available, speakers may self-censor rather than risk the perils of trial. There is a potential for extraordinary harm and a serious chill upon protected speech. The harm done from letting the injunction stand pending a trial on the merits, in contrast, will not be extensive. No prosecutions have yet been undertaken under the law, so none will be disrupted if the injunction stands.

Second, there are substantial factual disputes remaining in the case. As mentioned above, there is a serious gap in the evidence as to the effectiveness of filtering software.

Third, and on a related point, the factual record does not reflect current technological reality – a serious flaw in any case involving the Internet. The technology of the Internet evolves at a rapid pace. Yet the factfindings of the District Court were entered in February 1999, over five years ago. It is reasonable to assume that other technological developments important to the First Amendment analysis have also occurred during that time.

Remand will also permit the District Court to take account of a changed legal landscape. Since the District Court made its factfindings, Congress has passed at least two further statutes that might qualify as less restrictive alternatives to COPA – a prohibition on misleading domain names, and a statute creating a minors-safe "Dot Kids" domain. Remanding for trial will allow the District Court to take into account those additional potential alternatives.

On a final point, it is important to note that this opinion does not hold that Congress is incapable of enacting any regulation of the Internet designed to prevent minors from gaining access to harmful materials.

Or does it? Justice Breyer's dissent will address this point.

The parties, because of the conclusion of the Court of Appeals that the statute's definitions rendered it unconstitutional, did not devote their attention to the question whether further evidence might be introduced on the relative restrictiveness and effectiveness of alternatives to the statute. On remand, however, the parties will be able to introduce further evidence on this point. This opinion does not foreclose the District Court from concluding, upon a proper showing by the Government that meets the Government's constitutional burden as defined in this opinion, that COPA is the least restrictive alternative available to accomplish Congress' goal.

* * *

On this record, the Government has not shown that the less restrictive alternatives proposed by respondents should be disregarded. The District Court did not abuse its discretion when it entered the preliminary injunction.

It is so ordered.

CONCURRENCE: STEVENS, Justice:

When it first reviewed the constitutionality of the Child Online Protection Act (COPA), the Court of Appeals held that the statute's use of "contemporary community standards" to identify materials that are "harmful to minors" was a serious, and likely fatal, defect. I have already explained at some length why I agree with that holding. I continue to believe that the Government may not penalize speakers for making available to the general World Wide Web audience that which the least tolerant communities in America deem unfit for their children's consumption, and consider that principle a sufficient basis for deciding this case.

But COPA's use of community standards is not the statute's only constitutional defect.

In registering my agreement with the Court's less-restrictive-means analysis, I wish to underscore just how restrictive COPA is. COPA is a content-based restraint on the dissemination of constitutionally protected speech. It enforces its prohibitions by way of the criminal law, threatening noncompliant Web speakers with a fine of as much as $50,000, and a term of imprisonment as long as six months, for each offense. Speakers who "intentionally" violate COPA are punishable by a fine of up to $50,000 for each day of the violation.

Criminal prosecutions are, in my view, an inappropriate means to regulate the universe of materials classified as "obscene," since "the line between communications which 'offend' and those which do not is too blurred to identify criminal conduct." COPA's creation of a new category of criminally punishable speech that is "harmful to minors" only compounds the problem. But even with Justice Breyer's guidance, I find it impossible to identify just how far past the already ill-defined territory of "obscenity" he thinks the statute extends. Attaching criminal sanctions to a mistaken judgment about the contours of the novel and nebulous category of "harmful to minors" speech clearly imposes a heavy burden on the exercise of First Amendment freedoms.

COPA's criminal penalties are, moreover, strong medicine for the ill that the statute seeks to remedy. As a parent, grandparent, and great-grandparent, I endorse that goal without reservation. As a judge, however, I must confess to a growing sense of unease when the interest in protecting children from prurient materials is invoked as a justification for using criminal regulation of speech as a substitute for, or a simple backup to, adult oversight of children's viewing habits.

I join the opinion of the Court.

DISSENT: SCALIA, Justice:

[T]he Child Online Protection Act (COPA) is constitutional. Both the Court and Justice Breyer err, however, in subjecting COPA to strict scrutiny. Nothing in the First Amendment entitles the type of material covered by COPA to that exacting standard of review. "We have recognized that commercial entities which engage in 'the sordid business of pandering' by 'deliberately emphasiz[ing] the sexually provocative aspects of [their nonobscene products], in order to catch the salaciously disposed,' engage in constitutionally unprotected behavior."

There is no doubt that the commercial pornography covered by COPA fits this description. The statute applies only to a person who, "as a regular course of such person's trade or business, with the objective of earning a profit," and "with knowledge of the character of the material," communicates material that depicts certain specified sexual acts and that "is designed to appeal to, or is designed to pander to, the prurient interest." Since this business could, consistent with the First Amendment, be banned entirely, COPA's lesser restrictions raise no constitutional concern.

DISSENT: BREYER, Justice:

The Court recognizes that we should "'proceed . . . with care before invalidating the Act,'" while pointing out that the "imperative of according respect to the Congress . . . does not permit us to depart from well-established First Amendment principles." I agree with these generalities. Like the Court, I would subject the Act to "the most exacting scrutiny," requiring the Government to show that any restriction of nonobscene expression is "narrowly drawn" to further a "compelling interest" and that the restriction amounts to the "least restrictive means" available to further that interest.

Nonetheless, my examination of (1) the burdens the Act imposes on protected expression, (2) the Act's ability to further a compelling interest, and (3) the proposed "less restrictive alternatives" convinces me that the Court is wrong. I cannot accept its conclusion that Congress could have accomplished its statutory objective – protecting children from commercial pornography on the Internet – in other, less restrictive ways.

I

A

The Act's definitions limit the material it regulates to material that does not enjoy First Amendment protection, namely legally obscene material, and very little more. A comparison of this Court's definition of unprotected, "legally obscene," material with the Act's definitions makes this clear.

Material is legally obscene if

(a) . . . 'the average person, applying contemporary community standards' would find that the work, taken as a whole, appeals to the prurient interest . . . ; (b) . . . the work depicts or describes, in a patently offensive way, sexual conduct specifically defined by the applicable state law; and (c) . . . the work, taken as a whole, lacks serious literary, artistic, political, or scientific value.

The present statute defines the material that it regulates as material that meets all of the following criteria:

> (A) the average person, applying contemporary community standards, would find, taking the material as a whole *and with respect to minors,* [that the material] is designed to appeal to, or is designed to pander to, the prurient interest;
>
> (B) [the material] depicts, describes, or represents, in a manner patently offensive *with respect to minors,* an actual or simulated sexual act or sexual contact, an actual or simulated normal or perverted sexual act, or a lewd exhibition of the genitals or post-pubescent female breast; and
>
> (C) [the material] taken as a whole, lacks serious literary, artistic, political, or scientific value *for minors.*

The only significant difference between the present statute and *Miller's* definition consists of the addition of the words "with respect to minors," and "for minors". But the addition of these words to a definition that would otherwise cover only obscenity expands the statute's scope only slightly. That is because the material in question (while potentially harmful to young children) must, first, appeal to the "prurient interest" of, *i.e.,* seek a sexual response from, some group of adolescents or postadolescents (since young children normally do not so respond). And material that appeals to the "prurient interest[s]" of some group of adolescents or postadolescents will almost inevitably appeal to the "prurient interest[s]" of some group of adults as well.

The "lack of serious value" requirement narrows the statute yet further – despite the presence of the qualification "for minors." That is because one cannot easily imagine material that has serious literary, artistic, political, or scientific value for a significant group of adults, but lacks such value for any significant group of minors.

These limitations on the statute's scope answer many of the concerns raised by those who attack its constitutionality. Respondents fear prosecution for the Internet posting of material that does not fall within the statute's ambit as limited by the "prurient interest" and "no serious value" requirements; for example: an essay about a young man's experience with masturbation and sexual shame; "a serious discussion about birth control practices, homosexuality, . . . or the consequences of prison rape"; let alone Aldous Huxley's Brave New World, J. D. Salinger's Catcher in the Rye, or, as the complaint would have it, "Ken Starr's report on the Clinton-Lewinsky scandal."

These materials are *not* both (1) "designed to appeal to, or . . . pander to, the prurient interest" of significant groups of minors *and* (2) lacking in "serious literary, artistic, political, or scientific value" for significant groups of minors. Thus, they fall outside the statute's definition of the material that it restricts, a fact the Government acknowledged at oral argument.

I have found nothing elsewhere in the statute's language that broadens its scope.

B

The Act does not censor the material it covers. Rather, it requires providers of the "harmful to minors" material to restrict minors' access to it by verifying age.

I recognize that the screening requirement imposes some burden on adults who seek access to the regulated material, as well as on its providers.

In addition to the monetary cost, and despite strict requirements that identifying information be kept confidential, the identification requirements inherent in age-screening may lead some users to fear embarrassment. But this Court has held that in the context of congressional efforts to protect children, restrictions of this kind do not automatically violate the Constitution. And the Court has approved their use.

In sum, the Act at most imposes a modest additional burden on adult access to legally obscene material, perhaps imposing a similar burden on access to some protected borderline obscene material as well.

II

I turn next to the question of "compelling interest," that of protecting minors from exposure to commercial pornography. No one denies that such an interest is "compelling." Rather, the question here is whether the Act, given its restrictions on adult access, significantly advances that interest. In other words, is the game worth the candle?

The majority argues that it is not, because of the existence of "blocking and filtering software." The majority refers to the presence of that software as a "less restrictive alternative." But that is a misnomer. Conceptually speaking, the presence of filtering software is not an *alternative* legislative approach to the problem of protecting children from exposure to commercial pornography. Rather, it is part of the status quo, *i.e.*, the backdrop against which Congress enacted the present statute. It is always true, by definition, that the status quo is less restrictive than a new regulatory law. It is always less restrictive to do *nothing* than to do *something*. But "doing nothing" does not address the problem Congress sought to address – namely that, despite the availability of filtering software, children were still being exposed to harmful material on the Internet.

Thus, the relevant constitutional question is not the question the Court asks: Would it be less restrictive to do nothing? Of course it would be. Rather, the relevant question posits a comparison of (a) a status quo that includes filtering software with (b) a change in that status quo that adds to it an age-verification screen requirement. Given the existence of filtering software, does the problem Congress identified remain significant? Does the Act help to address it? These are questions about the relation of the Act to the compelling interest.

The answers to these intermediate questions are clear: Filtering software, as presently available, does not solve the "child protection" problem. It suffers from four serious inadequacies that prompted Congress to pass legislation instead of relying on its voluntary use. First, its filtering is faulty, allowing some pornographic material to pass through without hindrance. Just last year, in *American Library Assn.*, Justice Stevens described "fundamental defects in the filtering software that is now available or that will be available in the foreseeable future."

Second, filtering software costs money. Not every family has the $40 or so necessary to install it.

Third, filtering software depends upon parents willing to decide where their children will surf the Web and able to enforce that decision. As to millions of American families, that is not a reasonable possibility.

Fourth, software blocking lacks precision, with the result that those who wish to use it to screen out pornography find that it blocks a great deal of material that is valuable.

[A] "filtering software status quo" means filtering that underblocks, imposes a cost upon each family that uses it, fails to screen outside the home, and lacks precision. Thus, Congress could reasonably conclude that a system that relies entirely upon the use of such software is not an effective system. And a law that adds to that system an age-verification screen requirement significantly increases the system's efficacy. That is to say, at a modest additional cost to those adults who wish to obtain access to a screened program, that law will bring about better, more precise blocking, both inside and outside the home.

The Court's response – that 40% of all pornographic material may be of foreign origin – is beside the point. Even assuming (I believe unrealistically) that *all* foreign originators will refuse to use screening, the Act would make a difference in respect to 60% of the Internet's commercial pornography. I cannot call that difference insignificant.

Given the modest nature of [the] burden and the likelihood that the Act will significantly further Congress' compelling objective, the Act may well satisfy the First Amendment's stringent tests. Indeed, it does satisfy the First Amendment unless, of course, there is a genuine alternative, "less restrictive" way similarly to further that objective.

III

I turn, then, to the actual "less restrictive alternatives" that the Court proposes.

First, the Government might "act to encourage" the use of blocking and filtering software. The problem is that any argument that rests upon this alternative proves too much. If one imagines enough government resources devoted to the problem, then, of course, the use of software might become as effective and less restrictive. Obviously, the Government could give all parents, schools, and Internet cafes free computers with filtering programs already installed, hire federal employees to train parents and teachers on their use, and devote millions of dollars to the development of better software. The result might be an alternative that is extremely effective.

But the Constitution does not, because it cannot, require the Government to disprove the existence of magic solutions, *i.e.*, solutions that, put in general terms, will solve any problem less restrictively but with equal effectiveness. Otherwise, "the undoubted ability of lawyers and judges," who are not constrained by the budgetary worries and other practical parameters within which Congress must operate, "to imagine *some* kind of slightly less drastic or restrictive an approach would make it impossible to write laws that deal with the harm that called the statute into being." As Justice Blackmun recognized, a "judge would be unimaginative indeed if he could not come up with something a little less 'drastic' or a little less 'restrictive' in almost any situation, and thereby enable himself to vote to strike legislation down." Perhaps that is why no party has argued seriously that additional expenditure of government funds to encourage the use of screening is a "less restrictive alternative."

Second, the majority suggests decriminalizing the statute, noting the "chilling effect" of criminalizing a category of speech. To remove a major sanction, however, would make the statute less effective, virtually by definition.

IV

My conclusion is that the Act, as properly interpreted, risks imposition of minor burdens on some protected material – burdens that adults wishing to view the material may overcome at modest cost. At the same time, it significantly helps to achieve a compelling congressional goal, protecting children from exposure to commercial pornography. There is no serious, practically available "less restrictive" way similarly to further this compelling interest. Hence the Act is constitutional.

V

The Court's holding raises two more general questions. First, what has happened to the "constructive discourse between our courts and our legislatures" that "is an integral and admirable part of the constitutional design"? After eight years of legislative effort, two statutes, and three Supreme Court cases the Court sends this case back to the District Court for further proceedings. What proceedings? I have found no offer by either party to present more relevant evidence. What remains to be litigated? I know the Court says that the parties may "introduce further evidence" as to the "relative restrictiveness and effectiveness of alternatives to the statute." But I do not understand what that new evidence might consist of.

Moreover, Congress passed the current statute "[i]n response to the Court's decision in *Reno*" striking down an earlier statutory effort to deal with the same problem. Congress read *Reno* with care. It dedicated itself to the task of drafting a statute that would meet each and every criticism of the predecessor statute that this Court set forth in *Reno*. It incorporated language from the Court's precedents, particularly the *Miller* standard, virtually verbatim. And it created what it believed was a statute that would protect children from exposure to obscene professional pornography without obstructing adult access to material that the First Amendment protects. What else was Congress supposed to do?

I recognize that some Members of the Court, now or in the past, have taken the view that the First Amendment simply does not permit Congress to legislate in this area. There are strong constitutional arguments favoring these views. But the Court itself does not adopt those views. Instead, it finds that the Government has not proved the nonexistence of "less restrictive alternatives." That finding, if appropriate here, is universally appropriate. And if universally appropriate, it denies to Congress, in practice, the legislative leeway that the Court's language seems to promise. If this statute does not pass the Court's "less restrictive alternative" test, what does? If nothing does, then the Court should say so clearly.

For these reasons, I dissent.

∾

13. Pornography and Obscenity

Introduction

Pornography is protected speech under the First Amendment; obscenity is not. The point at which pornography goes too far and becomes obscenity is difficult to determine and, in fact, varies from community to community. The Supreme Court ultimately settled on a test that the Court articulated in the famous 1973 case of *Miller v. California.*

Pornography and Obscenity: Case 1

MILLER v. CALIFORNIA

No. 70-73

SUPREME COURT OF THE UNITED STATES

413 U.S. 15; 93 S. Ct. 2607; 37 L. Ed. 2d 419; 1973 U.S. LEXIS 149; 1 Media L. Rep. 1441

January 18-19, 1972, Argued
June 21, 1973, Decided

JUDGES: Burger, C. J., delivered the opinion of the Court, in which White, Blackmun, Powell, and Rehnquist, JJ., joined. Douglas, J., filed a dissenting opinion. Brennan, J., filed a dissenting opinion, in which Stewart and Marshall, JJ., joined.

OPINION: BURGER, Chief Justice:

This is one of a group of "obscenity-pornography" cases being reviewed by the Court in a re-examination of standards enunciated in earlier cases involving what Mr. Justice Harlan called "the intractable obscenity problem."

Appellant conducted a mass mailing campaign to advertise the sale of illustrated books, euphemistically called "adult" material. After a jury trial, he was convicted of violating California Penal Code § 311.2 (a), a misdemeanor, by knowingly distributing obscene matter, and the Appellate Department, Superior Court of California, County of Orange, summarily affirmed the judgment without opinion. Appellant's conviction was specifically based on his conduct in causing five unsolicited advertising brochures to be sent through the mail in an envelope addressed to a restaurant in Newport Beach, California. The envelope was opened by the manager of the restaurant and his mother. They had not requested the brochures; they complained to the police.

The brochures advertise four books entitled "Intercourse," "Man-Woman," "Sex Orgies Illustrated," and "An Illustrated History of Pornography," and a film entitled

"Marital Intercourse." While the brochures contain some descriptive printed material, primarily they consist of pictures and drawings very explicitly depicting men and women in groups of two or more engaging in a variety of sexual activities, with genitals often prominently displayed.

I

This case involves the application of a State's criminal obscenity statute to a situation in which sexually explicit materials have been thrust by aggressive sales action upon unwilling recipients who had in no way indicated any desire to receive such materials. This Court has recognized that the States have a legitimate interest in prohibiting dissemination or exhibition of obscene material[1] when the mode of dissemination carries with it a significant danger of offending the sensibilities of unwilling recipients or of exposure to juveniles. It is in this context that we are called on to define the standards which must be used to identify obscene material that a State may regulate without infringing on the First Amendment as applicable to the States through the Fourteenth Amendment.

The material we are discussing in this case is more accurately defined as "pornography" or "pornographic material." "Pornography" derives from the Greek (*porne*, harlot, and *graphos*, writing). The word now means "1: a description of prostitutes or prostitution 2: a depiction (as in writing or painting) of licentiousness or lewdness: a portrayal of erotic behavior designed to cause sexual excitement." Webster's Third New International Dictionary, *supra*. Pornographic material which is obscene forms a sub-group of all "obscene" expression, but not the whole, at least as the word "obscene" is now used in our language. We note, therefore, that the words "obscene material," as used in this case, have a specific judicial meaning which derives from the *Roth* case, *i.e.*, obscene material "which deals with sex."

In *Roth* v. *United States*, 354 U.S. 476 (1957), the Court sustained a conviction under a federal statute punishing the mailing of "obscene, lewd, lascivious or filthy . . . " materials. The key to that holding was the Court's rejection of the claim that obscene materials were protected by the First Amendment. Five Justices joined in the opinion stating:

> All ideas having even the slightest redeeming social importance – unorthodox ideas, controversial ideas, even ideas hateful to the prevailing climate of opinion – have the full protection of the [First Amendment] guaranties, unless excludable because they encroach upon the limited area of more important interests. But implicit in the history of the First Amendment is the rejection of obscenity as utterly without redeeming social importance.

> We hold that obscenity is not within the area of constitutionally protected speech or press.

---

[1] This Court has defined "obscene material" as "material which deals with sex in a manner appealing to prurient interest," *Roth* v. *United States, supra*, at 487, but the *Roth* definition does not reflect the precise meaning of "obscene" as traditionally used in the English language. Derived from the Latin *obscaenus, ob*, to, plus *caenum*, filth, "obscene" is defined in the Webster's Third New International Dictionary (Unabridged 1969) as "1a: disgusting to the senses . . . b: grossly repugnant to the generally accepted notions of what is appropriate . . . 2: offensive or revolting as countering or violating some ideal or principle." The Oxford English Dictionary (1933 ed.) gives a similar definition, "offensive to the senses, or to taste or refinement; disgusting, repulsive, filthy, foul, abominable, loathsome."

Nine years later, in *Memoirs* v. *Massachusetts*, 383 U.S. 413 (1966), the Court veered sharply away from the *Roth* concept and, with only three Justices in the plurality opinion, articulated a new test of obscenity. The plurality held that under the *Roth* definition "as elaborated in subsequent cases, three elements must coalesce: it must be established that (a) the dominant theme of the material taken as a whole appeals to a prurient interest in sex; (b) the material is patently offensive because it affronts contemporary community standards relating to the description or representation of sexual matters; and (c) the material is utterly without redeeming social value."

The sharpness of the break with *Roth*, represented by the third element of the *Memoirs* test was further underscored when the *Memoirs* plurality went on to state:

> The Supreme Judicial Court erred in holding that a book need not be 'unqualifiedly worthless before it can be deemed obscene.' A book cannot be proscribed unless it is found to be *utterly* without redeeming social value." (emphasis in original)

While *Roth* presumed "obscenity" to be "utterly without redeeming social importance," *Memoirs* required that to prove obscenity it must be affirmatively established that the material is "*utterly* without redeeming social value." Thus, even as they repeated the words of *Roth*, the *Memoirs* plurality produced a drastically altered test that called on the prosecution to prove a negative, *i.e.*, that the material was "*utterly* without redeeming social value" – a burden virtually impossible to discharge under our criminal standards of proof.

Apart from the initial formulation in the *Roth* case, no majority of the Court has at any given time been able to agree on a standard to determine what constitutes obscene, pornographic material subject to regulation under the States' police power.

The case we now review was tried on the theory that the California Penal Code § 311 approximately incorporates the three-stage *Memoirs* test, *supra*. But now the *Memoirs* test has been abandoned as unworkable by its author, and no Member of the Court today supports the *Memoirs* formulation.

II

This much has been categorically settled by the Court, that obscene material is unprotected by the First Amendment. We acknowledge, however, the inherent dangers of undertaking to regulate any form of expression. State statutes designed to regulate obscene materials must be carefully limited. As a result, we now confine the permissible scope of such regulation to works which depict or describe sexual conduct. That conduct must be specifically defined by the applicable state law, as written or authoritatively construed. A state offense must also be limited to works which, taken as a whole, appeal to the prurient interest in sex, which portray sexual conduct in a patently offensive way, and which, taken as a whole, do not have serious literary, artistic, political, or scientific value.

The basic guidelines for the trier of fact must be: (a) whether "the average person, applying contemporary community standards" would find that the work, taken as a whole, appeals to the prurient interest; (b) whether the work depicts or describes, in a patently offensive way, sexual conduct specifically defined by the applicable state law; and (c) whether the work, taken as a whole, lacks serious literary, artistic, political, or scientific value. We do not adopt as a constitutional standard the "*utterly* without redeeming social value" test of *Memoirs* v. *Massachusetts*, [T]hat concept has never commanded the adherence of more than three Justices at one time.

We emphasize that it is not our function to propose regulatory schemes for the States. That must await their concrete legislative efforts. It is possible, however, to give a few plain examples of what a state statute could define for regulation under part (b) of the standard announced in this opinion, *supra*:

(a) Patently offensive representations or descriptions of ultimate sexual acts, normal or perverted, actual or simulated.
(b) Patently offensive representations or descriptions of masturbation, excretory functions, and lewd exhibition of the genitals.

Sex and nudity may not be exploited without limit by films or pictures exhibited or sold in places of public accommodation any more than live sex and nudity can be exhibited or sold without limit in such public places. At a minimum, prurient, patently offensive depiction or description of sexual conduct must have serious literary, artistic, political, or scientific value to merit First Amendment protection. For example, medical books for the education of physicians and related personnel necessarily use graphic illustrations and descriptions of human anatomy.

Query: Is the Court suggesting that such books are "patently offensive depictions or descriptions of sexual conduct" that would require such an exception?

In resolving the inevitably sensitive questions of fact and law, we must continue to rely on the jury system, accompanied by the safeguards that judges, rules of evidence, presumption of innocence, and other protective features provide, as we do with rape, murder, and a host of other offenses against society and its individual members.

Under the holdings announced today, no one will be subject to prosecution for the sale or exposure of obscene materials unless these materials depict or describe patently offensive "hard core" sexual conduct specifically defined by the regulating state law, as written or construed. We are satisfied that these specific prerequisites will provide fair notice to a dealer in such materials that his public and commercial activities may bring prosecution. If the inability to define regulated materials with ultimate, god-like precision altogether removes the power of the States or the Congress to regulate, then "hard core" pornography may be exposed without limit to the juvenile, the passerby, and the consenting adult alike, as, indeed, MR. JUSTICE DOUGLAS contends. In this belief, however, MR. JUSTICE DOUGLAS now stands alone.

It is certainly true that the absence, since *Roth*, of a single majority view of this Court as to proper standards for testing obscenity has placed a strain on both state and federal courts. But today, for the first time since *Roth* was decided in 1957, a majority of this Court has agreed on concrete guidelines to isolate "hard core" pornography from expression protected by the First Amendment.

This may not be an easy road, free from difficulty. But no amount of "fatigue" should lead us to adopt a convenient "institutional" rationale – an absolutist, "anything goes" view of the First Amendment – because it will lighten our burdens. Nor should we remedy "tension between state and federal courts" by arbitrarily depriving the States of a power reserved to them under the Constitution, a power which they have enjoyed and exercised continuously from before the adoption of the First Amendment to this day.

III

Under a National Constitution, fundamental First Amendment limitations on the powers of the States do not vary from community to community, but this does not mean that there are, or should or can be, fixed, uniform national standards of precisely what appeals to the "prurient interest" or is "patently offensive." These are essentially questions of fact, and our Nation is simply too big and too diverse for this Court to reasonably expect that such standards could be articulated for all 50 States in a single formulation, even assuming the prerequisite consensus exists. The adversary system, with lay jurors as the usual ultimate factfinders in criminal prosecutions, has historically permitted triers of fact to draw on the standards of their community, guided always by limiting instructions on the law. To require a State to structure obscenity proceedings around evidence of a *national* "community standard" would be an exercise in futility.

During the trial, both the prosecution and the defense assumed that the relevant "community standards" in making the factual determination of obscenity were those of the State of California, not some hypothetical standard of the entire United States of America. Defense counsel at trial never objected to the testimony of the State's expert on community standards or to the instructions of the trial judge on "statewide" standards.

We conclude that neither the State's alleged failure to offer evidence of "national standards," nor the trial court's charge that the jury consider state community standards, were constitutional errors.

It is neither realistic nor constitutionally sound to read the First Amendment as requiring that the people of Maine or Mississippi accept public depiction of conduct found tolerable in Las Vegas, or New York City.[2]

In other words, the Court is arguing that the use of community standards instead of a national standard to define obscenity permits less strict application of obscenity law, since those communities with more liberal standards will be able to access the materials they deem acceptable that would not be available if a stricter community's standards were applied.

Ironically, in the context of the Internet, the reverse may be true. That is, the universal accessibility of material on the Net may lead to the imposition of the standards of the strictest community.

Where do you think a "national standard" would fall in the spectrum of community standards?

IV

The dissenting Justices sound the alarm of repression. But, in our view, to equate the free and robust exchange of ideas and political debate with commercial exploitation of obscene

---

[2] In *Jacobellis* v. *Ohio*, 378 U.S. 184 (1964), two Justices argued that application of "local" community standards would run the risk of preventing dissemination of materials in some places because sellers would be unwilling to risk criminal conviction by testing variations in standards from place to place. The use of "national" standards, however, necessarily implies that materials found tolerable in some places, but not under the "national" criteria, will nevertheless be unavailable where they are acceptable. Thus, in terms of danger to free expression, the potential for suppression seems at least as great in the application of a single nationwide standard as in allowing distribution in accordance with local tastes.

material demeans the grand conception of the First Amendment and its high purposes in the historic struggle for freedom. The First Amendment protects works which, taken as a whole, have serious literary, artistic, political, or scientific value, regardless of whether the government or a majority of the people approve of the ideas these works represent. But the public portrayal of hard-core sexual conduct for its own sake, and for the ensuing commercial gain, is a different matter.

There is no evidence, empirical or historical, that the stern 19th century American censorship of public distribution and display of material relating to sex in any way limited or affected expression of serious literary, artistic, political, or scientific ideas. On the contrary, it is beyond any question that the era following Thomas Jefferson to Theodore Roosevelt was an "extraordinarily vigorous period," not just in economics and politics, but in *belles lettres* and in "the outlying fields of social and political philosophies." We do not see the harsh hand of censorship of ideas – good or bad, sound or unsound – and "repression" of political liberty lurking in every state regulation of commercial exploitation of human interest in sex.

One can concede that the "sexual revolution" of recent years may have had useful byproducts in striking layers of prudery from a subject long irrationally kept from needed ventilation. But it does not follow that no regulation of patently offensive "hard core" materials is needed or permissible; civilized people do not allow unregulated access to heroin because it is a derivative of medicinal morphine.

In sum, we (a) reaffirm the *Roth* holding that obscene material is not protected by the First Amendment; (b) hold that such material can be regulated by the States, subject to the specific safeguards enunciated above, without a showing that the material is "*utterly* without redeeming social value"; and (c) hold that obscenity is to be determined by applying "contemporary community standards," not "national standards." The judgment of the Appellate Department of the Superior Court, Orange County, California, is vacated and the case remanded to that court for further proceedings not inconsistent with the First Amendment standards established by this opinion.

Vacated and remanded.

DISSENT: DOUGLAS, Justice:

I

Today we leave open the way for California to send a man to prison for distributing brochures that advertise books and a movie under freshly written standards defining obscenity which until today's decision were never the part of any law.

In other words, under the *Memoirs* test, Miller might not be in trouble unless the State could prove that the materials he distributed were utterly without redeeming social value.

The impossibility of knowing what material may be obscene before a court declares it so has long been a problem.

In *Ginzburg* v. *United States*, 383 U.S. 463, a publisher was sent to prison, not for the kind of books and periodicals he sold, but for the manner in which the publications were advertised. The "leer of the sensualist" was said to permeate the advertisements. The Court said, "Where the purveyor's sole emphasis is on the sexually provocative

aspects of his publications, that fact may be decisive in the determination of obscenity."
As Mr. Justice Black said in dissent, ". . . Ginzburg . . . is now finally and authoritatively
condemned to serve five years in prison for distributing printed matter about sex which
neither Ginzburg nor anyone else could possibly have known to be criminal." That
observation by Mr. Justice Black is underlined by the fact that the *Ginzburg* decision was
five to four.

But even those members of this Court who had created the new and changing standards
of "obscenity" could not agree on their application. Some condemn it if its "dominant
tendency might be to 'deprave or corrupt' a reader." Others look not to the content of the
book but to whether it is advertised "'to appeal to the erotic interests of customers.'" Some
condemn only "hardcore pornography"; but even then a true definition is lacking. It has
indeed been said of that definition, "I could never succeed in [defining it] intelligibly,"
but "I know it when I see it."

Today we would add a new three-pronged test. Yet how under these vague tests can
we sustain convictions for the sale of an article prior to the time when some court has
declared it to be obscene?

Today the Court retreats from the earlier formulations of the constitutional test and
undertakes to make new definitions. This effort, like the earlier ones, is earnest and
well intentioned. The difficulty is that we do not deal with constitutional terms, since
"obscenity" is not mentioned in the Constitution or Bill of Rights. And the First Amendment makes no such exception from "the press" which it undertakes to protect nor, as I
have said on other occasions, is an exception necessarily implied, for there was no recognized exception to the free press at the time the Bill of Rights was adopted which treated
"obscene" publications differently from other types of papers, magazines, and books. So
there are no constitutional guidelines for deciding what is and what is not "obscene." The
Court is at large because we deal with tastes and standards of literature. What shocks me
may be sustenance for my neighbor. What causes one person to boil up in rage over one
pamphlet or movie may reflect only his neurosis, not shared by others. We deal here with
a regime of censorship which, if adopted, should be done by constitutional amendment
after full debate by the people.

Obscenity cases usually generate tremendous emotional outbursts. They have no
business being in the courts. If a constitutional amendment authorized censorship, the
censor would probably be an administrative agency. Then criminal prosecutions could
follow as, if, and when publishers defied the censor and sold their literature. Under that
regime a publisher would know when he was on dangerous ground.

The requirement of "fair warning" is due here. The present case involves rights earnestly
urged as being protected by the First Amendment. In any case – certainly when constitutional rights are concerned – we should not allow men to go to prison or be fined when
they had no "fair warning" that what they did was criminal conduct.

II

If a specific book, play, paper, or motion picture has in a civil proceeding been condemned as obscene and review of that finding has been completed, and thereafter a
person publishes, shows, or displays that particular book or film, then a vague law
has been made specific. There would remain the underlying question whether the First
Amendment allows an implied exception in the case of obscenity. I do not think it does
and my views on the issue have been stated over and over again. But at least a criminal

prosecution brought at that juncture would not violate the time-honored void-for-vagueness test.[3]

No such protective procedure has been designed by California in this case. Obscenity – which even we cannot define with precision – is a hodge-podge. To send men to jail for violating standards they cannot understand, construe, and apply is a monstrous thing to do in a Nation dedicated to fair trials and due process.

III

There is no "captive audience" problem in these obscenity cases. No one is being compelled to look or to listen. Those who enter newsstands or bookstalls may be offended by what they see. But they are not compelled by the State to frequent those places; and it is only state or governmental action against which the First Amendment, applicable to the States by virtue of the Fourteenth, raises a ban.

The idea that the First Amendment permits government to ban publications that are "offensive" to some people puts an ominous gloss on freedom of the press. That test would make it possible to ban any paper or any journal or magazine in some benighted place. The First Amendment was designed "to invite dispute," to induce "a condition of unrest," to "create dissatisfaction with conditions as they are," and even to stir "people to anger." The idea that the First Amendment permits punishment for ideas that are "offensive" to the particular judge or jury sitting in judgment is astounding. No greater leveler of speech or literature has ever been designed. To give the power to the censor, as we do today, is to make a sharp and radical break with the traditions of a free society. The First Amendment was not fashioned as a vehicle for dispensing tranquilizers to the people. Its prime function was to keep debate open to "offensive" as well as to "staid" people. The tendency throughout history has been to subdue the individual and to exalt the power of government. The use of the standard "offensive" gives authority to government that cuts the very vitals out of the First Amendment. As is intimated by the Court's opinion, the materials before us may be garbage. But so is much of what is said in political campaigns, in the daily press, on TV, or over the radio. By reason of the First Amendment – and solely because of it – speakers and publishers have not been threatened or subdued because their thoughts and ideas may be "offensive" to some.

If there are to be restraints on what is obscene, then a constitutional amendment should be the way of achieving the end. There are societies where religion and mathematics are the only free segments. It would be a dark day for America if that were our destiny. But

---

[3] The Commission on Obscenity and Pornography has advocated such a procedure:

> The Commission recommends the enactment, in all jurisdictions which enact or retain provisions prohibiting the dissemination of sexual materials to adults or young persons, of legislation authorizing prosecutors to obtain declaratory judgments as to whether particular materials fall within existing legal prohibitions....
>
> A declaratory judgment procedure ... would permit prosecutors to proceed civilly, rather than through the criminal process, against suspected violations of obscenity prohibition. If such civil procedures are utilized, penalties would be imposed for violation of the law only with respect to conduct occurring after a civil declaration is obtained. The Commission believes this course of action to be appropriate whenever there is any existing doubt regarding the legal status of materials; where other alternatives are available, the criminal process should not ordinarily be invoked against persons who might have reasonably believed, in good faith, that the books or films they distributed were entitled to constitutional protection, for the threat of criminal sanctions might otherwise deter the free distribution of constitutionally protected material.

the people can make it such if they choose to write obscenity into the Constitution and define it.

We deal with highly emotional, not rational, questions. To many the Song of Solomon is obscene. I do not think we, the judges, were ever given the constitutional power to make definitions of obscenity.

DISSENT: BRENNAN, Justice:

In my dissent in *Paris Adult Theatre I* v. *Slaton*, decided this date, I noted that I had no occasion to consider the extent of state power to regulate the distribution of sexually oriented material to juveniles or the offensive exposure of such material to unconsenting adults. I need not now decide whether a statute might be drawn to impose, within the requirements of the First Amendment, criminal penalties for the precise conduct at issue here. For it is clear that under my dissent in *Paris Adult Theatre I*, the statute under which the prosecution was brought is unconstitutionally overbroad, and therefore invalid on its face. "The transcendent value to all society of constitutionally protected expression is deemed to justify allowing 'attacks on overly broad statutes with no requirement that the person making the attack demonstrate that his own conduct could not be regulated by a statute drawn with the requisite narrow specificity.'" Since my view in *Paris Adult Theatre I* represents a substantial departure from the course of our prior decisions, and since the state courts have as yet had no opportunity to consider whether a "readily apparent construction suggests itself as a vehicle for rehabilitating the [statute] in a single prosecution," I would reverse the judgment of the Appellate Department of the Superior Court and remand the case for proceedings not inconsistent with this opinion.

In other words, the California statute in question is overbroad and should be unconstitutional on that ground.

~

The *Miller* test is still good law today. Justice Douglas's dissent, of course, underlines what to many seems a fatal flaw in all obscenity law: a person cannot know whether material he or she is distributing is obscene until the person has been convicted.

With the development of the Internet, a new flaw emerged. The *Miller* test's reliance on "community standards" is, at best, problematic in the context of the borderless world of cyberspace, as illustrated by the next case.

Pornography and Obscenity: Case 2

UNITED STATES OF AMERICA, Plaintiff-Appellee, v. ROBERT ALAN THOMAS (94-6648) and CARLEEN THOMAS (94-6649), Defendants-Appellants.

Nos. 94-6648/94-6649

UNITED STATES COURT OF APPEALS FOR THE SIXTH CIRCUIT

74 F.3d 701; 1996 U.S. App. LEXIS 1069; 1996 FED App. 0032P (6th Cir.); 43 Fed. R. Evid. Serv. (Callaghan) 969; 24 Media L. Rep. 1321; 96 Cal. Daily Op. Service 609

October 11, 1995, Argued
January 29, 1996, Decided
January 29, 1996, Filed

JUDGES: Before: MARTIN and BATCHELDER, Circuit Judges; EDMUNDS, District Judge.

OPINION: EDMUNDS, Judge:

Defendants Robert and Carleen Thomas appeal their convictions and sentences for violating 18 U.S.C. §§ 1462 and 1465, federal obscenity laws, in connection with their operation of an electronic bulletin board. For the following reasons, we AFFIRM Robert and Carleen Thomas' convictions and sentences.

I.

Robert Thomas and his wife Carleen Thomas began operating the Amateur Action Computer Bulletin Board System ("AABBS") from their home in Milpitas, California in February 1991. The AABBS was a computer bulletin board system that operated by using telephones, modems, and personal computers. Its features included e-mail, chat lines, public messages, and files that members could access, transfer, and download to their own computers and printers.

Information loaded onto the bulletin board was first converted into binary code, i.e., 0's and 1's, through the use of a scanning device. After purchasing sexually-explicit magazines from public adult book stores in California, Defendant Robert Thomas used an electronic device called a scanner to convert pictures from the magazines into computer files called Graphic Interchange Format files or "GIF" files.

Note the likely copyright infringement here.

The AABBS contained approximately 14,000 GIF files. Mr. Thomas also purchased, sold, and delivered sexually-explicit videotapes to AABBS members. Customers ordered the tapes by sending Robert Thomas an e-mail message, and Thomas typically delivered them by use of the United Parcel Service ("U.P.S.").

Persons calling the AABBS without a password could view the introductory screens of the system which contained brief, sexually-explicit descriptions of the GIF files and adult videotapes that were offered for sale. Access to the GIF files, however, was limited to members who were given a password after they paid a membership fee and submitted a signed application form that Defendant Robert Thomas reviewed. The application form requested the applicant's age, address, and telephone number and required a signature.

After they established membership by typing in a password, members could then select, retrieve, and instantly transport GIF files to their own computer. A caller could then view the GIF file on his computer screen and print the image out using his printer. The GIF files contained the AABBS name and access telephone number; many also had "Distribute Freely" printed on the image itself.

In July 1993, a United States Postal Inspector, Agent David Dirmeyer ("Dirmeyer"), received a complaint regarding the AABBS from an individual who resided in the Western District of Tennessee.

Dirmeyer used an assumed name and sent in $ 55 along with an executed application form to the AABBS. Defendant Robert Thomas called Dirmeyer at his undercover telephone number in Memphis, Tennessee, acknowledged receipt of his application, and authorized him to log-on with his personal password. Thereafter, Dirmeyer downloaded the GIF files listed in counts 2–7 of the Defendants' indictments. Dirmeyer also ordered six sexually-explicit videotapes from the AABBS and received them via U.P.S. at a Memphis, Tennessee address. Dirmeyer also had several e-mail and chat-mode conversations with Defendant Robert Thomas.

On January 10, 1994, a search warrant was issued by a U.S. Magistrate Judge for the Northern District of California. The AABBS' location was subsequently searched, and the Defendants' computer system was seized.

On January 25, 1994, a federal grand jury for the Western District of Tennessee returned a twelve-count indictment charging Defendants Robert and Carleen Thomas with the following criminal violations: one count under 18 U.S.C. § 371 for conspiracy to violate federal obscenity laws (Count 1), six counts under 18 U.S.C. § 1465 for knowingly using and causing to be used a facility and means of interstate commerce for the purpose of transporting obscene, computer-generated materials (the GIF files) in interstate commerce (Counts 2–7), three counts under 18 U.S.C. § 1462 for shipping obscene videotapes via U.P.S. (Counts 8–10), one count of causing the transportation of materials depicting minors engaged in sexually explicit conduct in violation of 18 U.S.C. § 2252(a)(1) as to Mr. Thomas only (Count 11), and one count of forfeiture under 18 U.S.C. § 1467 (Count 12).

Defendant Robert Thomas was found guilty on all counts except count 11 (child pornography). Defendant Carleen Thomas was found guilty on counts 1–10. Robert and Carleen Thomas were sentenced on December 2, 1994 to 37 and 30 months of incarceration, respectively.

II.

A.

Defendants' challenge to their convictions under counts 1–7, rests on two basic premises: 1) Section 1465 does not apply to intangible objects like the computer GIF files at issue here,[1] and 2) Congress did not intend to regulate computer transmissions such as those involved here because 18 U.S.C. § 1465 does not expressly prohibit such conduct.

In support of their first premise, Defendants cite a Tenth Circuit dial-a-porn decision which holds that 18 U.S.C. §§ 1462 and 1465 prohibit the interstate transportation of tangible objects; not intangible articles like pre-recorded telephone messages. *See United States v. Carlin Commun., Inc.*, 815 F.2d 1367, 1371 (10th Cir. 1987). Defendants claim *Carlin* is controlling because transmission of the GIF files at issue under counts 1–7

---

[1] Section 1465 provides:

> Whoever knowingly transports in interstate or foreign commerce for the purpose of sale or distribution, or knowingly travels in interstate commerce, or uses a facility or means of interstate commerce for the purpose of transporting obscene material in interstate or foreign commerce, any obscene, lewd, lascivious, or filthy book, pamphlet, picture, film, paper, letter, writing, print, silhouette, drawing, figure, image, cast, phonograph recording, electrical transcription or other article capable of producing sound or any other matter of indecent or immoral character, shall be fined under this title or imprisoned not more than five years, or both.
>
> The transportation as aforesaid of two or more copies of any publication or two or more of any article of the character described above, or a combined total of five such publications and articles, shall create a presumption that such publications or articles are intended for sale or distribution, but such presumption is rebuttable.

involved an intangible string of 0's and 1's which became viewable images only after they were decoded by an AABBS member's computer. We disagree.

The subject matter in *Carlin* – telephonic communication of pre-recorded sexually suggestive comments or proposals – is inherently different from the obscene computer-generated materials that were electronically transmitted from California to Tennessee in this case. Defendants erroneously conclude that the GIF files are intangible, and thus outside the scope of § 1465, by focusing solely on the manner and form in which the computer-generated images are transmitted from one destination to another. *United States v. Gilboe*, 684 F.2d 235 (2nd Cir. 1982) illustrates this point.

In *Gilboe*, the Second Circuit rejected the argument that the defendant's transmission of electronic impulses could not be prosecuted under a criminal statute prohibiting the transportation of money obtained by fraud. The *Gilboe* court reasoned that:

> electronic signals in this context are the means by which funds are transported. The beginning of the transaction is money in one account and the ending is money in another. The manner in which the funds were moved does not affect the ability to obtain tangible paper dollars or a bank check from the receiving account. The same rationale applies here. Defendants focus on the means by which the GIF files were transferred rather than the fact that the transmissions began with computer-generated images in California and ended with the same computer-generated images in Tennessee. The manner in which the images moved does not affect their ability to be viewed on a computer screen in Tennessee or their ability to be printed out in hard copy in that distant location.

The record does not support Defendants' argument that they had no knowledge, intent or expectation that members of their AABBS would download and print the images contained in their GIF files. They ran a business that advertised and promised its members the availability and transportation of the sexually-explicit GIF files they selected. In light of the overwhelming evidence produced at trial, it is spurious for Defendants to claim now that they did not intend to sell, disseminate, or share the obscene GIF files they advertised on the AABBS with members outside their home and in other states.

We also disagree with Defendants' corollary position, raised at oral argument, that they were prosecuted under the wrong statute and that their conduct, if criminal at all, falls within the prohibitions under 47 U.S.C. § 223(b) rather than 18 U.S.C. § 1465. As recognized by the Supreme Court, Section 223(b) of the Communications Act of 1934, was drafted and enacted by Congress in 1982 "explicitly to address 'dial-a-porn.'" 47 U.S.C. § 223(b) addresses commercial dial-a-porn operations that communicate sexually-explicit telephone messages; not commercial computer bulletin boards that use telephone facilities for the purpose of transmitting obscene, computer-generated images to approved members.

Why did the defendants argue this? Because they wanted a two-step reduction in their sentences due to "special circumstances." The details are explained at the end of the case.

Defendants' second premise, that Congress did not intend to regulate computer transmissions because the statute does not expressly prohibit such conduct, is faulty as well. We have consistently recognized that when construing federal statutes, our duty is to "'construe the language so as to give effect to the intent of Congress.'" The Supreme Court observed this principle when it rejected an argument similar to one Defendants raise here, i.e., that Congress could not possibly have intended to include conduct not expressly prohibited in the statute. See *United States v. Alpers*, 338 U.S. 680, 94 L. Ed. 457, 70 S. Ct. 352 (1950).

In *United States v. Alpers*, the Court held that the rule of *ejusdem generis*[2] should not be "employed to render general words meaningless" or "be used to defeat the obvious purpose of legislation." It recognized that "the obvious purpose of [Section 1462] was to prevent the channels of interstate commerce from being used to disseminate" any obscene matter. The Court further recognized that Section 1462 "is a comprehensive statute, which should not be constricted by a mechanical rule of construction." Accordingly, the Court rejected the defendant's argument that the general words "other matter of indecent character" could not be interpreted to include objects comprehensible by hearing (phonographic recordings) rather than sight; an argument similar to the tangible/intangible one raised here, and held that obscene records fell within the scope of the criminal statute.

Likewise, we conclude that Defendants' conduct here falls within the plain language of Section 1465. Moreover, our interpretation of Section 1465 is consistent with Congress' intent to legislate comprehensively the interstate distribution of obscene materials.

B.

Defendants also challenge venue in the Western District of Tennessee for counts 2–7 of their indictments.

> **The Court says that the statute does not require that the defendants have specific knowledge of the destination of each transmission, just that they knowingly use their facilities for the purpose of distributing obscene materials.**

"Venue lies in any district in which the offense was committed," and the Government is required to establish venue by a preponderance of the evidence.

That is, venue lies in any district into which the material was sent.

A Net problem: "Venue for federal obscenity prosecutions lies in any district from, *through*, or into which the allegedly obscene material moves."

How can a person know, on the Net, the venues through which information moves? For example, e-mail in transmission follows the "path of least resistance" and might conceivably pass through *any* jurisdiction. Is venue proper anywhere?

C.

Defendants further argue that their convictions under counts 1–7 of their indictments violate their First Amendment rights to freedom of speech.

---

[2] This rule of statutory construction "limits general terms which follow specific ones to matters similar to those specified."

1. Defendants' Right to Possess the GIF Files in their Home

Defendants rely on *Stanley v. Georgia*, 394 U.S. 557, 22 L. Ed. 2d 542, 89 S. Ct. 1243 (1969), and argue they have a constitutionally protected right to possess obscene materials in the privacy of their home. They insist that the GIF files containing sexually-explicit material never left their home. Defendants' reliance on *Stanley* is misplaced.

The Supreme Court has clarified that *Stanley* "depended not on any First Amendment Right to purchase or possess obscene materials, but on the right to privacy in the home." It has also recognized that the right to possess obscene materials in the privacy of one's home does not create "a correlative right to receive it, transport it, or distribute it" in interstate commerce even if it is for private use only. Nor does it create "some zone of constitutionally protected privacy [that] follows such material when it is moved outside the home area."

Defendants went beyond merely possessing obscene GIF files in their home. They ran a business that advertised and promised its members the availability and transportation of the sexually-explicit GIF files they selected. In light of the overwhelming evidence produced at trial, it is spurious for Defendants to claim now that they did not intend to sell, disseminate, or share the obscene GIF files they advertised on the AABBS with members outside their home and in other states.

2. The Community Standards to Be Applied When Determining Whether the GIF Files Are Obscene

In *Miller v. California*, the Supreme Court set out a three-prong test for obscenity. It inquired whether (1) "the average person applying contemporary community standards' would find that the work, taken as a whole appeals to the prurient interest"; (2) it "depicts or describes, in a patently offensive way, sexual conduct specifically defined by applicable state law"; and (3) "the work, taken as a whole, lacks serious literary, artistic, political, or scientific value."

Under the first prong of the *Miller* obscenity test, the jury is to apply "contemporary community standards." Defendants acknowledge the general principle that, in cases involving interstate transportation of obscene material, juries are properly instructed to apply the community standards of the geographic area where the materials are sent. *Miller*, 413 U.S. at 15, 30-34. Nonetheless, Defendants assert that this principle does not apply here for the same reasons they claim venue was improper. As demonstrated above, this argument cannot withstand scrutiny. The computer-generated images described in counts 2–7 were electronically transferred from Defendants' home in California to the Western District of Tennessee. Accordingly, the community standards of that judicial district were properly applied in this case.

3. The Implications of Computer Technology on the Definition of "Community"

Defendants and *Amicus Curiae* appearing on their behalf argue that the computer technology used here requires a new definition of community, i.e., one that is based on the broad-ranging connections among people in cyberspace rather than the geographic locale of the federal judicial district of the criminal trial. Without a more flexible definition, they argue, there will be an impermissible chill on protected speech because

BBS operators cannot select who gets the materials they make available on their bulletin boards. Therefore, they contend, BBS operators like Defendants will be forced to censor their materials so as not to run afoul of the standards of the community with the most restrictive standards.

Defendants' First Amendment issue, however, is not implicated by the facts of this case. This is not a situation where the bulletin board operator had no knowledge or control over the jurisdictions where materials were distributed for downloading or printing. Access to the Defendants' AABBS was limited. Membership was necessary and applications were submitted and screened before passwords were issued and materials were distributed. Thus, Defendants had in place methods to limit user access in jurisdictions where the risk of a finding of obscenity was greater than that in California. They knew they had a member in Memphis; the member's address and local phone number were provided on his application form. If Defendants did not wish to subject themselves to liability in jurisdictions with less tolerant standards for determining obscenity, they could have refused to give passwords to members in those districts, thus precluding the risk of liability.

> **Query: Is this really feasible? Do Net bulletin board system operators and other "distributors" of information on the Net have to know *all* community standards?**

Thus, under the facts of this case, there is no need for this court to adopt a new definition of "community" for use in obscenity prosecutions involving electronic bulletin boards. This court's decision is guided by one of the cardinal rules governing the federal courts, i.e., never reach constitutional questions not squarely presented by the facts of a case.

I.

> **Now we find the details of the reason the Thomases argued for a different statute.**

Defendants' final argument challenges the district court's denial of a two-level reduction in their sentences for acceptance of responsibility. They claim they are entitled to the reduction because they fully acknowledged their conduct in running the AABBS. The sentencing court's finding regarding acceptance of responsibility is entitled to great deference and is reversed only if found to be clearly erroneous.

U.S.S.G. § 3E1.1(a) provides for a two-level reduction for a defendant who "clearly demonstrates acceptance of responsibility." To qualify for this reduction, Defendants were required to show by a preponderance of the evidence that they had accepted responsibility for the crime committed. U.S.S.G. 3E1.1(a), comment, n.2 clarifies that the reduction is "not intended for a defendant who puts the government to its burden of proof at trial by denying the essential factual elements of guilt, is convicted, and only then admits guilt and expresses remorse." This comment further clarifies that only in "rare situations" will the adjustment apply after a trial and verdict of guilt, e.g., where the defendant makes a challenge to the applicability of a statute to his conduct. Defendants assert that they fit the "rare situation" and should not have been denied the reduction.

The sentencing judge, however, stated more than one ground for denying the two-level reduction. She noted that neither Defendant acknowledged the character of the materials found to be obscene. In addition, she found no indication that either of them had put aside making their living through the same means. This court has recognized that the two-level adjustment is properly denied under circumstances where the defendant continues conduct that is the same type as the underlying offense. Accordingly, we hold that the sentencing court's denial of the two-level reduction was not clearly erroneous.

III.

For the foregoing reasons, this court Affirms Robert and Carleen Thomas' convictions and sentences.

So, the *Thomas* case does not really answer the fundamental question about whether the Net will be considered its own community for purposes of "community standards" analysis. But the case makes it clear that the courts are aware of this issue and will have to grapple with it, probably soon.

∼

While pornography is a form of expression protected by the First Amendment, *child* pornography is not. Even obscene material may be possessed in the privacy of the home, although it is illegal to create or distribute it. Child pornography (at least in its visual form) is *not* speech that is protected under the First Amendment. It is illegal to create it, disseminate it, and to possess it, even in your own home.

Laws illegalizing child pornography have historically relied for their "compelling interest" on the harm done to the children used in making child pornography.

Pornography and Obscenity: Case 3

NEW YORK v. FERBER

No. 81-55

SUPREME COURT OF THE UNITED STATES

458 U.S. 747; 102 S. Ct. 3348; 73 L. Ed. 2d 1113; 1982 U.S. LEXIS 12; 50 U.S.L.W. 5077; 8 Media L. Rep. 1809

April 27, 1982, Argued
July 2, 1982, Decided

JUDGES: WHITE, J., delivered the opinion of the Court, in which BURGER, C. J., and POWELL, REHNQUIST, and O'CONNOR, JJ., joined. O'CONNOR, J., filed a concurring opinion. BRENNAN, J., filed an opinion concurring in the judgment, in which MARSHALL, J., joined. BLACKMUN, J., concurred in the result. STEVENS, J., filed an opinion concurring in the judgment.

OPINION: WHITE, Justice:
At issue in this case is the constitutionality of a New York criminal statute which prohibits persons from knowingly promoting sexual performances by children under the age of 16 by distributing material which depicts such performances.

Note that the statute attacks the problem at the *distribution end*, not at its creation. That is so because the *creation* of child pornography is usually extremely clandestine, whereas distribution inherently requires at least some visibility.

I

In recent years, the exploitative use of children in the production of pornography has become a serious national problem. The Federal Government and 47 States have sought to combat the problem with statutes specifically directed at the production of child pornography. At least half of such statutes do not require that the materials produced be legally obscene. Thirty-five States and the United States Congress have also passed legislation prohibiting the distribution of such materials; 20 States prohibit the distribution of material depicting children engaged in sexual conduct without requiring that the material be legally obscene.

New York is one of the 20. In 1977, the New York Legislature enacted Article 263 of its Penal Law. N. Y. Penal Law, Art. 263 (McKinney 1980). Section 263.05 criminalizes as a class C felony the use of a child in a sexual performance:

> A person is guilty of the use of a child in a sexual performance if knowing the character and content thereof he employs, authorizes or induces a child less than sixteen years of age to engage in a sexual performance or being a parent, legal guardian or custodian of such child, he consents to the participation by such child in a sexual performance.

At issue in this case is § 263.15, defining a class D felony:

> A person is guilty of promoting a sexual performance by a child when, knowing the character and content thereof, he produces, directs or promotes any performance which includes sexual conduct by a child less than sixteen years of age.

To "promote" is also defined:

> 'Promote' means to procure, manufacture, issue, sell, give, provide, lend, mail, deliver, transfer, transmute, publish, distribute, circulate, disseminate, present, exhibit or advertise, or to offer or agree to do the same.

This case arose when Paul Ferber, the proprietor of a Manhattan bookstore specializing in sexually oriented products, sold two films to an undercover police officer. The films are devoted almost exclusively to depicting young boys masturbating. Ferber was indicted on two counts of violating § 263.10 and two counts of violating § 263.15, the two New York laws controlling dissemination of child pornography. After a jury trial, Ferber was acquitted of the two counts of promoting an obscene sexual performance,

Why? Because the jury applied community standards and found the films not to be "obscene." That is, they are pornography, but not obscene.

but found guilty of the two counts under § 263.15, which did not require proof that the films were obscene. Ferber's convictions were affirmed without opinion by the Appellate Division of the New York State Supreme Court.

The New York Court of Appeals reversed, holding that § 263.15 violated the First Amendment. The court began by noting that in light of § 263.10's explicit inclusion of an obscenity standard, § 263.15 could not be construed to include such a standard. Therefore, "the statute would . . . prohibit the promotion of materials which are traditionally entitled to constitutional protection from government interference under the First Amendment."

Although the court recognized the State's "legitimate interest in protecting the welfare of minors" and noted that this "interest may transcend First Amendment concerns," it nevertheless found two fatal defects in the New York statute. Section 263.15 was underinclusive because it discriminated against visual portrayals of children engaged in sexual activity by not also prohibiting the distribution of films of other dangerous activity.

Like what? Taking drugs? Seems to have been an odd decision.

It was also overbroad because it prohibited the distribution of materials produced outside the State,

That is, it covered materials that would not harm New York children in the production process. Frankly, this point of view is startlingly parochial. Imagine how this "out of state materials" argument applies in cyberspace!

as well as materials, such as medical books and educational sources, which "deal with adolescent sex in a realistic but nonobscene manner."

Two judges dissented. We granted the State's petition for certiorari, presenting the single question:

"To prevent the abuse of children who are made to engage in sexual conduct for commercial purposes, could the New York State Legislature, consistent with the First Amendment, prohibit the dissemination of material which shows children engaged in sexual conduct, regardless of whether such material is obscene?"

Notice the emphasis on abuse of the children used in making the pornography.

II

The Court of Appeals proceeded on the assumption that the standard of obscenity incorporated in § 263.10, which follows the guidelines enunciated in *Miller* v. *California*, constitutes the appropriate line dividing protected from unprotected expression by which to measure a regulation directed at child pornography. It was on the premise that "nonobscene adolescent sex" could not be singled out for special treatment that the court found § 263.15 "strikingly underinclusive." Moreover, the assumption that the constitutionally permissible regulation of pornography could not be more extensive with respect to the distribution of material depicting children may also have led the court to conclude that a narrowing construction of § 263.15 was unavailable.

The Court of Appeals' assumption was not unreasonable in light of our decisions. This case, however, constitutes our first examination of a statute directed at and limited to depictions of sexual activity involving children. We believe our inquiry should begin with the question of whether a state has somewhat more freedom in proscribing works which portray sexual acts or lewd exhibitions of genitalia by children.

That is, whether a state has more freedom to apply lower standards than those the state must apply in proscribing *adult* pornography.

[Section A is omitted.]

B

Like obscenity statutes, laws directed at the dissemination of child pornography run the risk of suppressing protected expression by allowing the hand of the censor to become unduly heavy. For the following reasons, however, we are persuaded that the States are entitled to greater leeway in the regulation of pornographic depictions of children.

First. It is evident beyond the need for elaboration that a State's interest in "safeguarding the physical and psychological well-being of a minor" is "compelling." "A democratic society rests, for its continuance, upon the healthy, well-rounded growth of young people into full maturity as citizens." Accordingly, we have sustained legislation aimed at protecting the physical and emotional well-being of youth even when the laws have operated in the sensitive area of constitutionally protected rights. In *Prince* v. *Massachusetts, supra,* the Court held that a statute prohibiting use of a child to distribute literature on the street was valid notwithstanding the statute's effect on a First Amendment activity. In *Ginsberg* v. *New York, supra,* we sustained a New York law protecting children from exposure to nonobscene literature. Most recently, we held that the Government's interest in the "well-being of its youth" justified special treatment of indecent broadcasting received by adults as well as children. *FCC* v. *Pacifica Foundation,* 438 U.S. 726 (1978).

Second. The distribution of photographs and films depicting sexual activity by juveniles is intrinsically related to the sexual abuse of children in at least two ways. First, the materials produced are a permanent record of the children's participation and the harm to the child is exacerbated by their circulation. Second, the distribution network for child pornography must be closed if the production of material which requires the sexual exploitation of children is to be effectively controlled. Indeed, there is no serious contention that the legislature was unjustified in believing that it is difficult, if not impossible, to halt the exploitation of children by pursuing only those who produce the photographs and movies. While the production of pornographic materials is a low-profile, clandestine industry, the need to market the resulting products requires a visible apparatus of distribution.

Respondent does not contend that the State is unjustified in pursuing those who distribute child pornography. Rather, he argues that it is enough for the State to prohibit the distribution of materials that are legally obscene under the *Miller* test. While some States may find that this approach properly accommodates its interests, it does not follow that the First Amendment prohibits a State from going further. The *Miller* standard, like all general definitions of what may be banned as obscene, does not reflect the State's particular and more compelling interest in prosecuting those who promote the sexual exploitation of children. Thus, the question under the *Miller* test of whether a work, taken as a whole, appeals to the prurient interest of the average person bears no connection to the issue of whether a child has been physically or psychologically harmed in the production of the work. Similarly, a sexually explicit depiction need not be "patently offensive" in order to have required the sexual exploitation of a child for its production.

That is, *obscenity* is not the relevant standard.

Third. The advertising and selling of child pornography provide an economic motive for and are thus an integral part of the production of such materials, an activity illegal throughout the Nation. We note that were the statutes outlawing the employment of children in these films and photographs fully effective, and the constitutionality of these laws has not been questioned, the First Amendment implications would be no greater than that presented by laws against distribution: enforceable production laws would leave no child pornography to be marketed.

Fourth. The value of permitting live performances and photographic reproductions of children engaged in lewd sexual conduct is exceedingly modest, if not *de minimis.* We consider it unlikely that visual depictions of children performing sexual acts or lewdly exhibiting their genitals would often constitute an important and necessary part of a literary performance or scientific or educational work. As a state judge in this case observed, if it were necessary for literary or artistic value, a person over the statutory age who perhaps looked younger could be utilized. Simulation outside of the prohibition of the statute could provide another alternative.

So the Court, surely unwittingly, is setting itself up for its decision twenty years later in the next case below.

Fifth. Recognizing and classifying child pornography as a category of material outside the protection of the First Amendment is not incompatible with our earlier decisions. "The question whether speech is, or is not, protected by the First Amendment often depends on the content of the speech." When a definable class of material, such as that covered by § 263.15, bears so heavily and pervasively on the welfare of children engaged in its production, we think the balance of competing interests is clearly struck and that it is permissible to consider these materials as without the protection of the First Amendment.

C

There are, of course, limits on the category of child pornography which, like obscenity, is unprotected by the First Amendment. As with all legislation in this sensitive area, the conduct to be prohibited must be adequately defined by the applicable state law, as written or authoritatively construed. Here the nature of the harm to be combated requires that the state offense be limited to works that *visually* depict sexual conduct by children below a specified age. The category of "sexual conduct" proscribed must also be suitably limited and described.

The test for child pornography is separate from the obscenity standard enunciated in *Miller*, but may be compared to it for the purpose of clarity. The *Miller* formulation is adjusted in the following respects: A trier of fact need not find that the material appeals to the prurient interest of the average person; it is not required that sexual conduct portrayed be done so in a patently offensive manner; and the material at issue need not be considered as a whole. We note that the distribution of descriptions or other depictions of sexual conduct, not otherwise obscene, which do not involve live performance or photographic or other visual reproduction of live performances, retains First Amendment protection. As with obscenity laws, criminal responsibility may not be imposed without some element of scienter on the part of the defendant.

D

Section 263.15's prohibition incorporates a definition of sexual conduct that comports with the above-stated principles.

We hold that § 263.15 sufficiently describes a category of material the production and distribution of which is not entitled to First Amendment protection. It is therefore clear that there is nothing unconstitutionally "underinclusive" about a statute that singles out this category of material for proscription. It also follows that the State is not barred by the First Amendment from prohibiting the distribution of unprotected materials produced outside the State.

III

It remains to address the claim that the New York statute is unconstitutionally overbroad because it would forbid the distribution of material with serious literary, scientific, or educational value or material which does not threaten the harms sought to be combated by the State. Respondent prevailed on that ground below, and it is to that issue that we now turn.

The court [found] that § 263.15 was fatally overbroad: "[The] statute would prohibit the showing of any play or movie in which a child portrays a defined sexual act, real or simulated, in a nonobscene manner. It would also prohibit the sale, showing, or distributing of medical or educational materials containing photographs of such acts. Indeed, by its terms, the statute would prohibit those who oppose such portrayals from providing illustrations of what they oppose."

A

What has come to be known as the First Amendment overbreadth doctrine is predicated on the sensitive nature of protected expression: "persons whose expression is constitutionally protected may well refrain from exercising their rights for fear of criminal sanctions by a statute susceptible of application to protected expression." It is for this reason that we have allowed persons to attack overly broad statutes even though the conduct of the person making the attack is clearly unprotected and could be proscribed by a law drawn with the requisite specificity.

The scope of the First Amendment overbreadth doctrine must be carefully tied to the circumstances in which facial invalidation of a statute is truly warranted. Because of the wide-reaching effects of striking down a statute on its face at the request of one whose own conduct may be punished despite the First Amendment, we have recognized that the overbreadth doctrine is "strong medicine" and have employed it with hesitation, and then "only as a last resort." We have, in consequence, insisted that the overbreadth involved be "substantial" before the statute involved will be invalidated on its face.

The requirement of substantial overbreadth is directly derived from the purpose and nature of the doctrine. While a sweeping statute, or one incapable of limitation, has the potential to repeatedly chill the exercise of expressive activity by many individuals, the extent of deterrence of protected speech can be expected to decrease with the declining reach of the regulation.

This requirement of substantial overbreadth may justifiably be applied to statutory challenges which arise in defense of a criminal prosecution as well as civil enforcement or actions seeking a declaratory judgment. Indeed, the Court's practice when confronted with ordinary criminal laws that are sought to be applied against protected conduct is not to invalidate the law *in toto*, but rather to reverse the particular conviction. We recognize, however, that the penalty to be imposed is relevant in determining whether demonstrable overbreadth is substantial. We simply hold that the fact that a criminal prohibition is involved does not obviate the need for the inquiry or *a priori* warrant a finding of substantial overbreadth.

B

Applying these principles, we hold that § 263.15 is not substantially overbroad. We consider this the paradigmatic case of a state statute whose legitimate reach dwarfs its arguably impermissible applications. New York, as we have held, may constitutionally prohibit dissemination of material specified in § 263.15. While the reach of the statute is directed at the hard core of child pornography, the Court of Appeals was understandably concerned that some protected expression, ranging from medical textbooks to pictorials in the National Geographic, would fall prey to the statute. [W]e seriously doubt, and it has not been suggested, that these arguably impermissible applications of the statute amount to more than a tiny fraction of the materials within the statute's reach.

IV

Because § 263.15 is not substantially overbroad, it is unnecessary to consider its application to material that does not depict sexual conduct of a type that New York may restrict consistent with the First Amendment. The judgment of the New York Court of Appeals is reversed, and the case is remanded to that court for further proceedings not inconsistent with this opinion.

So ordered.

JUSTICE BLACKMUN concurs in the result.

CONCURRENCE: O'CONNOR, Justice:

Although I join the Court's opinion, I write separately to stress that the Court does not hold that New York must except "material with serious literary, scientific, or educational value" from its statute.

Justice O'Connor is taking a VERY hard line.

The compelling interests identified in today's opinion suggest that the Constitution might in fact permit New York to ban knowing distribution of works depicting minors engaged in explicit sexual conduct, regardless of the social value of the depictions.

That is, even if the alleged child pornography – and remember the work need not be taken as a whole – has some serious literary, artistic, political, or scientific value, it might STILL be considered child pornography and its distribution prohibited by this law.

For example, a 12-year-old child photographed while masturbating surely suffers the same psychological harm whether the community labels the photograph "edifying" or "tasteless."

As drafted, New York's statute does not attempt to suppress the communication of particular ideas. The statute permits discussion of child sexuality, forbidding only attempts to render the "[portrayals] somewhat more 'realistic' by utilizing or photographing children." Thus, the statute attempts to protect minors from abuse without attempting to restrict the expression of ideas by those who might use children as live models.

CONCURRENCE: BRENNAN, Justice:

I agree with much of what is said in the Court's opinion.

But in my view application of § 263.15 or any similar statute to depictions of children that in themselves do have serious literary, artistic, scientific, or medical value, would violate the First Amendment. As the Court recognizes, the limited classes of speech, the suppression of which does not raise serious First Amendment concerns, have two attributes. They are of exceedingly "slight social value," and the State has a compelling interest in their regulation. The First Amendment value of depictions of children that are in themselves serious contributions to art, literature, or science, is, by definition, simply not "*de minimis*." At the same time, the State's interest in suppression of such materials is likely to be far less compelling. For the Court's assumption of harm to the child resulting from the "permanent record" and "circulation" of the child's "participation" lacks much of its force where the depiction is a serious contribution to art or science. The production of materials of serious value is not the "low-profile, clandestine industry" that according to the Court produces purely pornographic materials.

With this understanding, I concur in the Court's judgment in this case.

CONCURRENCE: STEVENS, Justice:

Two propositions seem perfectly clear to me. First, the specific conduct that gave rise to this criminal prosecution is not protected by the Federal Constitution; second, the state statute that respondent violated prohibits some conduct that is protected by the First Amendment. The critical question, then, is whether this respondent, to whom the statute may be applied without violating the Constitution, may challenge the statute on the ground that it conceivably may be applied unconstitutionally to others in situations not before the Court. I agree with the Court's answer to this question but not with its method of analyzing the issue.

Before addressing that issue, I shall explain why respondent's conviction does not violate the Constitution. The two films that respondent sold contained nothing more than lewd exhibition; there is no claim that the films included any material that had literary, artistic, scientific, or educational value. Respondent was a willing participant in a commercial market that the State of New York has a legitimate interest in suppressing. The character of the State's interest in protecting children from sexual abuse justifies the imposition of criminal sanctions against those who profit, directly or indirectly, from the promotion of such films.

A holding that respondent may be punished for selling these two films does not require us to conclude that other users of these very films, or that other motion pictures containing similar scenes, are beyond the pale of constitutional protection. Thus, the exhibition of these films before a legislative committee studying a proposed amendment to a state law, or before a group of research scientists studying human behavior, could not, in my opinion, be made a crime. The question whether a specific act of communication is protected by the First Amendment always requires some consideration of both its content and its context.

Even assuming that the Court's empirical analysis is sound, I believe a more conservative approach to the issue would adequately vindicate the State's interest in protecting its children and cause less harm to the federal interest in free expression.

A hypothetical example will illustrate my concern. Assume that the operator of a New York motion picture theater specializing in the exhibition of foreign feature films is offered a full-length movie containing one scene that is plainly lewd if viewed in isolation but that nevertheless is part of a serious work of art. If the child actor resided abroad, New York's interest in protecting its young from sexual exploitation would be far less compelling than in the case before us.

The federal interest in free expression would, however, be just as strong as if an adult actor had been used.

My reasons for avoiding overbreadth analysis in this case are more qualitative than quantitative. When we follow our traditional practice of adjudicating difficult and novel constitutional questions only in concrete factual situations, the adjudications tend to be crafted with greater wisdom. Hypothetical rulings are inherently treacherous and prone to lead us into unforeseen errors; they are qualitatively less reliable than the products of case-by-case adjudication.

Moreover, it is probably safe to assume that the category of speech that is covered by the New York statute generally is of a lower quality than most other types of communication. Today the Court accepts this view, putting the category of speech described in the New York statute in its rightful place near the bottom of this hierarchy. Although I disagree with the Court's position that such speech is totally without First Amendment protection, I agree that generally marginal speech does not warrant the extraordinary protection afforded by the overbreadth doctrine.

Because I have no difficulty with the statute's application in this case, I concur in the Court's judgment.

∾

According to this decision, if no minors are used, child pornography production and distribution laws are not constitutional because the compelling interest – protecting the children used in making the pornography – is not present. So, sketches from the imagination are pornography, but not illegal child pornography. Similarly textual descriptions of sexual activities by minors are not illegal, although such materials not involving the use of actual children might rise to the level of obscenity.

This approach to the issue worked for a long time because the only way to create photographic images of children engaged in sexual activity was to use real children. However, with the advent of advanced digital technology and "virtual child pornography," that changed.

Pornography and Obscenity: Case 4

JOHN D. ASHCROFT, ATTORNEY GENERAL, ET AL., PETITIONERS v. THE
FREE SPEECH COALITION ET AL.

No. 00-795

SUPREME COURT OF THE UNITED STATES

535 U.S. 234; 122 S. Ct. 1389; 152 L. Ed. 2d 403; 2002 U.S. LEXIS 2789; 70
U.S.L.W. 4237; 30 Media L. Rep. 1673; 2002 Cal. Daily Op. Service 3211; 2002
Daily Journal DAR 4033; 15 Fla. L. Weekly Fed. S 187

October 30, 2001, Argued
April 16, 2002, Decided

JUDGES: KENNEDY, J., delivered the opinion of the Court, in which STEVENS, SOUTER, GINSBURG, and BREYER, JJ., joined. THOMAS, J., filed an opinion concurring in the judgment. O'CONNOR, J., filed an opinion concurring in the judgment in part and dissenting in part, in which REHNQUIST, C. J., and SCALIA, J., joined as to Part II. REHNQUIST, C. J., filed a dissenting opinion, in which SCALIA, J., joined except for the paragraph discussing legislative history.

OPINION: KENNEDY, Justice:

We consider in this case whether the Child Pornography Prevention Act of 1996 (CPPA), 18 U.S.C. § 2251 et seq., abridges the freedom of speech. The CPPA extends the federal prohibition against child pornography to sexually explicit images that appear to depict minors but were produced without using any real children. The statute prohibits, in specific circumstances, possessing or distributing these images, which may be created by using adults who look like minors or by using computer imaging. The new technology, according to Congress, makes it possible to create realistic images of children who do not exist.

By prohibiting child pornography that does not depict an actual child, the statute goes beyond *New York* v. *Ferber*, 458 U.S. 747, 73 L. Ed. 2d 1113, 102 S. Ct. 3348 (1982), which distinguished child pornography from other sexually explicit speech because of the State's interest in protecting the children exploited by the production process.

Like the law in *Ferber*, the CPPA seeks to reach beyond obscenity, and it makes no attempt to conform to the *Miller* standard. For instance, the statute would reach visual depictions, such as movies, even if they have redeeming social value.

The principal question to be resolved is whether the CPPA is constitutional where it proscribes a significant universe of speech that is neither obscene under *Miller* nor child pornography under *Ferber*.

I

Before 1996, Congress defined child pornography as the type of depictions at issue in *Ferber*, images made using actual minors. The CPPA retains that prohibition at 18 U.S.C. § 2256(8)(A) and adds three other prohibited categories of speech, of which the first, § 2256(8)(B), and the third, § 2256(8)(D), are at issue in this case. Section 2256(8)(B) prohibits "any visual depiction, including any photograph, film, video, picture, or computer or computer-generated image or picture" that "is, or appears to be, of a minor engaging in sexually explicit conduct." The prohibition on "any visual depiction" does not depend at all on how the image is produced. The section captures a range of depictions, sometimes called "virtual child pornography," which include computer-generated images, as well as images produced by more traditional means. For instance, the literal terms of the statute embrace a Renaissance painting depicting a scene from classical mythology, a "picture" that "appears to be, of a minor engaging in sexually explicit conduct." The statute also prohibits Hollywood movies, filmed without any child actors, if a jury believes an actor "appears to be" a minor engaging in "actual or simulated . . . sexual intercourse." § 2256(2).

These images do not involve, let alone harm, any children in the production process; but Congress decided the materials threaten children in other, less direct, ways. Pedophiles might use the materials to encourage children to participate in sexual activity.

Furthermore, pedophiles might "whet their own sexual appetites" with the pornographic images, "thereby increasing the creation and distribution of child pornography and the sexual abuse and exploitation of actual children." Under these rationales, harm flows from the content of the images, not from the means of their production. In addition, Congress identified another problem created by computer-generated images: Their existence can make it harder to prosecute pornographers who do use real minors. As imaging technology improves, Congress found, it becomes more difficult to prove that a particular picture was produced using actual children. To ensure that defendants possessing child pornography using real minors cannot evade prosecution, Congress extended the ban to virtual child pornography.

Respondents challenge § 2256(8)(D). Like the text of the "appears to be" provision, the sweep of this provision is quite broad. Section 2256(8)(D) defines child pornography to include any sexually explicit image that was "advertised, promoted, presented, described, or distributed in such a manner that conveys the impression" it depicts "a minor engaging in sexually explicit conduct." One Committee Report identified the provision as directed at sexually explicit images pandered as child pornography. The statute is not so limited in its reach, however, as it punishes even those possessors who took no part in pandering. Once a work has been described as child pornography, the taint remains on the speech in the hands of subsequent possessors, making possession unlawful even though the content otherwise would not be objectionable.

The District Court granted summary judgment to the Government. The court dismissed the overbreadth claim because it was "highly unlikely" that any "adaptations of sexual works like 'Romeo and Juliet,' will be treated as 'criminal contraband.'"

The Court of Appeals for the Ninth Circuit reversed. The court reasoned that the Government could not prohibit speech because of its tendency to persuade viewers to commit illegal acts. The court held the CPPA to be substantially overbroad because it bans materials that are neither obscene nor produced by the exploitation of real children as in *New York* v. *Ferber*, 458 U.S. 747, 73 L. Ed. 2d 1113, 102 S. Ct. 3348 (1982). Judge Ferguson dissented on the ground that virtual images, like obscenity and real child pornography, should be treated as a category of speech unprotected by the First Amendment.

While the Ninth Circuit found the CPPA invalid on its face, four other Courts of Appeals have sustained it. We granted certiorari.

II

The First Amendment commands, "Congress shall make no law . . . abridging the freedom of speech." The government may violate this mandate in many ways, but a law imposing criminal penalties on protected speech is a stark example of speech suppression. The CPPA's penalties are indeed severe. A first offender may be imprisoned for 15 years. While even minor punishments can chill protected speech, this case provides a textbook example of why we permit facial challenges to statutes that burden expression. With these severe penalties in force, few legitimate movie producers or book publishers, or few other speakers in any capacity, would risk distributing images in or near the uncertain reach of this law. The Constitution gives significant protection from overbroad laws that chill speech within the First Amendment's vast and privileged sphere. Under this principle, the CPPA is unconstitutional on its face if it prohibits a substantial amount of protected expression.

Congress may pass valid laws to protect children from abuse, and it has. The prospect of crime, however, by itself does not justify laws suppressing protected speech.

As a general principle, the First Amendment bars the government from dictating what we see or read or speak or hear. The freedom of speech has its limits; it does not embrace certain categories of speech, including defamation, incitement, obscenity, and pornography produced with real children. While these categories may be prohibited without violating the First Amendment, none of them includes the speech prohibited by the CPPA.

As we have noted, the CPPA is much more than a supplement to the existing federal prohibition on obscenity. The CPPA extends to images that appear to depict a minor engaging in sexually explicit activity without regard to the *Miller* requirements. The materials need not appeal to the prurient interest. Any depiction of sexually explicit activity, no matter how it is presented, is proscribed. The CPPA applies to a picture in a psychology manual, as well as a movie depicting the horrors of sexual abuse. It is not necessary, moreover, that the image be patently offensive. Pictures of what appear to be 17-year-olds engaging in sexually explicit activity do not in every case contravene community standards.

The CPPA prohibits speech despite its serious literary, artistic, political, or scientific value. The statute proscribes the visual depiction of an idea – that of teenagers engaging in sexual activity – that is a fact of modern society and has been a theme in art and literature throughout the ages. Under the CPPA, images are prohibited so long as the persons appear to be under 18 years of age. This is higher than the legal age for marriage in many States, as well as the age at which persons may consent to sexual relations.

Both themes – teenage sexual activity and the sexual abuse of children – have inspired countless literary works. William Shakespeare created the most famous pair of teenage lovers, one of whom is just 13 years of age.

Contemporary movies pursue similar themes. Last year's Academy Awards featured the movie, Traffic, which was nominated for Best Picture. The film portrays a teenager, identified as a 16-year-old, who becomes addicted to drugs. The viewer sees the degradation of her addiction, which in the end leads her to a filthy room to trade sex for drugs.

Our society, like other cultures, has empathy and enduring fascination with the lives and destinies of the young. Art and literature express the vital interest we all have in the formative years we ourselves once knew, when wounds can be so grievous, disappointment so profound, and mistaken choices so tragic, but when moral acts and self-fulfillment are still in reach. Whether or not the films we mention violate the CPPA, they explore themes within the wide sweep of the statute's prohibitions. If these films, or hundreds of others of lesser note that explore those subjects, contain a single graphic depiction of sexual activity within the statutory definition, the possessor of the film would be subject to severe punishment without inquiry into the work's redeeming value. This is inconsistent with an essential First Amendment rule: The artistic merit of a work does not depend on the presence of a single explicit scene. For this reason, and the others we have noted, the CPPA cannot be read to prohibit obscenity, because it lacks the required link between its prohibitions and the affront to community standards prohibited by the definition of obscenity.

The Government seeks to address this deficiency by arguing that speech prohibited by the CPPA is virtually indistinguishable from child pornography, which may be banned without regard to whether it depicts works of value. Where the images are themselves the product of child sexual abuse, *Ferber* recognized that the State had an interest in stamping it out without regard to any judgment about its content. The production of the work, not its content, was the target of the statute.

Ferber upheld a prohibition on the distribution and sale of child pornography, as well as its production, because these acts were "intrinsically related" to the sexual abuse of children in two ways.

In contrast to the speech in *Ferber*, speech that itself is the record of sexual abuse, the CPPA prohibits speech that records no crime and creates no victims by its production. Virtual child pornography is not "intrinsically related" to the sexual abuse of children, as were the materials in *Ferber*. 458 U.S. at 759. While the Government asserts that the images can lead to actual instances of child abuse, the causal link is contingent and indirect. The harm does not necessarily follow from the speech, but depends upon some unquantified potential for subsequent criminal acts.

Ferber not only referred to the distinction between actual and virtual child pornography, it relied on it as a reason supporting its holding. *Ferber* provides no support for a statute that eliminates the distinction and makes the alternative mode criminal as well.

III

The CPPA is inconsistent with *Miller* and finds no support in *Ferber*. The Government seeks to justify its prohibitions in other ways. It argues that the CPPA is necessary because pedophiles may use virtual child pornography to seduce children. There are many things innocent in themselves, however, such as cartoons, video games, and candy, that might be used for immoral purposes, yet we would not expect those to be prohibited because they can be misused.

Here, the Government wants to keep speech from children not to protect them from its content but to protect them from those who would commit other crimes. The principle, however, remains the same: The Government cannot ban speech fit for adults simply because it may fall into the hands of children.

The Government submits further that virtual child pornography whets the appetites of pedophiles and encourages them to engage in illegal conduct. This rationale cannot sustain the provision in question. The mere tendency of speech to encourage unlawful acts is not a sufficient reason for banning it.

Without a significantly stronger, more direct connection, the Government may not prohibit speech on the ground that it may encourage pedophiles to engage in illegal conduct.

The Government next argues that its objective of eliminating the market for pornography produced using real children necessitates a prohibition on virtual images as well. Virtual images, the Government contends, are indistinguishable from real ones; they are part of the same market and are often exchanged. In this way, it is said, virtual images promote the trafficking in works produced through the exploitation of real children. The hypothesis is somewhat implausible. If virtual images were identical to illegal child pornography, the illegal images would be driven from the market by the indistinguishable substitutes. Few pornographers would risk prosecution by abusing real children if fictional, computerized images would suffice.

Finally, the Government says that the possibility of producing images by using computer imaging makes it very difficult for it to prosecute those who produce pornography by using real children. The argument, in essence, is that protected speech may be banned as a means to ban unprotected speech. This analysis turns the First Amendment upside down.

Protected speech does not become unprotected merely because it resembles the latter. The Constitution requires the reverse.

In sum, § 2256(8)(B) covers materials beyond the categories recognized in *Ferber* and *Miller*, and the reasons the Government offers in support of limiting the freedom of speech have no justification in our precedents or in the law of the First Amendment. The provision abridges the freedom to engage in a substantial amount of lawful speech. For this reason, it is overbroad and unconstitutional.

IV

Respondents challenge § 2256(8)(D) as well. This provision bans depictions of sexually explicit conduct that are "advertised, promoted, presented, described, or distributed in such a manner that conveys the impression that the material is or contains a visual depiction of a minor engaging in sexually explicit conduct." The parties treat the section as nearly identical to the provision prohibiting materials that appear to be child pornography. In the Government's view, the difference between the two is that "the 'conveys the impression' provision requires the jury to assess the material at issue in light of the manner in which it is promoted." The Government's assumption, however, is that the determination would still depend principally upon the content of the prohibited work.

We disagree with this view. The CPPA prohibits sexually explicit materials that "convey the impression" they depict minors. While that phrase may sound like the "appears to be" prohibition in § 2256(8)(B), it requires little judgment about the content of the image. Under § 2256(8)(D), the work must be sexually explicit, but otherwise the content is irrelevant. Even if a film contains no sexually explicit scenes involving minors, it could be treated as child pornography if the title and trailers convey the impression that the scenes would be found in the movie. The determination turns on how the speech is presented, not on what is depicted.

The Government does not offer a serious defense of this provision, and the other arguments it makes in support of the CPPA do not bear on § 2256(8)(D).

The First Amendment requires a more precise restriction. For this reason, § 2256(8)(D) is substantially overbroad and in violation of the First Amendment.

V

For the reasons we have set forth, the prohibitions of §§ 2256(8)(B) and 2256(8)(D) are overbroad and unconstitutional. Having reached this conclusion, we need not address respondents' further contention that the provisions are unconstitutional because of vague statutory language.

The judgment of the Court of Appeals is affirmed.

It is so ordered.

CONCURRENCE: THOMAS, Justice:

In my view, the Government's most persuasive asserted interest in support of the Child Pornography Prevention Act of 1996 (CPPA), 18 U.S.C. § 2251 *et seq.*, is the prosecution rationale – that persons who possess and disseminate pornographic images of real children may escape conviction by claiming that the images are computer-generated, thereby raising a reasonable doubt as to their guilt. At this time, however, the Government asserts only that defendants *raise* such defenses, not that they have done so successfully. In fact, the Government points to no case in which a defendant has been acquitted based on a "computer-generated images" defense. While this speculative interest cannot support the broad reach of the CPPA, technology may evolve to the point where it becomes impossible to enforce actual child pornography laws because the Government cannot prove that certain pornographic images are of real children. In the event this occurs, the Government should not be foreclosed from enacting a regulation of virtual child pornography that contains an appropriate affirmative defense or some other narrowly drawn restriction.

[I]f technological advances thwart prosecution of "unlawful speech," the Government may well have a compelling interest in barring or otherwise regulating some narrow category of "lawful speech" in order to enforce effectively laws against pornography made through the abuse of real children. The Court does leave open the possibility that a more complete affirmative defense could save a statute's constitutionality, implicitly accepting that some regulation of virtual child pornography might be constitutional.

DISSENT: REHNQUIST, Chief Justice:

Congress has a compelling interest in ensuring the ability to enforce prohibitions of actual child pornography, and we should defer to its findings that rapidly advancing technology soon will make it all but impossible to do so.

I also agree that serious First Amendment concerns would arise were the Government ever to prosecute someone for simple distribution or possession of a film with literary or artistic value, such as "Traffic" or "American Beauty." I write separately, however, because the Child Pornography Prevention Act of 1996 (CPPA), 18 U.S.C. § 2251 et seq., need not be construed to reach such materials.

We normally do not strike down a statute on First Amendment grounds "when a limiting instruction has been or could be placed on the challenged statute." This case should be treated no differently.

Other than computer generated images that are virtually indistinguishable from real children engaged in sexually explicitly conduct, the CPPA can be limited so as not to reach any material that was not already unprotected before the CPPA. The CPPA's definition of "sexually explicit conduct" is quite explicit in this regard. It makes clear that the statute only reaches "visual depictions" of:

> Actual or simulated ... sexual intercourse, including genital-genital, oral-genital, anal-genital, or oral-anal, whether between persons of the same or opposite sex; ... bestiality; ... masturbation; ... sadistic or masochistic abuse; ... or lascivious exhibition of the genitals or pubic area of any person.

The Court and JUSTICE O'CONNOR suggest that this very graphic definition reaches the depiction of youthful looking adult actors engaged in suggestive sexual activity, presumably because the definition extends to "simulated" intercourse. Read as a whole, however, I think the definition reaches only the sort of "hard core of child pornography" that we found without protection in *Ferber*. So construed, the CPPA bans visual depictions of youthful looking adult actors engaged in *actual* sexual activity; mere *suggestions* of sexual activity, such as youthful looking adult actors squirming under a blanket, are more akin to written descriptions than visual depictions, and thus fall outside the purview of the statute.

Indeed, we should be loath to construe a statute as banning film portrayals of Shakespearian tragedies, without some indication – from text or legislative history – that such a result was intended. In fact, Congress explicitly instructed that such a reading of the CPPA would be wholly unwarranted.

This narrow reading of "sexually explicit conduct" not only accords with the text of the CPPA and the intentions of Congress; it is exactly how the phrase was understood prior to the broadening gloss the Court gives it today. Indeed, had "sexually explicit conduct" been thought to reach the sort of material the Court says it does, then films such as "Traffic" and "American Beauty" would not have been made the way they were. "Traffic" won its Academy Award in 2001. "American Beauty" won its Academy Award in 2000. But the CPPA has been on the books, and has been enforced, since 1996. The chill felt by the Court ("Few legitimate movie producers . . . would risk distributing images in or near the uncertain reach of this law"), has apparently never been felt by those who actually make movies.

The First Amendment does not protect the panderer. Thus, materials promoted as conveying the impression that they depict actual minors engaged in sexually explicit conduct do not escape regulation merely because they might warrant First Amendment protection if promoted in a different manner.

The Court says that "conveys the impression" goes well beyond *Ginzburg* to "prohibit [the] possession of material described, or pandered, as child pornography by someone earlier in the distribution chain." The Court's concern is that an individual who merely possesses protected materials (such as videocassettes of "Traffic" or "American Beauty") might offend the CPPA regardless of whether the individual actually intended to possess materials containing unprotected images.

This concern is a legitimate one, but there is, again, no need or reason to construe the statute this way.

In sum, while potentially impermissible applications of the CPPA may exist, I doubt that they would be "substantial . . . in relation to the statute's plainly legitimate sweep." The aim of ensuring the enforceability of our Nation's child pornography laws is a compelling one. The CPPA is targeted to this aim by extending the definition of child pornography to reach computer-generated images that are virtually indistinguishable from real children engaged in sexually explicit conduct. The statute need not be read to do any more than precisely this, which is not offensive to the First Amendment.

For these reasons, I would construe the CPPA in a manner consistent with the First Amendment, reverse the Court of Appeals' judgment, and uphold the statute in its entirety.

CONCURRENCE AND DISSENT: O'CONNOR, Justice:

The Child Pornography Prevention Act of 1996 (CPPA), 18 U.S.C. § 2251 *et seq.*, proscribes the "knowing" reproduction, distribution, sale, reception, or possession of images that fall under the statute's definition of child pornography, § 2252A(a).

The CPPA provides for two affirmative defenses. First, a defendant is not liable for possession if the defendant possesses less than three proscribed images and promptly destroys such images or reports the matter to law enforcement. Second, a defendant is not liable for the remaining acts proscribed in § 2252A(a) if the images involved were produced using only adult subjects and are not presented in such a manner as to "convey the impression" they contain depictions of minors engaging in sexually explicit conduct.

This litigation involves a facial challenge to the CPPA's prohibitions of pornographic images that "appear to be . . . of a minor" and of material that "conveys the impression" that it contains pornographic images of minors. While I agree with the Court's judgment that the First Amendment requires that the latter prohibition be struck down, I disagree with its decision to strike down the former prohibition in its entirety. The "appears to be . . . of a minor" language in § 2256(8)(B) covers two categories of speech: pornographic images of adults that look like children ("youthful-adult pornography") and pornographic images of children created wholly on a computer, without using any actual children ("virtual-child pornography"). The Court concludes, correctly, that the CPPA's ban on youthful-adult pornography is overbroad. In my view, however, respondents fail to present sufficient evidence to demonstrate that the ban on virtual-child pornography is overbroad. Because invalidation due to overbreadth is such "strong medicine," I would strike down the prohibition of pornography that "appears to be" of minors only insofar as it is applied to the class of youthful-adult pornography.

[Section I is omitted.]

II

I disagree with the Court that the CPPA's prohibition of virtual-child pornography is overbroad. Before I reach that issue, there are two preliminary questions: whether the ban on virtual-child pornography fails strict scrutiny and whether that ban is unconstitutionally vague. I would answer both in the negative.

The Court has long recognized that the Government has a compelling interest in protecting our Nation's children. This interest is promoted by efforts directed against sexual offenders and actual-child pornography. These efforts, in turn, are supported by the CPPA's ban on virtual-child pornography. Such images whet the appetites of child molesters. Of even more serious concern is the prospect that defendants indicted for the production, distribution, or possession of actual-child pornography may evade liability by claiming that the images attributed to them are in fact computer-generated. Respondents may be correct that no defendant has successfully employed this tactic. But, given the rapid pace of advances in computer-graphics technology, the Government's concern is reasonable.

Respondents argue that, even if the Government has a compelling interest to justify banning virtual-child pornography, the "appears to be . . . of a minor" language is not narrowly tailored to serve that interest. They assert that the CPPA would capture even cartoon-sketches or statues of children that were sexually suggestive. Such images surely could not be used, for instance, to seduce children. I agree. A better interpretation of "appears to be . . . of" is "virtually indistinguishable from" – an interpretation that would not cover the examples respondents provide. Not only does the text of the statute comfortably bear this narrowing interpretation, the interpretation comports with the language that Congress repeatedly used in its findings of fact.

Reading the statute only to bar images that are virtually indistinguishable from actual children would not only assure that the ban on virtual-child pornography is narrowly tailored, but would also assuage any fears that the "appears to be . . . of a minor" language is vague. The narrow reading greatly limits any risks from "discriminatory enforcement."

The Court concludes that the CPPA's ban on virtual-child pornography is overbroad. The basis for this holding is unclear. Respondents provide no examples of films or other materials that are wholly computer-generated and contain images that "appear to be . . . of minors" engaging in indecent conduct, but that have serious value or do not facilitate child abuse. Their overbreadth challenge therefore fails.

III

I would strike the "appears to be" provision only insofar as it is applied to the subset of cases involving youthful-adult pornography.

In sum, I would strike down the CPPA's ban on material that "conveys the impression" that it contains actual-child pornography, but uphold the ban on pornographic depictions that "appear to be" of minors so long as it is not applied to youthful-adult pornography.

So the Supreme Court has not been willing to accept as a "compelling" interest to support child pornography legislation the idea that the very existence of child pornography encourages the molestation of children. The Court explicitly underlines the fact that the apparent age of the participants in visual depictions of sexual activities can be factored into the question of whether the material is obscene. That is, the apparent age of the participants can be considered in applying "contemporary community standards." So the material might still be regulated under obscenity law. Even this suggestion, however, did not satisfy those who wished to illegalize all visual depictions of child pornography, because obscenity may still be possessed in the home.

14. Advertising and Spam

Introduction

Generally any action designed to draw public attention to an organization, product, or service is considered "advertising." Certainly web pages qualify as an advertising medium.

Advertising is "speech" and is protected by the First Amendment. However, recall from Chapter 12 on Constitutional Law that commercial speech may be regulated or even prohibited if it is misleading or pertains to an illegal product, or if regulation of the commercial speech directly advances a substantial (i.e., not necessarily compelling) state interest. Examples include the regulation of ads about cigarettes, about whiskey, and about gambling. Television and radio networks screen proposed ads to weed out those that are "offensive." Will such regulations apply equally on the Net? It's still too early to be sure.

The following Supreme Court case addresses one particular type of advertising – by attorneys – and illustrates the criteria applied in decisions regarding whether advertising may be regulated or even prohibited.

Advertising and Spam: Case 1

BATES ET AL. v. STATE BAR OF ARIZONA

No. 76-316

SUPREME COURT OF THE UNITED STATES

433 U.S. 350; 97 S. Ct. 2691; 53 L. Ed. 2d 810; 1977 U.S. LEXIS 23; 1977-2 Trade Cas. (CCH) P61,573; 51 Ohio Misc. 1; 5 Ohio Op. 3d 60; 2 Media L. Rep. 2097

Argued January 18, 1977

June 27, 1977; as amended Petition for Rehearing Denied October 3, 1977

BLACKMUN, J., delivered the opinion of the Court, in which BRENNAN, WHITE, MARSHALL, and STEVENS, JJ., joined, and in Parts I and II of which BURGER, C.J., and STEWART, POWELL, and REHNQUIST, JJ., joined. BURGER, C.J., filed an opinion concurring in part and dissenting in part. POWELL, J., filed an opinion concurring in part and dissenting in part, in which STEWART, J., joined. REHNQUIST, J., filed an opinion dissenting in part, post.

OPINION: BLACKMUN, Justice:

As part of its regulation of the Arizona Bar, the Supreme Court of that State has imposed and enforces a disciplinary rule that restricts advertising by attorneys. This case presents two issues: whether §§ 1 and 2 of the Sherman Act, 15 U.S.C. §§ 1 and 2, forbid such state regulation, and whether the operation of the rule violates the First Amendment, made applicable to the States through the Fourteenth.

I

Appellants John R. Bates and Van O'Steen are attorneys licensed to practice law in the State of Arizona. As such, they are members of the appellee, the State Bar of Arizona. After admission to the bar in 1972, appellants worked as attorneys with the Maricopa County Legal Aid Society.

In March 1974, appellants left the Society and opened a law office, which they call a "legal clinic," in Phoenix. Their aim was to provide legal services at modest fees to persons of moderate income who did not qualify for governmental legal aid. In order to achieve this end, they would accept only routine matters, such as uncontested divorces, uncontested adoptions, simple personal bankruptcies, and changes of name, for which costs could be kept down by extensive use of paralegals, automatic typewriting equipment, and standardized forms and office procedures. More complicated cases, such as contested divorces, would not be accepted. Because appellants set their prices so as to have a relatively low return on each case they handled, they depended on substantial volume.

After conducting their practice in this manner for two years, appellants concluded that their practice and clinical concept could not survive unless the availability of legal services at low cost was advertised and, in particular, fees were advertised. Consequently, in order to generate the necessary flow of business, that is, "to attract clients," appellants on February 22, 1976, placed an advertisement in the Arizona Republic, a daily newspaper of general circulation in the Phoenix metropolitan area. [T]he advertisement stated that appellants were offering "legal services at very reasonable fees," and listed their fees for certain services.

Appellants concede that the advertisement constituted a clear violation of Disciplinary Rule 2-101(B), incorporated in Rule 29(a) of the Supreme Court of Arizona, 17A Ariz. Rev. Stat., p. 26 (Supp. 1976). The disciplinary rule provides in part:

> (B) A lawyer shall not publicize himself, or his partner, or associate, or any other lawyer affiliated with him or his firm, as a lawyer through newspaper or magazine advertisements, radio or television announcements, display advertisements in the city or telephone directories or other means of commercial publicity, nor shall he authorize or permit others to do so in his behalf.

After the filing of a complaint initiated by the president of the State Bar, a hearing was held before a three member Special Local Administrative Committee. Although the committee took the position that it could not consider an attack on the validity of the rule, it allowed the parties to develop a record on which such a challenge could be based. The committee recommended that each of the appellants be suspended from the practice of law for not less than six months. Upon further review by the Board of Governors of the State Bar, the Board recommended only a one-week suspension for each appellant, the weeks to run consecutively.

Appellants, as permitted by the Supreme Court's Rule 37, then sought review in the Supreme Court of Arizona, arguing, among other things, that the disciplinary rule violated §§ 1 and 2 of the Sherman Act because of its tendency to limit competition, and that the rule infringed their First Amendment rights. The court rejected both claims. The plurality may have viewed with some skepticism the claim that a restraint on advertising might have an adverse effect on competition. But, even if the rule might otherwise violate the Act, the plurality concluded that the regulation was exempt from Sherman Act attack because the rule "is an activity of the State of Arizona acting as sovereign." The regulation thus was held to be shielded from the Sherman Act by the state-action exemption of *Parker v. Brown*, 317 U.S. 341 (1943).

Turning to the First Amendment issue, the plurality noted that restrictions on professional advertising have survived constitutional challenge in the past. The plurality held that Disciplinary Rule 2-101(B) passed First Amendment muster. Because the court, in agreement with the Board of Governors, felt that appellants' advertising "was done in good faith to test the constitutionality of DR 2-101(B)," it reduced the sanction to censure only.

Of particular interest here is the opinion of Mr. Justice Holohan in dissent. In his view, the case should have been framed in terms of "the right of the public as consumers and citizens to know about the activities of the legal profession," rather than as one involving merely the regulation of a profession. Observed in this light, he felt that the rule performed a substantial disservice to the public:

> Obviously the information of what lawyers charge is important for private economic decisions by those in need of legal services. Such information is also helpful, perhaps indispensable, to the formation of an intelligent opinion by the public on how well the legal system is working and whether it should be regulated or even altered.... The rule at issue prevents access to such information by the public.

Although the dissenter acknowledged that some types of advertising might cause confusion and deception, he felt that the remedy was to ban that form, rather than all advertising. Thus, despite his "personal dislike of the concept of advertising by attorneys," he found the ban unconstitutional.

II

The Sherman Act

In *Parker v. Brown*, 317 U.S. 341 (1943), this Court held that the Sherman Act was not intended to apply against certain state action. We agree.

Of course, Parker v. Brown has not been the final word on the matter. In two recent cases the Court has considered the state-action exemption to the Sherman Act and found it inapplicable for one reason or another. *Goldfarb v. Virginia State Bar*, 421 U.S. 773 (1975); *Cantor v. Detroit Edison Co.*, 428 U.S. 579 (1976). Goldfarb and Cantor, however, are distinguishable, and their reasoning supports our conclusion here.

In *Goldfarb* we held that § 1 of the Sherman Act was violated by the publication of a minimum-fee schedule by a county bar association and by its enforcement by the State Bar. The schedule and its enforcement mechanism operated to create a rigid price floor for services and thus constituted a classic example of price fixing. This Court concluded that the action was not protected, emphasizing that "we need not inquire further into the state-action question because it cannot fairly be said that the State of Virginia through its Supreme Court Rules required the anticompetitive activities of either respondent." In the instant case, by contrast, the challenged restraint is the affirmative command of the Arizona Supreme Court. That court is the ultimate body wielding the State's power over the practice of law and, thus, the restraint is "compelled by direction of the State acting as a sovereign."

Appellants seek to draw solace from *Cantor*. The defendant in that case, an electric utility, distributed light bulbs to its residential customers without additional charge, including the cost in its state-regulated utility rates. The plaintiff, a retailer who sold light bulbs, brought suit, claiming that the utility was using its monopoly power in the distribution of electricity to restrain competition in the sale of bulbs. The Court held that the utility could not immunize itself from Sherman Act attack by embodying its challenged practices in a tariff approved by a state commission. Since the disciplinary rule at issue here is derived from the Code of Professional Responsibility of the American Bar Association, appellants argue by analogy to Cantor that no immunity should result from the bar's success in having the Code adopted by the State. They also assert that the interest embodied in the Sherman Act must prevail over the state interest in regulating the bar. Particularly is this the case, they claim, because the advertising ban is not tailored so as to intrude upon the federal interest to the minimum extent necessary.

We believe, however, that the context in which *Cantor* arose is critical. First, and most obviously, *Cantor* would have been an entirely different case if the claim had been directed against a public official or public agency, rather than against a private party. Here, the appellants' claims are against the State. The Arizona Supreme Court is the real party in interest; it adopted the rules, and it is the ultimate trier of fact and law in the enforcement process.

Second, the Court emphasized in *Cantor* that the State had no independent regulatory interest in the market for light bulbs. In contrast, the regulation of the activities of the bar is at the core of the State's power to protect the public. Federal interference with a State's traditional regulation of a profession is entirely unlike the intrusion the Court sanctioned in *Cantor*.

The disciplinary rules reflect a clear articulation of the State's policy with regard to professional behavior. Moreover, the rules are subject to pointed re-examination by the policy maker – the Arizona Supreme Court – in enforcement proceedings.

We conclude that the Arizona Supreme Court's determination that appellants' Sherman Act claim is barred by the *Parker v. Brown* exemption must be affirmed.

BUT, the Supreme Court says the Arizona Supreme Court was *wrong* about the First Amendment claim.

III

The First Amendment

A

Last Term, in *Virginia Pharmacy Board v. Virginia Consumer Council*, 425 U.S. 748 (1976), the Court considered the validity under the First Amendment of a Virginia statute declaring that a pharmacist was guilty of "unprofessional conduct" if he advertised prescription drug prices. The pharmacist would then be subject to a monetary penalty or the suspension or revocation of his license. The statute thus effectively prevented the advertising of prescription drug price information. We recognized that the pharmacist who desired to advertise did not wish to report any particularly newsworthy fact or to comment on any cultural, philosophical, or political subject; his desired communication was characterized simply: "'I will sell you the X prescription drug at the Y price.'" Nonetheless, we held that commercial speech of that kind was entitled to the protection of the First Amendment.

Our analysis began with the observation that our cases long have protected speech even though it is in the form of a paid advertisement. [A] consideration of competing interests reinforced our view that such speech should not be withdrawn from protection merely because it proposed a mundane commercial transaction. Even though the speaker's interest is largely economic, the Court has protected such speech in certain contexts. The listener's interest is substantial: the consumer's concern for the free flow of commercial speech often may be far keener than his concern for urgent political dialogue. Moreover, significant societal interests are served by such speech. Advertising, though entirely commercial, may often carry information of import to significant issues of the day. And commercial speech serves to inform the public of the availability, nature, and prices of products and services, and thus performs an indispensable role in the allocation of resources in a free enterprise system. In short, such speech serves individual and societal interests in assuring informed and reliable decisionmaking.

Arrayed against these substantial interests in the free flow of commercial speech were a number of proffered justifications for the advertising ban. Central among them were claims that the ban was essential to the maintenance of professionalism among licensed pharmacists. It was asserted that advertising would create price competition that might cause the pharmacist to economize at the customer's expense. Moreover, it was said, advertising would cause consumers to price-shop, thereby undermining the pharmacist's effort to monitor the drug use of a regular customer so as to ensure that the prescribed drug would not provoke an allergic reaction or be incompatible with another substance the customer was consuming. Finally, it was argued that advertising would reduce the image of the pharmacist as a skilled and specialized craftsman.

Although acknowledging that the State had a strong interest in maintaining professionalism among pharmacists, this Court concluded that the proffered justifications were inadequate to support the advertising ban. High professional standards were assured in large part by the close regulation to which pharmacists in Virginia were subject. [W]e observed that "on close inspection it is seen that the State's protectiveness of its citizens rests in large measure on the advantages of their being kept in ignorance." But we noted the presence of a potent alternative to this "highly paternalistic" approach: "That alternative is to assume that this information is not in itself harmful, that people will perceive their own best interests if only they are well enough informed, and that the best means to that end is to open the channels of communication rather than to close them." The choice between the dangers of suppressing information and the dangers arising from its free flow was seen as precisely the choice "that the First Amendment makes for us."

We have set out this detailed summary of the *Pharmacy* opinion because the conclusion that Arizona's disciplinary rule is violative of the First Amendment might be said to flow a fortiori from it. Like the Virginia statutes, the disciplinary rule serves to inhibit the free flow of commercial information and to keep the public in ignorance. Because of the possibility, however, that the differences among professions might bring different constitutional considerations into play, we specifically reserved judgment as to other professions.

In the instant case we are confronted with the arguments directed explicitly toward the regulation of advertising by licensed attorneys.

B

The issue presently before us is a narrow one. First, we need not address the peculiar problems associated with advertising claims relating to the quality of legal services. Appellee does not suggest, nor do we perceive, that appellants' advertisement contained claims, extravagant or otherwise, as to the quality of services. Second, we also need not resolve the problems associated with in-person solicitation of clients – at the hospital room or the accident site, or in any other situation that breeds undue influence – by attorneys or their agents or "runners." Third, we note that appellee's criticism of advertising by attorneys does not apply with much force to some of the basic factual content of advertising: information as to the attorney's name, address, and telephone number, office hours, and the like. We recognize, however, that an advertising diet limited to such spartan fare would provide scant nourishment.

The heart of the dispute before us today is whether lawyers also may constitutionally advertise the prices at which certain routine services will be performed. Numerous justifications are proffered for the restriction of such price advertising. We consider each in turn:

1. The Adverse Effect on Professionalism

It is claimed that price advertising will bring about commercialization, which will undermine the attorney's sense of dignity and self-worth. Advertising is also said to erode the client's trust in his attorney: Once the client perceives that the lawyer is motivated by profit, his confidence that the attorney is acting out of a commitment to the client's welfare is jeopardized. And advertising is said to tarnish the dignified public image of the profession.

At its core, the argument presumes that attorneys must conceal from themselves and from their clients the real-life fact that lawyers earn their livelihood at the bar. We suspect that few attorneys engage in such self-deception. And rare is the client, moreover, even one of modest means, who enlists the aid of an attorney with the expectation that his services will be rendered free of charge. In fact, the American Bar Association advises that an attorney should reach "a clear agreement with his client as to the basis of the fee charges to be made," and that this is to be done "[a]s soon as feasible after a lawyer has been employed." If the commercial basis of the relationship is to be promptly disclosed on ethical grounds, once the client is in the office, it seems inconsistent to condemn the candid revelation of the same information before he arrives at that office.

Moreover, the assertion that advertising will diminish the attorney's reputation in the community is open to question. Bankers and engineers advertise, and yet these professions are not regarded as undignified.

In fact, it has been suggested that the failure of lawyers to advertise creates public disillusionment with the profession. The absence of advertising may be seen to reflect the profession's failure to reach out and serve the community: Studies reveal that many persons do not obtain counsel even when they perceive a need because of the feared price of services or because of an inability to locate a competent attorney. Indeed, cynicism with regard to the profession may be created by the fact that it long has publicly eschewed advertising, while condoning the actions of the attorney who structures his social or civic associations so as to provide contacts with potential clients.

It appears that the ban on advertising originated as a rule of etiquette and not as a rule of ethics. Early lawyers in Great Britain viewed the law as a form of public service, rather than as a means of earning a living, and they looked down on "trade" as unseemly.

In other words, they were all from wealthy families.

Eventually, the attitude toward advertising fostered by this view evolved into an aspect of the ethics of the profession. But habit and tradition are not in themselves an adequate answer to a constitutional challenge. In this day, we do not belittle the person who earns his living by the strength of his arm or the force of his mind. Since the belief that lawyers are somehow "above" trade has become an anachronism, the historical foundation for the advertising restraint has crumbled.

2. The Inherently Misleading Nature of Attorney Advertising

We are not persuaded that restrained professional advertising by lawyers inevitably will be misleading. Although many services performed by attorneys are indeed unique, it is doubtful that any attorney would or could advertise fixed prices for services of that type. The only services that lend themselves to advertising are the routine ones: the uncontested divorce, the simple adoption, the uncontested personal bankruptcy, the change of name, and the like – the very services advertised by appellants. Although the precise service demanded in each task may vary slightly, and although legal services are not fungible, these facts do not make advertising misleading so long as the attorney does the necessary work at the advertised price.

The appellee State Bar itself sponsors a Legal Services Program in which the participating attorneys agree to perform services like those advertised by the appellants at standardized rates. We thus find of little force the assertion that advertising is misleading because of an inherent lack of standardization in legal services.

It is unlikely that many people go to an attorney merely to ascertain if they have a clean bill of legal health. Rather, attorneys are likely to be employed to perform specific tasks. Although the client may not know the detail involved in performing the task, he no doubt is able to identify the service he desires at the level of generality to which advertising lends itself.

Advertising does not provide a complete foundation on which to select an attorney. But it seems peculiar to deny the consumer, on the ground that the information is incomplete, at least some of the relevant information needed to reach an informed decision. Moreover, the argument assumes that the public is not sophisticated enough to realize the limitations of advertising, and that the public is better kept in ignorance than trusted with correct but incomplete information. We suspect the argument rests on an underestimation of the public. In any event, we view as dubious any justification that is based on the benefits of public ignorance. If the naivete of the public will cause advertising by attorneys to be misleading, then it is the bar's role to assure that the populace is sufficiently informed as to enable it to place advertising in its proper perspective.

3. The Adverse Effect on the Administration of Justice

Advertising is said to have the undesirable effect of stirring up litigation. The judicial machinery is designed to serve those who feel sufficiently aggrieved to bring forward their claims. Advertising, it is argued, serves to encourage the assertion of legal rights in the courts, thereby undesirably unsettling societal repose.

Although advertising might increase the use of the judicial machinery, we cannot accept the notion that it is always better for a person to suffer a wrong silently than to redress it by legal action.

That is, "so what?"

As the bar acknowledges, "the middle 70% of our population is not being reached or served adequately by the legal profession." Among the reasons for this underutilization is fear of the cost, and an inability to locate a suitable lawyer. Advertising is the traditional mechanism in a free-market economy for a supplier to inform a potential purchaser of the availability and terms of exchange. The disciplinary rule at issue likely has served to burden access to legal services, particularly for the not-quite-poor and the unknowledgeable. A rule allowing restrained advertising would be in accord with the bar's obligation to "facilitate the process of intelligent selection of lawyers, and to assist in making legal services fully available."

4. The Undesirable Economic Effects of Advertising

It is claimed that advertising will increase the overhead costs of the profession, and that these costs then will be passed along to consumers in the form of increased fees. Moreover, it is claimed that the additional cost of practice will create a substantial entry barrier, deterring or preventing young attorneys from penetrating the market and entrenching the position of the bar's established members.

These two arguments seem dubious at best. Neither distinguishes lawyers from others, see *Virginia Pharmacy Board v. Virginia Consumer Council*, 425 U.S., at 768, and neither appears relevant to the First Amendment. The ban on advertising serves to increase the difficulty of discovering the lowest cost seller of acceptable ability. As a result, to this extent attorneys are isolated from competition, and the incentive to price competitively is reduced. It is entirely possible that advertising will serve to reduce, not advance, the cost of legal services to the consumer.

In the absence of advertising, an attorney must rely on his contacts with the community to generate a flow of business. In view of the time necessary to develop such contacts, the ban in fact serves to perpetuate the market position of established attorneys. Consideration of entry-barrier problems would urge that advertising be allowed so as to aid the new competitor in penetrating the market.

5. The Adverse Effect of Advertising on the Quality of Service

It is argued that the attorney may advertise a given "package" of service at a set price, and will be inclined to provide, by indiscriminate use, the standard package regardless of whether it fits the client's needs.

Restraints on advertising, however, are an ineffective way of deterring shoddy work.

6. The Difficulties of Enforcement

Finally, it is argued that the wholesale restriction is justified by the problems of enforcement if any other course is taken. After-the-fact action by the consumer lured by such advertising may not provide a realistic restraint because of the inability of the layman to assess whether the service he has received meets professional standards. Thus, the vigilance of a regulatory agency will be required. But because of the numerous purveyors of services, the overseeing of advertising will be burdensome.

It is at least somewhat incongruous for the opponents of advertising to extol the virtues and altruism of the legal profession at one point, and, at another, to assert that its members will seize the opportunity to mislead and distort. We suspect that, with advertising, most lawyers will behave as they always have: They will abide by their solemn oaths to uphold the integrity and honor of their profession and of the legal system.

For every attorney who overreaches through advertising, there will be thousands of others who will be candid and honest and straightforward.

In sum, we are not persuaded that any of the preferred justifications rise to the level of an acceptable reason for the suppression of all advertising by attorneys.

C

Is, then, appellants' advertisement outside the scope of basic First Amendment protection? Aside from general claims as to the undesirability of any advertising by attorneys, a matter considered above, appellee argues that appellants' advertisement is misleading, and hence unprotected, in three particulars: (a) the advertisement makes reference to a "legal clinic," an allegedly undefined term; (b) the advertisement claims that appellants offer services at "very reasonable" prices, and, at least with regard to an uncontested divorce, the advertised price is not a bargain; and (c) the advertisement does not inform the consumer that he may obtain a name change without the services of an attorney. On this record, these assertions are unpersuasive. We suspect that the public would readily understand the term "legal clinic" – if, indeed, it focused on the term at all – to refer to an operation like that of appellants' that is geared to provide standardized and multiple services. And the clinical concept in the sister profession of medicine surely by now is publicly acknowledged and understood.

As to the cost of an uncontested divorce, appellees counsel stated at oral argument that this runs from $150 to $300 in the area. Appellants advertised a fee of $175 plus a $20 court filing fee, a rate that seems "very reasonable" in light of the customary charge. Appellee's own Legal Services Program sets the rate for an uncontested divorce at $250. Of course, advertising will permit the comparison of rates among competitors, thus revealing if the rates are reasonable.

As to the final argument – the failure to disclose that a name change might be accomplished by the client without the aid of an attorney – we need only note that most legal services may be performed legally by the citizen for himself.

We conclude that it has not been demonstrated that the advertisement at issue could be suppressed.

IV

In holding that advertising by attorneys may not be subjected to blanket suppression, and that the advertisement at issue is protected, we, of course, do not hold that advertising by attorneys may not be regulated in any way. We mention some of the clearly permissible limitations on advertising not foreclosed by our holding.

Advertising that is false, deceptive, or misleading of course is subject to restraint. [W]e recognize that many of the problems in defining the boundary between deceptive and nondeceptive advertising remain to be resolved, and we expect that the bar will have a special role to play in assuring that advertising by attorneys flows both freely and cleanly.

As with other varieties of speech, it follows as well that there may be reasonable restrictions on the time, place, and manner of advertising. Advertising concerning transactions that are themselves illegal obviously may be suppressed. And the special problems of advertising on the electronic broadcast media will warrant special consideration.

What kind of "special consideration"? This is an important question, of course, but one the Court does not address.

The constitutional issue in this case is only whether the State may prevent the publication in a newspaper of appellants' truthful advertisement concerning the availability and terms of routine legal services. We rule simply that the flow of such information may not be restrained, and we therefore hold the present application of the disciplinary rule against appellants to be violative of the First Amendment.

The judgment of the Supreme Court of Arizona is therefore affirmed in part and reversed in part.

It is so ordered.

DISSENT: BURGER, Chief Justice:

I am in general agreement with MR. JUSTICE POWELL's analysis and with Part II of the Court's opinion. I particularly agree with MR. JUSTICE POWELL's statement that "today's decision will effect profound changes in the practice of law." Although the exact effect of those changes cannot now be known, I fear that they will be injurious to those whom the ban on legal advertising was designed to protect – the members of the general public in need of legal services.

Some Members of the Court apparently believe that the present case is controlled by our holding one year ago in *Virginia Pharmacy Board v. Virginia Consumer Council*, 425 U.S. 748 (1976). However, I had thought that we made most explicit that our holding there rested on the fact that the advertisement of standardized, prepackaged, name-brand drugs was at issue. In that context, the prohibition on price advertising, which had served a useful function in the days of individually compounded medicines, was no longer tied to the conditions which had given it birth. The same cannot be said with respect to legal services which, by necessity, must vary greatly from case to case. Indeed, I find it difficult, if not impossible, to identify categories of legal problems or services which are fungible in nature. Because legal services can rarely, if ever, be "standardized" and because potential clients rarely know in advance what services they do in fact need, price advertising can never give the public an accurate picture on which to base its selection of an attorney. Indeed, in the context of legal services, such incomplete information could be worse than no information at all. It could become a trap for the unwary.

The Court's opinion largely disregards these facts on the unsupported assumptions that attorneys will not advertise anything but "routine" services – which the Court totally fails to identify or define – or, if they do advertise, that the bar and the courts will be able to protect the public from those few practitioners who abuse their trust. The former notion is highly speculative and, of course, does nothing to solve the problems that this decision will create; as to the latter, the existing administrative machinery of both the profession and the courts has proved wholly inadequate to police the profession effectively. To impose the enormous new regulatory burdens called for by the Court's decision on the presently deficient machinery of the bar and courts is unrealistic; it is almost predictable that it will create problems of unmanageable proportions. To be sure, the public needs information concerning attorneys, their work, and their fees. At the same time, the public needs protection from the unscrupulous or the incompetent practitioner anxious to prey on the uniformed. It seems to me that these twin goals can best be served by permitting the organized bar to experiment with and perfect programs which would announce to the public the probable range of fees for specifically defined services and thus give putative clients some idea of potential cost liability when seeking out legal assistance.

[T]he organized bar has recently made some reforms in this sensitive area and more appear to be in the offing. Rather than allowing these efforts to bear fruit, the Court today opts for a Draconian "solution" which I believe will only breed more problems than it can conceivably resolve.

CONCURRENCE AND DISSENT: POWELL, Justice:

I agree with the Court that appellants' Sherman Act claim is barred by the *Parker v. Brown* exemption. But I cannot join the Court's holding that under the First Amendment "truthful" newspaper advertising of a lawyer's prices for "routine legal services" may not be restrained.

I

[T]he question before us is whether the application of the disciplinary rule to appellants' advertisement violates the First Amendment.

[T]he Court [assumes] that what it calls "routine" legal services are essentially no different for purposes of First Amendment analysis from prepackaged prescription drugs. In so holding, the Court fails to give appropriate weight to the two fundamental ways in which the advertising of professional services presents a different issue from that before the Court with respect to tangible products: the vastly increased potential for deception and the enhanced difficulty of effective regulation in the public interest.

A

[T]he Court's basic response in view of the acknowledged potential for deceptive advertising of "unique" services is to divide the immense range of the professional product of lawyers into two categories: "unique" and "routine." The only insight afforded by the opinion as to how one draws this line is the finding that services similar to those in appellants' advertisement are routine: "the uncontested divorce, the simple adoption, the uncontested personal bankruptcy, the change of name, and the like." What the phrase "the like" embraces is not indicated. But the advertising of such services must, in the Court's words, flow "both freely and cleanly."

This definitional problem is well illustrated by appellants' advertised willingness to obtain uncontested divorces for $195 each. A potential client can be grievously misled if he reads the advertised service as embracing all of his possible needs. A host of problems are implicated by divorce. They include alimony; support and maintenance for children; child custody; visitation rights; interests in life insurance, community property, tax refunds, and tax liabilities; and the disposition of other property rights. The processing of court papers – apparently the only service appellants provide for $100 – is usually the most straightforward and least demanding aspect of the lawyer's responsibility in a divorce case. More important from the viewpoint of the client is the diagnostic and advisory function: the pursuit of relevant inquiries of which the client would otherwise be unaware, and advice with respect to alternative arrangements that might prevent irreparable dissolution of the marriage or otherwise resolve the client's problem.

The advertising of specified services at a fixed price is not the only infirmity of the advertisement at issue. Appellants also assert that these services are offered at "very reasonable fees." That Court finds this to be an accurate statement since the advertised fee fell at the lower end of the range of customary charges. But the fee customarily charged in the locality for similar services has never been considered the sole determinant of the reasonableness of a fee. This is because reasonableness reflects both the quantity and quality of the service. Whether a fee is "very reasonable" is a matter of opinion, and not a matter of verifiable fact as the Court suggests. One unfortunate result of today's decision is that lawyers may feel free to use a wide variety of adjectives – such as "fair," "moderate," "low-cost," or "lowest in town" – to describe the bargain they offer to the public.

B

Even if one were to accept the view that some legal services are sufficiently routine to minimize the possibility of deception, there nonetheless remains a serious enforcement problem.

The Court seriously understates the difficulties, and overestimates the capabilities of the bar – or indeed of any agency public or private – to assure with a reasonable degree of effectiveness that price advertising can at the same time be both unrestrained and truthful. There are some 400,000 lawyers in this country.

And there are far more today.

In view of the sheer size of the profession, the existence of a multiplicity of jurisdictions, and the problems inherent in the maintenance of ethical standards even of a profession with established traditions, the problem of disciplinary enforcement in this country has proved to be extremely difficult. There are serious difficulties in determining whether the advertised services fall within the Court's undefined category of "routine services"; whether they are described accurately and understandably; and whether appellants' claim as to reasonableness of the fees is accurate. Even if public agencies were established to oversee professional price advertising, adequate protection of the public from deception, and of ethical lawyers from unfair competition, could prove to be a wholly intractable problem.

II

The Court observes, and I agree, that there is nothing inherently misleading in the advertisement of the cost of an initial consultation. Indeed, I would not limit the fee information to the initial conference. Where the price content of the advertisement is limited to the finite item of rate per hour devoted to the client's problem, the likelihood of deceiving or misleading is considerably less than when specific services are advertised at a fixed price.

[Section III is omitted.]

IV

I am apprehensive, despite the Court's expressed intent to proceed cautiously, that today's holding will be viewed by tens of thousands of lawyers as an invitation – by the public-spirited and the selfish lawyers alike – to engage in competitive advertising on an escalating basis. Until today, in the long history of the legal profession, it was not thought that this risk of public deception was required by the marginal First Amendment interests asserted by the Court.

DISSENT: REHNQUIST, Justice:

I dissent from Part III because I cannot agree that the First Amendment is infringed by Arizona's regulation of the essentially commercial activity of advertising legal services.

I continue to believe that the First Amendment speech provision, long regarded by this Court as a sanctuary for expressions of public importance or intellectual interest, is demeaned by invocation to protect advertisements of goods and services. I would hold quite simply that the appellants' advertisement, however truthful or reasonable it may be, is not the sort of expression that the Amendment was adopted to protect.

I therefore join Parts I and II of the Court's opinion, but dissent from Part III and from the judgment.

～

The *Bates* decision opened the floodgates for advertising by lawyers. Such advertising is so common today in so many media that it is hard to believe that it was once routinely prohibited by State Bar Associations.

False or misleading advertising is not protected by the First Amendment. The federal Lanham Act prohibits "commercial ads" that are misleading. So misleading political ads, for example, are not prohibited by the Lanham Act, nor is editorial comment.

Federal Regulators

Advertising involves a number of federal agencies. These include the Federal Trade Commission, which regulates advertising in general; the Federal Communications Commission, which shares in the FTC's regulation of advertising in the broadcast media; the Food and Drug Administration; the Department of Transportation; and the Bureau of Alcohol, Tobacco, and Firearms. In addition to the federal agencies, most states have their own regulatory agencies, so this is a regulatory jungle that can be a nightmare for the advertiser.

But it is a nightmare that is easily dispelled if the advertiser adheres to a simple principle: tell the truth, and tell the whole truth. Run ads that are straightforward and positive, and that could not mislead in any way. Do not omit relevant information about the product or service. Make sure that all claims can be substantiated.

However, it is often difficult to tell what a court might find is a misleading advertisement. This next case illustrates that point with what seems a very close call regarding misleading visual images in an ad.

Advertising and Spam: Case 2

The COCA-COLA COMPANY, Plaintiff-Appellant, v. TROPICANA PRODUCTS, INC., Defendant-Appellee

No. 82-7422, No. 1524 – August Term, 1981

UNITED STATES COURT OF APPEALS FOR THE SECOND CIRCUIT

690 F.2d 312; 1982 U.S. App. LEXIS 25203; 216 U.S.P.Q. (BNA) 272

July 16, 1982, Argued
September 29, 1982, Decided

OPINION: CARDAMONE, Judge:

A proverb current even in the days of ancient Rome was "seeing is believing." Today, a great deal of what people see flashes before them on their TV sets. This case involves a 30-second television commercial with simultaneous audio and video components. We have no doubt that the byword of Rome is as valid now as it was then. And, if seeing something on TV has a tendency to persuade a viewer to believe, how much greater is the impact on a viewer's credulity when he both sees and hears a message at the same time?

In mid-February of 1982 defendant Tropicana Products, Inc. (Tropicana) began airing a new television commercial for its Premium Pack orange juice. The commercial shows the renowned American Olympic athlete Bruce Jenner squeezing an orange while saying "It's pure, pasteurized juice as it comes from the orange," and then shows Jenner pouring the fresh-squeezed juice into a Tropicana carton while the audio states "It's the only leading brand not made with concentrate and water."

Soon after the advertisement began running, plaintiff Coca-Cola Company (Coke, Coca-Cola), maker of Minute Maid orange juice, brought suit against Tropicana for false advertising in violation of section 43(a) of the Lanham Act. The statute provides that anyone who uses a false description or representation in connection with goods placed in commerce "shall be liable to a civil action by [anyone] . . . who believes that he is or is likely to be damaged by the use of . . . such false description or representation." Coke claimed the commercial is false because it incorrectly represents that Premium Pack contains unprocessed, fresh-squeezed juice when in fact the juice is pasteurized (heated to about 200 degrees Fahrenheit) and sometimes frozen prior to packaging. The court below denied plaintiff's motion for a preliminary injunction to enjoin further broadcast of the advertisement pending the outcome of this litigation. In our view preliminary injunctive relief is appropriate.

I

Scope of Review

A party seeking issuance of a preliminary injunction in this Circuit must always show that it is likely to suffer possible irreparable harm if the requested relief is not granted. In addition, it must demonstrate either (1) a likelihood of success on the merits of its case or (2) sufficiently serious questions going to the merits to make them a fair ground for litigation and a balance of hardships tipping decidedly in its favor.

The grant or refusal to grant interlocutory injunctive relief rests in the sound discretion of the district court judge. Upon appeal, the order granting or denying a preliminary injunction will not be disturbed unless it results from an abuse of judicial discretion, or is contrary to some rule of equity.

As so often is the case, the rule is easily stated; its precise meaning is more elusive.

Note how the appellate Court wrestles with the problem raised by being limited to reversal only if the lower court decision resulted from an "abuse of discretion."

The Court spends a fair amount of time explaining why it really should be able to overturn the lower court's decision in this case.

In reviewing the action of a trial court, an appellate court is not limited to reversing only when the lower court's action exceeds any reasonable bounds and to rubber-stamping with the imprimatur of an affirmance when it does not. Congress surely did not envision that appellate review should be limited to a choice between the monster Scylla and the abyss of Charybdis. The scope of review over the exercise of a trial court's discretion is broader, lying between – not relegated to – these two extremes. Thus, as Learned Hand defined it, abuse of discretion "means no more than that we will not intervene, so long as we think that the [discretion exercised] is within permissible limits."

An abuse of discretion may consist of an error of law, an error of fact, or an error in the substance or form of the trial court's order.

Upon review, if an error is found which did not actually form the basis for the determination whether the injunction issued or not, no abuse of discretion will have occurred because such an error will be deemed harmless. However, when the error, whatever its nature, is the *predicate* for the trial court's order, an appellate court must reverse because in such case the order would plainly result from an improvident exercise of the trial court's discretion.

But doesn't this more or less mean the review is "de novo"? It seems this Court clearly wants to review this case with an eye toward reversal of the lower court.

A trial court's discretion should not be disturbed where a question as to its validity is perched precariously, as though on a swaying aerial catwalk, subject to doubt and uncertainty.

We believe that the outlined scope of review and the authorities cited suffice for us to reverse in the instant case where the trial court, by a misapplication of the irreparable injury standard, concluded that Coca-Cola had failed to show an essential requirement for injunctive relief. This error of law constitutes an abuse of discretion which mandates reversal. In addition, we conclude that the trial court's finding of no facial falseness in defendant's TV commercial was an error of fact.

II

Irreparable Injury

Perhaps the most difficult element to demonstrate when seeking an injunction against false advertising is the likelihood that one will suffer irreparable harm if the injunction does not issue.

The Lanham Act plaintiff must offer something more than a mere subjective belief that he is likely to be injured as a result of the false advertising; he must submit proof which provides a reasonable basis for that belief, *Vidal Sassoon, Inc. v. Bristol-Myers Co.*, 661 F.2d 272, 278 (2d Cir. 1981). The likelihood of injury and causation will not be presumed, but must be demonstrated in some manner. *Johnson & Johnson*, 631 F.2d at 190.

Two recent decisions of this Court have examined the type of proof necessary to satisfy this requirement. Relying on the fact that the products involved were in head-to-head competition, the Court in both cases directed the issuance of a preliminary injunction under the Lanham Act. *Vidal Sassoon*, 661 F.2d at 227; *Johnson & Johnson*, 631 F.2d at 189-91.[1] In both decisions the Court reasoned that sales of the plaintiffs' products would probably be harmed if the competing products' advertising tended to mislead consumers in the manner alleged. Market studies were used as evidence that some consumers were in fact misled by the advertising in issue. Thus, the market studies supplied the causative link between the advertising and the plaintiffs' potential lost sales, and thereby indicated a likelihood of injury.[2]

Obviously this case more closely resembles *Vidal Sassoon*.

Applying the same reasoning to the instant case, if consumers are misled by Tropicana's commercial, Coca-Cola probably would suffer irreparable injury. Tropicana and Coca-Cola are the leading national competitors for the chilled (ready-to-serve) orange juice market. If Tropicana's advertisement misleads consumers into believing that Premium Pack is a more desirable product because it contains only fresh-squeezed, unprocessed juice, then it is likely that Coke will lose a portion of the chilled juice market and thus suffer irreparable injury.

Evidence in the record supports the conclusion that consumers are likely to be misled in this manner. A consumer reaction survey conducted by ASI Market Research, Inc. measuring recall of the commercial after it was aired on television [was] admitted into evidence. We note that the district court ruled that there were at least a small number of *clearly* deceived ASI interviewees. Our examination of the test results leads to the same conclusion, i.e., that a not insubstantial number of consumers were clearly misled by the defendant's ad.

So Coca-Cola will suffer at least *some* harm.

Together these tests provide sufficient evidence of a risk of irreparable harm because they demonstrate that a significant number of consumers would be likely to be misled. Coke, therefore, demonstrated that it is likely to suffer irreparable injury.

---

[1] In *Vidal Sassoon* it was assumed that two different shampoos competed for the same market, but in *Johnson & Johnson* the element of competition had to be proven because the two products, baby oil and a depilatory containing baby oil, were not obviously competing for the same consumer dollars.

[2] In *Vidal Sassoon* consumers were allegedly misled to believe that Body on Tap shampoo was an all-around superior product. In *Johnson & Johnson* consumers were allegedly misled into thinking that using NAIR depilatory with baby oil would obviate the need for using baby oil alone to moisturize the skin after shaving.

III

Likelihood of Success on the Merits

Once the initial requisite showing of irreparable harm has been made, the party seeking a preliminary injunction must satisfy either of the two alternatives regarding the merits of his case. We find that Coca-Cola satisfies the more stringent first alternative because it is likely to succeed on the merits of its false advertising action.

Coke is entitled to relief under the Lanham Act if Tropicana has used a false description or representation in its Jenner commercial. When a merchandising statement or representation is literally or explicitly false, the court may grant relief without reference to the advertisement's impact on the buying public.

We find that the squeezing-pouring sequence in the Jenner commercial is false on its face. The visual component of the ad makes an explicit representation that Premium Pack is produced by squeezing oranges and pouring the freshly-squeezed juice directly into the carton. This is not a true representation of how the product is prepared. Premium Pack juice is heated and sometimes frozen prior to packaging. Additionally, the simultaneous audio component of the ad states that Premium Pack is "pasteurized juice as it comes from the orange." This statement is blatantly false – pasteurized juice does not come from oranges. Pasteurization entails heating the juice to approximately 200 degrees Fahrenheit to kill certain natural enzymes and microorganisms which cause spoilage. Moreover, even if the addition of the word "pasteurized" somehow made sense and effectively qualified the visual image, Tropicana's commercial nevertheless represented that the juice is only squeezed, heated and packaged when in fact it may actually also be frozen.

Hence, Coke is likely to succeed in arguing that Tropicana's ad is false and that it is entitled to relief under the Lanham Act. The purpose of the Act is to insure truthfulness in advertising and to eliminate misrepresentations with reference to the inherent quality or characteristic of another's product.

Because Tropicana has made a false representation in its advertising and Coke is likely to suffer irreparable harm as a result, *we reverse the district court's denial of plaintiff's application and remand this case for issuance of a preliminary injunction preventing broadcast of the squeezing-pouring sequence in the Jenner commercial.*

∼

The Internet has become increasingly commercialized, a trend that is sure to continue. The Net is now as much a vast virtual shopping mall as it is a forum for ideas and expression and a medium for communication. Advertising on the Net takes many forms, including websites for products or services and, of course, the "pop-up ad." Perhaps the most ubiquitous, bothersome, and harmful form of advertising on the Net, however, is unsolicited and unwanted e-mail advertising, or spam. According to CBR Enterprise Performance Management, a company that monitors the effects of spam on the Net, in the period from September 2007 to March 2008, the volume of spam rose by 135% and now accounts for about 93% of all e-mail.

Two of the earliest cases regarding spam, both involving a company named "Cyber Promotions, Inc.," illustrate the nature of the problem as well as a novel approach to dealing with it.

Advertising and Spam: Case 3

CYBER PROMOTIONS, INC. VS. AMERICA ONLINE, INC.; AMERICA ONLINE, INC. VS. CYBER PROMOTIONS, INC.

C.A. NO. 96-2486, C.A. NO. 96-5213

UNITED STATES DISTRICT COURT FOR THE EASTERN DISTRICT OF PENNSYLVANIA

948 F. Supp. 456; 1996 U.S. Dist. LEXIS 17771; 1997-1 Trade Cas. (CCH) P71,675; 25 Media L. Rep. 1144

November 26, 1996, Decided

OPINION: WEINER, Judge:

A mere two days after this Court ruled in a Memorandum Opinion and Order dated November 4, 1996 that Cyber Promotions, Inc. ("Cyber") does not have a right under the First Amendment to the United States Constitution to send unsolicited e-mail advertisements over the Internet to subscribers of American Online, Inc. ("AOL"), Cyber filed a motion for leave to amend its First Amended Complaint to assert an entirely different yet equally untenable theory which it claims gives it the right to use AOL's private property free of charge to send millions of e-mail advertisements to AOL subscribers: that AOL's blocking of Cyber's e-mail advertisements in favor of its own advertising violates the federal antitrust laws. Specifically, Cyber contends that AOL has obtained a monopoly in the market for providing direct marketing advertising material via electronic transmission to AOL's own subscribers in violation of Section 2 of the Sherman Act, 15 U.S.C. § 2. Not only has Cyber sought leave to file a Second Amended Complaint alleging its monopolization theory, it has also moved for injunctive relief in the form of a temporary restraining order on that claim. Cyber, however, has not cited nor has our research disclosed a single case which has granted a temporary restraining order in a Sherman Act case. In any event, after reviewing the parties' submissions and hearing oral argument by telephone, we will grant the motion to amend but deny the motion for a temporary restraining order.

Cyber, an advertising agency incorporated in 1996, provides advertising services for companies and individuals wishing to advertise their products and services via e-mail.

Cyber sends its e-mail via the Internet to members of AOL, members of other commercial online services and other individuals with an Internet e-mail address.

The motivation behind Cyber's assertion of its latest theory which it claims entitles it to send unsolicited e-mail advertisements over the Internet to subscribers of AOL appears to be AOL's implementation of a system "tool" which it calls "PreferredMail – The Guard Against Junk E-Mail." This "tool" allows access to Cyber's e-mail advertisements to those AOL subscribers who wish to receive these advertisements. Cyber objects to this tool because, according to Cyber, it places the onus on the AOL subscriber to take affirmative steps to *access* Cyber's e-mail by checking off a box on the screen captioned "I want junk e-mail!" and because it groups legitimate advertisers such as Cyber with pornographic advertisers thereby discouraging the subscriber to choose to receive Cyber's e-mail. Cyber likens "PreferredMail" to a "virtual black list" because it "contains the names of Internet advertisers who are responsible for sending the vast majority of unsolicited advertising through the Internet to AOL subscribers."

Cyber points out in its Memorandum that AOL does not automatically block its own unsolicited advertising which it transmits to its subscribers under the label "marketing 'pop-up' messages." Instead, it places the onus on its subscribers to *block* these messages by entering an area of AOL called "Marketing Preferences". The Marketing Preferences area advises AOL subscribers that AOL sells the right to target electronic advertising to its subscribers and sells the subscribers names to direct mail advertisers who use the U.S. Postal Service to send unsolicited advertisements. Cyber contends that the "striking distinctions between the means by which an AOL subscriber can receive or block unsolicited advertising from AOL and its competitors was intended by AOL to secure, and has in fact secured, AOL's monopoly in the market for providing targeted electronic advertising to its subscribers." Cyber requests that we temporarily enjoin AOL from implementing its PreferredMail blocking tool, or from otherwise blocking system-wide, or interfering with, the electronic transmission of Cyber's advertising material sent to AOL subscribers.

The well-established factors we must consider when ruling on a motion for a temporary restraining order or preliminary injunction are (1) the likelihood that the applicant will prevail on the merits at a final hearing; (2) the extent to which the plaintiff is being irreparably harmed by the conduct complained of; (3) the extent to which the defendants will suffer irreparable harm if the preliminary injunction is issued; (4) the public interest. "All four factors should favor preliminary relief before the injunction will issue." Because Cyber cannot satisfy the first factor – a likelihood of success on the merits at a final hearing – the motion for injunctive relief in the form of a temporary restraining order must be denied.

Cyber contends that the ability to advertise to AOL's subscribers over the Internet via electronic mail is an "essential facility" and that AOL has "refused to deal" with Cyber in violation of Section 2 of the Sherman Act. The irony of this contention is that AOL has *not* actually excluded Cyber from having access to AOL's system. Cyber is continuing to send its e-mail advertisements to AOL's servers. By implementing its PreferredMail system, AOL has given its own subscribers the option of viewing Cyber's e-mail without them having to pay to erase the e-mail every time they go online. Thus, Cyber is only being denied the access to AOL's system in a manner which *it prefers*, i.e., that AOL's customers should be able to view Cyber's e-mail without having to take affirmative steps to view the e-mail.

In any event, under the "essential facilities" or "bottleneck" doctrine, "a business or group of businesses which controls a scarce facility has an obligation to give competitors reasonable access to it."

In order to make out a claim under the essential facilities doctrine, Cyber must show "(1) control of the essential facility by a monopolist; (2) the competitor's inability practically or reasonably to duplicate the essential facility; (3) denial of the use of the facility to a competitor; and (4) the feasibility of providing the facility."

With regard to the first factor, there is little likelihood that Cyber will be able to demonstrate that AOL is a monopolist. In order to show AOL is a monopolist, Cyber must show that AOL possessed monopoly power in a relevant market and "the willful acquisition or maintenance of that power as distinguished from growth or development as a consequence of a superior product, business acumen, or historic accident."

Cyber defines the product market as the service of transmitting commercial advertising by electronic means to AOL's subscribers and defines the geographic market as AOL's subscribers themselves, a type of "electronic island to which AOL controls the only bridge." Even without the benefit of discovery or a hearing, the market as defined by Cyber appears to us to be unrealistically narrow and tailored solely for Cyber's own purpose.

The first problem with Cyber's definition of the market is that AOL and Cyber are not competitors.

AOL's business is that of a private commercial online service. Cyber, on the other hand, is not in the business of providing commercial online service but instead is an advertising agency which provides advertising services for companies and individuals wishing to advertise their products and services via e-mail.

AOL has the right to control the advertisements which reach its own subscribers. After all these individuals became AOL subscribers by paying AOL a monthly fee. AOL has no problem accepting advertisements from advertisers as long as these advertisers pay AOL and therefore provide AOL with a source of revenue. Cyber, however, refuses to pay AOL for sending approximately 1.9 million e-mail advertisements to AOL servers each day.

The Court uses a nice analogy to explode Cyber's market definition:

The problems with Cyber's market definition can best be revealed by the following analogy: Suppose that an advertising agency (Cyber) promises that for a fee it can get an advertiser's advertisements for get-rich-quick schemes, health aid promises and phone sex services in a daily newspaper or magazine for dissemination to that publication's subscribers without having to pay any fee to the publication. When the publication refuses to carry the ads, the advertising agency sues the publication claiming it has a monopoly over the market of advertising access to its own subscribers by means of the pages of its newspaper. The likelihood of success on such a theory would be slim indeed.

Cyber has not, at least at this stage of the proceedings, made any showing that because AOL has restricted the manner in which Cyber may send its e-mail advertisements to AOL's subscribers, AOL has charged other potential advertisers supracompetitive prices for the right to advertise on its system or would desire to do so in the future. Indeed, it would be against AOL's economic best interests for it to even attempt to charge supracompetitive prices to advertisers on its system. As mentioned above, there are numerous commercial online services which compete for AOL's customer base, including CompuServe, the Microsoft Network and Prodigy. Were AOL to charge supracompetitive prices for advertising on its system, advertisers would only have to switch to any of these competing services or to other parts of the Internet such as the World Wide Web to disseminate their advertisements to online users.

Cyber correctly points out that the test for determining the relevant product market is one of "reasonable interchangeability."

In the case *sub judice*, there are numerous competitive methods for advertisers such as Cyber to reach AOL subscribers including, but not limited to, the World Wide Web as well as direct mail, billboards, television, newspapers and leaflets. AOL does not do business in these alternative advertising methods. If these additional advertising methods are ultimately found to be reasonably interchangeable with electronic mail and included as part of the relevant product market, AOL would not control a large enough percentage of the relevant product market to justify a finding of monopoly power.

Even if Cyber could prove AOL is a monopolist in the relevant market, there is little likelihood that Cyber could prove that AOL monopolizes an "essential facility."

"An 'essential facility' is one which is not merely helpful but vital to the claimant's competitive viability." The essential facility Cyber contends that AOL monopolizes is advertising to AOL's own subscribers via electronic mail. We believe there is little likelihood that Cyber will be able to show that the ability to advertise to AOL's subscribers is vital to Cyber's competitive ability.

Cyber can send its advertisements to the subscribers of the many other online services which compete with AOL, including CompuServe, the Microsoft Network and Prodigy.

Notice how the Court here oddly suggests CompuServe as an alternative target for Cyber's spam.

Cyber can send its advertisements to AOL members over the Internet through the World Wide Web which would allow access by AOL subscribers who want to receive Cyber's advertisements. Cyber, as an advertising agency, can disseminate its advertisements to AOL subscribers and others by non-Internet means including the United States mail, telemarketing, television, cable, newspapers, magazines, billboards and leaflets. And, of course, Cyber could attempt to lure AOL subscribers away from AOL by developing its own commercial online system or advertising web site and charging a competitive rate.

In sum, we find that there is little likelihood that Cyber will be able to establish the necessary elements of its claim under the "essential facilities" or "bottleneck" doctrine and that AOL has "refused to deal" with Cyber in violation of Section 2 of the Sherman Act. As there is little likelihood that Cyber will prevail on the merits of its antitrust claim at a final hearing or that it will be irreparably harmed in the absence of a temporary restraining order, its motion for injunctive relief in the form of a temporary restraining order must be denied.

Order

The motion of Cyber Promotions, Inc. to amend its Complaint is Granted.

It is so ordered.

Advertising and Spam: Case 4

CompuServe Incorporated, Plaintiff, vs. Cyber Promotions, Inc. and Sanford Wallace, Defendants.

Case No. C2-96-1070

UNITED STATES DISTRICT COURT FOR THE SOUTHERN DISTRICT OF OHIO, EASTERN DIVISION

962 F. Supp. 1015; 1997 U.S. Dist. LEXIS 1997; 25 Media L. Rep. 1545

February 3, 1997, Decided
February 3, 1997, FILED

OPINION: GRAHAM, Judge:

This case presents novel issues regarding the commercial use of the Internet, specifically the right of an online computer service to prevent a commercial enterprise from sending unsolicited electronic mail advertising to its subscribers.

So this is the opposite of the question asked in *Cyber v. AOL.*

Plaintiff CompuServe Incorporated ("CompuServe") is one of the major national commercial online computer services. Defendants Cyber Promotions, Inc. and its president Sanford Wallace are in the business of sending unsolicited e-mail advertisements on behalf of themselves and their clients to hundreds of thousands of Internet users, many of whom are CompuServe subscribers. CompuServe has notified defendants that they are prohibited from using its computer equipment to process and store the unsolicited e-mail and has requested that they terminate the practice. Instead, defendants have sent an increasing volume of e-mail solicitations to CompuServe subscribers. CompuServe has attempted to employ technological means to block the flow of defendants' e-mail transmission to its computer equipment, but to no avail.

This matter is before the Court on the application of CompuServe for a preliminary injunction which would extend the duration of the temporary restraining order issued by this Court on October 24, 1996 and which would in addition prevent defendants from sending unsolicited advertisements to CompuServe subscribers.

For the reasons which follow, this Court holds that where defendants engaged in a course of conduct of transmitting a substantial volume of electronic data in the form of unsolicited e-mail to plaintiff's proprietary computer equipment, where defendants continued such practice after repeated demands to cease and desist, and where defendants deliberately evaded plaintiff's affirmative efforts to protect its computer equipment from such use, plaintiff has a viable claim for trespass to personal property and is entitled to injunctive relief to protect its property.

I

Internet users often pay a fee for Internet access. However, there is no per-message charge to send electronic messages over the Internet and such messages usually reach their destination within minutes. Thus electronic mail provides an opportunity to reach a wide audience quickly and at almost no cost to the sender. It is not surprising therefore that some companies, like defendant Cyber Promotions, Inc., have begun using the Internet to distribute advertisements by sending the same unsolicited commercial message to hundreds of thousands of Internet users at once. Defendants refer to this as "bulk e-mail," while plaintiff refers to it as "junk e-mail." In the vernacular of the Internet, unsolicited e-mail advertising is sometimes referred to pejoratively as "spam."

E-mail sent to CompuServe subscribers is processed and stored on CompuServe's proprietary computer equipment. Thereafter, it becomes accessible to CompuServe's subscribers, who can access CompuServe's equipment and electronically retrieve those messages.

Over the past several months, CompuServe has received many complaints from subscribers threatening to discontinue their subscription unless CompuServe prohibits electronic mass mailers from using its equipment to send unsolicited advertisements.

CompuServe asserts that the volume of messages generated by such mass mailings places a significant burden on its equipment which has finite processing and storage capacity. CompuServe receives no payment from the mass mailers for processing their unsolicited advertising. However, CompuServe's subscribers pay for their access to CompuServe's services in increments of time and thus the process of accessing, reviewing and discarding unsolicited e-mail costs them money, which is one of the reasons for their complaints. CompuServe has notified defendants that they are prohibited from using its proprietary computer equipment to process and store unsolicited e-mail and has requested them to cease and desist from sending unsolicited e-mail to its subscribers. Nonetheless, defendants have sent an increasing volume of e-mail solicitations to CompuServe subscribers.

In an effort to shield its equipment from defendants' bulk e-mail, CompuServe has implemented software programs designed to screen out the messages and block their receipt. In response, defendants have modified their equipment and the messages they send in such a fashion as to circumvent CompuServe's screening software. Allegedly, defendants have been able to conceal the true origin of their messages by falsifying the point-of-origin information contained in the header of the electronic messages.

Defendants assert that they possess the right to continue to send these communications to CompuServe subscribers. CompuServe contends that, in doing so, the defendants are trespassing upon its personal property.

II

In determining whether a motion for preliminary injunction should be granted, a court must consider and balance four factors: (1) the likelihood that the party seeking the preliminary injunction will succeed on the merits of the claim; (2) whether the party seeking the injunction will suffer irreparable harm without the grant of the extraordinary relief; (3) the probability that granting the injunction will cause substantial harm to others, and (4) whether the public interest is advanced by the issuance of the injunction. None of these individual factors constitute prerequisites that must be met for the issuance of a preliminary injunction, they are instead factors that are to be balanced.

III

This Court shall first address plaintiff's motion as it relates to perpetuating the temporary restraining order filed on October 24, 1996. That order enjoins defendants from:

(i) Using CompuServe accounts or CompuServe's equipment or support services to send or receive electronic mail or messages or in connection with the sending or receiving of electronic mail or messages;

(ii) Inserting any false reference to a CompuServe account or CompuServe equipment in any electronic message sent by Defendants; and

(iii) Falsely representing or causing their electronic mail or messages to bear the representation that any electronic mail or message sent by Defendants was sent by or originated from CompuServe or a CompuServe account.

The behavior described in subsections (ii) and (iii) of the temporary restraining order would be actionable as false representations or descriptions under § 43(a) of the Lanham Act, 15 U.S.C. § 1125(a).

Defendants argue that the restrictions in the temporary restraining order are no longer necessary because defendants no longer have a CompuServe account. That being the case, a preliminary injunction perpetuating the proscribed activity articulated in subsection (i) of the temporary restraining order will present no hardship at all to defendants. Next, it does not appear that defendants would need to have a CompuServe account to perpetrate the proscribed acts articulated in subsections (ii) and (iii) of the temporary restraining order. Therefore, the fact that defendants no longer have an account with plaintiff does not vitiate the need which CompuServe has demonstrated for an injunction proscribing the acts set forth in those subsections.

For the foregoing reasons and the reasons articulated in the temporary restraining order issued by this Court, defendants Cyber Promotions, Inc. and its president Sanford Wallace are hereby enjoined from performing any of the acts therein described during the pendency of this litigation.

IV

This Court will now address the second aspect of plaintiff's motion in which it seeks to enjoin defendants Cyber Promotions, Inc. and its president Sanford Wallace from sending any unsolicited advertisements to any electronic mail address maintained by CompuServe.

CompuServe predicates this aspect of its motion for a preliminary injunction on the common law theory of trespass to personal property or to chattels, asserting that defendants' continued transmission of electronic messages to its computer equipment constitutes an actionable tort.

Trespass to chattels has evolved from its original common law application, concerning primarily the asportation of another's tangible property, to include the unauthorized use of personal property.

Its chief importance now, is that there may be recovery . . . for interferences with the possession of chattels which are not sufficiently important to be classed as conversion, and so to compel the defendant to pay the full value of the thing with which he has interfered. Trespass to chattels survives today, in other words, largely as a little brother of conversion.

Both plaintiff and defendants cite the Restatement (Second) of Torts to support their respective positions.

The Restatement § 217(b) states that a trespass to chattel may be committed by intentionally using or intermeddling with the chattel in possession of another. Restatement § 217, Comment e defines physical "intermeddling" as follows: . . . intentionally bringing about a physical contact with the chattel. The actor may commit a trespass by an act which brings him into an intended physical contact with a chattel in the possession of another[.]

Electronic signals generated and sent by computer have been held to be sufficiently physically tangible to support a trespass cause of action. It is undisputed that plaintiff has a possessory interest in its computer systems. Further, defendants' contact with plaintiff's computers is clearly intentional. Although electronic messages may travel through the Internet over various routes, the messages are affirmatively directed to their destination.

Defendants argue that they did not, in this case, physically dispossess plaintiff of its equipment or substantially interfere with it. However, the Restatement (Second) of Torts § 218 defines the circumstances under which a trespass to chattels may be actionable:

> One who commits a trespass to a chattel is subject to liability to the possessor of the chattel if, but only if,
>
> (a) he dispossesses the other of the chattel, or
> (b) the chattel is impaired as to its condition, quality, or value, or
> (c) the possessor is deprived of the use of the chattel for a substantial time, or
> (d) bodily harm is caused to the possessor, or harm is caused to some person or thing in which the possessor has a legally protected interest.

Therefore, an interference resulting in physical dispossession is just one circumstance under which a defendant can be found liable.

An unprivileged use or other intermeddling with a chattel which results in actual impairment of its physical condition, quality or value to the possessor makes the actor liable for the loss thus caused. In the present case, any value CompuServe realizes from its computer equipment is wholly derived from the extent to which that equipment can serve its subscriber base. Michael Mangino, a software developer for CompuServe who monitors its mail processing computer equipment, states by affidavit that handling the enormous volume of mass mailings that CompuServe receives places a tremendous burden on its equipment. Defendants' more recent practice of evading CompuServe's filters by disguising the origin of their messages commandeers even more computer resources because CompuServe's computers are forced to store undeliverable e-mail messages and labor in vain to return the messages to an address that does not exist. To the extent that defendants' multitudinous electronic mailings demand the disk space and drain the processing power of plaintiff's computer equipment, those resources are not available to serve CompuServe subscribers. Therefore, the value of that equipment to CompuServe is diminished even though it is not physically damaged by defendants' conduct.

Next, plaintiff asserts that it has suffered injury aside from the physical impact of defendants' messages on its equipment. Plaintiff asserts that defendants' messages are largely unwanted by its subscribers, who pay incrementally to access their e-mail, read it, and discard it. Also, the receipt of a bundle of unsolicited messages at once can require the subscriber to sift through, at his expense, all of the messages in order to find the ones he wanted or expected to receive. These inconveniences decrease the utility of CompuServe's e-mail service and are the foremost subject in recent complaints from CompuServe subscribers. Patrick Hole, a customer service manager for plaintiff, states by affidavit that in November 1996 CompuServe received approximately 9,970 e-mail complaints from subscribers about junk e-mail, a figure up from approximately two hundred complaints the previous year.

Many subscribers have terminated their accounts specifically because of the unwanted receipt of bulk e-mail messages. Defendants' intrusions into CompuServe's computer systems, insofar as they harm plaintiff's business reputation and goodwill with its customers, are actionable under Restatement § 218(d).

Plaintiff CompuServe has attempted to exercise [its] privilege to protect its computer systems. However, defendants' persistent affirmative efforts to evade plaintiff's security measures have circumvented any protection those self-help measures might have provided. The foregoing discussion simply underscores that the damage sustained by plaintiff is sufficient to sustain an action for trespass to chattels. However, this Court also notes that the implementation of technological means of self-help, to the extent that reasonable measures are effective, is particularly appropriate in this type of situation and should be exhausted before legal action is proper.

Under Restatement § 252, the owner of personal property can create a privilege in the would-be trespasser by granting consent to use the property. A great portion of the utility of CompuServe's e-mail service is that it allows subscribers to receive messages from individuals and entities located anywhere on the Internet. Certainly, then, there is at least a tacit invitation for anyone on the Internet to utilize plaintiff's computer equipment to send e-mail to its subscribers. However, in or around October 1995, CompuServe employee Jon Schmidt specifically told Mr. Wallace that he was "prohibited from using CompuServe's equipment to send his junk e-mail messages."

Defendants argue that plaintiff made the business decision to connect to the Internet and that therefore it cannot now successfully maintain an action for trespass to chattels. Their argument is analogous to the argument that because an establishment invites the public to enter its property for business purposes, it cannot later restrict or revoke access to that property, a proposition which is erroneous under Ohio law. See, e.g., *State v. Carriker*, 5 Ohio App. 2d 255, 214 N.E.2d 809 (1964) (the law in Ohio is that a business invitee's privilege to remain on the premises of another may be revoked upon the reasonable notification to leave by the owner or his agents).

In other words, it's legal to throw someone out.

On or around October 1995, CompuServe notified defendants that it no longer consented to the use of its proprietary computer equipment. Defendants' continued use thereafter was a trespass.

Further, CompuServe expressly limits the consent it grants to Internet users to send e-mail to its proprietary computer systems by denying unauthorized parties the use of CompuServe equipment to send unsolicited electronic mail messages.

As a general matter, the public possesses a privilege to reasonably use the facilities of a public utility, but Internet service providers have been held not to be common carriers. CompuServe is not a public utility as that status is defined under Ohio law and defendants can not be said to enjoy a special privilege to use CompuServe's proprietary computer systems.

In response to the trespass claim, defendants argue that they have the right to continue to send unsolicited commercial e-mail to plaintiff's computer systems under the First Amendment to the United States Constitution.

Very recently, in an action filed by Cyber Promotions, Inc. against America Online, Inc. ("AOL") the United States District Court for the Eastern District of Pennsylvania held that AOL, a company selling services that are similar to those of CompuServe, is private actor. *Cyber Promotions, Inc. v. America Online, Inc.*, 1996 U.S. Dist. LEXIS 19073, 1996 WL 633702. The court held that Cyber Promotions had no such right and that, *inter alia*, AOL was not exercising powers that are traditionally the exclusive prerogative of the state, such as where a private company exercises municipal powers by running a company town. This Court agrees with the conclusions reached by the United States District Court for the Eastern District of Pennsylvania.

Defendants do not argue that CompuServe is anything other than a private actor. Instead, defendants urge that because CompuServe is so intimately involved in this new medium it might be subject to some special form of regulation. No such legislation yet exists that is applicable to CompuServe. Further, defendants' discussion concerning the extent to which the Internet may be regulated (or should be regulated) is irrelevant because no government entity has undertaken to regulate the Internet in a manner that is applicable to this action.

Defendants in the present action have adequate alternative means of communication available to them. Not only are they free to send e-mail advertisements to those on the Internet who do not use CompuServe accounts, but they can communicate to CompuServe subscribers as well through online bulletin boards, web page advertisements, or facsimile transmissions, as well as through more conventional means such as the U.S. mail or telemarketing.

In the present case, plaintiff is physically the recipient of the defendants' messages and is the owner of the property upon which the transgression is occurring. As has been discussed, plaintiff is not a government agency or state actor which seeks to preempt defendants' ability to communicate but is instead a private actor trying to tailor the nuances of its service to provide the maximum utility to its customers.

Defendants' intentional use of plaintiff's proprietary computer equipment exceeds plaintiff's consent and, indeed, continued after repeated demands that defendants cease. Such use is an actionable trespass to plaintiff's chattel. The First Amendment to the United States Constitution provides no defense for such conduct.

Plaintiff has demonstrated a likelihood of success on the merits which is sufficient to warrant the issuance of the preliminary injunction it has requested.

Plaintiff has shown that it will suffer irreparable harm without the grant of the preliminary injunction.

It is improbable that granting the injunction will cause substantial harm to defendant. Even with the grant of this injunction, defendants are free to disseminate their advertisements in other ways not constituting trespass to plaintiff's computer equipment. Further, defendants may continue to send electronic mail messages to the tens of millions of Internet users who are not connected through CompuServe's computer systems.

Finally, the public interest is advanced by the Court's protection of the common law rights of individuals and entities to their personal property. High volumes of junk e-mail devour computer processing and storage capacity, slow down data transfer between computers over the Internet by congesting the electronic paths through which the messages travel, and cause recipients to spend time and money wading through messages that they do not want. It is ironic that if defendants were to prevail on their First Amendment arguments, the viability of electronic mail as an effective means of communication for the rest of society would be put at risk.

Having considered the relevant factors, this Court concludes that the preliminary injunction that plaintiff requests is appropriate.

V

Based on the foregoing, plaintiff's motion for a preliminary injunction is GRANTED. The temporary restraining order filed on October 24, 1996 by this Court is hereby extended in duration until final judgment is entered in this case. Further, defendants Cyber Promotions, Inc. and its president Sanford Wallace are enjoined from sending any unsolicited advertisements to any electronic mail address maintained by plaintiff CompuServe during the pendency of this action.

It is so ordered.

The use of the tort of Trespass to Chattels was a startlingly original idea. It is a wonderful example of applying existing law in an unusual way in the new context of cyberspace. Today, Trespass to Chattels is frequently used in this way.

Spam, however, continues to be a major problem for Internet users and service providers. Whether this activity can be regulated or prevented is questionable. Behavioral control issues in general are very problematic in cyberspace.

15. Jurisdiction

Introduction

Before a court can hear a case, two types of jurisdiction are required: subject matter jurisdiction and personal jurisdiction.

Subject Matter Jurisdiction

Subject matter jurisdiction is the power to decide the particular type of dispute. *Only* state courts have subject matter jurisdiction over civil suits between citizens of the same state. *Every* state has at least one court of *general* jurisdiction. (That is, it can hear *any* kind of claim between *any* parties – unless specifically prohibited from hearing certain types of cases, for example probate or family law cases, for which special courts are provided.)

Federal courts are all courts of *limited* jurisdiction (as opposed to general). That is, federal courts can hear cases only as specifically authorized by the statutes creating the court. For federal courts, the outer bounds of jurisdiction are set by the Constitution, Article III, Sec. 2. Congress can limit federal courts to *less* subject matter jurisdiction, but cannot grant more than allowed in the Constitution.

Federal courts have subject matter jurisdiction in three instances:

1. when there is jurisdiction based on "diversity" of the parties;
2. when the case involves a federal question; and
3. when the court has supplemental jurisdiction (which permits a defendant with a counter-claim to bring it in federal court if the court would have had jurisdiction over the original claim).

Federal courts have subject matter jurisdiction based on diversity of the parties ("Diversity Jurisdiction") in several instances:

1. when the suit is between citizens of different states,
2. when the suit is between a citizen of a state and a subject of a foreign country,
3. when the suit is between states, and
4. whenever the United States is a party.

There is also a requirement that the amount in controversy must be greater than $75,000. This figure does not include interest and costs. The total claims against one defendant can be added to calculate the amount in controversy, but the claims against multiple defendants cannot be added in that way. There must simply be a *good faith* allegation of the amount in controversy in the complaint filed to initiate the suit. The plaintiff's *recovery* can be less than $75,000. It is the amount in controversy that matters.

Certain types of cases are excluded from diversity jurisdiction, such as those regarding divorces, alimony, child custody, or estate probates.

A "state citizen" for diversity jurisdiction purposes is a citizen of the United States, or alien permanent resident of the United States, who is *domiciled* in a state. A person's "domicile" is the place where he or she has established a residence with *no present intention* of leaving for the foreseeable future. A person has only *one* domicile, and therefore, for purposes of determining whether a federal court has subject matter jurisdiction based on diversity, is a citizen of only one state.

Unlike individuals, corporations can have multiple "citizenships" for diversity purposes. Corporations are citizens, for diversity jurisdiction purposes, of the state or states in which they are incorporated and of the state in which the corporation has its principal place of business. Usually a corporation's principal place of business is the state in which the company has its corporate headquarters. This is the so-called nerve center test to determine the location of a company's principal place of business. In rare instances, when a corporation does virtually *all* its business in one state, that state might be considered the company's principal place of business. This is referred to as the "muscle center test."

It is important to remember that for a federal court to have subject matter jurisdiction based on diversity of the parties, there must be *complete* diversity. Many cases involve multiple plaintiffs and defendants. If even one of the plaintiffs and one of the defendants are from the same state then there is no diversity jurisdiction.

Federal courts also have subject matter jurisdiction if the case involves a federal question. In those cases, citizenship of the parties is irrelevant. The issue is whether the plaintiff's claim depends on federal law. That is, does the claim, the "cause of action," arise from a federal law? For example, trademark infringement suits brought under the federal Lanham Act would qualify as cases arising from a federal question, and of course, any case involving a claim based on the Constitution would be a case over which a federal court would have subject matter jurisdiction.

A defendant in a case brought in a state court, but in which diversity jurisdiction is present, can *remove* the proceedings to the federal court whose territory encompasses the state court in which the suit was brought. If the defendant chooses to "remove" the case to federal court, it must be done within thirty days of the case becoming removable, which is usually when the complaint initiating the suit is filed.

Why would a defendant choose to remove the case to federal court? Historically, federal courts were thought to be less locally biased than state courts. Jurors in a federal court are selected from a wider jury pool and the defendant might feel the federal rules of procedure are more favorable to the defendant than state rules of procedure. If there are multiple defendants they must *all* agree to the removal.

Only defendants may remove a case from state to federal court. It is presumed that if a plaintiff preferred a case to be brought in federal court the plaintiff would have initiated the action there. In a case in which diversity of the parties is present, a defendant *cannot* remove the case to federal court if the defendant is a citizen of the state in which the action is brought (or if any defendant is a citizen of that state). That is, removal by a defendant is possible only if the action is brought in the plaintiff's state, or in some state other then the defendant's home state. For example, if a Montana plaintiff sues a Wyoming defendant in state court in Wyoming, the Wyoming defendant cannot remove the case to federal court. The assumption is that if the defendant is a citizen of the state in which the action is brought, the defendant would prefer to be in state, rather than federal court. If a case cannot be removed based on diversity jurisdiction, it may still be removed by the defendant if the case contains a separate and independent claim based on a federal question.

Personal Jurisdiction

A court that has subject matter jurisdiction over a case must also have personal jurisdiction over the defendant. Personal jurisdiction is the power to enforce a decision. Winning a suit in a court that does not have the power to enforce the decision would be pointless.

Residents of a state are subject to suit in that state's court for *any* type of claim. It is important to be aware of the distinction between *citizenship* for determining when subject matter jurisdiction based on diversity is present and *residency* for determining when a court has personal jurisdiction over a defendant.

Recall that for diversity jurisdiction purposes corporations can be *citizens* of multiple states. Similarly, they can be *residents* of multiple states for purposes of determining if a court has personal jurisdiction over them. However, there is a slight, but extremely significant difference. Personal jurisdiction over a defendant – whether a defendant is a *resident* of a state – is determined by whether the defendant has sufficient "minimum contacts" with the state. (The "minimum contacts" rule is discussed more fully later.) So corporations are *residents* of the state or states in which they are incorporated, the state in which they have their principal place of business, *and any state in which the corporation is "doing business" – including those states in which its employees live and regularly work, so, for example, including "telecommuters."* So corporations can be *residents* for personal jurisdiction purposes of many more states than they are *citizens* of for diversity jurisdiction purposes. Doing business in a state automatically satisfies the minimum contacts rule and subjects a company to personal jurisdiction in that state.

Individuals too, under the "minimum contacts" rule, can be *residents* of any number of states even though they can be *citizens* of only one – the state in which they have their domicile. For example, a person whose domicile is in New York, and who is therefore a *citizen* of New York (and only New York) for diversity jurisdiction purposes, might own vacation homes in Vermont and Florida and therefore be *resident* and subject to personal jurisdiction in New York, Vermont, and Florida.

The distinction between a corporation's states of *citizenship* and its states of *residency* has practical significance. Consider the following three hypothetical situations.

1. A company incorporated in Delaware, with its principal place of business in New York and doing business in New York, is sued by a citizen of New York in a New York state court.
   - The state court will have subject matter jurisdiction since every state has a court of general jurisdiction (i.e., a court that can hear *any* type of case).
   - The state court will have personal jurisdiction over the defendant corporation since the corporation does business in the state and is thus a "resident."
   - The defendant *cannot* remove the proceedings to federal court in New York since the defendant, like the plaintiff, is a "citizen" of New York for diversity

jurisdiction purposes. That is, a federal court would not have subject matter jurisdiction based on diversity of the parties.

2. The same company is sued by a New Jersey citizen in a New Jersey state court. The company does business in New Jersey.
   - The New Jersey state court will have subject matter jurisdiction because New Jersey, like every other state, has a court of general jurisdiction.
   - The state court will have personal jurisdiction over the defendant corporation since the corporation does business in the state and is thus a "resident."
   - But the defendant *can* remove to federal court in New Jersey since there *is* diversity because the defendant corporation is *not* a "citizen" of New Jersey for diversity purposes.

3. The same company is sued by a New Jersey citizen in a New Jersey state court. The company does *not* do business in New Jersey.
   - The New Jersey state court will have subject matter jurisdiction because New Jersey, like every other state, has a court of general jurisdiction.
   - A federal court *would* have subject matter jurisdiction based on diversity of the parties because the plaintiff is a *citizen* of New York and Delaware, whereas the plaintiff is a *citizen* of New Jersey, so the defendant corporation *could* remove the case to a federal court in New Jersey – but only *if* New Jersey has personal jurisdiction over the defendant.
   - However, since the defendant corporation does not do business in New Jersey it is not a *resident* of New Jersey and is therefore not subject to personal jurisdiction in New Jersey.
   - Thus, the New Jersey citizen cannot bring the suit in either state or federal court in New Jersey. The plaintiff will have to bring the suit in a state that has personal jurisdiction over the defendant, probably in either New York or Delaware. Most likely the New Jersey citizen will bring the suit in federal court in one of those states since federal court would have subject matter jurisdiction based on diversity of the parties and, presumably, the New Jersey plaintiff will feel that federal court in one of the defendant's "home" states would be preferable to a state court in one of those states.

A claim against a state resident need *not* have arisen in the defendant's home state. For example, a Connecticut resident involved in a car accident in Florida with an Oklahoma resident is subject to suit in Connecticut as a resident of Connecticut. It is also likely that the Connecticut resident could be sued by the Oklahoma resident in Florida since the occurrence of the accident is likely to satisfy the "minimum contacts" rule. However, unless the Connecticut resident has sufficient minimum contacts with Oklahoma, a suit could not be brought there.

To Clarify

*Non*residents of a state are subject to a state's jurisdiction if they have "submitted themselves to the state's jurisdiction by some act." Usually the analysis amounts to this question: Is the defendant's alleged act over which the state asserts personal jurisdiction covered under the state's "long-arm statute"?

Every state has a "long-arm" statute, a law that defines the kinds of activities by nonresidents that the state claims permits the state to assert personal jurisdiction over a nonresident. Long-arm statutes, however, are limited by United States constitutional concerns based on the Constitution's Due Process clause. That is, long-arm statutes cannot claim personal jurisdiction to an extent that would violate the Constitution. Therefore, very often a state long-arm statute will simply say something like, "The state asserts personal jurisdiction over nonresident defendants to the extent permitted by the United States Constitution." Some long-arm statutes, however, such as New York's, as will be seen in the *Bensusan* case later, are quite specific.

In general, in order to satisfy constitutional concerns, nonresidents are subject to a state's personal jurisdiction if they have had certain "minimum contacts" with the state.

Application of the "minimum contacts" rule in cyberspace has been hotly litigated, as will be illustrated by several cases in this chapter, but first, examine the case that established the rule, a case with which *every* lawyer becomes familiar in law school.

Jurisdiction: Case 1

INTERNATIONAL SHOE CO. v. STATE OF WASHINGTON ET AL.

No. 107

SUPREME COURT OF THE UNITED STATES

326 U.S. 310; 66 S. Ct. 154; 90 L. Ed. 95; 1945 U.S. LEXIS 1447; 161 A.L.R. 1057

November 14, 1945, Argued
December 3, 1945, Decided

JUDGES: Stone, Black, Reed, Frankfurter, Douglas, Murphy, Rutledge, Burton; Jackson took no part in the consideration or decision of this case.

OPINION: STONE, Chief Justice:

The questions for decision are (1) whether, within the limitations of the due process clause of the Fourteenth Amendment, appellant, a Delaware corporation, has by its activities in the State of Washington rendered itself amenable to proceedings in the courts of that state to recover unpaid contributions to the state unemployment compensation fund exacted by state statutes, Washington Unemployment Compensation Act, Washington Revised Statutes, § 9998-103a through § 9998-123a, 1941 Supp., and (2) whether the state can exact those contributions consistently with the due process clause of the Fourteenth Amendment.

> **The Appellant (International Shoe) Wants: No enforcement of the statute requiring payment to state's unemployment compensation fund because the company is not legally "present" in the state for such purposes.**
>
> *The Appellee (State of Washington) Wants:* **Enforcement of statute.**

The statutes in question set up a comprehensive scheme of unemployment compensation, the costs of which are defrayed by contributions required to be made by employers to a state unemployment compensation fund. The assessment and collection of the contributions and the fund are administered by appellees. Section 14 (c) of the Act authorizes appellee Commissioner to issue an order and notice of assessment of delinquent contributions upon prescribed personal service of the notice upon the employer if found within the state, or, if not so found, by mailing the notice to the employer by registered mail at his last known address. That section also authorizes the Commissioner to collect the assessment by distraint if it is not paid within ten days after service of the notice.

In this case notice of assessment for the years in question was personally served upon a sales solicitor employed by appellant in the State of Washington, and a copy of the notice was mailed by registered mail to appellant at its address in St. Louis, Missouri. Appellant appeared specially before the office of unemployment and moved to set aside the order and notice of assessment on the ground that the service upon appellant's salesman was not proper service upon appellant; that appellant was not a corporation of the State of Washington and was not doing business within the state; that it had no agent within the state upon whom service could be made; and that appellant is not an employer and does not furnish employment within the meaning of the statute.

The assessment against the company was initially made by the state's commissioner charged with such activities. International Shoe appealed to a review tribunal, which affirmed the commissioner's ruling. That ruling was affirmed again by both the State Superior Court and the State Supreme Court.

The facts are not in dispute. Appellant is a Delaware corporation, having its principal place of business in St. Louis, Missouri, and is engaged in the manufacture and sale of shoes and other footwear. It maintains places of business in several states, other than Washington, at which its manufacturing is carried on and from which its merchandise is distributed interstate through several sales units or branches located outside the State of Washington.

Appellant has no office in Washington and makes no contracts either for sale or purchase of merchandise there. It maintains no stock of merchandise in that state and makes there no deliveries of goods in intrastate commerce. During the years from 1937 to 1940, now in question, appellant employed eleven to thirteen salesmen under direct supervision and control of sales managers located in St. Louis. These salesmen resided in Washington; their principal activities were confined to that state; and they were compensated by commissions based upon the amount of their sales. The commissions for each year totaled more than $ 31,000. Appellant supplies its salesmen with a line of samples, each consisting of one shoe of a pair, which they display to prospective purchasers.

The salesmen transmit the orders to appellant's office in St. Louis for acceptance or rejection, and when accepted the merchandise for filling the orders is shipped f. o. b. from points outside Washington to the purchasers within the state. All the merchandise shipped into Washington is invoiced at the place of shipment from which collections are made. No salesman has authority to enter into contracts or to make collections.

Appellant's argument, renewed here, that the statute imposes an unconstitutional burden on interstate commerce need not detain us. It is no longer debatable that Congress, in the exercise of the commerce power, may authorize the states, in specified ways, to regulate interstate commerce or impose burdens upon it.

Appellant also insists that its activities within the state were not sufficient to manifest its "presence" there and that in its absence the state courts were without jurisdiction, that consequently it was a denial of due process for the state to subject appellant to suit. It refers to those cases in which it was said that the mere solicitation of orders for the purchase of goods within a state, to be accepted without the state and filled by shipment of the purchased goods interstate, does not render the corporation seller amenable to suit within the state. And appellant further argues that since it was not present within the state, it is a denial of due process to subject it to taxation or other money exaction. It thus denies the power of the state to lay the tax or to subject appellant to a suit for its collection.

Historically the jurisdiction of courts to render judgment *in personam* is grounded on their de facto power over the defendant's person. Hence his presence within the territorial jurisdiction of a court was prerequisite to its rendition of a judgment personally binding him. *Pennoyer v. Neff*, 95 U.S. 714, 733. But now that the *capias ad respondendum* has given way to personal service of summons or other form of notice, due process requires only that in order to subject a defendant to a judgment *in personam*, if he be not present within the territory of the forum, he have certain minimum contacts with it such that the maintenance of the suit does not offend "traditional notions of fair play and substantial justice."

Since the corporate personality is a fiction, although a fiction intended to be acted upon as though it were a fact it is clear that unlike an individual its "presence" without, as well as within, the state of its origin can be manifested only by activities carried on in its behalf by those who are authorized to act for it. For the terms "present" or "presence" are used merely to symbolize those activities of the corporation's agent within the state which courts will deem to be sufficient to satisfy the demands of due process. Those demands may be met by such contacts of the corporation with the state of the forum as make it reasonable, in the context of our federal system of government, to require the corporation to defend the particular suit which is brought there. An "estimate of the inconveniences" which would result to the corporation from a trial away from its "home" or principal place of business is relevant in this connection.

"Presence" in the state in this sense has never been doubted when the activities of the corporation there have not only been continuous and systematic, but also give rise to the liabilities sued on, even though no consent to be sued or authorization to an agent to accept service of process has been given. Conversely it has been generally recognized that the casual presence of the corporate agent or even his conduct of single or isolated items of activities in a state in the corporation's behalf are not enough to subject it to suit on causes of action unconnected with the activities there. To require the corporation in such circumstances to defend the suit away from its home or other jurisdiction where it carries on more substantial activities has been thought to lay too great and unreasonable a burden on the corporation to comport with due process.

It is evident that the criteria by which we mark the boundary line between those activities which justify the subjection of a corporation to suit, and those which do not, cannot be simply mechanical or quantitative. The test is not merely, as has sometimes been suggested, whether the activity, which the corporation has seen fit to procure through its agents in another state, is a little more or a little less. Whether due process is satisfied must depend rather upon the quality and nature of the activity in relation to the fair and orderly administration of the laws which it was the purpose of the due process clause to insure.

But to the extent that a corporation exercises the privilege of conducting activities within a state, it enjoys the benefits and protection of the laws of that state. The exercise of that privilege may give rise to obligations, and, so far as those obligations arise out of or are connected with the activities within the state, a procedure which requires the corporation to respond to a suit brought to enforce them can, in most instances, hardly be said to be undue.

Applying these standards, the activities carried on in behalf of appellant in the State of Washington were neither irregular nor casual. They were systematic and continuous throughout the years in question. They resulted in a large volume of interstate business, in the course of which appellant received the benefits and protection of the laws of the state, including the right to resort to the courts for the enforcement of its rights. The obligation which is here sued upon arose out of those very activities. It is evident that these operations establish sufficient contacts or ties with the state of the forum to make it reasonable and just, according to our traditional conception of fair play and substantial justice, to permit the state to enforce the obligations which appellant has incurred there. Hence we cannot say that the maintenance of the present suit in the State of Washington involves an unreasonable or undue procedure.

Appellant having rendered itself amenable to suit upon obligations arising out of the activities of its salesmen in Washington, the state may maintain the present suit in personam to collect the tax laid upon the exercise of the privilege of employing appellant's salesmen within the state.

Affirmed.

DISSENT: BLACK, Justice:

Congress, pursuant to its constitutional power to regulate commerce, has expressly provided that a State shall not be prohibited from levying the kind of unemployment compensation tax here challenged. We have twice decided that this Congressional consent is an adequate answer to a claim that imposition of the tax violates the Commerce Clause. Two determinations by this Court of an issue so palpably without merit are sufficient. Consequently that part of this appeal which again seeks to raise the question seems so patently frivolous as to make the case a fit candidate for dismissal. Nor is the further ground advanced on this appeal, that the State of Washington has denied appellant due process of law, any less devoid of substance. It is my view, therefore, that we should dismiss the appeal as unsubstantial, and decline the invitation to formulate broad rules as to the meaning of due process, which here would amount to deciding a constitutional question "in advance of the necessity for its decision."

[I]t is unthinkable that the vague due process clause was ever intended to prohibit a State from regulating or taxing a business carried on within its boundaries simply because this is done by agents of a corporation organized and having its headquarters elsewhere. To read this into the due process clause would in fact result in depriving a State's citizens of due process by taking from the State the power to protect them in their business dealings within its boundaries with representatives of a foreign corporation. Nothing could be more irrational or more designed to defeat the function of our federative system of government. Were the Court to follow this principle, it would provide a workable standard for cases where, as here, no other questions are involved. The Court has not chosen to do so, but instead has engaged in an unnecessary discussion in the course of which it has announced vague Constitutional criteria applied for the first time to the issue before us. It has thus introduced uncertain elements confusing the simple pattern and tending to curtail the exercise of State powers to an extent not justified by the Constitution.

The criteria adopted insofar as they can be identified read as follows: Due Process does permit State courts to "enforce the obligations which appellant has incurred" if it be found "reasonable and just according to our traditional conception of fair play and substantial justice." And this in turn means that we will "permit" the State to act if upon "an 'estimate of the inconveniences' which would result to the corporation from a trial away from its 'home' or principal place of business," we conclude that it is "reasonable" to subject it to suit in a State where it is doing business.

I believe that the Federal Constitution leaves to each State, without any "ifs" or "buts," a power to tax and to open the doors of its courts for its citizens to sue corporations whose agents do business in those States. Believing that the Constitution gave the States that power, I think it a judicial deprivation to condition its exercise upon this Court's notion of "fair play," however appealing that term may be. Nor can I stretch the meaning of due process so far as to authorize this Court to deprive a State of the right to afford judicial protection to its citizens on the ground that it would be more "convenient" for the corporation to be sued somewhere else.

There is a strong emotional appeal in the words "fair play," "justice," and "reasonableness." But they were not chosen by those who wrote the original Constitution or the Fourteenth Amendment as a measuring rod for this Court to use in invalidating State or Federal laws passed by elected legislative representatives. No one, not even those who most feared a democratic government, ever formally proposed that courts should be given power to invalidate legislation under any such elastic standards. Superimposing the natural justice concept on the Constitution's specific prohibitions could operate as a drastic abridgment of democratic safeguards they embody, such as freedom of speech, press and religion, and the right to counsel. This has already happened. For application of this natural law concept, whether under the terms "reasonableness," "justice," or "fair play," makes judges the supreme arbiters of the country's laws and practices. This result, I believe, alters the form of government our Constitution provides. I cannot agree.

True, the State's power is here upheld. But the rule announced means that tomorrow's judgment may strike down a State or Federal enactment on the ground that it does not conform to this Court's idea of natural justice.

~

In general, the question asked in determining whether personal jurisdiction over a nonresident defendant is proper is whether the defendant "purposely availed" him or herself of the privilege of conducting activities in the forum state such that he or she should be "on notice" that a suit might be possible in that state.

So, what types of activities qualify?

- Personal presence when the actions were committed (regardless of the defendant's location when the suit is filed).
- Conduct specified in a long-arm statute, so long as the long-arm statute's "reach" does not violate the Constitution's Due Process clause. Typical activities specified in long-arm statutes are activities such as "transacting business" or committing tortious acts. "Transacting business" can be things like telephone solicitations, direct mail, or even advertising (if some part of the defendant's performance in response to the ad would have occurred in state).

Can an operator of an online service be subject to jurisdiction in a state or country where the service is accessible but illegal? The Minnesota Attorney General answered this question affirmatively and issued an Internet warning to the public that Minnesota intended to enforce its anti-gambling statutes against online gambling websites based outside Minnesota but accessible to Minnesota citizens. The Minnesota long-arm statute says that such personal jurisdiction is proper if the nonresident person or corporation in question "intentionally causes a result within the state that is prohibited by its laws." The following case resulted.

Jurisdiction: Case 2

State of Minnesota by its Attorney General Hubert H. Humphrey, III, Respondent, vs. Granite Gate Resorts, Inc., d/b/a On Ramp Internet Computer Services, et al., Appellants.

C6-97-89

COURT OF APPEALS OF MINNESOTA

568 N.W.2d 715; 1997 Minn. App. LEXIS 1053

September 5, 1997, Filed

JUDGES: Considered and decided by Willis, Presiding Judge, Crippen, Judge, and Harten, Judge.

OPINION: WILLIS, Judge:

Respondent State of Minnesota filed a complaint against appellants Granite Gate Resorts, Inc., d/b/a On Ramp Internet Computer Services, and Kerry Rogers, individually and as principal officer of Granite Gate Resorts, Inc., alleging that appellants engaged in deceptive trade practices, false advertising, and consumer fraud on the Internet. Appellants challenge the district court's denial of their motion to dismiss for lack of personal jurisdiction. We affirm.

Facts

Rogers, a Nevada resident, is president of Granite Gate, a Nevada corporation that does business as On Ramp. Until August 1995, On Ramp provided Internet advertising on the site located at http://www.vegas.com, which provides Nevada tourist information. Among the sites advertised was WagerNet, an on-line wagering service planned to be available internationally in the fall of 1995, whose page enabled Internet users to subscribe for more information about the service.

The WagerNet site, designed by Rogers, stated:

On-Line sports wagering open to International markets, Fall of 1995

Global Gaming Services Ltd, based in the country of Belize, is pleased to introduce *WagerNet*, the first and only on-line sports betting site on the Internet. *WagerNet* will provide sports fans with a legal way to bet on sporting events from anywhere in the world . . . 24 Hours a Day!

How it Works

First, there is a $ 100 setup fee, for necessary hardware and software. For security and privacy, all members are issued a card system linked to their personal computer to access *WagerNet*. Once on-line, the bettor selects the team/s and amount/s they wish to wager. *WagerNet* then matches your bet with an opposing bettor or bettors to cover your wager. *WagerNet* charges each bettor a transaction fee of ONLY 2.5% as opposed to the 10% fee charged by most bookmakers.

The website invited Internet users to put themselves on a mailing list for WagerNet information and included a form for that purpose. It gave a toll-free number for WagerNet and also told Internet users to contact On Ramp at a Nevada telephone number for more information. A note on the page advised users to consult with local authorities regarding restrictions on offshore sports betting by telephone before registering with WagerNet.

A "disclaimer" of sorts.

A linked web page listed the terms and conditions to which an Internet user assented by applying for the private access card and special hardware and software required to access WagerNet's services. This page stated that any claim against WagerNet by a customer must be brought before a Belizian court, but that WagerNet could sue the consumer in his or her home state to prevent the consumer "from committing any breach or anticipated breach of this Agreement and for consequential relief."

On July 5, 1995, Jeff Janacek, a consumer investigator for the Minnesota Attorney General's office, telephoned the toll-free number shown on an On Ramp site that advertised All Star Sports, a sports handicapping service, and asked how to bet on sports events. An On Ramp employee told Janacek to call Rogers directly. Janacek dialed the number he was given, which was the same number that the WagerNet site directed Internet users to call to receive more information, and spoke with an individual who identified himself as Rogers. Janacek identified himself as a Minnesotan interested in placing bets. Rogers explained how to access WagerNet, told Janacek the betting service was legal, and stated that he hoped the service would be up and running by the 1995 football season.

In July 1995, the attorney general filed a complaint alleging that appellants had engaged in deceptive trade practices, false advertising, and consumer fraud by advertising in Minnesota that gambling on the Internet is lawful. In October 1995, Janacek subscribed to the WagerNet mailing list under a fictitious name and received an on-line confirmation stating that he would be sent updates on the WagerNet service. Appellants filed a motion to dismiss for lack of personal jurisdiction. The district court allowed limited discovery to determine the quantity and quality of appellants' contacts with the state. Rogers refused to produce the names of the persons on the WagerNet mailing list, claiming that the information is the sole property of a Belizian corporation. As a sanction, the court found that it is established as a fact for this action that the WagerNet mailing list contains the name and address of at least one Minnesota resident. In December 1996, the district court denied appellants' motion to dismiss for lack of jurisdiction.

Issue

Did the district court err in denying appellants' motion to dismiss for lack of personal jurisdiction?

Analysis

This is the first time a Minnesota court has addressed the issue of personal jurisdiction based on Internet advertising. We are mindful that the Internet is a communication medium that lacks historical parallel in the potential extent of its reach and that regulation across jurisdictions may implicate fundamental First Amendment concerns. It will undoubtedly take some time to determine the precise balance between the rights of those who use the Internet to disseminate information and the powers of the jurisdictions in which receiving computers are located to regulate for the general welfare. But our task here is limited to deciding the question of personal jurisdiction in the instant case, and on the facts before us, we are satisfied that established legal principles provide adequate guidance.

Minnesota's long-arm statute, Minn. Stat. § 543.19 (1996), "permits courts to assert jurisdiction over defendants to the extent that federal constitutional requirements of due process will allow." To satisfy the Due Process Clause of the Fourteenth Amendment, a plaintiff must show that the defendant has "minimum contacts" with the forum state "such that the maintenance of the suit does not offend 'traditional notions of fair play and substantial justice.'" There must be "some act by which the defendant purposefully avails itself of the privilege of conducting activities within the forum State, thus invoking the benefits and protections of its laws."

Appellants allege that the district court erred in denying their motion to dismiss because a nonresident defendant that places information on the Internet has not purposefully availed itself of the privilege of conducting activities within every state from which that information may be accessed. The assertion of personal jurisdiction in Minnesota, appellants argue, would not comport with the traditional notions of fair play and substantial justice.

A court must consider five factors in determining whether a defendant has established minimum contacts with the forum state: (1) the quantity of the defendant's contacts; (2) the nature and quality of the defendant's contacts; (3) the connection between the cause of action and the defendant's contacts; (4) the state's interest in providing a forum; and (5) the convenience of the parties. The first three factors are of primary importance. In close cases, "doubts should be resolved in favor of retention of jurisdiction."

1. Quantity of Contacts

The quantity of contacts here supports the contention that appellants purposefully availed themselves of the privilege of conducting commercial activities in Minnesota. The district court found that (1) computers located throughout the United States, including Minnesota, accessed appellants' websites, (2) during a two-week period in February and March 1996, at least 248 Minnesota computers accessed and "received transmissions from" appellants' websites, (3) computers located in Minnesota are among the 500 computers that most often accessed appellants' websites, (4) persons located throughout the United States, including persons in Minnesota, called appellants at the numbers advertised on its websites, and (5) the WagerNet mailing list includes the name and address of at least one Minnesota resident.

In *Maritz, Inc. v. Cybergold, Inc.*, 947 F. Supp. 1328 (E.D. Mo. 1996), a Missouri federal court exercised personal jurisdiction over the California operator of an Internet site that provided information on a forthcoming service that would charge advertisers for access to a mailing list of Internet users.

2. Quality of Contacts

Even where the quantity of contacts with a state is minimal, the nature and quality of the contacts may be dispositive. Advertising in the forum state, or establishing channels for providing regular advice to customers in the forum state, indicates a defendant's intent to serve the market in that state.

Appellants argue that they "have not directed their activities at the citizens of Minnesota" because they "only placed information on the internet." An Internet site, however, can be viewed as an "advertisement" by which [the foreign corporation] distributes its pictorial images throughout the United States. That the local user "pulls" these images from [the corporation's] computer, as opposed to [the corporation] "sending" them to this country, is irrelevant.

The *Maritz* court also rejected the view that Internet advertising is a passive activity:

> [Defendant's] posting of information about its new, up-coming service through a website seeks to develop a mailing list of internet users, as such users are essential to the success of its service. Clearly, [the defendant] has obtained the website for the purpose of, and in anticipation that, internet users, searching the internet for websites, will access [the defendant's] website and eventually sign up on [the defendant's] mailing list. Although [the defendant] characterizes its activity as merely maintaining a "passive website," its intent is to reach all internet users, regardless of geographic location.

Minnesota courts have concluded that defendants who know their message will be broadcast in this state are subject to suit here. Other states have held that direct mail solicitation into the state is sufficient contact to justify personal jurisdiction.

Internet advertisements are similar to broadcast and direct mail solicitation in that advertisers distribute messages to Internet users, and users must take affirmative action to receive the advertised product. Here, the WagerNet site itself stated that it was "open to International markets," indicating an intent to seek customers from a very broad geographic area. The presence of the disclaimer on the site may be relevant to the merits of the consumer fraud action, but appellants' clear effort to reach and seek potential profit from Minnesota consumers provides minimum contacts of a nature and quality sufficient to support a threshold finding of personal jurisdiction.

3. Connection Between Cause of Action and Contacts

If the cause of action arises from the nonresident defendant's contacts with the forum state, even a single transaction can be sufficient to establish personal jurisdiction over the defendant. Advertising contacts justify the exercise of personal jurisdiction where unlawful or misleading advertisements are the basis of the plaintiff's claims. [T]he causes of action against appellants arise out of the information that appellants posted on their website inviting Internet users to use the on-line gambling service when it becomes operational, which, as discussed, was directed toward Minnesota and received here.

4. State's Interest

The state has an interest in enforcing consumer protection statutes and regulating gambling. The state's interest in providing a forum to enforce its consumer protection laws weighs in favor of exerting jurisdiction over appellants.

5. Convenience of Parties

The convenience of the parties is "of minor interest in comparison to the first three factors."

As technological progress has increased the flow of commerce between States, progress in communications and transportation has made defense of a suit in a foreign tribunal less burdensome.

"Foreign" corporations that seek business in Minnesota and reserve the right to sue Minnesota customers in courts here cannot claim inconvenience as an excuse to avoid personal jurisdiction here, particularly in light of the state's interest in regulating advertising and gambling. Appellants, an American corporation and its officer, who facilitated WagerNet's solicitation of business in Minnesota, have not shown that the inconvenience of defending themselves in Minnesota would be so great, by itself, as to offend traditional notions of due process.

Decision

For these reasons, we hold that appellants are subject to personal jurisdiction in Minnesota because, through their Internet activities, they purposefully availed themselves of the privilege of doing business in Minnesota to the extent that the maintenance of an action based on consumer protection statutes does not offend traditional notions of fair play and substantial justice.

Affirmed.

Note that these decisions regarding "minimum contacts" and "transacting business" are very fact-dependent. Slight variations in the facts might radically change the outcome.

Vendors who advertise and process orders online might find themselves subject to suit *anywhere.*

Many long-arm statutes specify that one instance in which the state will assert personal jurisdiction over a nonresident defendant is when the defendant has committed "tortious acts." This includes both negligent and intentional torts.

- **Negligence.** The classic case is one in which an Illinois court is found to have personal jurisdiction over an Ohio manufacturer of a safety valve installed in a water heater at a plant in Pennsylvania and then sold to a customer in Illinois. The *tort* (the injury) occurred in Illinois. However, the fact that a nonresident defendant might be able to foresee that a product, such as an automobile, *may* be carried by the stream of commerce into a forum state is not enough to assert personal jurisdiction. There must be an action "purposefully directed toward the forum state."
- **Intentional torts.** Knowingly causing injury to another always subjects a party to jurisdiction in the victim's home state.

The following case is an example of assertion of personal jurisdiction over a nonresident defendant based on the commission of an intentional tort, in this instance via the Internet.

Jurisdiction: Case 3

CALIFORNIA SOFTWARE, INC., a California corporation; and RELIACOMM CORP., Plaintiffs, v. RELIABILITY RESEARCH, INC., a Nevada corporation; JAMES J. WHITE, and LARRY MARTIN, Defendants

No. CV 85-6569 AHS

UNITED STATES DISTRICT COURT FOR THE CENTRAL DISTRICT OF CALIFORNIA

631 F. Supp. 1356; 1986 U.S. Dist. LEXIS 27269

April 2, 1986, Decided
April 2, 1986, Filed

OPINION: STOTLER, Judge:

On October 4, 1985, plaintiffs California Software, Inc. and Reliacomm, Inc. filed a complaint alleging that defendants Reliability Research, Inc. (hereinafter referred to as "RRI"), James White and Larry Martin made false statements through the use of the telephone, the mails, and a nationwide computer network concerning plaintiffs' right to market a software program. Defendants moved to dismiss the complaint for lack of personal jurisdiction. The issue presented is whether defendants' utilization of the foregoing means of communicating with plaintiffs' prospective customers both in and out of California for the purpose stated supports an exercise of jurisdiction in this forum. By this Order, the Court finds limited jurisdiction over two of these defendants. Accordingly, defendants RRI and White's motion is denied and defendant Martin's motion is granted.

I. Background

In 1985, Reliacomm employed California Software to provide marketing and consulting services for a new system of computer software known as resCue/MVS ("the product"). Under the employment contract, California Software agreed to promote and sublicense the product on behalf of Reliacomm. Both plaintiffs are California corporations having their principal places of business in California.

Reliability Research, Inc. ("RRI"), a Nevada corporation with its principal place of business in Vermont, has as its sole business the development of a single software program. RRI employs two individuals, Larry Martin, a citizen of Connecticut, the corporation's president and vice-president, and James White, a citizen of Vermont, its treasurer.

Plaintiffs brought this action as a result of defendants' allegedly tortious communications with certain business entities throughout the United States and Canada. Their claims arise out of two sets of communications made by defendant White with potential purchasers of the resCue/MVS software.

First, White communicated directly with three California residents, each of whom had seriously considered sublicensing plaintiffs' software. White told these companies of a title dispute over the product in a New York action and that, if successful, RRI would cancel all sublicenses to the product marketed by California Software and seek damages from plaintiffs and their sublicensees.

Second, on July 23, 1985, White placed a message on a nationally disseminated computer based information service known as the Computer Reliability Forum (the "CRF"), which is operated by defendants. Operators of large computer installations, having a license from UCCEL, utilize the CRF to share information regarding computer hardware and software. Although one may use the CRF to respond to a specific inquiry, the system acts as a bulletin board, its messages being available and visible to all its users.

White's CRF message stated that RRI was currently attempting to establish its ownership of the resCue/MVS software in a lawsuit filed in New York against California Software. The message further stated that RRI would hold any licensee of the product financially responsible for its use if RRI prevailed in the lawsuit. White's message was received by at least three users of the CRF network: Pacific Northwest Bell in the State of Washington; Marine Midland Bank in Buffalo, New York; and Canada Trust in Ontario, Canada. White placed the message on the CRF in response to inquiries made by these prospective purchasers of the product. The message was also made available to ARCO in California, although no evidence indicates that this CRF message influenced ARCO's decision not to purchase the product.

Plaintiffs claim that these communications contained false and malicious information which discouraged those who received the messages from purchasing plaintiffs' product. Prior to White's interference, the prospective customers had expressed interest in the resCue/MVS software.

II. Discussion

This Court has diversity jurisdiction over the instant matter pursuant to 28 U.S.C. § 1332. In diversity actions, California courts exert personal jurisdiction over non-resident defendants to the fullest extent permissible under the Fourteenth Amendment to the U.S. Constitution. Thus, it must be determined whether defendants have sufficient contacts with the State of California to satisfy due process requirements such that it is appropriate to exercise general or limited jurisdiction.

In order for this Court to assert jurisdiction, the non-resident defendants' contacts with the forum state, though minimal, must be of such quality and quantity that "maintenance of the suit does not offend traditional notions of fair play and substantial justice." A finding of minimum contacts satisfies the due process requirement that the non-resident defendants have "fair warning that a particular activity may subject [them] to the jurisdiction of a foreign sovereign." The defendants' "conduct and connection with the forum State [must be] such that [they] should reasonably anticipate being haled into court there."

A. General Jurisdiction

Plaintiffs failed to meet their burden in demonstrating general jurisdiction over any defendant. A defendant may be haled into a forum state's courts to defend against causes of action unrelated to his conduct there if his activities in the state are "substantial" or "continuous and systematic."

The evidence submitted indicates that neither the corporate defendant nor the two individual defendants maintain sufficient contacts with the State of California to support a finding of general jurisdiction. RRI is not licensed to do business in California and has no offices, agents, employees, telephone listings, bank accounts, or property within the State. Admittedly, RRI is a user of the CRF network and presumably maintains regular communications with California users. The mere act of transmitting information through the use of interstate communication facilities is not, however, sufficient to establish jurisdiction over the sender.

B. Limited Jurisdiction

On the other hand, this Court may assert limited jurisdiction over the non-resident defendants if their activities in the forum give rise to or are related to the litigation. The Court's inquiry must focus on the "relationship among the defendant, the forum, and the litigation." In examining this relationship, the Ninth Circuit applies the following three-prong test to evaluate whether the nature and quality of those contacts justify the assertion of limited jurisdiction:

1. The non-resident defendant must do some act or consummate some transaction within the forum or perform some act by which he purposefully avails himself of the privilege of conducting activities in the forum, thereby invoking the protections and benefits of its laws.
2. The claim must be one which arises out of or results from the defendant's forum-related activities.
3. Exercise of jurisdiction must be reasonable.

In the present case, defendants RRI and White's intentional conduct which gives rise to this litigation justifies assertion of limited jurisdiction over those two defendants.

[A] Court may assert jurisdiction over defendants who conduct their activities outside the physical boundaries of the forum state.

A defendant who purposefully directs his actions at a resident of the forum has "fair warning" that he may have to litigate there.

1. Communications by Mail to California Residents

In the present case, both sets of communications by defendant White subject himself and RRI to the jurisdiction of this Court. First, White contacted three California residents and allegedly employed defamatory statements to dissuade them from purchasing plaintiffs' software. White's statements influenced the receiver's conduct in the State of California, and caused injury there. Plaintiffs' causes of action arise out of statements directed to Californians (ARCO, Gibraltar, and Southern California Gas Company) and expressly aimed at injuring California residents (plaintiffs). Given the purposeful nature of White's conduct, he should have foreseen answering for the effects of his communications in California, reasonable.

2. Communications Over the CRF to Non-California Residents

a. The First Two Prongs of the *Data Disc* Test

This Court may also assert limited jurisdiction over defendants White and RRI as a result of the communications made through the CRF network. Defendants made tortious statements which, though directed at third persons outside California, were expressly calculated to cause injury in California. [T]he defendants knew that plaintiffs would feel the brunt of the injury, i.e., the lost income, in California.

It is significant that defendants acted intentionally. Plaintiffs do not charge defendants with untargeted negligence, the result of which fortuitously injured plaintiffs. Rather, defendants allegedly intentionally manipulated third persons to interrupt their plans to purchase plaintiffs' product.

This suggests, perhaps, that negligently posting information on the Net that happens to injure a party might not be a sufficient basis for personal jurisdiction.

Although the unilateral activity of the plaintiff or a third person cannot subject a non-resident defendant to the forum state's jurisdiction, the recipients of White's CRF message did not act unforeseeably or unilaterally. As a consequence of White's influence, they acted as conduits for defendants' express intention to injure California residents by diminishing plaintiffs' business. Accordingly, such intentional "manipulation" of third persons who thereby refrain from consummating a contemplated transaction in California constitutes a forum-related activity by the defendants. As such, they subject themselves to the laws of the State of California and avail themselves of the privilege of doing business there. This intentional tortious contact, which gives rise to this litigation, satisfies the first two prongs of the *Data Disc* test.

The fact that defendants directed their conduct through third parties does not insulate them from jurisdiction when it is the defendants' own activity that creates the injury in the forum state. The recipients of White's message acted, in a sense, as RRI's alter ego, deflecting business away from California. Not only did defendants intend that these third parties act in such a manner, but they anticipated benefitting therefrom by maintaining their customers and possibly obtaining new ones.

Defendants argue that, although they acted intentionally, they merely responded to inquiries made through the CRF. The conversational format, however, does not affect the jurisdictional analysis. Defendants intentionally responded to the inquiries with allegedly libelous statements and economic threats directed at plaintiffs in California. As explained above, this Court's inquiry must focus on the defendants' actions and not the independent conduct of a third party.

Not only did defendants act intentionally but, by communicating through the CRF network, they made their messages available to an audience wider than those requesting the information. Through the use of computers, corporations can now transact business and communicate with individuals in several states simultaneously. Unlike communication by mail or telephone, messages sent through computers are available to the recipient and anyone else who may be watching. Thus, while modern technology has made nationwide commercial transactions simpler and more feasible, even for small businesses, it must broaden correspondingly the permissible scope of jurisdiction exercisable by the courts.

b. The Third Prong of the *Data Disc* Test

Finally, this Court's assertion of limited jurisdiction over the defendants in relation to their communication over the CRF satisfies the requirement of reasonableness under *Data Disc*. The relevant factors bearing on reasonableness here dictate that this Court find limited jurisdiction.

The State of California has a strong interest in protecting the rights of its injured citizens. Plaintiffs are resident corporations which felt the brunt of the harm from defendants' out-of-state acts in California. It would be both unfair, in light of the forum-related activity, and inefficient to require plaintiffs who have suffered an economic injury as a result of defendants' intentional conduct to sue in defendants' home states (Nevada and Vermont) or in the three jurisdictions in which the known recipients of the CRF message reside (Washington, New York, and Canada).

Assertion of jurisdiction does not unduly burden defendants. Many of the witnesses are located in California while, except for the defendants themselves, none of the witnesses or evidence is located in Vermont.

In conclusion, defendants purposefully injected themselves into California through third parties. Although the defendants did not induce reliance in California itself through the CRF message, they intentionally directed the effects of their conduct into the forum, making jurisdiction in this case reasonable.

White's status as an RRI employee or agent does not insulate him from jurisdiction. Id. at 813. This Court must assess the contacts of each defendant individually, *Rush v. Savchuk*, 444 U.S. 320, 332, 100 S. Ct. 571, 62 L. Ed. 2d 516 (1980), and, as discussed above, the intentional conduct by White on behalf of RRI subjects both defendants to this Court's jurisdiction.

There is no personal jurisdiction over Martin, only over RRI and White. This is because the plaintiffs did not present any evidence of minimum contacts between *him* and California. The Court says it cannot exercise jurisdiction over a nonresident defendant because of the activities of his employer.

Note also that there is no discussion of the California long-arm statute. That is because California uses a "we'll go as far as the Constitution will allow us" model.

Accordingly, defendants RRI and White's Motion to Dismiss for Lack of Personal Jurisdiction is denied, and defendant Martin's Motion is granted.

It is so ordered.

The next case provides an example of how "transacting business" via the Internet can lead to a state asserting personal jurisdiction over a nonresident defendant. In this instance, "transacting business" is entering into a contract.

Jurisdiction: Case 4

COMPUSERVE, INCORPORATED, Plaintiff-Appellant, v. RICHARD S. PATTERSON, individually, and FLASHPOINT DEVELOPMENT, Defendants-Appellees.

No. 95-3452

UNITED STATES COURT OF APPEALS FOR THE SIXTH CIRCUIT

89 F.3d 1257; 1996 U.S. App. LEXIS 17837; 1996 FED App. 0228P (6th Cir.); 39 U.S.P.Q.2D (BNA) 1502; 24 Media L. Rep. 2100

June 14, 1996, Appellant Argued
July 22, 1996, Decided
July 22, 1996, Filed

OPINION: BROWN, Judge:

In a case that requires us to consider the scope of the federal courts' jurisdictional powers in a new context, a computer network giant, CompuServe, appeals the dismissal, for lack of personal jurisdiction, of its complaint in which it sought a declaratory judgment that it had not infringed on the defendants' common law copyrights or otherwise engaged in unfair competition. The district court held that the electronic links between the defendant Patterson, who is a Texan, and Ohio, where CompuServe is headquartered, were "too tenuous to support the exercise of personal jurisdiction." The district court also denied CompuServe's motion for reconsideration. Because we believe that CompuServe made a prima facie showing that the defendant's contacts with Ohio were sufficient to support the exercise of personal jurisdiction, we REVERSE the district court's dismissal and REMAND this case for further proceedings consistent with this opinion.

I. Background

CompuServe is a computer information service headquartered in Columbus, Ohio. It contracts with individual subscribers, such as the defendant, to provide, *inter alia*, access to computing and information services via the Internet, and it is the second largest such provider currently operating on the so-called "information superhighway."

CompuServe also operates as an electronic conduit to provide its subscribers computer software products, which may originate either from CompuServe itself or from other parties. Computer software generated and distributed in this manner is, according to CompuServe, often referred to as "shareware." Shareware makes money only through the voluntary compliance of an "end user," that is, another CompuServe subscriber who may or may not pay the creator's suggested licensing fee if she uses the software beyond a specified trial period. The "end user" pays that fee directly to CompuServe in Ohio, and CompuServe takes a 15% fee for its trouble before remitting the balance to the shareware's creator.

Defendant, Richard Patterson, is an attorney and a resident of Houston, Texas who claims never to have visited Ohio. Patterson also does business as FlashPoint Development. He subscribed to CompuServe, and he also placed items of "shareware" on the CompuServe system for others to use and purchase. When he became a shareware "provider," Patterson entered into a "Shareware Registration Agreement" ("SRA") with CompuServe. Under the SRA, CompuServe provides its subscribers with access to the software, or shareware, that Patterson creates. The SRA purports to create an independent contractor relationship between Patterson and CompuServe, whereby Patterson may place software of his creation on CompuServe's system. The SRA does not mention Patterson's software by name; in fact, it leaves the content and identification of that software to Patterson.

The SRA incorporates by reference two other documents: the CompuServe Service Agreement ("Service Agreement") and the Rules of Operation, both of which are published on the CompuServe Information Service. Both the SRA and the Service Agreement expressly provide that they are entered into in Ohio, and the Service Agreement further provides that it is to "be governed by and construed in accordance with" Ohio law. These documents appear to be standardized and entirely the product of CompuServe. It bears noting, however, that the SRA asks a new shareware "provider" like Patterson to type "AGREE" at various points in the document, "in recognition of your online agreement to all the above terms and conditions." Thus, Patterson's assent to the SRA was first manifested at his own computer in Texas, then transmitted to the CompuServe computer system in Ohio.

From 1991 through 1994, Patterson electronically transmitted 32 master software files to CompuServe. These files were stored in CompuServe's system in Ohio, and they were displayed in different services for CompuServe subscribers, who could "download" them into their own computers and, if they chose to do so, pay for them. Patterson also advertised his software on the CompuServe system, and he indicated a price term in at least one of his advertisements. CompuServe asserts that Patterson marketed his software exclusively on its system. Patterson, for his part, stated that he has sold less than $ 650 worth of his software to only 12 Ohio residents via CompuServe.

Patterson's software product was, apparently, a program designed to help people navigate their way around the larger Internet network. CompuServe began to market a similar product, however, with markings and names that Patterson took to be too similar to his own. Thus, in December of 1993, Patterson notified CompuServe (appropriately via an electronic mail or "E-mail" message) that the terms "WinNAV," "Windows Navigator," and "FlashPoint Windows Navigator" were common law trademarks which he and his company owned. Patterson stated that CompuServe's marketing of its product infringed these trademarks, and otherwise constituted deceptive trade practices. CompuServe changed the name of its program, but Patterson continued to complain. CompuServe asserts that, if Patterson's allegations of trademark infringement are correct, they threaten CompuServe's software sales revenue with a loss of approximately $ 10.8 million.

After Patterson demanded at least $ 100,000 to settle his potential claims, CompuServe filed this declaratory judgment action in the federal district court for the Southern District of Ohio, relying on the court's diversity subject matter jurisdiction. CompuServe sought, among other things, a declaration that it had not infringed any common law trademarks of Patterson or FlashPoint Development, and that it was not otherwise guilty of unfair or deceptive trade practices. Patterson responded *pro se* with a consolidated motion to dismiss on several grounds, including lack of personal jurisdiction. Patterson also submitted a supporting affidavit, in which he denied many jurisdictional facts, including his having ever visited Ohio. CompuServe then filed a memorandum in opposition to Patterson's consolidated motion, along with several supporting exhibits.

The district court, considering only these pleadings and papers, granted Patterson's motion to dismiss for lack of personal jurisdiction in a thorough and thoughtful opinion. At various points in its consideration of the case, however, the district court expressly relied on Patterson's affidavit. The court below then denied CompuServe's motion for a rehearing, which it construed as a motion for reconsideration under Federal Rule of Civil Procedure 59(e). CompuServe timely appealed. Patterson, however, filed no appellate brief, and he did not appear at oral argument.

II. Analysis

A. Standards of Review

We conduct a plenary review of personal jurisdiction issues.

B. Personal Jurisdiction

This case presents a novel question of first impression: Did CompuServe make a prima facie showing that Patterson's contacts with Ohio, which have been almost entirely electronic in nature, are sufficient, under the Due Process Clause, to support the district court's exercise of personal jurisdiction over him?

[T]here is less perceived need today for the federal constitution to protect defendants from "inconvenient litigation," because all but the most remote forums are easily accessible for the pursuit of both business and litigation. The Court has also, however, reminded us that the due process rights of a defendant should be the courts' primary concern where personal jurisdiction is at issue.

The Internet represents perhaps the latest and greatest manifestation of these historical, globe-shrinking trends. It enables anyone with the right equipment and knowledge – that is, people like Patterson – to operate an international business cheaply, and from a desktop. That business operator, however, remains entitled to the protection of the Due Process Clause, which mandates that potential defendants be able "to structure their primary conduct with some minimum assurance as to where the conduct will and will not render them liable to suit." Thus, this case presents a situation where we must reconsider the scope of our jurisdictional reach.

To determine whether personal jurisdiction exists over a defendant, federal courts apply the law of the forum state. "The defendant must be amenable to suit under the forum state's long-arm statute and the due process requirements of the Constitution must be met."

The Ohio long-arm statute allows an Ohio court to exercise personal jurisdiction over nonresidents of Ohio on claims arising from, *inter alia*, the nonresident's transacting any business in Ohio. It is settled Ohio law, moreover, that the "transacting business" clause of that statute was meant to extend to the federal constitutional limits of due process, and that as a result Ohio personal jurisdiction cases require an examination of those limits.

Further, personal jurisdiction may be either general or specific in nature, depending on the nature of the contacts in a given case. In the instant case, because CompuServe bases its action on Patterson's act of sending his computer software to Ohio for sale on its service, CompuServe seeks to establish such specific personal jurisdiction over Patterson.

As always in this context, the crucial federal constitutional inquiry is whether, given the facts of the case, the nonresident defendant has sufficient contacts with the forum state that the district court's exercise of jurisdiction would comport with "traditional notions of fair play and substantial justice."

We conclude that Patterson has knowingly made an effort – and, in fact, purposefully contracted – to market a product in other states, with Ohio-based CompuServe operating, in effect, as his distribution center. Thus, it is reasonable to subject Patterson to suit in Ohio, the state which is home to the computer network service he chose to employ.

1. The "purposeful availment" Requirement

This requirement does not mean that a defendant must be physically present in the forum state. The soliciting of insurance by mail, the transmission of radio broadcasts into a state, and the sending of magazines and newspapers into a state to be sold there by independent contractors are all accomplished without the physical presence of an agent; yet all have been held to constitute the transaction of business in a state.

There is no question that Patterson himself took actions that created a connection with Ohio in the instant case. He subscribed to CompuServe, and then he entered into the Shareware Registration Agreement when he loaded his software onto the CompuServe system for others to use and, perhaps, purchase. Once Patterson had done those two things, he was on notice that he had made contracts, to be governed by Ohio law, with an Ohio-based company. Then, he repeatedly sent his computer software, via electronic links, to the CompuServe system in Ohio, and he advertised that software on the CompuServe system. Moreover, he initiated the events that led to the filing of this suit by making demands of CompuServe via electronic and regular mail messages.

The real question is whether these connections with Ohio are "substantial" enough that Patterson should reasonably have anticipated being haled into an Ohio court.

Patterson entered into a written contract with CompuServe which provided for the application of Ohio law, and he then purposefully perpetuated the relationship with CompuServe via repeated communications with its system in Ohio. And Patterson was far more than a purchaser of services; he was a third-party provider of software who used CompuServe, which is located in Columbus, to market his wares in Ohio and elsewhere.

In fact, it is Patterson's relationship with CompuServe as a software provider and marketer that is crucial to this case. The district court's analysis misses the mark because it disregards the most salient facts of that relationship: that Patterson chose to transmit his software from Texas to CompuServe's system in Ohio, that myriad others gained access to Patterson's software via that system, and that Patterson advertised and sold his product through that system. Though all this happened with a distinct paucity of tangible, physical evidence, there can be no doubt that Patterson purposefully transacted business in Ohio.

Moreover, this was a relationship intended to be ongoing in nature; it was not a "one-shot affair." Patterson sent software to CompuServe repeatedly for some three years, and the record indicates that he intended to continue marketing his software on CompuServe. Patterson deliberately set in motion an ongoing marketing relationship with CompuServe, and he should have reasonably foreseen that doing so would have consequences in Ohio.

Admittedly, merely entering into a contract with CompuServe would not, without more, establish that Patterson had minimum contacts with Ohio. By the same token, Patterson's injection of his software product into the stream of commerce, without more, would be at best a dubious ground for jurisdiction. Because Patterson deliberately did both of those things, however, and because of the other factors that we discuss herein, we believe that ample contacts exist to support the assertion of jurisdiction in this case, and certainly an assertion of jurisdiction by the state where the computer network service in question is headquartered.

Further, we must reject the district court's reliance on the *de minimis* amount of software sales which Patterson claims he enjoyed in Ohio. As this court recently stated, "It is the **'quality'** of [the] contacts," and not their number or status, that determines whether they amount to purposeful availment. Patterson's contacts with CompuServe here were deliberate and repeated, even if they yielded little revenue from Ohio itself.

Moreover, we should not focus solely on the sales that Patterson made in Ohio, because that ignores the sales Patterson may have made through CompuServe to others elsewhere.

In the instant case, the record demonstrates that Patterson not only purposefully availed himself of CompuServe's Ohio-based services to market his software, but that he also "originated and maintained" contacts with Ohio when he believed that CompuServe's competing product unlawfully infringed on his own software. Patterson repeatedly sent both electronic and regular mail messages to CompuServe about his claim, and he posted a message on one of CompuServe's electronic forums, which outlined his case against CompuServe for anyone who wished to read it. Moreover, the record shows that Patterson demanded at least $ 100,000 to settle the matter.

Thus, we believe that the facts which CompuServe has alleged, viewed in the light most favorable to CompuServe, support a finding that Patterson purposefully availed himself of the privilege of doing business in Ohio. He knowingly reached out to CompuServe's Ohio home, and he benefitted from CompuServe's handling of his software and the fees that it generated.

2. The Requirement that the Cause of Action Arises from Patterson's Activities in Ohio

Even though we have found that Patterson purposefully availed himself of Ohio privileges, we must also find that CompuServe's claims against him arise out of his activities in Ohio if we are to find the exercise of jurisdiction proper. If a defendant's contacts with the forum state are related to the operative facts of the controversy, then an action will be deemed to have arisen from those contacts.

The cause of action in the instant case concerns allegations of trademark or trade name infringement and unfair competition. Patterson's contacts with Ohio are certainly related to the operative facts of that controversy. He placed his software on CompuServe's Ohio-based system. He used that system to advertise his software and sell it. The proceeds of those sales flowed to him through Ohio. According to CompuServe's allegations, Patterson has marketed his product exclusively on their system.

As the district court points out, Patterson could have placed his software anywhere and had the same result. Nevertheless, it is uncontroverted that Patterson placed, marketed, and sold his software **only** on Ohio-based CompuServe. Thus, any common law trademark or trade name which Patterson might have in his product would arguably have been created in Ohio, and any violation of those alleged trademarks or trade names by CompuServe would have occurred, at least in part, in Ohio.

Moreover, as noted heretofore with regard to the purposeful availment test, CompuServe's declaratory judgment action arose in part because Patterson threatened, via regular and electronic mail, to seek an injunction against CompuServe's sales of its software product, or to seek damages at law if CompuServe did not pay to settle his purported claim. Thus, Patterson's threats – which were contacts with Ohio – gave rise to the case before us.

3. The Reasonableness Requirement

Here, we have an entrepreneur who purposefully employed CompuServe to market his computer software product. It may be burdensome for Patterson to defend a suit in Ohio, but he knew when he entered into the Shareware Registration Agreement with CompuServe that he was making a connection with Ohio, and presumably he hoped that connection would work to his benefit. Further, Ohio has a strong interest in resolving a dispute involving an Ohio company, which will involve the Ohio law on common law trademarks and trade names. CompuServe alleges that more than $ 10 million could be at stake in this case, and it also contends that this case will have a profound impact on its relationships with other "shareware" providers like Patterson, who also directed their activities toward Ohio-based CompuServe. We have no reason to believe otherwise.

Someone like Patterson who employs a computer network service like CompuServe to market a product can reasonably expect disputes with that service to yield lawsuits in the service's home state.

Finally, because of the unique nature of this case, we deem it important to note what we do not hold. We need not and do not hold that Patterson would be subject to suit in any state where his software was purchased or used; that is not the case before us. We also do not have before us an attempt by another party from a third state to sue Patterson in Ohio for, say, a "computer virus" caused by his software, and thus we need not address whether personal jurisdiction could be found on those facts. Finally, we need not and do not hold that CompuServe may, as the district court posited, sue any regular subscriber to its service for nonpayment in Ohio, even if the subscriber is a native Alaskan who has never left home. Each of those cases may well arise someday, but they are not before us now.

III. Conclusion

Because we believe that Patterson had sufficient contacts with Ohio to support the exercise of personal jurisdiction over him, *we Reverse the district court's dismissal and Remand this case for further proceedings consistent with this opinion.*

∾

Judicial decisions regarding personal jurisdiction based on activities in cyberspace have been mixed. In particular, courts have differed over whether the creation of a "passive website" should be enough to assert personal jurisdiction over a nonresident defendant. Most courts try to sidestep the question any time they have something more tangible on which to base their decisions. The following cases are a sampling of personal jurisdiction cases involving cyberspace issues.

Jurisdiction: Case 5

BENSUSAN RESTAURANT CORPORATION, Plaintiff, -against- RICHARD B. KING, individually and d/b/a THE BLUE NOTE, Defendant.

96 Civ. 3992 (SHS)

UNITED STATES DISTRICT COURT FOR THE SOUTHERN DISTRICT OF NEW YORK

937 F. Supp. 295; 1996 U.S. Dist. LEXIS 13035; 40 U.S.P.Q.2D (BNA) 1519

September 9, 1996, Decided
September 9, 1996, FILED

OPINION: STEIN, Judge:

Plaintiff Bensusan Restaurant Corp. ("Bensusan") brought this action against defendant Richard King, individually and doing business as The Blue Note, alleging that King is infringing on Bensusan's rights in its trademark "The Blue Note." King has moved to dismiss the complaint for lack of personal jurisdiction pursuant to Fed. R. Civ. P. 12(b)(2). The issue raised by that motion is whether the existence of a "site" on the World Wide Web of the Internet, without anything more, is sufficient to vest this Court with personal jurisdiction over defendant pursuant to New York's long-arm statute and the Due Process Clause of the United States Constitution. For the reasons that follow, the motion to dismiss the complaint is granted.

I. Background

Bensusan, a New York corporation, is the creator of a jazz club in New York City known as "The Blue Note." It also operates other jazz clubs around the world. Bensusan owns all rights, title and interest in and to the federally registered mark "The Blue Note." King is an individual who lives in Columbia, Missouri and he owns and operates a "small club" in that city which is also called "The Blue Note."

In April of 1996, King posted a "site" on the World Wide Web of the Internet to promote his club. This Web site, which is located on a computer server in Missouri, allegedly contains "a fanciful logo which is substantially similar to the logo utilized by [Bensusan]." The Web site contains general information about the club in Missouri as well as a calendar of events and ticketing information. The ticketing information includes the names and addresses of ticket outlets in Columbia and a telephone number for charge-by-phone ticket orders, which are available for pick-up on the night of the show at the Blue Note box office in Columbia.

At the time this action was brought, the first page of the Web site contained the following disclaimer: "The Blue Note's Cyberspot should not be confused with one of the world's finest jazz club[s] [the] Blue Note, located in the heart of New York's Greenwich Village. If you should find yourself in the big apple give them a visit." Furthermore, the reference to Bensusan's club in the disclaimer contained a "hyperlink" which permits Internet users to connect directly to Bensusan's Web site by "clicking" on the link. After Bensusan objected to the Web site, King dropped the sentence "If you should find yourself in the big apple give them a visit" from the disclaimer and removed the hyperlink.

Bensusan brought this action asserting claims for trademark infringement, trademark dilution and unfair competition. King has now moved to dismiss the action for lack of personal jurisdiction pursuant to Fed. R. Civ. P. 12(b)(2).

II. Discussion

At this stage of the litigation – prior to an evidentiary hearing or discovery – Bensusan may defeat a motion to dismiss the complaint for lack of personal jurisdiction by making merely a *prima facie* showing of jurisdiction.

In that regard, Bensusan is entitled to have its complaint and affidavits interpreted, and any doubts resolved, in the light most favorable to it.

Knowing that personal jurisdiction over a defendant is measured by the law of the jurisdiction in which the federal court sits, Bensusan relies on subdivisions (a)(2) and (a)(3)(ii) of N.Y. C.P.L.R. § 302, New York's long-arm statute, to support its position that personal jurisdiction exists over King in this action. Each provision will be addressed in turn.

A. C.P.L.R. § 302(a)(2)

C.P.L.R. § 302(a)(2) permits a court to exercise personal jurisdiction over any nondomiciliary who "commits a tortious act within the state" as long as the cause of action asserted arises from the tortious act. [T]he issue that arises in this action is whether the creation of a Web site, which exists either in Missouri or in cyberspace – *i.e.*, anywhere the Internet exists – with a telephone number to order the allegedly infringing product, is an offer to sell the product in New York.

Even after construing all allegations in the light most favorable to Bensusan, its allegations are insufficient to support a finding of long-arm jurisdiction over plaintiff. A New York resident with Internet access and either knowledge of King's Web site location or a "search engine" capable of finding it could gain access to the Web site and view information concerning the Blue Note in Missouri.

It takes several affirmative steps by the New York resident, however, to obtain access to the Web site and utilize the information there. First, the New York resident has to access the Web site using his or her computer hardware and software. Then, if the user wished to attend a show in defendant's club, he or she would have to telephone the box office in Missouri and reserve tickets. Finally, that user would need to pick up the tickets in Missouri because King does not mail or otherwise transmit tickets to the user. Even assuming that the user was confused about the relationship of the Missouri club to the one in New York, such an act of infringement would have occurred in Missouri, not New York. The mere fact that a person can gain information on the allegedly infringing product is not the equivalent of a person advertising, promoting, selling or otherwise making an effort to target its product in New York. Here, there is simply no allegation or proof that any infringing goods were shipped into New York or that any other infringing activity was directed at New York or caused by King to occur here.

Accordingly, C.P.L.R. § 302(a)(2) does not authorize this Court to exercise jurisdiction over King.

B. C.P.L.R.§ 302(a)(3)(ii)

Bensusan also contends that personal jurisdiction is established pursuant to C.P.L.R. § 302(a)(3)(ii), which permits a court to exercise personal jurisdiction over any non-domiciliary for tortious acts committed outside the state that cause injury in the state if the non-domiciliary "expects or should reasonably expect the act to have consequences in the state and derives substantial revenue from interstate or international commerce."

As an initial matter, Bensusan relies on arguments that King participates in interstate commerce by hiring and showcasing bands of national stature. Section 302(a)(3)(ii), however, explicitly states that substantial "revenue" is required from interstate commerce, not mere participation in it. King has submitted an affidavit stating that 99% of his patronage and revenue is derived from local residents of Columbia, Missouri (primarily students from the University of Missouri) and that most of the few out-of-state customers have either an existing or a prior connection to the area, such as graduates of the University of Missouri.

Moreover, Bensusan's allegations of foreseeability, which are based solely on the fact that King knew that Bensusan's club is located in New York, is insufficient to satisfy the requirement that a defendant "expects or should reasonably expect the act to have consequences in the state."

Finally, Bensusan's conclusory allegation of a loss in New York is nothing more that an allegation of an "indirect financial loss resulting from the fact that the injured person resides or is domiciled in New York," which is not the allegation of a "significant economic injury" required by section 302(a)(3).

Accordingly, C.P.L.R. § 302(a)(3) does not authorize this Court to exercise jurisdiction over King.

Bensusan's primary argument in support of both statutory bases for personal jurisdiction is that, because defendant's Web site is accessible in New York, defendant could have foreseen that the site was able to be viewed in New York and taken steps to restrict access to his site only to users in a certain geographic region, presumably Missouri. Regardless of the technical feasibility of such a mere foreseeability of an in-state consequence and a failure to avert that consequence is not sufficient to establish personal jurisdiction.

C. Due Process

Furthermore, even if jurisdiction were proper under New York's long-arm statute, asserting personal jurisdiction over King in this forum would violate the Due Process Clause of the United States Constitution. Due process requires "that the non-resident defendant has purposefully established 'minimum contact' with the forum state such that the 'maintenance of the suit does not offend 'traditional notions of fair play and substantial justice'."

As set forth above, King has done nothing to purposefully avail himself of the benefits of New York. King, like numerous others, simply created a Web site and permitted anyone who could find it to access it. Creating a site, like placing a product into the stream of commerce, may be felt nationwide – or even worldwide – but, without more, it is not an act purposefully directed toward the forum state. There are no allegations that King actively sought to encourage New Yorkers to access his site, or that he conducted any business – let alone a continuous and systematic part of its business – in New York. There is in fact no suggestion that King has any presence of any kind in New York other than the Web site that can be accessed worldwide. Bensusan's argument that King should have foreseen that users could access the site in New York and be confused as to the relationship of the two Blue Note clubs is insufficient to satisfy due process.

The Court then distinguishes *CompuServe v. Patterson*.

Although *CompuServe Inc. v. Patterson*, 89 F.3d 1257 (6th Cir. 1996), a recent decision of the United States Court of Appeals for the Sixth Circuit, reached a different result, it was based on vastly different facts. In that case, the Sixth Circuit found personal jurisdiction proper in Ohio over an Internet user from Texas who subscribed to a network service based in Ohio. The user, however, specifically targeted Ohio by subscribing to the service and entering into a separate agreement with the service to sell his software over the Internet. Furthermore, he advertised his software through the service and repeatedly sent his software to the service in Ohio. Id. at 1264-65. This led that court to conclude that the Internet user "reached out" from Texas to Ohio and "originated and maintained" contacts with Ohio. Id. at 1266. This action, on the other hand, contains no allegations that King in any way directed any contact to, or had any contact with, New York or intended to avail itself of any of New York's benefits.

Accordingly, the exercise of personal jurisdiction over King in this case would violate the protections of the Due Process Clause.

III. Conclusion

For the reasons set forth above, defendant's motion to dismiss the complaint pursuant to Fed. R. Civ. P. 12(b)(2) for lack of personal jurisdiction is granted and the complaint is dismissed.

~

So if Bensusan wants to pursue this matter further, it would have to bring suit in some state that has personal jurisdiction over the defendant, presumably Missouri.

Note that the parties in this case shared the same trademark without conflict for quite some time. It was the Internet and the Web that created a problematic situation.

Note also that the District Court here analyzes the "passive website" issue and finds that, under the Constitution's Due Process clause, the creation of a passive website would not, by itself, provide a sufficient basis for asserting personal jurisdiction over a nonresident defendant. The Court did not have to address that question since it had already decided that New York's long-arm statute did not cover the activities engaged in the Missouri club. However, the Court was anticipating the possibility that the case might be appealed and, if the appellate court disagreed with the District Court on the long-arm statute question, the case would have to be remanded to the District Court to answer the constitutional issue. And, indeed, the District Court's decision was appealed. Here is the appellate court's decision.

Jurisdiction: Case 6

BENSUSAN RESTAURANT CORPORATION, Plaintiff-Appellant, v. RICHARD B. KING, Individually and doing business as The Blue Note, Defendant-Appellee.

Docket No. 96-9344

UNITED STATES COURT OF APPEALS FOR THE SECOND CIRCUIT

126 F.3d 25; 1997 U.S. App. LEXIS 23742; 44 U.S.P.Q.2D (BNA) 1051

April 9, 1997, Argued
September 10, 1997, Decided

OPINION: VAN GRAAFEILAND, Judge:

Bensusan Restaurant Corporation, located in New York City, appeals from a judgment of the United States District Court for the Southern District of New York (Stein, J.) dismissing its complaint against Richard B. King, a Missouri resident, pursuant to Fed. R. Civ. P. 12(b)(2) for lack of personal jurisdiction. We affirm.

In addition to seeking trebled compensatory damages, punitive damages, costs and attorney's fees, Bensusan requests that King be enjoined from:

using the mark "The Blue Note," or any other indicia of the Blue Note in any manner likely to cause confusion, or to cause mistake, or to deceive, or from otherwise representing to the public in any way that [King's club] is in any way sponsored, endorsed, approved, or authorized by, or affiliated or connected with, Plaintiff or its CABARET, by means of using any name, trademark, or service mark of Plaintiff or any other names whatsoever, including but not limited to removal of Defendant's website....

The district court dismissed the complaint in a scholarly opinion. Although we realize that attempting to apply established trademark law in the fast-developing world of the internet is somewhat like trying to board a moving bus, we believe that well-established doctrines of personal jurisdiction law support the result reached by the district court.

In diversity or federal question cases the court must look first to the long-arm statute of the forum state, in this instance, New York. If the exercise of jurisdiction is appropriate under that statute, the court then must decide whether such exercise comports with the requisites of due process. Because we believe that the exercise of personal jurisdiction in the instant case is proscribed by the law of New York, we do not address the issue of due process.

The New York law dealing with personal jurisdiction based upon tortious acts of a non-domiciliary who does not transact business in New York is contained in sub-paragraphs (a)(2) and (a)(3) of CPLR § 302, and Bensusan claims jurisdiction with some degree of inconsistency under both sub-paragraphs. The legislative intent behind the enactment of sub-paragraphs (a)(2) and (a)(3) best can be gleaned by reviewing their disparate backgrounds. Sub-paragraph (a)(2), enacted in 1962, provides in pertinent part that a New York court may exercise personal jurisdiction over a non-domiciliary who "in person or though an agent" commits a tortious act within the state. As recently as 1996, another of our district judges flatly stated:

> To subject non-residents to New York jurisdiction under § 302(a)(2) the defendant must commit the tort while he or she is physically in New York State.

Bensusan has failed to allege that King or his agents committed a tortious act in New York as required for exercise of personal jurisdiction under CPLR § 302(a)(2). The acts giving rise to Bensusan's lawsuit – including the authorization and creation of King's web site, the use of the words "Blue Note" and the Blue Note logo on the site, and the creation of a hyperlink to Bensusan's web site – were performed by persons physically present in Missouri and not in New York. Even if Bensusan suffered injury in New York, that does not establish a tortious act in the state of New York within the meaning of § 302(a)(2).

Bensusan's claims under sub-paragraph (a)(3) can be quickly disposed of. Sub-paragraph (a)(2) left a substantial gap in New York's possible exercise of jurisdiction over non-residents because it did not cover the tort of a non-resident that took place outside of New York but caused injury inside the state. Accordingly, in 1966 the New York Legislature enacted sub-paragraph (a)(3), which provides in pertinent part that New York courts may exercise jurisdiction over a non-domiciliary who commits a tortious act without the state, causing injury to person or property within the state. However, once again the Legislature limited its exercise of jurisdictional largess. Insofar as is pertinent herein it restricted the exercise of jurisdiction under sub-paragraph (a)(3) to persons who expect or should reasonably expect the tortious act to have consequences in the state and in addition derive substantial revenue from interstate commerce. To satisfy the latter requirement, Bensusan relies on the arguments that King participated in interstate commerce by hiring bands of national stature and received revenue from customers – students of the University of Missouri – who, while residing in Missouri, were domiciliaries of other states. These alleged facts were not sufficient to establish that substantial revenues were derived from interstate commerce, a requirement that "is intended to exclude non-domiciliaries whose business operations are of a local character." King's "Blue Note" cafe was unquestionably a local operation.

For all the reasons above stated, we affirm the judgment of the district court.

∼

So the Second Circuit Court of Appeals says that merely creating a "passive" website that can be accessed by New Yorkers does not amount to the type of contact that satisfies the New York long-arm statute. However, it is important to note that the appellate Court specifically does *not* address the issue of whether the creation of a passive website by a nonresident defendant satisfies the minimum contacts rule for personal jurisdiction.

The Connecticut long-arm statute contains the same language as the New York statute, asserting personal jurisdiction over a nonresident defendant who "commits a tortious act within the state." However, as the next cases shows, courts in different states can interpret identical language in different ways.

Jurisdiction: Case 7

COLIN M. CODY, Plaintiff, V. KEVIN M. WARD, Defendant.

CASE NO. 3:95CV169 (RNC)

UNITED STATES DISTRICT COURT FOR THE DISTRICT OF CONNECTICUT

954 F. Supp. 43; 1997 U.S. Dist. LEXIS 1496

February 4, 1997, Decided

OPINION: CHATIGNY, Judge:

Ruling and Order on Motion to Dismiss for Lack of Personal Jurisdiction

This case presents interesting issues of personal jurisdiction. Plaintiff Colin M. Cody, a resident of Connecticut, alleges that he invested almost $ 200,000 in common stock of E. N. Phillips Company ("ENP"), an installer of video bingo games in casino-style bingo halls in Louisiana, in reliance on fraudulent misrepresentations by defendant Kevin M. Ward, a resident of California. Claiming that the stock is now worthless, he seeks damages and other relief against the defendant under the Connecticut Uniform Securities Act. The defendant has moved to dismiss the action pursuant to Fed. R. Civ. P. 12(b)(2) for lack of personal jurisdiction on the ground that he engaged in no activities that would make him susceptible to suit in Connecticut. For reasons explained below, I conclude that a nonresident's transmission of fraudulent misrepresentations to a Connecticut resident by telephone and electronic mail for the purpose of inducing him to buy and hold securities renders the nonresident subject to suit in Connecticut in an action based on the misrepresentations. Accordingly, the motion to dismiss is denied.

1. Background

Plaintiff alleges that the defendant communicated with potential investors concerning ENP stock via Prodigy, an on-line computer service, which maintains a forum for discussion of financial matters known as "Money Talk." Plaintiff alleges that between

August 1993 and May 1994, the defendant posted 225 messages on Prodigy encouraging people to buy or hold ENP shares. Most of the messages were addressed to current and potential ENP investors as a group but some were addressed specifically to particular individuals, including the plaintiff, who was known to the defendant to be a Connecticut user of "Money Talk."

The defendant's Prodigy messages purported to provide reliable factual information concerning ENP that the defendant had obtained as a result of personal contacts with the President of ENP and others intimately familiar with the company.

Plaintiff alleges that in August and September 1993, he purchased 101,000 shares of ENP stock for $ 196,000 in reliance on materially false and misleading statements by the defendant. Plaintiff does not claim that his purchases were based solely on the Prodigy messages. Rather, he alleges that in early September 1993, while he was in the process of purchasing ENP shares, the defendant telephoned him in Connecticut four times to discuss ENP stock. He further alleges that between September 1993 and May 1994, the defendant sent him at least 15 messages regarding ENP stock by electronic mail directed to his personal computer in Connecticut, which caused him to hold his ENP shares.

2. Discussion

a. Long Arm Jurisdiction

Plaintiff contends that the defendant is subject to suit under Connecticut's long arm statute on the ground that a person who sends false representations into Connecticut by wire "commits a tortious act within the state" as that phrase is used in Conn. Gen. Stat. § 52-59b(a)(2), the subsection of the statute applicable to nonresident individuals. Defendant contends that the long arm statute does not apply to him because he was not physically present in Connecticut when the alleged misrepresentations were made.

The Connecticut Supreme Court has not addressed the issue whether § 52-59b(a)(2) applies to a nonresident who sends oral and written misrepresentations into Connecticut. However, I believe the court would conclude that the statute does apply to the tortious acts alleged in the amended complaint even though the defendant was not physically present in the state when those acts occurred.

In making this prediction, I am guided by *David v. Weitzman*, 677 F. Supp. 95, 98 (D. Conn. 1990), where Judge Cabranes held that transmitting fraudulent misrepresentations into Connecticut by mail and telephone in connection with the sale of a condominium in Florida was conduct "within the state" for purposes of both § 52-59b(a)(2) and § 33-411(c)(4).

A more restrictive interpretation of § 52-59b(a)(2) is suggested by case law construing the tortious act provision of New York's long arm statute. Since *Feathers v. McLucas*, 15 N.Y.2d 443, 446-64, 261 N.Y.S.2d 8 (1965), the New York provision has been interpreted to mean that a nonresident does not "commit a tortious act within the state" unless he is physically present in the state while the tort is committed. Consistent with that interpretation, most courts sitting in New York have declined to exercise jurisdiction over nonresidents who transmitted misrepresentations into New York from outside the state.

Cases construing New York's tortious act provision would be of interest to the Connecticut Supreme Court but they would not be viewed as controlling. Many states assert jurisdiction over a nonresident when, as in this case, oral and written misrepresentations are directed specifically to the forum. Interpreting Connecticut's long arm statute to reach this type of intentional tort is consistent with the statute's remedial purpose of providing Connecticut residents with a convenient forum to seek redress for losses they suffer here as a result of a nonresident's tortious actions. This interpretation of the statute is also consistent with Connecticut's traditional adherence to the doctrine that tort cases are governed by the law of the place of injury.

b. Due Process

Because the defendant is amenable to suit under the long arm statute, his motion to dismiss must be denied unless exercising personal jurisdiction over him would offend due process.

I conclude that the defendant's contacts with the plaintiff in Connecticut were substantial enough that he should reasonably have anticipated being sued here. Crediting the allegations of the amended complaint, the defendant made fraudulent misrepresentations to the plaintiff in a series of telephone calls and e-mail messages for the purpose of causing the plaintiff to purchase and hold ENP shares. Given the nature and number of the defendant's telephone calls and e-mail messages to the plaintiff, he could reasonably expect to be sued in Connecticut if the plaintiff lost the nearly $ 200,000 he invested in ENP stock.

Because the threshold requirement of purposeful minimum contacts with Connecticut is satisfied, jurisdiction is proper unless exercising specific personal jurisdiction over the defendant on the basis of his contacts with Connecticut would be unfair. The defendant has not shown that litigating in Connecticut would be so costly or inconvenient for him that for all practical purposes he would be deprived of his day in court. Connecticut has a strong interest in adjudicating this dispute and the plaintiff has an obvious interest in obtaining convenient and effective relief, which would be impaired if he were required to sue the defendant in California. Weighing all these factors, I am not persuaded that exercising jurisdiction over the defendant would be unjust.

Accordingly, the defendant's motion to dismiss is hereby denied.

So ordered.

∾

Some courts have been willing to confront the "passive website" question head-on. The final two jurisdiction cases are examples of how the courts have differed.

Jurisdiction: Case 8

INSET SYSTEMS, INC., Plaintiff, v. INSTRUCTION SET, INC., Defendant.

Civil No. 3:95CV-01314 (AVC)

UNITED STATES DISTRICT COURT FOR THE DISTRICT OF CONNECTICUT

937 F. Supp. 161; 1996 U.S. Dist. LEXIS 7160; 155 A.L.R. Fed. 745

April 17, 1996, Decided
April 17, 1996, FILED

OPINION: COVELLO, Judge:

Memorandum of Decision on Motion to Dismiss

This is an action for damages and injunctive relief based upon an alleged infringement of a trademark.

The defendant, Instruction Set, Inc., now moves pursuant to Rules 12(b)(2) and 12(b)(3) of the Federal Rules of Civil Procedure to dismiss the complaint in its entirety based upon a lack of personal jurisdiction over the defendant and for the further reason that venue is set in the wrong forum.

Facts

The plaintiff, Inset Systems, Inc. ("Inset"), is a corporation organized under the laws of the state of Connecticut, with its office and principal place of business in Brookfield, Connecticut. Inset develops and markets computer software and other related services throughout the world. The defendant, Instruction Set, Inc. ("ISI"), is a corporation organized under the laws of the state of Massachusetts, with its office and principal place of business in Natick, Massachusetts. ISI provides computer technology and support to thousands of organizations throughout the world. ISI does not have any employees, nor offices within Connecticut, and it does not conduct business in Connecticut on a regular basis.

On August 23, 1985, Inset filed for registration as the owner of the federal trademark INSET. On October 21, 1986, Inset received registration number 1,414,031.

Thereafter, ISI obtained "INSET.COM" as its Internet domain address. ISI uses this domain address to advertise its goods and services.

The Internet is a global communications network. If a company uses a domain which is identical to the name or trademark of a company, an Internet user may inadvertently access an unintended company. Thereafter, the Internet user may not realize that the advertisement is actually from an unintended company, or the Internet user may erroneously assume that the source of information is the intended company. As a result, confusion in the marketplace could develop.

Unlike television and radio, in which advertisements are broadcast at certain times only, or newspapers in which advertisements are often disposed of quickly, advertisements over the Internet are available to Internet users continually, at the stroke of a few keys of a computer. At this time there are at least 10,000 Internet connected computer users in the state of Connecticut.

Inset first learned of ISI's Internet domain address in March, 1995 when attempting to obtain the same Internet domain address. ISI also uses the telephone number "1-800-US-INSET" to further advertise its goods and services. Inset did not authorize ISI's use of its trademark, "INSET," in any capacity. ISI continues to use "INSET" in relation to both its Internet domain address and its toll-free number. On June 30, 1995, the plaintiff filed the within action.

Discussion

1. Connecticut Long-Arm Statute

ISI, the defendant, in the within motion does not specifically address whether the Connecticut long-arm statute, C.G.S. § 33-411(c) has been satisfied in the present instance.

Inset, the plaintiff, on the other hand, argues that the requirement of the Connecticut long-arm statute has been satisfied because ISI has repeatedly solicited business within Connecticut via its Internet advertisement and the availability of its toll-free number.

The Connecticut long-arm statute, C.G.S. § 33-411(c)(2) states that "Every foreign corporation shall be subject to suit in this state, by a resident of this state . . . on any cause of action arising . . . (2) out of any business solicited in this state . . . if the corporation has repeatedly so solicited business, whether the orders or offers relating thereto were accepted within or without the state . . . "

In *McFaddin v. National Executive Search, Inc.*, 354 F. Supp. 1166, 1169 (D.Conn. 1973), the court held that "the placing of at least six franchise ads over a six-month period in a newspaper whose circulation clearly includes Connecticut (citation omitted) demonstrates a sufficiently repetitious pattern to satisfy subsection (c)(2)" of the Connecticut long-arm statute. See also *Whelen Eng'g Co.*, 672 F. Supp. 659 (advertising in 30 publications known to have been circulated in Connecticut over the course of a year and a half, plus delivery of 30 allegedly infringing catalogs to Connecticut residents, plus two sales of the allegedly infringing products to Connecticut residents, which may or may not have been due to the solicitation activities, satisfies C.G.S. § 33-411(c)(2)).

Similarly, since March, 1995, ISI has been continuously advertising over the Internet, which includes at least 10,000 access sites in Connecticut. Further, unlike hard-copy advertisements noted in the above two cases, which are often quickly disposed of and reach a limited number of potential consumers, Internet advertisements are in electronic printed form so that they can be accessed again and again by many more potential consumers.

The court concludes that advertising via the Internet is solicitation of a sufficient repetitive nature to satisfy subsection (c)(2) of the Connecticut long-arm statute, C.G.S. § 33-411, thereby conferring Connecticut's long-arm jurisdiction upon ISI.

2. Minimum Contacts

The defendant claims that personal jurisdiction is lacking here because it does not have sufficient minimum contacts within Connecticut to satisfy constitutional precepts concerning due process. Minimum contacts are lacking, according to the defendant, because it is a Massachusetts corporation with its office and principal place of business in Natick, Massachusetts, "it does not conduct business in Connecticut on a regular basis," and it "does not maintain an office in Connecticut, nor does it have a sales force or employees in the State."

The plaintiff responds that minimum contacts comporting with due process have been satisfied because the defendant has used the Internet, as well as its toll-free number, to try to conduct business within the state of Connecticut.

a. Reasonably Anticipate

Instruction has directed its advertising activities via the Internet and its toll-free number toward not only the state of Connecticut, but to all states. The Internet as well as toll-free numbers are designed to communicate with people and their businesses in every state. Advertisement on the Internet can reach as many as 10,000 Internet users within Connecticut alone. Further, once posted on the Internet, unlike television and radio advertising, the advertisement is available continuously to any Internet user. ISI has therefore, purposefully availed itself of the privilege of doing business within Connecticut.

The court concludes that since ISI purposefully directed its advertising activities toward this state on a continuing basis since March, 1995, it could reasonably anticipate the possibility of being haled into court here.

b. Fair Play and Substantial Justice

Since the defendant contends that no minimum contacts exist, it did not address the fairness of such a finding.

The plaintiff states that it is fair to adjudicate the present case in Connecticut because travel time between Natick, Massachusetts and Hartford, Connecticut is less than two hours, and the defendant has retained counsel within the state of Connecticut.

In the present case, the distance between Connecticut and Massachusetts is minimal. Further, since the present action also concerns issues of Connecticut common and statutory law, Connecticut has an interest in adjudicating the dispute. This being the case, adjudication in Connecticut would dispose of this matter efficiently. Therefore, the court concludes that its finding of minimum contacts in this case comports with notions of fair play and substantial justice.

3. Venue

The defendant next claims that, according to 28 U.S.C. § 1391(b), venue is improper because the defendants reside in different states, the events or omissions giving rise to this claim took place in Massachusetts, and this action, therefore, should be prosecuted in Massachusetts.

The plaintiff responds that subsection (1) of 28 U.S.C. § 1391(b) which states that "a civil action . . . may . . . be brought only in (1) a judicial district where any defendant resides, if all defendants reside in the same state . . . ," has been satisfied in this case. This is because 28 U.S.C. § 1391(c) provides that: "a defendant that is a corporation shall be deemed to reside in any judicial district in which it is subject to personal jurisdiction at the time the action is commenced. . . . " Since the defendant, ISI, a corporation, is subject to personal jurisdiction in Connecticut, then for venue purposes, it is deemed to reside in Connecticut.

The court concludes, therefore, that the provisions of § 1391(b)(1) having been complied with, Connecticut venue is proper.

Conclusion

For the foregoing reasons, the motion to dismiss is denied.

Jurisdiction: Case 9

CYBERSELL, INC., an Arizona corporation, Plaintiff-Appellant, v.
CYBERSELL, INC., a Florida corporation; WEBHORIZONS, INC., a Florida corporation; WEBSOLVERS, INC., a Florida corporation; SAMUEL C. CERTO, husband; JANE DOE CERTO, wife; MATT CERTO, husband; JANE DOE II CERTO,

wife; CYBERGATE, INC., a corporation; SPRINTNET, a corporation,
Defendants-Appellees.

No. 96-17087

UNITED STATES COURT OF APPEALS FOR THE NINTH CIRCUIT

130 F.3d 414; 1997 U.S. App. LEXIS 33871; 44 U.S.P.Q.2D (BNA) 1928; 97 Cal. Daily
Op. Service 9006; 97 Daily Journal DAR 14545

November 6, 1997, Argued, Submitted, San Francisco, California
December 2, 1997, Filed

OPINION: RYMER, Judge:

We are asked to hold that the allegedly infringing use of a service mark in a home page
on the World Wide Web suffices for personal jurisdiction in the state where the holder of
the mark has its principal place of business. Cybersell, Inc., an Arizona corporation that
advertises for commercial services over the Internet, claims that Cybersell, Inc., a Florida
corporation that offers web page construction services over the Internet, infringed its
federally registered mark and should be amenable to suit in Arizona because cyberspace
is without borders and a web site which advertises a product or service is necessarily
intended for use on a world wide basis. The district court disagreed, and so do we.
Instead, applying our normal "minimum contacts" analysis, we conclude that it would
not comport with "traditional notions of fair play and substantial justice," for Arizona
to exercise personal jurisdiction over an allegedly infringing Florida web site advertiser
who has no contacts with Arizona other than maintaining a home page that is accessible
to Arizonans, and everyone else, over the Internet. We therefore affirm.

I

Cybersell, Inc. is an Arizona corporation, which we will refer to as Cybersell AZ. It
was incorporated in May 1994 to provide Internet and web advertising and marketing
services, including consulting. The principals of Cybersell AZ are Laurence Canter and
Martha Siegel, known among web users for first "spamming" the Internet.

On August 8, 1994, Cybersell AZ filed an application to register the name "Cybersell"
as a service mark. The application was approved and the grant was published on October
30, 1995. Cybersell AZ operated a web site using the mark from August 1994 through
February 1995. The site was then taken down for reconstruction.

Meanwhile, in the summer of 1995, Matt Certo and his father, Dr. Samuel C. Certo,
both Florida residents, formed Cybersell, Inc., a Florida corporation (Cybersell FL), with
its principal place of business in Orlando. Matt was a business school student at Rollins
College, where his father was a professor; Matt was particularly interested in the Internet,
and their company was to provide business consulting services for strategic management
and marketing on the web. At the time the Certos chose the name "Cybersell" for their
venture, Cybersell AZ had no home page on the web nor had the PTO granted their
application for the service mark.

As part of their marketing effort, the Certos created a web page at http://www.
cybsell.com/cybsell/index.htm. The home page has a logo at the top with "CyberSell"
over a depiction of the planet earth, with the caption underneath "Professional Services
for the World Wide Web" and a local (area code 407) phone number. It proclaims in

large letters "Welcome to CyberSell!" A hypertext link allows the browser to introduce himself, and invites a company not on the web – but interested in getting on the web – to "Email us to find out how!"

Canter found the Cybersell FL web page and sent an e-mail on November 27, 1995 notifying Dr. Certo that "Cybersell" is a service mark of Cybersell AZ. Trying to disassociate themselves from the Canters, the Certos changed the name of Cybersell FL to WebHorizons, Inc. on December 27 (later it was changed again to WebSolvers, Inc.) and by January 4, 1996, they had replaced the CyberSell logo at the top of their web page with WebHorizons, Inc. The WebHorizons page still said "Welcome to CyberSell!"

Cybersell AZ filed the complaint in this action January 9, 1996 in the District of Arizona, alleging trademark infringement, unfair competition, fraud, and RICO violations. On the same day Cybersell FL filed suit for declaratory relief with regard to use of the name "Cybersell" in the United States District Court for the Middle District of Florida, but that action was transferred to the District of Arizona and consolidated with the Cybersell AZ action. Cybersell FL moved to dismiss for lack of personal jurisdiction. The district court denied Cybersell AZ's request for a preliminary injunction, then granted Cybersell FL's motion to dismiss for lack of personal jurisdiction. Cybersell AZ timely appealed.

The Arizona Supreme Court has stated that under Rule 4.2(a), "Arizona will exert personal jurisdiction over a nonresident litigant to the maximum extent allowed by the federal constitution." Thus, Cybersell FL may be subject to personal jurisdiction in Arizona so long as doing so comports with due process.

Cybersell AZ concedes that general jurisdiction over Cybersell FL doesn't exist in Arizona, so the only issue in this case is whether specific jurisdiction is available.

Cybersell AZ argues that trademark infringement occurs when the passing off of the mark occurs, which in this case, it submits, happened when the name "Cybersell" was used on the Internet in connection with advertising. Cybersell FL, on the other hand, contends that a party should not be subject to nationwide, or perhaps worldwide, jurisdiction simply for using the Internet.

A

Since the jurisdictional facts are not in dispute, we turn to the first requirement, which is the most critical. We recently explained in *Ballard* that the "purposeful availment" requirement is satisfied if the defendant has taken deliberate action within the forum state or if he has created continuing obligations to forum residents. "It is not required that a defendant be physically present within, or have physical contacts with, the forum, provided that his efforts 'are purposefully directed' toward forum residents."

We have not yet considered when personal jurisdiction may be exercised in the context of cyberspace, but the Second and Sixth Circuits have had occasion to decide whether personal jurisdiction was properly exercised over defendants involved in transmissions over the Internet, see *CompuServe, Inc. v. Patterson*, 89 F.3d 1257 (6th Cir. 1996); *Bensusan Restaurant Corp. v. King*, 937 F. Supp. 295 (S.D.N.Y. 1996), *aff'd*, 126 F.3d 25, 1997 WL 560048 (2d Cir. 1997), as have a number of district courts. Because this is a matter of first impression for us, we have looked to all of these cases for guidance. Not surprisingly, they reflect a broad spectrum of Internet use on the one hand, and contacts with the forum on the other.

Patterson subscribed to CompuServe and placed items of "shareware" on the CompuServe system pursuant to a "Shareware Registration Agreement" with CompuServe which provided, among other things, that it was "to be governed by and construed in accordance with" Ohio law. The court found that Patterson's relationship with CompuServe as a software provider and marketer was a crucial indicator that Patterson had knowingly reached out to CompuServe's Ohio home and benefitted from CompuServe's handling of his software and fees. Because Patterson had chosen to transmit his product from Texas to CompuServe's system in Ohio, and that system provided access to his software to others to whom he advertised and sold his product, the court concluded that Patterson purposefully availed himself of the privilege of doing business in Ohio.

The Court then discusses the *District* court decision in *Bensusan*, without making it clear that the question of "passive" website jurisdiction is not addressed by the Second Circuit Court of Appeals. The citation provided above, which indicates that the Court of Appeals affirmed the District Court's decision, without noting that it did so only on the question of New York's long-arm statute, is very misleading and has led to a great deal of confusion in the cyberlaw community.

By contrast, the defendant in *Bensusan* owned a small jazz club known as "The Blue Note" in Columbia, Missouri. He created a general access web page that contained information about the club in Missouri as well as a calendar of events and ticketing information. Tickets were not available through the web site, however. The district court distinguished King's passive web page, which just posted information, from the defendant's use of the Internet in *CompuServe* by observing that whereas the Texas Internet user specifically targeted Ohio by subscribing to the service, entering into an agreement to sell his software over the Internet, advertising through the service, and sending his software to the service in Ohio, King has done nothing to purposefully avail himself of the benefits of New York. King, like numerous others, simply created a Web site and permitted anyone who could find it to access it. Creating a site, like placing a product into the stream of commerce, may be felt nationwide – or even worldwide – but, without more, it is not an act purposefully directed toward the forum state.

"Interactive" web sites present somewhat different issues. Unlike passive sites such as the defendant's in *Bensusan*, users can exchange information with the host computer when the site is interactive. Courts that have addressed interactive sites have looked to the "level of interactivity and commercial nature of the exchange of information that occurs on the Web site" to determine if sufficient contacts exist to warrant the exercise of jurisdiction.

Cybersell AZ points to several district court decisions which it contends have held that the mere advertisement or solicitation for sale of goods and services on the Internet gives rise to specific jurisdiction in the plaintiff's forum. However, so far as we are aware, no court has ever held that an Internet advertisement alone is sufficient to subject the advertiser to jurisdiction in the plaintiff's home state. Rather, in each, there has been "something more" to indicate that the defendant purposefully (albeit electronically) directed his activity in a substantial way to the forum state.

But then the Court discusses the *Inset Systems* case, in which the Court held specifically that an Internet advertisement alone is sufficient to subject a nonresident defendant to personal jurisdiction!

Inset Systems, Inc. v. Instruction Set, Inc., 937 F. Supp. 161 (D. Conn. 1996), is the case most favorable to Cybersell AZ's position. Inset learned of ISI's domain address when it tried to get the same address, and filed suit for trademark infringement in Connecticut. The court reasoned that ISI had purposefully availed itself of doing business in Connecticut because it directed its advertising activities via the Internet and its toll-free number toward the state of Connecticut (and all states); Internet sites and toll-free numbers are designed to communicate with people and their businesses in every state; an Internet advertisement could reach as many as 10,000 Internet users within Connecticut alone; and once posted on the Internet, an advertisement is continuously available to any Internet user.

Some courts have given weight to the number of "hits" received by a web page from residents in the forum state, and to other evidence that Internet activity was directed at, or bore fruit in, the forum state.

In sum, the common thread is that "the likelihood that personal jurisdiction can be constitutionally exercised is directly proportionate to the nature and quality of commercial activity that an entity conducts over the Internet."

B

Here, Cybersell FL has conducted no commercial activity over the Internet in Arizona. All that it did was post an essentially passive home page on the web, using the name "CyberSell," which Cybersell AZ was in the process of registering as a federal service mark. While there is no question that anyone, anywhere could access that home page and thereby learn about the services offered, we cannot see how from that fact alone it can be inferred that Cybersell FL deliberately directed its merchandising efforts toward Arizona residents.

Cybersell FL did nothing to encourage people in Arizona to access its site, and there is no evidence that any part of its business (let alone a continuous part of its business) was sought or achieved in Arizona. There is no evidence that any Arizona resident signed up for Cybersell FL's web construction services. It entered into no contracts in Arizona, made no sales in Arizona, received no telephone calls from Arizona, earned no income from Arizona, and sent no messages over the Internet to Arizona. The only message it received over the Internet from Arizona was from Cybersell AZ. No money changed hands on the Internet from (or through) Arizona. In short, Cybersell FL has done no act and has consummated no transaction, nor has it performed any act by which it purposefully availed itself of the privilege of conducting activities, in Arizona, thereby invoking the benefits and protections of Arizona law.

We therefore hold that Cybersell FL's contacts are insufficient to establish "purposeful availment." Cybersell AZ has thus failed to satisfy the first prong of our three-part test for specific jurisdiction. We decline to go further solely on the footing that Cybersell AZ has alleged trademark infringement over the Internet by Cybersell FL's use of the registered name "Cybersell" on an essentially passive web page advertisement. Otherwise, every complaint arising out of alleged trademark infringement on the Internet would automatically result in personal jurisdiction wherever the plaintiff's principal place of business is located.

[Section III is omitted.]

IV

We conclude that the essentially passive nature of Cybersell FL's activity in posting a home page on the World Wide Web that allegedly used the service mark of Cybersell AZ does not qualify as purposeful activity invoking the benefits and protections of Arizona. As it engaged in no commercial activity and had no other contacts via the Internet or otherwise in Arizona, Cybersell FL lacks sufficient minimum contacts with Arizona for personal jurisdiction to be asserted over it there. Accordingly, its motion to dismiss for lack of personal jurisdiction was properly granted.

Affirmed.

The issue of whether the creation of a "passive website" subjects a nonresident defendant to personal jurisdiction in any state from which the site is accessible – which is to say all states – has still not been definitively answered. For policy reasons, most commentators seem to believe that the answer should be that personal jurisdiction based on a passive website is not reasonable.

However, the opposite point of view is not entirely without merit. As we have seen earlier, doing business in any jurisdiction will subject a nonresident to personal jurisdiction there. It might be argued that anyone who creates a website for the purpose of doing business is intentionally taking advantage of the broad Web-wide availability of the website and *wants* to do business in every jurisdiction. If successful, the creator of the website, doing business in all jurisdictions, would be subject to personal jurisdiction in all states. It is not completely unreasonable to say that a person soliciting business on a continuous basis in all jurisdictions should be subject to personal jurisdiction just as if he or she had succeeded in a bid to do business everywhere.

Afterword

Unlike most inventions and technologies, the development of computing is a story of unintended consequences. The elevator was invented to permit the vertical growth of cities; the automobile was invented to speed transportation; the telegraph and telephone to enhance communication across distances. Those inventions have retained their original purpose. The computer, on the other hand, was devised as a machine to speed up mathematical calculations. No one foresaw that it would ultimately become the single most ubiquitous communication device known and the portal for each computer user on the Net to a vast new world called cyberspace, with its own social norms and, consequently, a significant impact on law.

Perhaps the single most critical issue we must confront in foreseeing (for we may in the end be powerless to *decide*) the future of cyberspace and its effect on the legal system is the issue of accountability versus anonymity. Traditional notions of personal jurisdiction, for example, rely on being able to identify the party over whom jurisdiction is asserted; conduct, such as gambling, cannot be effectively regulated absent the ability to identify the party whose conduct is to be controlled, or sovereignty over the place in which the conduct is "happening." The level of protection accorded to personal privacy is, and always has been, a balancing act between society's interest in promoting freedom of personal expression and activity versus society's interest in protecting itself and its members from harm, with the latter goal predicated on identification.

Think of the issue as a spectrum. At one end is total anonymity and thus total lack of accountability. At the other, total accountability and therefore total lack of anonymity. In the physical world it has been relatively easy to isolate discrete areas in which to apply standards located at varying points on the spectrum so that anonymity and accountability can co-exist. Anonymous political speech is protected as a Constitutional right; anonymous defamatory speech or infringement of intellectual property rights is not. Society insists on personal accountability for activities that violate its laws. While personal privacy is a socially recognized expectation that is considered legally reasonable in appropriate circumstances, its protection is excepted once society's interests begin to outweigh those of the individual. The United States Supreme Court underlined this tension in *McIntyre v. Ohio Elections Commission*, which appears in Chapter 9, and in which the Court said, "Anonymity is a shield from the tyranny of the majority," but also that, "The right to remain anonymous may be abused when it shields fraudulent conduct."

Cyberspace presents us with a world in which it is much harder to draw lines around different types of conduct, one in which it is presently impossible to restrict the use of anonymity to certain specific contexts. To be sure, recent innovations in tracking technology suggest at least some possibility of enforcing personal accountability in cyberspace. However, it is unclear how effective this approach might ultimately prove, given that every technological attempt to defeat anonymity on the Net to date has been relatively easily undone by a counter-technology aimed at preserving a "right" of anonymity. And tracking technologies generate objections from those who believe that the scale should tip toward personal privacy, not surveillance.

Thus it is uncertain how (or even *if*) we might transfer to cyberspace our real-world understanding that anonymity and personal accountability are *both* socially valuable. If it proves impossible to do so, how will our legal system evolve as cyberspace becomes the dominant arena for social and commercial interaction? Which of our customary legal paradigms will have to be modified or even abandoned? In a world that will incorporate innovation from day-to-day, if not hour-to-hour, how will the Common Law and its practitioners keep pace?

These are some of the fundamental questions that cyberlawyers must consider and the background against which they must work, as they continue to move into a new century, and perhaps a new age of law.

Index